I0820409
HAUNTING
468.46
3
AXELLE CAROLYN
JAMES KNIEST
The Final Girl Returns
ROLL
SCENE
TAKE
2
4
2
DIRECTOR Alex Perez
CAMERA Rob Bennett
DATE
DAY NIGHT INT EXT MOS
ΠΕΔ
58 A
1
A/B
23.98
William Butler/
Brinke Stevens
Josh Apple
Ø5 Sep22
CENSOR
TAKE
SLATE
DIR:
DOP: Annika Summerson
DATE 30.09.201

5B
1
23.97
19.11.35.10
A
WONDERFUL WORLD
A. ASAKURA
TOSHING
3/18/12
00.26.02.02
A030
147A
2
MY ANIMAL
24
Jacqueline Castel
A
Bryn McCashin
FEB 22 2022
A
THE SACRIFICE GAME
35mm
SCÈNE
PLAN
PRISE
3
V3
1
RÉAL:
J.WEXLER
CAM:
A01
D.P.:
A.BUSSIERE
SON:
01

HEIDI HONEYCUTT

HEADPRESS

A HEADPRESS BOOK
First published by Headpress in 2024, Oxford, United Kingdom
< headoffice@headpress.com >

I SPIT ON YOUR CELLULOID
The History of Women Directing Horror Movies

Cover design: LUKE INSECT (featuring scenes from Roberta Findlay's *A Woman's Torment*, Anna Biller's *The Love Witch*, and Kei Fujiwara's *ID*, with color inspiration from Prano Bailey-Bond's *Censor*, Jill Gevargizian's *The Stylist*, and Nia D'Acosta's *Candyman*)
Layout: MARK CRITCHELL < mark.critchell@gmail.com >

The Publisher thanks Gareth Wilson, Jen Wallis and Leigh Bushell

10 9 8 7 6 5 4 3 2 1

A CIP catalogue record for this book is available from the British Library

ISBN 978-1-915316-29-5 paperback
ISBN 978-1-915316-30-1 ebook

HEADPRESS. POP AND UNPOP CULTURE

Exclusive NO-ISBN special edition hardbacks and other items of interest are available at **HEADPRESS.COM**

CONTENTS

FOREWORD

I AM DEVOTED TO THE WORLD of fantasy, so I don't know why any sane writer of expositional nonfiction would come to me for an introduction to her work. Heidi, you should know better than to ask to have your one desire granted by a demented female filmmaker. Be careful what you wish for ... What follows is the story as it was told to me:

Heidi Honeycutt, a beautiful young woman with red hair, wishes to know the meaning of life. She decides to seek enlightenment from horror movies, and although her friends and family priest try to dissuade her, she embarks on a quest, seeking out the makers of these horror films. She watches many films filled with terror, dread, supernatural plots, and expensive special FX. Some of these films are made by prestigious male directors, but she finds herself strangely drawn to the (mostly lower budget) films made by women, and she makes it her lifelong quest to understand what these women are trying to say.

She watches our films, and she listens to us.

What is a horror movie anyway?

For me, a truly great horror film has some supernatural element or unsolvable mystery at the core of the narrative.

Sometimes a frightening thriller will be deemed a horror movie. *Psycho* is an early example of this trend, which was refined by movies like *Silence of the Lambs* (1991), and in the 1990s by movies like *Zodiac* (2007). These are all movies directed by men. Sometimes a disturbing fantasy movie will be deemed horror—there were fans who felt that the *Harry Potter* franchise was headed in that direction. Unfortunately, no women were ever chosen to helm a *Harry Potter* movie.

Religious mythology is often an inspiration for supernatural themes. The Bible, Catholic dogma, or Christian superstitions with dark themes are used to create a force or a character that threatens other sympathetic characters. Witches, usually female witches, are frequent figures in horror stories, as is the theme of the priestess or goddess who gives birth to Satan or the Anti-Christ.

Christianity, which started as a belief system based on love and self-sacrifice, vilified the goddess from the very beginning or at least from the moment that the resurrected Christ ascended to heaven and left his female followers at the mercy of a male-dominated society. There is much evidence that Jesus respected female disciples, whose gospels were later destroyed by the early Church Fathers. And when women continued to demand a voice in spiritual matters of the church, bishops and priests, aided and, in some cases, controlled by emperors and kings, tightened the reins and set forth a complicated system of beliefs deeming blasphemy and heresy punishable by dire means. Women who wanted agency over their bodies and spiritual lives became blasphemers and heretics, punished with torture and death. Sound familiar?

From my lesser knowledge of Judaism and Islam, I see the same issues of women being subjugated by a male priesthood and denied direct spiritual access to the godhead. Satan seems to be the only Supreme Being who can speak directly to women. Satan, a man and the supreme embodiment of evil, dominates the horror landscape with or without a credible religious theology. It is no consolation that the ultimate villain is usually portrayed as a binary male because the villain is often the most interesting character in the story. Female filmmakers often wonder why both the villain (Satan) and the hero (God) should claim the male gender. Granted, there are female protagonists in horror movies, but too often, they are the victim, and the protagonist who drives the action is a man.

Why does the patriarchy fear women and seek to subjugate them? Because women have the power to give birth? Because they see more easily into forbidden realms of emotion and spirit? The spiritual world, which is naturally the habitat of women, is difficult to control, so the easiest way to disenfranchise women spiritually used to be to label them witches and burn them at the stake. This only happens very rarely in modern times, but the urge to deny agency to women is still strong in many societies and industries, including the film industry.

The nature of horror films has changed over the course of my lifetime. Horror has gained respectability as a genre, and more films are being directed by women. The big-budget films still seem to be helmed by men, but perhaps because of general frustration with the limitations set on them, a large number of female directors have chosen horror as their medium. Another reason for the increasing number of female horror directors might be found in the subject matter of many of their films. An astonishing number of them are about revenge (supernatural or otherwise) on a society that punishes, restricts, or mistreats women.

A male friend of mine has suggested that because horror films frequently have plots where the protagonist believes herself powerless against the prevailing evil, there is an affinity for women, both as audience and as auteurs, who feel powerless against society. Are we (women) powerless? Recent decisions by the Supreme Court on *Roe v. Wade*[1] would suggest that we are. Peaceful protests and legal remedies don't seem to make a difference when it comes to abortion rights or the Equal Rights Amendment. Metaphors and subversive works of art sometimes seem like the only lights flickering in the dark.

Breaking taboos and expressing subversive opinions about society and religion have long been the domain of horror. Ghosts and supernatural beings have inhabited the stories of human civilization since ancient times. Films are a relatively new medium for tales of terror.

Horror is scarier if it is unexpected, and older horror films tend to be less frightening than modern ones to modern audiences. We are more comfortable with the ungodly creatures that inhabit them, and the taboos they break seem inevitable as we look back to these early stories and metaphorical monsters.

I would state that the three most iconic supernatural creatures to enter the world of horror in modern times are zombies, vampires, and Frankenstein's monster. Zombies existed in Haitian and African folklore but were brought into popular culture by George Romero in *Night of the Living Dead*. Vampires were first popularized by the novel *Dracula*, written by Bram Stoker. *Frankenstein* was created by a woman named Mary Shelley, the wife of Percy Shelley, a famous nineteenth-century poet. (Few people read his poems for pleasure today, but *Frankenstein* is known to all.) Mary Shelley believed in the power and promise of nature and feared the consequences of industrialization on the natural world, a fear that has proven to be well-founded. The irony is that Frankenstein's monster lives in the imagination of the world as a frightening monster when, in fact, he is a blameless innocent, the creation of an ambitious scientist, Victor Frankenstein, who embodies the concept of unrestrained technology and harnesses the powers of science for personal gain. Mary Shelley might say that Frankenstein the monster is the conscience of his creator, Victor.

Women hold up half of the sky—so claims an ancient Chinese proverb. And they witness horror just as keenly as men. Women see clearly that, just as there is no dark without the existence of light, the existence of evil allows for the existence of good. Tales of supernatural terror give me the power to break taboos and raise my voice. They inspire me to believe in the mysteries of the spiritual world.

Thank you, Heidi, for telling the simple story of each woman and allowing the subtext to speak for itself. Read between the lines of her book into the hearts and souls of the directors who long to tell their stories, even if those stories don't fit the mold that society has in mind for the gentle sex.

Like a really good horror movie, Heidi attempts with her book to explain the unexplainable.

PREFACE

THIS BOOK FIRST SPARKED AS an idea in my head in 2005, thanks to a man named Christopher K. Philippo. He began a list of horror films directed by women and enthusiastically shared his knowledge with me, a list that I have maintained to this day. Seventeen years later, I was able to write this book.

I tell myself that it took so long to write because I had to live it to know what I was talking about. Since 2005, I have written numerous articles, interviewed multiple women horror directors and their actors, producers, and screenwriters, and watched the phenomenon of women horror directors grow from a small, misunderstood minority to an incredible movement on equal footing with other genders and minorities in the film industry.In 2003, when I was a writer for Bloody-Disgusting.com, I noticed that the only women in horror culture were actresses. Amazing actresses were celebrated, and rightly so, but only actresses. I would go to giant horror conventions, such as the *Fangoria* Convention in New Jersey, and they would be the only women signing autographs or participating in panel discussions. Many beloved male horror actors were there, but fans also celebrated male horror directors, writers, authors, and artists. George Romero, Dario Argento, and Tobe Hooper all appeared at horror conventions, but never would one see Mary Lambert, Katt Shea, Kathryn Bigelow, or Mary Harron. Were they not invited? Did they decline the invitations to attend? Certainly, the truth is a little of both.

When an average horror convention attendee was asked to name five horror films directed by women, they could get to about three (*Pet Sematary*, *Near Dark*, and *American Psycho*). Sometimes they'd get to five and mention *Ravenous* and *Stripped to Kill*. After that? Fans, men and women, couldn't name any more. But I knew there were many, and now I know that there were thousands, and what a shame it was that that information was so cryptic fifteen years ago.

INTRODUCTION

W*HO AM I?* I'M HEIDI Honeycutt. I'm a journalist, film programmer, and producer. I hope writing this book contributes to the history of horror film studies by accurately describing the contributions of women film directors to the horror film genre.

Why did I write this book? Learning about women making horror films doesn't have to be boring! Movies are made to be watched, enjoyed, and shared. Filmmakers make them for people like me to write about and watch. Books and articles about women film pioneers and modern women's films tend to overemphasize women filmmakers' political and social importance while never treating their films *like films*. Overly academic, well-meaning authors have made the history of women directors boring to mainstream film fans. Film fans don't want to learn about social and Freudian feminism in *Stripped to Kill* (1986). Authors writing from this point of view are writing for themselves and other academics rather than for audiences who watch movies and are responsible for films' artistic success or failure.

Why women? There is misinformation in the collective film fan consciousness about which woman was 'the first' to direct or write a specific genre, which person is or is not a woman, which out-of-print films that no one can watch are horror or not, and why women did or didn't participate in horror directing until the twenty-first century. It's time to clarify some of that. In the twenty-first century, information about women directors and their horror films has become far easier to access and understand than before the 1980s. There is so much information available about movies such as *Jennifer's Body* (2009), for instance, that my task in later chapters is the complete opposite of what it is in the earliest chapters of this book: to narrow down the discussion to the most influential films, and the information that one should know to fully understand the importance and meaning of these horror films and their directors. Later chapters will be more selective about specific films. Many will be left out of the deep discussion to create a more robust and understandable narrative about the evolution of horror films. In several instances, women co-directors received no credit initially, and some still haven't. Irene Wong (*Love Me Vampire*, 1986), Giuseppina Marotta (*La Casa del Buon Ritorno*, 1986), and Claire Hagen (*Reel Horror*, 1985) are all finally getting their credit as co-directors, either officially or via fans and researchers. Some films are obscure and out of print, and there is almost no way to watch them. *Red* (1976) by Astrid Frank and Sofia Waldi's *Badai-Selatan* (1962) are unavailable and were never distributed outside their initial theatrical run. I have devoted fifteen years to independently researching this subject, and this book is the result of that research.

Andrew Hubatsek as the terrifying Zelda in *Pet Sematary* (1987), directed by Mary Lambert.

Who is a woman? Helia Colombo (*The Police Are Blundering in the Dark*, 1975), Marian Dora (*Melancholie der Engel*, 2009), Dominique Othenin-Girard (*The Omen IV*, 1991), Lauri Haukkamaa (*The Kin*, 2004), Rosa von Praunheim (*Horror Vacui*, 1984), and anyone from France or Italy named Michele or Andrea are not women. In addition, Tiffany Kilbourne (*Shower of Blood*, 2004), Sylvia St. Croix (*Gingerdead Man 2: Passion of the Crust*, 2008), Mary Crawford (*My Stepbrother Is a Vampire!?!*, 2013), Victoria Sloane (*Prison of the Dead*, 2000), and Ellen Cabot (*Puppet Master III: Toulon's Revenge*, 1991) are pseudonyms.

What is horror? Mary Lambert, the director of the famous horror movie *Pet Sematary* (1989), once told me that her definition of horror was something terrifying and supernatural. Ghosts, magic, demons, monsters, reanimation of the dead, and witchcraft are all recurring popular themes in some of the best horror films in the world, such as *Dracula* (1931), *A Nightmare on Elm Street* (1984), *Hellraiser* (1987), and *Child's Play* (1988). However, I consider the non-supernatural terror film most deserving of the 'horror' label. *Psycho* (1960), *The Texas Chain Saw Massacre* (1974), the first installments of *Friday the 13th* (1980) and *Halloween* (1978), and all of the *Scream* films are equally as revered as their supernatural counterparts. It's a bit fluid. People's opinions about what is and isn't a 'horror' film will differ.

In the early chapters of this book, I cover films that are not traditional horror films. These early films had horror elements and laid the groundwork for future films in the horror genre. Scenes, directing techniques, and storylines are attractive to any horror fan and essential in film history. Some movies directed by women labeled 'horror' are nothing of the sort. Samantha Lang's *The Well* (1997) was on an early list of horror films directed by women for research for this book. But then I saw it. It has some dark moments, but I wouldn't include them in this book. Mai Zetterling's *Night Games* (1966), Anja Breien's *The Witch Hunt* (1981), Marleen Gorris's *A Question of Silence* (1982), and *Broken Mirrors*

(1984) are all films that were initially on my list of horror films directed by women. After watching them, it is clear that they don't belong in a book about horror movies, though they are disturbing. Some films are not horror but try to trick you into thinking they are with their names or poster art. *Hellcab* (1997), co-directed by Mary Cybulski, is not horror despite the name and the lettering on the front of the initial VHS release giving every indication that it is. It was subsequently re-released as *Chicago Cab,* so no one else is likely to be fooled. On the other hand, Julie Taymor's 'drama' *Titus* (1999) has some of the most brutal horror imagery I have ever seen, yet fans and critics rarely call it a horror film.

Do women and men make different horror films? During Barbara Peeters' dispute with Martin Cohen and Roger Corman over the added nudity and rape scenes in the final cut of the 1980 horror film *Humanoids from the Deep*, Cohen said to the male *Los Angeles Times* reporter, "What's too much T&A? How do you argue that? You and I are men, and we look at women differently. A woman director just has a different point of view toward sexuality."[1] Author Molly Haskell asked the question, "Are Women Directors Different?" in 1977:

> It is expectations that are at the root of the problem, prescriptive definitions of masculine and feminine that have become self-fulfilling prophecies. Better not to expect or ask for, only observe and describe. Polarities do exist, but they don't necessarily correspond to gender. All we can do is hope that women filmmakers become, like their counterparts in the other arts, merely filmmakers.[2]

But are they different? Yes. And no. There is no answer; differences are up to the viewer to observe and discuss. This book is an in-depth, non-fiction examination of the thousands of women who have directed horror movies from the beginnings of film and the silent era through to the rise of television, from the impact of the sexual revolution and the civil rights movement of the 1960s and 1970s to their careers in the twenty-first century. This book considers social, political, and artistic movements and their effect on women's films while focusing on their horror movies' exciting, fun, and popular innovations. From the obscure to the mainstream, all women horror film directors are part of the cultural phenomenon we know as the modern horror film. This book is their story.

ACKNOWLEDGMENTS

THIS BOOK WOULD NEVER HAVE been possible without the help of the AFI Directing Workshop for Women, Adam K. Hart, Alice Lowe, Ama Lea, Amanda Reyes, Amanda Rossi, Amber Benson, Amelia Moses, Amy Holden Jones, Amy Lynn Best, Ana Clavell, Ana Lily Amirpour, Anastasia Elfman, Andrea Giner, Andrew Shearer, Andrew van den Houten, Anna Biller, Anna Gawrilow, Anna Thomas, Anne Goursaud, Annette Kasch, Antonio Lázaro-Reboll, April Wolfe, Art Ettinger, Arunaraje Patil, Ashley Fester, Ashley Maria, Astrid Frank, Avalon Fast, Axelle Carolyn, Barbara Peeters, Barbara Scharres, Bill George, Bill Kopp, Bola Ogun, Bob Murawski, Brad Miska, Bradley Harding, Brea Grant, Brian Buzz Jeurgens, Brian Gant, Brian Pulido, Brian S. Gross, Brinke Stevens, Briony Kidd, Caroline Golum, Caroline du Potet, Catherine Hardwicke, Celeste Yarnall, Chelsea Stardust, Chere Aprecino, Chloe Okuno, Chris Alexander, Chris Poggiali, Chris Woodrich, Christiane Cegavske, Christopher K. Philippo, Christopher Toyne, Cliff MacMillan, Concepcion Carmen Cascajosa Virino, Craig Mullins, DJ Perry, Dame Darcy, Danielle Harris, Danica McKellar, Danis Goulet, Danishka Esterhazy, Darla Enlow, Darrin Ramage, Dayna Noffke, Debbie Rochon, Deborah Brock, Denice Duff, Deryn Warren, Devi Snively, Donna Davies, Donna McRae, Ed Baran, Elizabeth Stanley, Elza Kephart, Emily Hagins, Emma Bell, Emma Tammi, Erica Fox, Erin Brown, Erin Li, Gabrielle Beaumont, Gala Goliani, Gale Anne Hurd, Giannalberto Bendazzi, Gigi Saul Guerrero, Grant Moninger, Gregory Hakatana, Guinevere Turner, Hanelle M. Culpepper, Heather Buckley, Heidi Lee Douglas, Heidi Moore, Holly Dale, Hope Perello, Isabel Peppard, Izzy Lee, Jackie Kong, Jaclyn Chessen, James Morgart, Jane Clark, Jane Rose, Janet Greek, Jacqueline Castel, Jen Soska, Jenn Page, Jenn Wexler, Jennifer Blanc-Biehn, Jennifer Kent, Jennifer Lynch, Jennifer M. Kroot, Jennifer Thym, Jessica Gallant, Jessica Larocca, Jessica Sherif, Jessie Seitz, Jill Gevargizian, Jill Killington, Joanna Angel, Joe Dante, Joe Rubin, Joey Ally, Joseph Ziemba, Josh Goldbloom, Jovanka Vuckovic, Judith Beauvallet, Julia Ostertag, Julia Walter, Julie Corman, Kaitlin Tinker, Kansas Bowling, Karen Barragan, Karen Lam, Karyn Kusama, Kasia Kowalcyk, Katia von Garnier, Katt Shea, Kayoko Asakura, Kier-La Janisse, Kitty Pie, Kirsten Carthew, Kriscinda Meadows, Krishna Sen, Kristina Klebe, Laura Lau, Laura Moss, Laura Whyte, Lawrence Russell, Leigh Bushell, Leigh Janiak, Lesley Manning, Leslie Delano, Lexi Alexander, Lily Grote, Lily Mariye, Linda Hassani, Lindsay Denniberg, Lisa Hammer, Lisa Palenica, Liz Adams, Liz Tabish, Lloyd Kaufman, Lola Rocknrolla, Lola Wallace, Lordi/Tomi, Luis Deltell Escolar, Mae Catt, Maegan Houang, Mai Nakanishi, Marina de Van, Mark Edward Heuck, Mark Quigley, Martha Colburn, Mary Harron, Mary Lambert, Mattie Do, Maude Michaud, Maya M. Smuckler, Megan Riakos, Melanie Light, Melantha Blackthorne, Melinda Merroquin

Fontino, Meosha Bean, Mercedes the Muse, Meredith Berg, Michelle Fatale, Mike Hein, Milady Flores, Monique Parent, Natalie Erika James, Natasha Halevi, Natasha Kermani, Novi Kurnia, Olga Osorio, Paige K. Davis, Paula Haifley, Paulette Victor-Lifton, Penelope Spheeris, Peter Dendle, Petra Haffter, Prano Bailey-Bond, Rachel Samuels, Rachel Talalay, Rae Dawn Chong, Rebecca Thomson, Rebekah McKendry, Rena Riffel, Richard Elfman, Robert Dassanowsky, Roberta Findlay, Roger Corman, Rolfe Kanefsy, Ron Bonk, Rose McGowan, Roseanne Liang, Roxanne Benjamin, Roxy Shih, Sarah Appleton, Sandy Chukhadarian, Sarah Doyle, Scott Phillips, Sean Redlitz, Shade Rupe, Shayna Connelly, Sid Haig, Siri Rødnes, Sofia Carrillo, Sonia Lupher, Sophia Cacciola, Staci Layne Wilson, Stacie Ponder, Stacy Pippi Hammon, Stacy Title, Stéphanie Cabdevila, Stephanie Rothman, Stewart Thorndike, Sue Corcoran, Susannah Gent, Suzanne Osten, Sylvia Soska, Tammi Sutton, Tara Anaïse, Tara K. Clark, Tara Perry, Tara Price, Terry Curtis Fox, Taryn O'Neill, The Final Girls Berlin Film Festival, The University of Pittsburgh, Thomas Duke, Tiffany Warren, Tim Sullivan, Tina Krause, Tony Brown, Toy Lei, UCLA Film and Television Archive, Ursula Dabrowsky, Victoria Angell, Venita Ozols-Graham, Veronika Franz, Vivienne Vaughn, WENCH Film Festival, William Hellfire, William Wright, Yamuna Sharma, Dejan Ognjanović, and Yfke Van Berckelaer and every woman who has ever directed a horror movie, short or long, good or bad.

DEDICATION

I dedicate this book to my parents and my sister,
without whom I would have finished it at least a decade earlier.

And to the best horror lifer Kelly Barlow for being my unwavering
friend and cemetery kitty sister forever.

CHAPTER 1

Mother of All Evil

1896 THROUGH 1945

A nightmarish geometry composes the hallway in Germaine Dulac 's *The Seashell and the Clergyman*.

"It surprises a lot of people to find out that there were more women working behind the scenes in motion pictures in influential positions before 1920." — Ally Acker, Reel Cinema[1]

AS WE KNOW THEM TODAY, horror films did not exist until the second half of the twentieth century. The things we associate with horror, like slasher films, 'Final Girls,' gore, excessive blood, nudity and sex, visual computer effects, and practical makeup effects, were not the norm for cinema with horrific or fantastic premises. It wasn't until the 1920s that feature-length 'horror' films became recognizable, and not until the 1930s that classic icons like Dracula and Frankenstein's monster became known to audiences in a meaningful way. It wasn't until the 1960s that films like *Psycho* (1960), *Blood Feast* (1963), and *Night of the Living Dead* (1968) ushered in an entirely new type of horror cinema unfettered by the chains of the studio code, theatrical monopolies, and traditional, conservative Victorian sensibilities.

Like most fantastic movies made during the silent era through World War II, the films covered in this chapter are thrillers, science fiction, fantasies, and mysteries that introduce the familiar themes, tropes, and plots used in later horror films. Most books about the history of the horror genre include early fantasy, suspense, and science fiction. For example, academics and film journalists had Weine's *The Cabinet of Doctor Caligari* (1920) and Browning's *Dracula* (1931) in the pantheon of early horror movies. However, they lack the gore and violence that horror audiences of the late twentieth and early twenty-first centuries would come to expect. Likewise, suspense thrillers, mysteries, and fantasy films directed by women before the 1950s are vital to understanding women directors' roles in the evolution of modern horror films.

Most of the suspense and thriller films of Alice Guy-Blaché have been lost or destroyed except for a few reels and still images, some preserved digitally and online in the public domain. In this section, the suspense and fantasy films directed by Guy-Blaché between 1896 and 1920 provide an insight into the drastically changing technology of the film industry in the early twentieth century and the implications those changes had for independent and female filmmakers.

In 1896, no film studios, movie stars, professional film actors, or cinematographers existed. Film was a brand-new technology, wholly pliable to those possessed of creative industry. The director was in charge of the entire scenario and chose the actors, decorators, costumes, and furnishings while overseeing rehearsals, stage direction, lighting, and editing of the finished film.[2] It was not prestigious to be a film director, which is probably why, in 1895, Alice Guy-Blaché, while working as a secretary in the offices of the French photography company Gaumont Studios, was instructed to pick up a camera and direct a film at a time when most women were not allowed to vote. A young woman who spent most of her early life in Chile, twenty-two-year-old Alice Guy-Blaché knew nothing about cameras when she started working for Gaumont. She worked to support her family, which had suffered a severe financial loss, by doing secretarial work—one of the only jobs a woman could respectably perform. What would become an illustrious career began by filing papers, making appointments, and running errands, but she was smart and soon began to run the office as a trusted employee.

At the time, films had only one requirement: motion. Thus, scenes of dancers, boxers, horses, strongmen, and everyday events were filmed without narrative structure or dialogue. They were 'living pictures' of existing people and events. The film was used to record information already there, not to create new stories. After watching some of the films her company had produced for a client, Alice Guy-Blaché decided to ask if she could direct a movie for the company:

> I had done a little amateur theatricals and thought that one might do better than these demonstration films. Gathering my courage, I timidly proposed to Gaumont that I might write one or two little scenes and have a few friends perform in them. If the future development of motion pictures had been foreseen at this time, I should never have obtained his consent.[3]

With that request, she became the first woman to direct a film. *La Feé aux Choux* (*The Cabbage Fairy*) was a fantasy-themed narrative short featuring costumed actresses as fairies in a garden. It's unclear exactly which year she made it, but Guy-Blaché said it was in 1896. French film historian Francis Lacassin (using the Gaumont Film Catalog as reference) places it in 1900. If she made it in 1896, she could very well be the inventor of the narrative film.

In *A History of Narrative Film* by David A. Cook, and most film histories, the credit for the first narrative film is given to Georges Méliès, the French director of the science fiction adaptations *A Trip to the Moon* (1902) and *Twenty Thousand Leagues Under the Sea* (1907). Cook doesn't mention Alice Guy-Blaché until he discusses the twentieth century, and then only briefly. While Cook awarded early male filmmakers detailed histories in his book, Guy-Blaché's one-sentence mention indicates how historians have forgotten women's early accomplishments in the film industry. Ally Acker mentions this discrepancy in her documentary study of women pioneers of early film, *Reel Herstory: The Real Story of Reel Women* (2014). According to her, history presents Guy-Blaché in a subcategory, a 'woman director.' Therefore, Méliès is given the official credit as the first narrative 'film director.' According to Acker, traditional film scholars treat Guy-Blaché as a novelty act.[4]

Alice Guy-Blaché was interested in filming action, drama, and suspense from the beginning of her career. Few of her films survive, but many that have are early examples of suspense, thrillers, science fiction, and fantasy. Her experiments in genre film include depictions of grotesque images such as doctors amputating limbs and holding up the (fake) severed arms and waving them about. One shocking short portrays an armed assault by a group of men on a person's home (*Surprise Attack on a House at Daybreak*, 1898).

Based on the poem by Goethe, the opera by Gounod, and the play by Marlowe, *Faust et Méphistophélès* is a short 1903 narrative made by Guy-Blaché under Gaumont's banner. It is the first fantastical film directed by a woman in history. The story of Faust is well known:

Denise Becker as Esmeralda in the lost horror film *Esméralda* (1905).

Faust conjures the demon in *Faust et Méphistophélès* (1903).

a young scholar in sixteenth-century Germany makes a pact with the Devil, exchanging his soul for untold earthly knowledge and delights. Unfortunately, Satan calls for his payment at the end of the story, and Faust is dragged down to Hell to endure an eternity of agonies. Guy-Blaché's two-minute version fits on only forty-four meters of film stock and focuses on Faust's succumbing to the Devil's (Mephistopheles) temptations.

Faust et Méphistophélès is not a sophisticated-looking film. Shot entirely on a raised platform stage, the actors wear comical, even cartoonish, beards and costumes, and pantomime into one static camera, as early silent actors were wont to do. Faust and Mephistopheles are compelling because Guy-Blaché's fancy editing tricks made her characters appear and disappear magically. Like most of Guy-Blaché's films, *Faust* is comical and meant to inspire awe of a fantastic sort rather than fear. It seems more like a short stage play than a film to modern audiences, and typical of the casual manner in which she shot short films.

The first film Guy-Blaché directed at the upgraded Paris Gaumont Studio facilities, completed in 1905 (with new sets, stages, equipment, and increased personnel), was *La Esmeralda*, a short version of Victor Hugo's *The Hunchback of Notre Dame*. It was co-directed with Victorin-Hippolyte Jasset and consisted of eight scenes starring Denise Becker as the title character Esmeralda and Henry Vorins as the hunchback Quasimodo. The most popular 1923 film version stars Lon Chaney as Quasimodo, but Guy-Blaché's was the first film version of the story. Her ten-minute black-and-white short reel depicted the torture of poor Quasimodo. She relates her difficulty in creating the gruesome scene:

> Coming on the stage, I stopped, perplexed. The décor represented an old corner of Paris, all right, but my painter was certainly a futurist. The lop-sided houses were ringed with corkscrew spirals right up under their painted bonnets. The goat that I had tried to tame during a whole week followed me faithfully, refusing the company of Esmeralda. Mounted on the torture rack, the unhappy Quasimodo tried to steady the balls of cotton with which he had stuffed his costume for realism, but they moved in all directions, turning the drama to farce ... the torture was all mine! There could be no question of beginning over, the overall costs were running up and when the cost of a film passed ten thousand francs, I would be summoned by the Board of Directors and asked if I intended to ruin the company![5]

While rare still images of *La Esmeralda* survive in *Moving Picture World* and *Motion Picture News* archives, the film is lost.

By 1910, Alice Guy-Blaché and her husband Herbert Blaché had split from Gaumont Studios. They formed their own movie studio, Solax, across the Atlantic in New Jersey. Solax made over three hundred films, some directed by Alice, some by her husband, and others intended for American audiences with American actors. Guy-Blaché was excited about the freedom women seemed to enjoy in the American film industry: "The attitude towards women in America is very different," she said. "It is a constant conflict when a woman in a French studio attempts to handle and superintend men in their work. They don't like it, and they are not averse to showing their feelings."[6] It wasn't long after Guy-Blaché made her first feature-length narrative films through Solax that she realized what audiences at the turn of the century truly wanted: terror, romance, and adventure.

> Films [reels] had now attained the length of 30,000 feet. In each of the reels, the public demanded a 'punch' or suspense ... this genre of the film put me in touch with the daredevils who made a specialty of doubling the stars in perilous moments. *The Shadows of the Moulin Rouge*, *A Terrible Night*, *The Rogues of Paris*, and many others were all of this genre. The abduction of rich heiresses (always young and pretty), pursuit by a lover or detective, entrapment in boats, flooded dungeons, quicksands, etc. Anything went if only there was a happy ending.[7]

In 1913, through Solax, Alice Guy-Blaché was responsible for the first horror film directed by a woman: an adaptation of Edgar Allan Poe's *The Pit and the Pendulum*. The film stars

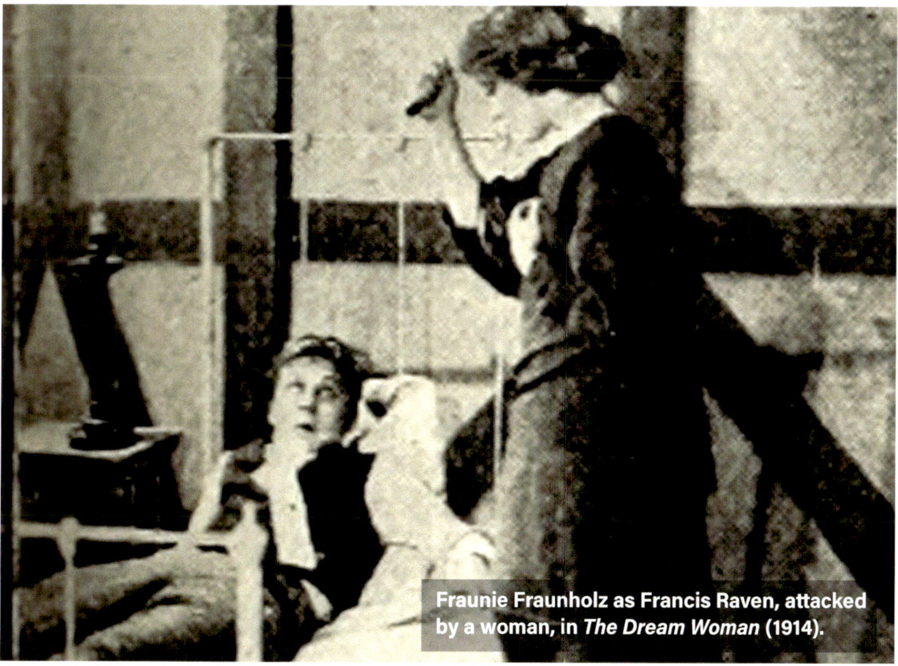

Fraunie Fraunholz as Francis Raven, attacked by a woman, in *The Dream Woman* (1914).

Darwin Karr as the hero Dr. Alonzo, Blanche Cornwall as his love interest Isabella, and Fraunie Fraunholz as the villain. Edgar Allan Poe's short story is a first-person narrative tale set during the Spanish Inquisition, wherein a man accused of a crime is condemned to death. In the story, the man, strapped securely to a table in a dank dungeon, must endure the slow pendulous movements of a giant blade that swings lower and lower with each stroke and will eventually disembowel him. Guy-Blaché's version added melodrama and expanded on the love story by having the evil Pedro, a monk in love with the beautiful Isabella, frame her lover Alonzo for the theft of his monastery's jewels and place him under the judgment of corrupt inquisitors. Alonzo is imprisoned and forced to endure the pendulum torture.

Only the first reel survives (in the Library of Congress; digitized versions also exist) and stills survive in the publication *Moving Picture World*. However, we know that the monks torture Alonzo and Isabella until Alonzo confesses, at which point he is tied to a table to await death by the pendulum. Miraculously, rats chew through his bonds and free him, but the monks then heat the metal walls of his prison to red hot, and the walls begin to close in on him. Just when it seems that Alonzo will surely die, Isabella arrives with soldiers to release him, and all is well.[8]

The elaborate sets and costumes in the first reel, for which Guy-Blaché had become famous at this point, convey an exaggerated expressionist attitude. The oversized Gothic windows effused with light usually accompany Pedro's evil plotting. A human skull sits on Dr. Alonzo's desk, always a reminder of the looming specter of death. The unsophisticated theatrics kill any real suspense: the flimsy cardboard door of Alonzo's house is comical; the fact that Pedro's church keeps its most remarkable treasures in an unlocked top drawer of a dresser in the central hallway makes little sense; the candlesticks in the candelabra at the monastery always seem in danger of falling because they don't fit in their sockets; Fraunie Fraunholz plays a cartoonish Pedro. However ridiculous some of the acting, plot points, and props seem, *The Pit and the Pendulum* is a morality tale designed to elicit an emotional reaction from the audience. Guy-Blaché remembers that the rats were persuaded to chew through Alonzo's bonds because the crew smeared the ropes holding down the actor, Darwin Karr, with food:

> They fulfilled their role marvelously, but a few preferred fresh meat, came sniffing at the nose of the actor and even penetrated the legs of his trousers. When at last, the ropes broke he was not slow to jump to his feet, swearing there would be no retake. The film had enormous success. I went incognito at the first showing, and I had great pleasure in observing the shivers and anguished sighs of the public.[9]

Solax released the entire three-reel film in theaters on August 18, 1913.

By 1913, Guy-Blaché's studio Solax had become virtually defunct after her husband, Herbert Blaché, started his own company, Blaché Features, in direct competition with hers. Under the Blaché Features banner, Guy-Blaché directed several straight suspense films, including *Shadows of the Moulin Rouge* (1913), a story about a woman named DuPont kidnapped and taken to the Moulin Rouge nightclub by a villain named Chevrele. Chevrele has killed a prostitute and substituted her body in Mrs. DuPont's bed, so her husband will assume she's dead. The husband is sent to an insane asylum when he tries to uncover the truth, and much dark drama ensues before the husband and wife are reunited.[10]

Two more Guy-Blaché-directed, feature-length suspense films made through Blaché Features are *The Dream Woman*[11] and *The Woman of Mystery*, both from 1914. Both are Gothic tales involving murder and the supernatural, and star Fraunie Fraunholz (*The Pit and the Pendulum*) and Claire Whitney.

In *The Dream Woman,* based on Wilkie Collins's short story of the same name,[12] recurring nightmares plague Francis Raven (Fraunholz). In these nightmares, he is stabbed to death by a strange woman. He marries an alcoholic woman (Claire Whitney) against his mother's wishes, and their relationship becomes abusive. One night, after he hits her in disgust at her drunken stupor, she vows to kill him, just like the woman in his dream. He takes her knife to ensure she won't, and they part ways. Years later, still in terror of his recurring stabbing nightmares, Francis begs his friend to guard him on his birthday. The friend, named Rigobert, ties him up and gags him, presumably for safekeeping, at the insistence of a prostitute Rigobert has brought home. Once Rigobert leaves the room, the prostitute reveals herself as Alicia, the alcoholic ex-wife, and stabs Francis in the heart. Francis's employers find his corpse and follow the murderer's footprints down to the nearby river, where they vanish.[13]

The Woman of Mystery is about an actress named Norma and the mysterious Hindu princess who attempts to kill her by sending her a box filled with venomous snakes. Detective Nelson (Fraunie Fraunholz) investigates the crime and jails the villainess. The Hindu princess uses her powerful psychic magic to force Detective Nelson to commit armed robbery. When he finds his scarf at the crime scene the next day, he is baffled. With the help of Norma and his mother, Nelson can clear himself of the crime and pursue the criminal princess, who has escaped her jail cell. When they capture her, the princess commits suicide by drinking poison from a secret compartment in her ring. With Nelson free from her evil magic and Norma free from the threat of murder, the two fall in love.[14] Claire Whitney is credited in some documents as playing Norma and in others as playing the princess. Since the film is lost, there is no reliable method of determining which actress played which character.[15]

Many of Guy-Blaché's lost films have sensational titles that hint at the horror or suspense genres. Some of these more promising missing titles include her early Gaumont films *Le Mort Qui Ressuscite* (*The Dead that Live Again*, 1905), *Les Druides* (*The Druids*, 1906), *Le Portrait de Mme X* (*The Portrait of Madame X*, 1906), and her later Solax and Blaché Features American films *The Witch's Necklace* (1912), *A Message from Beyond* (1912), *The Blood Stain* (1912), and *The Eyes of Satan* (1913). Her violent Western, *Two Little Rangers* (1912), features a brutal death scene.

Several of Guy-Blaché's last American films starred Olga Petrova, an actress who typified the seductive vamp ideal of the 1910s and 1920s: a morally corrupt, beautiful, and evil woman that sucks the life out of those who love her. Olga Petrova's memoirs included some sad musings on why Guy-Blaché stopped directing, "Why Madame Blaché didn't continue to direct me after these four [films], I don't know, but I do know I missed her sorely."[16]

The closing of Solax Studios eventually led to Guy-Blaché's early retirement from film directing. Unable to find work in the United States as a director, Guy-Blaché returned to France. Devastatingly, all prints of her American films seem to have disappeared from the Solax and Blaché Features studios. Guy-Blaché spent most of the rest of her life trying to correct the mistakes of film scholars who consistently incorrectly cataloged her films. She died unknown in New Jersey without so much as an obituary.

The French actress and director known only as Musidora (born Jeanne Roques in 1889) starred in a series of silent thriller serials directed by Louis Feuillade titled *Les Vampires* (1915) as Irma Vep (an anagram of Vampire), and was known for having created the original seductive 'vamp' silent screen persona. Musidora worked closely with Feuillade and directed at least ten films during the 1910s and 1920s, but unfortunately, all her films as director are lost except for two: *Soleil et Ombre* (1922) and *La Terre des Taureaux* (1924). Her lost Gothic thriller, *Vincenta* (1920), is about murder and passion in the Basque region of Spain. In Vincenta, a prince named Romano seduces a waitress named Vincenta and then callously discards her to announce his engagement to a wealthy American heiress. When Vincenta causes a scene because of her heartache, a man named Morenito violently kills him out of love for Vincent. Musidora played the role of Vincenta, Jean Guitry in the part of the prince, Marcel de Garcon as Morenito, and Ginette Chrysias as the American. It was filmed at the Château de Madame du Barry in France. It had elaborate nineteenth-century costumes and art direction heavily inspired by the Basque country in France and the work of sculptor Maurice Guiraud-Rivière. Elaborate masks with feathers and other artistic touches were used in several scenes. Musidora cited the story of Princess Badourah from *The Arabian Nights* as one of her main influences for Vincenta.[17]

Rosa Porten, born in 1884, was one of Germany's first female directors. By 1910, she was writing screenplays and co-directing films with her husband, Franz Eckstein. It's difficult to catalog all the films she was involved with as a director because Porten often used the pseudonym Dr. R. Portegg, which confused archives and led to the loss of most of her films. She primarily made dramas and comedies for the production company Treumann-Larsen-Film GmbH, but several of her films seem to be early horror films. *Der nicht vom Weibe Geborene*, aka *Not of the Woman Born* (1918), co-directed with Eckstein, stars expressionist German horror cinema star Conrad Veidt (*The Cabinet of Doctor Caligari*, 1920, and *The Man Who Laughs*, 1928) as Satan. The synopsis and all film images are lost, along with the film itself. Another suspiciously horror-sounding film she directed is *Das Geschenk der Norne,* AKA *The Gift of the Norn* (1916). The Norn are three supernatural entities in Norse mythology that control the fate of all humans, much like the Fates of Greek Mythology. Again, there is no film copy or any available descriptive information.

Louise Kolm-Fleck (also known as Luise Kolm, Luise Kolm-Fleck, Luise Veltee, and Luise Fleck) was an Austrian director whose horror films are not well-known to horror fans. As a filmmaker, Kolm-Fleck's work spanned the days of the Austrian Empire to the fall of Hitler. Her first husband, Anton Kolm, and their cameraman, Jacob Fleck, formed their partnership in 1906 and their studio, Österreichisch–Ungarische Kino–Filmsindustrie

Ges.m.b.H (Austrian–Hungarian Cinema Film Company Ltd.), in 1910. The only existing description of Kolm-Fleck comes from her son, Austrian film director Walter Kolm-Veltée (1910–1999). He describes her as "energetic and full of humor. She loved fantasy but also desired to comment on the problems of society and the relationships between men and women."[18]

Kolm co-directed the horror anthology film *Trilby,* AKA *Three Tales of Terror* (1912)[19] with Jacob Fleck, Anton Kolm and Claudius Veltée based on the 1894 story by George du Maurier about a beautiful young singer named Trilby O'Ferrall and her evil, manipulative mentor, Svengali. Svengali takes the tone-deaf Trilby under his masterful wing and uses hypnotism to turn her into a fabulous opera singer. Trilby is always in a hypnotic trance, unable to ask for help or leave Svengali, and under a constant dark spell until her master has a heart attack during one of her performances. This story was also the inspiration for Gaston Leroux's *Phantom of the Opera* (itself the basis of a classic silent horror film).[20] Two years later, another version of the same film (*Svengali*, AKA *Svengali, Der Hypnotiseur*, 1914) was released in Europe.[21]

The feature-length silent ghost story *Die Ahnfrau,* AKA *The Ancestress* (1919), is one of the first actual horror films directed by a woman. The hour-long film is a Gothic supernatural story set in a semi-medieval/Renaissance fantasy world. Graf (Count) Zdenko von Borotin (Karl Ehmann) and his daughter Berta (Liane Haid, Austria's first movie star) live in the ancient castle of their family and are the last members of the family line. A ghost haunts the castle: a medieval ancestor forced to marry against her will. When her husband caught her in her lover's arms, she was murdered ruthlessly as punishment. Now, the ghost visits family members when a tragedy occurs.

Based on a play and filmed earlier in 1910 by Jacob Fleck, *Die Ahnfrau* embodies everything a Gothic horror story should: it features a large, ancient castle; a tragic heroine; an ancient curse; a ghost; unheeded warnings of impending doom, and suicide. Despite static camerawork and a slow-burn plot, *Die Ahnfrau* contains some exemplary special effects, such as the ghost fading in and out with a supernatural wind streaming its long dress and shawl in a windless room. The film also has some bleak imagery: one scene shows the hanged bodies of robbers dangling from long poles in the distance. The rest of the scenery lacks any expressionist artistry that other German horror films employed and is reasonably dull.

After its initial release, *Die Ahnfrau* was long-neglected, and some pieces of the film are lost and unrecoverable. A partial print was restored and digitized by the San Paolo film library in Brazil and screened to the public in 2019, for the first time since its original theatrical run, at the Austrian film festival Diagonale.[22]

Some of Kolm-Fleck's other genre feature films as co-director with Jacob are the crime thriller *Mir kommt keiner aus,* AKA *The Black Hand* (1917); the expressionist film with a fever-induced nightmare, *Die Schlange der Leidenschaft* (1917);[23] the Victor Hugo story and opera-adaptation *Rigoletto,* AKA *Der König amüsiert sich* (1918); the fantasy horror *Die Zauberin am Stein* (1919); horror film *Der tanzende Tod* (1920), and the thriller *Revanche* (1922), most of which also starred Haid in a leading role. Kolm-Fleck's 1920 horror film *Anita*, also known as *Trance* and co-directed with Jacob Fleck,

The only known surviving image from Louise Fleck's horror film *Anita* (1920).

had a similar plot about a young woman under a hypnotist's evil spell.[24] No surviving copies of these films exist.

Kolm-Fleck would go on to direct the violent 1927 thriller *Yacht of the Seven Sins*: a feature-length serial killer mystery co-directed with her husband starring Brigitte Helm, a superstar of Weimar Germany silent cinema. In the film, singer Leonie Storm (Rina Marsa) and dancer Olga Petrowna (Brigitte Helm) find themselves aboard the luxury cruise ship Yoshiwara during a harrowing murder mystery complete with an onboard detective and psychopathic killer. The final missing reel, all of act six, is described as having scenes of police boats overtaking the ship and the detective revealing himself, resulting in the killer's arrest.[25]

Elvira Notari was one of the first woman directors in Italy. Beginning her career in photography in 1905, by 1912, she had her own production studio, founded an acting school, and directed several short fantasy films, *The Sunflower*, *The Fool's Goodbye*, and three feature-length thriller films. *Il nano rosso,* AKA *The Red Dwarf* (1917), was a film version of the 1905 novel by prolific Italian romance author Carolina Invernizio, *Raffaella o i misteri del vecchio mercato,* also known as *Raffaella, or the Mysteries of the Old Market*. Raffaella's lead character is an innocent young woman kidnapped by criminals and sold to different people. She goes insane and spends most of the story drugged by quack doctors to keep her docile.[26] This synopsis is different from the one described in the Women's Film Pioneers Project, which says that the film is about "a deformed wealthy man who becomes enamored with a chorus girl and then depletes his fortune to conquer her affections, only to be betrayed when she leaves him. When he discovers the truth, he kills himself."[27] According to the same source, *Il nano rosso* was re-released in 1924 as *La Fata di Borgo Loreto*. Notari would make several mystery/thriller/crime films adapted from romantic literature: *Carmela, La Sartina di Mo* and *La Medea di Portamedina* (1919),

A still image from the set of Marion Wong's film *The Curse of Quon Wong* (1917). Only two of the original nine reels have been found.

based on novels by the nineteenth-century Italian author Francesco Mastriani.

Marion Wong was a Chinese-AmericanChinese American actress living in Hollywood. At twenty-one, she wrote, produced, and directed a thirty-five-minute film with Chinese-American actors titled *The Curse of Quon Gwon* (1916). Wong's film is described by contemporary writers as a love story more than anything else, but it has fantastic elements. What is described as the most impressive effect of the surviving film is a scene in which the heroine, played by Marion Wong's sister Violet Wong, is wearing a necklace and bracelets that dissolve into chains as if, by magic, imprisoning her. Marion Wong herself played "the Villainess," though what that means in terms of the storyline is lost today. Only two reels of the original seven or eight have survived, so the plot and relationships between all the characters are messy in modern viewings. However, star Violet Wong's daughters remember the film's happy ending.

Marion Wong was interviewed about *The Curse of Quon Gwon* in an article in the July 17, 1917, issue of *Moving Picture World*:

> I had never seen any Chinese movies, so I decided to introduce them to the world. I first wrote the love story. Then I decided that people who are interested in my people and my country would like to see some of the customs and manners of China. So I added to the love drama many scenes depicting these things. I do hope it will be a success.[28]

Unfortunately, it was not a success financially. Ultimately, Wong left a career in Hollywood to raise her family, fading into obscurity until film historian Arthur Dong resurrected her contribution to Chinese-American and women's film history in his 2007 documentary, *Hollywood Chinese.*

Eloyce Gist, along with her husband James, was an African American filmmaker when Black people were actively barred from the mainstream film industry and experienced segregation in almost every other area of society. The Gists made their films with all-black cast for a black audience. In particular, they were evangelist Christians using cinema to spread their religious message. One of their films is *Hell-Bound Train* (1930). Considered a full feature at only fifty minutes, *Hell-Bound Train* is an allegorical film with low-budget symbolism: a speeding train is shown intermittently throughout the story of the various sinners and their sins. The Devil wears a Halloween mask and red cape, cutting a cartoonish rather than a hellish figure. He announces he's giving away free one-way trips on his train (in exchange for one's soul, of course).

Each group of sinners (gamblers, promiscuous women, bootleggers, those who don't attend church each Sunday, etc.) is described in vignettes acting out their specific sins. The first train car has dancers, which the film reminds us are indecent. The second contains bootleggers. The other train cars include single women with babies being led astray by the whispers of a man; the train becomes so rowdy and drunken that one woman stabs another out of jealousy. Women are raped, and men are mugged. Jazz music is evil! Stealing is wrong! At the end of most vignettes, the Devil laughs because he has acquired more souls for Hell. All on the train, these souls are hell-bound, and as they approach death (literally a man dressed in black holding a sign that says "Welcome to Hell"), their train enters a cave and bursts into flames. The film's interstitial title tells us that a sermon inspires this story.[29]

Cinema historians often cite Lois Weber as the most important female silent film director. Weber was an American director with a career spanning from the 1910s through to her retirement in 1934. Her prominence in the collective consciousness of the film industry inspired Alice Guy-Blaché's bitterness when she said, "She had watched me direct the first little films and doubtless thought it was not difficult. She got a directing job, and certain Americans pretend that she was the first woman director. My first film dated from 1896."[30]

Satan in *Hellbound Train* (1930), directed by Eloyce King Patrick Gist. Image courtesy of Kino Lorber.

A split-screen technique innovated by Weber in *Suspense* that would come to be used by filmmakers like David Cronenberg. Image courtesy of Kino Lorber.

Like many filmmakers before 1920, Weber was an actress, director, producer, and screenwriter, a veritable Jill-of-all-trades, as were many women in film at the time. Weber was also one of the few women to direct mainstream theatrical films after the 1920s.[31] She had begun her career at the new Gaumont studio in New Jersey in 1908, working directly under Guy-Blaché's husband at the time, Herbert Blaché. Weber discovered the appeal of the suspense thriller elements despite focusing on exploitation films about challenging issues such as abortion and racism during her early days at Gaumont and later at Universal Studios.

Though most of Weber's films are lost, her 1913 short *Suspense* has been restored.[32] Based loosely on the 1901 French play *Au Telephone* (*At the Telephone*) by Grand Guignol's most famous playwright André de Lorde, *Suspense* is a sophisticated example of early high-tension genre films. The one-reel, ten-minute thriller co-directed with Weber's husband, Phillips Smalley, is about a homeless man who stalks a woman and her child in an isolated farmhouse in Los Angeles. Weber herself stars as the woman, and Sam Kaufman plays the hobo. Despite widespread rumors to the contrary, a young Lon Chaney does not appear in the film.

Historians and critics laud *Suspense* for its innovative cinematography and editing.[33] Weber and Smalley used a three-way split-screen technique, simultaneously showing the frantic wife phoning her husband, the husband's appalled and worried reaction, and the attacker entering the home and cutting the telephone wires. Scenes of the mother caring for her child are shown through keyholes, making the audience voyeurs. During the husband's frantic race home, the police and indignant car owner are visible through his rear-view mirror. The most intense image in *Suspense* might be the scene in which the prowler, long knife poised and ready to plunge, slowly walking up the stairs, his face a blank, sociopathic visage of pure evil, is stalking his prey. Modern slasher films like John Carpenter's *Halloween* (1978) reinvent these images: the prowler's face seen peeping through the window and the cutting of phone wires mid conversation would become clichés when victims were home alone. The split-screen technique that shows three characters in different rooms was one that other directors would use, such as Brian De Palma in *Carrie* (1976).

Weber made other films with supernatural themes, like *The Mysterious Mrs. Musslewhite* (1917),[34] based on a short story by Thomas Edgelow[35] about fortune tellers and psychic predictions.[36] Her short *A Cigarette—That's All* (1915) features a pair of magical glasses delivered by a Hindu priest to an ordinary man, allowing him to see everything, including the sources of his unhappiness.[37] Kingsley reported that star J. Warren Kerrigan quit while filming Lois Weber's *The Mysterious Mrs. Musselwhite* when his contract with Universal expired. They hadn't agreed on a new contract because Kerrigan wanted more money than they offered. According to *Variety*, Universal sued Kerrigan for $8,000 for breach of verbal agreement, but they never reported on the outcome. The suit was probably dropped.[38] The film survives in the Library of Congress, albeit incomplete. Reels one and two survive. Reels three, four, and five are lost.[39]

According to the Internet Movie Database and Wikipedia, Weber's lost mystery film *The Eye of God* was released in 1913 or 1916. It starred Tyrone Power, Sr. Weber was also the co-writer of the first feature film adaptation of Edgar Rice Burroughs' adventure story *Tarzan of the Apes* (1918). Weber stopped directing in the 1930s and died in obscurity in 1939, penniless at fifty-eight, leaving Dorothy Arzner as the only working female director in the United States. Arzner continued to direct mostly romantic comedies until the early 1940s when her career fizzled out.

Ida May Park, a prolific Hollywood screenwriter considered one of the Universal Women,[40] began directing her scenarios in 1917.[41] Contemporary news articles explain that her husband, Joseph De Grasse, had been unable to complete a film starring the actress Dorothy Phillips. Hence, the production company hired Park as his replacement. Park happened to be experienced with assisting in her husband's films already.[42] After Lois Weber left Universal to head her own production company, Weber Productions, Universal promoted Park to the director for their Bluebird Photoplays brand to keep a female presence. Weber's popularity undoubtedly made Universal believe that another woman director's films would be equally profitable.[43]

On May 17, 1917, released by Universal/Bluebird Photoplays, Park's five-reel feature-length thriller *Flashlight* starred horror favorite Lon Chaney in dual roles as Henry Norton and Porter Brixton. The film also starred Dorothy Phillips (as Delice Brixton), William Stowell (Jack Lane), Alfred Allen (John Peterson), George Berrell (Barclay), Evelyn Selbie (Mrs. Barclay), Clyde Benson (Deputy), Orin C. Jackson (Howard), and Marc Fenton (Judge). Park wrote the screenplay from a story by Albert M. Treynor. The film's original title was *The Flashlight Girl*, but it was changed before the theatrical release. An official synopsis has been pieced together by film historian and Lon Chaney expert Jon Mirsalis based on trade publications and copyright filings: the lead character, Jack Lane, is a photographer camping in the mountains who has a rigged camera flash set up to take a photograph when an intruder comes near his camp. The developed photo shows a girl walking around with a rifle in the middle of the night. Also, that night, a man named Porter Brixton was murdered in his cabin. Jack is the main suspect. At his trial, the identity of the girl and several twists, as well as the real murderer, are revealed.[44]

Motography praised *Flashlight* for its locations in California's Sierra Nevada mountains, beautiful setting, and "flavor of adventure and mystery."[45] The film seems to have been generally well-received by critics and audiences as an intriguing mystery using still photography flash to add a dramatic flair to the darkness of the woods in which it was set. One Mrs. M. M. McFadden, when asked by a reporter outside the Lincoln Theater, presumably where she had just watched the film, said it was "splendid entertainment, beautiful scenery, and an altogether interesting picture. Patrons were well pleased." Unfortunately, the film is lost, and no footage survives.

When describing her career trajectory from writer to director to *Photoplay* magazine, Park told her changing attitude towards whether 'director' was an appropriate job for a woman:

> It was because directing seemed so utterly unsuitable for a woman that I refused the first company offered me. I don't know why I looked at it that way, either. A woman can bring to this work splendid enthusiasm and imagination; a natural love of detail

> and an intuitive knowledge of character. All of these are supposed to be feminine traits, and yet they are all necessary to the successful director.[46]

By 1920, Park's career as a director was over. Ironically, that same year, she wrote about film directing as a viable and open career for women in Hollywood in an article entitled "Careers for Women" (1920).[47]

Poster for Ida May Park's mystery/thriller *The Flashlight* (1917).

Mexican filmmaker Mimi Derba was the first woman director in Mexico. Her 1917 feature film *La Tigresa* (*The Tigress*), co-directed with Enrique Rosas, is a silent thriller about a young woman, Eva, who falls in love with a working man named Bruno. Eva decides to be more prosperous, leaving Bruno for a millionaire. Bruno goes insane and is committed to an asylum, where he has nightmares of a tiger with Eva's face attacking and murdering him. *La Tigresa* is a lost film, with only one small fragment of about thirty seconds surviving and preserved, which tells us little about the characters or the plot; it's a scene of a party with guests dancing. *La Tigresa* was written by Maria Teresa Farias de Issasi and starred Salvador Arnaldo, Manuel Arvide, and Juan Barba.

At times also known as Harriet Mildred Jeffries, Mrs. Jack Shannon, and "The Master Pen," Grace Cunard (born in 1893) was an immensely popular actress and screenwriter in early silent Hollywood. Paired as an actress and writer with director Francis Ford (the brother of director John Ford) at Universal, she was able to co-direct with him on five different projects between 1913 and 1917. Cunard and Ford were a famous team in the 1910s, co-starring in and co-directing many of their collaborations. In 1915, Cunard was interviewed in *Motion Picture* magazine by writer Richard Willis and said of her desire to direct,

> As to the directing, I have done a good deal of it and often put on a photoplay while Mr. Ford is cutting and assembling a picture. I believe that I best like it in the way I do it—that is occasionally. I hardly believe I would take it as a steady diet. Later on, when I feel I am too old to take leads, I guess I will direct entirely, because I will never give up motion pictures—I am too wrapped up in them.[48]

The same article notes that the films she has written, in which she always stars, "embrace mystery stories, and both Miss Cunard and Francis Ford are particularly fond of tales of mystery."[49]

Only two images remain of Lottie Lyell's lost mystery/thriller *Blue Mountains Mystery* (1921).

Cunard directed the action/adventure silent serial, *The Purple Mask*. The series premiered in theaters in December 1916 and ran for sixteen episodes. Unfortunately, of the thirty-three reels, episodes one ("The Vanished Jewels"), three ("The Capture"), six ("The Silent Feud"), nine ("A Strange Discovery"), ten ("House of Mystery"), and fifteen ("Floating Signal"), all of which Cunard co-directed, are lost. Indeed, all the films Cunard co-directed have been lost except for the crime thriller *Unmasked* (1917) and the western *A Daughter of the Law* (1921).[50]

Fun sleight of hand, with a bit of dashing *Arsene Lupin*-style mystery, *Unmasked* is a fun, romantic take on the crime thriller popular in the 1910s, in novels and on screen. Two notable moments: The opening scene when The Man and The Woman meet — as the camera pulls out from a woman's neck adorned with a pearl necklace, it slowly reveals the hands, and then masked faces, of both thieves. Another is when Cunard is caught breaking into The Man's house for the first time, and he aims a gun at her. It's not particularly innovative, but it is a sophisticated story with a fast pace that could be called the culmination of the 'Gentleman Thief' genre. Cunard and Ford made *Unmasked* together as co-directors, and in 2014 it was selected by the United States National Film Preservation Board for the National Film Registry. Cunard also directed the short crime thriller *The Black Masks* (1913), the murder mystery *The Mysterious Leopard Lady* (1914), and its sequel *Lady Raffles Returns* (1916).

Like *Unmasked*, writer/director Julia Crawford Ivers' silent crime thriller *The Majesty of the Law* (1915) is about theft. Ivers' take on crime is less romanticized. William Desmond plays Jackson Kent, the son of a judge, who assumes the blame for a diamond theft even though he is innocent. The United States Library of Congress has a 35mm print of *The Majesty of the Law,* and the film has been restored and released on Blu-ray.

Flames of Wrath (1923) by Maria P. Williams is a crime drama about murder, theft, jail, and courtroom trials. As an African American woman and a filmmaker, Williams is, like Eloyce King Patrick Gist, an essential part of early American film history overlooked by mainstream studies. As with many other women filmmakers of her time, the word "director" wasn't always used to describe her work; she is referred to as a "producer," though her duties were definitely in the directing wheelhouse.[51]

Williams plays the role of prosecuting attorney in *The Flames of Wrath*.[52] She and her husband, Jessie L. Williams, made the film and created their production and distribution company, the Western Film Producing Co. and Booking Exchange, to distribute to movie theaters. Williams was a dedicated activist for African American rights and a teacher in Kansas City. In her autobiographical book, *My Work and Public Sentiment* (1916), she details her work as a journalist and feminist and her devotion to charity. In 1932, Williams was found shot dead near her home. Her murder was never solved, and there is very little information about how she died or the investigation.[53] *Flames of Wrath* is considered a lost film.

There were no less than sixteen feature films in Australia directed or produced by women by 1920.[54] As in Europe and the United States, women directors disappeared in Australia after the 1920s. At that time, Australian films, less in demand than Hollywood pictures, became less marketable, and the Australian film industry died between the 1920s and 1950s. Lottie Lyell was an actress who, in the 1910s, teamed up with an actor named Raymond Longford to make their films under the production banner Southern Cross Feature Film Company. Lyell and Longford were two of the most successful silent-era filmmakers in Australia.[55]

In 1921, Lyell co-directed the silent feature *The Blue Mountains Mystery* with Longford. Based on the 1919 novel *The Mount Marunga Mystery* by Harrison Owen and shot entirely in Katoomba, New South Wales, Lyell moved the film's setting from the fictitious Marunga of Owen's story to the very real Blue Mountains. When one journalist wondered why Lyell was directing and not acting in the film, Lyell replied, "I love the acting, but I was too interested in the directing work to get in front of the cameras myself."[56] Many scenes were shot at the Blue Mountains' Carrington Hotel; some production photos show the sweeping ballroom and large rooms lit and art directed by the film crew. The rest was shot in studios in Sydney later. The author of the original novel upon which the screenplay was based, Harrison Owen, attended a private screening before its release. He didn't seem to care for the cinematography or the action. The film needed to be re-edited and re-subtitled in the United States before being screened in front of Australian and International audiences, which annoyed Owen.[57] Considered a lost film, *The Blue Mountains Mystery* is the story of Henry Tracey, a murdered businessman. The usual suspects include his wife, his ward Pauline, her fiancé Hector, and Hector's rival Richard Maxim. After accusations and finger-pointing, Henry Tracey is alive, a kidnapping victim, while the dead man is one Stephen Rodder. The latter happens to look almost precisely like Henry Tracey. Lyell died of tuberculosis at age thirty-five; her gravestone says she was a "Photo Play Artiste."[58]

Germaine Dulac was born at the end of the nineteenth century to a wealthy family and was thrust into the Parisian world of art and social and political activism of the early 1900s. As an adult, Dulac embarked on a career in writing, journalism, photography, and film (both narrative and surrealist) that laid the foundation for European women directors

Disorienting camera angles skew our dimension in Germaine Dulac's *The Seashell and the Clergyman* (1928).

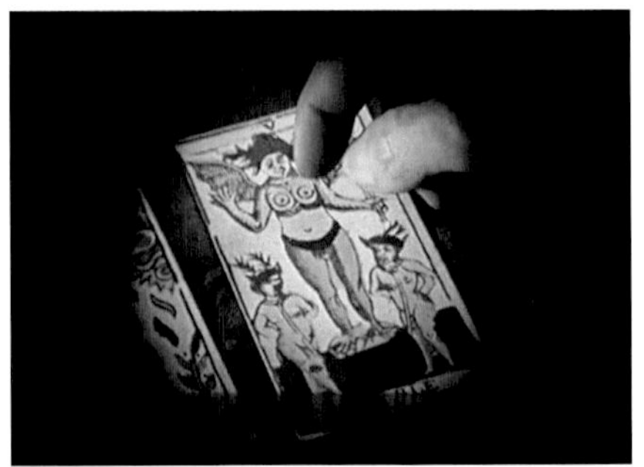
Ominous signs from the Tarot cards in *Le diable dans la ville* (1925), directed by Germaine Dulac.

to be respected and embraced as part of a primarily male artistic movement. There's a marvelous biography of Dulac by Professor Tami Williams titled *Germaine Dulac: A Cinema of Sensations* (part of the Women and Film History International series) that explores Dulac's entire body of work in all mediums,[59] but we will concentrate the 1925 period thriller *Le diable dans la ville,* AKA *The Devil in the City,* which contains dark imagery and narrative experimentation that would heavily influence the work of later filmmakers such as Alfred Hitchcock and Maya Deren.

In the fourteenth century, in the French town of Pimprelune, there was a grey tower abandoned and crumbling. Infested with rats and other crawling creatures, the only person there is L'illuminé (The Enlightened), a hermit who can make medicines and tell the future. Blanche (Jacqueline Blanc) and Rose (Michelle Clairfont) are the two beautiful wards of the nobleman and archivist Bonifacius (Albert Mayer), who is also a superstitious tarot card reader. A stranger in town, Marc Herner (Léon Mathot), purchases the tower and moves in. He is a nobleman and an alchemist, and when he sees the beautiful Blanche, he immediately falls in love with her. L'illuminé must vacate the tower, and he objects strongly, but the mayor and town guards drive him out. As an act of revenge, L'illuminé prophesies that Marc Herner is the Devil Himself and that great evil will befall the town if he does not leave the Grey Tower.

A narrative successor to *The Cabinet of Doctor Caligari* (1920), *Le diable dans la ville* takes the unreliable narrative further than its expressionist predecessor. Carefully questioning traditional film narratives by making the audience unsure which version of the story to believe, Dulac plays with the inconsistency of human memory and experience, hinting that such accounts, especially those heavily infused with emotion, are not always to be trusted as fact. Dulac believed that film should show the reality of life rather than artificial sound stages. She preferred to set her films in actual outdoor settings, so *Le diable dans la ville* features a naturalistic atmosphere wherever possible.[60]

Dulac creates a beautiful, Gothic, medieval setting, much like in Blaché's *The Pit and the Pendulum*, though less stylized and more reliant on shadows and landscapes to create a feeling of moody, romantic places. Some genuinely striking visuals weave throughout the film, especially during the scenes of 'madness.' The breaking angel statue, the scenes at

The only existing image from Cleo de Verberena's thriller film *O Mistério do Dominó Preto* (1931).

Leni Riefenstahl did all of her own stunt work as Junta leaping across crevasses on real mountaintops in *The Blue Light*.

the ballroom dance, the black-cloaked 'phantoms,' and the shadowy, intimate interactions between characters are eerie and intricate. The Grey Tower is one of the first images in the film, and the dilapidated, crumbling tower with its rats is something—well, something out of a horror film. A 35mm print of *Le diable dans la ville* is preserved by the Cinémathèque Française and used worldwide for retrospective screenings of Dulac's work.

Cleo de Verberena is Brazil's first woman director. Her first (and only) film as director is the mystery/thriller *O Mistério do Dominó Preto,* AKA *The Mystery of the Black Domino* (1931).[61] The film is lost, but recently the short story upon which it is based has been discovered, and comparisons between that story and press clippings from the time about the film allow for a basic understanding of what the film was like.

The 'Domino' in *O Mistério do Dominó Preto* refers to a long black costume of the Italian Commedia dell'arte tradition that includes gloves, a mask, and a long cloak, making the wearer completely unrecognizable. The film's plot differs from that of the short story in many ways, de Verberena having made it less conservative, a bit racier, and a bit more fun. The story centers on the murder of a married woman named Cleo, played by de Verberena, who dressed in a black Domino costume during the carnival in São Paulo. On her way to see her lover, Cleo is poisoned by someone pretending to be him, also dressed as a Domino. Although killed early, Cleo appears alive throughout the film through flashbacks, which set up her relationships with various characters in the story, while an ex-lover leads the investigation into her murder.[62]

Murder, poison, mystery, detectives, several lovers, and a murderer on the loose are a recipe for a good time. Still, in 1931, American films were far more popular than Brazilian films in Brazil, so after the film magazines' big hype, the discussion of the movie ended. *O Mistério do Dominó Preto* screened in five theaters in São Paulo but then disappeared. It was a significant financial loss for de Verberena and her husband, and he passed away from stress at the age of thirty-one shortly after. De Verberena never directed another film.

Leni Riefenstahl is more famously known as the Nazi propagandist who made *Triumph of the Will* (1935). With an eye for the camera, Riefenstahl's work is renowned for its beauty, but few people recognize how much she could practice this delicate art with her narrative features, which she stopped making after the Nazis rose to power in Germany in 1933. History has disparaged Riefenstahl for her role as a Nazi collaborator and propagandist. In the 1930s, she was appropriated by the Nazi party to make propaganda films. She was treated well, she was able to make films, which she loved, and it was the only way she could have been able to continue in the film industry without leaving the country for the United States, which was not friendly to women who wanted to direct feature-length narrative films. Working for the Nazi party destroyed any other film career she could have had.

Das Blaue Licht (1932) is a fairy tale, a mystery, and a tragedy. It's also a 'mountain film,' a genre that was quite popular in the 1920s and 1930s in Germany. Characters spend time in the wild natural world of mountains, surviving and sometimes experiencing an existential reformation or gaining esoteric wisdom. Set in turn-of-the-twentieth-century Italy, in a remote mountain village far from the big cities where a beautiful young woman named Junta lives, alone and among the wildness of the mountains surrounding the town. Junta (played by Riefenstahl) is harassed by the local populace, who has decided she is a witch—she can ramble along the cliffs and mountains like a mountain goat while full-grown men fall to their deaths trying to follow the same paths. Her only solace is a secluded mountain cave filled with thousands of glittering crystals. The mountain cave is illuminated on full moon nights and shines with a breathtaking blue light reflected through the crystals. The light fascinates the townsfolk, and young men feel compelled to climb the mountain to find the source of this mysterious blue light. The treacherous mountain climbing usually results in these men falling to their deaths before discovering the secret of the crystal cave. Junta is blamed for these deaths and the blue light too.

Rather than follow the lead of the German expressionist filmmakers of the time, such as Fritz Lang, Riefenstahl's *Das Blaue Licht* is a purely romantic view of the world, as in the naturalistic, romantic movement from the previous century that depicted nature as a brooding, dominant character in an emotional manner. Riefenstahl's brilliant landscape shots are punctuated with great shadows and silhouettes. The crystal cave, the mountain, the characters, and the moon are framed poetically and deliberately with stunning camera work. Junta is alternately in shadow and light, pictured against the wild backdrop of the waterfalls and rocks. Her loose shirt and skirt cling to her body in daylight on the hillside. Everything roars with naturalism. The narrative isn't incredibly strong, nor is the love story, but the visuals are an awesome experience.

Everything in *Das Blaue Licht* is Riefenstahl's vision. Filming on location in the mountains, Riefenstahl put herself and her crew in dangerous situations to get the perfect shots she wanted. Riefenstahl performed all her stunts in the film, including numerous jumps across rocks and waterfalls. Though it was her first film as director, she co-wrote the script and produced it. Unlike anything else she ever made, this film alone gives us an accurate idea of what a Riefenstahl film would be like without the fascist influence of the Nazi propaganda wing dictating the style and substance of her art. Though it is set in Italy, *Das Blaue Licht* embodies the nostalgia that collective German culture was developing in the early twentieth century for Germanic folklore, mythology, and a medieval and mystical past that transcended the borders of the Weimar Republic to which they were confined after World War I.

Dorothy Davenport was a silent movie actress in the 1910s from an established theater family. Her directing career began when her husband, Wallace Reid, died of a morphine overdose in 1923, prompting her to direct a whirlwind of social message films under the name Mrs. Wallace Reid (extolling the evils of drug use while also capitalizing on her husband's death). Compared by film scholars with Lois Weber, the two are often called "sensational moralists" who doled out large doses of melodrama in their social message movies.[63] However, as soon as the silent era was over, Davenport began directing talking pictures and abandoned her social crusade in favor of exploitation and suspense. For Poverty Row producer Willis Kent Productions, Davenport directed ultra-low-budget movies that were not bound by the Production Code of the day since they were not distributed by The Motion Pictures Producers and Distributors of America.[64]

Poster for Dorothy Davenport's thriller *A Woman Condemned* (1934).

In 1934, Davenport directed two films; the exploitation flick *The Road to Ruin* and the mystery/thriller *The Woman Condemned*. *The Road to Ruin* features bad-girl exploitation behavior such as booze, drugs, nudity, and even strip poker, but it is *The Woman Condemned* (1934) that ventures into the arena of thrilling violence.

The Woman Condemned stars Lola Lane as Jane Merrick, a radio star who takes a quick vacation because she is blackmailed by a creepy man with an accent who makes sure to tell her, "Remember—I do not accept checks" when asking for his next payment. Merrick's concerned boyfriend hires intrepid girl detective Barbara Hammond (Claudia Dell). When she witnesses Merrick's murder, she can't explain why she was secreted behind a curtain in the same room where Merrick was killed, or her cover as an intrepid girl detective will be blown. Next is a convoluted display of plucky reporters, an unsolved murder, more intrepid girl detective sleuthing, and, unfortunately, some painfully forced romantic comedy, all eventually culminating with a deranged criminal doctor at his hospital of crime at gunpoint.

The available film prints of *The Woman Condemned* are terrible at best, with low-quality sounds and sad scratches due to age and mishandling, but the film has been digitally preserved and is in the public domain. Some unexciting car chases around New York City and a gaggle of slang-speaking jazz-era hipsters can't save the film from its intensely low budget, though the twisted ending does lend some charm. Most notable is the murder scene with Dell hidden behind a curtain and Lane mugging her gunshot death in a mirror rather than facing the camera. *The Woman Condemned* was Davenport's

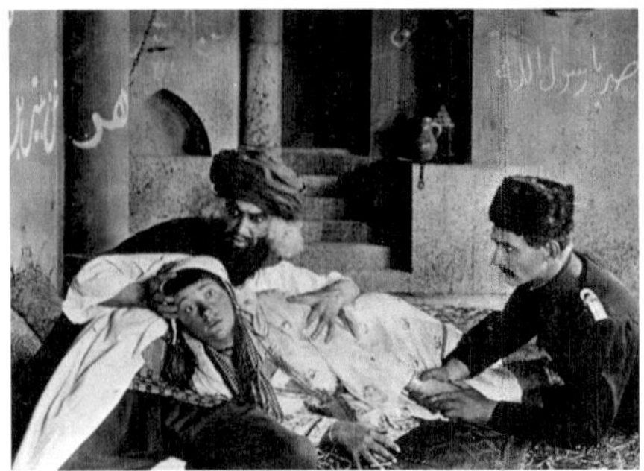

A still image from Marie Louise Droop's lost thriller/adventure film *Die Teufelsanbeter* (1921).

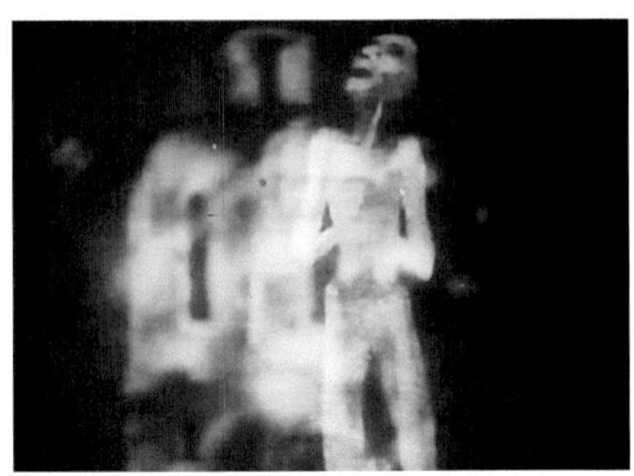

A grotesque figure in *A Night on Bald Mountain* (1934), co-directed by Claire Parker.

last film as director, though she did enjoy a career as a producer and writer well into the 1950s, particularly in television.

German director Marie Louise Droop was mainly known for screenwriting in the silent teens and twenties, penning dozens of romantic thrillers and adventure tales. *Die Teufelsanbeter,* AKA *The Devil Worshippers* (1920), was Droop's directorial debut and also featured a then-unknown Bela Lugosi.

The Devil Worshippers is a feature-length adventure/thriller involving murder, revenge, evil satanic cults, and morbid punishments. The film tells of Kara Ben Nemsi (played by Carl de Vogt), a brave adventurer, his faithful companion, Hadschi Halef Omar (Meinhart Maur), and their encounter with The Jesidi, or Devil worshippers: a secret sect rumored to worship Satan in the form of an angelic peacock that commits hideous crimes, including human sacrifice, at the shrine of Sheik Adi. Bela Lugosi appears as Pir Kamek, who is forced to carry the dead body of his granddaughter in a coffin on his back throughout a city as punishment for his part in a massacre.

The Devil Worshippers features beautiful young women tortured in prisons, people sacrificed on ritual altars, corrupt Sheiks, necrophilia, and people buried to their necks in the sand to be devoured by wild animals.[65] No existing film copies exist; however, an extensive plot outline and several still images featuring Bela Lugosi have been recovered.

That same year Droop co-directed with E. Mouhssin-Bey a film version of *Das Fest der schwarzen Tulpe* (*The Festival of the Black Tulip*) by Alexandre Dumas. This shortest Dumas novel is a brutally violent love story and detective thriller set in 1672. The film lacked action because the lead character spends much of his time in prison in this faithful adaptation. The resulting deficient box office draw may have been the cause of Droop's production company's bankruptcy later that year.[66]

Animation is one of the most expressive and dynamic art technologies and bridges the gap between art and consumable media. In the 1920s, it wasn't just Walt Disney experimenting with innovative animation techniques; many women artists found animation to be the perfect conduit for their non-commercial expressions. Animation also included experimentation with narrative and story, allowing artists to take extreme liberties with surreal and experimental film aspirations.

Claire Parker was a young American woman living in Paris in the early 1930s. From a wealthy, prominent Boston family, she sought creative outlets in the city of lights, love, and artists. Finding the latter two in a man named Alexandre Alexeieff, Parker became involved in an innovative film technique known as pinscreen animation. Pinscreen was a movable engraving: a screen is filled with moveable pins and is lit so that the pins all cast a shadow, creating a chiaroscuro effect of volume and depth. When an object is placed on the pins, they take the shape of that object (or can be manipulated to create images and scenes by hand). A time-consuming process (and ultimately very unpopular among animators), the pinscreen technique was the method of choice for the six short films Alexeieff and Parker made over their fifty years of collaboration.

Their first pinscreen film, made in 1933, was *A Night on Bald Mountain* (1934): an animated interpretation of the musical piece by nineteenth-century Russian composer Modest Mussorgsky. Mussorgsky originally envisioned the piece as a lyrical poem describing a witches' Sabbath and their cavorting with Satan on St. John's Night. In 1940, Walt Disney would also pay homage to the composition with his own *A Night on Bald Mountain* segment in Disney's *Fantasia* feature animated film. Still, Parker and Alexeieff's original piece was far darker in imagery and tone than Disney's version.[67] Painstaking to make, *A Night on Bald Mountain* was synchronized to a phonographic recording of Mussorgsky's music to an accuracy of a twenty-fourth of a second.[68]

A Night on Bald Mountain took eighteen costly months to complete. It made absolutely no money, as it was an art film with no distribution possibilities[69] despite being hailed as a "masterly adaptation" by film critics:

> When the spectral beings arranged in a circle hold hands then raise and drop their arms, or the moment when the music surges like a rocket and then falls like rain, what is achieved is a reinforcement of musical emotion of extremely rare quality ... This film marks a day to remember.[70] (*Le Temps*)

> There are hags and demons on horseback, there are witches' Sabbaths that combine musicians and birds, horses and fireworks, landscapes and calm one moment and stormy the next, in one oneiric vision.[71] (*Regards*)

> Every art house cinema should show this film. It is the most brilliant, astonishing short that you will come across.[72] (*Quarterly*)

As animators, Parker and Alexeieff were neither considered real artists nor real filmmakers by the artistic community and were an anomaly. Unable to pay the bills doing pet projects like *A Night on Bald Mountain* (despite Parker's wealthy Boston family's contributions), they went to work in graphic design for advertising. They would use the pinscreen technique only a few more times.[73]

Parker often remarked that Alexeieff was the "true genius" behind the technique and the Russian folkloric imagery of witches and goblins. Still, his working relationship with Claire Parker is described as "happy, loving, creative and, above all else, inextricably linked."[74] Parker and her Boston wealth did finance the artistic endeavors and helped foster Alexeieff's creative genius. Still, witnesses to their filmmaking process saw her executing and rejecting many of his ideas, and they witnessed Alexeieff expanding on creative suggestions she had imagined. Parker herself was the one under whose name the patent for the pinscreen apparatus was filed and granted on October 3, 1935.

Although she worked equally as a co-creator of the machine and the creative results, she was not credited with Alexeieff's later work.[75] However, Claire Parker's biographer Cecile Starr points out that in articles written by Parker, she states that they made the illustrations and the animated films as a team:

Claire's role in all five of their pinboard productions included all the still and motion picture camera work, timing of the movements, soundtrack analysis, and synchronization, and, of course, drawing the negative side of the images in tune with Alexeieff's sensitivity.[76]

It wasn't until the 1980s, when Cecile Starr redistributed *A Night on Bald Mountain* in art house theaters and university classrooms, that the talent of Parker and Alexeieff truly began to be appreciated by the entertainment industry at large.[77]

American artist Mary Ellen Bute made short, experimental films from 1934 to 1954 and was one of the first abstract female filmmakers in the world. Her movies never involved straightforward narratives but focused on the kinetic and dynamic movement of objects and music. Bute used mirrors, three-dimensional objects, and even oscilloscopes in her work, but she also worked in animation and usually set her films to classical music pieces. As a young art student in Philadelphia, Bute was struck by the blossoming abstract art movement in museums:

> [So] when I went to Philadelphia, I was ... deeply impressed by the wonderful Picassos, the African art, the [Paul] Klees, the Braques, the Kandinskys ... He [Kandinsky] used abstract, nonobjective elements so you could experience a canvas the way you experience a musical composition ... Well, I thought it was terrific ... [but] these things should be unwound in time continuity. It was a dance. That became my [objective] ...[78]

Spook Sport (1939) was Bute's experimental animated short with horror and Halloween imagery. In color and only eight minutes in length, it screened as an opener to major motion pictures in mainstream theaters in the United States. Not exactly a horror film, *Spook Sport* was made with hand-drawn animation cells directly on the filmstrip. Set to the music of *Danse Macabre* by Saint-Saëns, it is very abstract, with 'ghosts' and 'bats' represented by figures that look nothing like ghosts or bats moving dynamically to the music.

Not exactly a horror filmmaker, Bute nevertheless was part of an explosive experimental movement in which women directors found great acceptance and dynamic support from the artistic community. Like the work of Lotte Reininger, Claire Parker, and Maya Deren, the lines between emotion and imagery in Bute's short *Spook Sport* blur. Bute enjoyed pretentiously describing the art of the abstract film with words like "Abstronics" (a combination of abstract and electronic)[79] and "The Absolute Film" (light, form, and sound are in dynamic balance with kinetic space, devoid of association with religion,

MUSIC MADE VISIBLE IN WEIRD MOVIE

FUTURISTIC patterns of light and shadow are projected upon a movie screen to accompany the music of Wagner's "Song to the Evening Star," in a unique sound film recently completed for exhibition in a New York theater. Marching rhymically across the audience's field of view, the odd designs were produced by trick photography, with the aid of bracelets, toy balls, silks, and crushed tissue ribbons.

Ellen Bute, director, and Ted Nemeth, photographer, who made a movie of a song. Left, a "scene" from the film

Bute, co-director of *Spook Sport* (1939), profiled in the November 1936 issue of *Popular Science*.

ethics, literature, or, basically, meaning of any kind).[80] What she essentially means by all this is that her films are not about any cohesive story but are meant to be experienced as music, sound, and movement only.

In a contemporary article about *Spook Sport*, film authority Cecile Starr made sure to mention that the person behind the film was a woman. Describing Bute as a wife and mother and referring to the studio as Bute's husband's, it is apparent Starr wanted to feminize Bute to audiences to make her more likable as an artist:

> When wifely and motherly duties permitted, she concentrated on work (in her husband's commercial animation studio) and has come up with an impressive number of items. This year her *Spook Sport* and *Color Rhapsodie* were shown at the Music Hall, while a third film, *Polka Grap*, won mention at the Venice Film Festival. Granted that the familiar acceptability of the music (Liszt, Grieg, etc.) is a good basis for audience and theatre approval, still this is no minor triumph for Miss Bute, her work, and the experimentalists who follow hopefully.[81]

Starr would be a lifelong supporter of Bute, even distributing her films through the Women's Independent Film Exchange organization. Of Bute as a person, Starr said:

> She was a character ... She was about five feet tall and she wore about four-inch high-heel shoes and had a ton of energy and a southern accent from Texas that she never lost. It was one of her trademarks. I was brought up in Louisiana and lost my accent about three days after I moved to New York. So I was amazed. People didn't know whether to take her seriously or not.[82]

Bute's section would be much longer in a book about experimental film or animation. However, her section in a book about women horror directors is necessarily short. Norman McLaren, a Canadian/U.K. animator, painted the animation cels and did all of the art for *Spook Sport*. Bute is credited as the director, but the consensus among animation experts seems to be that McLaren was directly responsible for all of his direction, though perhaps his collaboration with Bute meant she guided the process somewhat.[83] Bute made one largely unknown feature-length film, *Passages from Finnegans Wake*, which won an award at the 1965 Cannes Film Festival. She passed away in New York City at seventy-six in 1983.

Peter Foldes was a prolific British animator and artist, originally from Hungary, who made incredibly influential surreal and experimental animated films with his wife, Joan Foldes. One of these films, *A Short Vision* (1956), had a significant impact on audiences when it aired on May 27, 1956, to television watchers' horror, awe, and confusion across the United States. For various reasons, Ed Sullivan had watched the film and agreed to screen it on his show.[84]

Airing at the height of the Cold War and fear of atomic war, *A Short Vision* was both a cautionary tale about the horrors of the nuclear holocaust and a straightforward story that cuts to the core with no politics in mind.

A narrator tells the story: an atomic bomb appears over a city and mountains in the night sky—a swift and noiseless bomb noticed by no one. Animals like an owl, a deer, and a rat notice it. Humans in their beds asleep don't notice it, but the leaders of the people, and the wise men, see it, but it's "too late." The bomb explodes in a magnificent eruption of orange and yellows, and the face of the leader melts into bone and ash in an incredibly gruesome manner. The animals' faces dissolve the same way, melting and turning into skeletal remains in seconds. The mountains are gone, and the only thing left is a small flame in a sea of complete darkness, but even that, too, eventually goes out, and there is just darkness.

The accompanying score is a haunting and dramatic piece reminiscent of sirens and screams. The artwork is rudimentary, the animals animated as cutouts, and the cityscape is a simple background drawing that barely alters until the bomb falls. The simplicity of the pictures in this six-minute animation makes it as creepy as it is: it's innocent and childlike. It's the way a child would describe the scenes and the story. The narrator tells us what happened almost as if they were a parent reading a fairy tale to children.

To say that this animated horror frightened the children is an understatement. One child's hair allegedly turned white when they watched it alone in their living room.[85] The general attitude in the art world was that *A Short Vision* had created the most significant reaction to media since Orson Welles' 1938 *War of the Worlds* radio broadcast.[86]

Funded by the British Film Institute's Experimental Film Fund, *A Short Vision* was a joint venture between Peter and Joan Foldes. *A Short Vision* was the second film Peter and Joan worked on and the last. Joan Foldes was interviewed about *A Short Vision* in an online article about the short film and its legacy. She said:

> The poem [theme/story] that runs through *A Short Vision* was Peter's. He came up to me on the ship that was bringing us back from Australia in October 1954. He asked me what I thought of it. I said we HAD to do it. He was the creative artist; otherwise, it was the same as for *Animated Genesis*. I helped in setting up the stand, deciding on some of the figures, the timing of the animation lighting, and the easier part of the animation.[87]

By 1968, Peter Foldes had moved to Paris, France, where he made animated surrealist films. But Joan Foldes disappeared from recorded history at this time. In an article about Peter Foldes' animation, one film writer laments that there isn't enough information about Peter Foldes, let alone Joan. "Joan Foldes is even more buried. I wonder what she's done."[88] *A Short Vision* has been digitized from its original 35mm film stock and made publicly available online through the British Film Institute.

Experimental film in the 1920s paved the way for experimental artists through the present. 'Experimental' film rejects mainstream narrative and commercial film practices and often draws on other art forms, such as poetry or dance. Avant-garde, expressionist art, and surrealism heavily influenced the movement. In the late 1920s, Germaine Dulac experimented with surrealism while pursuing a more mainstream career with films like *Le diable dans la ville*. Before *Le diable dans la ville*, Dulac directed the shorts *The Cigarette* (1919) and *The Smiling Madame Beudet* (1923). Both are about unhappily married couples and plots to kill spouses and feature a level of violence that could qualify them for discussion.

However, her truly unsettling, horrific work comes with her surrealist explorations in the *Eraserhead* (1977) of early twentieth-century cinema: the forty-minute collaboration between Dulac and Antonin Artaud, *The Seashell and the Clergyman* (1927) was the first actual surrealist film ever made. It premiered with other short films at the Studio des Ursulines in Paris, France, on February 9, 1928. The film's legacy includes causing a riot when it screened and causing breaks between Artaud and Dulac as collaborators and Artaud from the entire surrealist movement in Paris. Artaud was notoriously unstable and was effectively kicked out of the movement by his colleagues for his irrational behavior and actions.

The riot that ensued at the first screening was organized by an angry Artaud, with other surrealists there to support him. The collaborators had exchanged a series of communications about how the film should be. Still, ultimately Artaud hated it for deviating too strongly from his original screenplay and rejected the final cut. Dulac's more musical, rhythmic experiential vision was counter to Artaud's fierce surrealist bombardment of imagery, and they disagreed over the result. In any case, when the screening began, he incited verbal abuse towards the film while others, taking offense, defended it.[89]

Dulac utilizes numerous special effects and camera transitions and plays with light and shadow, and movement in such a way in this film that all sense of time and space essentially vanish. There is a vague storyline, seemingly about a tortured clergyman (Alex Allin) obsessed with a married woman (Genica Athanasiou), but his torment is shown rather than explained through the narrative as we experience his inner turmoil—a prominent artistic function of the surrealist movement. In the first moments of the film, Dulac uses slow motion to differentiate the images of the clergyman and the woman's husband, a general (Lucien Bataille); the general moves slowly while the priest repetitively and swiftly repeats his task of pouring out liquid from a large seashell into glass containers. The priest's anger and fear grip him, shown by the superimposition of images and movement upon the character, reflections, and changing light.

With horror imagery neatly unfolding, the film continues a violent turn. Like Nosferatu lurking in the shadows, with eyes that penetrate and pierce the darkness, the priest's hands, claw-like, emerge from behind a pillar, and he strangles the general in cold blood out of jealousy for his wife. The priest will not let go of the general, even when his head splits in half for an uncomfortable moment. As if they were dancing, the priest and the general float lightly above the church's floor, phantom-like. The characters seem trapped in their timelines and spatial areas; they float, rotate, and seem immune to the effects of gravity and physics.

The priest hangs from a rope as the wife makes erotic and vile movements with her tongue. The wife floats in a fog in her white dress in the recurring, dark, haunted hallway, coming finally to a door. The priest walks in reverse through that door and into a room where a glittering, gleaming orb sits on a pedestal. He walks again down seemingly maze-like hallways while holding a key, trying to find the right door for the key to unlock. He's trapped; the doors lead nowhere, and the key unlocks nothing but more confusion. He walks with purpose but is aimless in spirit.

Shadows, light, movement, water, and physics-defying spatial relationships define the essence of *The Seashell and the Clergyman*. Dark and deep shadows exist alongside

Bloody eye holes in Joan Foldes' animated film *A Short Vision* (1956).

Deren, wearing thick sunglasses, carries a knife throughout the strange dimensions of *Meshes of the Afternoon*. Image courtesy of Kino Lorber.

and in sharp contrasts to light and motion. More than gloomy, the hallways and endless doors are creepy. Water reflections often appear, providing movement and a source of sunshine in the otherwise dark, sharp, and disorienting world of the priest's psyche. *The Seashell and the Clergyman* was restored and digitized in 2004 by the Filmmuseum in Amsterdam, Netherlands.

I wonder whether the famous surrealist filmmaker Maya Deren was influenced by *The Seashell and the Clergyman*, especially concerning patterns of disorientation and recurring symbolic imagery. She would undoubtedly have been aware of it, probably had seen it, and was likely sufficiently inspired to make her surreal masterpiece *Meshes of the Afternoon* (1943). To this day, the dark, nightmarish imagery of that short black-and-white spectacle still haunts viewers, and it established Deren as an innovator of the surrealist horror film. Though she directed eight other films, one of which was a documentary on Haitian Voodoo called *Divine Horsemen: The Living Gods of Haiti* (1954), *Meshes of the Afternoon* is the film for which she is most famous. Like Claire Parker, Deren was an independent filmmaker that collaborated on projects with her husband(s).[90] Unlike Parker, she was an experimental intellectual more concerned with the process of filmmaking than the final product.

Deren consistently sought abstraction over accessibility in her film projects. Born in Russia in 1917, she fled with her wealthy, intellectual family to the United States, where she began to pursue filmmaking and art shortly after graduate school. Known for favoring 16mm (considered 'amateur' at the time) over 35mm film, she is referred to by film scholars by such lofty titles as "Mother of the Independent Film" and "Goddess of the Experimental Film."[91]

"My films might be called experimental, referring to the use of the medium itself," she wrote:

> In these films, the camera is not an observant, recording eye in the customary fashion. The total medium's full dynamics and expressive potentials are ardently dedicated to creating the most accurate metaphor for the meaning.[92]

Meshes of the Afternoon (1943) is ambitious, silent, jarring, and deeply disturbing, depicting startling violence. Deren designed it to disorient the viewer. It is an experimental film with no logical storyline; it is far from mainstream narrative, a flowing series of images that arouse fear and inspire emotions. The audience is introduced to the protagonist as a shadow against the sunlight, an arm held out or feet detached from an off-screen body, and they experience the film through her. As *Meshes* progresses, she takes on a more fully realized personality: her face is shown, and her expressions and fear focus.

A series of events are repeated, each time in more detail. The woman follows a hooded figure up a winding, sunny driveway. Unable to catch the figure, she finds a small key that grants her access to a nearby house. Once inside, she invariably sees a telephone, a knife, and a record player, and then she ascends the stairs. She often holds, notices, or picks up a white blossom on a long stem. Light curtains swirl in the wind over a bed up the stairs and in the bedroom. The knife, record player, and blossom are also in the bedroom. Back down the stairs, she sits in a comfortable chair to sleep or sees herself sleeping in the chair and glances out the window, where she sees a dark figure hurrying up the drive and herself following it.

The cycle repeatedly begins, becoming darker, more detailed, and more disturbing. It ends with a shocking scene: knives and broken glass are scattered all over the living room floor. The woman is lying in the chair, her neck slashed and bloodied by the mirror shards. Was it suicide? Some delusional paranoid gesture? Or was she murdered, and the ordeal a metaphor for what happened? *Meshes* provides no answers—only more questions—as was intended by its director.

Film students, scholars, and artists often interpret the meaning behind the images and cinematic choices Deren made in *Meshes*; few have ever made a compelling argument. The best person to explain the film is Deren herself. She left extensive notes and synopses (she was an avid and persuasive author, documenting extremely complex and academic philosophies on filmmaking, art, and all of her films) in which she describes her goal with *Meshes*:

> The film is concerned with the inner realities of an individual and with the way the sub-conscious will develop, interpret, and elaborate an apparently simple and casual occurrence into a critical emotional experience. It is culminated by a double-ending in which it would seem that the imagined is achieved, for the protagonist, with such force that it became reality. Using cinematic techniques to achieve dislocations of inanimate objects, unexpected simultaneities, etc., this film establishes a reality which, although somewhat based on dramatic logic, can exist only on film.[93]

To Deren's surprise, audiences found it difficult to understand the film. Lacking a narrative structure and rife with symbolism, many didn't know what to make of the disjointed images and incoherent storyline (much as audiences don't today). "When it was made," she wrote,

> ... there was no anticipation of the general audience and no experience of how the dominant cultural tendency towards personalized psychological interpretation could impede the understanding of the film.[94]

In 1959, sixteen years later, Deren had then-lover/soon-to-be husband Teiji Ito write a musical score for *Meshes*, which had been silent up until then, to make the film a bit easier to understand or at least, to inspire the audience to understand what they were supposed to be feeling at particular moments throughout the film:

> This music, with its dramatic intensity and its archaic austerity (a surprisingly contemporary sound), is not only extraordinarily pertinent to the film but, in its impersonal, mythological character, underscores and illuminates that original intent of the film itself.[95]

A black-cloaked figure with a mirror for a face stalks Maya Deren in her avant garde horror film *Meshes of the Afternoon* (1943). Image courtesy of Kino Lorber.

Deren claws her way up the stairs as the laws of physics don't work in her terrifying dream-state in *Meshes of the Afternoon*. Image courtesy of Kino Lorber.

While not her favorite film, Deren was proud of *Meshes of the Afternoon* as a visual poem and an expressionist film: a clash between her own internal and external worlds, poetry and the world of the physical, the inner realities of the individual.[96]

Meshes is vital as a horror film because, while eschewing the narrative in favor of the symbolic, it allowed Deren to explore some creative camera and visual tricks that make *Meshes* the unique and exotic experience it remains today. Deren enjoyed manipulating space and time with camera trickery. She describes the stairway scene in *Meshes* in which the woman navigates the gravity-shifting, Escheresque stairs to reach the upstairs bedroom:

> The length of a stairway can be enormously extended if three different shots of the person ascending it (filmed from different angles so that it is not apparent that the identical area is being covered each time) are so edited together that the action is continuous and results in an image of enduring labor toward some elevated goal.[97]

Time and space lose all meaning for the character and the audience. The woman finds herself falling; the stairs rotate, and up and down are reversed as she struggles to hold on to the railing. Complete disorientation takes hold. Deren believed this to be one of the most compelling sequences in all of her films, " ... so real that, at times, members of the audience who are particularly susceptible to sea-sickness have had to close their eyes."[98] Likewise, Deren uses slow motion to increase the helplessness and desperation of the girl as she tries to catch the mirror-white-faced version of herself up the drive. Deren referred to this "portability of the camera" as a resource to be exploited in the manipulation of time and space, such as when numerous versions of the girl sit across from one another at the dinner table, or one comes across her sleeping self:[99]

> There is a very, very short sequence in that film—right after the three images of the girl sit around the table and draw the key until it comes up knife—when the girl with the knife rises from the table towards the self which is sleeping in the chair. As the girl

> with the knife rises there is a close-up of her foot as she begins striding. The first step is in sand (with suggestion of sea behind), the second stride (cut in) is in grass, third is on pavement, and the fourth is on the rug, and then the camera cuts up to her head with the knife descending towards the sleeping girl. What I meant when I planned that sequence was that you have to come a long way—from the very beginning of time—to kill yourself, like the first life emerging from the primeval waters. Those four strides, in my intention span all time.[100]

Throughout *Meshes*, Deren was aware of her own "cinematic thinking"[101] and thoroughly planned the uncomfortable feeling from the curtains, wind, light, shadow, and odd, sharp camera angles. Her style is evident in the slow reveal of the woman's face and features.

Meshes of the Afternoon has been cited as an inspiration for everything from David Lynch's *Lost Highway* (1997) to actress/singer Milla Jovovich's mid-1990s music videos, and indeed, it is pretty famous as one of the most disturbing, disorienting, and dedicated examples of twentieth-century avant-garde film. While *Meshes of the Afternoon* was a success (intellectually, if not commercially), Deren never made a film shown in mainstream theaters.

Mordets melodi (1944) is a serial killer-themed thriller directed by Bodil Ipsen, a Danish director with a prolific career in post-World War II Copenhagen. Based on a famous Danish stage play written by Tavs Neiiendam, *Mordets melodi* crosses over from film noir into a disturbing mystery/thriller about a serial killer murdering young women in the world of seedy nightclubs in the dark, rainy streets of Copenhagen. French singer Odette Margot (Gull-Maj Norin) is known for her signature song, "Si Petite," which she sings in the best Copenhagen nightclubs. Her abusive ex-husband Louis Valdini (Angelo Bruun) is also in the city and has a strange power over Odette. The Copenhagen police force investigates a shocking murder. Still, it can't stop the second and third murders from happening, and witnesses claim that the killer was singing Odette's song, which soon became famous throughout the city. Her love interest, Max Stenberg Poul Reichhardt), is there for the grand finale, which takes place at a creepy, abandoned mansion outside the city. From the grotesque and fantastic performance of Bruun to the stormy nights that never end, *Mordets melodi* is an intense story of a psychopath's abusive relationship with his victim and how she barely escapes death after he has vindictively and chillingly stalked her for six years.

Another woman director from Denmark, Alice O'Fredericks, worked with Lau Lauritzen's ASA Films. Originally from Sweden, O'Fredericks began working in the Danish film industry in the 1920s and played the role of a nun in the controversial horror docudrama *Häxan* (1921) by director Benjamin Christensen. But it's her solo-directing credit, *Hr. Petit* (1948) about a serial killer who targets lonely, rich women, first seducing them and then murdering them for their money, which makes her one of the critical women thriller film directors of the first half of the twentieth century. Based on the Danish true crime novel of the same name written by Alice Guldbrandsen, which was based on the murder spree and subsequent trial of French serial killer Henri Desirè Landru (who was nicknamed "Bluebeard of Gambais" by French newspapers), the same story was filmed in the United States and released in 1947, starring Charlie Chaplin as the killer, *Monsieur Verdoux*. That version was a black comedy rather than a chilling story about a calculated series of cold-blooded murders.

Bárbara Virgínia, Portugal's pioneering female director, also held the distinction of being the country's first director in the genre film realm. Her gothic thriller, *Três Dias Sem Deus* (1945), marked a significant cinematic achievement. The film premiered at the prestigious Cinema Ginásio in Lisbon, Portugal, in August 1945, and later graced the inaugural Cannes Film Festival in 1946.[102] Unfortunately, a fire led to the partial loss of the film, leaving only twenty-six minutes without sound. However, the Cinemateca Portuguesa undertook the task of restoring and digitizing this surviving footage.

Inspired by a lost novel by Gentil Marques titled *Mundo Perdido*, the film revolves around Virgínia's character, Lídia, a young countryside schoolteacher. At the age of twenty-two during the film's release, Virgínia co-wrote the script and portrayed Lídia. The narrative unfolds as Lídia, visiting the mansion of local lord Paulo Belforte to address bullying concerns, becomes trapped there overnight due to inclement weather. Subsequently, she discovers from villagers that Belforte is accused of murder and has made a pact with the devil, leaving her cursed as well.

The restored footage captures Lídia's arrival at the foreboding mansion and her unsettling night's stay. The imagery is evocative, with moody, dark, and chilling scenes. Notably, the portrayal of Belforte's deranged wife, Izabel, confined to a creaking wheelchair and scenes of a crying child, Pedro, being carried away by a housekeeper, adds to the eerie atmosphere. The shadowy, imposing mansion and ominous lighting underscore the deliberate intent to create a terrifying sequence within what was likely a disturbing film.[103]

Despite this groundbreaking contribution, Bárbara Virgínia did not pursue further directorial projects. Nevertheless, she retained her popularity as an actress in Portugal.

One more film belongs in this chapter: an incredibly odd and grotesque short film called *La Cravate/Les têtes interverties* (*The Transposed Heads*) (1957), Alejandro Jodorowsky's (*The Holy Mountain*, 1973) first film as director. The twenty-minute color film was co-directed by Saul Gilbert and Ruth Michelly—two filmmakers with no other credits.

An experiment in lighthearted horror, *La Cravate* shows a young man changing his appearance to win the love of a woman. He lives in a world where shops sell human heads, and a person can change their head anytime. The film is entirely mimed and stars a young Jodorowsky. It was filmed over four years in France, and the very loose plot is based on Thomas Mann's novella *The Transposed Heads* (*Die vertauschten Köpfe*) (1940).

Gilbert and Michelly were equally involved in the film as Jodorowsky, though Michelly was not a filmmaker usually—she was a children's book illustrator. Her art career went as far back as 1944. A few of the titles she illustrated include the children's books *Als Sabinchen 'Lotte' war. Ein Bilderbuch für alle Puppenmütter* (1948) written by Juliane Trendelenburg and *Mein liebstes Geschichtenbuch* (1966), written by James Krüss.

Michelly's whimsical and surreal artistry must have contributed to the look and feel of *La Cravate*, a colorful dance of expression and emotion. Even the severed heads are still uniquely human, played by actors, and lend themselves to Jodorowsky's surreal style very well.

La Cravate premiered at Rome's Cinema Auteur Festival in 1957 and won "Best Film." Saul Gilbert, an American, died soon after making the film. Ruth Michelly, his wife, took the only copy of the film print with her when she returned to Germany, and the film remained in her attic until it was rediscovered in 2006.

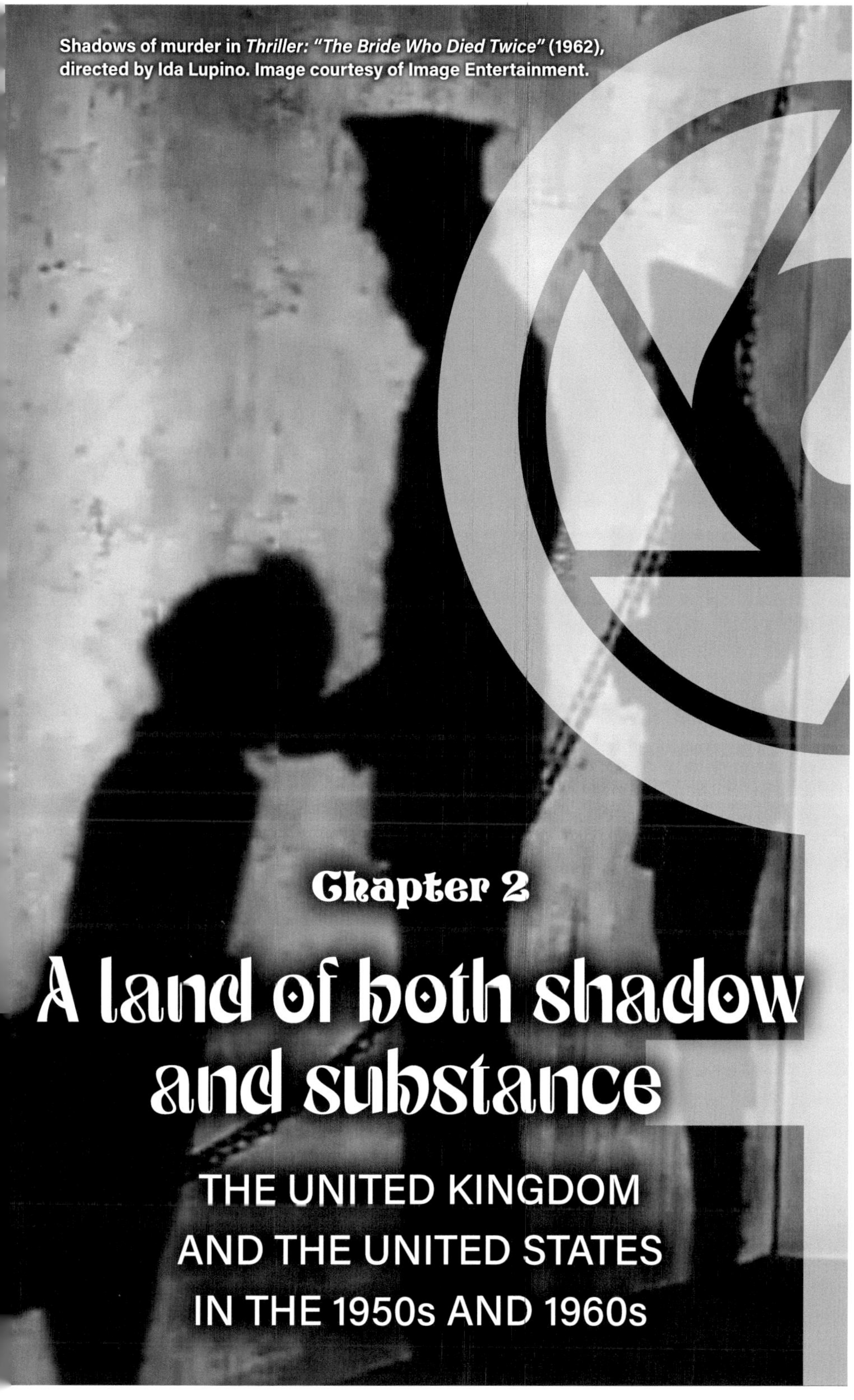

Shadows of murder in *Thriller: "The Bride Who Died Twice"* (1962), directed by Ida Lupino. Image courtesy of Image Entertainment.

Chapter 2

A land of both shadow and substance

THE UNITED KINGDOM AND THE UNITED STATES IN THE 1950s AND 1960s

WOMEN HAD ALL BUT DISAPPEARED as directors by the 1920s. Except for a handful of Hollywood films directed by Dorothy Arzner and several independent filmmakers and animators in Europe, women did not direct films once sound technology came to theaters. The advent of the television series changed that forever.

It wasn't just the popularity of television and the sudden need for numerous skilled directors churning out weekly episodic series at a fast pace that prompted the hiring of women as directors. As mentioned in the previous chapter, several other significant events, socially and legally, made this possible. First, the Supreme Court of the United States ruling on the Hollywood Antitrust Case of 1948 (*United States v. Paramount Pictures, Inc.*) stated that Hollywood studios had violated the Sherman Antitrust Act of 1890 by owning the theaters where their films were screened. As a result, studios had to relinquish control over theaters, meaning independently produced films could be distributed theatrically for the first time. Small, independent theaters could now opt to screen arthouse, independent, and innovative films that violated the strict Hays Code content standards because they were not subject to its jurisdiction.

As a result, movies became more graphic, violent, and likely to involve a woman or person of color behind the camera. These changes caused repercussions throughout the film industry in the United States and other English-speaking countries. In the United Kingdom, Italy, France, Argentina, and Mexico, women directed numerous television series and made-for-television movies, many of them horror and thrillers.

During World War II, opportunities for women in all professions opened up in the United Kingdom in film and the brand-new world of television. Originally a ballet choreographer known for her avant-garde style, Wendy Toye was one of the first women to break into mainstream film and television directing in Britain in the second half of the twentieth century.

The 1952 short film *The Stranger Left No Card* was part of an anthology created by George Arthur in the United Kingdom. His friend Wendy Toye, a successful musical stage director and choreographer, suggested to Arthur that he ask director David Lean to direct one particular segment that Arthur, and Toye, believed to be very good indeed. When Lean was unavailable, Arthur asked Toye to direct.

"Now, I had never thought of directing a film in my life," said Toye of that moment. She liked "doing what I'm asked to do and doing what I choose to do." Her one real ambition in life was to be a choreographer, which she had done. When Arthur presented her with a film directing job, Toye was surprised but jumped in immediately:[1]

> George K. Arthur and his wife and he showed me three short stories and said, "What do you think of them?" I said, "Well, I think this one, *Stranger in Town*, is one of the best stories I've ever read." He asked me who I thought should do it. And I said, obviously Alan Badel would be wonderful ... And I said Muir Mathieson ought to control the music and Jean Barker would be lovely to edit it because she was so good. And I would take it to David Lean, I said ... because it is such a wonderful story. And he came back in a week's time and he said, "I've got everybody." So I said, "Have you got

David Lean?" So he said, "Well I've always wanted you to do it", and he put the script on my lap and said "Get on with it."[2]

The short is based on a story by Sidney Carroll (who also wrote the segment "You Killed Elizabeth" in *Three Cases of Murder*, another anthology horror that Toye directed). It is more ballet than drama, showcasing Toye's talent for putting movement into music. As Hugo Alfvén's *Swedish Rhapsody No. 1* repeats nearly incessantly throughout the film's first half, a devilish-looking man (played by Alan Badel) emerges from the train station. Comical and whimsical, both he and the music narrate the story. He's a stranger, and he knows the townspeople are looking at him, thinking him odd. At the local hotel, he requests a room, quite belligerently, under the name Napoleon Bonaparte, a sure sign he's nuts, and the townspeople begin to endearingly refer to him as such (both as nuts and as "Napoleon").

On the tenth day, he begins to enact his sinister purpose. Finding Mr. Latham at work just before going home for the night, Napoleon demands to show him some card tricks. Humoring the town crazy, Mr. Latham unwittingly plays into Napoleon's hands. Napoleon's fake beard, eyebrows, eccentric clothes, and odd demeanor begin to fall off as it is revealed that he is, in fact, one Jason Smith, come to avenge himself on Mr. Latham. Smith just spent fifteen years in prison for a crime his former boss, Mr. Latham, committed. He is in town for bitter revenge. Having cleverly arranged for Napoleon to have entered the office in full view of other people but not to be Napoleon when leaving, Smith may have just committed the perfect crime as he boards the 6:20 train out of town.

The whimsical aspect of *The Stranger Left No Card* contrasts sharply with the bitter and gruesome murder at the end. Viewers get two extremes, two dire distinctions: a cloying silly musical score that mutates into dark and ominous tones when the stranger's true intentions are revealed. Toye closes the film with a close-up of a child's face, pondering whether Napoleon and the stranger are one and the same person. The innocent child, holding handfuls of Napoleon's faux-magic confetti, appears immediately after Smith conceals his bloody knife in his bag and wipes his fingerprints from the office door.

"We did it in thirteen days," said Toye, "and it cost something like three thousand pounds. We didn't have any money. We got expenses plus minimum wage, and that was all. I got a fifty pound gold coin as a bonus for finishing on time."[3]

The most striking aspects of *The Stranger Left No Card* are the music, which repeats dramatically for effect, and the way the characters seem to effortlessly careen to the soundtrack without actually dancing. Toye had an affinity for and long career in choreography:

> Almost the whole of *The Stranger Left No Card* I'd worked out to music before we went to shoot it. And in those days, we couldn't afford audiotape for the playback on the set, so I had a little wind-up gramophone on all the location sets. And we had to do it with a metronome because I knew exactly what bits of music I wanted to fit into the shots. It was all very planned out.[4]

Toye didn't believe anyone would ever see *The Stranger Left No Card*. After all, it was a two-reel short, and she thought she'd be lucky to hear about it ever playing anywhere in the United States. It was film producer Alexander Korda who championed the short and Toye's further directing career:

> Alex Korda was having a party and showing a film to some of his guests; they were quite important people ... And that was *The Stranger Left No Card*. And Alex saw it and was so impressed by it that he asked if he could send it to the Cannes Festival under the banner of London Films, it was British Lion by then, and he asked to send it to Cannes which he did and won an award of course for the short film of that year.[5]

Jean Cocteau presented Toye with the award. Toye was very happy with the look and feel of the film:

> And it was exactly what I wanted it to look like, I wanted it to look a bit like a documentary and in those days that sort of thing didn't happen with films of that sort. They were much glossier looking. And that was part of the success of it, his wonderful photography. And of course Alan Badel who was so marvelous in it.[6]

"I did some things in *Stranger* which I, probably two or three years later, wouldn't have attempted," she later said of the short,[7]

Korda next asked Toye to direct a thriller. *The Teckman Mystery* (1954) was a remake of the British television series *The Teckman Biography*, a BBC whodunit based on the writings of Francis Durbridge, which aired for two seasons in 1953. Toye admits that she was young and scared of Korda, so she wouldn't refuse despite her reservations about directing the film. Toye describes her reluctance in her memoirs:

> One of the excuses that I used was that I thought I wasn't experienced enough to do that subject. I didn't think I could do it in six weeks. But he insisted, so I jumped in. I had a lovely cast because Korda let me have who I wanted. Margaret Leighton played the lead. So I said yes to that at last and then shot it, and that's why I did that.[8]

Toye may have been wise to listen to her misgivings, as *The New York Times* called the movie a "decidedly not so hot" "obvious fly-by-night" that is a "slow, contrived and exasperatingly arch puzzler that sets some sort of record for meandering banality. The new director," said the reviewer, " would be wise to take more pains next time."[9] The main problem with *The Teckman Mystery* is that Toye's instincts always lead towards the whimsical rather than the scary. Her cinematic style is far better suited to adapt Roald Dahl or *Grimms' Fairy Tales* than a straight thriller. Her attention to detail and set design are meticulous and ornate. Her characters are choreographed rather than directed, and fiendish scenes are subverted with silly music. The characters bounce through the frames rather than sneak, and the cinematography is abandoned in favor of sets and symbolism, serving only the scenes, never the actors.

Alan Badel as Stranger in *The Stranger Left No Card* (1952), directed by Wendy Toye.

Mr. X ascends the staircase inside the painting in *Three Cases of Murder*. Image courtesy of Criterion.

Toye's best work, and most macabre, is her short "In the Picture," the first segment of the anthology film *Three Cases of Murder* (1955). It is a supernatural masterpiece. This horror/thriller anthology was comprised of three separate and distinct stories with the common theme of, well, *murder*. All three segments starred Alan Badel (the star of *The Stranger Left No Card*) in separate roles, though Orson Welles, who only appeared in the last segment, "Lord Mountdrago," was given top billing. Actor Eamonn Andrews introduces the anthology and each story in a tuxedo with witticisms and warnings of the horrors awaiting the audience.

"In the Picture" is decisively Toye's style in her whimsical way of using music to tell the story. At a museum, Mr. Jarvis (Hugh Pryse) mistakes a strange man (Alan Badel) for one of the museum trustees and finds himself engaged in a detailed conversation about a gorgeous old painting. The painting is large, depicting an old desolate house on a moor, beaten by wind and fog, with dark windows and only the moaning trees for company. The stranger beckons Jarvis to look closely at the painting. Then, the mysterious, strangely-dressed man leads Mr. Jarvis literally into the picture: into the twisted, broken trees and the fog and up to the wild house in one of the most beautiful shots contrived by cinematographer Georges Périnal. The scene combines masterful synchronization between the dialogue and the intense close-up of the painting with Toye's characteristic fantasy elements (with some help from rear projection). Jarvis and Mr. X do, indeed, literally walk into the painting before our eyes.

Once inside the old mansion, Dutch angles set off the striking aspect of the manor: ragged curtains sweep across a collection of dust-laden paintings, sculptures, and artifacts, all proudly stolen from the museum itself by Mr. X. While accepting a warm drink from the stranger, Jarvis is poisoned and is at the mercy of the stranger's friends in the paintings. He will endure a gruesome procedure that will sever his spinal column and make him a new part of the painting forever. The artist, Mr. X, steps out of the painting and admires his handiwork.

Toye's sense of comedic timing, as in *The Stranger Left No Card*, is based on the odd, the strange, and the uncomfortable. Fast-paced, the short only gives the viewer enough time to absorb the elaborate scenery and delicate story with a growing sense of dread, to store and process later. At its completion, "In the Picture" is understood as a study of sociopathic obsession. The artist, so fixated on his work that he decided to stay with his painting even after death, is always looking for new ways to perfect it. The sad and apparent horror is that it will never be completed to his satisfaction, and numerous innocent museumgoers will continue to die for his vanity.

Toye choreographed the first portion of "In the Picture" to a score by Doreen Carwithen, though the film is sans music for a time during the sequence when Jarvis is inside the painting. Toye's creative style would have lent itself incredibly well to more modern absurdities like Tim Burton's *The Nightmare Before Christmas* (1993) and *Edward Scissorhands* (1990), making the cute horrible and the horrible adorable.

Though compared to *The Twilight Zone* in tone and style by modern horror film fans for being fantastically morbid and with a devilish twist, "In the Picture" was not appreciated at the time of its release. *The New York Times* called it "a mild exercise in the fantastic which, frankly, we did not dig ... The idea is fascinating, but it doesn't particularly jell, and the obvious attempt to make it funny doesn't quite come off."[10] *Three Cases of Murder* is a testament to British Gothic and was at the early forefront of supernatural film and television, paving the way for anthology television series such as *The Outer Limits* and Boris Karloff's *Thriller* only a few years later.

Toye's last film project as director was a remake of her own short, *The Stranger Left No Card*, for an episodic British television series called Roald Dahl's *Tales of the Unexpected*. Hosted by Dahl, who also wrote many episodes, the story was re-titled *A Stranger in Town* (1982). Toye adamantly did not want to direct this remake; she believed she could never do it as well as she had initially and that it was far better as a black-and-white film. She finally consented because the producer told her it would be remade, with or without her. "So I thought, "Well, I must do it. I can't let somebody else do it."[11] Shot on videotape rather than film (another aspect of the production that irked Toye; she believed that video strips everything down and made it seem too real),[12] "A Stranger in Town"[13] aired as a half-hour episode and starred Derek Jacobi (*I, Claudius*, 1976) as The Stranger. A veritable shot-for-shot remake of *The Stranger Left No Card*, "A Stranger in Town" differs from the original mainly in that it has a new musical score, was shot in entirely new locations, and is in color rather than black and white. Certain scenes differ slightly as well. The Stranger's cane resembles a serpent rather than a bird, and The Stranger writes his name at the hotel as "Christopher Columbus" instead of "Napoleon."

In addition to being one of Britain's most beloved filmmakers, Toye was also one of Britain's only women directors at the time:

> I like to think that I paved the way for other women to work in film. I thought I had a job to do, and I had to stick to it. I like to think that, because of that, perhaps I did help other women get jobs. People say, "You've never been a feminist, and you never fight for women." Well, I don't, really, but I think an example of doing something and getting on with it and not being a crashing bore about things is probably better than getting onto a platform and making some speech about it all.[14]

In December 1991, Toye was surprised by the British television series *This is Your Life* which ambushed unsuspecting celebrities and brought them face-to-face with people who had worked with them and perhaps not seen them for many years on live television. Her nephew, Peter Toye, recounts his aunt's experience on the show, saying that she was a private person who had never allowed biographies to be written about her. "She refused to let any details of her private life get out," he said. While he felt that she should have been recognized by British royalty with a title (such as Dame Wendy Toye, perhaps), he knows she was highly regarded in her profession. "Everybody thought she was the tops. And she was."[15] Notoriously modest and insisting on her lack of ambition in the film industry (and in general), Toye nevertheless loved making films and thought she was good at it. She reminisced,

> A lot of people ask me now, "As a woman, did you find it very tricky in those times?" I didn't at all. Some of the women who worked in Britain—I mean, even Muriel Box—she hated every minute of what she was doing. Where I had a blazingly happy time in my career and absolutely enjoyed every moment of it, she really had a rotten time. And she was brilliant.[16]

Toye suffered crippling arthritis towards the end of her life and increasing frailty, which may have forced her to retire before she was ready. She passed away in 2010 at the age of ninety-two, having continued directing for the stage and a few television projects well into her early eighties.

Muriel Box, like Wendy Toye, is a beloved figure in British film history. Also, like Wendy Toye, Box was already well-established in film and entertainment when she began directing. A sometime actress and screenwriter beforehand, Box started directing feature films in 1950 at the age of forty-five (though she did direct short documentaries a few years before that). And, like Toye, she began by directing narrative short films for British production companies. Unlike Toye, she was a staunchly outspoken feminist.[17] Toye was not incorrect in saying that Box had a "rotten time" of it. Beginning her directing career a few years before Toye did hers, Box often faced explicit sexual discrimination. One of her very first directing jobs for the British Ministry of Information was the short *Road Safety for Children*, which was taken out of her hands by a man named Arthur Elton, head of the Film Division at the ministry.

> The reason, he informed Sydney [the executive producer], was that he did not feel it was the type of picture suitable for a woman to direct! Sydney asked to suggest an alternative, and Ken Annakin, who had just directed his first documentary, *English Justice*, found favor in Elton's eyes and was given the job instead. This was the first time I had been discriminated against in my work on the grounds of sex. I regret to say it was by no means the last.[18]

Box noticed an industry preference for male directors throughout her entire career, through to her last film projects:

> You can bet your bottom dollar, if you're recommended and a man whose got an equal record of what they've done, you can be absolutely certain the man will get the job. It's so odd why they can't have the grace to say, "We know we have all the good opportunities as men to direct and do everything." Why they can't give women a chance, they haven't any confidence at all in them, they never say to women let us try and see what she's done. Right into my last film, which is interesting, they didn't want a woman director on that last one, so Sydney dug his heels in, and he said, "I'm very sorry"—he was approaching the starting date—"If Muriel's not going to direct it I'm afraid I'm not going to make the film." If you don't have support as strong as that you don't get any jobs. Fortunately, they gave in.[19]

Longtime collaborator Sydney Box (her husband) produced the short and narrative feature films that Box directed in the 1940s and 1950s, including the mystery/thriller *Eyewitness* (1956). The only movie of Box's that belongs in this chapter, *Eyewitness* is a thriller about a woman who witnesses a murder and is subsequently stalked by the killers.

In *Eyewitness,* two criminals, Wade (Donald Sinden) and Barney (Nigel Stock), rob a movie theater safe during a busy film screening. Unhappy Lucy (Muriel Pavlow), a young woman who has just argued with her husband Jay (Michael Craig) about finances, decides to treat herself to a screening of the new film *Desperados* only to witness the robbery in progress inadvertently. Running from the theater like a mad woman, Lucy is hit by a double-decker British bus and knocked unconscious. Reckless Wade waits until Barney leaves the safe room and then puts two bullets in the theater manager's body. The two criminals calmly walk away, following the ambulance to the hospital to await Lucy's diagnosis. If Lucy wakes up and talks to the police, Wade and Barney have a big problem, so Wade is determined to murder her in her sick bed before she gets a chance.

The critics were right in saying it was a damp squib: the defining characteristic of *Eyewitness* is that it shows people often getting in and out of cars and bars. A few excellent noir angles and shadow-lit shots contribute to an eerie effect (as does the constant theremin soundtrack), but there's a lack of real tension about Lucy's predicament. Janet Green's original screenplay is somewhat less well-paced than her later endeavors[20] and chock-full of a giddy dark comedy that doesn't do much for creating or maintaining tension.

Aside from some of the cinematography (by Reginald H. Wyer) and the grating and intermittent theremin (thank you to musician Bruce Montgomery), *Eyewitness* has at least one more redeeming quality in that it features three extremely violent scenes: the initial murder of the theater manager, Belinda Lee's attack in the ward kitchen by Wade, and Wade's final attempt to strangle Lucy (thwarted by a redeemed Barney, who strangles Wade with razor wire). You won't see any blood, but you will get a good dose of criminal brutality. In a contemporary interview with *Australian Women's Weekly*, star Donald Sinden said of his character, Wade, "I've been reading the files of Neville Heath, the woman-slayer. I'm modeling the part a lot on him."[21] With a stark scar on his face and villainous mustache, Sinden certainly looked (and acted) the part.

While Box may not have considered *Eyewitness* an important film[22], it is part of the pantheon of mid-twentieth-century thrillers directed by women. These thrillers would soon translate well to television: a dynamic new medium in which creative roles were slightly less rigidly divided by the sexes.

In 1948 the United States Supreme Court ruled against studio monopolies on film distribution in the case *United States v. Paramount Pictures, Inc.*, opening the possibility for independent films to be screened publicly in theaters. In 1952, after the First Amendment of the United States Constitution was officially extended to protect film, The Hollywood Production Code, which had previously so cautiously censored films for nudity and "inappropriate" content since 1934, began to relax its stranglehold on artistic expression. This relaxation was an industry response to the modern television set, a new medium whose content was unpredictable, fresh, and full of endless possibilities. These combined events led to women stepping behind the camera as directors in an entirely socially accepted, studio-approved manner. Amidst this blaze of this new technology and film industry upheaval, World War II had put women into the conventional workforce, and some were loathe to leave it.

Ida Lupino was the first female mainstream American filmmaker to make movies within the Hollywood system since Dorothy Arzner[23] and is often cited by feminist film scholars as one of the two prominent female directors of the mid-twentieth century making women-oriented, independent films in Hollywood.

An actress initially and throughout her career, Lupino never quite achieved the massive success that some of her contemporaries did.[24] The well-known story of how she began directing is credited to a mishap during pre-production on the set of the movie *Not Wanted*, which Lupino co-wrote and co-produced independently of any studio with then-husband Collier Young. Director Elmer Clifton suffered a heart attack right before production began, and Lupino stepped in at the last minute to save the picture. Clifton was on set during the production, and his name remained on the film out of respect to his career, but Lupino was the director of the low-budget, unwanted-pregnancy exploitation flick.[25]

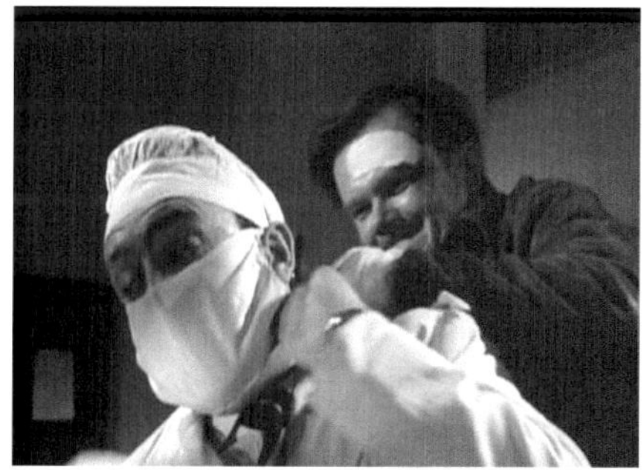

Barney (Nigel Stock) strangles psychopath Wade (Donald Sinden) in Muriel Box's thriller *Eyewitness* (1956). Image courtesy of VCI Entertainment.

Simon (Richard Lupino) is strangled by a giant chicken in *Thriller: "Trio for Terror — The Extra Passenger"* (1961), directed by Ida Lupino. Image courtesy of Image Entertainment.

An original lobby card for Ida Lupino's serial-killer noir *The Hitch-Hiker* (1953). Image courtesy of Kino Lorber.

While Lupino's resume of films as a director is a lush landscape of semi-feminist, B-movie, and low-budget foliage, her significant contributions to the thriller genre and the later horror phenomenon on television make her one of the most critical women horror directors. In the 1950s, Lupino was the first American woman to direct a film noir. Like the Western, it was initially a uniquely American phenomenon.[26] Unlike the Western, it developed from an increasingly nihilistic and desperate view of post-war social upheaval and rampant corruption and crime in modern American cities. Beginning in the early 1940s and tapering off in the late 1950s, film noir is epitomized by dramatic shadows, unnerving camera angles, and highly stylized lighting and outlines. Plots tend towards heists-gone-wrong, murder, and dangerous, abusive, obsessive love stories. By the late 1940s, noir had spread as a visual and thematic style to many other Western countries in many variations.

The first film noir directed by a woman was *Death is a Caress,* AKA *Døden er et kjærtegn*, a 1949 Norwegian film that marked the debut feature of Edith Carlmar,[27] depicting a young newlywed couple and their disturbing relationship. Carlmar and French director Jacqueline Audry were only two of the many European women breaking into mainstream film directing at the same time as Lupino. The first noir film directed by a woman in the United States was Lupino's dramatic 1950 film *Outrage,* about the violent rape and subsequent psychological unraveling of a young woman in the shameful and terrifying aftermath of her attack. Like Lupino's other films as director,

Outrage presented an alternative to mainstream Hollywood with its controversial topic but was heavily influenced by the current trends in suspenseful cinema. Using angular, encroaching shadows, Lupino designed a composition to accentuate the protagonist's psychological isolation and inner turmoil. Ultimately, *Outrage* ends on a happier note, with few suspenseful scenes.

"When was the last time you invited death into your car?" read the original tagline for Ida Lupino's now-famous desert noir *The Hitch-Hiker* (1953). Unlike other noir films of the day, *The Hitch-Hiker* features an all-male cast. There are no femme fatales, no cityscapes or gangsters or powerful, corrupt overlords forcing the hands of troubled but generally good World War II veterans who have fallen in love with the wrong girl. Instead, *The Hitch-Hiker* is a story of deviance and isolation, conformity and horror, and disturbed unseated identity.

Originally titled *The Difference,* and then *The Persuader,* before being changed to its final title, *The Hitch-Hiker* is loosely based on the true story of William Edward Cook, Jr., a serial killer who dominated United States news headlines in January 1951 with a three-week murder spree that wound throughout the highways of the American Southwest and ended in the tragic deaths of six people.[28]

Using the (sensationalized) news discourse as a starting point for the story, screenwriter Daniel Mainwaring crafted a character named Emmet Myers. Like Cook, he was unwanted from an early age and abandoned by uncaring parents. Like Cook, he has a disfigured eye and a cold, sociopathic attitude toward the world around him. Like Cook, he hitches rides with unsuspecting innocents on stretches of long, dark highways in isolated parts of the country.

The Hitch-Hiker makes much of its "based on a true story"[29] preamble, counting on audiences' love of sensational violence to boost intensity and popularity. It begins with a text screen that says:

> This is the story of a man and a gun and a car. The gun belonged to the man. The car might have been yours—or that young couple across the aisle. What you will see in the next seventy minutes could have happened to you. For the facts are actual.

The "based on a true story" angle has long served sensational film, from true-crime retellings to far-fetched horror and fantasy stories.[30] Emmett Myers is based on a real serial killer; leaving that tidbit out of the press releases (and the opening credits) would have been a serious public relations failure.

The opening credits overlay a sunny highway with black shadows against the bright asphalt. An anonymous man, his head cut off by the camera, walks deliberately and slowly while distressing music plays. Despite the searing heat of the day, he wears a black leather jacket. When he sticks out his thumb in the classic hitchhiking pose, the audience knows that the man they are looking at is the eponymous hitchhiker. Soon after, a woman's high-pitched scream and a series of gunshots tell us that this man, the killer, has just claimed another victim. His face is still hidden, and the woman screams completely off-camera, but the effect is chilling: the audience is a helpless bystander witnessing extreme violence.

After a lawman discovers the bodies, spinning newspapers appear, confirming what we already knew: "Couple Found Murdered." Then, the newspapers tell us there is a nationwide search for the killer, Myers, and a picture of his ugly, cold-eyed face stares back at us from the front page. Now that we know what we're facing, we see the killer rifling through his victims' wallets and purses, utterly undisturbed by what he has just done. These people are things to him. In Lupino's own words,

> I wanted hard-hitting scenes in the opening on *The Hitch-Hiker* with the audience seeing hard packed drama illustrated with facts! An image appears on the screen, no this is not the hitch-hiker slayer but the film viewer will think he is. This was used to build suspense. The viewer then sees shadows and the spinning image of a newspaper which winds down like the wheel of fortune. I keep the victims faceless to enhance fear that the next murder victim could be anybody—even the film viewer watching the film or the person sitting next to them.[31]

Lupino shifts from this montage to a quiet, calm car ride interior, introducing us to the protagonists: Roy Collins (Edmond O'Brien), a mechanic, and Gilbert Bowen (Frank Lovejoy), a more white-collar sort (a draftsman), are driving a 1949 Plymouth to a guys-only weekend fishing trip in the Chocolate Mountains on the California-Mexico border. Bored and feeling a little rebellious, Collins suggests they head instead to the city of Mexicali, then go fishing at San Felipe, Mexico, after a bit of fun. Their wives will never know the difference.

Very casually, Bowen stops for a hitchhiker beside a stalled car at the edge of the highway. Assuming the guy has run out of gas, Bowen says, "*Hop in*." And that's where their terror begins. Emmett Myers, darkly played by William Talman, is a silent, murky shadow in the back seat of the car and unresponsive to Bowen's friendly chatter. When the hitchhiker pulls a gun on the two men, they and the audience face the facts: no one knows where they are, and no one expects them home for at least a few days.

Instead of murdering Collins and Bowen as he did his previous victims, Myers decides to keep them alive as hostages and chauffeurs. Though it may seem out of character for Myers not to immediately kill both men and steal their car, the real-life killer on which the character of Emmett Myers is based also kidnapped people he didn't kill for a ride, and it allows for seventy minutes of pure tension. The claustrophobic mise-en-scène, tightly cluttered by Bowen, Myers, and Collins crammed into the dark car, often with only the rear-view mirror to connect their eye lines, purposely suffocates.

Citing the stark shadows in *The Hitch-Hiker* as a tie that binds the film to classic, city-set noir films of the time, film writer Lauren Rabinovitz observes that "Myers is a shadowy figure, made possible by the post-war highway system."[32] Myers is a construct of modern corruption, disappointment, and technology: a killer that has adapted to the new social expectations of people calmly settling down into suburban sprawl, connected by brand-new expensive freeways that facilitate housing developments and long work commutes and leaving long, lonely stretches of uninhabited country marred only by telephone poles, concrete, and cars. While in earlier noir films, the city itself is a haven for corrupt cops, crooked politicians, and hard-boiled femme fatales that smother disappointed and cynical war veterans, in *The Hitch-Hiker*, the city is a comfortable nest where job, family, and home are protected from the shocking and harsh wilderness of the outside world. Bowen and Collins are conformist, 1950s Cold War culture husbands looking for excitementand escape; instead of reveling in gritty adventure, they find that they've "*gone soft*," as Myers says. He enjoys pointing out their inadequacies, particularly Collins,' saying,

"*You're up to your necks in IOUs. You're suckers. You're scared to get out on your own. You always had it good, so you're soft.*"

Rabinovitz suggests that *The Hitch-Hiker* studies masculinity and power in the modern world. I agree but posit, however, that *The Hitch-Hiker* is a precursor to many of the violent horror and thriller films of the late twentieth and early twenty-first centuries in which everyday modern citizens become victims of dangerous, backward 'others' that still live outside of the known, safe, and comforting city.

The seeds planted by *The Hitch-Hiker* would blossom into the anti-rural culture sentiment later seen in 1970s horror films such as *The Hills Have Eyes* (1977) and *The Texas Chainsaw Massacre* (1974). 'Classier' mainstream pictures, such as *Straw Dogs* (1971) and *Deliverance* (1972), reinforced the continued perception that civilization equals good, and countryside/wilderness/small town equals bad. Even in the U.K., the remote island of Summerisle in *The Wicker Man* (1973) is dangerously pagan and old-world. Into the 2000s, horror film screenwriters universally contrived ways to have their characters' cellular phones and mobile devices systematically lose wireless signals anytime the setting shifted to a remote cabin or cornfield to keep their characters as isolated from safety and civilization as Lupino kept Collins and Bowen.

As Robin Wood observes in his essay "The American Nightmare: Horror in the 70s," a history of cultural repression created numerous monsters for the modern horror film to exploit: female sexuality, other cultures, ethnic groups, and children are often the monsters of 1970s horror films, but in the cases of *The Texas Chainsaw Massacre* and Lupino's *The Hitch-Hiker*, the proletariat, or working-class, non-bourgeois possessed of backward ideologies, sexualities, or moralities is a danger to us all. Myers is that amoral 'other'[33] that threatens the post-war, nuclear-family stability that Bowens and Collins have carved out for themselves (Bowen more successfully than Collins). "Central to the effect and fascination of horror films," says Wood, "is their fulfillment of our nightmare wish to smash the norms that oppress us and which our moral conditioning teaches us to revere."[34] It is not pure horror at Myers' exploits alone that drives the audience's fascination with *The Hitch-Hiker;* it is also their secret desire to see him destroy Bowen and Collins' civilized, family-man lifestyle by turning them into violent monsters like himself (in which he almost succeeds with Collins). 'Dangers of the road' films owe much to *The Hitch-Hiker*; the ominous hitchhiker in *The Texas Chainsaw Massacre* (1974) and the horror film *The Hitcher* (1986) are all reminders of the lonely, deadly stretches of highway on which no one can hear you scream.

A contemporary review of *The Hitch-Hiker* admits that it gives "one of the less likely dangers of travel in the motorized twentieth-century" a "vigorous, if grim treatment." Unfortunately, the reviewer also refers to the "obvious conclusion" and Lupino's initial cinematic tension that she is "incapable of maintaining ... throughout ... However, Miss Lupino's brisk direction and the solid portrayals by the three principals overcome, to a large degree, the film's cops-versus-killer format."[35]

Not the most critically acclaimed film to come out in 1953, *The Hitch-Hiker* nevertheless did receive immediate press, mainly from United Press International, which came out to photograph Lupino directing in the desert during a set visit.[36] Modern-day film scholars and fans of classic cinema hold *The Hitch-Hiker* in high regard as an entry into the film noir pantheon, often as the pinnacle of Lupino's feature film directing career. *The Hitch-Hiker* may have been too violent, not violent enough, too slow, too sensational, or too cheap for RKO (who released it theatrically) and audiences to take seriously. Perhaps the idea of a woman director making films independently still carried a stigma that condemned the film to the B-list. Or perhaps it was, in reality, a B-movie that belonged on the bottom half of the double bill.

The official press notes for *The Hitch-Hiker* contained an interview with Lupino entitled, "Ida Lupino Retains Her Femininity as Director." It was presumably written as a first line of defense against critics, professional and peanut gallery alike, that didn't like the idea of a woman directing films:

> While I've encountered no resentment from the male of the species for intruding into their world, I give them no opportunity to think I've strayed where I don't belong. I assume no masculine characteristics, which can often be a fault of career women rubbing shoulders with their male counterparts, who become merely arrogant or authoritative.[37]

While to feminists and historians alike, Lupino's charmed directing career can be seen as a beacon of equality in a time when women in the United States were genuinely confined to highly rigid gender roles, the above interview serves as a stoic reminder that Lupino probably faced incredible hurdles as a female director in what was a man's business, to the point of publicly promising not to stray "where she doesn't belong." Unfortunately for the sexists in Hollywood, she was probably insincere, as she continued to stray into men's territory for the rest of her working career. Lupino later said that during the filming of *The Hitch-Hiker*, she realized suspense was indeed her element;[38] author Barbara Scharres writes that "Lupino's larger curiosity about human behavior equally found expression in sexual triangles and stories of the supernatural."[39]

Lupino's film directing had earned her the nickname "The Female Hitch" (as in Hitchcock) not only because of her ability to direct action and suspense sequences but because she usually insisted on calling all the shots on set as Hitchcock himself was wont to. Having crafted masterpieces like *Rebecca* (1940), *Strangers on a Train* (1951), and *Dial M for Murder* (1954), Hitchcock was revered as a master of suspense. First airing in the United States on October 2, 1955, his television series *Alfred Hitchcock Presents* ran for ten years, first in a twenty-five-minute format. Then, in 1962, the show expanded

Ursula Andress ss the stunning Luana, in *Thriller: "La Strega"* (1962), directed by Ida Lupino. Image courtesy of Image Entertainment.

Lucy (Jennifer Raine) found the cursed knife in *Thriller: "The Closed Cabinet"* (1961), directed by Ida Lupino. Image courtesy of Image Entertainment.

to fifty-minute episodes and was retitled *The Alfred Hitchcock Hour*. The show's opening sequence featured a cartoon caricature of Hitchcock's profile and a decidedly unforgettable, plodding tune, making it one of the most iconic television series images of the twentieth century.

Hitchcock first approached Ida Lupino in 1960 to star in the sixth season episode "Sybilla." Lupino turned Hitchcock down and told him that instead of starring in it, she'd love to direct it (despite a pay reduction from the actor's salary to that of the director).[40] Hitchcock cast actress Barbara Bel Geddes (she worked for Hitchcock in 1958's *Vertigo*) in the role originally intended for Lupino and hired Lupino as the episode's director.

Beginning with a darkly humorous monologue from Hitchcock, "Sybilla" (which aired December 6, 1960) is a decidedly anticlimactic story about a newly married Edwardian couple and the groom's immediate regret at getting married. Horace (Alexander Scourby) feels smothered by his lovely new bride Sybilla (Barbara Bel Geddes). He plots her murder by poison, which doesn't succeed, and then believes Sybilla knows he tried to kill her. When Sybilla describes a mystery novel she's reading in which a murderer is caught because the victim left documents implicating them behind, Horace thinks Sybilla has done the same and resolves never to harm her lest he goes to prison. After many years of happy marriage, it turns out that Sybilla never did any such thing and was only relating to him the premise of her novel.

Starring Claire Trevor, one of the most prominent actresses in film noir of the 1940s and 1950s opposite Biff Elliot (best-known as television's hard-boiled detective Mike Hammer), "A Crime for Mothers" (which aired January 24, 1961) was Lupino's second and last episode of *Alfred Hitchcock Presents*. Trevor had previously starred in the episode "Safe Conduct" and was perfect for the role of blackmailer Lottie Mead. Trevor portrays an unsavory character who had given up her daughter for adoption years ago only to return demanding money from the parents. When they refuse, she, with the help of an unscrupulous private detective, kidnaps the child and holds her for $25,000 ransom. It turns out, however, that the child is the wrong one, the private detective works for the parents, and Lottie Mead was set up as a kidnapper. Aside from the brilliance of Trevor's drunk and crooked Lottie Mead, this featureless episode lacks any real suspense, even in light of the twist ending.

When asked what of her work she thought was the best as director, Lupino responded with, "A few on *Thriller,* I think, are pretty good."[41] Like *Alfred Hitchcock Presents* and *The Twilight Zone*, *Thriller* was an anthology series, and each episode was introduced by Boris Karloff, as Hitchcock and Rod Serling introduced their series' episodes. Because she directed so many episodes in *Thriller*'s first and second seasons, it is perhaps the television series Lupino had the most influence shaping as director.[42] Karloff believed Lupino to be one of the most vital directors in his series.[43]

"Trio for Terror" (March 14, 1961) was Lupino's first episode of *Thriller*. Three short stories, set in 1905 in London, are connected by a local pub which all the characters visit as they are introduced. The first story, "The Extra Passenger,"[44] shows a man (played by Lupino's brother, Richard Lupino) murdering his warlock uncle for his money so he can impress a gold-digging woman. An ingenious plan involves the nephew pretending to be aboard a train while killing his uncle at home. Unfortunately, the uncle returns to life, and his familiar (a giant rooster) pecks the nephew to death in his train compartment. The second story, "A Terribly Strange Bed,"[45] involves a casino desperate to get back its gold from a drunk winner. After surviving a near-fatal night in one of the casino's hotel rooms, the gambler believes he has beaten the system only to find that one of the hotel employees stole all his gold. The last story, "The Mask of Medusa," is set in a museum where the main attraction is stone statues of serial killers. A serial killer stumbles in and discovers that the statues are not statues at all but the actual killers turned into stone by the head of Medusa herself.

While the stories in "Trio for Terror" are somewhat lackluster compared to their competition (the stirring episodes of *The Twilight Zone*, for instance), they show off some of Lupino's strengths. Her element is black and white, and she dramatically uses the claustrophobic train compartment in the first segment. As she proved in *The Hitch-Hiker*, Lupino is deft at using only a small space to increase drama and tension, and she cleverly avoids having to show a giant rooster pecking someone to death by choosing to work with shadows.[46]

"Mr. George" (May 9, 1961) was based on another short story by August Derleth.[47] It starred child actress Gina Gillespie[48] as Priscilla, a young woman plagued by money-grubbing relatives desperate to get their hands on the fortune left to her by one George Craig, who had intended to marry her mother but died before he could. With Pricsillia's mother gone as well, it is left to second cousins Edna, Jared, and Adelaide to raise Priscilla on a small allowance until she reaches maturity. Naturally, they feel cheated and scheme to murder Priscilla. However, the ghost of George Craig, whom Priscilla calls "Mr. George," always seems to be there to protect her.

Virginia Gregg as Edna Leggett is not entirely unsympathetic; she's a solid on-screen presence, and Lupino is quite good at directing desperate female characters. "Mr. George" is a fairy tale horror story; an innocent child is at the mercy of several hard-hearted adults and, like Sleeping Beauty or Snow White, has supernatural guardians protecting her from evil adults. As can be expected, the would-be villains are thwarted by the ghost of Mr. George; their murder attempts backfire, and they all suffer the gruesome accidents intended for Priscilla.

"What Beckoning Ghost?" (September 18, 1961) is a gaslighting affair in which a rich wife is systematically broken down by her cheating husband and sister in the name of money. Judith Evelyn[49] plays Mildred Beaumont, a talented concert pianist recovering from a heart attack. Her husband Eric and sister Lydia dote over her, making sure she takes her medication and rests well, but they have sinister plans for Mildred. As Mildred hears strange music downstairs, she wanders down her home's staircase and sees a terrifying sight: a repeating vision of her funeral staged in the sitting room. Each time she sees it, Mildred has a breakdown, not knowing that her husband and sister produced it to scare her to death. When Mildred passes, and Eric starts receiving condolence cards and flowers about his death, it's clear Mildred is not going quietly to the grave without revenge.

"What Beckoning Ghost?" is based on a short story written by Harold Lawlor[50] and embodies the creepy, twisted television morality tale pioneered by *The Twilight Zone*. Easily one of the best of Lupino's *Thriller* episodes, due mainly to Evelyn's delicate ability to appear terrified, it also features the most developed female protagonist of all her episodes. An inspired monologue towards the end of the episode that breaks the fourth wall is unusual for Lupino but has a masterful effect.

"Guillotine" (September 26, 1961) was written for the screen by Charles Beaumont.[51] Despite this promising source, it suffers from the same glaring problems as Lupino's later episodes "La Strega" (January 15, 1962) and "The Bride Who Died Twice" (March 19, 1962). All three take place in non-English speaking countries (France, Italy, and an unnamed South American nation, respectively) but feature thickly-accented characters speaking English.

"Guillotine" is set in nineteenth-century France. Starring Robert Middleton as Monsieur de Paris, a professional executioner, it is a long and often dull episode compared to the brooding and moody manse-set stories of Lupino's other episodes. In the incredible resource, *This Is a Thriller: An Episode Guide, History and Analysis of the Classic 1960s Television Series* by Alan Warren, Warren criticizes the acting in "Guillotine" but praises Lupino's heavy-handed cut scenes by saying she directs with her "customary skill."[52] He seems to hold Lupino in especially high regard as far as the series' directors go and believes that "Guillotine" and "La Strega" are perhaps her two best episodes.

"La Strega" stars Ursula Andress as a beautiful young woman named Luana who has run away from her evil grandmother, La Strega (The Witch, played by Jeanette Nolan). Harassed by villagers who believe she, too, is a witch, Luana is saved by big-city Spaniard Tonio Bellini, a handsome young man who is instantly attracted to her and does not believe in witches. He invites Luana to stay with him at his apartment in town, where he is attempting a career in painting. Unfortunately, Luana's grandmother comes looking for her, and when she finds Tonio unwilling to return her granddaughter, she curses him. Antonio begins to fear that the curse is real and succumbs to terror. Eventually hallucinating (or does he?), he kills Luana in a nightmarish episode because he believes her to be her grandmother.

Andress is not particularly powerful as an actress, but in inches of makeup, Nolan is a superbly sinister witch. A cameo from Ramon Novarro as Tonio's painting teacher adds another masterful actor to the mix to counteract Andress. Lupino's decision to include a midnight black Sabbath of witches doing modern interpretive dance routines is regrettable: that scene, which could have been powerful, is painful to watch.

"The Bride Who Died Twice" is a meandering story[53] with a Gabriel Garcia Marquez-like magical realism set in an unnamed South American nation under the iron grip of a dictator. Played by Joe De Santis, the powerful and corrupt Colonel Sangriento focuses all his energy on forcing the innocent young Consuelo to marry him. Consuelo is the daughter of General De La Varra, Sangriento's superior, and is already affianced to the young soldier Antonio. To break up the engagement, Sangriento blackmails De La Varra into sending Antonio on a suicide mission. What ensues is a bit of a mess and a mystery simultaneously.

"The Last of the Sommervilles" (November 6, 1961), written by Lupino with her brother Richard, could easily have been included as a smaller segment in Lupino's last *Thriller* episode, "The Lethal Ladies." Along with "Mr. George," "The Closed Cabinet," and "What Beckoning Ghost?", "The Last of the Sommervilles" takes place in a large, oppressive mansion with strong familial themes. Like "Mr. George," it involves a plot to murder a wealthy family member and a crafty female lead. Warren again praises Lupino's directorial "flourishes" as one of the major highlights of "The Last of the Sommervilles" along with the photography, the mansion itself, and the darkly clever opening scene in which Ursula (played by Phyllis Thaxter) is fast at work burying a body in the front yard of the family estate. Considering the similarities to other *Thriller* episode plot lines and that Lupino penned this script herself, it may be that Lupino felt that "The Last of the Sommervilles" combined the best elements of several previous episodes she'd directed.

"The Closed Cabinet" (November 27, 1961) is easily the most traditionally enjoyable horror story of Lupino's episodes. A ghost story set in a haunted castle features a ghost named Lady Beatrice Mervyn (played by Patricia Manning), who is doomed to walk the castle grounds after killing herself. Her mother-in-law, Dame Alice Mervyn, decides this is an excellent reason to set a family curse on all her son's descendants. Fast-forward three hundred years to the present, and Evie Bishop (Olive Sturgess), is now staying at Castle Mervyn because her cousin Lucy (Jennifer Raine) is married to the current Lord George Mervyn (Peter Forster). His attractive brother Alan (David Frankham) is also there, and it seems like romance is blooming.

Unfortunately, the mysterious curse on the Mervyns has something to do with the men having hideous tempers. Alan is reluctant to pursue Evie and warns George against marrying Lucy with the curse still hanging over their heads. Lucy is immediately visited by the ghost of Beatrice Mervyn and is led first to her tomb in the basement and then to the locked cabinet in her bedroom that contains the knife that must be used to kill the ghost of Lord Hugh Mervyn. Of course, Lucy breaks the curse by solving the mystery of the locked cabinet (it seems shockingly simple once she solves it), and all is well for the poor ghost of Lady Beatrice. It doesn't make much logical sense, but this episode is full of ghostly apparitions, atmospheric storms, and beautiful haunted sets.

"The Lethal Ladies" (April 16, 1962), Lupino's last episode of *Thriller*, benefits from a genuinely strong performance by leading lady Rosemary Murphy in two different roles. The two segments of "The Lethal Ladies" are titled "Murder on the Rocks" and "Goodbye, Dr. Bliss" and are based on the short stories, respectively, "The Pool" and "Goodbye, Dr. Bliss" by Joseph Payne Brennan. *Thriller* scholar Warren praises Lupino's camera angles in "Murder on the Rocks," which he considers the inferior of the two episodes, and refers to "Goodbye, Dr. Bliss" as "gripping," but spends most of his analysis dissecting the career of Brennan rather than focusing on Lupino's direction or Murphy's acting.[54]

Lupino continued to direct episodic series for other shows as well. Perhaps the most influential horror anthology television series of all time, *The Twilight Zone* first aired on CBS television on October 2, 1959, and solidified a long tradition of anthology horror and science fiction on television that would only a few years later include *The Outer Limits*, *Night Gallery*, and the aforementioned *Thriller*. Rod Serling asked Lupino to direct "The Masks" (March 20, 1964), an episode he had himself written.[55] She had previously acted in "The Sixteen Millimeter Shrine," the first season's fourth episode. "The Masks," a fifth-season episode, became the only original *Twilight Zone* episode directed by a woman. Lupino enjoyed the script, which depicted a tense and ghastly evening in a New Orleans mansion during Mardi Gras as four ungrateful family members eagerly anticipate the death of their patriarch.

Robert Keith was cast as Jason Foster, a wealthy old man on the brink of death. His daughter Emily (Virginia Gregg), son-in-law Wilfred (Milton Seltzer), and two grandchildren, Paula (Brooke Hayward) and Wilfred Jr. (Alan Sues) arrive at his mansion because of his imminent death. Though they are there supposedly to provide strength and ease his passing, it's evident that they're more interested in inheriting his large fortune than making sure he spends his last hours in comfort.

When they go up to see Foster, Paula focuses on her reflection in a mirror. Her grandfather promptly points out her vanity. Wilfred Jr. is a brute. Emily is a hypochondriac. Wilfred is greedy. He doesn't love his family any more than they love him. Unshaken by his insults or perhaps eager to remain in his will, the family humors the old man's ill temper. They even agree to wear special masks he has bought from an old Cajun in celebration of Mardi Gras. The creepy, simplistic masks were designed by famous makeup artist William Tuttle and made of Styrofoam to look like carved wood.[56]

Foster's mask is merely a skull, the face of Death. "*Because I am alive*," he explains. They must wear the masks until midnight, after which Foster promises they have fulfilled their agreement and will inherit everything he owns.

The most impressive scene in "The Masks" is a heated conversation between Emily, Wilfred, Jr., and Paula five minutes before midnight. Their facial expressions are hidden, but nowhere are their personalities, fears, greed, and anger more apparent than when they speak their lines beneath the stoic, hideous visages. They have been wearing the grotesque masks for hours, suffocating under their heat and abrasive annoyance; they've been forced to look at one another's horrible features while enduring increasing boredom and anxiety. Their voices grate, and their patience is stretched thin. They finally beg to remove the masks, betraying their inability to cooperate. It's a moment of genius for

Lupino, which might surpass all her other television work.

Jason's mask represents not only his death but the end of his family's joy—he is a bringer of a sort of death for them. "*You're caricatures*," he exclaims before he suddenly perishes in his chair with a small and understated jerk. Free at last from the tyranny of Jason Foster, Wilfred Sr. is the first to remove his mask; what he finds is horrifying. His face has molded itself into monstrous features. The rest of his family follows, and one by one, they are revealed as grotesques doomed to enjoy Foster's money as outcasts and monsters. However, Foster's face, under his skull mask, is the same as it was in life.

While at first "The Masks" seems to mete out just punishment to weak people, Foster seems just as greedy and weak as his daughter's family. He can't stand the idea of giving away his money, of his family getting to live on and enjoy his estate after he has gone. He spends the entire episode insulting his family and alienating them rather than attempting to reconcile. "Why must you always say such cruel and miserable things to me?" begs his daughter at one point before midnight, after he has insulted her appallingly. Emily feels the lack of her father's love keenly. She is not without feeling. How much influence Foster had on the outcome of his daughter's personality and her family's should be considered before placing the blame squarely on them. Having one's face molded into that of a monster as lifelong punishment for being the shallow, unhappy daughter of a despotic old man does not seem just in many ways. Perhaps the real moral of "The Masks" is not that the superficial and weak are to be punished but that those with the power often unjustly and cruelly wield it over the spineless for perceived injustices.

Lupino came close to creating her own anthology horror series; in the early 1960s, she pitched her television show to different networks. It was called *Ida Lupino Presents This is Murder* or *Theatre of Crime Classics*. Lupino described it this way: "It's about when people love too much. Or hate too much. Or lust too much. It's about murder. All kinds of murders. In every land. From every time. And the difference is: they are all true."[57] That series never materialized, and Lupino never quite fully identified as a director. When asked about her acting career, she always said she was directing television in between film roles, but she acted less and less as time went on and directed more. By the 1970s, however, she had stopped both acting and directing for the most part, choosing instead to focus on her family and husband.

In 1950, Lupino was the first woman to join the Director's Guild of America—no small accomplishment. While she wasn't the first woman director in the United States, she was the first to establish a career in the post-World War II television revolution, leading many women, both in the United States and the United Kingdom, to direct professionally. Perhaps the most telling example of Lupino's personality as a director is not the oft-quoted statement that as an actress, she was "the poor man's Bette Davis," but instead that as a director, she was considered, and considered herself "the poor man's Don Siegel."[58]

Lela Swift was one of the first women, after Lupino, to direct United States television and one of the most prolific horror television directors of her time. She began as an assistant director to Worthington Miner as early as 1948 on the CBS hour-long show *Studio One* and was quickly promoted to become part of the CBS family. Despite her rapid ascent up the ladder at CBS, Swift felt she was held back from directing. She said, of her first promotion to director,

What happened was the head of the programming department called me in and said, "They're going to make you a director." My eyes lit up. I was really delighted, 'cause I didn't know it would ever happen to me. And he said, "But, I think that you know you'll only be doing cooking shows 'cause you're only a girl."[59]

She never did direct a cooking show, however. After directing dramatic television serials for nearly twenty years, she became a core team member in making the Gothic soap opera *Dark Shadows* in 1966.

The brainchild of Dan Curtis, *Dark Shadows* (1966-1971) was set in the Maine town of Collinsport and, for the first season, focused on family secrets, murder, and other traditional soap opera fare. Swift was signed on to direct episodes from the beginning when the working title was still *Shadows on the Wall.*[60] After six months of dismal ratings, elements of the supernatural began to creep into the storyline. Ghosts of long-dead relatives, witches, and finally vampires (in the form of the two-hundred-year-old Barnabas Collins, played to perfection by the unsettling Jonathan Frid) and even time travel emerged throughout 1966. By 1967, *Dark Shadows* was American television's first supernatural horror-themed soap opera. With the addition of charismatic Grayson Hall as Julia Hoffman, a doctor intending to cure the vampires of Collinsport, the show became successful with viewers. Fan mail began pouring in, and frenzied fans sought autographs and mobbed their favorite actors from the show. "The show, in my memory," said Swift,

> Didn't really take off with the audience till we got the vampire story going. It was much better; the ratings rose immediately once we became supernatural. But the fanaticism and the love and the hunger of the audience for this show didn't really begin, I think, until we got the vampire story going ... I do think that no one has really found out why the show was so popular when it became a vampire show. I thought about it and I think one of the reasons is that the vampire story itself is such a complex one. It is involved in all kinds of sexual feelings.[61]

Barnabas Collins (Jonathan Frid) stands below a painting of himself in a promotional photo from *Dark Shadows* (1966–1971).

Lela Swift directing on the set of *Dark Shadows*.

As the series progressed, flashbacks to the Collinsport of 1795 allowed for a dramatic and elaborate back story to Barnabas' vampirism and a dramatic Gothic love story involving New England witchcraft in the tradition of Hawthorne.

Swift directed 580 of 1,225 episodes of the series, including both the first and last episodes of the show. She also took over as producer in 1970. Dan Curtis himself directed twenty episodes under the tutelage of Swift. Actress Kathryn Leigh Scott, who played Maggie Evans, described Swift as well-respected on set:

> A remarkable, seasoned, award-winning woman director who was a pioneer in the era of live television ... Dan became her protégé. She stood by, mentoring Dan when he directed his first episodes of the show, and advised him on his first feature *House of Dark Shadows*.[62]

In episode #191, the season finale aired on March 20, 1967, the character of Laura Collins (played by Diana Millay) burns in a fiery phoenix-like death in a small fishing shack in front of her young son, David. It was shot on March 7, 1967, at ABC Studio 16 in New York because of the complicated pyrotechnics involved. The raw footage of the scene reveals discussions between the technical director Lupatkin, director Swift, and actress Millay as they create the live, in-camera effect. The entire scene is at once hectic and finely tuned; you can hear Swift giving orders and the actors and crew responding almost like clockwork. Tense, effects-heavy episodes like that one prompted Swift to describe *Dark Shadows* as "the kind of show where you could lose your mind because every week you had to keep that door creaking."[63]

In an interview for the *Dark Shadows* original series DVD release, when asked if she could remember any funny stories that had taken place on set, Swift replied, laughing,

> I don't think anything was funny at the time it happens. I remember once we sent the old house, which was one of our major sets, out to be repaired. And they instead sent it to the dump, and it was burned. And you can imagine what this did to the writers and the whole storyline ... So it sounds like a funny story, but at the time it was anything but to all of us.[64]

There are dozens more stories like this one—trivia from the set that reveals the peculiarities of the cast and crew, stories for posterity cherished by fans of the original series—like the time Joan Bennett brought Fritz Lang down to the set, and he sat in the control room watching Swift direct. Later, Lang sent Swift a fan letter, which she kept framed. Besides being one of the most famous film directors of all time, he was an avid fan of *Dark Shadows* and would watch it every day.[65]

Even though Swift once had to chastise a crew member for taking a nap in an on-set coffin prop,[66] she seems to have been extremely fond of the people she worked with on *Dark Shadows*. In particular, Joan Bennett "left her with nothing but wonderful memories."[67] She genuinely liked the actors, saying:

A ghostly encounter in Swift's horror TV pilot *Dead of Night:* "A Darkness at Blaisedon" (1969).

Heroine Angela Martin (Marj Dusay) looking out the window of the haunted house in "A Darkness at Blaisedon."

> The *Dark Shadows* cast members were an unusual group of people. They were just as dramatic in their own personas as the characters they played. So every rehearsal was like an adventure. It was just wonderful. They all were fun to work with. They were special. There wasn't an ordinary person in the whole cast.[68]

Unfortunately, Swift was not always as beloved by her *Dark Shadows* cast. Actor Jonathan Frid, Barnabas Collins himself, described the other directors of the series quite favorably, but when asked about Swift, he had this to say:

> Lela Swift got on my nerves after a while. She was too noisy, but, however, she got results, and most of the time we were fine ... one time I said, "Lela Swift will you shut up!" and I stopped everything ... I was very mad that day, and I thought I was going to get canned, because I was very rude. However, she forgave me, she had a good sense of humor. As a matter of fact, we became quite good friends after that. Sort of.[69]

A fifty-two-minute pilot for a new Dan Curtis-produced series, *Dead of Night: A Darkness at Blaisedon,* AKA *Dark of Night,* aired on ABC in 1969 but failed to gain steam as an actual series. It now exists as a bonus feature on the DVD release of the Dan Curtis-directed anthology horror feature *Dead of Night*, released by Dark Sky Films.

Shot on video during the time *Dark Shadows* was still on the air, Thayer David and Louis Edmonds, who both appeared in *Dark Shadows*, have roles. The series was titled *Dead of Night,* and "A Darkness at Blaisedon" was to be the first episode, introducing the three main characters and the premise of an ongoing paranormal investigation. We are introduced to Angela Martin (Marj Dusay), a beautiful woman from San Francisco who has just inherited a vast, broken-down mansion named Blaisedon in New England with its candelabras, classic Gothic romance exterior, misty grounds dotted with graveyards, and evocative portraits of her ancestor Commodore Nicholas Blaise (Louis Edmonds). It is also haunted.

An intrepid skeptic, former secretary Angela travels to New York City (where some 16mm city footage is erroneously mixed in the film) to meet with paranormal investigators

A television newspaper listing advertising *The Satan Murders* (1974), directed by Lela Swift for ABC's *Wide World of Mystery* program.

Jonathan Fletcher (Kerwin Matthews, who played the lead in 1958's *The 7th Voyage of Sinbad*) and his assistant Sajid Rowe (Cal Bellini). Once at Blaisedon, the three spend the next forty-five minutes navigating the Matheson-esque story (it's not too dissimilar from *The Legend of Hell House,* 1973) amid séances and haunted paintings. Angela is possessed by the Commodore and tries to kill Fletcher with an old rusty knife. They dig up graves in the cemetery yard. Fletcher conducts a séance while Angela becomes possessed by the ghost of Melinda, Blaise's wife.

By the end of the episode, Sajid, Angela, and Jonathan decide to continue their adventures as paranormal investigators together. Angela seems to have some untapped potential as a medium, so they set up the ongoing series by wrapping the darkness at Blaisedon up neatly and forever. The dozens of constantly-lit candles shine a way-too-bright light on the cast and set, and despite the gorgeous statuary, candelabras, and decent art direction, the cheap skeleton used to represent the decaying body of Melinda Blaise, as well as an organ playing Bach's Toccata and Fugue in D minor, are just too cheesy to be enjoyed.

IN THE EARLY 1970S, the ninety-minute anthology series became popular with television viewers in the United States. One of the most popular was *ABC Afternoon Playbreak* (which debuted on October 31, 1973, and ran until February 13, 1975). Airing only once a month, these made-for-television movies earned United States television network ABC eighteen Daytime Emmy Awards, the highest honor a non-prime-time series can receive. The films usually aired on weekdays during a 3:00 p.m. to 4:30 p.m. Eastern Standard Time slot, making it accessible to kids after school as well as homemakers. A heady mix of dramas, coming-of-age stories, and both Gothic and horror thrillers, the most popular episodes were often given nighttime encores.

The Gift of Terror (aired April 5, 1973), the seventh episode of the first season of *ABC Afternoon Playbreak*, won Lela Swift a Daytime Emmy for directing. Most episodes of *Playbreak* are lost, including *The Gift of Terror*. All that remains is the chilling synopsis of this supernatural episode, Swift's first foray into television directing after the end of *Dark Shadows*:

A young woman starts having premonitions of her friends dying. Once her friends begin to die, she starts having premonitions of her own death.

Another late-night anthology television movie series from ABC was *The Wide World of Mystery*, AKA *ABC's Wide World of Mystery* (1973 to 1978). The feature-length movies in this series were of the horror, thriller, and even science fiction variety. Swift's first episode of the series, *Deadly Visitor*, aired July 3, 1973. In the film, a boarding house is haunted by the ghost of a former resident, a fierce spirit (played by Ann Miles) who drives everyone else away except the young writer she has set her heart on (Perry King). *The Satan Murders* (aired on January 11, 1974), another of her horror episodes, boasts the following horrific synopsis: *a woman enters into a pact with the Devil to murder her husband.*

The Two Deaths of Sean Doolittle (aired on April 4, 1975) was another of Swift's supernatural films in the series. The story, in which a man believes he can achieve immortality through medical science and thus has no fear of dying, was based on a somewhat less interesting actual event. Actress Grayson Hall's biographer describes it as "the film no one wants to remember" and interviewed the screenwriter Sam Hall about what was to be Hall's last film:

> There was this famous man who disappeared in South America, and he had pretended to commit suicide and then sailed or something. He was discovered in South America ten years later, alive and well, living under another name. That is what it was based on.[70]

According to R.J. Jamison, Grayson Hall's biographer, Lela Swift, did not recall directing *The Two Deaths of Sean Doolittle* when he asked her about it. Co-star George Grizzard, who played the title role of Sean Doolittle, said to Jamison:

> If the director can't remember *The Two Deaths of Sean Doolittle*, you can imagine how impressive it was! I only remember I had frozen myself, came to, and was then burned to death. Barnard Hughes played my father, and we promised never to mention it.[71]

Indeed, according to Jamison, screenwriter Sam Hall readily admitted that "It wasn't any good."[72] Jamison did preserve through his interviews that Clovis Productions, Jacqueline Babbin's company, which also produced the soap opera *All My Children,* made the episode. Only two photos from the film have survived as a testament to its existence.

While four of Swift's *Wide World of Mystery* films are lost, hopefully not forever, three remain in circulation and have been digitized. *The Haunting of Rosalind* (1973) is a feature-length film episode of a series within the *Wide World of Mystery* programming called *The Classic Ghosts.*[73] This film has been preserved by the UCLA Film & Television Archive, has been digitized and restored, and screened publicly as part of the Archive's official programming.[74]

The Haunting of Rosalind stars a young Susan Sarandon and Pamela Payton-Wright as sisters Perdita and Rosalind, respectively. Beatrice Straight (best known as the female paranormal investigator in *Poltergeist*, 1982) co-stars as their mother. When handsome

Arthur Lloyd (Frank Converse) marries Perdita, Rosalind imagines the ghost of Arthur's first wife, Helen, haunts them and will soon kill Perdita, driving her pregnant sister insane and setting off a chain of events that destroys their lives and opens them up to hauntings by vengeful spirits.

The vibrancy of the costume and background colors are remarkable; the house itself is dark, but the yellow, red, blue, and green dresses, curtains, and window lighting are shockingly bright. Images of Rosalind standing in windows and mirror reflections are a go-to transition between scenes, as they were for Swift in both *Dark Shadows* and *Dead of Night: A Darkness at Blaisedon*. Because this is a Gothic ghost story, Swift was familiar with the subject matter and setting and knew how to perfectly pace the drama and scares so that the short run time of seventy minutes is enough.

The source material for *The Haunting of Rosalind* is the Henry James short story "The Romance of Certain Old Clothes," a Gothic tale that was first published in 1868 and then republished in 1885 with some minor changes to the characters' names. It is also the basis of the 2020 television horror miniseries *The Haunting of Bly Manor,* episode number eight, "The Romance of Certain Old Clothes," directed by Axelle Carolyn (*Soulmate*, 2014), which is used as a backstory to explain some of the hauntings at the mansion. Unlike Swift's version, the episode is black and white as an homage to Gothic horror films of the 1930s to 1950s. Of the 2020 episode, show creator Mike Flanagan said:

> That comes from a time when it was about atmosphere and dread and character development and not about jump scares and gore and special effects ... and Axelle Carolyn, who directed that episode, is also a student of classic black-and-white horror cinema and came to it with so many exciting ideas of how she wanted to tell it when it came to the costume design for that episode, which was this juggernaut compared to the rest of the season.[75]

Alien Lover (1975) was another George Lefferts *Wide World of Mystery* script and boasted the opening credit "Introducing Kate Mulgrew," an actress who would go on to be best-known to genre fans as Captain Kathryn Janeway on *Star Trek: Voyager* in the 1990s. Mulgrew plays Susan, a teenager who comes to live with her aunt and uncle after her parents die. She suffers a mental breakdown before finding an old television set in their attic—a television set that shows her the face of a handsome, lonely young man named Marc. She doesn't know that Marc is an alien bent on the destruction of the human race and is hoping to find a way to cross from their world into ours.

Alien Lover is a Gothic story with the classic premise of a young, troubled girl wandering the darkened halls of an unfamiliar home and navigating familial mysteries. Marc is the Gothic romance lover—a man who usually overcomes his demons to be worthy of the heroine's true love—but in this case, Marc slowly reveals himself as ominous and Susan's love, even in the face of an alien takeover. Though the true nature of the death of Susan's parents is never stated, it is hinted that Susan feels guilty and that she may have been responsible for it. The theme of loving, or hating, one's parents is revisited continuously throughout the story, like when Marc tells Susan that in his dimension, parents are removed from their children immediately after birth so that they can't "poison" them with their misguided parenting. In a psychiatric evaluation, Susan insists that she loved her parents, though the psychiatrist seems to be prompting her to say otherwise. And when Susan's aunt and uncle, her new parental figures, tell her they are having her committed again, she tells them, "*I just want you to know I hate you*." Was Susan originally committed after her parent's death because she was suspected of murdering them out of hate? *Alien Lover* doesn't make this clear either way.

Playful, creative camera angles, like framing characters through the open spaces in hanging chandeliers, using characters' reflections in mirrors, and switching to point-of-view shots whenever possible (Swift's modus operandi on her *Dark Shadows* episodes) add spice to what is otherwise a static play taking place mainly in three rooms: the living room, Susan's bedroom, and the attic. Kate Mulgrew gives a very sophisticated performance as the possibly-deranged, thoughtful, lonely young teenager who has just lost her family. The story is not only about insanity and loss; it's about young love and the fiction of television and fantasy instead of actual physical and emotional relationships. As television-movie blogger Amanda Reyes puts it so eloquently in her review of the film,

> *Alien Lover* makes an interesting comment on the phenomenon of finding solace on the small screen. Susan has a hunky love interest, but she constantly turns to the man in the television because he claims to understand the lack of wholeness within her. He recites poetry with her and plies her with compliments, creating the fantasy of the perfect man, while making himself seem unthreatening because the television screen holds him back from initiating physical contact. The natural awkwardness and fear of going into a first romantic relationship after the loss of a great love is captured rather nicely ... [76]

One reviewer believes that George Lefferts used the short Ray Bradbury story "Zero Hour" as his main inspiration for *Alien Lover*.[77] In it, children talk to an alien race through their television, and none of the adults believe them. The aliens end up invading Earth with the help of the children. Lefferts adapted "Zero Hour" into a thirty-minute teleplay in 1955 for the television series *Star Tonight*, so he was undoubtedly familiar with it. While it does share some story elements, there are just as many similarities between *Alien Lover* and the 1982 feature film *Poltergeist*: both have children hearing voices from another dimension through the television, and both have paranormal events manifest themselves as very bright lights behind closed doors in which children are trapped with malignant entities. Swift passed away on August 4, 2015. She was ninety-six.

Gloria Monty, like Swift, had a long and prolific career directing daytime television soap operas and horror/thriller films for *ABC's Wide World of Mystery*. However, she is far less known to horror film fans than Swift, whose devoted *Dark Shadows* fans have preserved her memory. In 1978, she famously revamped the soap opera *General Hospital* as a producer, having the character of Spencer (played by Anthony Geary) rape Laura Baldwin (played by Genie Francis) on a dance floor, only to have Laura fall in love with him afterward.

Monty has the distinction of being the first woman television executive at ABC and thus felt she had to prove herself far more than her male contemporaries did:

> Sexism was absolutely appalling. They waited for you to fail. I had to know twice as much as everyone else, especially the technical part. I had a good theatrical background, which made it easier. I tried not to be assertive at the beginning—a man in my position could have gotten much further. I just hung in and kept on learning. Any slight mistake was really exaggerated: "Well, that's a woman for you." Gals have taken tremendous strides forward since then ... But I learned one thing: keep on being a woman rather than try to be one of the guys. I watched a woman do that, and it was abysmally unsuccessful.[78]

Those who worked under Monty called her many things: "Mother," "a genius," and "a Hitler figure, incapable of allowing credit to anyone else." She was the model for the motherly producer of the fictional soap opera in the 1982 film *Tootsie*. In contrast, critics of her work on *General Hospital* say she turned it into "a trashy electronic comic strip."[79] An intimidating micromanager, despite being five foot two and "85 pounds after a big meal,"[80] Monty could be quite antagonistic herself. She once said to the cast of *General Hospital*, after watching an episode they worked on together, "The only thing I could think of doing was to put you all in a plane and crash it."[81]

Like Swift, Monty directed several episodes of *ABC's Wide World of Mystery* before joining *General Hospital*. Unfortunately, three out of four of her episodes are currently considered lost. Monty's first ABC television movie is *The Classic Ghosts: The Screaming Skull* (1973): an adaptation of the short horror story of the same name by Francis Marion Crawford. Not to be confused with the 1958 horror B-movie *The Screaming Skull* (though it is loosely based on the same short story), the film is the founder of the National Society of Film Critics Hollis Alpert's only film credit. Like the other episodes of ABC's late-night *Wide World of Mystery*, it was shot on videotape, giving it that 'soap opera' feel. Though it was originally shot and aired in color, the video-to-film kinescope transfers to 16mm were made in black and white, so all color versions are lost.

A drawing-room thriller with a heady mix of psychedelia, *The Screaming Skull* is littered with choppy dream sequences and ornate cathedral windows of stained glass. It bears an uncanny resemblance to episodes of *Dark Shadows*. It's a less imaginative version of Poe's "The Tell-Tale Heart" with a moaning, clearly fake, and polished skull instead of a beating floorboard. *The Screaming Skull* episode was created as part of a larger series titled *The Classic Ghosts*, developed in the United Kingdom by Hollis Alpert and produced by Specter Productions. It is unclear whether that series had other episodes and whether they initially aired in the United Kingdom; by 1974, it was on American television sets as part of the ABC *Wide World of Mystery*.

The House and the Brain was Monty's second *Wide World of Mystery* film and aired on March 16th, 1976, but possibly for the first time as early as 1973. Listed in *Creature Features Movie Guide Strikes Again* by John Stanley, it's about a woman possessed by the spirit of a warlock: she lures men to their death in an old castle. Very loosely inspired by the short horror story "The House and the Brain" by Victorian author Edward Bulwer-Lytton, the screenwriter, John Vlahos, took liberties when adapting it for the screen. We're lucky enough to have a contemporary review/preview of the episode:

> *The House and the Brain*—a bizarre story of the occult about a young woman who is held a virtual prisoner by her satanic guardian, and a sympathetic young army officer who takes lodging in their house. Hurd Hatfield stars as the guardian 'Constantine St. Mai,' Carol Williard as the girl 'Marianna Gallatin,' and Keith Charles as 'Lt. David Vaughan.' Vaughan is charmed by the eighteenth-century mansion in which he has rented quarters and by the portrait of Marianna's ancestor, whom she so closely resembles. But he's mystified when Marianna tells him she never leaves the house, and by her refusal of his offer to take her away. Later, Vaughan hears a conversation between a sobbing Marianna and a man coming from her room. Investigation shows that the room is unoccupied. Then Marianna tells him he heard only the ghosts who inhabit the house. That night he dreams he is a Union Army captain who comes to the house for a rendezvous with Marianna. In the dream, a man detains her, ordering that she kill her lover. When she refuses, he murders the officer. Vaughan recalls his dream for an uneasy Marianna the next morning. His story is interrupted by his first meeting with St. Mai. Vaughan is amazed when he recognizes St. Mai as the killer in his dream.[82]

Sorority Kill (1974) is another Monty episode of *Wide World of Mystery* that was long thought lost. Like Swift's *The Haunting of Rosalind* (1973), it resurfaced in 2020 and was made available for public viewing (though the surviving version is from a VHS recording and has numerous tracking flaws). It was described in contemporary television listings as a "suspense story of a group of people held captive by a psychotic killer."[83] Alternately, it is described as *"a chilling story of a psychotic killer who holds six people captive in a*

A moment of terror as Martha Scott, portraying the housemother to a college sorority house, receives rough treatment at the hands of Tony Geary, who plays an accused rapist in Screen Gem's *Sorority Kill* (1974).

David McCallum is Dr. Pratt in Gloria Monty's episode of *The Classic Ghosts:* "The Screaming Skull" (1973).

sorority house, each of them realizing that their captor's mind is like a defective time bomb and could go off at any moment." It was written by Fletcher Beaumont and Wilford Lloyd Baumes and was based on a story originally written by Baumes. Baumes also produced, and Douglas S. Cramer was Executive Producer.[84]

Sorority Kill stars Anthony Geary, with whom Monty would work extensively on *General Hospital* in just a few years, as the psychotic maniac.

Sorority Kill is written like a 1950s noir; the plot is very similar to 1948's William Holden film *The Dark Past*, which is a remake of *Blind Alley* (1939), which is similar in many ways to *The Petrified Forest* (1936). *Sorority Kill* is the unsophisticated, and sometimes very silly, television version of these stories. There's no real tension (Monty doesn't seem good at that, nor at any scenes where her actors have to move around the screen or perform action sequences). The acting is over-the-top, the pacing never really sells the urgency of the hostage situation, and Geary's Kurt, while extremely intense, doesn't seem to have any clear motivation. Together, Geary and Monty would fine-tune his dark and absorbing intensity and go on to create one of the most sensational daytime soap opera characters of all time: Luke Spencer. Geary also appears in the 1972 fantasy horror film *Blood Sabbath,* directed by Brianne Murphy, covered in Chapter 3 of this book.

If Ida Lupino paved pathways for women directors in United States television, Wendy Toye cleared roadways for women directors in anthology horror and science fiction on BBC television in the 1960s. Numerous women directed BBC television in the late 1950s and through the 1960s when Lupino was the only one directing for American television. Rosemary Hill, Chloe Gibson, and Julia Smith were among several women who directed episodes of the BBC mystery/crime series *Suspense* ("Wormwood," "The Edge of Discovery," and "Letter to a Soldier" respectively, all of which aired in 1963). Smith would go on to be the first woman to direct the cult science fiction series *Doctor Who* (she directed eight episodes from 1966-1967),[85] while Hill's 1960 miniseries *The Haunted House* was a film version of the ancient comedic Roman play *Mostellaria* by the Roman author Plautus in which a house is said to be haunted by the ghost of a man killed there. It is also the basis of the twentieth-century musical *A Funny Thing Happened on the Way to the Forum*.[86] The crime/thriller series *Thirty-Minute Theatre* featured more than a dozen episodes directed by women: Elsa Bolam, Anne Head, Elizabeth Small, Suzanne Neild, and June Wyndham-Davies (who also directed the television horror movie *Christmas Spirits*, 1981, and an episode of the horror anthology series *Shades of Darkness*: "Agatha Christie's The Last Séance" in 1986).

Naomi Capon was a British television producer and director (born 1921) who began her career working for the BBC's North American Service in the United States in 1947. Mostly remembered for co-directing the miniseries *The Six Wives of Henry VIII* (1970) and other lavish, romantic, and historical television productions, Capon directed several episodes of BBC anthology horror and thriller television in the 1960s, making her the first woman to do so after Wendy Toye's shorts aired in the 1950s.[87]

Though she began by directing historical series for children, at some point in the 1960s, Capon moved on to more adult content. Like her contemporaries Rosemary Hill, Chloe Gibson, and Julia Smith, Capon contributed to the BBC series *Suspense*; Capon's

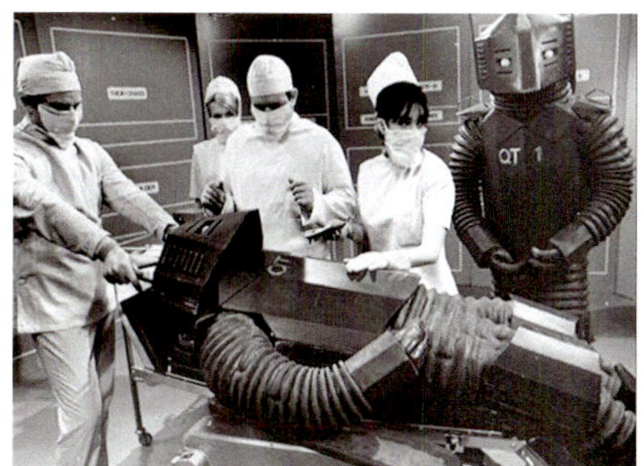

A still image from Naomi Capon's *Out of the Unknown* episode "The Prophet" (1967).

One of the only known photos from Naomi Capon's lost episode of *Late Night Horror: "The Bells of Hell"* (1968).

episode was "The Light Trap" (May 21, 1962). "The House," the first season opener of the anthology series *The Wednesday Thriller* (August 4, 1965), was directed by Capon. In it, a little girl is given a Victorian doll's house to play with, and she obsesses over the elaborate dolls in period clothing. The girl constructs an elaborate fantasy around the two dolls, presumably with deadly or unhappy results. Unfortunately, the series ran only eight episodes, and none survived. Capon directed three episodes of the 1960s science fiction anthology series *Out of the Unknown* ("The Prophet," "The World in Silence," and "Sucker Bait"), but it is her episode of the horror anthology series *Late Night Horror*, "The Bells of Hell" (May 17, 1968) which is best remembered by fans of 1960s British horror television.

Late Night Horror is said to be "a bit of a misnomer" by contemporary fans of the show, as the plots "put sinister twists on apparently ordinary situations." The subject matter of the now lost "The Bells of Hell" episode, on paper, appears to fall nicely into the category of a horror story.[88] Based on the short story "Ringing the Changes" by Robert Aickman,[89] the title was changed to appeal more to horror fans. The screen adaptation by Hugh Whitemore remained relatively faithful to the original short story; Whitemore was a fan of Aickman's and hoped to achieve some "poetic ambiguity" with his script. Of the title change, he said:

> I thought "The Bells of Hell" was a cheap, vulgar, and dumbing down title for what I still think of as a strange and subtle story. I much preferred "Ringing the Changes." I forget who thought of the new title; it may have been the story editor, Richard Davis. It certainly seemed silly to muck about with the title of a thirty-minute story that would be screened very late, as the size of the audience must have been minuscule. I didn't approve at all, and I remember arguments—which, of course, I eventually lost![90]

The finished script was offered to Naomi Capon after she had already turned down directing the *Late Night Horror* episode "Party Games" (aired as "The Corpse Can't Play"). She was impressed with the new script and said it presented "the most exciting possibilities." Capon decided on the town of Wivenhoe in Essex to represent the fictional Holihaven and used a local pub and inn as the main set locations. The official

BBC television listing synopsis for the episode described the plot:

> Three months after their marriage, Phrynne and Gerald Banstead decide to stay at "The Bell," a picturesque pub in East Anglia ... At first, the place seems strangely deserted—the only sound they can hear is the desolate tolling of a church bell. Mr. and Mrs. Pascoe, who run "The Bell," and Commander Shotcroft, the only other guest, seem desperately frightened of something vague and indefinable. Later, when the young couple is in bed, all the bells of the village, which have been ringing loudly, suddenly stop. A single cry rings out along the streets, a cry which is to involve the Bansteads in a hideous night of unbelievable horror.[91]

Throughout the episode, Gerald Banstead (Ronald Hines) is unnerved by the clamoring bells, which seem to herald some horrible catastrophe. In contrast, his wife Phrynne (Michele Dotrice) seems to enjoy their clanging. As the night progresses, the couple is warned by Commander Shotcroft, another guest at The Bell, that the town of Holihaven rings the bells to arouse their dead and reunite with them and that they will do so again this evening. When the bells stop ringing and the dead rise to see their loved ones, the townspeople begin an eerie chanting song and drag Phrynne away from her husband to join their revelry. The following day, when he finds her again, Phrynne seems to have enjoyed the experience while Gerald is terrified.

Capon was adamant that the musical chanting, performed by the BBC's Radiophonic Workshop at Maida Vale, should be a "weird and partly distorted chant" with "tramping, shuffling and dancing" feet of the townspeople. The only music in the entire episode is the chanting of the locals as they reunite with their dead because Capon felt that "all the 'noise' should emanate from the bells and the rhythm that they establish."[92]

A contemporary review of the episode in *The Sunday Telegraph* said that "The Bells of Hell" had "come closer than anything recently to fulfilling the proper requirements of a ghost story," that it had a "disquieting atmosphere," and "a genuinely macabre climax as the dead awoke to go dancing and chanting through the streets." The last scene, in which the lead actress seems to be excited by the site of gravediggers in a cemetery, is described as "a note of erotic equivocation as Miss Dotrice, eyeing some vaguely familiar gravediggers, licked little pink tongue around little pink lips."[93]

The first horror television series in color, *Late Night Horror* was something of an experiment in new color technology for BBC television. The series initially ran between April 19 and May 24, 1968, and then again in December 1969 through March 1970, before the footage was erased from the master tapes. *Late Night Horror's* archived episodes are all lost, except for "The Corpse Can't Play," rumored to be in a private collector's hands but not publicly available. The time-coded wraparound title sequence was found in 2009 on a VHS tape made of old BBC television showreels and digitized for online viewing; the soundtrack and shockingly creepy imagery are perhaps more intense than modern viewers would have expected from the 1960s. All that is left of "The Bells from Hell" are the production files, the camera script, and a tape of sound effects used in the episode.[94]

Much of Capon's work has been lost; all but two of her episodes of the dramatic series

Theatre 625 were never recovered, and it was only in 2011 that her episode of the crime series *Thirteen Against Fate* ("The Judge," July 17, 1966) was located in the British Film Institute archives.

Joan Kemp-Welch was another successful BBC television director in the 1960s. When she began directing for television in the 1950s, Kemp-Welch found herself shoehorned into directing segments to appeal solely to female viewers. "And, I was very upset at doing women's programmes," she said, "because I thought, you know, I'd fought against—I'd fought to be accepted in the theatre, and now I'm back again, you know, in women's programmes."[95]

In 1955 she was approached by the first independent television production company servicing London, Associated-Rediffusion, to be one of their directors; she immediately signed on. This association would lead to a varied and thriving television directing career, including her episode of the fantastic anthology series *Mystery and Imagination*, "The Open Door" (1966).

Mystery and Imagination was a successful supernatural and horror anthology series that ran for five seasons on ITV in the United Kingdom from 1966 through 1970. Relying on ghost and horror stories from classic Victorian literature rather than newer science fiction from current authors, *Mystery and Imagination* embodied a Gothic sensibility with its versions of stories by Edgar Allen Poe, Sheridan Le Fanu, Mary Shelley, and M. R. James, unlike anything else airing on television at the time. The series was famous for using sensational tag lines for its episodes; the one written for "The Open Door" was *Please hurry home, father—mother and I are frightened out of our senses*. Of the original twenty-four episodes, sixteen are lost (or currently missing); fortunately, Kemp-Welch's episode, "The Open Door," is not one of them.

Based on the short story by Margaret Oliphant,[96] "The Open Door" is preceded by opening credits peppered with swirling tarot cards, satanic imagery, and a montage of seductive, Gothic imagery before being introduced by Beckett, the Byronesque host of the black-and-white *Mystery and Imagination* television series.

"The Open Door" is a relatively static piece taking place in (mainly) two sets: a Victorian country house and the ruined remains of a mansion on the same property. After being called home because his sick son Roland (Henry Beltran) is having nightmarish fits, Colonel Mortimer (Jack Hawkins) leaves London hurriedly and attends to the boy's bedside while his wife (Rachel Gurney) and daughter Jeanie (Jill Mai Meredith) look on. Roland is bedridden and complains of hearing anguished voices crying in the night outside his window, coming from the ruins. Colonel Mortimer investigates the ruins during the day and finds nothing.

With Corporal Jones (Derek Tansley), Mortimer uncovers a legend that there are things on the estate grounds that "*are neither man nor woman.*" Mortimer and Jones, creeping along alone, are bombarded by natural sounds at midnight. Just as Mortimer and Jones doubt they will find anything, a whispering, breathing groan begins to sound. At last, a bloodcurdling scream rings out and turns into a pitiful crying, "*Mother, let me in!*" Mortimer connects the spirit to Roland's illness and sets about freeing the spirit from the ruins.

The evocative sound design and off-camera voice acting in "The Open Door" was the first thing about the episode that struck Helen Wheatley in her thorough book on the *Mystery and Imagination* series:

> This sound was intentionally 'uncanny,' distorted and without a visible (diegetic) origin within an inherently visual medium. As a drama built around the actors' reactions to that which, though clearly audible, is visually 'not there,' the production's emphasis on audio rather than visual 'haunting' allows a description of "The Open Door" as a 'radio play with pictures.' By emphasizing sound over image the episode appears to 'borrow' from the sound design of the radio ghost-play.[97]

Wheatley notes how sound was not used to tell the story of the haunting in the ruins but to indicate changes from day to night, in which birds, wind, and other ambient noises are employed:

> This was an episode of *Mystery and Imagination*, which attempted to answer the call of critics such as Denis Thomas to "show less and suggest more" by revisiting ghost-story broadcasting on domestic radio.[98]

A *Television Times* article accompanying "The Open Door" television premiere also focused on the sounds; the show's publicists knew its selling points and wanted to ensure prospective audiences were geared up. In the article, actress Amanda Walker, the off-screen voice of the ghost of Willy, is the center of attention rather than the onscreen actors or the literary origins of the story:

> She is thirty-year-old Amanda Walker. Amanda told me: "I was told that my sobs and screams had to be really uninhibited, so the first thing I did was to take off my shoes. Then, to avoid self-consciousness, I turned my back on the faces in the control room ... the script only gave instructions like 'moan and sigh,' 'low moan,' 'moan and cry,' and 'sob softly.'" So how did she do it? Amanda, who is married to actor Patrick Godfrey, said: "I'll let you into my secret. I thought of my four-year-old son, Richard. I thought of his agonised cries and heartrending sobs when he pricks his finger or falls down or suffers some other misfortune."[99]

Walker is the most memorable performer and frightening aspect of the entire episode.

Kemp-Welch continued to direct for BBC television, including an episode of the show *Haunted* ("Through a Glass Darkly," aired on January 13, 1968), a series about a paranormal investigator. The series is lost. She did work in the crime/thriller genre early in the 1980s, mainly on the true crime show *Lady Killers* (1980 to 1981), directing what would be her last two television episodes: "Miss Madeline Smith," about a nineteenth-century poisoner, and "A Smile is Sometimes Worth a Million Dollars" about a 1922 prostitute murderer.

Another woman who made her career as a BBC television director in the 1960s and 1970s was Anthea Browne-Wilkinson. Like Moira Armstrong, she directed episodes of the adventure series *Adam Adamant Lives!* and the crime thrillers *Detective* and *Menace*, but her 1976 television movie *The Witches of Pendle* has a supernatural slant.

Based on the story of the 1612 witch trials and executions in Lancaster, England,[100] Browne-Wilkinson's film stays reasonably close to historical records. The protagonist is teenage Alizon Device (pronounced Alison Day-vis), played by the remarkable Cathryn Harrison, granddaughter of actor Rex Harrison. Harrison had previously starred in the surreal 1975 fantasy movie *Black Moon*, and *The Witches of Pendle* is no less surreal or startling in imagery than that film. Set in 1612, Alizon Device is accused of witchcraft by a local peddler. Her mother, Elizabeth, holds coven meetings and believes that Alizon has supernatural powers. Alizon believes herself to be a witch. She talks with ravens, even calling one by the name of Jim Crow and ordering it to do her bidding. She speaks of dreams, visions, hallucinations, and premonitions that have come true. Whether she is truly insane or truly a witch is never understood; it is made clear that she is the product of an abusive family born to poverty, incest, and rape. She confesses to giving birth to two stillborn children (the result of rape by her older brother). She has fits, the intensity of which even makes the judges in the courtroom hallucinate to the point of whipping her bloody. Her family is also put on trial, and eventually, as in real life, her mother, brother, and several other local coven members are put to death by hanging. Browne-Wilkinson depicts this with a very expressionist shot of hanging human shadows against a deep, bright blue background—a cold and silent death for such a furiously loud and manic group.

Despite the dark and overbearing transfer (the only one preserved), the colors are remarkably vibrant. Browne-Wilkinson alternates between bright deep reds and natural

A surreal moment in Anthea Browne-Wilkinson's TV movie *The Witches of Pendle* (1966).

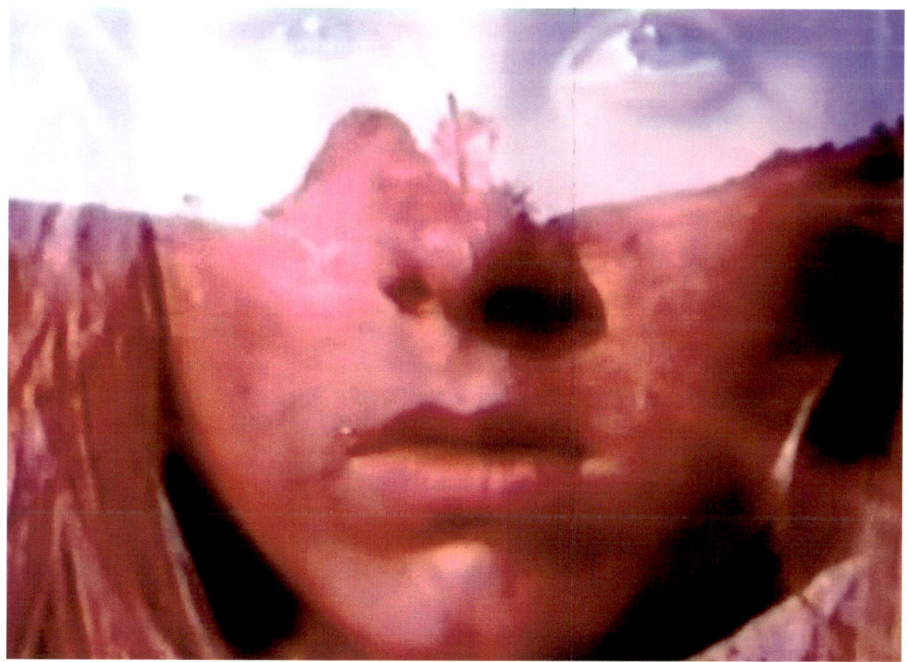

A little boy is subjected to dreadful psychic experiments in *The Omega Factor* episode "Child's Play" (1979), directed by Fiona Cummings.

Tom Crane (James Hazeldine) hovers over a dead person in *The Omega Factor* episode "Child's Play".

lighting, one conveying the stifling confines of jail cells and the other the natural beauty of the countryside.

The Witches of Pendle is no documentary or even realistic reenactment for historical posterity. It is surreal and experimental, with a tense sexual undertone to the proceedings against Alizon. Ultimately, Alizon is a tragic victim of violence, mental illness, and sexism that needlessly murdered hundreds of women in England between the fifteenth and eighteenth centuries.

Scottish director Fiona Cumming is best known for her involvement in the original BBC science fiction series *Doctor Who*, of which she directed sixteen episodes in the 1980s and worked with five separate actors playing The Doctor. She also directed two episodes of the science fiction series *Blake's 7* in 1980 and an episode of the popular science fiction/horror series *The Omega Factor* (1979), "Child's Play," about a journalist named Tom Crane (James Hazeldine), who writes mainly about the occult and paranormal phenomena. A mysterious government agency called "Department 7" conscripts him, as they believe he has true psychic powers. Department 7 is searching for something called "The Omega Factor," which can only be described as the untapped psychic potential of the human brain. Crane helps them investigate paranormal phenomena while also investigating his wife's untimely death in a car accident that may have been planned. He is joined by investigator Anne Reynolds (Louise Jameson) on his adventures.

Only ten episodes of the shot-on-video *The Omega Factor* were aired. The series was called "thoroughly evil" by British Christian values campaigner Mary Whitehouse, who believed that the supernatural references were bad influences on the minds of the British public, particularly in the episode "Powers of Darkness."[101] Many twenty-first-century genre fans consider it a precursor to the 1990s American science fiction/mystery series *The X Files*: both are about government agencies researching paranormal activity, and both have a conspiracy-obsessed male and red-headed female partnered in investigations (Louise Jameson, of *Doctor Who* fame, played Dr. Anne Reynolds, Tom Crane's investigative partner).[102] Whether the BBC was pressured to cancel the series or decided to for other, unrelated reasons, it is commonly believed that *The Omega Factor* was taken off the air due to government intervention.[103]

Chapter 3

A woman's place is in exploitation films

DRIVE-INS, ART FILMS AND FEMINISM

The haunted voodoo doll can manifest in the middle of the street in Doris Wishman's film *Indecent Desires* (1968). Image courtesy of the American Genre Film Archive.

Alison Nastasi (writing for Flavorwire): "In recent years, there's been a big push to reevaluate films from the Golden Age era, both mainstream movies and adult films, and reframe the works of women—to recognize the contributions of women from the time period."

Roberta Findlay: "I wasn't aware that it was a Golden Age era."[1]

IN 1960, IDA LUPINO WAS the only working female director in either film or television. By 1980, roughly fifteen women had made mainstream films distributed by major studios, and dozens more had found a niche in low-budget exploitation, art films, and pornography. These stories of female horror and exploitation directors are often left out of the mainstream discourse about women in the film industry, especially regarding the significant milestones women directors reached in the 1970s. Instead, film historians and feminists prefer to talk about French New Wave pioneer Agnès Varda, for instance, shunning the dirtier, less classy struggles of women who eked out an existence making violent, often profoundly sexual, horror films. Female horror film producers to come out of this era (Gale Anne Hurd and Debra Hill, for example) are respected as businesswomen who made wise financial decisions catering to audiences, but women horror directors are often ignored as part of a seedy underground populated by exploitation films while historians focus mainly on their non-horror accomplishments. These women deserve to have their stories placed within the more powerful framework of the rise of women in the film industry rather than relegated to retrospectives in cult movie magazines.

The late 1960s through the early 1980s was an important and impressive time for women directors, producers, writers, editors, and cinematographers. There were once again as many working in Hollywood as there had been in the silent film era. The formation of special women's film organizations reflected this rise in numbers as well as the understanding that women faced some significant obstacles to success in the mainstream film industry: Women in Film formed in 1973; in 1974, the American Film Institute began the first intensive lab for women directors, the Directing Workshop for Women (of which horror director Karen Arthur, the first women to join the Director's Guild, was an inaugural participant, along with Brianne Murphy in 1977, Lesli Linka Glatter and Mary Neema Barnette in 1982, and *The Slumber Party Massacre* screenwriter Rita Mae Brown in 1991, among many other horror directors after that); the Directors Guild of America (DGA), Screen Actors Guild (SAG), and Writers Guild of America (WGA) were actively involved in debates about sexism within the industry, prompting SAG and WGA to form Women's Committees in 1972 and the DGA in 1979; in 1980, Brianne Murphy was the first woman to join the Hollywood faction of the International Cinematographers Guild. In 1976, Lina Wertmüller was the first woman nominated for a Best Director Oscar by the Academy of Motion Pictures Arts and Sciences for her film *Seven Beauties*. In the United Kingdom, the Edinburgh Film Festival featured a women filmmakers section for the first time in 1972; that same year, the London Women's Film Group was organized.

In the early 1970s, the feminist and civil rights movements had brought women to the forefront of film theory and art; suddenly, women appeared behind the camera in droves while the women in front of the camera became more varied and complex. "Many girls growing up today do not understand the extent of the impact of the 1960s, and there's a story to be told that isn't only flower children and drugs, but about the power of passionate youth," said horror/genre director Rachel Talalay in an interview about her long career.[2] It was a time for art and politics when both women and men filmmakers explored sexuality and gender. "In the 1960s," explained surreal animator Caroline Leaf,

> Filmmaking was undergoing a democratization process similar to the one that happened a few decades later with digital technology: the popularization of cheaper 16 and 8mm film stock meant that filmmaking was almost affordable for everyone. It began to be taught in liberal arts colleges.[3]

Directors like Věra Chytilová (*Daisies*, 1966), Mai Zetterling (*Night Games*, 1966), Jane Arden (*The Other Side of the Underneath*, 1972), Christina Hornisher (*Hollywood 90028*, 1973), Valie Export (*Invisible Adversaries*, 1977), and Helma Sanders-Brahms (*No Mercy, No Future*, 1981) were pioneers of modern art, avant-garde, New Wave, and surrealist horror films. Shirley Clarke was an early independent art film director whose surreal films (like 1964's *The Cool World*) make her a direct descendant of Maya Deren's provocative, individualist legacy. *The Plastic Dome of Norma Jean* (1966) by independent director Juleen Compton uses fantasy to showcase a story of female independence.

With the breakdown of the restrictive censorship of the Hays Code and the break up of the studio monopoly on theatrical distribution in the 1960s, violent, independent films of the 1970s found a home in art house theaters in the United Kingdom and Europe and drive-in and grindhouse theaters in the United States. As a result, new films were being made for a variety of budgets and a variety of audiences. Numerous women directors began making low-budget, sexual, sensual, and often very violent horror films featuring an assortment of female characters either entirely independently or for new independent production companies finally able to compete in Hollywood. Author Graeme Harper, in his discussion of female characters and women's stories in 1970s horror films, says,

> It is no surprise to find this kind of horror film appearing on drive-in screens in the 1970s. Not only did a new mode of family living, more open to secular 'marriages,' increasingly inclined to question paternal autocracy and to promote such ideals as 'doing your own thing,' mean a disintegration of traditional ideas about the constitution of the Western family unit, but the birth of modern feminism meant the role of women in the family was in the process of being redefined. To find a 'hip young director' making 'trendy, youth-orientated' horror films where women are focal, and their psychological states are powerful was entirely in keeping with this.[4]

In Alex Stapleton's 2011 documentary *Corman's World: Exploits of a Hollywood Rebel*, directors, actors, producers, and screenwriters as famous as Jack Nicholson, Peter Fonda, Joe Dante, Martin Scorsese, Bruce Dern, and William Shatner all describe how Roger Corman gave them their first big breaks. These filmmakers went to what they collectively refer to as "The Corman Academy." Corman allowed inexperienced filmmakers to cut their teeth on low-budget and exploitation films in the 1960s and 1970s, ultimately preparing them for successful careers in mainstream Hollywood. A touching documentary about a remarkable man's career and directed by a woman, *Corman's World: Exploits of a Hollywood Rebel* abruptly ends with the release of *Star Wars* in 1977, despite Corman having a lucrative and prolific career as a producer throughout the 1980s.

"I interviewed all of the Cormanites, as many as I could," said Stapleton in a 2011 interview when the documentary was released.[5] There is a six-hour cut in which she claims she delves deeply into Corman's films of the 1980s, but this version has not been distributed. In Stapleton's documentary's standard, feature-length version, the only woman director interviewed was Penelope Spheeris. Spheeris' 1984 film about homeless teenage punk rockers, *Suburbia*, was produced by Corman and distributed by his company New World Pictures. Surprisingly, many women Corman hired to direct horror, action, and science fiction movies throughout the 1970s and 1980s did not appear in the documentary. Stephanie Rothman (*Terminal Island*, 1974), Katt Shea (*Stripped to Kill*, 1987), Barbara Peeters (*Bury Me an Angel*, 1971), Amy Holden Jones (*The Slumber Party Massacre*, 1982), Catherine Cyran (*Sawbones*, 1995), and Bettina Hirsch (*Munchies*, 1987), among others, were either directly or indirectly hired as directors by the Cormans. In Chapter 5, we'll discuss the legacy of *The Slumber Party Massacre* series and the Cormans' company Concorde-New Horizons. In this chapter, it is Corman's work on one particular picture for American International Pictures and his subsequent role as a producer with his wife and partner Julie at their company New World Pictures, which launched in 1970 and closed in 1983, that launched the careers of several women horror movie directors.

The formation of New World Pictures allowed Roger Corman to take a step back from directing and focus on production and distribution. The new, much looser censorship laws in the United States and the still successful drive-in theater distribution model made more violent, sexy, and gory films available for public consumption. As a result, many aspiring actors, producers, and directors could make between five and ten films each year on limited schedules and budgets under Corman's watchful eye. Women, often beginning in other departments and working their way up to director, found Corman willing to hire anyone, regardless of gender, who could meet his schedule and budget demands while crafting a profitable horror, exploitation, or science fiction film.

Despite new opportunities for women filmmakers in low-budget films, those that began in exploitation and horror films were not provided the same opportunities as their avant-garde and more commercial counterparts. Attitudes towards women making films in which other women are brutalized were not encouraging. In 1982 prolific *Los Angeles Times* film writer Linda Gross, who contemporarily reviewed films directed by Stephanie Rothman and Barbara Peeters in a column titled "Gross' Sleaze Favorites," wrote, "I confess that I lost my real objectivity a long time ago. Sexual sadism scares me. In the wake of the Hillside Strangler, I find violence against women particularly menacing."[6] In the early years of low-budget exploitation movies, women horror directors had a hard time gaining the respect of mainstream audiences and studios, ultimately preventing many of them from going on to mainstream success.

The first woman to direct a 'modern' horror movie, Stephanie Rothman, was an anomaly at a time when women were not genre film directors. Not only did Rothman tackle subversive, often feminist themes in her films, she indulged in wild settings and surreal atmospheres, not shying away from horror or dystopian genres but embracing them fully. Stephanie Rothman met producer Roger Corman when she was a recent graduate of the University of Southern California's master's film program and had responded to his call for an assistant at his production company, The Filmgroup. She had just won the Director's Guild Award as an outstanding director at an American university. Rothman remembers with gratitude:

> USC got a call from Roger Corman, asking them to send over somebody to interview to be his assistant, and they sent me over. I'm very grateful to USC; otherwise, I don't know how I would have gotten launched as a filmmaker in that time in that world. We're talking 1964 or 1965. A long, long time ago.[7]

"There was no way I could not hire Stephanie," said Corman of his decision. "Stephanie began a fine career that led to several directorial efforts for me."[8]

A detailed description of the inception and final release of Stephanie Rothman's directorial debut *Track of the Vampire* (1966) is given by Tim Lucas in a three-part article in his film magazine *Video Watchdog*,[9] but a condensed version of the initial versions of the movie are worth noting here. In 1963, Roger Corman bought the rights to a Yugoslavian film called *Operacija Ticijan* (*Operation Titian*) and assigned a young Francis Ford Coppola to oversee the additional production shoot in Yugoslavia. The film, a crime thriller about a stolen Titian painting, starred William Campbell (who also appeared in Coppola's *Dementia 13* (1963), also made for Corman) and Pat Magee. Corman declared the final cut of *Operacija Ticijan* "unreleasable" because it had no exploitation elements, everyone in it was over thirty, and the action consisted primarily of people walking and talking. Worse, it was in black and white when color was in demand in drive-in theaters in North America. Perhaps in anticipation of just such a disaster, Corman had made sure the producers shot as much scenic footage as possible so that, if necessary, a new film could be cut from the footage. Corman re-dubbed the dialogue, inserted a few new scenes, and briefly released the film as *Portrait in Terror* with fake, Americanized credits.

Determined to salvage the film, Corman hired another young filmmaker named Jack Hill to film brand-new footage and edit it into *Portrait in Terror* using actor William Campbell again, but this time Campbell played an artist named Sordi. Hill was also told to use at least thirty minutes of the original footage from *Operacija Ticijan*, and he was asked to do it all in only five days on a budget of $900. Hill delivered, re-setting the film in Venice Beach, California, and shooting new scenes with not only Campbell but a new troupe of beatniks, one of which is played by Sid Haig, who would later star in Hill's most famous film *Spider Baby* (1967). For numerous reasons, including other projects getting in the way and the obvious discrepancy between the original Yugoslavian footage and Hill's Venice Beach footage, *Blood Bath* was never released theatrically as a stand-alone film.

Having previously worked as Associate Producer for Corman on *Voyage to the Prehistoric Planet* (1965) and *Queen of Blood* (1966), Stephanie Rothman seemed like an ideal candidate to salvage the film. She had become known as Corman's go-to person for "patchwork filmmaking" at The Filmgroup. Corman handed her all of the footage from Jack Hill's *Blood Bath* and the original footage from *Operacija Ticijan/Portrait in Terror*, along with some extra scenic footage of the Yugoslavian city of Dubrovnik, and asked her if she could make it into a new film. Rothman embarked on this new project and decided she could turn this crime thriller about a stolen painting into a vampire film. Giving her another impossible schedule and roughly $900, Corman set her loose on her first directing job. William Campbell was unavailable for reshoots, so a new actor was brought in to play the vampire; his visage was introduced as it dissolved onto William Campbell's face using an optical effect. Rothman also shot two new outdoor attack sequences in broad daylight in which the vampire assaults women. More obviously, Rothman altered the storyline to include actress Sandra Knight as the character Daisy's sister, who investigates her disappearance at the hands of Sordi/the vampire along with a character Jack Hill had created, an artist and former boyfriend of Daisy, named Max.

The film stayed on the shelves at The Filmgroup for another year until it was finally released in theaters by American International Pictures on a double bill with *Queen of Blood* in March 1966. In a 1978 *Los Angeles Times* article about women and exploitation films, Rothman doesn't mention the film at all and instead says that she worked on "a few foreign films" for Corman: "I wrote new sections, shot them, and edited my material in with the original."[10] She refers to it as a "mish-mash" of several films and estimates that she shot about thirty minutes of new footage that made it into the final film.[11] This doesn't mean Rothman didn't appreciate the chance that Corman had given her. "Working for Roger was really wonderful," she recalls,

> He just threw me into the swimming pool and I had to swim. He was very encouraging. I know that some people came away from their experience with him a little bitter, but I personally found him to be very encouraging. Really, he gave me the self-confidence to do what I needed to do. He was thoroughly behind me. He was, as I've said before, the only mentor I ever had, and until my last breath I will be very grateful to him for that.[12]

In 1966, Corman decided that The Filmgroup would no longer produce films for American International Pictures to distribute; he would form his own company, New World Pictures, and not only produce but distribute his series of exploitation, horror, science fiction, and drama films. New World Pictures' first film production directed by Rothman was 1970's *The Student Nurses*. *The Student Nurses* followed a strict formula Corman had created and wanted to continue to follow: "Contemporary dramas with a liberal to a left-wing viewpoint and some R-rated sex and humor. But they were not to be comedies." Corman goes on to say,

> I frankly doubt the left-wing bent, or message, was crucial to the success of the films we would do. But it was important to the filmmakers and to me that we have something to say within these films. One nurse was Black; another was involved in street protests ... We had four very attractive nurses; I insisted each work out her problems without relying on a boyfriend. Stephanie Rothman directed *The Student Nurses* in three weeks on a budget of $150,000.[13]

Charles Swartz, Rothman's husband who also worked for Corman, produced and co-wrote the story with Rothman. Upon the film's release, the Private Duty Nurses Association sent the film's producer, Larry Woolner, a scathing letter saying they felt that the film depicted nurses in an inappropriate sexual manner. As a response, Corman told Woolner, "They've just given us the title of our first sequel—*Private Duty Nurses*."[14] Despite this, *The Student Nurses* was recognized as the liberal film that it was by many critics. One reviewer called it "the first exploitation picture about the Chicano revolution."[15] Corman gave Rothman the freedom to write and direct the films she wanted "as long as they have a lot of sex or violence and action with material that is sufficiently strong enough to receive an R rating."[16]

Rothman's next film was the beautiful, surreal vampire tale *The Velvet Vampire* (1971). Starring Celeste Yarnall, who previously had performed opposite Elvis Presley in *Live a Little, Love a Little* (1968), it is a Gothic horror film about a female vampire living in a beautiful house out in the desert. When she invites an attractive young couple to stay with her for the weekend, they both enjoy sexual relationships with the mysterious woman (who also enjoys visiting desert cemeteries and doesn't fear the sunlight). It wouldn't be a horror film without a few dead bodies and some iconic coffin imagery, and sadly Yarnall's Diane meets a brutal and almost tragic end. Jack Hill felt that Rothman borrowed a lot of shots from *Blood Bath.*[17] While Hill's mirror scenes are stationary shots with little movement, Rothman's are far grander in scope and color and evoke a surreal warping of time and space. Rothman also engages the viewer in a surrealistic play of colors. For example, Diane, dressed in a blood-red dress against the blue-tinged desertscape background of the dream sequences, is one of the most glorious images from any vampire film. When Diane is not wearing red, she's dressed stylishly or in sparkling silver like ice. The dream sequences alone put *The Velvet Vampire* on a pedestal above other vampire films of the early 1970s. Diane has a blatantly sexual relationship with both Lee (Michael Blodgett) and Susan (Sherry Miles) throughout the film, creating a love triangle that shifts and causes jealousy and unfulfilled sexual frustration between Michael and Sherry. "I wanted to make a vampire film that dealt explicitly with the sexuality implicit in the vampire legend,"[18] explains Rothman:

> While in the *Dracula* films, both men and women were the victims of vampires; it was the women who always seemed to endure the ecstasy of having their blood sucked while lying passively in their beds. If men were assaulted by vampires, it was usually while battling them ... So I decided to reverse this convention, and have

A surreal dream sequence (and also perhaps the most beautiful moment in a horror movie of all time) in *The Velvet Vampire*. Image courtesy of Shout! Factory.

Celeste Yarnall as Diane the vampire in Stephanie Rothman's stunning horror fantasy *The Velvet Vampire* (1971). Image courtesy of Shout! Factory.

the man enjoy a masochistic orgasmic death by vampire while the woman battled back.[19]

Though a contemporary reviewer wrote that *The Velvet Vampire* was unintentionally funny in places, Rothman insists that it "was obviously intended to be funny."[20] Yarnall saw the humor in some of the scenes as well. "Though the part was a bit corny," she remembered, "I got into playing a vampire."[21] Yarnell dyed her hair black for the role and embraced playing Diane wholeheartedly as her character ate raw chicken innards and sucked rattlesnake poison from Susan's shapely, sun-tanned thigh.

Shot entirely in Joshua Tree in the California desert for $165,000, the production was not easy. Celeste Yarnall was unhappy about having nude scenes, which she'd never done before, but admits that she was having financial trouble at the time and needed the money to help her get through a tough divorce. She'd just had a child she needed to support, so she was willing to compromise regarding what she would and wouldn't do on camera. She was lucky to have a completely closed set with just Rothman, Swartz, and the cinematographer, Daniel Lacambre. Yarnall also remembers working with Sherry Miles fondly but has a more troubling opinion about her co-star Michael Blodgett:

> He was drinking heavily throughout the shoot ... In the scene where I have to stab him and he dies, he's laying on top of me. Michael had his hand behind me and didn't realize that as he was acting he was closing his hand around my spine. He really hurt me—my whole back was bruised, but he had no clue what he was doing. He had been drinking the night before. Consequently, it was difficult for me to work with him and retain my air of professionalism.[22]

The Velvet Vampire managed to do well at the box office, well enough to inspire other studios to create similar films. This didn't translate into more directing jobs for Rothman, however. She was shut out of the horror genre by major studios rather than included and allowed to create new feature film success:

I was called in to meet an executive at MGM after I'd made *The Velvet Vampire*, in fact it was perhaps three or four years later. And this person said to me "Oh, you know, we were talking about you the other day in a meeting, because we've hired the younger brother of Ridley Scott to make a film, and we think we'd like it to be a vampire film, and we were talking about how we would like it to sort of be like *The Velvet Vampire*." And my response was, "Well, if you want a film like *The Velvet Vampire*, why don't you get Stephanie Rothman to make it?"[23]

At this point, Rothman, her husband Charles Swartz, and Larry Woolner formed Dimension Pictures and left behind Roger Corman and New World. Despite rumors that Rothman and Jack Hill had bickered over the 1971 film *The Big Doll House*, which Hill would direct, Rothman insists that is not why she left New World to join Dimension. In 2010, Rothman wrote an online letter to counter Hill's version of why she left New World Pictures in 1971:

When I read this Jack Hill-centric version of why we left New World Pictures, I laughed. No, it was not all about Jack. Nor were we "still smarting" from a dispute with him. Charles and I left New World with Larry Woolner to start Dimension Pictures because Larry offered us a small percentage of the company and more money than we were paid at New World. In other words, we were offered a promotion. Then there is the tiresome claim Jack has made through the years that I had a dispute with him about who would direct *The Big Doll House*. This, too, is simply false.[24]

Unfortunately, being a partner at Dimension and having more control over her work (and higher pay) than at New World did not turn out to be the boon for which Rothman had hoped. She explained in 1978 in a *Los Angeles Times* interview:

The limitations that we encountered making films at New World extended into our work for Dimension Pictures ... The freedom that existed was the freedom to take the genre expectations and do unexpected things with them. Do things that would make them seem relevant to a wider audience than the usual fans of exploitation films. So we included political opinions and we tried to make the stories have more psychological depth.[25]

Rothman's first feature as director (and writer) for Dimension was *Group Marriage* (1972), a sex comedy about the formation of an unconventional family, including a gay marriage. The film was screened in suburban theaters after a run in drive-ins because of how well the mainstream public received it. Her next film was a science fiction thriller/action film with distinctly feminist overtones and a feminine-focused storyline, *Terminal Island* (1973).[26] Rothman was inspired to write this near-future, violent, dystopian thriller by real-life public outcry over the cost of keeping convicted criminals fed and healthy throughout their life sentences. *Terminal Island* was made on a meager budget and lacked notable special effects or production design. "Many scenes occur in outdoor settings designed solely by the last ice age,"[27] remarked Rothman in an essay she wrote for the

1984 issue of *Omni's Screen Flights*. Shot during a light rainstorm, which made production rather difficult, Rothman liked the resulting heavy and brooding natural atmosphere: "It gave the land a verdant look that is uncharacteristic of Southern California where it was shot," she explained. "We were intending to make a 'Devil's Island' picture."[28] Pitting men against women in a battle of the sexes that ultimately ends in naturally-occurring equality, Rothman intended to tell a story in which men and women needed each other for survival and therefore had to cast off traditional sex-role behaviors in favor of staying alive and safe behavior. *Terminal Island* was also Rothman's first opportunity to shoot significant action sequences and direct a large cast, about which she was very excited.

The basic storyline of *Terminal Island* would inspire John Carpenter's *Escape from New York* (1981) and even Ana Lily Amirpour's *The Bad Batch* (2016); both are films with the same general setting. While *Terminal Island* does have some feminist leanings, and it is easy to interpret the storyline as anti-men, it's not a film about men versus women, per se. It is a film about fighting for freedom and survival and how the weaker must use tools of solidarity and intelligence to create a more fair and sustainable society that includes both men and women as equals.

Rothman felt restricted by her low-budget and exploitation reputation while making *Terminal Island*. She felt obligated, by unofficial 'exploitation' rules, to make the women appear sexier than she felt the story called for:

> Perhaps the one stereotypical element in the film that I have never been comfortable with is some of the costuming and makeup of the women prisoners. One of the exploitation rules I had to follow strictly was that the women must always look very attractive and 'sexy,' which meant they couldn't look the way women really would as prisoners on an island with harsh living conditions. I have watched *Terminal Island* several times in recent years with audiences who have an interest in seeing revivals programs. When they first see the women prisoners on the island, there is sometimes laughter at their unrealistic appearance. I don't take any offense at this, because it just validates my own uneasiness with the message sent by the way the women look.[29]

In an interview in 2006, *Terminal Island* actress Barbara Leigh described Rothman on set: "She was calm, knew exactly what she wanted from an actor for each role, and relayed that to us. She was easygoing yet strong in her direction. She saw in her mind's eye what she thought each character should be. She got that across with no trouble."[30] Leigh was not excited about her role. She had only one speaking line ("not speaking in the film until the last frame where I say 'I want to go home' didn't give me much to think about") and her new watch was stolen by one of the cast or crew (she never did find out by whom).[31]

Though it may not seem shocking to twenty-first-century film audiences, in 1973, the MPAA wanted to give *Terminal Island* an X rating. Rothman defended the violence in her film: "It was necessary for me to be very strong and graphic to show the full awfulness. I think it's irresponsible to show violence as painless."[32] While there is lots of death, blood, beating, and subjugation of women in *Terminal Island*, all of the rape is implied. "Rape was the only thing I ever refused to do in a film," explained Rothman:

Carmen (Ena Hartman) doesn't take any shit in *Terminal Island* (1973), directed by Stephanie Rothman. Image courtesy of Vinegar Syndrome.

> In *Terminal Island*, I indicated that the women were forced to have sexual relations with the men, but I never showed it. I couldn't bring myself to film it—even to show it as a reprehensible act. I would not want to be responsible in any way for showing how it could be done.[33]

Perhaps Rothman's films are considered 'feminist' exploitation films because of her attitude toward female nudity. In most exploitation films from the 1960s through the present, naked women are on display far more often than males and usually in unhappy rather than erotic situations. "In my films," said Rothman,

> There is as much male nudity as there is female, sometimes more. I won't allow women to be put in that kind of vulnerable position and men left with the honor of their clothing. It's all in the way you handle it.[34]

"A Stephanie Rothman film deals with questions of self-determination," the director said of her work: "My characters try to forge a humane and rational way of coming to grips with the vicissitudes of life. My films are not always about succeeding, but they are always concerned with fighting the good fight."[35]

Rothman reiterated this message many times to reject the notion that she was merely an exploitation director. The term 'exploitation' was distasteful to Rothman;

> It underlined that I was making films of no status that would not get any kind of serious recognition from reviewers, certainly not in the papers or magazines. And it certainly would not be taken seriously in Hollywood in any way and it would not open up great employment opportunities for me in terms of the tools I would have to work with as a filmmaker.[36]

In 1974, she directed her last film for Dimension, *The Working Girls*, and wouldn't direct again. The Museum of Modern Art in New York City has prints of *The Velvet Vampire* and *The Student Nurses,* as does The Academy Film Archive in Los Angeles. There is a digital restoration of *Terminal Island* by the company Vinegar Syndrome and a digital version of *The Velvet Vampire* with the American Genre Film Archive in Austin, Texas.

Roberta Findlay is one of the most well-known female exploitation filmmakers of the 1960s, 1970s, and 1980s. Her lengthy resume includes credits on numerous soft-core, horror, and hardcore films throughout these decades, in roles as actress, cinematographer, co-director, director, producer, writer, and editor. Findlay did not direct horror films until 1977's *A Woman's Torment*, long after she had ended her relationship with Michael Findlay and had embarked on her directing career. Researching Findlay on mainstream film databases, it is impossible to establish her actual directing credits before 1977 due to misinformation.

When Roberta and Michael Findlay's partnership began in the mid-1960s, there was a new movement of low-budget filmmakers creating arthouse, avant-garde, and exploitation films. Michael was in the middle of it. With several of his male colleagues, Findlay made 'roughies,' films incorporating many sex scenes, often very violent ones. These films would screen in grindhouse theaters in the city. Michael shot, edited, lit, wrote, and acted in numerous movies in the 1960s under his name and several pseudonyms, often adding Roberta Findlay's name to the credits, as Julian Marsh, Anna Riva, Robert West, Marshall Smith, and more. One of the first films to which Roberta is supposed to have creatively contributed is the violent sexploitation movie *Body of a Female* (1964). This 'nudie roughie' stars Roberta Findlay under the pseudonym Anna Riva (which she would use numerous times). *Body of a Female* is a lost film. However, much of it is used as additional footage in John Amero's film *Lusting Hours* (1967).

The second film Roberta Findlay is incorrectly said to have co-directed is the strange, avant-garde rape film *Satan's Bed* (1965) (originally an earlier, unfinished film starring Yoko Ono called *Judas City* by a director known as Tamijian before Michael shot new footage and edited it into the existing film). Findlay is credited as Marshall Smith, having worked on the lighting and cinematography, and she appears briefly, nude, tied to a pool table. Roberta Findlay's only comment on the final version of *Satan's Bed* is that it is "so unwatchable. A badly-made, non-sex picture."[37]

Another film on which Roberta Findlay is credited as co-director is the violent thriller *Take Me Naked* (1966); she is often listed as having co-directed it with Michael Findlay under the pseudonym Anna Riva. Again, she acts in the film (she suspects she may have written it but doesn't entirely remember).[38] The same is true for the rape-revenge fantasy *Mnasidika* (1969), which was set in ancient Greece:

> I was not involved. People say I am in the credits of these pictures; I don't think I've even seen one ... I was just hanging around. I had nothing to do with those pictures. Michael shot everything. Why would he make me do it? When and if I did shoot for Michael, I was just a tool. That is, I don't remember ever knowing how to change a lens, change a magazine, nothing. He did all that. I was just a button-presser ... I never saw any of them.[39]

In another interview, Findlay confirmed that she never worked on any of Michael Findlay's films except as an occasional actress and assistant:

> I never saw any of these films completed [except for *Take Me Naked*], and I certainly didn't write any of them. I was not the co-producer or anything. He did everything. Why he put me on as co-producer, I don't know.[40]

As noted by Findlay scholar Lisa Petrucci of Something Weird Video, this seems incredibly hard to believe, considering Roberta Findlay not only appears in many of the films but is credited as the cinematographer. Petrucci notes a distinct change in style in the films *Take Me Naked* and *Mnasidika* from the Findlays' regular sleaze; the films are (loosely) inspired by *The Collected Works of Pierre Louÿs*, a rather highbrow collection of stories from the French author originally published in 1932. These films stand out as twisted art films rather than violent roughies, possibly inspired by the magical aspects of Joe Sarno's *Sin You Sinners* (1963), which had a significant impact on other low-budget sleaze filmmakers of the time. Overtly poetic and highly symbolic, they used a Vaseline-lens technique to create a surreal quality that is notably absent in any of Michael's earlier works. In *Mnasidika,* it is generally understood that Michael directed the opening and closing scenes while Roberta directed the sexual content.[41]

The allure of the Findlays' work in the 1960s and early 1970s is its highly violent nature; extreme film connoisseurs find the work dark, misogynistic, strange, and highly unusual for that period, even in the world of low-budget exploitation films. Michael Findlay was not only deeply interested in films of all kinds, but he was making films highly unlikely to find mainstream viewership, even at a drive-in theater. For this, he has attained a cult status among horror and exploitation film fans and critics. The Findlay partnership represents an era of genre filmmaking exploring previously-set limits placed on film by censorship and prohibitively expensive technology. Michael Findlay was making some genuinely shocking films for the time. Despite being a part of this renegade art film creation, Roberta Findlay purports that she had no great love of their work nor of making it:

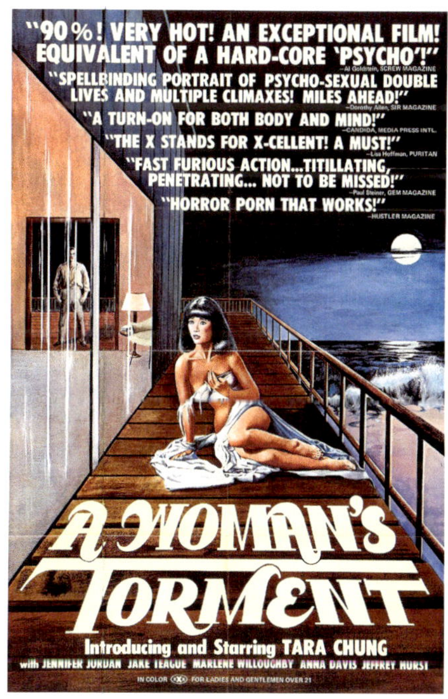

The original promo poster for Roberta Findlay's *A Woman's Torment* (1977). Image courtesy of Vinegar Syndrome.

> I don't know anything about this genre. I was a tag-along. I was just there ... I didn't have the maturity to psychoanalyze what he was doing. I knew there was something amiss. I can't tell you who would see these films. Just people as sick and tormented as he was ... I think he really did think he was making a statement. It was sordid and crazed, but I think he thought it was more than exploitation. I think he was trying to say something ... If he had visualized his sick mind in reality, he would have been executed.[42]

In the 1970s, the Findlays began working as an actual team, with Michael writing and directing and Roberta working the camera and lighting. Roberta was the cinematographer on Michael's horror films *Shriek of the Mutilated* (1974) and *Slaughter* (later released as *Snuff*, 1976). "The first film I remember shooting was *Snuff*," said Roberta Findlay:

> What he [Michael] said to me was, "Aim and shoot. That's all you have to do." That was about it. I noticed that the lighting that he did was terrible on *Snuff*, and I became mostly interested in lighting. He just blasted light in; it wasn't aimed, it wasn't purposeful.[43]

The Findlays parted ways artistically and intimately shortly after *Snuff* was completed in 1972 or 1973. "I ran away," she explained:

> I just left. I left during the time he went to California trying to sell *Snuff* to a distributor. He was gone a long time because he was terrified of flying and he wouldn't do it, so he took a bus to California and a bus back. It took him about a month. I hated being married. That's why I left.[44]

Michael Findlay died in a helicopter accident on May 16, 1977. By then, Roberta Findlay had been making her films as a writer and director for a few years. Allan Shackleton, who initially distributed *Snuff*, produced five films directed by Michael Findlay in the 1970s. After the release of *Snuff*, Roberta Findlay approached Shackleton and said, "I can make these pictures." He invested several thousand dollars in the making of *Altar of Lust* (1971), a soft-core pornography film, followed by the supernatural soft-core *Angel on Fire,* AKA *Angel Number 9* (1974), which had a supernatural storyline about gender-switching. Findlay worked as a writer, director, editor, cinematographer, and more on all of the films she made for Shackleton, mainly because the low budgets did not provide for an entire crew on set or in post-production. "I don't know how I knew how to edit," she marveled. "I never saw Michael edit or paid any attention to it when he did."[45]

Despite making five films together, producer Allan Shackleton seemed never to want to pay Findlay for her work. Several times during this tumultuous business relationship, he physically assaulted her. Finally, with a black eye, she pressed charges, ending their partnership forever. Before this happened, she had met producer and composer Walter Sear, owner of Sear Studios in New York City, in Shackleton's office one day. He invited her to make her next picture with him, and shortly after her falling out with Shackleton, she did. Findlay and Walter Sear began a romantic relationship that would last for years, and their production partnership would last until 1989 and through all of Findlay's 1980s horror films. In the 1970s, however, Sear and Findlay concentrated on making the shift from soft-core pornography to hardcore pornographic films. By the late 1970s, Findlay had formed a production partnership with Dave Darby and Walter Sear. Together, they made seven films with Findlay directing; the first was *A Woman's Torment* (1977), a hardcore pornography film with a dark, psychotic, and artistic undertone.

Compared by some critics as a worthy companion to Roman Polanski's *Repulsion*,[46] *A Woman's Torment* is "the story of my life," according to Findlay.[47] It was her first solo horror directing attempt, and she credited herself as Robert W. Norman. On set, Findlay described herself as "bossy and assertive. I had no problem while shooting anything." When she wasn't directing, she had a very different attitude: "Outside of that narrow aspect of living, I was unassuming, self-deprecating, and had no self-esteem whatsoever. Zero."[48]

A Woman's Torment is a not-very-erotic mix of slasher imagery and hardcore sex. Findlay mixed the story of a mentally ill woman suffering from hallucinations with some very graphic sex scenes, resulting in an unpleasant viewing experience. She made another film during the same shooting period called *Mystique* (1979), with the same dichotomy of story elements. "We did this a couple of times," explained Findlay at a live screening of the film in 2017. "*Mystique* is about a woman dying of cancer ... Some sex picture! It's just not very erotic."[49] A mentally ill woman named Karen (Tara Chung) is sent to live alone in her sister's beach house while relatives determine her fate. While she stays alone, she has hallucinations of a man with a knife trying to stab her in the shower. She also hears voices and has trouble relating to other people meaningfully. Wandering around the beach house in a white satin nightgown, having sex with virtually everyone she meets, Karen spirals out of control and murders everyone she sleeps with or fantasizes about so they will stay with her as her "friends" forever. Her murders are discovered by her sister, who gut-wrenchingly realizes that Karen is far sicker than she ever knew, while Karen walks out into the ocean to drown herself. There are about thirty minutes of an actual storyline, and everything else is pure hardcore sex, full penetration, and cum shots galore. There's something ugly about not only the way the sex is filmed but the relationships between the characters. The whole movie is a big turn-off, which seems to be a misfire for a director making a pornography film and hoping to make money, but it's highly tempting to analyze the strange choices Findlay made and try to find some feminist or psychological meaning in them. There isn't any. The surreal quality of the movie is not purposeful. Chung walked off of the set after only a few days of shooting, leaving Findlay with many scenes that needed to be patched together in the editing room with extra inserts shot later:

> One of the other cast members had overheard her say that the place was like a morgue and there was no fun to be had on our shoot, there were no drugs, there was no sex outside of the stuff that we were shooting, and she found it horribly boring and a giant pain. And we patched this stuff together somehow. All the back two shots, all the shots of hands, cutaways, and so on, is me. She left her dress, the costume. She left her wig (she was totally bald), so we shot me in an attempt to patch the thing together with pieces of hands and arms. I think there's one scene with a poker killing someone—that was me. You don't see her face at all. What could we do?[50]

A bloody moment in Roberta Findlay's *A Woman's Torment* (1977). Image courtesy of Vinegar Syndrome.

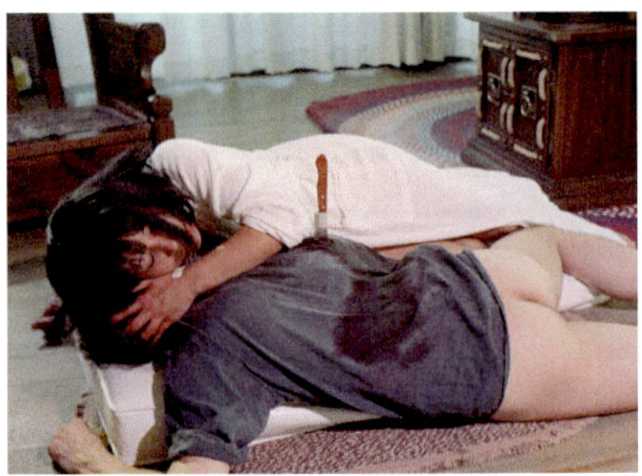

Karen (Tara Chung) has a problem with murdering people in *A Woman's Torment*. Image courtesy of Vinegar Syndrome.

Karen's story's intensity is undermined by the long sequences of hardcore sex, which Findlay didn't enjoy shooting. She was far more interested in framing shots of the actors and their dialogue, the beach house, and the ocean itself, but with genitals being the main focus of the sex scenes, she had to move in on them more closely with the camera:

> The direction I gave was non-verbal. I'd walk around and try to find interesting angles. My famous technique was a ninety mackerel which was a very tight telephoto lens that focused within an inch or two [of the subject]. It was a really cheap way of using up film time. I'd pan up and down for a few minutes ... the whole thing became symbolic, unreal, it didn't look like anything ... It was totally abstract, but it used up a lot of film time. I didn't speak. I hated it, I found it very distasteful.[51]

The sex in *A Woman's Torment* seems designed to show women in a different light than in regular pornographic films. This may partly be because Findlay claims she never actually watched any other pornography films, but it could be that Findlay wanted her women characters to sound like real people when they spoke and to have relatable thoughts about the sex they were having. Though Findlay said the film is "the story of her life," maybe she means it's the story of her *sex* life.

Findlay directed actress Sandi Foxx in the adult films *Angel Number 9* (1974) and *Slip Up* (1975). Foxx seemed to believe Findlay did have, at least in an unconscious manner, an agenda of sorts when it came to her female characters, even in pornography, "Roberta was smart and knew what she was doing," Foxx said in an interview. "I remember she didn't want to have women portrayed as being dumb. In those days, many of the films portrayed women as sex objects."[52] But Findlay denies any political, social, or even artistic leanings in any of her work from this period:

> I was consumed with two things while shooting all these films. I was consumed with making a good frame, that is, lighting, the shot. And I was also consumed with editing. With making things match. My interest was purely technical. If stuff shines through, integrity or some ulterior motive, it's unconscious.[53]

She said in another interview,

> Invariably and inevitably, anyone who creates something has got themselves in that work. Whether they deny it or accept it or whatever. It can't be avoided ... there's no way to divorce yourself from subconscious feelings. I wrote the thing. I can deny it, I guess, all I like, or say it's not feminist, but whatever I am is in that picture.[54]

With Dave Darby as the distributor, *A Woman's Torment* played in some drive-in theaters but never at the Pussycat Theaters, the biggest venue for pornographic films at the time. Darby and the booker of the Pussycat Theaters did not get along, so the film was never able to get a wide release. Like her business relationship with Shackleton, Findlay's partnership with Dave Darby ended badly after seven films. In one of the only feminist things Findlay ever said, she was upset by Darby's dismissal of her equal share of the film profits because she was a woman. "He said, 'One man is on one side, and the other man is on the other side, and you're part of the other man.'"[55] After suing Darby for an equal third of the money, Findlay was awarded ownership of all seven films they had made together, including *A Woman's Torment*, while Darby kept all the money.

Unlike some of her contemporaries, Findlay had no desire to make any feminist commentary through her work:

> I had no particular ax to grind. I'm not a feminist of any sort. I never thought to support my sisters or to support womanhood in general. That never occurred to me. I myself never had a problem in the world with sexism. I just went in and did my job. And by the time I was making films in the 1980s, I was very skilled technically. I had no problem with anybody in distribution or shooting; they never thought of me as a woman doing a man's job.[56]

A Woman's Torment was restored from the original 35mm print and released on Blu-ray disc and DVD by Vinegar Syndrome in 2017. At the time of the publication of this book, she has attained a respected cult status among cinephiles and exploitation film connoisseurs and is alive and living in New York, U.S.A.

Doris Wishman is the most enigmatic and preposterous woman director in exploitation history. She makes Roberta Findlay look like David Lean. Most of her life before she made films is obscure at best. She may have been born in 1912 and died on August 10, 2002, at eighty-nine or ninety. Wishman made almost thirty features in four decades and didn't begin making films until she was in her forties. She had had some experience working with exploitation films; she had worked for her cousin Max Rosenberg, a producer of exploitation films in the 1940s and 1950s, and she was working for Walter Bibo, who made the notorious nudist film *Garden of Eden* (1954). She decided she would make movies and asked her sister to finance the first one, *Hideout in the Sun*, for $10,000. Filmmaker Mark Boswell recalls how Wishman learned to make films:

What she always said, and we all remember this, was she got her start doing clerical work for a movie producer. She would look at all the films made by the producer, and because she studied acting, she had a basic sense of what narrative structure was. When her husband died, she had a slight mental collapse and kept fantasizing that her husband was still alive. She felt like this obsession was unhealthy and so to keep herself occupied she started making films. She had the formula early on: work a story in which you can show a bunch of nudity.[57]

Wishman had, initially, wanted to be an actress, but having never seriously acted and well into middle age by the 1960s, she focused instead on all other aspects of the filmmaking process:

I made twenty-four films. Why in heaven's name didn't I act in them? ... I can't answer that. I think I was so busy doing everything else. Producing, directing, casting, and writing. But I know I look back and ... I just must have been an idiot. In a couple of films, I appeared for a second, but that's not acting. I could have been anything I wanted ... too late.[58]

When Wishman moved on from 'nudie' films, she started making 'roughies' (as had Roberta and Michael Findlay during the same period). She shot in black and white, as opposed to color like her nudie films, and used a handheld camera. These were provocative exploitation films featuring violence and some sexual depravity (though little nudity) and eroticism.[59] "After a while, nudist pictures were passé," Wishman relates:

So there was calm sex, you know, very slight sex, not too hot. I went along with that. And then sex became ... hotter, shall we say? But I couldn't bring myself to do hardcore, not that it's anybody's business if people want to see it, but I couldn't do it. So I just kept making films.[60]

Wishman's 'roughies' were *Bad Girls Go To Hell* (1966), *A Taste of Flesh* (1967), and *Indecent Desires* (1967). Michael Bowen points out in his contribution to *Underground U.S.A.: Filmmaking Beyond the Hollywood Canon* that Wishman's mid-1960s roughie films have many things in common with the concurrent New Wave, avant-garde Cinéma Vérité; in particular, black-and-white realism and handheld cameras. He also notes a documentary-like realism resulting from these stylistic (and economical) choices.[61] A contemporary of Wishman's, filmmaker John Amero was a close friend of Roberta and Michael Findlay and said that *Bad Girls Go To Hell* was one of his and Michael's "favorite of those awful Doris Wishman films."[62] *Bad Girls Go To Hell*, *A Taste of Flesh*, and *Indecent Desires* all have violence with their sexual content. *Indecent Desires* has elements of fantasy and magic with its dreamy voodoo dolly molestation and sudden, violent climax. *Bad Girls Go To Hell* has a dream cycle in which the lead character is doomed to repeat the horror of her rape and subsequent self-destruction as if she first saw it in a premonition. These films have genre elements, but they are usually not considered horror films by fans. Most lists of genre films directed by women don't include her first films as horror, usually choosing instead to list *The Amazing Transplant* and *The Haunted Pussy*. I believe most people making these lists have not watched all of Wishman's films and are going by word of mouth from lists they find online; otherwise, either all of these films or none of them would be considered "horror directed by a woman."

By 1970, as with nudies, Wishman tired of making roughies:

> After a while, those films just weren't acceptable anymore, they weren't commercial, and so I had to go on to other things, and I started making regular features, which of course was more fun, more challenging, and more costly. But every time I made a film, the budget was a little higher, which is just the way it goes.[63]

I'm not sure which films Wishman was referring to when she said she started making "regular" films because the next film she made was the roughie/rape film *The Amazing Transplant* (1970). I don't believe any film Wishman ever made could be considered "regular." Wishman also once said that "they" (critics? fans?) compared her work to that of Alfred Hitchcock, which couldn't be true except as a joke.[64] If it was a joke, Wishman didn't get it.

Wishman (as Louis Silverman) directed *The Amazing Transplant* and wrote it under the pseudonym Dawn Whitman. With a supposed $250,000 budget and in vivid full color, it was a step up from Wishman's previous attempts at subversive cinema. But that isn't saying very much. And I honestly do not believe that the film had a $250,000 budget unless most of it went to the cocaine needed to get the actors to show up. That number has been thrown around on the internet, but Wishman never provided any documentation for this budget that can be found in the twenty-first century. It's cheaply made, comparable to early John Waters films such as *Multiple Maniacs*, but without any sense of the authentic style or engaging character creation found even in Waters' most obscene films.

The Amazing Transplant is a crime thriller with graphic rape scenes. A young man named Arthur has a history of attacking and raping women. Soon, Dr. Meade, Arthur's psychiatrist, confesses that he transplanted Arthur's dead friend's penis onto Arthur because Arthur was always jealous of his friend's sexual prowess, which has caused his propensity for rape and murder. Arthur's uncle Bill, a detective in the police department, puts an end to his crimes.

The Amazing Transplant offers little to cinema history except for the most hardcore cinema masochists. There's one consensual sex scene in *The Amazing Transplant*, but the rest are violent, long rape scenes verging on hardcore (though I don't believe there is actual penetration). Random, bad filmmaking choices make *The Amazing Transplant* hard to watch. As a fan or cinephile, one can search hard for some stylistic meaning to the odd editing and weird framing, but there's nothing behind it.

A video version of *The Amazing Transplant* was released by distributor Electric Video VHS in 1981, marketing it as a regular slasher film, from whence the confusion about Wishman's film classifications comes. When Joe Bob Briggs, famed film reviewer,

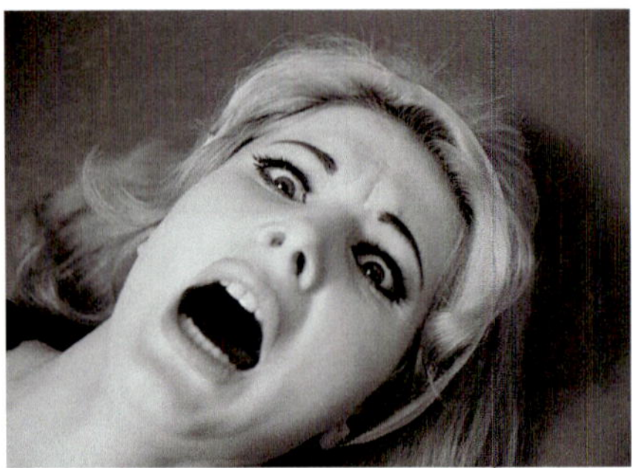
Ellen (Gigi Darlene) descends into sexual hell after she is raped by her building manager in Doris Wishman's *Bad Girls Go To Hell* (1965). Image courtesy of the American Genre Film Archive.

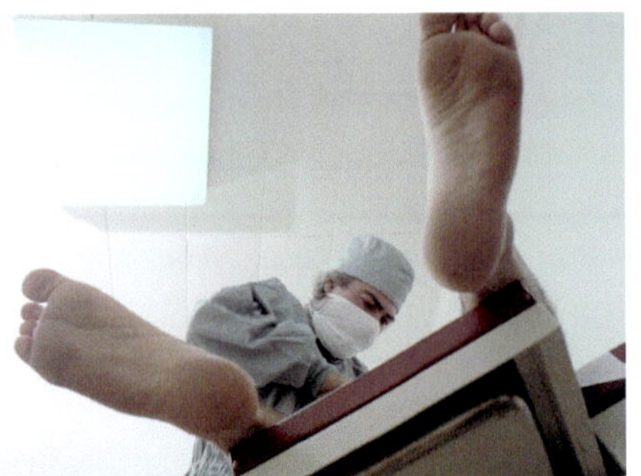
An unintentionally nicely-composed moment from Doris Wishman's penis horror film *The Amazing Transplant* (1970). Photo courtesy of the American Genre Film Archive.

wanted to include it in his "Sleaziest Movies in the History of the World" video series, the producers found *The Amazing Transplant* too sleazy.[65] DVD Distributor Something Weird Video eventually released the film, along with many of Wishman's other features, though they've not been restored.

Wishman made hardcore pornography at various points throughout her career, but she claims that she left the room when sex scenes were being shot. "She was actually rather sexually naïve," Bowen said in an article. "She personally thought someone's hand caressing your face was more erotic than sex itself."[66] Contemporary filmmaker Dave Friedman confirms that "Doris would be embarrassed. Entirely different for a woman than a man. Doris was a very respectable nice little lady."[67] Wishman even wanted the world to know that, while she shot hardcore pornography, among other less offensive forms of cinema, "I've had two husbands and a lover, and that's my quota."[68]

While *The Amazing Transplant* is unwatchable, it's far better than her next film, *Come With Me My Love,* AKA *The Haunted Pussy*, released in 1976. Wishman directed this hardcore ghost story as Luigi Manicottale. For someone who didn't want to make hardcore pornography, Wishman sure made a lot of hardcore pornography. There are horror films that cross over into pornography, and many pornography films have horror-based storylines (usually as parodies or for fun costume reasons). *The Haunted Pussy* is a pornography film with some horror elements. Abby (Ursula Austin), a young woman renting the apartment in which horrific murders happened in 1925, is seduced not only by various friends and acquaintances but by the ghost of the murderer.

While Wishman's films were remarkably, objectively terrible, she sometimes had pretensions that she was good at what she did, and at other times seemed incredibly humble. She never understood when people claimed her films had a distinct style. Her style was a complete and total lack of style with repetitive poor choices and mistakes. Wishman didn't know that her films were so bad that they were artistically recognizable as hers:

> I don't think I have a style, and yet people will look and go, "Ah, that's Wishman." And I really don't know what they mean because nothing's deliberate. Sometimes I did things because I had no money, and they'll say, "Isn't that great, look what she did," and I only did it because I had to.[69]

While Wishman's films have been studied in-depth in recent years by enthusiastic film students and feminist explorers of past art, she denied any feminist or political subtext to anything she made. She genuinely was making fun, silly sexploitation films. She even expressed doubt that women, in general, could do things as well as men could:

> Of course, it's very exciting, but in many areas, I don't feel that women are as capable as men...I don't think I should speak this way because I'll have the women down on me! I think men are more enterprising. I think women are much more cautious because they have to be, I suppose. I don't believe in Women's Lib. I really don't.[70]

In a later interview, Wishman was asked to compare what making genre and exploitation films was like in the 1960s and 1970s to making those films as a woman in the twenty-first century. She never expressed any disdain for "the system" or complained about unfair opportunities in the film industry:

> I never thought of it like that, but I must say I was always treated very fairly, and it never became ... I mean, it just didn't matter. You know, these days it's completely different, but then it was a bit of a novelty, but the other producers and directors and so on were extremely nice and really tried to be cooperative. I had no problems, and I never thought of myself as the only woman director. I just didn't think about it; I just wanted to work and make movies.[71]

Wishman would release another horror film in the 1980s and one in the 2000s before her death. Until the day she died, she was known and loved as a vital exploitation director at a time when women exploitation filmmakers were few and far between. Though arguably untalented and artistically dense, Wishman accomplished what many people in Western culture find incredibly gutsy and challenging: she made many films, released them, and never gave up on her dream of being a filmmaker. "I don't really care," she told one interviewer. "I know that what I did, I did to the best of my ability. I was fair with everybody, and that's all that counts."[72]

There seems to be a disagreement between several film history sources about whether or not Brianne Murphy co-directed the 1961 black-and-white horror cheapie *Teenage Zombie* with her then-husband Jerry Warren or if Warren directed alone. Acker's *Reel Women* interview with Murphy states that "she ... wrote and directed" it.[73] *The St. James Women Filmmakers Encyclopedia* distinctly describes her as a director on both: "Suddenly, she found herself in the driver's seat on *Virgins from Venus* and *Teenage Zombies*. Murphy delivered, and one of a select few female directors—even if the material was not exactly classic."[74]

Despite these sources claiming the contrary, Murphy did not direct *Teenage Zombies*, though she was heavily involved in all aspects of its production. In a *Fangoria* magazine interview from 1996, Murphy remembers the horror films *Man Beast* (1956) and *Teenage Zombies,* plainly saying that Jerry Warren directed both. Murphy stated that she did not begin directing until the late 1960s. Another of Murphy's film credits, the obscure science fiction film *Virgins from Venus* (about which little is known), is often listed as having been released in 1957. In the same *Fangoria* interview, Murphy confirms that *Virgins from Venus* was not a 1957 release at all but was shot immediately after she directed *Blood Sabbath* (1972) with the same cast of women ("none of whom were virgins," she joked).[75]

Even if her first and only directing credit in a horror film was dated 1972 and not 1957, Murphy was a significant figure in the 1960s and 1970s because of her pioneering work as a woman cinematographer. Murphy was the first female member of the American Society of Cinematographers (ASC), the first female member of the International Alliance of Theatrical Stage Employees (IATSE), and the first female member of the International Cinematographers Guild (ICG). As the first female cinematographer for a major studio film—Anne Bancroft's directorial debut *Fatso* (1980),[76] Murphy is a celebrated figure of the film industry's feminist movement. In a famous story, Murphy was allowed to join the ICG in 1973 only because feminist and activist Gloria Steinem demanded a female camera crew to shoot an NBC television documentary about the women's movement in the United States.[77] In 1979, Murphy was again in demand at NBC for a documentary about breast cancer, and a male cinematographer was not allowed to film topless cancer patients.[78]

In 1953, twenty-one-year-old Brianne Murphy met Jerry Warren, a low-budget B-movie director, and she immediately began working as his camerawoman, script supervisor, production supervisor, and actress. Her first film as a cinematographer was the 1955 monster movie production *Man Beast*, but she became the camera person accidentally. Originally hired to do makeup, props, and wardrobe, she was also asked to wear the monster costume when it finally came time to shoot. The suit didn't fit Murphy; the only person who could fit in was the cinematographer Vic Fisher. So, Fisher and Murphy switched roles: Fisher became the suited monster, and Murphy was handed the camera.[79] The sixty-three-minute *Man Beast*, filmed in Arizona and featuring an abominable snowman, has been referred to by critics as a "cheap horror hodgepodge from the redoubtable Jerry Warren."[80] The same article also suggests that while Murphy shot parts of *Man Beast*, it "consists largely of footage from a forgotten Mexican production."[81] Murphy never mentioned this salvaged footage or what film it may have come from originally. The critic does not mention his source of information, but fans of Warren's suggest that he was in the habit of buying the rights to Mexican films, adding in the footage, and re-editing them as brand-new films for release in the United States (something not uncommon, as seen in several of Roger Corman's foreign re-cuts).[82]

While on the set of *Man Beast*, Murphy met the film's investor. She boasted to him that she could shoot two low-budget horror films for what it cost to shoot *Man Beast* ($30,000). The investor took her up on that offer, and Murphy and Warren's next monster movie was *Teenage Zombies*. Many sources confusedly say that she directed *Virgins from Venus* next, but that isn't truthful, as that film was shot in 1972, not 1957.[83] On *Teenage*

Zombies, she was paid $50 a week and worked as script supervisor, makeup and wardrobe designer, and still photographer, but not as director.

By 1959, Murphy and Warren divorced, ending their B-movie filmmaking partnership. Murphy continued to work in film, and in 1962, she was credited as Director of Photography for the first time on two different films. She became a founding member of Women in Film and a founding member of an organization for female cinematographers called Behind the Lens. Often praised for these fairly impressive accomplishments by the mainstream film industry, her 1972 horror film *Blood Sabbath* doesn't get much attention.

Blood Sabbath was written by William Allen Bairn, who also produced the film. *Blood Sabbath*'s cast comprises seasoned television and film actors, which seems out of place with the meager budget. Sam Gilman (Lonzo) had been acting on television since 1954, most notably as Doc Holliday in the 1968 *Star Trek* episode "Spectre of the Gun." He would go on to star in the action exploitation movie *'Gator Bait* (1973), co-directed by Beverly and Ferd Sebastian. Anthony Geary is the young lead, David, years before he played Luke Spencer on the soap opera *General Hospital*. Geary also worked with another woman director, Gloria Monty, in the 1974 television horror film *Sorority Kill*.[84] Steve Gravers (the Padre), like Gilman, had a prolific television acting career dating back to 1950. Dyanne Thorne plays Alotta, the queen of the witches, but is best known to horror and exploitation fans as Ilsa of the *Ilsa: She Wolf of the SS* film series. With this impressive cast, Murphy made an amateurish and sometimes ridiculous horror movie.

David (Geary) is a Vietnam veteran who wants to find happiness and peace in the seclusion of nature. Unfortunately, he can't seem to avoid the nude orgies and all the hippies, so he looks for an even more secluded part of the wilderness to recuperate. David meets and falls in love with a swimming woman named Yyala (Susan Damante), a member of a witch's coven in the forest. She loves David back, but they can't be together because he has a soul, and she does not; this torments David. The head witch of the nearby coven, Alotta (Thorne), now wants David for herself. She takes David's soul away in a witchcraft ritual, freeing him to be with Yyala, but David is drawn back to the witch's rituals and forced to drink human blood. When Yyala sees him with blood dripping from his mouth and all over his hands, she runs away, screaming. Rejected, David returns to Alotta, who is incredibly happy about this turn of events. But when David kisses her, he stabs her with a concealed knife. Alotta curses him on her deathbed, saying he will be killed by "his kind." David and Yyala are now free to try to be happy again, but the film's last scene is a van filled with hippies chasing David down and killing him. Weird.

There is a considerable lack of sets, props, and costume design (most of the witches are naked most of the time), but Murphy managed to create a few beautiful images with what she had. When Yyala and David first meet, she is coming out of the water and hovering over his sleeping body and face like the Waterhouse painting *Hylas and the Nymphs*. The magic rituals and dances of the witches are beautiful, too, and Murphy has a way of filming Thorne that accentuates her charisma and beauty to a ridiculous degree. But the story is childish, the characters feel empty and shallow, and the dialogue is high school play quality. The film is mysteriously set in Mexico, as everyone in the village seems to speak Spanish, and the restaurant is filled with Spanish music. But none of the witches speak Spanish or appear to be Mexican. There's some struggle between good and evil that's supposed to be taking place, but the story is flimsy. Yes, Alotta does kill a young woman and make David drink her blood, but as a whole, the coven seems pretty benign as far as covens go.

As for the writing of this film, there is no restoration of the original film print. As a result, all available digital files are blown out and faded. Several different film stocks seem to have been used, causing a discrepancy in color vibrancy and clarity. In 2007, an Internet Movie Database user left a review comment on the listing for *Blood Sabbath,* claiming to have worked on the film. They said the film was shot on 16mm, then transferred to 35mm, and made on location in the San Fernando Valley in Los Angeles, California, and the Gower Street Studios in Hollywood.[85]

Murphy and Jerry Warren, like Roberta and Michael Findlay and Beverly and Ferd Sebastian, were filmmaking teams in which the woman was allowed to direct (often out of necessity). There were numerous other low-budget and horror filmmaking male/female duos in the 1960s, the 1970s, and the 1980s, some romantic, but many professional like Gale Anne Hurd and James Cameron and Debra Hill and John Carpenter.

There has been some confusion about one particular filmmaking duo, Gloria Katz and Willard Huyck, regarding whether Katz acted as co-director on their 1973 horror film *Dead People,* AKA *Messiah of Evil.*

In *Fangoria* magazine #338 and #339, author Bradley Steele Harding recounts the history of the strange horror film *Messiah of Evil* (1973) with expertise.[86] William Huyck and Gloria Katz were a young writing team fresh out of film school who had just written *American Graffiti* (1973) for a not-yet-famous George Lucas when they made a horror film together. Both were equal writing partners on the script, initially titled *Blood Virgin*, then *The Second Coming*, and finally, *Messiah of Evil*. The film, shot in 1971, was released into relative obscurity until brought back into mainstream horror fandom in 2014 with a digital restoration and re-release.

When it came to creative and artistic choices, Huyck seems to have been in control and collaborated mainly with cinematographer Stephen Katz (Gloria's brother) and production designer Jack Fisk. Katz and Huyck were partners on the film, but the particular roles they took on set make Huyck the "director" of this low-budget film in ways that Gloria, though equally present, was not. Both co-wrote the script, produced, edited, and "directed" the low-budget film. Katz and Huyck were approached as a team to write the script, which they could then make for $100,000. They hadn't much experience in horror. Said Katz in her Fangoria interview, "The only influence was H.P. Lovecraft. I had always loved his writing."[87]

Like Christina Hornisher's *Hollywood 90028* (1973), which we'll discuss later in this chapter, and like Hornisher herself, Katz and Huyck emerged from the burgeoning Los Angeles art and film movement of the late 1960s and early 1970s. Instead of the University of California, Katz had studied at the University of Southern California, where an entirely different crop of students and artists, just as hungry for creation as Hornisher's gang, developed their friendships and sense of style as a movement:

"We knew we wanted to make something about Los Angeles, and we thought it would be interesting to use the San Fernando Valley as a setting for a horror film because it's very mundane."[88]

Other Los Angeles locations, such as Echo Park and Redondo Beach, make appearances in *Messiah of Evil*. Like *Hollywood 90028*, it is a love letter to Southern California and the innovative new film industry.

Messiah of Evil is an art film filled with Technicolor imagery, surreal moments, artwork, visions, dreams, and a sense that nothing is real. This art is mixed with cheap-looking zombies eating people. It's a trip. Katz was an equal partner in casting and minor creative choices. She told Harding,

> And we put in all of our relatives as ghouls and, you know, anyone we knew. That's why we have a strange assortment of people in it. The person that runs in the beginning of the movie is Walter Hill, the director.[89]

In favor of Katz being co-director on *Messiah of Evil*, star Anitra Ford does remember Katz working with her on acting for a particular scene: "I do recall Willard and Gloria working with me a bit during the motel scene, when Joy, Michael and I were in the room together. I don't remember the exact dialogue, but I do recall them gently coaxing me in a particular direction. They were really, really kind."[90] However, Ford also remembers "the director," not "the directors." "The death scene in the supermarket was quite simple," she says.

> The gang converged on me, I sank to the floor screaming, and the director called, "Cut!" There was no blood or extensive makeup. The scene I shot was all implied and went to fade out. I saw a photo online connected to the film, and it looked like a peep show shot up my skirt with someone's hand on my thigh. I was stunned. We did nothing like that in *Messiah*.[91]

Katz also refers to herself mainly in terms of producing while she was on set: "I had a nervous breakdown as a producer because we were making this movie for zero money, and it was an incredible amount of tension just to get the film as far as it got."[92]

Katz also recalls that horror critic Robin Wood ran into Katz and Huyck "and he said, 'Oh my god, Willard Huyck—you made *Messiah of Evil!*'"[93] Katz didn't correct Wood, either then or when recounting the incident. Katz's importance to the creation of *Messiah of Evil* and on set during production is not in question, but her involvement in creating the moment-to-moment look, design, and experience of the film as a director, isn't convincing enough to give her the full credit.

In 1973, a heavily edited and shortened version of *Messiah of Evil* was released in theaters, but it wasn't until 2009 that the film was digitally remastered and released on DVD by distributor Code Red.

Louise Sherrill, also known as Frances L. Durkin, and Louise S. Durkin, better known as "Edna Masters," appears as a prostitute who is murdered with her client/lover in the opening scene of the 1971 horror film *Blood and Lace*. The other victim in that scene was Joseph Durkin, Jr., Sherrill's real-life husband, and producer of the 1968 feature horror film

The Ghosts of Hanley House—Sherrill's only directing credit. An obscure haunted house film, it was rumored to have been filmed in Victoria, Texas and was spoofed on the 1985 television show *The Texas 27 Film Vault* because of this assumption. *The Ghosts of Hanley House* was shot in Los Angeles, California, with a local cast and crew, using the same house as in *Blood and Lace*. Intrepid film fans on the Internet have determined that *The Ghosts of Hanley House* was filmed sometime between January 1966 and June 1967, at which point the Durkins lived at 498 St. Pierre Road, Los Angeles, a home built initially for Al Jolson in 1929.[94] The 2015 Blu-ray release of *Blood and Lace* features a commentary with film historian and critic Richard Harland Smith in which he reveals that the two films were shot in the exact location.

Louise and Joseph Durkin seem to have been deeply embroiled in the emerging horror and science fiction film and television fan and filmmaker scene in Los Angeles in the 1960s: they were members of The Count Dracula Society, which met annually to discuss horror and science fiction films. The Durkins hosted the organization's events at their (supposedly) haunted, historic house.[95] *The Ghosts of Hanley House* is a genuine attempt by Louise and Joseph Durkin to rip off the haunted house movie *The Haunting* (1963), directed by Robert Wise. The storyline is directly stolen from *The Haunting*, as is the representation of the house itself and the ghostly apparitions that appear (or don't) within it. The characters are similar, and Durkin shot on black and white film.

In an almost experimental opening montage, superimposed lightning on a red filter strikes *over* a house exterior, and the opening credits begin. Barbara Chase plays "Sheila" in *The Ghosts of Hanley House* and is actress Florence Henderson's daughter. The opening credits contain several tongue-in-cheek pseudonyms, including actor Nosmo King, editor Frances Durkin (Louise Sherrill's first name is Frances), and set decorator Francesca Sherrill.

A group of young people, including Hank (Leonard Shoemaker), Dave (Wilkie de Martel), Gabby (Roberta Reeves), Sheila (Barbara Chase), and Sam Morgan (Cliff Scott), break into the Hanley House mansion. Sheila is the sensitive one affected by the ghosts first and most intensely. Gabby is a medium who can speak to the dead. Cliff is a former friend of the Hanleys.

Sheila has her first dangerous encounter with the ghosts of Hanley House when she is suddenly strangled from behind by invisible hands, believing it must be Gabby who is playing a joke. "*Your hands are like ice!*" she exclaims. Then Sheila realizes it is a ghost and fights and screams until she is free. The group comforts her as she tries to explain what happened.

If you're thinking, "Hey, that sounds just like the scene in *The Haunting* (1963) where Julie Harris's character Eleanor believes she is holding Theodora's hand in the middle of the night when they hear horrible, terrifying noises, but Theo's hand is icy cold, and then after you find out, it wasn't even Theo's hand she was holding, it was a ghost hand," it's because it is similar. The similarities to *The Haunting* ("copied from" is probably the correct term) don't end there. Sheila is blonde and suddenly affected by the ghosts, just like Eleanor is. Theo is a brunette and a medium, just like Gabby is. Ghosts use noise and sound to scare, from behind closed doors, in both films. In both films, the impetus of the visit to the house is about proving whether ghosts are real. In addition, in a direct redo of a scene from *The Haunting*, Sheila is terrorized by pounding on her bedroom door and entities whispering her name.

Between the stolen scenes from *The Haunting* to the awkward staging, *The Ghosts of Hanley House* is somewhat unbearable as far as films go. The glaring issues, such as the exterior house not matching the interior and the kitchen not matching the rest of the house inside, are distracting and sad. There is some incredibly awkward staging in which the tablecloth doesn't fit over the dining room table. Later, the partiers confine themselves to using the cramped white kitchen's breakfast table rather than the large dining room table, which seats four. An insert of stock footage of a cougar walking around the backyard during the attempted escape adds two seconds of action.

The Ghosts of Hanley House is unintentionally experimental. The rapid editing of various clocks, artwork, objects, people, eyes, doors, lighting, bushes, and drawn-out scenes with no one speaking for far too long and people wandering around without any direction or sense of time make this movie seem like a surreal experiment. Sherrill made a wholly unwatchable film by trying to copy the fine cinematography and exquisite use of light and sound in *The Haunting*. *The Ghosts of Hanley House* never had a theatrical release, but it appeared on television beginning in 1975. As of 2016, Louise Sherrill was disabled and could not comment on her career.

JANE ARDEN IS ONE of British cinema and theater's most enigmatic female figures.[96] She was born in 1927 as Norah Patricia Morris, and in the 1940s, worked as an actress and a writer in mainstream comedy theater. In the 1960s, she became involved with the growing feminist movement, inspiring her to create a radical feminist theater troupe called Holocaust, populated with artists and musicians also involved in the counterculture of the 1960s. She wrote, and they performed the plays *Vagina Rex and the Gas Oven*, *A New Communion for Freaks, Prophets and Witches*, and finally, *Holocaust*, an extreme live performance that was the basis for Arden's only solo-directed film *The Other Side of the*

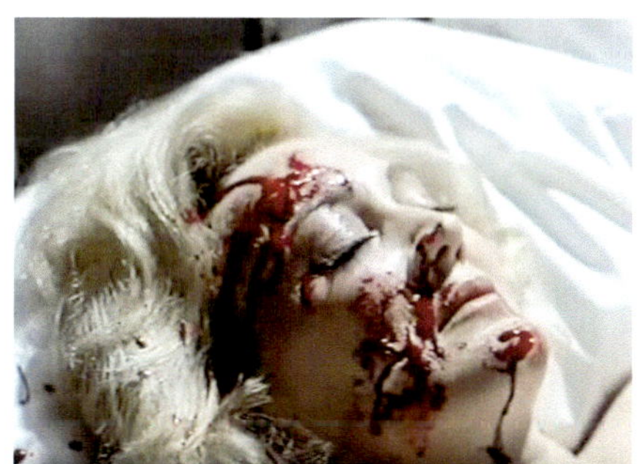

An image of Louise Sherrill in *Blood and Black Lace* (1971) which was shot in the same location as *The Ghosts of Hanley House*.

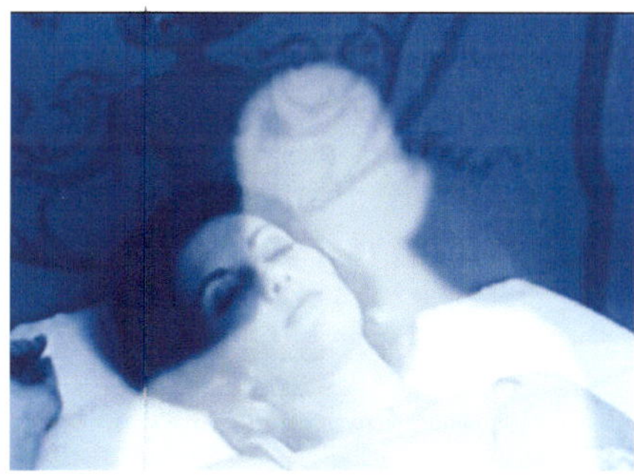

A ghostly chroma key spirit visits Sheila in her bed in Louise Sherrill's *The Ghosts of Hanley House* (1971).

Underneath (1972). Fascinated by the anti-psychiatry movement spearheaded by Jacques Lacan, Arden incorporated themes of exploitation, oppression, feminism, sexuality, and psychiatry in her theater and film work, as well as shocking imagery, violence, and experimental storylines.

The British Film Institute says *The Other Side of the Underneath* is the only woman-directed (solo) feature film made in the 1970s in the United Kingdom. It is the only *independent* feature film made by a woman in the 1970s in the United Kingdom. Numerous women-directed feature films were made during the 1970s, but their films aired on or were funded by BBC television. For instance, Anthea Browne-Wilkinson's 1976 historical thriller *The Witches of Pendle*.

The Other Side of the Underneath stars Susanka Fraey, Sheila Allen, Jane Arden, Ann Lynn, and Penny Slinger, with dozens of extras. It was filmed in the Welsh countryside and screened at the 1972 London Film Festival. Arden's husband, Jack Bond, was the cinematographer (as well as an actor), and David Mingay, the film's editor, worked very closely with Arden and Bond through filming and editing. Critics, and even the actors in the film, compare *The Other Side of the Underneath* to films like Jodorowsky's *The Holy Mountain* (1973)[97] and, probably more accurately, to Niki De Saint Phalle and Peter Whitehead's *Daddy* (1973).[98] Its surreal quality is like that in Louis Malle's *Black Moon* (1975): a bleak and eerie landscape interspersed with uncomfortable human interactions. It is a long, persistent, well-crafted, unpleasant piece of art created using film. It is not a narrative feature and is not made for mainstream audiences.

There's a thread of a storyline: a woman is rescued from a suicide drowning attempt and taken to a mental institution where she endures arduous therapy sessions with her psychiatrist and fellow inmates. It's an onslaught of disturbing cello music, a court jester speaking cryptically, red-stained concrete walls, white nightgowns, religious iconography, sexual revulsion and exploration, and human emotional suffering. Space and time sometimes don't work the way we expect them to. Frenzied ceremonies take place, like the wedding/funeral procession to a cemetery, after which a woman is buried alive in a coffin. As she agonizes, buried, footage of World War II soldiers singing a triumphal song is projected onto the gravestones. Arden creates a grueling crucifixion of a woman and leaves her to die. There are echoes of Maya Deren's films in the scene in which Penny Slinger and Susanka Fraey play with broken mirror shards; their game eventually becomes emotionally heated, and they threaten one another, then kiss, and a bloody mirror shard with a reflection takes their place. At one point, while waiting endlessly for her turn in therapy, Fraey bursts through the office door, ignoring a sign that says "Knock and Wait": she does neither. Her frustration is palpable. In the group therapy sessions, there seems to be one real revelation: "Under each of us is all the pain and all the love," says one patient, letting us know what is "underneath." All of this artistic imagery is actually about something. The main question of the film is, what is schizophrenia? Is it diagnosed differently by different doctors? And are women in an exploitative and oppressive system that drives them insane? *The Other Side of the Underneath* doesn't answer these questions, but it asks them repeatedly.

Arden fostered a strange community at the Welsh farmhouse during the film shoot. The

Susanka Fraey and Meg (Sheila Allen) in *The Other Side of the Underneath* (1972).

methods of making the film were unorthodox. Arden asked her actors to feel the pain and trauma that she expected them to play on camera. "The making of was a journey of self-exploration and self-discovery," says actress Penny Slinger, "an experiment on many levels—in community, in co-creativity, in identity."[99] Actor Natasha Morgan, who had never acted before, was also affected deeply by the methods and madness of Arden as a filmmaker:

> Visually, it was stunning, and it had this quality which I'd always been after where people spoke from themselves. They were autobiographical pieces, narrative pieces that were threaded together by a brilliant intellect in a way that was visually innovative. Musically exciting, lights were used, there was a woman who played the cello, somebody sang. There was some very, very fine performances, and it was about ... the topic was women's pain.[100]

Slinger describes the way Arden would rehearse their scenes:

> Nothing about our approach was traditional—our rehearsals were more like workshops. The basic brief was to delve into ourselves to discover our deepest traumas and denials, then pull them out to shape and crystallize them into creative offerings. It was gut-wrenching and cathartic. It was meant to be. Our aim was to unearth all the pain and anger that was bottled up inside and reveal the seething underbelly of our own psyches and, by extension, the collective community consciousness/unconsciousness. There were a couple of professional actresses in the group, but otherwise, most of us had not performed before.[101]

Circumstances just as bizarre as the scenes they were filming plagued the crew. There was a live brown bear in the farmhouse they were shooting, which would terrorize the cast and threaten to come into their living quarters. Roughly fifty severely mentally and physically challenged people from government institutions used as extras would run away,[102] others were exploited as extras during the Gypsy caravan party scenes (which included an actual Gypsy caravan that had come through the property during the film shoot) and almost all the actors and crew were tripping on LSD (excepting actress Sheila Allen). Natasha Morgan was hesitant to join the cast under these circumstances but finally relented. Arden herself drank and was chain-smoking throughout much of the shoot. She plays the role of the psychiatrist.

The cast and crew were to live on set this way, in the old farmhouse that is the main location, always staying in their costumes (most notably their nightgowns). Their unabashed method of filmmaking was just as radical as the film itself; their rejection of most Western ideas of patriarchy and psychiatry translated directly into the free-for-all that the film shoot became. The artists became the art, acted in the art, and were a part of the art. It becomes impossible to separate Arden and her cast from the art of the film itself and its message.[103] Most disturbing is that shortly after the film was completed, cast member Martin Pullinger, the husband of Sally Minford, the cello player appearing throughout the film, committed suicide by setting himself on fire.[104]

Sheila Allen, who plays the court jester, gave up a role on television to make *The Other Side of the Underneath* and was shocked by the drug use and unconventional shooting methods on set. In the end, Allen and Arden argued endlessly, ending their work and personal relationship forever. Natasha Morgan felt that the film was embarrassing and believed that the women in the film were exploited like the mentally ill extras. She also claimed that several people died during the production of the film.[105]

The Other Side of the Underneath is neither fun nor easy to view. As with all artistic, unconventional films, some people will love them, and others will hate them. For instance, one reviewer says,

> I do not view it as a bad thing that I have had to watch Jane Arden's *The Other Side of the Underneath* three times before I could form a solid opinion. Quite the contrary, I love the fact that this film's complexities run so deep that it requires a great deal of thought.[106]

And another said,

> If, for some insane reason, you feel like watching 100 minutes of women working themselves up into hysteria, depression and madness, and perform provocative, symbolic, avant-garde pieces to convey radical, straw-man-patriarchy-hating-feminist thoughts, then this is the movie for you.[107]

Arden seemed darkly confused about the film and her internal struggles as an artist. She knew she was stomping on boundaries created by the mainstream film industry, but the nature of the ideas she was writing about was not happy. "I feel depressed by this concept of genius ... " she said in an interview,

> Any artist who has been courageous enough to relate between things that nobody dares relate ... anybody who crosses that line, in any field, has to be admired because it's a dangerous game to play.[108]

Arden committed suicide in 1982 at the age of fifty-five. She had made several other films, including the surreal science fiction film *Anti-Clock* (1979) with her husband Jack Bond, but when she died, he collected all the prints and copies of their films and stored them with the British Film Institute. They could keep the films, but he made the organization agree never to screen or release them. He explained in an interview,

> When Jane Arden committed suicide, it had such a violent effect on me that I put them away. I stored them away in a laboratory in the national film archive with orders on them that they weren't to be shown again or ever released. Strange reaction, isn't it? I find it hard to work out why I did that.[109]

In 2009, Arden's son finally convinced Bond to let them release the films. In 2009, Arden's films finally screened again publicly, and the British Film Institute set about restoring the prints and digitizing them for a DVD/Blu-ray release. For three decades, Arden's work was locked away from the public. Because of that, she is not very well known, especially to American audiences. As time passes, her work is rediscovered as a profoundly intense example of radical late 1960s feminism and surreal, experimental filmmaking methods and art.

The best available information about Christina Hornisher comes from a detailed 2015 blog post from film researcher Marc Edward Heuck, who contacted[110] Hornisher's ex-husband, classmates from UCLA, the lead actor Chris Augustine from *Hollywood 90028* (1973), Hornisher's close friend director Tom DeSimone, the family of her second husband, and her estranged sister to put together a detailed picture of Hornisher's film career. For the blog post, Heuck went in person to UCLA to watch Hornisher's short experimental student films and visited The Academy of Motion Pictures Arts and Sciences' Margaret Herrick Library to find any release details about *Hollywood 90028*. And he did. She got a film degree in 1966 from UCLA and her M.F.A. from UCLA in 1970. She went to film school with both *The Doors* members Jim Morrison and Ray Manzarek, *Lemora* (1973) director Richard Blackburn, and *American Graffiti* (1973) co-screenwriter Gloria Katz (who we also discuss in Chapter 3). Hornisher also had a law degree from Loyola Law School in Los Angeles and spent a few years in Europe before returning to Los Angeles for graduate school.[111] Thanks to Heuck's research, we know that the film was possibly released in theaters in 1973/74 as *Hollywood 90028* and had a second run at drive-ins via Hallmark Releasing Corp. in 1978 as *The Hollywood Hillside Strangler*. We know it was released in 1983 on VHS as *Insanity* (by United Kingdom distributor Go Video Ltd.).[112] At some point, the film was screened under *Twisted Throats* in drive-ins.[113] *Hollywood 90028* was screened in 2005 at the New Beverly Cinema in Los Angeles from a complete print in possession of distributor Grindhouse Releasing, which created a fully-restored Blu-ray version of the film in 2021. During the 1978 drive-in release, it screened on a

Poster art for Christina Hornisher's *Hollywood 90028* (1973). Image courtesy of Grindhouse Releasing.

double bill with a 1971 film called *Night of the Demon* (AKA *The Touch of Satan*).[114] When the film was released on VHS in 1983, it was reviewed in the January edition of *The Video Times*, which indicated that the VHS purchase came with a free light bulb (because it was so scary) and that the screenwriter, Craig Hansen, was writing from personal experience, had this to say:

> Set in the twilight world between normality and insanity, you have all the elements of a good horror film a psychotic killer who kills everything he loves and lots of passionate love scenes ending in murder. The man who wrote this film, Craig Hansen, actually spent several weeks inside a psychiatric hospital to do research for his film I hasten to add. Even if you don't like the film, you still benefit from your new light bulb![115]

There is no Craig Hansen: it was a pseudonym used by Hornisher, and the story about the mental asylum is a great gimmick to help sell the film. And this review is a bit misleading. There are only three deaths in the entire film; one is off-screen.

Hornisher's student films had all been experimental.[116] She was part of a movement of young, experimental filmmakers in the Los Angeles film scene in the 1970s.[117] Her short student film *4×8=16* (1966, shot on 16mm in color and only three minutes long) is widely recognized (among experimental film circles) as a great example of "Rock 'n roll and experimental films that were on parallel groundbreaking paths from the late 1960s to the early '70s, "and were

> Fueled by all of the ecstasy and anger of a vibrant and explosive California counterculture never to be replicated ... in that era, cinema's influence on music (and vice-versa) was on par with the holy pairing of sex and drugs ... loopy Zappa fare alongside Christina Hornisher's structuralist speculations, and George Lucas' prescient early work beside Chris Langdon's pared-down homage to '60s singer-songwriter Lou Christie ... the synesthetically powerful results of a compact cultural Big Bang.[118]

This affinity for the experimental may explain why long-time obscure film scholar Fred Adelman says that *Hollywood 90028* "barely qualifies as a horror film. It's actually a talky psychodrama (with a pro-feminist slant)."[119] Lots of audio-manipulated voice-overs, intense sounds, and montage-style narratives using music over motion rather than a traditional, straightforward narrative technique place *Hollywood 90028* firmly in the non-traditional style of 'horror.'

The story's main character is Mark (Chris Augustine, also in Ted V. Mikel's *The Doll Squad*, 1973). Mark is a pornographer, meaning he is the cameraman on the set of low-budget pornography films. He works for Jobal (credited as Dick Glass). Though he is passionate about photography and film, he finds himself in a creative, emotional, and mental slump from which he is having trouble emerging. Mark also strangles women during his sexual encounters. The rest of the time, Mark is quite nice, played extremely naturally by Augustine, and it's easy to sympathize with him despite us having seen him murder a nude woman in the opening scene. At a photography shoot, Mark meets Michele (Jeanette Dilger, who also appears briefly in *American Graffiti*), a woman who moved to Los Angeles to become an actress and now finds herself living with a sugar daddy and making pornography.

There's something beautiful and poetic about Mark's fascination with Michele. They get to know each other with dialogue set to panoramas of Los Angeles. They have existential discussions about their childhoods, dreams, hopes, and fears. When they walk around Los Angeles, they visit gorgeous Victorian homes on Bunker Hill, the natural setting of Griffith Park and the Hollywood Sign, and the clean streets of Century City. The rest of the film is set against the grimy, sleazy backdrop of Hollywood and Downtown, set to music when there's no character dialogue. In many ways, *Hollywood 90028* is a love letter to Los Angeles in the way that Agnès Varda's French new wave film *Cléo de 5 à 7* (1962) is a love letter to Paris, making the city itself and the movements of the characters within it a focal point of the story. There's an urban element in this movie that is usually left out of films about Los Angeles; instead of the green suburban lawns, we are given concrete and landlocked, traffic-stricken Downtown. As we see the Bunker Hill homes being demolished for new apartments, we experience the changing landscape of Los Angeles in the 1970s, when old neighborhoods disappeared and were remade entirely in the ugly and efficient manner that mars most modern cities. Mark cannot change, and the city's changing landscape bothers him. He likes what he does and the way things are, essentially.

Aside from his visits with Michele, Mark's entire life seems consumed by pornography. He films it for a living but also visits pornography theaters and often watches Michele's films. Hornisher always includes the signs and lights of strip clubs, pornography theaters, and pornography stores in Mark's path. We're invited to participate in the sleaze with Mark when he watches an entirely surreal striptease film in a pornography theater. Michele stands in front of an odd geometric design backdrop wearing a solid white outfit, slowly unbuttoning her shirt to the droning sound of the projector.

Most of the film is spent with this intense visual and auditory experience. There's a notable lack of narrative and explication dialogue, and the existing dialogue has a surreal element. The emphasis on pornography and voyeurism isn't offensive; it's titillating. For instance, as we watch Mark during a film shoot, we hear the director, his boss, wording instructions to the actress, and it's not difficult to understand that he is voicing the thoughts of the audience—us. This film within film adds another element of disorienting strangeness.

Hornisher also uses color and sound as significant components of her storytelling; voices echo and step on themselves. Lots of blues and reds and high-contrast lighting asks the audience to *feel* something and rejects the traditional narrative film style of telling you what's happening, creating an experience that feels very personal and intimate. It's not a pretty film, focused as it is on the sleaze and filth of Los Angeles' underbelly and exploitation industries, but it's beautiful as a piece of art.

When Hornisher doesn't have music playing over her montage scenes, the sounds of cars and traffic dominate the senses (except when they visit Griffith Park, the one natural refuge for the masses). Some of the dialogue truly is bizarre and fascinating. For instance, when Mark and Michele hike to the Hollywood Sign, they discuss their families and the mundane details of their lives. Michele asks him, "*Do you live alone?*" He replies, "*Everybody lives alone.*" Mark is pessimistic but still finds beauty in parts of the city and his relationship with Michele. "*I live in Los Angeles,*" he says to no one in particular, gazing out onto the city from the sign. "*In an ugly apartment surrounded by smog. And I make money by making marginal movies. But you know what? I have the feeling that I'm waiting for something.*" Michele's dialogue is less hard-boiled and a bit more tragic. "*The story is simple,*" she says:

> *Born in a little town in a Midwest state where everybody knows everybody, and there's nothing to do. You spend your time going to movies, watching television, dreaming of the city you keep hearing about. You save some money, just a little, but it's enough for a chance, and you can't let it go. So you say goodbye to everybody, and it's even sort of sad to leave the little town so early in the morning. But the city is fantastic like you knew it would be. It's big; it's powerful. It's exciting, until you get used to it.*

As she tells her story, Mark and Michele look like an album cover, strolling through Century City. Hornisher tarnishes and breaks up the monotony of the speech by

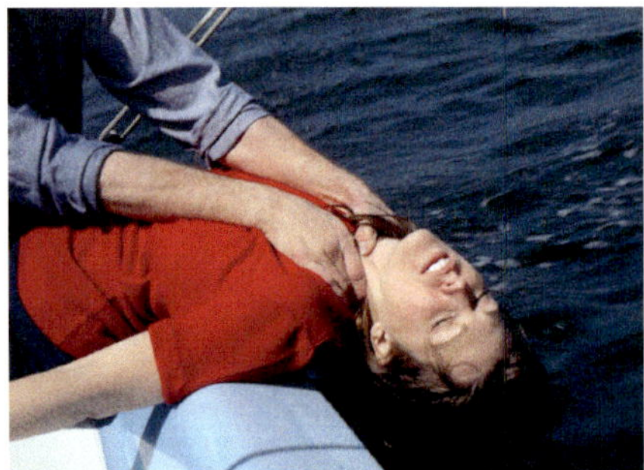

Just one of the shocking murders in *Hollywood 90028*. Image courtesy of Grindhouse Releasing.

You'll recognize the retro-futuristic buildings of Century City in Los Angeles from *Conquest of the Planet of the Apes* (1972) in *Hollywood 90028*. Image courtesy of Grindhouse Releasing.

inserting images of pawn shops and cheap loan stores, along with scenes of Michele working in pornography films. Michele describes how you fall into pornography and *"have no friends, no values, and you're alone with that obscene image of yourself on the screen."*

Despite this budding romance, Mark later picks up a hitchhiker on her way to the beach who excitedly tells him about how the water at the beach makes her feel the corpuscles traveling inside her bloodstream in a very poetic way. In this scene, like in the rest of the films, conversations start incredibly quickly, and the subject matter naturally changes abruptly. For instance, the hitchhiker says, *"I like myself now. Have you ever been to Mexico?"* Mark hangs out on the beach with her, discussing art (he once wanted to be a sculptor) while making sand castles. She discusses her invisible pet parrot to which she fed invisible bologna. Mark seems to enjoy her company, so he rents a boat from a rental shop on the marina and offers to take her out onto the ocean, as she has never been sailing. The sounds here are immense: the ocean waves, the seagulls, and the music. It's 'experiential.' When the hitchhiker comes on to Mark in the boat and mentions her (non-existent) brother again, Mark has another echoing voice-over attack of the mind. Her voice fades and echoes, and he becomes agitated. Mark can't handle the overwhelming emotions he experiences, and he strangles the hitchhiker and tosses her body in the water. He arrives back on shore alone with no trouble.

The bizarre nature of the film ramps up after this; we cut immediately to images of Mark curled up in a large dark room, watching a movie that seems to be someone moving film strips in front of the camera, every bit of him shrouded in darkness except his face. When Mark is home, he finds a recorded audio tape Michele has for him, breaking up with him. She says that she loves Mark, but he is too unpredictable. She says that Mark throws her off-balance and doesn't believe Mark wants to be happy, as if he's *"punishing himself for something."* She then plays him a song written by her boyfriend, Paul, as Mark, all in blue, sits and silently listens until he can no longer take it, and he shuts off the tape player. He drives across Los Angeles to Michele's house, where she answers the door completely naked. He enters the house, and they make love in another montage; this one is soft and warm with yellow and orange colors, soft shadows, and soothing music. Unlike the pornography shoots, there are no outright, still shots of genitalia; it's a moving, veiled moment, reflected in mirrors and glass, and patently different from the sexual scenes in the film so far. And it goes on for several minutes.

When it stops, Mark begins fantasizing verbally over montage photos of Michele, about living with Michele and being a legitimate photographer, the both of them being very happy. He mentions walks in the sun, the rain, and being together. He believes it's not too late for him as long as he can be with Michele. It's another poem set to music like so much of the written word in *Hollywood 90028*. It's a beautiful fantasy—one in which Michele can forget about her past in pornography, and he can get away from the murders he has committed. Michele lies silently in the bed next to him.

The spell is broken when Mark tries to wake her up, and she is dead. He must have strangled her during their sex session. He doesn't remember, we didn't see it, but there's no other explanation. The next thing we see is Mark hanging himself from the Hollywood

Sign, the camera slowly moving away, showing that not only is it the actual Hollywood Sign, but that somehow they were able to shoot someone committing suicide without any issues. The word "Hollywood" slowly fades away until it is unrecognizable, only a white spot on the hillside in a sea of houses and freeways.

It's a horror film, sort of. It's an art film, and frankly, a good one. It's not such a good horror film. It has horror, people dying in unpleasant ways, and we see the world's darker side. Changing the title from *Hollywood 90028* to *The Hollywood Hillside Strangler* or *Twisted Throats* was incredibly misleading to the distributors. It likely incurred the disappointment of drive-in goers who came expecting a gruesome, bloody horror slasher and instead got a poetic, dark story about two people ground down by the subversive nature of the city. Hornisher died in 2003 of ovarian cancer, not having pursued directing after *Hollywood 90028*.

FOR YEARS I PUT off watching *Alien Zone*, AKA *House of the Dead*, directed by Sharron Miller, for research for this book. It seemed utterly unappealing in every way. The copy I had on DVD was a bootleg from an old VHS, so it was almost impossible to watch. In 2018, Vinegar Syndrome restored the horror anthology feature from its original 35mm negative and put the restored digital version on Blu-ray. I bought it and knew that someday I would have to watch it, as Sharron Miller's film belongs in this chapter amongst the other films directed by women at the time. When I finally watched it, I realized that I had seen the film before and that *Elvira's Movie Macabre* featured it in the 1980s on television in Los Angeles. The last segment is the one that I remembered. It's the most intelligent and well-done part of the film, and I remember, even as a kid, really thinking hard about that story in particular.

Sharron Miller is a native of Oklahoma, born in the town of Enid. When she was thirteen, she knew she wanted to be a filmmaker. She'd seen Elia Kazan's tragic romance *Splendor in the Grass* (1961) and felt a calling to be a film director and make the world a better place.[120] In 1972, she moved to Hollywood, California, to begin a career in film. She worked first as a script supervisor and then as an editor before being hired to direct episodes of *The Life and Times of Grizzly Adams* in 1976.

In 1977, her friend William Jackson back home in Stillwater, Oklahoma, asked her to direct a feature film for him and producer Arthur Leonard. Unfortunately, the film fell through, and Jackson and Leonard asked her if she had any scripts she'd like to direct, as they still had funding in place and wanted to make something; they didn't know what.[121] Miller didn't, but her friend David O'Malley did. He had a few. The one he showed them was a horror anthology titled *Five Faces of Terror*, and with Miller set as director, the film went into production and was filmed in Stillwater, Oklahoma.

This was Miller's first and only feature film (except for television movies). It was not what she wanted to be doing, as horror was not her preferred genre. However, she told herself that there were opportunities to make this a great film: "I have spent a lifetime studying the films of great directors, so I could see possibilities of paying homage to Hitchcock. Unfortunately, we didn't have the budget to do what I would have liked."[122] Her

Burr DeBenning as a serial killer and his date in the found-footage segment in *House of the Dead* (1978). Image courtesy of Vinegar Syndrome.

One of the murderous children with bad teeth in *House of the Dead*. Image courtesy of Vinegar Syndrome.

cinematographer was a colleague from Los Angeles, Ken Gibb, who had previously shot the horror films *The Witch Who Came from the Sea* (1976) and *Drive-In Massacre* (1976). Her producer, Arthur Leonard, had directed the horror film *The Devil's Daughter* (1939), known for its all-Black cast and voodoo themes. Though he'd been actively making films in the 1930s and 40s, Leonard hadn't made a film in three decades, but he wanted to. He'd contacted William Jackson because he was a film professor at Oklahoma State University, who had contacted his old friend Sharron. With the student filmmakers at the University, Leonard had a very cheap crew to stretch a meager budget. Miller believes it was about $300,000.

In an article in *Fangoria* magazine from April 2009, journalists Michael Price and John Wooley wrote about the making of *House of the Dead* in which they interviewed a student crewmember of the film named Rick Scott. "We were the grips, the bottom feeders, and we did all the grunt work—but we were glad to do it," Scott told them. Scott recalls that it was freezing during the shoot, and lots of alcohol was consumed by the students late into the long evenings of shooting. "The students who were working on the film saw how exciting it could be, but we also found out there was a lot of hard work involved."[123]

David O'Malley, who would write the screenplay for the horror film *The Boogens* (1981), had structured his anthology after *The Twilight Zone*. The wraparound story was about an unfaithful man (played by John Ericson, who starred in *Seven Faces of Doctor Lao* in 1963) on a business trip, stumbling into a mortuary in the middle of a rainstorm. The mortician (Ivor Francis, who had a small part in *Splendor in the Grass*) invites him out of the cold, offers him coffee, and then shows him the four corpses he currently has in his workshop. Each corpse has a terrifying backstory that he tells Mr. Talmudge (and, therefore, the audience).

The first segment is about a schoolteacher named Miss Sibiler (Judith Novgrod) who hates children and is stalked and killed by monstrous, fanged supernatural ones as punishment. This strange and uninspired story is supposed to be a morality lesson. Still, Miss Sibiler's crime seems to be just that she doesn't like kids.

Burr DeBenning (recognizable as the star of 1977's *The Incredible Melting Man*) stars in the second segment as a serial killer fond of filming all of his murders. There's not much to the story, but the use of found footage, as most of the narrative, is pretty revolutionary for a horror film from 1978.[124] The entire segment is shot in an apartment with a static shot (except for a scene when Growski is being hauled off to prison by police). Using a real apartment as the set (no sound stages were used in any aspect of the film) created some creative difficulties. According to Scott,

> That was shot on the second story of a little apartment building in Stillwater, and Kenny Gibb, the cinematographer, realized he needed to get as far back in the corner as he could to get his establishing shot because it's all from the point of view of the camera in the apartment. In setting up the shot, Ken was looking through the viewfinder, backing the camera up—and he backed into the window and broke the glass with his rear end.[125]

The third story is an odd detective game between British detective Inspector McDowal (Bernard Fox, the most famous actor in the film, best known as Dr. Bombay on the 1960s television series *Bewitched*) and American sleuth Detective Malcolm Toliver (Charles Aidman, best known in the original *Twilight Zone* episodes "And When the Sky Was Opened" as Colonel Ed Harrington and as Bill, the physicist in "Little Girl Lost"), each vying for the title of World's Best Detective. They grudgingly respect one another's work, but they have a rivalry that is too strong for them to escape. The Maître' d hands Toliver a strange note during a fancy dinner with McDowal that suggests that someone will die unless he figures out whom and when. He is consumed with the mystery while McDowal "watches him work." Of course, we find out McDowal sent him the note and planned to murder Toliver, but Toliver had already solved the mystery and was only pretending not to know, and he had booby-trapped the chair McDowal sits in, so they both die. This story doesn't seem to have a moral, except that maybe both men were too proud of their skills, and so had to be punished for it. Fox and Aidman give the best performances in the film, and though the story doesn't make much sense, it's difficult not to admire their acting.

The fourth story stars Richard Gates as a man named Mr. Cantwell nearing the end of his frustrating day at work. He hates his job, the cubicle to which he is confined, and his annoying co-workers. As he leaves work during lunch, he is accosted by a homeless man asking for money. He coldly brushes him off, telling him to get a job. He walks into an empty store expecting to find chewing gum and can't open the doors to leave. Trapped inside, he tries to find another way out but finds himself lost even more in the bowels of the building. Almost impaled by spikes in a small, enclosed space, Cantwell realizes he may never get out. He has nothing to eat or drink, and no one knows where he is. But someone must because a small slot opens up in the bottom of the wall, and a bottle of alcohol is pushed through to Cantwell. It isn't said outright, but he is released after at least a few days, probably longer. His clothes are filthy, he's addicted to alcohol, and he can barely speak from the trauma he's been through. He grabs the first man he sees: a man in a nice suit just leaving work. That nice man tells him to get a job. This was the segment that I remembered as a little girl. This image of the man "being turned homeless" by some evil force has stuck with me for many years, and on a rewatch, I realize it's the most powerful story with the most effective visuals. Miller felt the same way, saying,

> It was the perfect marriage of style and performance, [Gates] was an actor I studied with in Los Angeles, from the Stanislavsky system. There wasn't much dialogue, so it had to be a stylistic approach that told the story. I thought I did the best job there.[126]

Miller says the entire shoot was only twenty to twenty-one[127] days, while Scott remembers a full four weeks of production.[128] The production was problematic for two reasons: the low budget and the fact that everything was shot in real locations, not on sound stages. The $300,000 budget didn't go very far because of the cost of film stock and development, though producer Leonard told the *Tri-City Herald* newspaper that the budget was $600,000.[129] Another newspaper article says the budget was $685,000.[130] While she didn't like the schoolteacher segment and felt that it suffered the most from these limitations, she found the fourth story the easiest to shoot:

> For some reason, that seemed to flow the best and was the easiest one to do. I think the story with the two detectives was probably the most complicated and complex and difficult in terms of locations and the amount of story there was, and it wasn't that it didn't turn out okay; it's that it took a lot of time and different places. And everything was on location, we didn't have any sets ... we didn't build any sets, everything was shot on location, and when you do that, it always makes it more complicated. That was the story that had the most sets, so it was difficult in that regard. The actors were great, but just the actual doing of it. The easiest one to do was the one with the camera because that was basically one set. Looking back on it, I wish I would have directed it differently. I would have made different choices today.[131]

Miller co-edited the film (she had worked as an editor on other films; she had even cut the sound effects into the horror movie *The Exorcist*, 1973), which was renamed from *Five Faces of Fear* to *Alien Zone*, probably to make it sound more like *The Twilight Zone*. At a screening of the rough cut in Oklahoma City at the Will Rogers Theatre, the entire film was over two hours long. It wasced and a genuine premiere took place in Stillwater, Oklahoma, before Jupiter Pictures of Burbank, California, officially released the film. Scott remembers that Miller and Bill Jackson showed up to the premiere in a hearse, and there were many people present and a sense of excitement along with rented searchlights.[132] On the other hand, Miller says she didn't attend the premiere.[133] There was a hearse, though, and some of the people that made the film arrived at the premiere in it.[134]

The film was released on VHS in the 1980s as *House of the Dead* and, later, on DVD as *Last Stop on 13th Street*. Miller is surprised the film has a fan base and still has a kind of cult following. She says they're mostly people "who don't like it but also love it. I find that fascinating. I think that's pretty nice, actually. It's nice when things you make for no money end up having a following."[135] Miller continued to direct television and won several notable awards for her work, including the Director's Guild of America Award and a Daytime Emmy award for the ABC *Afterschool Special* episode "The Woman Who Willed a Miracle." She would not make another feature film except for television.

Like Rothman and Hornisher, and another filmmaker we'll discuss later in this chapter named Anna Thomas, Karen Arthur came from...Thomas, and Hornisher, Karen Arthurcame from a new generation of women who attended film schools and created independent work with the hopes of breaking into mainstream filmmaking. She attended film school in 1971 at UCLA, where legendary director Penelope Spheeris (*The Decline of Western Civilization*, 1981) was a teaching assistant. Spheeris told Arthur, "You've got talent.[136] You're going places."[137]

Arthur is one of the directors interviewed many times by newspapers in the 1970s and 1980s, so there is an ongoing record of her film releases, critic reactions, and Arthur's changing outlook on the film industry over those twenty years preserved in print form. Arthur began her film career with *Legacy* and proceeded to *The Mafu Cage* with enthusiasm, a bright spirit of creativity, and a passion that every journalist notes. Young Arthur was reluctant to label herself as a feminist, much like earlier filmmakers like Ida Lupino and Doris Wishman were. Arthur evolved in the middle of the sexual revolution and movement for women's rights, which makes her stance stand out among filmmakers like Barbara Peeters and Stephanie Rothman. "I am not part of the Women's Movement as such," she claimed in an early interview: "It's so bloody boring the way they talk, endless dreary polemics nothing to do with people." A few sentences later, Arthur describes her actual feelings about being a woman in the film industry, and it turns out that she is a feminist; she doesn't know it. "Bigotry and chauvinism in the film world is bad," she points out, "and the industry has been notorious for the poor handling of women, both in the projection of image and in behind-the-scenes participation."[138] In 1986, in another article about the state of women directors in Hollywood, Dawn Steel, then-President of Production at Paramount, said to a reporter,

> Karen Arthur made a film, *The Mafu Cage,* ten years ago. I saw it and thought it was brilliant. If you don't have passion about your work, your work's not good. I'll never forget Karen. She was unbelievably passionate.[139]

Arthur's second feature film, *The Mafu Cage*, was independently financed with a budget of $1 Million. Her passionate nature convinced investor Gary Triano to put "unlimited funds" in *The Mafu Cage* budget. Museums and art galleries were taken by her enthusiasm and lent her artwork and artifacts as props for the mansion, the film's primary setting. Arthur first got the idea for *The Mafu Cage* in 1971 when she saw a play in Paris called *Toi et tes nuages* starring Anna Karina. It was a story about two sisters and the psychological breakdown of their unhealthy relationship. "It needed to be translated into cinema," she explained in an interview:

> By the time I brought the script to the screenwriter, I'd spent a year breaking things down visually, scene by scene, beat by beat. I think a director-writer collaboration at an early stage saves rewrites later.[140]

She spent time in mental hospitals to research patients with mental disorders. She immersed herself in the project, convincing the owners of a mansion in Los Angeles to allow her to shoot there for free. She had a completed script in 1975,[141] and by January 1977, she took the script to studios, which made offers, but she went with Triano to keep creative control of the project. By August 1, 1977, the five-week film shoot in Los Angeles, California, had begun.[142]

Lee Grant and Carol Kane star in the film as two sisters, Ellen and Cissy, respectfully, and live in a vast mansion as they have inherited unlimited funds from their father. They were raised in Africa, where their father conducted fieldwork (it's never clear if it was animal or human-related), but came back to the United States when their mother died. Now that their father has passed, the two of them live alone in the sprawling house living a lonely and weird life of unhealthy attachment with only their father's old friend Zom looking in on them occasionally. Cissy is mentally ill and has been for years. Ellen's father made her promise never to put Cissy in a mental institution, so out of guilt, Ellen devoted her adult life to caring for the spoiled, annoying, odd, frustrating, and insane Cissy. The only time she has away from Cissy is when Ellen works at the Griffith Observatory as an astronomic photographer. Her co-worker David (James Olson) has feelings for her, but Ellen can't return his affection because of Cissy. Cissy has an unhealthy obsession with Africa; she plays African music every day, wears African-inspired clothes, and does African-inspired dances. It's unclear whether any of this "African" stuff is actually African or just Arthur's white-person-idea-of-what-Africa-is, but it is deeply ingrained in their day-to-day lives. Cissy also has a pet primate called a "mafu." She spends her days with the pets until she breaks down and brutally kills them one day. So far, Ellen has always gotten her a replacement mafu, and after some convincing, she finally gets another one after the most recent incident. Unfortunately, Cissy beats the next one with a chain until it's dead. Instead of sending her to a psychiatrist as Zom insists, Ellen believes it would be better to leave Cissy alone in the house for a few days while Ellen goes on a work trip to take photos of the night sky. What could go wrong? Well, David stops by to see if Ellen has been in touch as she isn't available by phone, and Cissy at first charms him, then chains him up and beats him to death. When Ellen gets home, she doesn't know what Cissy has done at first, but when she figures it out, Cissy shackles her in the cage and makes her the new mafu. Having had a total breakdown, Ellen refuses to eat and starves to death. Cissy spends the movie's last moments gently rocking her and shrilly crying.

The Mafu Cage has a terrifying premise but is experienced as a frustrating study in filmed theater. It's reminiscent of *Whatever Happened to Baby Jane?* (1962) with Kane as the insane Cissy and Lee playing her trapped older sister, fearing for her life. There's a sad *Grey Gardens* (1975) aspect to the story; real people live like that, and it's highly romanticized in *The Mafu Cage*. Arthur enjoys arty, staged scenes with too much going on in them: too much noise, too much music, too much body paint, too many vases, and too many drawings. Arthur goes overboard on the atmosphere, enhancing their living situation and relationship claustrophobia. Kane and Grant act more like daughter and mother; age-wise, they seem to fit that dynamic better than sisters. There's an incredibly uncomfortable element of incest as Cissy is sexually obsessed with Ellen and implies they've had sex in the past. When Cissy isn't beating an ape to death or dancing around in an African costume play, she's drawing, which she seems to take very seriously and calls her "work." Her artwork plays a significant role in the plot. Ellen recognizes a sketch of David realizing that he's been to the house and that Cissy killed him. Cissy also paints on the wall above and around Ellen's unconscious body in the chair in the mafu cage.

The Mafu Cage is simultaneously fun to watch and a total drag of predictable art house nonsense. Some contemporary critics agreed: it's "Too concocted to work as 'serious' horror and too solemn to succeed as an item in the horror genre" with a "foolish plot" that was a "waste of time," said one.[143] Another called it not likable, "high pitched, screechy, and alienating."[144] It's not *that* bad. It's worth a watch to witness the powerful forces Karen Arthur conjured up for this movie: the solid acting talent, the exciting visuals, and the vile plot involving animal and human abuse and incest. The film's origin in a pretentious French play holds it back. Underneath the horror, an affected plot rings hollow.

Arthur tried to make the two sisters so different that they were two halves of the same person, "the traditional and the more primitive in all of us," she explained in an interview in Cannes, where the film premiered in 1978. She says, "The violence in the film represents the conflict of life," but that's a pretty hollow sentiment.[145] All violence in all horror movies represents the conflict of life. The violence in *The Mafu Cage* represents an abusive family relationship with an enabler who is ultimately killed when they try to leave the relationship.

The Mafu Cage was released in theaters in Europe and briefly in the United States, but it didn't do very well with American audiences. Arthur and Triano originally self-distributed the film to theaters, but they soon found that theaters were shortchanging them on ticket percentages. They found a distributor, hoping to have someone negotiate those problems, but the distributor changed the film's title to *Don't Ring the Doorbell* and advertised it as an exploitation horror film, disappointing audiences and going bankrupt. The rights were then sold to a new company that distributed it as an art house film. It was also released under *My Sister, My Love,* and *Deviation*. Eventually, it ended up on DVD in the 2000s, and in 2017, it was restored and given a 2K digital Blu-ray release with special features.

The Haunting of M (1979) is Anna Thomas's only film as director. It was her master's thesis from her graduate degree from the University of California, Los Angeles, where she was a student from 1972-1979. Born in Stuttgart, Germany, she moved to the United States with her family as a little girl. In 1972 she entered UCLA and partnered with fellow filmmaker (and future husband) Gregory Nava to write his directorial feature debut film and master's thesis, *The Confessions of Amans* (1976). He next co-produced *The Haunting of M*, and together they would write five more films as a team, including the acclaimed 2002 screenplay for the Frida Kahlo biopic *Frida*. In the early-to-mid-1970s, Thomas and Nava mixed with other young, independent, and rebellious filmmakers who wanted to create a new community. This small group formed IFP/West (Independent Feature Project), a non-profit organization dedicated to providing resources for independent filmmakers and supporting diversity in the film industry. That small organization became Film Independent, now one of the largest non-profit film organizations in Los Angeles and producing the annual Independent Spirit Awards. At the same time she began her

Carol Kane as the unhinged Cissy in a gorgeous shot from Karen Arthur's *The Mafu Cage* (1978). Image courtesy of Kino Lorber.

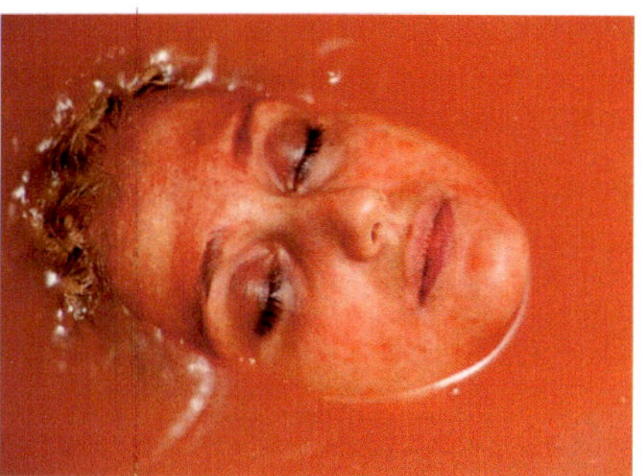

Cissy bathes in red water to make you think about blood in *The Mafu Cage*. Image courtesy of Kino Lorber.

film career in the early 1970s, Thomas wrote a vegetarian cookbook called *The Vegetarian Epicure,* which was a best-seller sensation, bringing her the funds she needed to complete her thesis film *The Haunting of M*.

Perhaps the most unexpected thing about *The Haunting of M* is that it was one of Roger Ebert's favorite films. In 1979, when it premiered at the Chicago Film Festival, he praised it as "the most audacious, ambitious, and generally successful debut film since *Citizen Kane*."[146] He meant "successful" because Thomas knew exactly what she wanted to make, a "joyous debut" that perfectly showcased Thomas' skills.[147] He continued to have respect for Thomas and all of her work throughout the rest of his career. Ebert had a great admiration for independent filmmakers that were artists who needed to tell their stories no matter what, like Thomas: "Maybe an independent film is one that tells a story that the filmmaker believes has to be told, no matter what," he wrote. "No matter whether it's 'commercial,' no matter whether Hollywood will finance it, no matter whether anyone will ever want to pay to see it, it has to be told."[148]

What Ebert enjoyed about the film itself was its approach to the classic ghost story: instead of being a modern horror film (and in 1979, many gory slasher films were saturating the horror film market), it channels the calm and mysterious magic of psychological horror the way nineteenth-century literature does, and the films that are (sometimes loosely) based on that literature. *The Innocents* (1961), *Eye of the Devil* (1966), *The Hound of the Baskervilles* (1939), and *The Woman in White* (1948) all share similarities with *The Haunting of M*. The slow and steady Gothic thriller perfectly encapsulates the feeling of reading a nineteenth-century ghost story. In her own words, Thomas called it a "kind of a Jamesian ghost story."[149]

Set in 1905, the film's Western world is on the brink of new technology and changing views about women's roles as wives and mothers. Halina (Nini Pitt) is a woman in her twenties who returns home to visit her family in their beautiful countryside mansion. Her little sister Marianna (Sheelagh Gilbey) is just coming out into the formal world of society, and her parents hope she'll marry family friend Stefan (Peter Austin) and become respectable. The family gathers for a family photograph, a very formal affair, and just as Stefan takes the picture, elderly Aunt Teresa (Jo Scott Matthews) falls over. The doctor is called, she is put in her bed, and the doctor tells them that it is only a matter of time before she dies. Aunt Teresa's heart is bad, and she has dementia.

While Teresa languishes upstairs in her bedroom, Marianna continues enjoying herself. Stefan develops the photograph and shows Marianna and Halina, saying he is upset by how blurry one of the figures turned out. The man in the photograph is wearing an old-fashioned jacket and is no one they recognize. Thinking it may have been a friend of Teresa, Halina shows her the photograph. When she sees it, Teresa names him only as "Marion."

This mystery takes the sisters deeper into a rabbit hole of family secrets as they discover that Marion was Aunt Teresa's lover fifty years ago, and he disappeared under mysterious circumstances. Now, his spirit has come to claim Aunt Teresa on her deathbed and wants Marianna for himself. Haunting and possessing Marianna, Marion both frightens and interests her, as she is disappointed in her life and what it will be like as a wife to an ordinary man. Marianna looks up to Halina, who has forged her path, despite their mother disapproving of the way she has chosen to live her life. Halina fights desperately to save her sister and learns that Aunt Teresa had been pregnant and eloped with Marion when she was Marianna's age, but her brother and father chased her down, brought her back, and her brother and Marion killed each other in an ensuing duel. Teresa's life was ruined after that. She lost the baby, she developed early onset dementia, and she never did anything with her life or went anywhere. Teresa may as well have died too. Marianna has to send Marion's ghost away and transform her ordinary life into something special, which she eventually does.

Like *Dracula*, *The Haunting of M* has a female character psychically drained by a supernatural entity. She languishes in bed, doctors prescribe rest, and her psychological state suffers. But unlike other Gothic stories set in the nineteenth century, the women have agency and save themselves. Marion haunts Marianna because she allows it and finds it exciting. Halina disregards her mother's criticism and decides to live her life her way.

The turn of the century changed things for women in a way that wouldn't fully manifest until after World War II: women could support themselves, had more rights, were allowed in bars, could live alone, and never marry if they chose. Halina is a member of the new generation of women who smokes and wants to vote while her mother and Aunt Teresa linger in an old-fashioned Victorian way of life out in the country. Marianna is caught in the middle: she worries that getting married will relegate her to a dull, uneventful life as a wife and mother, but Halina helps her see that the possibilities for her life are numerous and getting married to Stefan in no way limits what else she might do in this brave new century. "Halina is the independent woman, ahead of her time," said Thomas:

> And Marianna is struggling with more than just deciding whether or not to get married. She is struggling to move forward in her life in some way, doesn't know what that way should be, and doesn't want to let go of any possibilities—so she is paralyzed ... She wants something more than the ordinary world, so she is vulnerable to the spell of the ghost of Marion. And yes, when she breaks free, she is moving toward her actual future life, with all its pitfalls and ordinary problems. I don't know

> if destiny is the right word—but it is life in a new century. And it is frightening.[150]

Thomas's direction is precise and solid; the *Barry Lyndon*-esque lighting is always natural and feels authentic. "I was very influenced by impressionist painting," she said; "That was the look that I was trying to capture on film—and Scotland has such incredible light, it would be a crime not to use it to the greatest possible effect!"[151]

The Scottish castle in which the film was shot is a fantastic backdrop that Thomas used in every way possible for maximum atmosphere:

> Well, I had this moody, psychological ghost story that I wanted to make that was set in the turn of the century, and I wanted it to look amazing, and I knew I wasn't going to be building sets. So I went off to Britain to scout locations—I knew I had to shoot someplace where English was spoken; that was the single practical thought that crossed my mind. I just set off, completely unaware of what it took to scout locations and mount a production—I was a naïve kid, oblivious to reality ... Finally, I found my way to Scotland, and it was amazing. The beauty of the landscapes and the mood of the place were hypnotic; there was no turning back after that. In Scotland, I spoke to some very nice people at the National Trust, and little by little, I found my way to the places that completely captured my imagination—Kellie Castle, the countryside around St. Andrews. It was magical. I think we made a very modest donation to the National Trust, and they gave us full permission to shoot at Kellie Castle as long as we didn't interfere with the days it was open to the public.[152]

Thomas had a small crew and only shot for five weeks: Greg Nava was her cinematographer, a friend with whom she had previously worked on his thesis film, and Bob Yerington, another friend from film school who did all the audio sound work (and more). "That was it for the American team," said Thomas,

> I hired a young production manager in Britain and a film student who served as the AC, grip, and general support. For a while, we had a wonderful young woman who I believe was also a film student, and helped us for nothing, just for the experience. And wherever we were shooting, people involved with those locations got so interested and wanted to help—it was wonderful. I remember the woman who did all the flowers for Kellie Castle; she was very helpful and so kind to us. I was the director, but I also did the hair and make-up, and that was an experience! But it was great because I spent that time with my principal actors, and we could talk about the characters and the scene in an intimate but informal way. We shot long hours and worked so hard. I didn't have any idea then that we should have a decent turnaround time. We were all just students who had not had any training in how a professional set is run, so we broke rules and laws right and left, usually without even being aware of it. But we shot on two main locations for all the interiors and numerous exteriors, both at Kellie and in the different parts of the countryside.[153]

"It was made in Scotland for $100,000," she said in an interview in the *Los Angeles Times* in 1981:

> The film is slow-paced, with no known names but high production values. I don't even know how to approach a producer, so I went on my own. One thing I learned is never to go to a distributor with a 16-mm print—only with a 35mm.[154]

Originally shot on 16mm, the film was later blown up to 35mm for distribution. *The Haunting of M* premiered at the Edinburgh Film Festival and played at the Chicago International Film Festival. It then had a small theatrical run with a tiny independent distributor and was eventually sold to a German television network. Ebert himself lamented in 2010 that *The Haunting of M* had never been released on DVD.[155] Based on the success of her modest student film, Thomas was offered a chance to write the adaptation of Kate Chopin's great novel *The Awakening* for the screen. But then her writing partnership with her husband took off, and they made the film *El Norte* (1983), which was a big success for them, so Thomas didn't take *The Awakening* job offer, and she never directed another film. "All of that is true," said Thomas:

> But is it all the truth? I don't know. Maybe I was afraid to rock the boat once Greg and I started having a real career as a writing team. Maybe I somehow internalized the idea that directing a film was much harder than what I think now it is—because I was doing so many jobs at once. Making that movie was a thrilling experience but also exhausting. I was in my twenties and getting gray hair![156]

In an interview with Ebert, Thomas had this to say about vegetarianism food and the parallel to women directors:

> I don't believe in the us-and-them thing. I look forward to the day when there is no distinction made when the porcini pasta is not a "vegetarian meal" and Katherine Bigelow is not a "female director"—when good is good, and that's it. But these things take time. Habits only fade when they are replaced by new habits.[157]

Astrid Frank was born in 1944 in Germany as Eike Pulwer but made her films in the United Kingdom with British actors, and they were only distributed in the United Kingdom. A professionally trained actress, having studied in Hamburg at Schauspielschule der Hamburger Kammerspiele and in Berlin at the UFA Schule, she chose Astrid Frank as a stage name after marrying British actor Charles Frank. Her most well-known film as an actress is the United Kingdom production *Au Pair Girls* (1972), in which she co-starred with British actress Gabrielle Drake and Ferdy Mayne, best known to horror fans as Count von Krolock in Roman Polanski's *The Fearless Vampire Killers* (1967). *Au Pair Girls* was directed by Val Guest, who also directed numerous early Hammer films, including *The Quatermass Xperiment* (1955).

As an actress, Frank found that she was very interested in the camera work on the set of her films. Reluctantly, the crew would sometimes let her look through the camera in exchange for a crate of beer, which she paid them. She was unhappy with the quality of the films in which she acted. "There was a time in Germany when they only made really bad films," she says. "I just was thinking, well, I would do this better." Frank would star in numerous German soft-core sex comedies throughout the 1960s and 1970s and a few in France. It wasn't the subject matter of the soft-core movies that bothered Frank in any way. "I don't mind being naked," she explains, "but it is the stupidity that I can't take!"[158]

Wanting to learn about filmmaking, she applied to a film school in London but was rejected because she didn't have any filmmaking experience. "I haven't done anything!" she told the school admissions team. "I want to go to school to learn it. I sent them a picture of my baby and said this is my last production. They did not have a sense of humor. They said film anything, three minutes, five minutes, 8mm, and show us."[159] So Frank decided to make a short film to show the school and the world.

> I tell you something: a journalist who knew me as an actress; I told him, "I thought we were friends." I told him I wanted to direct, and he said, "You, as a woman?" I said yes, and he said, "People won't respect you." I said, "What, you don't respect me?" He said, "I didn't mean it like that." "Yes, you did say that! You don't respect me." Then he wasn't a friend anymore.[160]

Frank's first short film would be the twenty-four-minute horror movie *Red* (1976). She already had the idea, and she had friends and locations that she could use to make something exceptional. "I had a few ingredients: I have Ferdy Mayne, a good friend of mine (we were once lovers); Gabrielle [Drake], I knew her from *Au Pair Girls*, and I had Medmenham Abbey." Medmenham Abbey is a restored historic mansion in Buckinghamshire, England, right on the River Thames. It has a very dark history that inspired the story behind *Red*. The famous Hellfire Club of Sir Francis Dashwood held meetings in Medmenham Abbey, which Dashwood wholly restored from its medieval ruin and had the words "Do What Thou Will" written in stained glass at the entrance. Rumors of orgies, satanic rituals, and worse circulated about the Hellfire Club until they were eventually forced to leave Medmenham Abbey. Frank included an orgy scene and a violent beheading with a saber in her story that was directly inspired by this local history:

> The film was really very daring, I must say. But I dared. The censor wanted to forbid it. I had a big argument with him. "Why do I make a film and then not show it?" I asked. He said, "It's not because of the sex; it's because of the violence." It is symbolic! The head is on again! This is what men do to us, they cut our heads off, but our heads grow again.[161]

Frank's friend Brian Desmond Hurst, a famous Irish director who was ninety years old at the time, fully supported her desire to direct a film and helped her secure a cast and crew, including Australian cinematographer Robert Krasker who had won an Academy Award for his work on the famous noir thriller *The Third Man* (1949). They would shoot on 35mm film. *Red* was originally just the working title of the short, but it stuck. "Like Picasso had a blue period, this painter, played by Ferdy Mayne, he has his red period. Red for blood, lips, love, and red in paintings."[162] *Red* was based on a poem that Frank had written. The painter's voice-over narration is a recitation of her poem as he finds himself wandering to Medmenham Abbey:

> TO ART
> *When I was a young artist, I looked, yet I was rather blind*
> *A cloud was a cloud, a tree was a tree*
> *A woman was for my bed*
> *Beloved art, since I offered you my soul, you gave me other eyes*
> *The superficial world is changing in my eyes, your eyes*
> *A tale in the cloud*
> *A writing in the sky*
> *A face in a tree*
> *A woman on a pedestal*
> *The autumn forest is a girl, her long red hair blowing in the wind*
> *Beloved art, I follow you without wanting to know the answers to my questions*
> *Can there be color in the dark?*
> *Can there be beauty in evil?*
> *I follow you beyond the far horizon*
> *To meet whatever you have prepared for me*
> *Will it be the end? Is the end death? Is death the end? Is there a solution?*
> *Or, at least, peace?*

As the painter finds himself at Medmenham Abbey, he finds a group of three troubadours (played by Gabrielle Drake, Mark Wynter, and Roy North). Greeting them, he asks who they

"Fais ce que tu voudras" ("Do what thou wilt") etched in French on the fireplace mantel of Medmenham Abbey where Astrid Frank's short horror film *Red* (1976) was filmed. Image courtesy of Astrid Frank.

Glynis Barber is a young woman having a very unhealthy love affair with her mirror in Astrid Frank's horror/fantasy *The Jealous Mirror* (1982).

are. They tell him they are wanderers, and he says he is a wanderer too. He throws a bunch of coins at them, saying, "Catch." Drake puts the money in her bodice, and the troubadours sing a song for the painter. That evening, asleep in the castle, the painter has a horrific nightmare: Drake is tied nude to a table. Fully naked, North and Wynter both rape her. After they finish their assault, the men cut off Drake's head with a saber. At the last moment, before the saber comes down, Drake's character realizes that she is about to die and shows fear. "I only meant to please you!" she cries, then chop! Her head is off. There is a prosthetic head that rolls away, seeping blood. The painter shakes, sweats, and makes the sign of the cross on his chest. Then, he wakes up the following day and comes down for breakfast. The troubadours are all alive and happy. When the painter looks at Drake's neck, he sees a red scar across her neck! But only for a moment; the scar fades into a red choker necklace studded with rubies. The painter shivers in fear. Drake's character says to him, "But you said you like red? Red is your color." "I am no longer sure whether I like it," the painter answers her, thinking that he may try blue instead.

Red had a budget of £30,000 and fourteen shooting days over two weeks at Medmenham Abbey. "Everything went really lovely, and everybody helped me," says Frank. "I learned directing by doing it. Bob Krasker said to me, 'You must shout!' It is much faster when you shout."[163] On the morning of the shoot of the breakfast scene, Mayne came down the mansion's stairs and asked Frank how he looked. She replied that he looked awful, to which he said, "Oh good," because that's exactly how his character was supposed to look. Of Wynter, Frank says, "Mark looked good, he is good, he does everything that I as a director wants. He is fantastic material." The actors had no problem with the sex or the violence in the film. At the beginning of the shoot, Drake asked, "When is my head coming off?" Frank jokingly replied, "Well, on the last day, of course." The decapitated head prop was sculpted by "theater people." When Frank watched *Red* in a theater with an audience, they gasped when the head rolled. "That was my success," she said.[164]

Cinema International Corporation distributed *Red* (then United International Pictures as of 1981), and it played as an opening short film in front of all the major American horror films that came to United Kingdom theaters between 1976 and 1981, such as *The Omen II*. In a review of the film, one critic said, "The short film *Red* is better than the main feature," insists Frank.[165] Red never screened outside the United Kingdom except in a few film festivals: the San Sebastian Film Festival, where it won a Silver Shell award, then called a Silver Venus, and the 1975 Thessaloniki Film Festival in Greece. After five years, the film's rights lapsed back to Frank, and she never sold them to anyone except to the short-lived cable network Channel Z.

There is very little information publicly available about *Red*.[166] Most mentions of Astrid Frank herself are about the films she acted in, especially *Au Pair Girls*. Frank decided to make a second film after feeling that *Red* was a success. This one was titled *The Jealous Mirror*. It's listed only by the British Film Institute and with a release year of 1982, though Frank says that the film was made and released before then.[167] Like *Red*, *The Jealous Mirror* played in front of American horror films in British theaters and had been shot on 35mm film, but unlike *Red,* it never played at a film festival.

Shot in the local film school studio on a budget, *The Jealous Mirror* is a surreal fantasy horror love story every bit as edgy and dark as *Red*. A young woman (Glynis Barber) has a mirror that can communicate with her and that can feel love. They have an unhealthy relationship but ultimately can't live without one another, so the woman's sex life (with suitor Mark Wynter) suffers while the mirror is doomed to watch but never love her as a real person could. As Frank describes it,

> The mirror has a soul like a human soul and has thoughts. And the mirror is in love with the girl. And the girl has a boyfriend. And the mirror doesn't like the boyfriend. And so, when the boyfriend looks in the mirror, he looks ugly and untidy, and sweaty, so he gets quite mad and runs away. The girl talks to the mirror, but the mirror doesn't talk; it shows what he thinks. When she has a hairstyle up, he shows her a bird's nest on her head. She says, "Okay, you don't like it." Then it shows her with long, auburn wavy hair, and she says, "Fine." When her boyfriend wants to propose to her with a bottle of champagne, the cork flies into the mirror and the mirror cracks. She makes a big scene yelling, "My mirror!" and he [the boyfriend] says he will buy her a new mirror, but she says, "You can't replace my mirror!" and he runs away. She shouts at the mirror, "Why do you do this to me? I will never get a man because of you, jealous mirror!" And then she says sweetly, "He hurt you, didn't he, darling?'" and there is blood coming out of the mirror. In the end, her boyfriend has gone and never comes back, and she says, "I love you, we will stay together forever and ever and ever," and kisses and kisses and kisses the mirror.[168]

In *Red* and *The Jealous Mirror*, Frank explores the dark relationships between men and women and the complicated emotions that can result in violence. But she isn't making a statement about violence against women: "It's just a story," she explains. "Somehow, my personal view comes into it. When I am writing, I am all the persons. I am also the mirror. Like Agatha Christie, she is also the murderer."[169]

Unlike her American contemporaries Stephanie Rothman, Karen Arthur, and Brianne Murphy, Frank was not consistently interviewed about her filmmaking in newspapers, nor did her "being a woman" give her any publicity the way it did these other women. Unlike her German contemporary Helma Sanders-Brahms or the British Jane Arden, Frank wasn't given much attention by European film festivals and distribution companies after the initial run of the shorts in theaters.

Learning animation at Harvard University in 1968 was not a very structured endeavor for Caroline Leaf; instead of traditional animation, the students in her class were taught experimental animation. Leaf said it was not taught as professional training but "as a form of artistic self-expression, perhaps like writing poetry."[170] Her animation is experimental, with few mainstream gimmicks and, instead, primarily self-taught techniques. Leaf's short animated movie *The Metamorphosis of Mr. Samsa* (1977) is adapted from Franz Kafka's story *The Metamorphosis*; she was able to make it with a grant from the American Film Institute and produced by the National Film Board of Canada. In the existential, dark short, which has no dialogue, a man wakes up one day to find that he has been turned into a beetle. These experiments in darkness conjure up unsettling thoughts as the animation, made with sand, creates the unpredictable movement of the entities and is entirely unlike mainstream animation. Leaf's goal was to conjure up the images of alienation and anxiety that Kafka's original story recalls.

The Yellow Wallpaper (1977) by Marie Ashton deserves to be included in this section. The short film is based on the short story of the same name by Charlotte Perkins Gilman. In both the film and the story, a woman writer is forced against her will by her husband and doctor to isolate herself in her bedroom when she becomes ill. As the days go by, she begins hallucinating that a woman is trapped in the yellow wallpaper, and as a result, her condition deteriorates. *The Yellow Wallpaper*, the story, is a famous feminist commentary on women's agency regarding male guardians in the late 1800s. Ashton shot *The Yellow Wallpaper* on 16mm.

"Even in the mid- [19]70s, the kind of proto-feminist element was being written about," said Kathleen McHugh, director of the UCLA Center for the Study of Women:

> Feminist film scholars were writing about Roger Corman and Stephanie Rothman, locating a feminist impulse in the standard plot, where you have these powerful, self-assertive, one might even use the term "extremely aggressive" women who are wreaking vengeance against forces, people, men who are trying to keep them down.[171]

When asked in 2016 if second-wave feminism, civil rights, and the anti-war movement were relevant to her work, Rothman said,

> If I wasn't conscious of them, they wouldn't have occurred in my films. I was very conscious of them, and I was very interested in them. I wanted to have a conversation with a wider audience who might not encounter these ideas at all or might encounter them in a very narrow and stereotypical form. I wanted to open their minds as best as I could.[172]

The socially innovative horror and science fiction films directed by women in the 1960s and 1970s set the stage for even more experimental, deliberate, and hardcore feminist genre movies like *Born in Flames* (1983), directed by Lizzie Borden. Disagreeing with McHugh and Rothman, and writing three decades earlier, *Los Angeles Times* film writer Linda Gross, who wrote about Rothman, Peeters, and horror and exploitation films for the paper regularly, said,

> I admit that one man's sleaze is another woman's trash. I don't find violence against women cathartic. The same men who cheer during scenes in which women are gang-raped are the same ones who collectively moan and hiss when men are castrated on screen. You figure it out.[173]

Many women producers were coming into power in the late 1970s and early 1980s, like Gale Anne Hurd (*The Terminator*, 1984), Marilyn Tenser (*Galaxina*, 1980), Debra Hill

(*Halloween*, 1978), and Julie Corman (*Saturday the 14th*, 1981), but they didn't necessarily begin hiring more women to direct their projects. In 1978, Tenser was asked if she would hire more women directors:

> People say to me, "Aren't you going to hire a woman director?" Sure, if I find a woman director who has a feel for my project. But I'm not going to put a woman on a project just because that person happens to be a woman.[174]

What sounds harsh coming from Tenser sounds charitable coming from a male producer like Roger Corman. Corman's lawyer Barbara Boyle described his attitude towards hiring female directors in the 1970s: "There were always women at New World because we were cheaper and more loyal."[175] Some women directors didn't even like other women directors. Roberta Findlay said:

> I personally don't like women. I don't like women and children. They're an annoyance and generally in the way ... I hate horror films. I never watch them. They're all so bad; badly made, badly constructed.[176]

Whatever personal opinions of individual writers and directors may have been towards women, there was a general movement toward women, as a whole, being hired to direct horror movies in the 1970s and 1980s for many reasons, but with one consequence. As film writer Mark Olsen puts it,

> By working within the exploitation field, filmmakers such as Rothman, Peeters, and Holden Jones were largely following what was at the time the most viable career path to directing in Hollywood. Where many male filmmakers who worked the same route moved on to more respectable projects and acclaim, their female counterparts largely faded into obscurity.[177]

Whether these women wanted to be making horror films is another question. Sometimes, they didn't want to but found that those were the only genres that would hire them at that moment. Barbara Peeters (*Bury Me an Angel*, 1971) said,

> I don't know any director who wants to spend his whole life making low-budget exploitation movies, just as nobody wants to spend their whole life in kindergarten. You look forward to graduating to high school.[178]

Rothman replied, "I still hope to make a major motion picture. I never give up hoping ... If I hang in there long enough, my turn will come."[179] She later said in 2008,

> It was my fervent wish that I would be able to make mainstream films. I wanted to, I never got the opportunity. I tried for about ten years, and then I gave up and just decided to continue living my life, not making films anymore.[180]

Rothman expanded on that statement in a 2010 interview:

I had good agents, and together we tried very hard to get me work, but we repeatedly discovered I was stigmatized by the films I had made. The irony was that I made them in order to prove that I had the skills to make more ambitious films, but no one would give me the chance. Then there was the other reason, the so-called elephant in the room: I was a woman. No one told me directly, but I often learned indirectly that this was the decisive reason why many producers wouldn't agree to meet me. If that sounds exaggerated, remember that I worked in the American film industry from 1965 to 1974, and some of those years, I was the only woman directing feature films.[181]

As author Terry Curtis Fox wrote of Rothman,

It is hard to think of another contemporary American director of Rothman's talent and temperament who has remained trapped in grind films for as long as she has. The temptation is to blame it on misogyny, a temptation which Rothman refuses to do. She's probably right on factual grounds (if *Group Marriage* had been seen by the right people, Rothman might well have made her break) but wrong on promotional ones. The most bitter irony of Stephanie Rothman's career is that the one woman filmmaker of the Seventies with a consistent and solid body of work—a body of work that expresses the possibilities of American society—seems to have a better future as a cause than as a director.[182]

Some women directors had an incredibly positive attitude about their role in horror film directing. Doris Wishman believed that *nothing* held her back:

I think I could've gone to Hollywood. I was approached by Paramount. They called me into their office and asked me if I'd be interested in working with them. I said, "I'll let you know." And then—this is the truth, Bill—I forgot about it completely because I didn't want to work for anybody. I had already made three films, and I thought I didn't need anybody. *I* just didn't want to work for anybody, which is stupid. I really think I could've been a big producer, director, what have you. Are you doubting me?[183]

Unfortunately, the 1960s and 1970s left several mysteries regarding the fully realized history of women directing horror movies. Between Gabrielle Beaumont directing Viktors Ritelis' *Crucible of Horror,* AKA *Velvet House* (1971) and not receiving any credit, to the uncertainty about the deserved directing credit of Christina Hornisher and Gloria Katz, to statements that actress Marilyn Burns, star of the *Texas Chainsaw Massacre* (1974), covertly directed the majority of Toby Hooper's follow-up horror film *Eaten Alive* (1976), in which Burns also starred,[184] we may never know the entire truth about what happened on the set of some of these films.

Chapter 4
Obras maestras del terror

NON-ENGLISH LANGUAGE HORROR

Poster art for Isela Vega's *Lovers of the Lord of the Night* (1986).

DISCUSSIONS OF WOMEN HORROR FILM directors can be Anglocentric, meaning that films from the United States, the United Kingdom, and English-speaking nations like Canada and Australia are often the focus of most horror film studies because there are so many more of them than from other nations. They are well-covered compared to obscure or lost films from non-English speaking countries. I will give the reader a general description of the state of European cinema in the mid-twentieth-century and then focus on specific nations' cinema.

During the 1950s, 1960s, and 1970s, a new wave of film swept non-English-speaking countries, especially Europe. Identified in France as the French New Wave by film critics and the magazine *Cahiers du Cinema*, the movement was about rejecting traditional narrative filmmaking, embracing realism and truth, and experimenting with non-traditional stories. In Italy, it was called the Neo-Realist movement at first but morphed into its own New Wave of Italian films (Neorealismo). In the Soviet Union, it was known as Parallel Cinema. The New Wave was a reaction to many different events, including the lessening grip of communism over their nations' film industries, processing the horrors of World War II, a more modern, less uptight code of morality in movies, and a desire for more relatable truth in art, even in avant-garde films that evolved from post-war realism during this same time, which is roughly the late 1950s through the early 1980s—though, in Italy, it started in the late 1940s.

These New Wave film movements in Europe were dominated by male filmmakers like Jean-Luc Godard, François Truffaut, Louis Malle, Roger Vadim, Jaromil Jireš, Werner Herzog, Wim Wenders, and Roberto Rossellini. A few exceptions to these male directors were Agnès Varda (*Cléo de 5 à 7*, 1962) in France; Wanda Jakubowska (*Pożegnanie z diabłem*, 1956) in Poland; Věra Chytilová (*Daisies*, 1966) in Czechoslovakia; Margarethe von Trotta (*Die verlorene Ehre der Katharina Blum*, 1975), Helke Sander (*Brecht die Macht der Manipulateure*, 1967), Danièle Huillet (*Geschichtsunterricht*, 1972), and Helma Sanders-Brahms (*Germany Pale Mother*, 1980) in Germany; Mai Zetterling (*Nattlek*, 1967) in Sweden; and Lina Wertmüller (*Seven Beauties*, 1975) and Liliana Cavani (*The Night Porter*, 1974) in Italy.

In India, Bollywood films with musical numbers and fantasy romances were the mainstream industry output, and in Hong Kong, martial arts films had become a major export. Some of the women involved in these movements directed genre films, and others, often not included in the list of European New Wave filmmakers or critical Asian feminists, made actual horror films. Especially in The Philippines and Argentina, women directors made horror films in the early 1960s while women directors in the United States and the United Kingdom were still breaking down barriers. It wasn't until the mid-1960s that Western women filmmakers were openly making horror for theaters and television, while women in these two other nations were prolific in their output of horror.

Soviet Russia (1917-1991) had quite a robust film industry in which women excelled as directors. People may believe that Soviet Russia was no place for innovation and art, but the Soviet film industry prioritized arts and culture from its beginnings in 1918. Film, photography, and art were encouraged, and because of Soviet gender equality attitudes, women were never discouraged from film or animation direction the way that they were in Western nations.[1] The world's first film school, the VGIK (All-Union Film Institute of Cinematography), was founded in 1919 as the Moscow Film School, and it admitted women from all over the world to attend. Hungarian filmmaker Márta Mészáros (*Bye bye chaperon rouge*, 1989), Romanian filmmaker Kira Muratova (*Change of Fate*, 1987), Russian-born Leida Laius (*Libahunt*, 1968), Czech director Iris Gusner (*The Blue Light*, 1976), and Russian Irina Tarkovskaya (*Skazka, rasskazannaya nochyu*, 1981), among others, attended the school.

We've gone over early women genre directors in Germany in Chapter 1: Rosa Porten, Marie Louise Droop, and Leni Riefenstahl, but there was a break in Germany's film history when World War II occupied the country's artistic resources. It wouldn't be until the 1970s that a new artistic wave of women directors appeared in Germany, experimenting with horror, surrealism, and sexuality onscreen.

Helma Sanders-Brahms was a German filmmaker, active in the 1970s and 1980s, and recognized as an essential figure in the New German Cinema movement of that time. Two of her films, *No Mercy, No Future* (1981) and the made-for-television movie *Die letzten Tage von Gomorrha,* AKA *The Last Days of Gomorrah* (1974), have genre elements. *No Mercy, No Future* is a more familiar film to audiences, as it has been distributed internationally on DVD. It's a disturbing movie about a schizophrenic young woman who wanders around Berlin, having sex with strangers and hallucinating in between suicide attempts. There is blood, and in one scene, the protagonist has just had an abortion and is bleeding profusely but engages in sex anyway, creating an uncomfortable mess that disturbs most people who see it. In an interview in 1982, Sanders-Brahms said of that scene:

> I knew that this scene, in normal film terms, goes on "too long." But I did it deliberately. I wanted the audiences to become caught up in the spiral of suffering that Rita G. is in. In real life, that lovemaking actually lasted three hours. In my film, it's just three minutes. But the shock value, the relentlessness makes it seem more.[2]

Die letzten Tage von Gomorrha is a pure science-fiction critique of capitalism and consumerism. The film has screened since its original air date, most notably at The Museum of Modern Art in New York City. It is about a television that "satisfies every human craving."[3] Sanders-Brahms died in 2014, but before she did, she had a favor to ask of you: "Before I die, I'd just like to make one last attempt to rescue my films from oblivion in my country and say: at least have a look at them."[4]

Independent, underground filmmakers Ulrike Ottinger and Tabea Blumenschein collaborated on three fantastical low-budget art films: *Laokoon & Söhne* (1975), based on the Virginia Woolf story *Orlando*, an experimental fantasy about a siren killing soldiers *Die Betörung der blauen Matrosen* (1975), and a film about women running away to join a lesbian pirate ship and enjoy adventures, called *Madame X—Eine absolute Herrscherin* (1978). On her own, Ottinger made her Berlin trilogy, consisting of *Bildnis einer Trinkerin,* AKA *Ticket of No Return* (1979), *Freak Orlando* (1981), and *Dorian Gray im Spiegel der Boulevardpresse,* AKA *Dorian Gray in the Mirror of the Yellow Press* (1984) and the adventure film *Johanna D'Arc of Mongolia* (1989) which all have fantastical elements.

Madame X—Eine absolute Herrscherin is probably the most interesting to horror fans. It stars Tabea Blumenschein as Madame X, a pirate queen of the lesbian pirate ship Orlando who convinces women to leave their boring, regular lives and join her on epic quests for adventure.

West German musician Marianne Enzensberger was essential to Berlin's 1980s punk rock underground film scene. *Der Biß,* AKA *The Bite* (1984) Enzensberger wrote, produced, directed, and starred in the low-budget vampire rock musical that contemporary German film critics compared to German expressionist horror films like *Nosferatu*.[5] Shot on 16mm in New York City and West Berlin, *Der Biß* is unlike any other 1980s vampire film except, in some ways perhaps, *The Hunger* (1983), written and directed by Tony Scott.[6] In a deserted and claustrophobic New York City, a young woman named Sylvana (played by Enzensberger) wanders. Her voice-over narration describes her loneliness and anxiety and how she misses her lover David who never gives her enough attention. She collapses and is brought inside a house of vampires. There they happily live in darkness as a family. The seductive vampire Jason bites Sylvana and inducts her into the obscene and decadent world of vampirism, which the filmmaker shows us with a montage of black lace, candlelight, shirtless men, and sinister meetings. Unlike traditional vampires, Sylvana can walk in the sunlight (always wearing sunglasses), though she is more comfortable in the dark.

When she thinks she has found her place, Sylvana discovers that she's bored by the mundane bourgeois lifestyle in the castle. Sylvana is horrified and hitchhikes back to Berlin, where she walks in the sunset in the street and decides to be a vampire in her way, on her own.

Der Biß is a low-budget, independently made rock-and-roll musical vampire film. Enzensberger and her co-star Rosenberg were extremely popular musicians in the 1980s German music scene known as Neue Deutsche Welle: an electronic post-punk, new wave genre. The cast includes members of other bands and many of Enzenberger's friends. She had people from her real life do her favors by being in the film: her lawyer played the lawyer, her dentist played the dentist, etc. "This makes it a bit amateurish," admits Enzensberger, "but they played their roles with enthusiasm." The entire production was rushed, and

> We did not behave in an exemplary manner. We filmed fourteen to sixteen hours a day, then danced and talked through the night, and someone would set the alarm, and two hours later, everyone got up again. The makeup artists had to work really hard to get our faces in shape, and we just continued to work.[7]

Enzensberger was inspired to make *Der Biß* during a trip to New York City, where she watched the television series *Dark Shadows*. The goth scene was popular (called "Ruby Vampires" in Germany at the time), and she knew that the all-black eye makeup and white-powdered skin would make a stunning visual backdrop for a horror movie. A friend gave her some film stock as a gift, and she decided to make a film, beginning to shoot immediately in New York in her friends' homes and on the streets. Self-aware and often satirical, the film is about freedom and how to be happy living everyday life. Sylvana sacrifices her humanity to be extraordinary but finds herself alone as none of her friends will follow her, preferring to live their everyday lives. Sylvana begins to realize that she is the only one who isn't satisfied with her human life, and as a result, she is even more alone than ever. Being a vampire didn't relieve her existential dread, and not being a vampire didn't relieve it either. Reflecting on the chase for fame in the music industry, *Der Biß* shows the allure and the horror of fame and money while not offering reasonable solutions to people who crave those things. It's also quite funny; the movie mocks pretentious artists and their lives in nightclubs and rock shows. Early in the film, after Sylvana has just returned to Berlin, we're introduced to a band that plays in what looks like an abandoned building. This band is always there, always playing. When one of the musicians says that Sylvana is crazy for wanting to bite people, they are harshly reminded that being a musician in an abandoned building playing music at all times is crazy, too.

Enzensberger plays with German expressionism at the beginning of the film, modeling many of her shadows and light after the silent German horror films *The Cabinet of Doctor Caligari* and *Nosferatu*. Continuous music plays throughout *Der Biß*, a score made with a synthesizer and synthetic drums, combined with ominous sound effects and several songs by Enzensberger with her band Unlimited Systems and cult musician Marianne Rosenberg. The director made a concerted effort to exaggerate the expressionist aspect of her horror film with music and sound, even at one point playing "Toccata and Fugue in D Minor" as Enzensberger herself dramatically ascends a staircase wearing a black wedding dress. Looking back on her punk rock art film effort, Enzensberger sees the flaws and plot holes, but she says:

> I see that the film has its own language, its own aesthetic language, precisely because of these flaws. We had very little money. We couldn't properly light the scenes. We had to improvise ... it reminds me of theatrical silent films with the drama and poses and light and darkness. It has its own aesthetics, its own charm. Its own tension ... This parable, this social satire of society, was also important to me.[8]

Der Biß has more in common with the independent films of the 1960s than with commercial horror movies of the 1980s. It's a kindred spirit to Christina Hornisher's *Hollywood 90028* in that it's a piece of expressionist and surrealist horror art rather than a traditional narrative film. Voice-overs, music and sound, and quickly shifting scenes tell a story in a linear but unconventional way that doesn't conform to any popular style. "It's a niche film," says Enzensberger. "It's funny; it's photographed nicely and deserves to be looked at again."[9]

Comparing *Der Biß* to another rock music-based horror film directed by a woman, Beverly Sebastian's *Rocktober Blood* (1984), *Der Biß* is far more entertaining and thoughtful. *Rocktober Blood* is a cheap, badly made slasher film with uninspired music. It doesn't have any artistic touches that Enzensberger effortlessly put into her movie. After *Der Biß*, Enzensberger formed a new band with Marianne Rosenberg called La

Rouge et la Noire; Enzensberger went by Marianne Rouge (because of her dyed red hair) and Rosenberg as Marianne Noire. In 1987, Rosenberg starred in the German women-in-prison film *Komplizinnen*, directed by Margit Czenki. Enzensberger would write the scripts for two more horror films: *Horror Vacui* (1984) and *Anita: Dances of Vice* (1987), both directed by her friend Rosa von Praunheim (not a woman), who also appeared in *Der Biß*.[10]

Numerous women directors made genre films in Germany after Enzensberger released *Der Biß*. The best-known horror films directed by German women filmmakers are Petra Haffter's *A Demon in My View* (1991) starring Anthony Perkins, Katrina Gebbe's *Nothing Bad Can Happen* (2013), and Swedish-born but Berlin-based Carolina Hellsgård's German-language zombie movie *EndZeit*, AKA *Ever After* (2018). 2013's *Job Interview* by Julia Walter is a prime example of the ongoing evolution of thriller and horror films in the reunified German film industry. I'll be discussing more German directors in future chapters.

An early Czech genre director is Olga Rautenkranzová, whose short silent film is *Kozlonoh* (1918). The ten-minute-long fantasy is set in the 1700s with actors dressed in elaborate costumes and is about a young woman named Anisja (played by director Rautenkranzová) who is haunted by a jealous spirit who doesn't want her to marry the count's son Felix (Oldřich Kmínek). The spirit animates a satyr statue in the count's garden and invades Anisja's dreams, hoping to prevent her and Felix from being together. The spirit is unsuccessful, and Anisja wakes up from what seems like a dream determined to marry Felix. *Kozlonoh* was shot entirely in the Grébovka vineyard park in Prague.

Like East Germany, Czechoslovakia had a robust television industry under communism, and women directors made an astounding number of films of these two genres. Once television became accessible in the communist nation, dozens of Czechoslovakian woman directors made fantasy and crime/mystery thrillers for Czech television.

Meze Waltera Hortona, AKA, *The Limits of Walter Horton* (1969), directed by Jirina Pokorná-Makoszová, is a made-for-television horror mystery comedy based on the short story of the same name by John S. Sharnik. Walter Horton (Vlastimil Brodský) is an ordinary man who one morning sits down at his piano and plays perfect Chopin. His behavior is unusual because he never knew how to play the piano. His wife (Jiřina Jirásková) is baffled and concerned. But Walter is so good that he gets a manager, Gresham (Rudolf Hrušínský), and begins playing concerts. He's a huge success. It soon becomes apparent to Gresham that Walter never plays anything more than once and cannot commit to any piece of music as he plays it. His wife, too, is disillusioned by the unearned success her husband has found, and she drifts far from him emotionally. Eventually, Horton plays a sonata that he couldn't have heard before because it was Gresham's. Gresham realizes that everyone will believe that Horton created it and that he can't stop Horton from playing the music that is created. He can't stop creating music, so anything he ever creates (or that anyone ever creates) in the future will end up being Horton's. Horton's compulsion and the horror Gresham feels make this a particularly unnerving fantasy.

The most critical Czechoslovakian television horror film directed by a woman is Anna Procházková's *Hrabé Drakula,* AKA *Count Dracula* (1971). This faithful adaptation of Bram Stoker's work is shot entirely in black and white (color television wouldn't

Hana Maciuchová as Lucy Westerner in Anna Procházková's *Hrabě Drakula* (1971).

A surreal image from Věra Chytilová's thriller *Fruit of Paradise* (1970).

become prominent until the late 1970s in communist Czechoslovakia). It has a low-key charm that can be lost in other more opulent adaptations of the story. Procházková wrote the screenplay with Oldrich Zelezný, and the film stars Ilja Racek as Dracula. When Jonathan Harker (Jan Schánilec) arrives at Dracula's castle, it is not an opulent Gothic palace; it's a plain, Romanesque stone castle from the Middle Ages, devoid of flashy frills or elaborate set dressings. Count Dracula is an ordinary-looking man, strong and handsome in a rugged way, with a beard and mustache and a robust manner of speaking. The landscape around the castle is plain, with white snow and skeletal winter trees. Transylvania is a bit bleak but feels authentic. The graveyards, too, are real and not fabrications. All of the sets are as-is ruins and countryside with no set decoration needed. This kind of original filming would have been highly valued in a communist nation, where resources were not to be wasted on the frivolous and unnecessary trappings of lavish Western horror films. The only decorative elements are the brides: all three of them are dressed in gaudy gowns and sparkle with jewels in their elaborate hairstyles. They're from another era when nobility flaunted their wealth and, most likely, to the citizens of communist Czechoslovakia watching the movie, were distasteful displays of feudal wealth. Despite the austerity in set design, the film is a suspenseful and enjoyable version of the Dracula story. Procházková made the vampire brides translucent to accentuate their otherworldliness, a choice I have not seen in any other Dracula film adaptation. It's the film's only special effect, but it works marvelously.

Procházková's 1987 television horror film *Lokis* is based on the short story of the same name by French author Prosper Mérimée. Set in the nineteenth century, *Lokis* is about a professor of folklore who travels to the outskirts of the remote Baltic Lithuanian countryside to study the local legends. While there, he hears stories about a half-man, half-bear creature that roams the forests. He also hears that the local count's mother was raped by a bear on a hunting trip before he was born, implying that he is the monster and a result of the attack. Young women are being murdered, and the locals believe this man-bear monster is responsible. Based on a medieval Danish legend, the story has been adapted into film several times: the Russian film *Medvezhya svadba* (1925), the British Hammer film *The Curse of the Werewolf* (1961), the Polish horror film *Lokis* (1970), the French film *La Bête* (1975), and the American horror movie *The Beast Within*

(1982), directed by Philippe Mora. Procházková would go on to direct many thriller films for Czech television, ending her career only when the nation split into the Czech Republic and Slovakia and adopted a capitalist economy in 1992.

Ester Krumbachová directed the fantasy film *Vrazda ing. Certa,* AKA *The Murder of Mr. Devil* (1970), and co-wrote *Sedmikrásky,* AKA *Daisies* (1966) with Vera Chytilová. Krumbachová worked as a co-writer with Chytilová on two more films: the thriller parody *Ovoce stromů rajských jíme,* AKA *The Fruit of Paradise* (1969) and the drama *Faunovo velmi pozdní odpoledne,* AKA *The Very Late Afternoon of a Faun* (1983). She co-wrote the famous surreal Czech New Wave film *O slavnosti a hostech,* AKA *A Report on the Party and Guests* (1965), with the director (and her then-husband) Jan Němec. She co-wrote the well-known surreal fantasy/horror film *Valerie and Her Week of Wonders* (1970) with that film's director, Jaromil Jireš.

Krumbachová and Němec wrote the fantasy comedy film *The Murder of Mr. Devil* in 1969. The film was Krumbachová's first and only feature film as director. Němec never liked the script or the film itself: "We needed a screenplay, and we made easy money," he said in an interview. "I can't think of a more stupid film. I'm very ashamed to have been the co-writer and that I'm in it as an extra."[11] *The Murder of Mr. Devil* is about a lonely woman who desperately wants to find a man. She invites over an eligible bachelor Mr. Čert ("Devil" in Czech) and cooks him a fantastic meal. He's so off-putting that the woman realizes he's a demon and that his name is no joke. After trapping Mr. Čert in a bag of raisins, she uses her newfound magic to fund an expedition to Tibet to find an abominable snowman who, she believes, will be a kind and gentle man, unlike Mr. Čert. Krumbachová was at one time married to Němec, but she was married to film in her heart. In a letter she wrote to herself late in her life, she says that the only true love she has ever experienced is making films:

"One day, I found myself in a film studio, the fateful arrow of love pierced my heart, and that was it. I succumbed to film in the way some people do to alcohol."[12]

Věra Chytilová was a famous avant-garde Czech New Wave film director. Chytilová was the first woman to study film directing at the Film Academy in Prague, which became a prestigious institution for future Czech filmmakers. Their first film together, *Sedmikrásky,* AKA *Daisies* (1966), is about two young women, both named Marie, who trick men into giving them food and presents. Marie and Marie wander through a surreal pastiche of symbolism and color designed to critique consumerism and material greed. The girls engage in food fights, dance in fields, have a 1920s dance experience at a nightclub, and generally rebel against everything. It's a weird, cool, experimental movie that showcases the strangeness with which Chytilová imbued her films and the satire and absurdism that came so quickly to Krumbachová. The scenes of wasted food were abhorrent to the communist Czech government, which prevented the film from being released until 1969.[13] Chytilová's explanation of the film's symbolism is pretentiously challenging to understand. She says the film is supposed to "restrict [the spectator's] feeling of involvement and lead him to an understanding of the underlying idea or philosophy." *Daisies* has the elements of fantasy and comedy that Krumbachová would include in most of her future scripts and *The Murder of Mr. Devil.* Chytilová would develop these experimental storytelling techniques throughout the 1960s and 1970s.

The experimental, surreal thriller *Fruit of Paradise* (1970), also written by Krumbachová with Chytilová, was directed by Chytilová and based very loosely on the stories of Adam and Eve with elements from the story of Pandora's Box and serial killers. The film is about Eva (Jitka Nováková) and Josef (Karel Novak), a married couple who meets the mysterious stranger Robert (Jan Schmid). Robert may be the serial killer murdering women in the area. Cartoonish sound effects and over-the-top suspense music have caused some critics and viewers to believe that *Fruit of Paradise* is a "parody" of a thriller rather than an actual thriller film, but I believe that is not necessarily the case. The film has a loose narrative composed mainly of experimental and surreal scenes, including animation, stop-motion, and inspired lighting. *Fruit of Paradise* has much more in common with Arden's *The Other Side of the Underneath,* discussed in Chapter 3, than with a traditional thriller film. Like Arden, Chytilová rejects traditional filmmaking and instead creates a total experience to make the audience emote. The dream sequences in Rothman's *The Velvet Vampire*, also discussed in Chapter 3, have this same expressionist quality of combined sound, movement, colors, and camera effects that join as a total artistic expression. The Soviet invasion of Czechoslovakia happened in the middle of the filming of *Fruit of Paradise*, causing the crew to fear being trapped by military forces and unable to finish the film. But they did finish it. Everyone could leave, and the film premiered at the Cannes Film Festival in 1970, where critics and audiences hated it."[14 & 15]

In the 1980s, the communist government in Czechoslovakia no longer tolerated the creative expression of filmmakers and artists; in the previous two decades, freethinking and artistic expression had led to political unrest and citizens discussing leaving the Eastern Bloc of communist countries. Chytilová's style changed as a result. She no longer experimented recklessly with visuals or dialogue; her films became more grounded in recognizable narratives and traditional filming techniques. That doesn't mean they weren't still weird because they were, especially *Vlci bouda,* AKA *Wolf's Hole* (1987). A decade prior, in 1978, she said during an interview, "I want to direct science fiction or fantasy because it's the only way to show reality."[16] *Wolf's Hole* is an odd film designed to make the audience uncomfortable and expect horrific events that don't materialize. Eleven teenagers are specifically chosen for an elite ski camp in a remote mountainside slope during the dead of winter that happens to be operated by aliens from another world.

Several moments in the film highlight the surreal and disturbing nature of Chytilová's vision: characters roll around unnaturally in the snow at night; Babeta (Stepánka Cervenková) grotesquely overreacts when she holds a hot cup of tea, and finally when the instructors feel like the time is right, they sit the children down and tell them that they're aliens from another planet and are conducting a social experiment.

The snowy, drab environment and the narrative of the film showcase the communist values of Czechoslovakia's government in the 1980s: fierce competition exists among the kids to be the best, the smartest, the strongest, the fastest, and so they are pleased to be chosen for an exceptional ski workshop "for the best" skiers. No attention is paid to clothing or physical beauty as an indicator of status except as it occurs naturally in sexual attraction (the boys like Babeta, who has long blonde hair and is very pretty). The aliens treat the boys

Babeta (Stepánka Cervenková)'s dead body has been packed into the snowman in Věra Chytilová's *Wolf's Hole* (1987).

Babeta can't hold hot things because she's an alien.

and girls equally; no concessions are made for the women based on perceived weaknesses, and the aliens don't force the boys to act out masculinity unnaturally. There's no television, phone, or relics of consumerism anywhere in the cabin or on the mountain except for one flimsy nightgown brought by one of the girls, and they make fun of her for it. Social interaction is the only pastime aside from chores. The ending cements the idea that working together is better than sacrificing one for the comfort of the remaining: everyone should be willing to sacrifice for the greater good and do what is best for the team, not for the individual. Because of these aspects of the film, *Wolf's Hole* looks stark and devoid of modernity to Western viewers used to flashy displays of wealth and color, even in their horror films.

Chytilová defies the government of Czechoslovakia in two ways with *Wolf's Hole*. First, she uses some experimental techniques despite the orders from her government to make more "realistic" films. The premise of *Wolf's Hole* is wholly fantastic. Chytilová gets away with it by setting the story in a realistic location that requires special effects or sensational filmmaking techniques. Instead, she shows the aliens as "aliens" by employing the camera to capture their facial expressions and body movements: exaggerated in all ways to give off the unnerving impression that they are not human. From the actors writhing in the snow to the camera's close-ups of their twisted faces, Chytilová uses experimental filmmaking styles as she did with *Daisies* and *Fruit of Paradise*. She disguises the film as a straightforward pro-communism story. If they read between the lines, the audience can see the criticism of authoritarian governments and the encouragement to defy direct orders. She shows that the people in control do not have the nation's best interests in mind except for how it benefits them personally. The teenagers reject the order to kill a fellow student pointlessly; their leaders lie to them and don't represent their interests. As the film progresses, the growing sense of paranoia and unease among the teenagers and the viewer reflects the distrust of the Czech and Slovak peoples of their government, which would fall just six years later along with most of the other Eastern European communist governments.

Chytilová's 1998 rape-revenge film *Pasti, pasti, pasticky,* AKA *Traps,* was not subject to the same rigid government control as her work in the 1980s. The press and audiences heavily criticized it, but the new Czech government had little interest in controlling movie

Lucie Belohradska as the possessed princess in Zuzana Zemanová-Hojdová's 1998 TV horror fantasy *Spravedlivy Bohumil*.

Jitka Nemcová's made-for-television horror/comedy *O babe hladové* (1990).

messages. Chytilová was challenging to work with and even more difficult to befriend. She had a habit of saying pretentious but honest things in interviews with journalists, such as,

> If there's something you don't like, don't keep to the rules—break them. I'm an enemy of stupidity and simple-mindedness in both men and women, and I have rid my living space of these traits ... People are generally weak, cautious, and frightened of being embarrassed, whereas I'm merciless and impertinent.[17]

She would scream at her cast and crew on set, even physically assaulting her cameraperson during an on-set disagreement.[18]

O babe hladové (1990) is a made-for-television horror/comedy film directed by Jitka Nemcová. Described as a fairy tale for adults, it's about a woman (Ivana Chýlková) who desperately wants to commit suicide but has to deal with a lengthy administrative visit from death (Boleslav Polívka) before she can move on. It's a deadpan dark comedy that mostly takes place in one setting and feels like a small theater play. Nemcová also directed several thriller/crime films for Czech television: *Setkání v Praze, s vrazdou* (2009) and *Jses mrtvej, tak nebrec!* (2010).

Zuzana Zemanová-Hojdová directed one of the most whimsical films to come out of the Czech Republic: the made-for-television medieval fantasy horror *Spravedlivý Bohumil* (1998). Set in an ambiguous fairy tale, the film is about a dead princess possessed by a demonic spirit in this dark horror/fantasy. It's not quite terrifying, but it is grotesque and unnerving.

Pavlina Moskalykova began her Czech television career in 1987 writing the crime thriller *Ryba ve ctyrech*. That film's screenwriter, Lucie Belohradská, would direct one made-for-television horror film for the Czech Republic: *Specialita séfkuchare* (2000), adapted from the Stanley Ellin horror story *Specialty of the House*, about a lonely man named Laffler (Jiří Lábus) who invites his work friend Costain (Lukáš Hlavica) out to dinner at a strange restaurant where, unknowingly, they are consuming human flesh and are in danger of ending up on the menu. Belohradská has a large body of television film work in the crime/mystery/thriller genres throughout the 2000s.

Lidiya Ishimbaeva's 1969 television adaptation of the Faust story is the first horror

A witch is flogged to death in Ledia Laius' 1968 Soviet Union horror drama *Libahunt*.

Tiina (Ene Rämmeld) is accused of witchcraft by her fellow villagers in *Libahunt*.

film directed by a woman in Russia. Co-directed with Yevgeni Simonov, it stars Anatoli Katsinsky as Faust and Yuriy Yakovlev as Mephistopheles. Over three hours long, the film was produced by Tsentralnoe Televidenie.

Leida Laius's *Libahunt,* AKA *Forest Legend* (1968), is a Soviet thriller set in the early twentieth century and is based on the 1912 Estonian play *Libahunt* by August Kitzberg. In it, a baby named Tiina is adopted by a family when her true mother is flogged to death for witchcraft. Tiina (Ene Rämmeld) falls in love with her stepbrother Margus (Evald Hermaküla) when she grows up. Still, her new parents want their other adopted daughter, the timid and pretty Mari (Malle Klaassen), to marry Margus. Out of revenge for stealing Margus's heart on the night of the village's Midsummer Eve celebration, Mari claims that Tiina is a witch and a werewolf. Tiina runs away into the forest to escape death at the hands of the villagers. The film's last scene shows Tiina's parents, Margus, and Mari silently contemplating the horrors they have done to her and why they have done it. It's a genuinely brutal film, especially in the flashback scenes when we see Tiina's mother being whipped to death, tied to a stake, and a younger Tiina trying to free her and being dragged away by the villagers. A statement about paranoia and betrayal, *Libahunt* is a surprisingly beautiful story.

In 1950s communist Poland, director Wanda Jakubowska directed the mystery crime thriller *Pożegnanie z diabłem,* AKA *Farewell to the Devil* (1956). She'd been directing since the 1930s, primarily documentary films like her Academy Award-nominated short *The Sea* (1933), but her career was abruptly interrupted when she was placed in a concentration camp by the Nazis during World War II. Jakubowska survived and was released when the Soviet Union liberated the camp. She made a world-renowned film about the horrors she had witnessed titled *Ostatni etap,* AKA *The Last Stage* (1947). She wouldn't go on to direct any more genre films.

It was not until 2011 that Polish women directors made genre horror films again. Ewelina Lisek's *Haunted Poland* (2011) is a found footage supernatural horror involving a Ouija board. Agnieszka Smoczyńska's *The Lure* (2015) is about mermaids and the horrors they bring when they go on land. Smoczyńska has two new genre films in production at the time of the writing of this book: *Hot Spot* and *Silent Twins*. Agnieszka Holland, one of the most famous directors from Poland, co-directed the serial killer thriller *Spoor* (2017) with Kasia Adamik.

After Germaine Dulac (*Le diable dans la ville*, 1925) and Marie Louise Iribe (director of the fantasy film *Le Roi des aulnes*, 1931),[19] women took a back seat as genre film directors in the French film industry for a while. Marie Epstein co-directed the film *La Mort du cygne,* AKA *Ballerina* (1937), about a little girl who plans to kill a dancer to ensure her favorite ballerina isn't replaced. Epstein and Jean Benoît-Lévy wrote the screenplay together and co-directed, but he is officially credited as the sole director.[20]

Script supervisor Lucile Costa worked on 1946's Jean Cocteau fantasy *Beauty and the Beast* but directed five of her films. They were produced by Paul Ricard, a French wine tycoon, and all were fantasy films. Four were shorts based on fairy tales: *Peau d'ours, Le filleul de la mort, La boîte à musique, and Murs* (all 1953). Her feature *L'enfant et le lamentin* (1962) was an original fantasy script she had written herself.[21]

Jacqueline Audry, perhaps the most famous woman director from France before Agnès Varda, made three genre films: the Western *La caraque blonde* (1953, also produced by Paul Ricard); the claustrophobic fantasy *Huis-clos* (1954) written by Sartre about people trapped in a room in Hell together for all eternity, and the murder mystery *Cadavres en vacances* (1963).

Nadine Trintignant directed the crime thriller *Le Voleur de crimes,* AKA *Crime Thief* (1969). The film is about a woman who kills herself and a psychopath who writes to the police taking credit for her death. Trintignant is known for her thoughtful family dramas and early feminist work, so *Le Voleur de crimes* is usually not mentioned in profiles of the director as it deviates from her more socially conscious work in the 1960s and 1970s. The film is not widely distributed and is unavailable in the United States.[22] Her next thriller was *Défense de savoir* (1973), a murder mystery with political intrigue in which a woman is suspected of killing her husband.

Out 1, noli me tangere (1971) is a thirteen-hour-long film co-directed by Suzanne Schiffman with Jacques Rivette. It's experimental, but the narratives involve secret societies in politics and their nefarious plans.

Rachel Weinberg's 1974 surreal fantasy *L'ampélopède*, starring Isabelle Huppert, is about the urbanization of our world and how we long to escape it. A Jewish woman, played by Huppert, lives on a farm in France during the Nazi occupation, hiding. The farmer who owns the land has trapped a strange Bigfoot-like creature on his property and often kidnaps young women so that the creature can mate and reproduce with them. It's a bleak vision of wartime escapism.

The 1987 film *Le moine et la sorcière,* AKA *Sorceress*, directed by Pamela Berger and Schiffman, is a period drama about religious zealotry in the thirteenth century in France and women who were persecuted for being witches. It's an art house film with few genre elements.

Élisabeth Rappeneau directed numerous television thrillers in the late 1980s and the 1990s. Her thriller films *Fréquence meurtre* (1988), *Mieux vaut courir* (1989), and *Turbulences* (1992) all aired on French television. And since the 1990s, there have been dozens of French genre films directed by women. From horror anthologies (Anita Assal's *Wacko,* AKA *Parano*, 1994) to adult horror (Véronique Lefay's *Ensorceleuses: Le projet*

Blair Bitch, 1998), the 1990s set the stage for some of the most influential, confrontational, and revered horror films of the twenty-first century. The shocking rape-revenge horror *Baise-Moi* (2000) by Virginie Despentes, Claire Denis' disturbing *Trouble Every Day* (2001), and Marina de Van's body horror *In My Skin* (2002) would inspire an explosion of extreme and innovative horror films from France that include Coralie Fargeat's *Revenge* (2017) and Julia Ducournau's *Raw* (2016) and *Titane* (2021). We'll cover those films more in Chapter 7.

After Elvira Notari's several silent thrillers in the 1910s, Italy didn't produce any genre films by women directors until the 1970s. World War II had deeply scarred the lives of Italian filmmakers and the people around them, leading to several reflective thrillers inspired by the real-life atrocities of the war and the political systems that fueled it. *Blood Feud* (1978) was a fascist thriller directed by Lina Wertmüller, who was the first woman to be nominated for an Academy Award in 1975 (for the film *Seven Beauties*), and Liliana Cavani's 1974 thriller *The Night Porter* brought Nazisploitation films into the mainstream film industry disguised as a psychological drama. Wertmüller later made the crime thriller *Camorra* (1985).

In the early 1980s, a six-part Italian television miniseries called *I giochi del diavolo* (*The Devil's Game*), a highly ambitious set of feature films based on nineteenth-century Gothic literature, aired in 1981. The sixth episode "Il sogno dell'altro" was directed by Giovanna Gagliardo. Gagliardo worked as an actress in several films by director Miklós Jancsó, her husband, before directing her features. her sixty-minute episode of *I giochi del diavolo* is the first horror film directed by a woman in Italy. The episode is an adaptation of the short story "The Story of the Late Mr. Elvesham" by the English author H. G. Wells. It stars Stefano Madia as Edward Eden, a young man invited to dinner by a mysterious older man, famous philosopher Albert Elvesham (José Quaglio). At the end of their meal, Edward finds himself incredibly groggy, only to wake up realizing his consciousness has been transferred to Elvesham's body and that Elvesham is in his young body. Gagliardo shot the episode mainly on sound stages, so it has a muffled, soap opera feeling. Gagliardo used fantastic, surreal imagery to portray Edward's disorientation, such as an Escheresque staircase in Elvesham's mansion that seems to lead to places where physics does not apply and the Daliesque clouds in the sky. Like the original story, the episode is told mainly through a narrator, and most scenes are highly static (sitting at the dinner table or a desk).

The second horror film directed by a woman in Italy is the Giallo horror thriller *Delitti,* AKA *Crimes* (1987), co-directed by Giovanna Lenzi with Sergio Pastore. *Delitti* is a murder mystery about a masked serial killer who poisons his victims. It's a low-budget detective mystery that starts with Harry Francis (Gianni Dei) and his companion being found dead in their villa from an unknown poison after a wild night of partying and homemade pornography orgies. At first, the police suspect a drug overdose, then an accidental ingestion of uric acid with plain coffee (which they say forms cyanide!). But Susan (Deborah Ergas) and the criminal Rhett know it's only a matter of time before the police discover the truth. Intrepid reporter (and Giallo author) Bob Rawling (Saverio Vallone) and Inspector Sanders (Tony Valente) team up against the wishes of the chief of police

The wonderful, surreal horror imagery in Giovanna Gagliardo's episode of *I giochi del diavolo. "Il sogno dell'altro"* (1981).

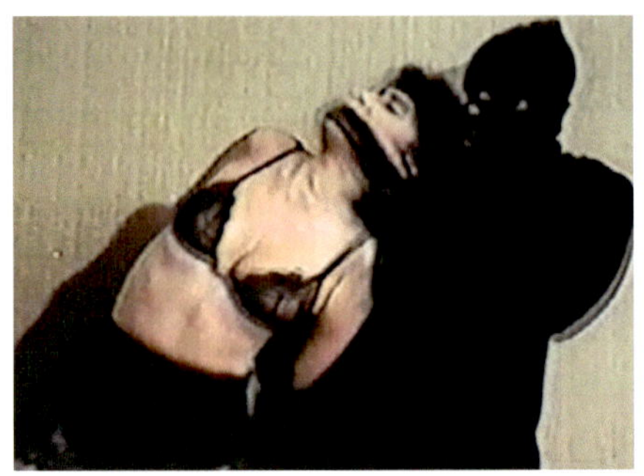

A woman is killed wearing her bra in in Giovanna Lenzi's *Delitti* (1987).

(George Ardisson) to interview and investigate aspiring actress Betty (Michela Miti), the mysterious Julie Garrett (played by Lenzi herself), an ex-girlfriend of the deceased, Jimmy the midget, Julie's friend Harriett (Solvi Stubing), Francis's sister Mirta (Laura Troschel) before they are all poisoned by the murderer. They learn that a pornographic film was made the night of the party at Francis's villa, and the murderer wants it before anyone else can see it. No one is safe in elevators, pompom factories, phone booths, or sawmills. The murderer switches to snake poison halfway through the film; when the little black snake bites its victims, their faces are transfixed into hideous, distorted masks made of paper-mâché. He also sends letters to the police using letters cut from magazines, inviting Rawling and Sanders to meet at the cemetery for a showdown. Cheesiness, 1980s hairdos, inappropriate aerobics, awkward staging, soap-opera lighting, and ugly sex scenes are balanced out by the random nudity, bad wigs, police brutality, and odd practical effects to form a collage of bad/good fun.

La Casa del buon ritorno, AKA *The House of the Blue Shadows,* is an Italian horror film directed by Beppe Cino (AKA Bob J. Ross). Giuseppina Marotta is said to be the uncredited co-director of the film on one website.[23] Her only other film credit is as Executive Producer of a film from 1996, *La Singora della citta*, and on the Internet Movie Database, she is credited as the Executive Producer of *La Casa del buon ritorno,*[24] with no other credits. But she is the Executive Producer of Cino's *Breath of Life* (1993).[25] On the DVD release from United Kingdom distributor TetroVideo from 2017, she is not listed as a director of *The House of the Blue Shadows.*[26]

In 1994, the Italian horror film anthology *DeGenerazione* was released with two segments directed by women. Asia Argento, the director/filmmaker and daughter of famous horror filmmaker Dario Argento, directed the segment "Prospettive," and Eleonora Fiorini directed the segment "Finalmente insieme." (Asia) Argento starred as "Alessia" in the segment "Consegna a domicilio", as "Se stessa" in her own segment "Prospettive", and "Lorna" in the segment "Squeak!" She also co-wrote all of the scripts and served as First Assistant Director. Argento would direct numerous feature and short film projects after her work on *DeGenerazione*. We'll talk more about anthology horror films in Chapter 8 and how they introduce women directors to horror fans.

Italian filmmaker Silvana Zancolò released two feature-length horror films in succession: the straight-to-video Giallo-esque thriller *La radice del male,* AKA *The Root of Evil* (2006) and the English-language supernatural horror film *The Shadow Within* (2007). Low-budget gorefest horror sequel *American Guinea Pig: Sacrifice* (directed by Poison Rouge, 2017) is an Italian production, as is Poison's horror feature follow-up *61: Scorecard Killer* (2020). Cristina Comencini's thriller *Tornare* and Emanuela Rossi's strange apocalyptic thriller *Darkness* were released in Italy in 2019. In 2021, the Italian horror thriller by Michela Cescon, *Occhi blu*, was released.

After the prolific Louise Kolm-Fleck, the Austrian film industry suffered, like many other European nations, during the 1930s rise of Nazism and Fascism and the subsequent war and recovery through the 1940s, 1950s, and into the 60s. After Leontine Sagan's Austrian drama films in the 1930s, women didn't emerge as contributors to the Austrian film industry in strength until the 1970s. Austrian artist and filmmaker Valie Export's directorial debut, *Unsichtbare Gegner,* AKA *Invisible Adversaries* (1977), is a black-and-white experimental film that loosely follows the plot of a schizophrenic woman who comes to believe that aliens called the Hyksos have taken over everyone's minds and increased human aggression towards one another. It's an avant-garde film described by one critic as a feminist remake of *Invasion of the Body Snatchers.*[27] That description is a stretch, as the film does not follow a clear-cut narrative path and is more focused on expressing emotions and sexuality than a true science fiction story.

In 2004, filmmaker Jessica Hausner released her horror thriller *Hotel*, about a young woman working in an isolated hotel who finds that her predecessor has mysteriously disappeared. That same year, director Sabine Derflinger's action thriller *Kleine Schwester,* AKA *Little Sister,* aired on Austrian television. In 2019, Hausner followed up *Hotel* with a science fiction creature feature called *Little Joe* (2019), in which a scientist takes home a genetically engineered plant experiment which, of course, turns out deadly. The other notable woman Austrian horror director is Veronika Franz. She co-directed the horror films *Goodnight Mommy* (2014) and *The Lodge* (2019) with her nephew Severin Fiala. They also directed a segment of the anthology horror television film *The Field Guide to Evil* in 2018, "Die Trud." *Goodnight Mommy* was nominated for a Foreign Language Oscar.[28]

Forfølgelsen, AKA *The Witch Hunt* (1981), is a Norwegian film directed by Anja Breien that screened at the 38th annual Venice International Film Festival. Like the Soviet film *Libahunt* (1968), the French film *Le moine et la sorcière* (1987), directed by Suzanne Schiffman, and the British film *The Witches of Pendle* (1976), directed by Anthea Browne-Wilkinson discussed in Chapter 2, *Forfølgelsen* is a period film about witch trials and the women affected by them. Unlike *The Witches of Pendle*, it is a drama with no supernatural elements. The film is about a young woman in 1630 who survives the black plague as a child and returns to her village years later as an adult. She has an independent attitude, has an affair outside of marriage, and heals people with herbs. The other villagers decide that she must be a witch and torment and torture her during a deeply unsettling trial. Breien is a prolific filmmaker. Her thriller *Papirfuglen,* AKA *Paper Bird* (1984), which won an award at the 1984 Chicago International Film Festival, is her only other experiment with genre elements.

Women have directed only two more horror films from Norway at the time of the writing of this book: the serial killer slasher thriller *1732 Høtten* , AKA *Bloody Angels* (1998) by director Karin Julsrud,[29] in which grisly murders are rumored by locals to be the acts of supernatural angels, and Nini Bull Robsahm's supernatural horror *De dødes tjern,* AKA *Lake of Death* (2019), which was streamed on the United States horror streaming service Shudder in 2021. *Lake of Death* is a loose remake of the 1958 Norwegian horror film *De dødes tjern,* AKA *Lake of the Dead*, which is considered the first modern Norwegian horror film. Robsahm also directed a thriller, *Amnesia* (2014), about a woman who must escape from an abusive psychopath when he unexpectedly loses his memory.

After the Danish noir horror films *Mordets melodi* (1944) by Bodil Ipsen and *Hr. Petit* (1948) by Alice O'Fredericks, it wouldn't be until 2016's experimental fan film *Fear of Silent Hill* by Svetlana Merlov Pittman that Denmark would produce another horror movie directed by a woman.

Actress Mai Zetterling made the shocking and grotesque Swedish surreal thriller *Nattlek,* AKA *Night Games,* in 1966. The black-and-white experimental film is about a man who brings his new wife to his family's mansion in the countryside, where he relives memories from his childhood, including the incestuous and emotionally and physically abusive relationship with his mother. *Nattlek* was first screened at the 1966 Venice Film Festival and was considered possibly the most disturbing and audacious film ever made, with only the judges allowed to view it behind closed doors.[30] Zetterling would continue to direct, and one of her three episodes of the American horror/mystery television series *The Hitchhiker*, "Hired Help," aired in 1985. It stars Karen Black as a ruthless and seductive businesswoman who falls for one of her employees, an illegal Mexican immigrant, and receives cold and hellish justice for her evil actions. Also in 1990, Zetterling appeared as an actress in the fantasy film *The Witches* (1990) as Helga.

Swedish director Susan Sontag made the psychosexual thriller *Duett för kannibaler,* AKA *Duet for Cannibals* (1969), and the thriller-y drama *Bröder Carl* (1971), and while they established Sontag as a strong art house director, her career failed to make an impact outside of Sweden's theaters at the time. In 1990, she directed two episodes of the horror/suspense television series *Chillers*.

Suzanne Osten is also a Swedish filmmaker. Her mother, Gerd Osten, was a filmmaker and a film critic who made the experimental shorts *Zigenardans* (1946) and *Antonius och Cleopatra* (1948). Gerd would inspire her daughter Suzanne Osten to become a filmmaker and experiment with her own ideas about narrative, reality, politics, and comedy. Osten's 1988 comedy/horror *Livsfarlig film,* AKA *Fatal Film,* examines the human psyche through horror movies and comedy. The story of a film crew trying to make a movie is the story of the film itself. In *Livsfarlig film*, Emil Frankenstein (Etienne Glaser, also the co-writer of the screenplay with Osten and Niklas Rådström) is a horror film director known for his highly gory, twisted movies with demented storylines. His brusque producers, Menaden (Stina Ekblad) and Görel Key (Agneta Ekmanner), like things the way they are because they know their audiences and make money from their cheap, disgusting horror movies. But Emil suddenly needs to make a different kind of film: about real people, starring real people (and not actors) and real human things. Despite Emil's desires to include "real" people as actors, the Keys push famous scream queen Ingrid Stromboli (Lena T. Hansson) into the cast, and Emil's daughter Ella (Zoie Finer) finds herself playing a child, even though she's now a grown woman, to help out her father. Emil, his cast, crew, and producers realize that they don't know what being a "real" person means and don't consider themselves real people. But the more they, and the audience, think about it, the more confused they become about what they're trying to do, who they are, and why they aren't just making a fun horror movie instead of their seemingly impossible realistic drama. Is the black-and-white realism film "for prestige? Or is it art?" Emil doesn't know and never did.

Livsfarlig film is about making horror movies more than an actual horror film, like Tatiana Bliss's *Scream Queen* (2002): the set of a horror film is the backdrop to a story about ordinary people working on an extraordinary project. In tone and spirit, it's similar to other existential comedies like *Zombie Strippers* (2008) and *Rosencrantz and Guildenstern are Dead* (1990): modern philosophy is an important aspect of the film, as the characters struggle to make sense of highbrow philosophy while also applying it to their everyday situations without fully comprehending that they're doing it. Actress Agneta Ekmanner was a horror actress in the 1970s (*The Garage*, 1975) and worked with Ingmar Bergman, one of Osten's main artistic antagonists.[31] Etienne Glaser and Lena T. Hansson collaborated with Osten on her other films *Mamma* (1982), *Bröderna Mozart* (1986), and *Tala! Det är så mörkt* (1993). Though not a straight horror film, *Livsfarlig* was nominated for Best Film at the international fantasy film festival, Fantasporto, in 1990, while Lena T. Hansson won the award for Best Actress at the 24th Guldbagge Awards (the Swedish Oscars).

What *Livsvarlig film* offers that makes it easily translate into both horror and comedy genres seamlessly is a combination of cheap horror film plots and people with inventively funny characters and situations. For instance, the Keys and Emil discuss his new movie ideas. They suggest a horror film about a born-again Catholic fundamentalist that is "*torching kindergartens in El Salvador*" because "*Catholic fundamentalism is a relatively unexploited theme.*" Another idea is "*a story about a worker and his baby. And it turns out the kid is a giant sperm, and lurking in his cute little room is a madman who collects babies' brains. And finally, the man has to kill the kid with scissors.*"

In contrast to industry humor are the rather endearing and engaging filmmakers who say things like, "*Real fear is worse than horror. Worse than the worst of horrors*" and "*I want to do something so that I won't have to be ashamed to exist ... I never did anything that was real.*" Osten describes *Livsfarlig film* as "a depiction of horror and the horror film industry. Reality versus manufactured entertainment horror." She says, "I can trace black humour, and my all-encompassing taste for all genres and things I wanted to try to do myself: comedic opera, drama, splatter farce, horror film, political thriller ... " and "dangers, thrillers and grotesque effects ... " because "It is the very dangerous reality that makes us the most vulnerable."[32]

Osten's semi-autobiographical thriller *Flickan, mamman och demonerna*, AKA *The Girl, the Mother and the Demons* (2016), was deemed too graphic and disturbing for younger viewers by the Swedish government. Still, after a battle explaining why the film is so relevant to children with mentally ill parents, the government approved the film for children as young as ten.[33] She is, as of 2021, going to direct an unproduced Ingmar Bergman script as her next project.[34]

Exposé (1998) by Daphna Edwards is the only genre film made by a Swedish woman after *Livsfarlig film* until 2015 when Beata Gårdeler's 2015 rape-revenge thriller *Flocken* came out in Swedish theaters. In 2021, the supernatural horror film *Knocking* by director Frida Kempff played in numerous international horror film festivals like Sitges in Spain, the Neuchâtel International Fantastic Film Festival in Switzerland, and Beyond Fest in California, and was widely seen by horror audiences around the world in theaters before being released on streaming services. The official synopsis is chilling:

> *After suffering a traumatic incident, Molly (Cecilia Milocco) moves into a new apartment to begin her path to recovery, but it's not long after her arrival that a series of persistent knocks and screams begin to wake her up at night. Molly's new life begins to unravel as the screams intensify, and no one else in the building believes or is willing to help her.*[35]

In 1991, Dutch Dorna X. van Rouveroy's horror movie *Intensive Care*, starring George Kennedy, was released in the United States. *Intensive Care* is described as a bad film, with plot holes, and possibly the worst Dutch film ever made. After *Intensive Care*, Esther Rots' thrillers *Kan door huid heen* (2009) and *Retrospekt* (2018), and Antoinette Beumer's thriller *Loft* (2010) are the only genre films made by women in the Netherlands until Madellaine Paxson's grisly horror thriller *Blood Punch* (2014), one of the most underrated thriller/horror films of the twenty-first century.

After the Golden Age of film in Greece in the 1950s and 1960s, a new wave of filmmakers began making movies in the 1970s in drastically different ways than their predecessors. *Ιωάννης ο Βίαιος/Ioannis o Viaios*, AKA *John the Violent* (1973), is a black-and-white thriller set on the dangerous streets of Athens in the early 1970s. Directed by Tonia Marketaki, it was her feature film directorial debut. Almost three hours long, the film tells the story of Ioannis Zahos (Manolis Logiadis), a twenty-year-old man, as he entertains violent fantasies, murders a woman, and then is arrested and tried for the murder. It's an engaging character study of a self-professed sociopath; Ioannis feels no empathy for his victims and any guilt or regret for his crimes. His murder trial becomes a public spectacle. The second half of the film argues whether psychopathy is mental illness and whether the truth is detectable in the confessions of a mentally ill criminal. Ioannis is found not guilty because of insanity and sent to a mental institution. Still, we're unsure if he truly belongs there, as he's been articulate and straightforward in his confessions and reasons for killing.

Marketaki was inspired to make *John the Violent* by American thriller films like *Psycho* (1960) and *In Cold Blood* (1967); it's loosely based on a true crime in Athens with a public murder trial.[36] Marketaki likes to frame her protagonist the way Hitchcock presents Anthony Perkins' Norman Bates at the end of *Psycho*: a straight-on portrait focusing on the eyes. There are shocking moments and discussions of taboo behavior: *John the Violent* is full of nudity and sex. There are scenes of Ioannis strangling and stabbing women, a man getting shot in the back as he runs away from police, violence-enticed press, homosexual relationships, masturbation, and a rational and cold-blooded account of his crime. It's a very violent film for 1973; it showcases the relationships between crime and insanity and sex and murder. Ioannis kills because he believes it makes him strong while the weak are killed; he's sexually impotent, misogynistic, and shallow. He does not value human life, especially female human life.

But Ioannis is also a cat lover; he cares for stray kittens. He's handsome and intelligent. He's not the typical horror movie psychopath, and if he hadn't killed anyone, he stood a chance of having a decent and fulfilling life. But something in Ioannis is broken. During his trial, he blames it on domestic violence, school bullying, and horror comics that he read as a child. He says a bad breakup ruined him mentally; he found out the woman wasn't a virgin, and that was the first time he felt the urge to kill. More importantly, his relationship with his aunt is unhealthy; she enables his behavior and defends him in the courtroom, while his other family members refuse to believe him when he confesses at home before the police arrive. The black-and-white photography combined with the realism of the courtroom strikes a contrast to Ioannis's dreamlike fantasies in which he, dressed as St. George, kills women with a spear as if they were the dragon of the legend. The bright sunlit, dusty streets of Athens and the night-drenched shadowy corners don't leave much room for fantastical imagery in Ioannis's real life.

Later, Marketaki directed the fantasy/horror film *Krystallines nyhtes* (1992) about reincarnation and psychic dream states set against a backdrop of the Nazi invasion of Greece. There are no other feature horror films directed by women in Greece. The 2004 historical thriller *Ecuba*, co-directed by Giuliana Berlinguer and Irene Papas, is the next closest thing. It's based on the play by Euripides in which Trojan queen Hecuba takes revenge against the Greeks for the murder of her son Polydorus; the film is rarely seen and almost entirely unknown outside of Greece.

In the 1960s, Turkey became one of the biggest exporters of films. Yeşilçam ("Green Pine"), the Turkish Film Industry's nickname for its film industry (like Hollywood, Bollywood, Lollywood, etc.), was a thriving industry with hundreds of actors and filmmakers churning out films throughout the 1960s and 1970s. One of the few women directors in Turkey during the golden age of Yeşilçam was Bilge Olgaç. Olgaç made crime thrillers, Westerns, and adventure films from 1965 to 1972. All are black and white; all are low-budget exploitation films with plenty of guns, spies, criminals, conspiracies, bar fights, and beautiful women to different degrees. These low-budget exploitation films were emulations of Western exploitation films screened in Turkey. There would be no women directing any genre films in Turkey after Olgaç until decades later when Yesim Ustaoglu directed the thriller *Iz* in 1995 and then nothing else for a few more decades until the fantasy movie *Bir Dilek Tut* from director Meta Akkus in 2019.

It wasn't until 2003 that independent filmmaker Desiré Dubounet would make the first real horror movie directed by a woman in Hungary, *Dracu* (2003). Born in the United States, Dubounet moved to the United Kingdom and then to Hungary to make independent genre films. She followed *Dracu* with a series of low-budget horror and science fiction, including *Illuminati* (2004), *Blood in the Water* (2006), and the sequels *Dracu 2* (2006) and *Illuminati 2: The Battle in Space* (2013). The most recent horror film directed by a woman to come out of Hungary (at the time of the writing of this book) is

The Girl in the Mirror (2016), co-directed by Ildiko Peli.

In communist Bulgaria, Binka Zhelyazkova was one of the few women working in the film industry. Her fantasy film *Привързаният балон*, AKA *The Tied-Up Ballon* (1967), was her only genre movie. After the Hungarian communist regime fell in 1989, she stopped directing films. Also making films under communism was Ivanka Grybcheva, who directed the wartime action thriller *Глутницата*, AKA *The Pack* (1972), the science fiction movies *Пришествие*, AKA *Advent* (1981) (based on the science fiction novel of the same name by Dimitar Delyan), and the fantasy/science fiction films *13та годеница на принца*, AKA *The Thirteenth Bride of the Prince* (1987), in which aliens interfere in a fairy tale kingdom, and *Карнавалът, AKA Carnival* (1990), in which sinister robots pretending to be human travel with a carnival. Grybcheva was allowed to study at the West German Film Institute in Bablesberg, Germany, where she graduated in 1966.

In a July 2021 article in an online news source *Digis Mak*, Spanish film director and president of the Acadèmia del Cinema Català Judith Colell, said of genre films in Spain directed by women,

> We are talking about almost thirty years ago, and the panorama was a desert. There were no women who made genre films, there were no references, and in the end, you think that women are not useful for making this type of film, and ... you abandon it.[37]

She's not altogether correct; women from Spain direct genre films. Aside from the better-known and more recent feature *Salvación* by Denise Castro (2016), Alice Waddington (*Paradise Hills*, 2018), Arantxa Echevarría (*De noche y de pronto*, 2012), Olga Osorio (*ReStart*, 2016), and Alexia Muiños (*Domestic Affairs*, 2015) are also examples of women directing genre films in Spain, among many others.

The first horror film directed by a woman in Spain is the short film *La Brujita* (1965) from director Cecilia Bartolomé made during her time as a student at the Escuela Oficial de Cinematografía (EOC) in Madrid. In the short black-and-white film, a young girl (Ana Martínez) feels isolated and upset at her family dynamic, which involves her father's new girlfriend, a missing mother, and a hovering aunt. Using voodoo witchcraft, which includes a voodoo doll with pins, and fresh blood, Irma casts a spell seeking rebellious revenge against her circumstances.[38]

On television, women directors in Spain had a remarkable success that horror fans and film historians ignore. There are essential sociocultural elements in Spain that affected the number of women working, in general, let alone in television, and it's important to note that the right-wing dictatorship under Franco was still strong when women began directing television. Even in Franco's Spain, the women's rights movement was in full swing and challenged traditional ideas about women's role in filmmaking. Escuela Oficial de Cine was the first film school in Madrid to allow women entry, and it was from this institution the first Spanish women directors graduated. In particular, Pilar Miró and Josefina Molina are two film directors with television horror resumes who entered the Escuela Oficial de Cine in 1964. Both directed episodes of the television series *Hora Once,* an anthology show adapted from literary works that aired at 11:00 p.m. every Monday from 1968 through 1974. Most importantly, like in the United States during the same time, television and made-for-television films targeted a mainly female audience: a genre into which women directors were allowed to take the helm.[39]

Though not all of the episodes were horror, after 1970, horror seemed to be the more popular genre on *Hora Once*:

> En *Hora Once*, los episodios fantásticos sólo representan una décima parte del total (...) pero su concentración a partir de 1971 demuestra un aumento del interés del género tanto en los autores como en los telespectadores (in *Hora Once*, the fantastic episodes only represent a tenth part of the total (...) but its concentration from 1971 shows an increase in the interest of the genre both in the authors and in the viewers).[40]

Directors shot the stand-alone episodes on small sets with a small crew and three or four cameras: not quite like a soap opera, but not visually complex either. Each episode's prologue told the audience which literary work they had adapted and the cultural period in which it had been written. Each episode ran between twenty to sixty minutes and followed a formula: a long first act introduced conflict, and there was a swift ending. There were rarely any subplots, and the characters were few. In many ways, it resembled the American formula of *ABC's Wide World of Mystery*, especially the *Classic Ghosts* episodes such as *The Haunting of Rosalind* (1973) and *The Screaming Skull* (1973), discussed in Chapter 2. Very little contemporary criticism of the series is available; it was referenced occasionally by newspapers or listed in upcoming television programming ads, but no substantial discussion of the series tells us more about it. It is considered a successful series, nonetheless, and one that gave women directing jobs.

Pilar Miró's episodes of *Hora Once* were not horror. However, she did direct an episode of the *Original* television series, "A verces occuran cosas" ("Sometimes Things Happen," 1975), a thriller about murder and the discovery of a dead body in a closet, and the episode "El platillo volante" ("The Flying Saucer," 1967) of the anthology television series *Los encuentros*. Her episode of another anthology series, *Teatro de misterio* (*Mystery Theater*), a purely horror/mystery/fantasy series, is titled "El sello de lacre" ("The Wax Seal," 1970). It was her later non-television work that she is better known for by the international film community. The government banned her politically charged historical film *La peticion* (1976) for violating censorship rules with its sexual violence and was upset by *El crimen de Cuenca* (1980), which had previously unheard-of torture scenes in mainstream Spanish cinema.[41]

Josefina Molina's first television directing job was for *Once Hora*. She directed four horror episodes. The first two were "La metamorfosis" (1968), adapted from the surreal story by Franz Kafka (as was Caroline Leaf's animated 1977 short *The Metamorphosis of Mr. Samsa* as discussed in Chapter 3) and "El hundimiento de la Casa Usher" (1970) based on *The Fall of the House of Usher* by Edgar Allan Poe. Her third episode, "Vera, un cuento cruel" (1971), she would adapt into an entire feature film released in 1973. Her fourth episode, "Eleonora" (1971), was based on the Poe short story of the same name, which has themes of cannibalism and necrophilia. As of 2020 there was a Spanish streaming distributor, RtelevisionE Play, the VOD services of RtelevisionE, containing numerous other episodes of the series, but the horror episodes directed by Molina are not among them. A digitized version of "La metamorfosis" has been unofficially distributed online, but it's unavailable to most potential viewers.

Vera, un cuenta cruel is the only Spanish feature-length theatrical horror movie directed and written by a woman during the last few years of Franco's dictatorship, a time when the horror and fantasy genres were at their most popular in Spanish film history. Salvador Maldonado (the pseudonym of Lola Salvador Maldonado) wrote both Molina's episode and its feature-length remake. Maldonado, a writer, and television producer, initially approached Molina about making an episode based on the Gothic novel *Vera* by Villiers de L'Isle-Adam about a young count who keeps the dead body of his deceased bride Vera in his castle. The television episode is lost, but sources tell us that Salvador Maldonado does not omit the novel's original Gothic and gloomy elements. On the contrary, the morbid necrophilia and sinister aspects of the original story are present in the television script. However, Salvador Maldonado's script version differs from the novel. The television story no longer focuses on the ghost of Vera (played by Enriqueta Carballeira, who starred in many episodes of *Hora Once*), who wants to destroy the count, but on the count's relationship with his butler. Maldonado and Josefina Molina's episode is mainly about the count (played by José Carlos Plaza), who gets his butler, Raymond (Fabio León), to accept and sympathize with his misery. As the story progresses, Raymond goes crazy, believing that Vera is still alive. The count is surprised when the butler prepares the fire in Vera's empty room and makes the bed. Madness moves from one person to another inside that gloomy house. The episode is about the count's psychosis transferring to the people around him. The television episode preserves classic elements of horror cinema at the time, such as some blood, specifically "the elongated shadows, the closed spaces, the characters, and the exaggerated acting."[42]

In 1972, a company called Etnos Films was founded by Gabriel Moralejo and José Sámano to make fantasy and horror films. Etnos offered Molina her first feature-length directing job: a full-length theatrical adaptation of her television episode "Vera". Etnos only made two films, one of which was *Vera, un cuenta cruel* (1973).[43] Before they offered the feature to Molina, the directing role was offered to three other filmmakers, Mario Camus, Pedro Olea, and Miguel Picazo, who all turned it down. Etnos hired Salvador Maldonado and horror writer Juan Tébar to adapt a feature-length script version of the existing television episode (though the final version of the script leaves their names off, which caused some friction between Molina and the writing team) to attract Molina to the film. As a result, the feature film's plot would retain the differences between the original story and the television episode's plot. Etnos sent the final script to the government film censors, who usually only censored political messages and had no interest in censoring nudity or violence, and the film was approved.[44]

The feature film *Vera, un cuenta cruel* is a more extended, drawn-out version of the television episode and has a few key differences. Like in the television version, the focus is on the relationship between the count (Víctor Valverde) and the butler Roger (Fernando

Fernán Gómez). Vera herself appears only in flashbacks and as a ghost.

Vera is a mystery in the television and feature versions: we know almost nothing about her except the count's idealized visual memories. Also, both versions are about psychology and mental illness and how it can result in mass delusions. The mental illness in *Vera, un cuenta cruel* is the inability to distinguish reality from fantasy; by the end of the film, the viewer also doesn't know what is fantasy and what is real. A difference between the television and the feature versions is that the feature film is excessively "beautiful" for horror. The ghost is beautiful. Her dead body is gorgeous. Even the spider webs on the crypt door are aesthetically, pleasingly, Gothic. The land around the castle is lovely. The lighting is beautiful. Cinematographer José Luis Alcaine focuses on making the ghostly scenes ethereal rather than shocking. Molina wanted a horror film that focused on the soul rather than the horror of the visual; it was her reaction to the overly-sensational, visually horrific horror fantasy films from Spain in the 1970s.[45] American horror fans will be reminded of Dan Curtis's *House of Dark Shadows* (1970) in tone and setting, if not in pacing and plot when they watch *Vera, un cuenta cruel*: far more cinematic than a soap opera, but written with the same sense of brooding period drama. *Vera, un cuenta cruel* attempts to build a complex interpersonal relationship between the count and the butler overshadowed by the cruelty of grief. It's a "cruel" and unfortunate tale. Contemporary reviewers weren't that impressed with *Vera, un cuenta cruel* mainly because they'd all seen the television episode, so they made many comparisons between the two. They expected justifications for the changes in the feature film version:

Poster art for *Vera, un cuenta cruel* (1973).

> The film doesn't justify its length as it doesn't do anything more profound than what Molina did with the short version. Nevertheless, *Vera, un cuenta cruel* is incredibly faithful to the Gothic literary tradition of stories like *Jane Eyre*, *Wuthering Heights*, and *Rebecca*: they're slower, they're terrifying, but they're not grotesque even when dealing with undead visions, violence, and terror.[46]

In 2019, Molina was honored with Spain's 2019 National Cinematography Prize at the San Sebastian Festival. At the ceremony, Spanish filmmaker Patricia Ferreira said that Molina's artistic technique in and of itself had political meaning:

The focus on the fate of female figures. Such is the subordination of Vera to the men in her life—her husband and her manservant—in *Vera, un cuento cruel* that they are quite able to carry on life as if she were alive even after her premature death. Their passion for her stronger than any sense of the reality of her existence.[47]

In 2012, Molina received an honorary Goya Award from the Academy of Motion Picture Arts and Sciences of Spain. At the ceremony, she made a statement about how making films was not only an artistic but a political act for feminism:

> I would say that I have always talked about freedom. Especially the freedom of women to make their own life. Deep down, it's what always concerned me since I was a child. To do what I wanted and to do it the way I wanted. This was not easy for women. And it still isn't.[48]

Like many women directors worldwide, Molina is spoken about purely in terms of her political and feminist film dramas. Her horror work, which launched her career, is rarely mentioned except in passing in any essays, interviews, and at any of her award ceremonies. It's the most interesting, fun thing that she directed and, sadly, remains relatively unknown to horror fans.[49]

As mentioned in Chapter One, the horror film *Três Dias Sem Deus* (1945) marked the directorial debut of Bárbara Virgínia. it wasn't until January 7, 1981, with the advent of Noémia Delgado's television mini-series, "Contos Fantásticos," that a woman once again helmed a horror or fantasy project in Portugal. Delgado, the creative force behind all seven episodes spanning two seasons for RTP - Rádio e Televisão de Portugal (which has digitized and preserved all of the episodes) - brought to life standalone fantastical narratives based on works by Portuguese authors.

Each episode, ranging from forty minutes to over an hour, showcased Delgado's unique perspective on horror and fantasy. The inaugural episode, "A Princesinha das Rosas," adapted from Fialho de Almeida's short story, intertwines the fateful love story of a mermaid and a fisherman. In the second season, "O canto da sereia," inspired by Júlio Diniz's short story, explores mermaids with a sinister agenda. Further captivating tales include "A Noite de Walpurgis," unveiling Satan-worshipping witches, and "A Estranha Morte do Professor Antena," delving into dark occult forces influencing daily lives. "O Defunto," based on Eça de Queiroz's short story, immerses viewers in medieval fantasy horror, while "Tiaga ou A Reencarnação Deliciosa" and "O Visconde" offer riveting narratives of possession and cannibalistic marriages, respectively.

Beyond her foray into horror and fantasy, Delgado's 1976 documentary, *Máscaras*, transcends conventional boundaries as a captivating work of visual anthropology. Although focusing on traditional Portuguese folk masks and their role in holiday rituals in the region of Trás-os-Montes, the documentary takes a fascinating turn by exploring their pagan origins and enduring significance. *Máscaras* is a notable inspiration to folk horror filmmakers.

In 1981, Solveig Nordlund, the Swedish-Portuguese filmmaker, unveiled her crime thriller *Dina e Django* to Portuguese audiences. This Bonnie-and-Clyde-esque narrative unfolds the tale of two teenagers entangled in a passionate love affair, embarking on a gripping crime spree of robbery and murder amidst the tumultuous backdrop of the Portuguese revolution of 1974. As the young protagonists take the life of a taxi driver, their destinies become irrevocably intertwined, evolving them into enigmatic "anti-heroes" as they attempt to elude capture and survive their passion for surviving.

Nordlund would also direct the 2002 science fiction thriller *Aparelho Voador a Baixa Altitude* and the 2003 horror movie *A Filha*.

Pakistan did not have a working film industry until the 1960s, when the first feature films and color films were being produced within the country. Shamim Ara, born Putli Bai, was a Pakistani actress who began her career in the 1950s. After starring in dozens of Pakistani films, she began directing in 1976. Ara is noteworthy for directing the exploitation/action "Miss" series: *Miss Hong Kong* (1979), *Miss Colombo* (1984), *Miss Singapore* (1985), *Miss Bangkok* (1986), and *Miss Istanbul* (1996). She also directed the action/thrillers *Lady Smuggler* (1987) and *Lady Commando* (1989), starring Babra Sharif, Pakistan's most famous Urdu actress. The "Miss" series always features a woman lead fighting hand-to-hand combat with men, wielding guns, having love affairs, and foiling international criminals. *Miss Hong Kong,* the first in the series, was shot in Hong Kong because director Ara wanted to appeal to martial arts/action film fans that already loved Hong Kong action movies. By setting these films in different cities, Ara also appealed to fans of the popular action/travel films coming out of Pakistan in the 1970s. Ara had been inspired to make an action film with a female lead after watching Taiwanese action star Angela Mao in the Bruce Lee film *Enter the Dragon* (1973).[50] *Miss Hong Kong* is about a female martial arts action star named Tina (played by Barbra Sharif), a Pakistani woman living in Hong Kong who must save her kidnapped father from a gang of Pakistani international drug dealers. Another director, Sangeeta, made the action films *Kelona* (1996) in Urdu and *Sher-e-Lahore* (2001) in Punjabi. In 1997, *Da Khwar Lasme Spogmay* by director Shehnaz Begum came out in Pakistan; it's about a woman who transforms into a deadly cat to get revenge on her rapists.

In the 1950s and 1960s in the Philippines, the first Golden Age of film began with Susana C. De Guzman and Fely Crisostomo. De Guzman's feature ghost film *Villa Milagrosa* (1958) stars Nestor de Villa, Charito Solis, Nita Javier, Eddie Rodriguez, Pianing Vidal, Dan Mesinas, and Florentino Ballecer. The production company LVN Pictures released the film on Filipino television between February 28 and March 9, 1958. The story, written by Luz del Mundo, isn't exactly horror, but it is a Gothic ghost story with genre elements. The official synopsis reads:

> Romy Penaflor (Nestor de Villa), a young physician in a Manila hospital, goes home to his paralytic old uncle who lives alone in Villa Milagrosa. The old man bequeaths the huge hacienda and the antiquated mansion to his nephew. Romy is stricken by the mysterious atmosphere of the Spanish mansion and is particularly intrigued by a room with its massive door locked against all inquisitive intruders. The young doctor meets a beautiful young woman in the garden of his uncle's mansion one moonlight night. He falls in love with her, but she disappears. When he meets her

Poster art for Susana C. De Guzman's ghost movie *Villa Milagrosa* (1958).

again, he manages to win her heart. But there is something mysterious about this girl who calls herself Virginia (Charito Solis). Romy can only see her in the garden on Wednesday nights when she would pick flowers for the Lady of Perpetual Help. Finally, he convinces her to attend a birthday party he was throwing. Virginia consents on condition that she could only be present up to twelve o'clock. At the appointed time, she arrives. But before she could be introduced to the crowd, the clock strikes twelve, and she disappears into the night. It was at this time that the old uncle learns of the true identity of Virginia. He tells Romy that she had died twenty years ago. She had been his sweetheart and had haunted him for years.[51]

Villa Milagrosa is as close as Guzman got to making horror movies. Despite not sounding very frightening, *Villa Milagrosa*'s synopsis possesses a fantastical, supernatural sadness reminiscent of films like *The Innocents* (1961).

Fely Crisostomo is better known to the Filipino and American film industries than Guzman. She was the first woman to win a Filipino Academy of Movie Arts and Sciences Award for best director in 1967 (for a drama/romance film). Her first job as a film director was on one of the four short horror segments in the 1960 Filipino horror anthology *Mga alamat ng sandaigdig*, AKA *Legends of the World*. It was one of the three horror anthologies that she would work on as a director. The other directors with segments in *Mga alamat ng sandaigdig* included the prolific genre filmmaker Jose Miranda Cruz, who also worked with Cristosomo on her second anthology horror film. *Mga Alamat ng Sandaigdig*, made by Tamaraw Productions, was released in Philippine Theaters in 1960 but also seems to have been released on radio and Philippine television from December 28, 1960, to January 6, 1961, as a serial, meaning it played in parts on the early DZAQ television network. Jose Miranda Cruz, Johnny Legarda, Manuel Silos, and Fely Crisostomo wrote and directed the four segments. Crisostomo's segment "Alamat ng Waterlily" starred Myrna Delgado, Gloria Sevilla, and Lilian Leonardo.[52] Crisostomo wrote and directed a segment in another horror anthology, *Katotohanan o guniguni?*, AKA *Fact or Fantasy?* which was also released in 1960, on June 28, from Tamaraw Productions. This time, her co-directors were Armando de Guzman, Jose Miranda Cruz, and Tommy C. David. The third segment, "Kadena de Amor," was directed by Crisostomo and starred Lilia Dizon, Norma Blancaflor, Bert Olivar, Pedro Faustino, Dadang Ortega, and Fred Cruzado.[53] In 1985, Jose

Miranda Cruz made a direct sequel to this anthology called *Katotohanan o guniguni? The Movie Part II*. Cruz directed that by himself. In 1967, Cristosomo once again was a part of a horror anthology titled *4 na daigdig ng lagim*, AKA *Four Worlds of Gloom*. The other directors were Martin Marfil, Felix Villar, and Jose Miranda Cruz. These are lost films, possibly existing in a vault, forgotten in the Philippines, having never been digitized or distributed outside their original theatrical run. The poster for *Katotohanan o guniguni?* advertises the segments as "blood-curdling horror mysteries," and all three films' posters claim an "all-star cast."

Poster art for the 1960 horror anthology *Mga Alamat ng sadaigdig*. Image courtesy of James D. Rosa/Pelikula Atbp.

In the 1970s, The Philippines was experiencing what film scholars call the Second Golden Age of their cinema. This era was characterized by several primary factors: films were now made in color (before the 1970s, all films made in the Philippines had been black and white); the nation was under a martial law dictatorship beginning in 1972 that had a strong influence over the industry including the subject matter, and a rebellious avant-garde attitude in the new filmmakers of that decade who tested the limits of sexuality and violence on-screen in the face of the new social order.

Magandang gabi sa inyong lahat, AKA *Good Evening to All* (1976), directed by Lupita Aquino-Kashiwahara (as Lupita A. Concio) is the first feature-length true horror film directed by a woman in the Philippines. Anna Carballo (Nora Aunor) returns to her rural home in Manila after many years to visit her older sister Sarah at their secluded family mansion on the outskirts of the mountain town of Baguio. A Gothic thriller complete with family secrets, ghosts, nightmares, and a decaying mansion, the film follows a Western formula in terms of horror. Still, it imbues it with a distinctly Filipino supernatural folklore flavor.

In one incredibly creepy sequence, Anna is sitting alone in a boat in the ocean. It's a dream, but we don't know that at first. Strained voices scream her name from all around her. A dead body floats before the surface, causing the seagulls to fly away in terror. The corpse, all in white, jumps out of the water and reaches for the boat with a decaying arm. Covering her ears to drown out the sound of the screaming and the birds, Anna suddenly finds herself in the garden of her family's mansion. The family consists of a mother, father, grandmother, grandfather, and brother, all seated waiting for Anna. When she enters the room, they all turn to greet her and at once cry, "Magandang gabi sa inyong lahat!" ("Good evening to all!"). This event would be a happy reunion if it weren't that all of these other family members are long dead. On the verge of panic,

Poster art for Lupita Aquino-Kashiwahara's ghost movie *Magandang gabi sa inyong lahat* (1976). Image courtesy Simon Santos/ Video 48.

Anna wakes up in her hotel room. It was all a bad dream.

Aquino-Kashiwahara makes Sarah alternately human and ghostly, with subtle changes to the lighting, camera angles, and direction that are impressive. The startling sound design of *Magandang gabi sa inyong lahat* stands out: the wails of the ghost Sarah are gut-wrenching, and there is a jarring telephone ring that slices the peaceful moments like a knife. *Magandang gabi sa inyong lahat* may follow the basic Western Gothic romance thriller storyline, but it is more about the inevitable intergenerational horrors ond family ties.

The story on which *Magandang gabi sa inyong lahat* is based was originally serialized in *The Weekly Superstar Komiks*, a comic and photo magazine dedicated to actress Nora Aunor named after her weekly television series.[54] Aunor was, at the time of shooting *Magandang gabi sa inyong lahat*, one of the most famous actors in the Philippines. Aunor's co-star Tirso Cruz III, who played Roy, was her co-star in many previous teen movies they'd made together in the early 1970s, so playing adult lovers in a darker story like *Magandang gabi sa inyong lahat* was a change for their images. Aunor also produced Aquino-Kashiwahara's first feature film as a director, *Alkitrang Dugo* (1975), a thriller based on the classic novel Lord of the Flies by William Golding.

Marilou Diaz-Abaya is another Filipino director that began making films in the 1980s. Her long career spanned decades, and before her death in 2012, she had directed the thriller features *Brutal* (1980) and *Of the Flesh,* AKA *Karnal* (1983) and the action films *Macho Gigolo* (1981) and *Muro-ami* (1999). Diaz-Abaya made *Brutal* a statement about women's suffering under oppression. There wouldn't be another horror movie from the Philippines directed by a woman until 2014's horror comedy *Da Possessed,* directed by Joyce Bernal.

In 1900, Indonesia was still a Dutch colony, and the colonial government restricted filmmaking to Dutch colonials. Between 1942 and 1945, Japan controlled all filmmaking in the country. At the end of World War II, the Allies returned Indonesia to the Dutch, but by 1949 the Indonesians had declared independence. Unlike in the West, it is only since 1949 that Indonesians have produced their own films. Before 1998, there were only four women directors from Indonesia. Ratna Asmara was the first woman director in India, with her 1951 debut of the racy melodrama *Sedap Malam,* AKA *Sweetness of the Night.*[55]

SofiaSmith Sutomo Waldi was the second woman filmmaker in Indonesian history. She had been acting since 1948 but wanted to step behind the camera after a decade. Sofia Waldi's *Badai Selatan,* AKA *Southern Storm* (1960), is the only horror directed by a woman in Indonesia until 1971. Thankfully, the Berlinale film festival preserved a record that *Badai Selatan* screened at the twelfth annual festival in 1962, nominating it for a Golden Bear award. The current synopsis from the British Film Institute is: "*In order to expiate, a young man comes to the loneliness of a poor village. There he is killed after many troubles, just at the moment when the man to whom he felt guilty, is ready to forgive,*" which vaguely leaves much to the imagination.[56] There are a few low-resolution posters on the Internet, with no accurate sources listed, no reviews, no still images, and no published interviews with Waldi about the film.

In 1965, the political regime changed in Indonesia from the more socialist-leaning Sukarno government to the more conservative Suharto government, which disrupted the film industry until about 1970. Waldi would only make a few more non-genre films but continued acting in several famous horror films through the 1980s, including *The Queen of Black Magic* (1981) and *Mystics in Bali* (1981). She passed away in 1986.

The other Indonesian woman filmmaker who made a horror film during this period was Chitra Dewi, whose real name was Roro Patma Dewi Tjitrohadikusumo. Like Waldi, she began working as an actress in the 1950s. In 1971, three films that she directed were released in theaters. Her work was highly sensational. The most extreme of her films as director, the action/horror *Penunggang Kuda dari Tjimande,* AKA *The Horserider of Tjimande* (1971), she co-directed with Sofyan Sharna. *Penunggang Kuda dari Tjimande* was a bloody, gory, dramatic film with plenty of murders:

> Riding a white horse, Purbaya, the horseman from Cimande, comes to Sukajadi in search of his parent's graves. There he runs into an old man who tells his past story. Purbaya is the son of Hamidah and Meureksa, who were murdered by Argasuta. Argasuta was in love with Hamidah, and he sent Hasan Botak and Bagus Bantar after her. Upon hearing this, Hamidah turns hysterical and tries to kill Argasuta. But he survives, and Hamidah instead dies in the hands of his underlings. Then the story returns to the present, where Purbaya takes his revenge on Argasuta. The film is filled with blood, castrated limbs, and exploding organs.[57]

Dewi's second film, a thriller/romance called *Bertjinta dalam Gelap,* AKA *Love in the Dark* (1971), which also had murders, poisonings, and gory traffic accidents:

> Sri Lestari and her fiancé, Joni, are invited to an empty house. Instead, he is met by a policeman who asks him to the police station for questioning. Joni then calls his future mother-in-law, Rahayu, who later on pays a visit. When Joni goes back to the police station, Rahayu had left behind a letter after taking poison. The letter tells her life story about her husband, Yono, who had many wives and liked to sleep around. This prompted Rahayu to get a divorce and start an affair with her former lover, Jufri.

But Yono is angry when he finds out about the affair. He fights with Jufri but ends up being killed by Jufri. In a panic, Jufri runs out of the house and is killed by an oncoming truck. Then Rahayu goes to her aunt's house, claiming that Yono has remarried. Frans, the maid, begins to blackmail Rahayu but Rahayu later poisons her. All of this happens when Lestari was five years old. The letter ends, and we return to the film, where we see Joni and Lestari drive off after their wedding ceremony.[58]

Her last film, *Dara Dara* (1971), is an erotic story about virgins having love affairs featuring plenty of gratuitous sex.[59] Audiences and critics looked down on Dewi's three films as a director, believing them to be pure exploitative trash, which they were, and Dewi did not continue to direct films,[60] though she did continue to act.

Since the end of President Suharto's New Order regime (1966–1998), there has been a significant increase in women working behind the camera in the Indonesian film industry. In the 1980s, the Indonesian film industry declined as the government focused on infrastructure and relaxed censorship rules, bringing in a flood of foreign films from the West. In 1998, the government regime changed again, and Western film trends ushered in new Indonesian independent films, including far more women-directed movies but not many horror and genre films. Sadly, none of these early Indonesian women-directed films are available to the public.

Vietnam's first woman horror director did not release a film until 1992 with *Mark of the Devil*, then in 1999 with *Chung cu*, which is set in an apartment building where the inhabitants are stalked by something dark and supernatural. Both films were directed by Linh Viet, a filmmaker about whom little is known or available.

Women filmmakers from India don't get that much attention in mainstream film news discussions. Women horror film directors from India get even less attention for several reasons: the first is that Indian horror is seen as very male-centric for a male audience, and the second is that India has only fostered women's filmmaking careers since the 1970s, meaning that there are far fewer than in Western nations. Fatma Begum made the fantasy film *Bulbul-e-Paristan* in 1926, but the first authentic Indian horror film directed by a woman was *Gehrayee,* AKA *Depth* in 1980, co-directed by one of India's most prolific women directors, Arunaraje Patil.

Terrie Samundra is an Indian horror film director. Her supernatural Hindi-language film *Kaali Khuhi* (2020) was distributed widely in the United States via the streaming service Netflix. Samundra describes Arunaraje Patil's place in modern Indian horror:

> I do think that she's known in more art-house film circles and among the progressive film community, especially women filmmakers. I can almost say that most of the population doesn't know her or her work. The film itself is little known. Horror is so rare there, and at the time she was making it, the only people making horror were men, and it was almost all slasher pornography/explòitive stuff ... She's of a generation where she was really working in the margins and an anomaly as an editor, literally the first woman editor there. Her film *Firebrand* was released on Netflix a few years ago. I know her horror film did not have the wide audience it deserved. I've never heard anyone mention it or her

name when the topic of women in horror in India comes up.[61]

Arunaraje Patil was born in 1946 in Pune, India, into a very sheltered childhood. She was obsessed with movies as a child. Originally enrolled in medical school, she switched to a film school in 1967 to learn to edit and direct. In film school, she met Vikas Desai, another film student, and together they made their thesis films. They were married and ended up having a long filmmaking partnership as co-directors, beginning in 1969 until their divorce in the late 1980s.

Original release poster for Aruna Raje's 1980 Indian possession film *Gehrayee*.

The second film they directed together was a horror film: *Gehrayee* (1980). "I have always been fascinated about black magic and witchcraft," admitted Raje in her autobiography, "the spooky and the mysterious, the unknown and the unpredictable, from childhood."[62] While working on their first film together, *Shaque* (1976), Raje shared this idea of a horror movie about the supernatural with Desai. He was excited, but their business partner/producer, Mr. Kamat, did not believe it was commercial enough to gain an audience when formulaic Bollywood films were the mainstream popular style. When *The Exorcist* (1973) was released in India in 1977, investors changed their minds and wanted to make an Indian horror film to take advantage of the buzz. Raje wanted *Gehrayee* to use common Indian folklore and mythology as a basis for its storyline, which would resonate deeply with Indian audiences. "We decided to make a real scary horror film, definitely not fantasy or make-believe," she said:

> Having the film grounded in reality meant doing a lot of research. We had to delve into the practices of witchcraft, mantra, and tantra and study their effects and implications ... Thus began our journey into the unknown ... we culled a handful of stories that we altered to create the backbone of our script for *Gehrayee*. The central theme, of a girl being possessed by another soul that had entered her body and have her take on a new persona, came from the [real] experiences of two people.[63]

Raje and Desai set *Gehrayee*, which means "depth" in English, in the south of India, in Bangalore, which they felt would be more believable. After a few months of research, they gave the story to playwright Vijay Tendulkar who wrote the script. They immediately started casting their ghost story at this point. Padmini Kolhapure plays Umakka, the adolescent girl who becomes possessed. Dr. Sriram Lagoo was cast as her father, Chennabasappa, Indrani Mukherjee as her religious mother, Saroja, Anant Nag was Umakka's older brother Nandu, Sudhir Dalvi as the good priest, Amrish Puri as the evil sorcerer, Suhas Bhalekar as the disloyal servant Basava, and Rita Bhaduri as Chenni, Basava's daughter. The city of Bangalore was perfect for what Raje wanted: they filmed in green Cubbon Park with hundred-year-old trees, providing the perfect spooky, rural forest setting.[64] One of their other locations, the Bangalore city house, became a problem when the owners demanded more money than they had agreed on after filming had begun. It was challenging for a low-budget movie to scrape up the extra money, but they completed the scenes they had left.[65]

Gehrayee focuses on the adolescent Umakka's demonic possession and her family's attempts to treat her medically and spiritually with exorcists. One afternoon she is chased by an invisible entity as she walks home from school. Raje describes this scene:

> We had the scene where Padmini is walking following her, and nobody is actually there in physical form. It gets so eerie that she drops her cycle and runs like the Devil is after her. The scene was shot with a handheld camera, and it was a challenge for the cameraman, who had to run not only forward but also backward ... adding sound to it intensified the feeling by several notches ... The scene looked perfect with the music and effects, but it is amazing how every single technician adds something to a scene.[66]

Chennabasappa and Saroja take Umakka to the doctor, but they can't find anything wrong with her. The family calls upon several different Hindu holy men to help them. The first is ineffective, while the second ends up being an evil priest using Umakka's body to invite the dark goddess Kali into the world. Raje says that Amrish Puri was so convincing and scary as the evil magician that Steven Spielberg cast him as the evil cult leader in *Indiana Jones and the Temple of Doom* (1984).[67] She goes on to describe the scene:

> A scene that drew a lot of attention was the one where Amrish Puri, as the evil black magician, had hypnotized Padmini through Vashikaran and was invoking the goddess in her so that he could have sex with the goddess, amassing enormous power in the process ... The background was a broken-down temple where the yoni pooja was being performed. Padmini was supposed to be nude in that scene, and though unintentional, a lot of curiosity got generated, the buzz being whether she was actually nude or not during the shoot ... And though she looked nude in the film, she was not actually so.[68]

Following a series of increasingly disturbing demonic encounters, the family must face that they have been cursed because of Chennabasappa's actions in the past, which are finally revealed. After the final scene, "The end?" appears on the screen. Raje explains the audience's reaction to watching the last part of the film for the first time:

> It was the scene in the cemetery where Anant Nag is trying to get a spirit to talk to him amidst the shrieking of ghosts. The scene was dark, and there was pin-drop silence in the theatre. It was very, very scary. For a moment, my heart stopped beating. It was as if I was all alone. I could not see anybody else in the audience—I seemed to

be stranded in the empty theatre with the ghosts. But it was only in the next scene that I breathed a sigh of relief when the picture was brighter, and I could make out the heads of the audience in silhouette. After the film, we got hundreds of calls from people asking for help, sharing their stories of how magic spells and hexes put on them had affected their lives. They asked for solutions and names of the magicians who could undo the bad effects of somebody's evil design.[69]

Was Raje hoping to make a sequel? I am not sure. The film is a ponderous two hours and fifteen minutes—it easily could have been edited down to a more concise story, but the length also provides in-depth character development and background story. The actual 'horror' only appears sporadically, in scenes of Umakka at the fire during the evil ceremony with the evil priest and when they speak to actual spirits at the end of the film. The rest of the film doesn't reinforce the supernatural; nothing that happens to Umakka, except the spirit speaking through her, can be considered supernatural or horrifying. There are no extreme possession scenes for the first three-quarters of the movie, and everything happening to Umakka could be chalked up to a mental disorder.

Unlike in *The Exorcist*, where Regan is disfigured, vomits green, and levitates, *Gehrayee* does not offer similar horror scares. It's a calm movie for the most part, with Umakka having crying fits and moments of split-personality as the only sign that she's possessed. Both men are also guilty of crimes against women (Nandu strangling Chenni and Chennabasappa leaving a pregnant girl) and risk karma getting even by attacking their families and loved ones. *Gehrayee* is about accepting the supernatural and religious despite scientific evidence to the contrary; it's about losing traditions and values, and beliefs as we move away from our ancestral homes and into big cities and forget the prayers, rituals, and superstitions that plague us in the countryside and small villages. Despite their skepticism, Nandu and even Chennabasappa both believe in ghosts and demons at the film's end.

Gehrayee premiered in Eros at Churchgate in Bombay, India, and was attended by celebrities. It did well at the box office; people found it scary and spellbinding.[70] *Gehrayee* has been referred to as the best horror movie to come out of India.[71] One of the reasons *Gehrayee* was well-received in India is the attention to cinematography, lighting, and sound that make it a well-made film. Desai and Raje found ways to innovate Indian cinema as they made this film:

Another tool we used effectively in *Gehrayee* was the crab dolly, which is a camera dolly that has the ability to move in any direction and does not need rails like conventional trolleys. There was only one available in Bombay, maybe in India at that time, and it belonged to Merchant Ivory Productions. Booking it was as difficult as getting a star's dates. We used it to move from room to room with speed when something was afoot (with the spirits).[72]

Real life echoes art in scary ways: Raje was warned by many people not to make a movie about witchcraft and religion because she'd be cursed for doing so:

> There were a lot of people who told us not to make the film. They warned us that dabbling in such subjects would have an adverse effect on us—it might even destroy us. Well, within the next few years, a lot that was precious to me was lost — my daughter, my marriage, etc. But I don't think it had anything to do with the subject or making a film on it.[73]

When their marriage broke up, so did their film partnership:

> My husband and I had been the Aruna–Vikas duo, a film-making team who wrote, directed and edited films together, and now ... ? I was not sure if as a woman I would get work on my own steam ... Who would give work to a woman in a male-dominated film industry? [74]

Arunaraje wouldn't direct again until the drama feature film *Rihaee* (1988), her solo directorial debut. In 2004, Arunaraje Patil directed the thriller *Tum: A Dangerous Obsession*. She has always wanted to make a film that she is sure others will refer to as an "art film": the story is non-linear, with dream sequences, past lives, "I don't see it happening," she says. "I don't know anyone who will fund a film like that."[75]

Though India is a nation of many different languages, all mainstream Indian films (and even many independent films) are made in the Hindi language. Still, Tamil, Telugu, and Malayalam-language film industries are also in the country's south. A woman in India would not direct another horror film until the twenty-first century when Jennifer Lynch's 2010 horror film *Hisss* was filmed in India against an Indian mythological backdrop. The documentary *Despite the Gods* (2012) is about the making of *Hisss*: it follows Lynch and her crew and cast on set (which we'll discuss in Chapter 8), disasters and all. Indian-American filmmaker Anam Syed made the short film *The Pink Sorrys* (2014) which blends Bollywood musicals with rape/revenge horror and is based on the true story of women in Mumbai who killed known rapists. Anvita Dutt Guptan's horror thrillers *Bulbbul* (2020) and *Qala* (2021) have supernatural horror themes, and Sapna Bhavnani's fantasy horror *My Dog is Sick* (2021) is about human desire and pushing sexual limits too far.

In the 1970s, Taiwan moved away from communism and towards its national identity. Taiwanese cinema is unique from other Chinese film industries because it developed independently of the communist People's Republic of China and mainstream Hong Kong cinema. In the 1960s, Taiwan underwent rapid modernization in almost all industries, including its film industry. Taiwanese slowly faded out in favor of films in Mandarin, and by the late 1970s, only Mandarin-language films were being made in mainland Taiwan. Taiwan imported both Western and Hong Kong movies to the island. Still, a particular Taiwanese underground film scene emerged in local low budget 'social realist' films about the everyday troubles facing people in an industrialized society: organized crime, rape, murder, gambling, prostitution, and drugs. Filmmakers and distributors claimed that these "realistic" movies (which were not realistic) dealt with critical social issues. They are thinly-veiled exploitation films that use sensational violence and nudity to compete for theatrical audiences with films from the United States and kung fu movies from Hong Kong. The phenomenon of social realist films was short-lived: it began in the late 1970s and, by 1982, had faded. Nevertheless, these Taiwanese pulp/Black movies were popular outside of Taiwan, and several women filmmakers began their careers working in this specific genre.

Chia-Yun Yang is considered one of the most influential filmmakers of this Black Movies movement and perhaps the first woman to direct an actual rape/revenge film. She made a few drama films before she made a Taiwan Black Film, but her exploitation movies brought her notoriety, attention, and fandom that lasted through the twenty-first century. In the late 1970s, Yang and her writing partner Hsuan Hsiao-fa set up Sunshine Film Company and made two comedy films before transitioning to thriller and horror films. When IFD distributed Yang's genre films overseas, her name was changed to "Karen Yang" on the credits to westernize her to American audiences. Yang's *Feng huang nu sha xing*, AKA *The Lady Avenger* (1981), is a rape/revenge thriller, and her horror film *Leng yan sha ji*, AKA *Exposed to Danger* (1982), is one of the only horror movies directed by a Taiwanese woman.

Feng huang nu sha xing came into being when producer Hsien-Cheng Chiang approached Yang about directing a Black Film for him. Chiang produced sixteen of these exploitation films, including Yang's *Leng yan sha ji*, and needed a director for a fast shoot for a new rape/revenge film starring Lu Hsiao-Fen. She had just become famous for starring in the shocking Chiang-produced film *On the Society File of Shanghai* (1981). Chiang made these films very quickly on tiny budgets (often with money financed by the Taiwanese mafia), and he wanted to exploit the success of his recent release, which meant he had to move fast. Yang said:

> Chang requested me to shoot a movie for him. The social realistic films were prosperous ... he planned to make more successful movies. So he asked for my cooperation. I thought for a while, and I wrote the outline. With that outline, we began our shoot. Without a full-text script, we shot and wrote the script at the same time. Within twenty working days, we finished the shooting and hurried the editing. All things were done within a month, and it opened just in time.[76]

The idea behind 'social realism' films was that filmmakers based their plots on the gritty crimes of the day; "When I make a social realistic movie, usually the subject was based on news, reported on the society pages," Yang explained. "But the script was more provocative. We made it more sensational."[77] It's very sensational. *Feng huang nu sha xing* is one of the most violent crime thrillers ever made. Yang pulls no punches in torturing her lead character, Wan-ching (Lu Hsiao-Fen), who is subject to physical and mental torture as her attackers pursue her in a scene upwards of almost fifteen minutes.

The intensity of the film comes from its extreme violence. For instance, there is a long, stressful sequence of Wan-ching running for her life, fighting off her assailants with anything she can get her hands on, and desperately screaming for help that won't come. After her rape, Wan-ching transforms into a new person. She's lost her relationship, she's lost her job, and she's lost her sense of security and identity. Now that she has nothing to lose, Wan-ching will seek revenge.

The rest of the film is Wan-ching seeking out and murdering the men who raped her, one by one. Having gotten a job at the meat-packing factory where one of her rapists works, she sends him a wrapped red present box with a raw pig's heart inside. Disgusted, he throws the container away, but Wan-ching is waiting in the shadows for him with a meat hook. She brutally beats him to death with it. After leaving a red box for him in his apartment, she follows another rapist to his workplace. She terrorizes him with a blowtorch at the construction site and then suspends him dozens of feet in the air by a cable before dropping him onto the hard concrete below, ignoring his cries for help. She follows the third rapist, Fuzzy, to his rustic cabin in the woods. Pretending to be a hunter, she aims at him with her rifle and fires. As he runs away, his foot is caught in a bear trap, and she fires again, but this time does not miss. The last rapist is an avid gambler, so she plays at his roulette table and agrees to go to bed with him. In a moment of passion, she bites his neck. She tells him who she is as she chases him through his apartment: "*You ruined my life. I'll kill you!*" Holding a katana, she runs him through with one push, blood gushing out of his wounds at the moment of impact. Last, there are eight minutes of frantic running and brutal violence as she and the remaining rapist fight to the death. Wan-ching faces him in a grueling, bloody showdown on a staircase in which her anger overcomes her fear, and she slashes him with a knife before jumping to the bottom story and stabbing him in the back. Dying, he stands up, gasps, and still tries to come after her. But he collapses, dead. The grandfather clock in the hallway rings out the time, reminding Wan-ching that she only has a few moments before the police arrive and her freedom is gone forever.

Yang made some pretty bold choices with her story and the gore, which did not go unnoticed by the censors' office. They marked numerous scenes for exclusion before allowing the film to play in Taiwan. But Yang, and other filmmakers in the same genre and underground scene, would often agree to the censor's rules and then completely ignore them:

> We didn't intend to stop because we wanted to present it whole. Also, we have to think about the overseas market. Such plots are not prohibited there. So, we only tried our best for the domestic release; you need to know where the critical points are. In post-production, those too-bloody should be cut out, too-sensational should be cut out, too rude lines need to be silenced. But these sequences were not really cut out. When the movie is released, they spliced them all back in.[78]

Some of the more involved action scenes, like the construction cable fall, were made up on the spot when they arrived at the site to shoot the scene. "There was a lot of action in it, and it was highly dramatic," said Yang, "especially when you saw a woman killing as if she had lost her reason. The audience seemed satisfied, so it nearly topped the box office."[79]

Other rape-revenge films of the time, like *They Call Her One Eye* (1973), *I Spit on Your Grave* (1978), *Last House on the Left* (1972), and *Ms .45* (1981), are made by men and are about men's fears of retribution from vengeful women. *Feng huang nu sha xing* focuses on women's anxiety about how society will treat them after they are raped and that they'll never get justice. *Feng huang nu sha xing* is an exploitation film about rape and murder, but it contains satire, poking fingers into the sexist nightmare that its female characters live. After Wan-ching is raped, the sexism becomes less amusing and more humiliating, depressing, and enraging as she loses her fiancé, self-confidence, and future. Wan-ching throws away any semblance of the life she may have left to exact revenge on her attackers. It's a pricey bargain, as she will spend the rest of her life in prison, or worse, for the systematic first-degree murders of five people. Most rape victims don't go on murder rampages to get revenge; Wan-ching makes a violent and horrific choice because she has nothing to lose. It's not a pretty sentiment, certainly not one to applaud. It's a horror movie, and it's pretty horrifying.

American horror films influenced Yang's decisions when making *Feng huang nu sha xing*. She steals a scene directly from *The Shining* (1980): when Wan-ching is running from rapist Mr. Li, she hides in a bathroom. He uses an ax to break through the wooden bathroom door, the camera framing the scene with the door and ax in the forefront and Wan-ching in the back, screaming, just like during the climax of *The Shining*. Likewise, Yang's next horror film, *Leng yan sha ji*, AKA *Exposed to Danger* (1982), also borrows from American horror, this time from *Friday the 13th* (1980) and its finale and canoe scenes.

Leng yan sha ji, AKA *Exposed to Danger* (1982), made after the exploitation surge of the late 1970s, has a higher production value and a more mature character dynamic than *Feng huang nu sha xing*. It also stars Lu Hsiao-Fen as the lead character Chou Tien-chi and follows her nightmare of obsession, murder, and violence. The characters in the United States dubbed versions (in theaters as *Exposed to Danger* and on DVD as *Breakout From Oppression*) have Western names. In the original Taiwan release, the film is in Mandarin, and the characters have Chinese names. Characters Chou Tien-chi (Lu Hsiao-Fen), Hsiao-tung (Alan Tam Wing-Lun), and Shih-yun (Fu-Mei Chang) find themselves in a nightmare of obsession, stalking, and life long grudges.

Director Chia-Yun Yang copies a scene from *The Shining* (1980) in her rape/revenge horror film *Lady Avenger* (1982).

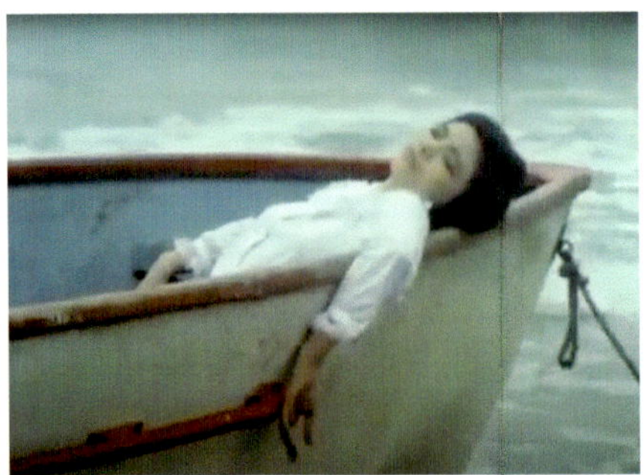

Director Chia-Yun Yang borrows the last scene from *Friday the 13th* (1980) in *Exposed to Danger*.

The only existing imagery from *Murder Case in Chinatown* (1961), directed by Esther Ng.

Yang again has her main characters endure brutal challenges for their survival. Shih-yun goes after Tien-chi in a showdown with a butcher knife that, like in the final fight between Mr. Li and Wan-ching in *Feng huang nu sha xing*, is a grueling minutes-long battle for survival. The two women end up on the beach shore when Tien-chi finally wrests the knife away from Shih-yun; in a dramatic and highly applaud-worthy moment, Tien-chi runs in slow motion towards the camera at Shih-yun and, in one fell swoop, slices her head off her body. Free at last from the horror of her past, Tien-chi lies down in a small boat, floats on the water, and falls asleep. She wakes up when help arrives. If, to horror fans, this sounds exactly like the ending of the original *Friday the 13th* (1980), you're right. Yang would have been very familiar with this film as she would have been *The Shining*, both popular Western horror films that came out around the same time, and she milked these famous moments for all she could. They're good moments.

Leng yan sha ji is a more sophisticated horror film than *Feng huang nu sha xing*. It explores the inner workings of pain and madness due to loneliness and anger in much the same way that films like *Fatal Attraction* (1987), *Single White Female* (1992), *The Hand that Rocks the Cradle* (1992), and *The Crush* (1993) do: through the eyes of demented female love. When horror films express the same sentiments in male characters, the men tend to be written as psychopaths, with their emotions always seen as perverse rather than explainable in, for example, *Maniac* (1980), *Silent Night, Deadly Night* (1984), *Terror Train* (1980), and *Prom Night* (1980). For a film from 1982, *Leng yan sha ji* seems to be a decade ahead of other slasher films from the same period in terms of character development and focus on the newly-interesting female psychopath. The early 1980s were a fascinating time in Taiwan's film history.[80] There would not be another horror film made by a woman director in Taiwan until 2015 with *Shi yi,* AKA *The Bride* by Lingo Hsieh.

History books say that the first woman film director in China was Shu Shuen Tong with her 1968 drama film *The Arch*. However, Esther Eng had directed films since the late 1930s when China entered World War II to repel the Japanese occupation. Originally from mainland Southern China, Eng moved to Hong Kong when the war began. At age twenty-two, she made her directorial debut: the adventure film *National Heroine* about a female military pilot joining the fight against the Japanese. Her crime thriller *Niuyue Tangrenjie suishian,* AKA *Murder Case in Chinatown* (1961) (co-directed with Wu Peng in Cantonese), was the first genre film directed by a Chinese woman. In 1960, Alfred Hitchcock's *Psycho* was a massive success, prompting Hong Kong filmmakers to cash in on the new Western trend of suspense/thrillers coming out of the U.S.A. *Murder Case in Chinatown* was one of several Cantonese-language thrillers to come out of Hong Kong then, along with Mandarin-language films by production companies such as The Shaw Brothers.[81]

As martial arts films developed in the 1960s and 1970s, martial arts actress Pao-Shu Kao directed the action movie *Lady with a Sword* (1970), her directorial debut, soon followed by martial arts movies *The Desperate Chase* (1971), *The Cannibals* (1972), *Win Them All* (1973), *Female Fugitive* (1975), *The Damned* (1977), *The Jade Fox* (1979), *The Master Strikes* (1980), and the thriller *Nie zhong* (1981). Before directing, Pao-Shu Kao had joined the famous Shaw Brothers film studio as an actress in 1958, and she appeared in eighty martial arts films, including her own. In 1971, she left the Shaw Brothers to form her own production company Park Films, where she made most of her films as director. The Chinese film industry under communism had fully embraced women directors and feminist ideas in their film industry.[82] Still, Hong Kong had its separate film industry in which the best martial arts films of all time were created, including Pao-Shu Kao's.

In 1979, one woman director, in particular, would emerge in Hong Kong's movie industry and enjoy a directing career well into the twenty-first century. Ann Hui's first film, *The Secret* (1979), is a true-crime suspense thriller based on the real-life 1970 Double Corpse Murder Case in the Mount Lung Fu area of Hong Kong. Along with other Hollywood-inspired, Western-style suspense films, *The Secret* was part of a film movement called the Hong Kong New Wave. Written by Joyce Chan, who would go on to collaborate with Hui on future films as well as write the script for the horror film *Love Massacre* (1981), *The Secret* flows like a modern suspense thriller; a murder is committed, two bodies found, a mystery ensues to catch the murderer. The depictions of the bloody bodies are graphic: they're dripping blood, tied up and hanging from trees. An autopsy scene shows everything, nude body and all, without hesitation. The police investigate the murders like a television procedural; we get a play-by-play of how the murders took place. Family members identify the brutally battered bodies of their loved ones in fluorescent morgue lighting. A few breathtaking shots of the dark woods where the bodies are found give the film an otherworldly look, while desolate streets almost glow with greens and blues. Hui makes poverty a complicated spectacle on the streets of Hong Kong. Lin Jeng-ming (Sylvia Chang) is haunted by the murder of her friend, Li Yuen (Angie Chiu), and her fiancé Ah Cho (Alex Man). She embarks on a personal quest to investigate their deaths that involves flashbacks, faded memories, and sleuthing. The audience solves the mystery along with Jeng-ming and witnesses the gruesome murders and the figures responsible. The plot jumps in time in a confusing way, but is not impossible to follow. Hui enjoyed true crime as a source for her films; she would make the thrillers *The Zodiac Killers* (1991) and *Night and Fog* (2009) based on real-life crimes.

Hui's second film, *The Spooky Bunch* (1980), also written by Joyce Chan, is a horror-comedy utterly different in tone from *The Secret. The Spooky Bunch* combines the supernatural with cartoonish, slapstick comedy. *The Spooky Bunch* is about Chinese ghosts seeking revenge for their deaths and their continually thwarted attempts to

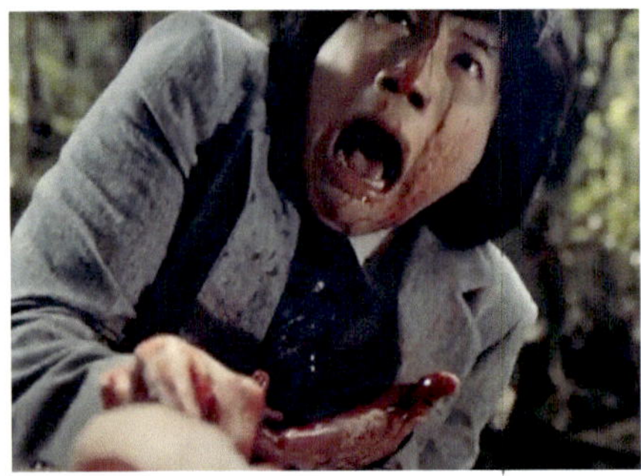

A violent twist in Ann Hui's *The Secret* (1979) results in lots of blood.

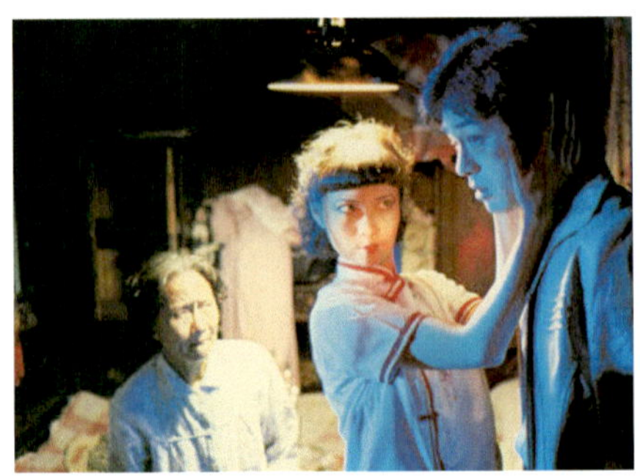

Ah Gee (Josephine Siao) talks to ghosts in Ann Hui's horror comedy *The Spooky Bunch* (1980).

obtain it. The main focus is a small-time Cantonese opera troupe whose member, Ah Gee (Josephine Siao), is a second-rate actress who happens to be the last member of the family line of her ghostly lieutenant grandfather, the focus of the hauntings.

Chaos and calamity punctuate the hauntings, for instance, when the actors are possessed by ghosts during their performance, causing them to wear the wrong costumes and break character in the middle of their performances. There's a running gag that Ah Gee has a gambling problem and is constantly challenging the ghosts to games; she even gambles with a group of little kids who keep popping up to distract the spirits. The ghosts are angry and menacing but continually thwarted by trickery or narrow escapes by the protagonists. Kung fu is used as physical comedy quite effectively. The ghosts are pale and creepy, but Hui smashes every scary moment with a joke. In many ways, *The Spooky Bunch* is like Sammo Hung's Hong Kong horror comedy *Encounters of the Spooky Kind* (1981), the most famous Hong Kong horror-comedy of the early 1980s. Other films such as Wu Ma's *The Dead and the Deadly* (1982), Ricky Lau's *Mr. Vampire* (1985), and Siu-Tung Ching's *A Chinese Ghost Story* (1987) join *The Spooky Bunch* and *Encounters of the Spooky Kind* as entries in the horror/fantasy/comedy subgenre of Hong Kong films lovingly referred to by fans and scholars as the Golden Age of Hong Kong Horror, and the only one of that genre directed by a woman. Her 2001 movie, *You ling ren jian,* AKA *Visible Secret,* returns to her horror comedy roots in a story about vengeful ghosts following and harassing human targets over past transgressions.

Lin tai, AKA *The Siamese Twins* (1984), is a horror movie produced by the Shaw Brothers and directed by Angela Mak (Mai Ling-tzu). Mak, who also wrote the film, made five films during the New Wave movement of the 1980s in Hong Kong. The film stars Po-Erh (Hong Kong television star Idy Chan, also known as Chen Yu-Lien) as a woman born with a Siamese twin named Bei-Erh, with whom she shared a brain. Dr. Fong (Kwan Hoi San) is the doctor that surgically separated them when they were young, causing Bei-Erh to die. There's some confusion as to why Po-Ehr wouldn't remember having such a necessary surgery at age five; she has flashbacks of being in the hospital but no real memories of ever having had a sister, let alone one attached to her brain. However, she begins to see Bei-Ehr's ghost, and the spirit lashes out to hurt Po-Ehr by possessing people close to her, seducing them, and killing them, not always in that order. Bei-Ehr wins in the end, and an entire airport full of people witnesses Po-Ehr beaten to death by her lover with a crutch he grabs from a passing man.

The Siamese Twins is a very bleak movie with a gloomy ending. It's never clear why Bei-Ehr is such an angry ghost, except that she was killed during the separation surgery (although Dr. Fong tried to save them both). Mak doesn't hold back from nudity, sex, and violence, nor does she hold back from showing blood: the film's last third is drenched in sex and violence in sharp contrasts to the first two-thirds of the film, which are relatively uneventful. In particular, Dr. Poon's rape scene is horrifying, and Mrs. Kei's suicide is explicit. Mak would only make one horror film in her directing career.

After *The Siamese Twins*, there was a break in the phenomenon of women directing horror out of Hong Kong. There have been misconceptions that the horror-comedy *Kai xin gui jing ling*, AKA *Love Me Vampire* (1987), was co-directed by an uncredited Irene Wang Chin-Hsiang. Wang was not the film director; she was a "presenter," which is a title that is customarily called "executive producer" in Western cinema. Clara Law is a New Wave Hong Kong director like Mak, and her 1989 feature film debut is the fantasy *The Reincarnation of Golden Lotus*. Still, her 2015 action/comedy *The Unbearable Lightness of Inspector Fan*, AKA *Shanghai Noir*, is much better known among genre fans.

In 2006, Hong Kong filmmaker Carol Miu-Suet Lai directed *The Third Eye*, a thriller about surveillance and voyeurism. She followed that with the horror film *Naraka 19* in 2007, about a supernatural phone texting game that forces users to travel through various levels of Hell to "win" the game and escape. *Naraka 19* is based on a novel published on the Internet, and "Naraka" is Sanskrit for "Hell" in Buddhist lore, of which there are eighteen levels. Targeted at a teen audience, Naraka 19 didn't make it onto the radar of any horror fans in the West. Chinese filmmaker Jennifer Thym wrote and directed the short proof-of-concept horror fantasy film *Bloodtraffick* and released it in 2011. The film stars Grace Huang as a human vigilante and Kirt Kishita as a vampire who kills angels; the short essentially launched Grace Huang's career as an action star in films like *The Man with the Iron Fists* (2012). Other women filmmakers from China and Hong Kong that would make horror, fantasy, and science fiction shorts in the twenty-first century include Yan Lu (who directed the superb science fiction film *Hard Drive*, 2018), Rosa Wang (*A Confession*, 2018), Chaoqun Wang (*Tale Of The Song*, 2019), Yunbing Li (*Evasion*, 2019), and Sangyi Zhao (*Radio Murmurs*, 2020).

Thailand's film industry is steeped in mystery regarding women directors. There are supposedly at least a dozen women directors, from the 1950s onward, that made their films in Thailand, but there is little to no information about most of them other than a short mention in the Thai Film Archives.[83] Pimpaka Towira's short experimental horror film *Mae Nak* (1992) is the first horror film directed by a Thai woman. It retells the folk ghost story Mae Nak Phra Khanong (Lady Nak of Phra Khanong) about a woman who dies in childbirth and becomes a vengeful, angry spirit. Towira's version is from the point of view of the ghost herself.

Because Japan's women horror film directors began in earnest in the 1960s only in the pornography/horror industry, those films will be discussed in Chapter 8.

Isela Vega's *Las amantes del señor de la noche,* AKA *Lovers of the Lord of the Night,* was released in 1983 in Mexico and the United States in 1986.[84] Vega was a very famous actress in Mexico. She started her career in the 1960s by starring in numerous Mexican horror and action films like *Verano violento* (1960), Jack Hill's *Fear Chamber* (1968), *La señora Muerte* (1969), *Enigma de muerte* (1969), *Pacto diabólico* (1969), and *The Bloody Monks* (1988). Her best-known role is "Elita" in Sam Peckinpah's *Bring Me the Head of Alfredo Garcia* (1974). Having made over 130 films in her lifetime, Vega was always working. Considered an outspoken public figure, Vega was a Mexican sex symbol (the first Latina woman featured in *Playboy* magazine) with aggressive political opinions. She never stopped working until her death in 2021.[85] Hugo Argüelles, a famous screenwriter, wrote the script for *Lovers of the Lord of the Night* with Vega. He'd previously written the scripts for the Mexican horror film *Doña Macabra* (1972) and the action-thriller *La primavera de los escorpiones* (1971). Vega stars as Amparo, the witchy housekeeper who takes care of teenage Venus (Elena de Haro) and her father, Don Venustiano (Emilio Fernández). Arturo Vázquez is Pedro, the wealthy young man that Venus loves.

Vega creates her folk horror ambiance by portraying witchcraft as a woman's craft in the story. Amparo casts innocent charms throughout the film using kitchen bowls and herbal recipes. Bad omens abound in the form of a wild, black horse that appears to Venus and Amparo on their first trip to the witch Saurina's and again right before Amparo's execution. One dramatic scene is a silhouette of Venus riding on her dark-shadowed horse against a deep orange sunset. The imagery is impressive any time Venus rides her horse or has visions. The increasing violence, which culminates in a beheading, is intense. *Lovers of the Lord of the Night* is a thoughtful, absorbing film, disorienting in all the right ways. There is a disturbing scene of an actual chicken being killed for a magic spell to caution sensitive viewers. In a 2007 interview with *Shock Cinema* writer Nicanor Loreti, Isela was asked what made her want to direct, write, and star in a film. Her answer was only, "That's a good question. Sincerely, I don't know how I decided to play writer, producer, director, and actress, but I won't do it again."[86] Vega would never direct another film, though she would continue to act until her last year of life, 2021.

María Luisa Alcalá is an even less well-known horror film director than Vega. Also an actress in Mexico, Alcalá mostly appeared in comedies and, in later years, in soap operas. She did co-direct three films relevant to this book: *La Alacrana,* AKA *The Scorpion Woman* (1986), *Violación* (1989), and *Investigador privado ... muy privado* (1990). *Investigador privado ... muy privado* is a sex comedy, but the other two are violent thrillers. Alcalá directed *La Alacrana* with José Luis Urquieta, and, like Vega, she also acted in it. The lead was played by Maribel Guardia, who began her acting career in low-budget horror genre films and is now famous for her television work. Urquieta had a career making low-budget action films and Westerns in Mexico before he worked with Alcalá on *La Alacrana*. *La Alacrana* is a gritty, sleazy film about a sexy Mexico City homicide police detective Eugenia (Maribel Guardia), nicknamed "La Alacrana" (The Female Scorpion), who must catch and stop a deranged, religious serial killer from murdering pornography filmmakers. *Violación* was co-directed with Mexican B-movie star Valentín Trujillo, and both act in the film as Garrido (Trujillo) and Agustina (Alcalá). It's an action thriller about a woman

Amparo (Isela Vega) gets her head chopped off by angry villagers in *Lovers of the Lord of the Night* (1986).

A still from the violent Mexican thriller *Violación* (1989), directed by María Luisa.

named Laura (Olivia Collins) who is raped in her apartment. Garrido is a social justice warrior fighting for women's rights against their rapists. When the police determine that no crime was committed and refuse to go after the rapist, Garrido decides that Laura will need to get her personal revenge and justice through violence. Alcalá is not credited as co-director on either *La Alacrana* or *Violación;* in the 2020s, she has been recognized for her directing work.

From the first film she directed in 1989 to the writing of this book, filmmaker Aurora Martinez would direct an astounding two hundred and seventeen films, most of them action thrillers about criminals and Mexican drug dealers. Martinez does have five horror films on her resume, however: *Tarot sangriento* (1990), *Sueños de muerte* (1995), *Homicida religioso* (1997), *La verdadera historia de la llorona* (2007), and *Volver de los infiernos* (2007). Despite her prolific work, Martinez is elusive and generally unknown to genre film festivals.

In 2012, Mexican/American director Eva Aridjis released her witchcraft horror film *The Blue Eyes* (not to be confused with the 2021 thriller film *Blue Eyes* by Italian director Michela Cescon), which she set in Mexico. In 2017, director Issa López released the horror fantasy film *Tigers Are Not Afraid*, also set in Mexico, about childhood trauma and the ghosts of the Mexican drug cartel's crimes. Yulene Olaizola directed the horror film *Selva trágica*, AKA *Tragic Jungle* (2020), set deep in the Mayan jungles and inspired by Mexican folklore and legends. In 2010, Mexican/Canadian director Gigi Saul Guerrero began making short horror films that would get worldwide attention for their gruesomeness and high-quality direction. In 2019, her horror film *Culture Shock* was produced by Blumhouse and released on the streaming service Hulu. Her next feature film, *Bingo Hell*, was also produced by Blumhouse and released on the streaming service Amazon in 2021. Since the 2010s, many Mexican women directors have created horror film shorts.

Of all the lost horror films directed by women, to me, none is more of a loss to the horror community and the entertainment industry's history as a whole than the forgotten television horror films of Argentinean director Marta Reguera. Born in 1932, she worked as a camera assistant, and her horror work was her first job as a director. One of the first women filmmakers working in television in the country, she directed nineteen feature-length miniseries episodes of horror for the series *Obras maestras del terror,* AKA *Masterworks of Terror,* between 1960 and 1962. Originally a stand-alone horror anthology film of the same title, the inaugural *Obras maestras del terror* was directed by Enrique Carreras and aired on August 3, 1959, on Argentinean television's Channel 9 (it was later released as a film called *Master of Terror* in 1965 in the United States with one of the three segments, "The Tell-Tale Heart," taken out). All three segments starred Narciso Ibañez Menta, nicknamed "The Spanish Lon Chaney." The television movie was so successful that it was turned into a three-season television show, each episode as a stand-alone feature horror film. Instead of Carreras, a new director named Marta Reguera was hired for all nineteen new episodes, though they still starred Menta.

During the second season, one episode was Reguera's adaptation of Gaston Leroux's *The Phantom of the Opera*, *El fantasma de la ópera*. Feature-length, it was broken into segments and aired as a miniseries of nine episodes. *Masterpieces of Terror:* "The Phantom of the Opera" premiered on Channel 9 Saturday, July 2, 1960, starring Narciso Ibáñez Menta as Eric, the Phantom, Beatriz Dia Quiroga as Cristina, and Noemí Laserre as Carlota. Narciso Ibáñez Serrador, Menta's son, wrote the script under Luis Peñafiel. This first episode cemented the series as one of the most popular Argentinean TV series. The nine chapters aired every Saturday night through August 27, 1960, at 10:00 p.m. In the Argentinean newspaper *La Nación*, an article stated that the first episode terrified viewers who had not taken the new series seriously, expecting something far less frightening and being shocked.[87] At the time, Menta was publicly credited as the director, while Reguera was credited as the "camera director" or presumably the cinematographer. More recently, as women's film history comes under more scrutiny, it is generally agreed that Reguera was the "director" and Menta had significant creative input into the entire series. Enrique Carreras is listed as a director of the series in *Dirigido* magazine,[88] but no episodes are credited to him as director by sources like IMDb; he is only the director of the original anthology television film that kicked off the series.

The episode "El muñeco maldito" (1962) was based on the two Gaston Leroux stories "La Poupée Sanglante" and "La Machine à Assassiner." It is the most famous episode of the series. Filmmaker Juan Manuel Fontanals recalled in 1975 that on the night it aired in Buenos Aires, the streets were empty as people were glued to their television sets:

> Me acuerdo que el 30 de junio de 1962, la misma noche en que se transmitía el último capítulo, se casaba mi colega Potín Domínguez. Era tanta la expectativa por el final que, en un momento, todos se fueron a ver un televisor cercano y dejaron absolutamente solos a los novios en un salon. (I remember that on June 30, 1962, the same night the last episode was broadcast, my colleague Potín Domínguez got married. At the end, everyone, at one point, everyone went to watch a nearby television and left the bride and groom absolutely alone in a room.)[89]

A cameraman named Roberto Monfort worked on the show for the first time on the episode "El muñeco maldito" and remembered, in 1999, the way the videotape editing was done:

En esa época no había empalme electrónico: directamente se empalmaba la cinta de videotape y se pegaba. Se tardaba muchísimo en grabar, más de veinticuatro horas a veces. (At that time there was no electronic splicing: the videotape tape was directly spliced and glued. It took a long time to record, sometimes more than twenty-four hours.)[90]

The episodes of each season, not necessarily in order, are:

Season 1 (1959): "El corazón delator," "El caso de Míster Valdemar," "Ligeia," "Berenice," "El tonel del Amontillado," "El hombre y la bestia"

Season 2 (1960): "Al caer la noche," "La mano," "La carreta fantasma," "La figura de cera," "El hacha de oro," "El fantasma de la ópera," "Donde está marcada la cruz," "¿Es usted el asesino?"

Season 3 (1962): "El muñeco maldito," "La pata del mono," "Un hombre encantador—Las aventuras de Landrú," "Las huellas del diablo," "La chica que comía los pecados"

A newspaper ad for *Obras maestras del terror:* "La Muñeca Maldita" (1962), directed by Marta Reguera, courtesy of the Archivo Narciso Ibáñez Menta.

Ligeia, *Berenice*, *El fantasma de la ópera*, *La figura de cera*, and *La chica que comía los pecados* are listed as separate television films from the *Obras maestras del terror* television series in *Dirigido* magazine.[91] It seems evident that these were episodes of the series and not separate, stand-alone films. The series has been mistaken for the original anthology film that Carreras directed and vice-versa; the episodes were aired as miniseries rather than episodic films, which has led to confusion about which titles were films and which were episodes from the series. The entire series has been the subject of online speculation for film detectives (especially the episode "El fantasma de la opera") who have uncovered rumors that because the series was shot on video, it was recorded over and lost or that it was burned in a fire, or that the Argentinean government destroyed it.[92] We may never know. It's doubtful that the films will be recovered. "¿Es usted el asesino?" is also listed in several sources as a separate nine-episode miniseries in and of itself, so whether it was remade as a series after first appearing as a single episode of *Obras maestras del terror* or not is unclear. Reguera would continue to work in horror and often with Narciso Ibáñez Menta on numerous television series and films, including the horror film and miniseries *Ceremonia secreta* (1981) and *El Pulp Negro* (1985). She died in 1991.

In 1959, Reguera was not the only Argentinean woman director to direct horror in television film anthology format. María Herminia Avellaneda, who had a similar career trajectory to Reguera, began as an assistant director in 1955 on Channel 7 Argentinean television series right after she graduated from film school. On Tuesday, October 13, 1959, an obscure television horror film anthology titled *Antología de miedo* aired on Channel 7 at 11:30 p.m. The four-part anthology series, directed entirely by Avellaneda, featured a different film for each episode and continued each week through November 1959. The first segment was called "Lugar el Reunion," but the names of the three following features are lost, much like the series itself. *La Nacion* reviewed the first episode and said that while the anthology was clearly an attempt to capitalize off of the popularity of Channel 9's *Obras maestras del terror*, it was nonetheless "una idea finamente desarrollada en el libreto y un ejercicio de imaginación feliz en su exposición (a finely developed idea as a script and a happy exercise of imagination in its presentation)."[93] But what was it about? What were the other three segments? Who was the screenwriter, Carlos Arcidiacono, and why does he seem to have no other writing credits? Why was there no season two? Were any artwork or posters created to advertise the series? The anthology is a rumor at this point. One day, hopefully, we'll see the horror anthology work from these Argentinean directors widely available to horror fans.

Horror in Brazil didn't become a true phenomenon until a filmmaker named José Mojica Marins began his long career in 1964 with the film À Meia-Noite Levarei Sua Alma (*At Midnight I'll Take Your Soul*). Marins invented and starred as a character named Zé do Caixão (Coffin Joe) and eventually made two more films that became the official "Coffin Joe Trilogy." What is less well-known about Marins is that he co-directed two films with actress/director Rosângela Maldonado: *A Deusa de Mármore-escravo do Diabo,* AKA *The Marble Goddess, Slave of the Devil* (1978) (Marins denied this and claimed to have directed that film alone)[94] and *A Mulher Que Põe a Pomba no Ar* (1978). Maldonado became an actress in 1950s Brazil and developed a close relationship with Marins when she appeared in his films *Finis Hominis* (1971) and *Sexo E Sangue na Trilha do Tesouro* (1972). 1964 through 1985 was a period of political dictatorship for Brazil, during which a government agency, Embrafilme, simultaneously provided funds for artistic development in film and somewhat censored/guided the direction of Brazilian cinema as the dictatorship saw fit. Usually, filmmakers were left alone to make horror films, and by 1975 the Brazilian film industry was more extensive than ever, with physical theaters growing and audiences devouring films.

A Deusa de Mármore-escrava do Diabo is an erotic fantasy horror film in which Maldonado starred, wrote, produced, and co-directed with Marins. Marin plays a demon named Seu Sete Encruzilhada, while Maldonado plays a two-thouand-year-old goddess who keeps herself young by sucking the energy life force out of them when she seduces and kisses them. The glamour is reminiscent of the 1940s, with plenty of glitter, a "Hispano-Luso-Afro-Brazilian" vibe, and an odd shot of feminism combined, it seems, to create a very feminine but dark and sexy horror film.[95] *A Deusa de Mármore-escrava do Diabo* is a lost film; only poster art and a few photographs remain. However, her erotic fantasy movie *A Mulher Que Põe a Pomba no Ar*, AKA *The Woman Who Puts the Dove in the Air* (1978), is available to viewers. In the film, a scientist named Adelaide devises a unique way to get even with cheating men. She finds a way to contact beings from outer space that give women the magical ability to turn into giant doves (complete with go-go boots and glitter), and they use their new form to interrupt the sexual liaisons of cheaters. An erotic comedy with nudity and sex, *A Mulher Que Põe a Pomba no Ar* is a ridiculous film with extravagant low-budget costumes and a burlesque appeal. Rosângela Maldonado is credited as writer, Executive Director, and Artistic Director, with Marins credited (as J. Avelar) as Technical Director.

Brazilian experimental artist Lygia Pape's elusive short horror film *Wampirou* (*Vampire*) (1974) is a metaphor for the blood-sucking nature of the film industry (supposedly). Also, a fan of cannibalism as a metaphor, Pape's film work involved a lot of fake blood and a sense of radical humor. A Spanish museum that hosted Pape's film work in its gallery says that *Wampirou* is art in the spirit of the "Cinema Novo" and is "anthropophagous fiction notable for [its] refreshing irony."[96] Another art critic, however, disagrees and says:

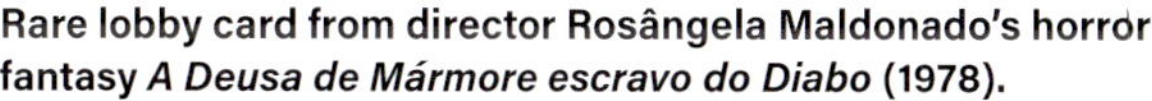
Rare lobby card from director Rosângela Maldonado's horror fantasy *A Deusa de Mármore escravo do Diabo* (1978).

> A silly film about a vampire in a black cape who roams around Rio biting people and reading copies of *The Hulk*. At one point, a man with a cross pops up and forces the bearded vampire, who looks like Russell Brand in a cloak, to retreat behind a curtain. Perhaps some sort of artistic attack on the role of the church in Brazilian politics is intended, à la Goya. Who knows?[97]

There were no true horror films made in Brazil by women directors in the last quarter of the twentieth century. It would not be until the horror movies *Trabalhar Cansa,* AKA *Hard Labor* (2011) and *As Boas Maneiras,* AKA *Good Manners* (2017), both co-directed by Juliana Rojas (with Marco Dutra), were made that another woman would direct a genre film in Brazil. Rojas was followed by a boom of horror films directed by women, such as Anita Rocha da Silveira's *Kill Me Please* (2015), Gabriela Amaral's *Friendly Beast* (2017), and Alice Furtado's *Sem Seu Sangue* (2019). Brazilian filmmaker Natalia Leite's thriller *M.F.A.* (2017) was an American production.

In other nations, such as Laos, Bolivia, Kazakhstan, Finland, Barbados, South Korea, Israel, Lebanon, Latvia, Lithuania, Colombia, Iran, Iceland, Benin, Ecuador, Egypt, Malaysia, the Dominican Republic, South Africa, Switzerland, Ireland, Bahrain, Belgium, Panama, Romania, Peru, Croatia, Montenegro, Uruguay, Zambia, Scotland and even the Maldives and the Faroe islands, women also did not direct feature-length genre films until the turn of the twenty-first century, give or take a decade in some cases. Nations not mentioned have no history of women directing genre films.

Chapter 5

Some nudity required

STRIPPERS, SEQUELS AND VHS

A haunting image from Denice Duff's vampire romance, *Song of the Vampire* AKA *Vampire Resurrection* (2003).

THE VHS REVOLUTION OF THE early 1980s created a new avenue of film distribution that would last until the late 1990s, when DVD technology made VHS tapes obsolete. Just as when television had sparked new directing roles for women in the 1960s, and independent theaters had increased demand for new content in the 1970s, in the 1980s, many women found themselves directing genre films that either went to theaters and then to VHS or directly to VHS, which was considered an utterly viable distribution strategy. Many specialized in low-budget horror films, and small production companies began releasing them.

There had previously been a shortage of directing jobs for women, there was now a flood of new films needing to be made, and women were making them. Women directors like Jackie Kong (*The Being*, 1983), Deryn Warren (*Mirror of Death*, 1988), Janet Greek (*Spellbinder*, 1988), and Amy Holden Jones (*The Slumber Party Massacre*, 1982) were in the middle of this revolution and began their careers in horror filmmaking then. Numerous horror episodic and anthology series required numerous directors, so women were hired to direct some of the most iconic and well-remembered horror television series of all time. Along with the rush of film sequels to successful horror films, television was again opening doors for women that they felt were closed.

By the 1990s, new women directors of horror didn't feel so out of place. When discussing her horror movie *Mirror Mirror* (1990) in a 1991 interview with *Fangoria* magazine, Marina Sargenti said at the time of the shooting that "no one is surprised anymore to find the producer is a woman, and women are directors are falling right in line," and continued, saying that working as a woman director with an all-male crew can seem intimidating at first, but "if you go in knowing what you're doing, let them know you know what you want and you understand what has to be done to get it, it all works out."[1]

When Roger Corman asked Stephanie Rothman to reshoot scenes for the horror film *Track of the Vampire* in 1966 (covered in Chapter 3), Corman opened the door to numerous women as filmmakers in his company, Concorde-New Horizons, and he and Julie Corman would continue to hire them as directors, producers, writers, and editors. Most female-directed, Corman-produced horror films are a product of Corman's company. After Rothman, women horror film directors with whom the Cormans worked include Barbara Peeters (*Humanoids from the Deep*, 1980), Amy Holden Jones (*The Slumber Party Massacre*, 1982), Deborah Brock (*The Slumber Party Massacre II*, 1986), Susan Shadburne (*Shadow Play*, 1986), Sally Mattison (*The Slumber Party Massacre III*, 1990), Carol Frank (*Sorority House Massacre*, 1986), Katt Shea (*Stripped to Kill*, 1985), Penelope Spheeris (*Suburbia*, 1983), Tina Hirsch (*Munchies*, 1987), Mary Ann Fisher (*Lords of the Deep*, 1989), Kristine Peterson (*Body Chemistry*, 1990), Talia Shire (*One Night Stand*, 1995), Victoria Muspratt (*Circuit Breaker*, 1996), Catherine Cyran (*Sawbones*, 1995), Rachel Samuels (*Running Woman*, 1998), and Gwyneth Gibby (*Black Scorpion Returns*, 2001). "The Corman School had an unusually high 'enrollment' of promising women writers, producers, editors, and directors in part because historically the industry had been and still was very difficult to crack for untested women," said Roger Corman in his career autobiography *How I Made a Hundred Movies in Hollywood and Never Lost a Dime*, "but I always felt inclined to give women an equal shot, even though not many women were eager to work in exploitation in those days."[2]

Along with Stephanie Rothman, Barbara Peeters was one of the most prominent women directors in exploitation and genre films in the 1970s. Peeters had previously written and directed an independent, soft-core lesbian exploitation film called *The Dark Side of Tomorrow,* AKA *Just the Two of Us* (1970), and a biker/Western revenge film titled *Bury Me an Angel* (1971). She had worked for Corman as a production manager, second unit director, and location manager on films like *Night Call Nurses* (1972) when he hired her to direct the exploitation sex comedy *Summer School Teachers* (1974), her third film as director. Peeters also directed the 1978 science fiction film *Star Hops* (from a modified script written by Stephanie Rothman) for Corman before being hired to helm the monster movie *Humanoids from the Deep* (1980).

In the September 2010 issue of *Fangoria* magazine, editor Chris Alexander posed the following question to Roger Corman: "*Humanoids* is full of sex, nudity, and sexual violence. Having a woman—Barbara Peeters—direct it was unusual. Did you hire a woman because the subject matter was potentially volatile?" to which Corman responded, "No, I brought Barbara on board because she was a good director."[3] Peeters, however, in a different interview, said that he " offered it to all the boys, but the boys turned it down. It was a terrible script. So he offered it to me."[4]

Humanoids from the Deep is a creature feature with aquatic amphibian monsters (men in suits) that come on shore to the fishing town of Noyo, California, to rape the local women to continue their race. The basic plot follows the cookie-cutter creature-feature outline: a hero must save people from a monster in the water during a major festival that is the town's biggest source of income. An evil corporation had experimented with growth hormones for salmon and contaminated the local waters, causing the fish to mutate into hideous creatures with an insatiable sex lust. *Humanoids* has a gloriously awful scene of a mutant baby popping out of a raped woman's belly.

Peeters seems to have had a high opinion of Corman during the filming of *Summer School Teachers* and *Star Hops*. "God bless Norman Lear and Roger Corman," said Peeters in an interview in 1978,

> They are two of the few people who are serious about letting women direct ... As long as you open big and close big and try to resolve three stories in the end, Roger lets you do what you want. Just be sure you put in either a sex scene or an action sequence every fifteen minutes.[5]

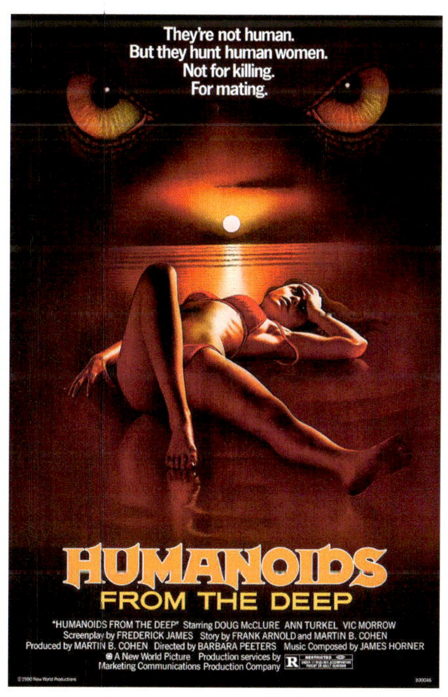

Humanoids from the Deep (1980) poster.

Despite this mutual respect, Peeters and Corman would ultimately disagree strongly over the outcome of *Humanoids from the Deep*. Filming commenced on the low-budget horror film, and what followed was a monster movie rife with feminist subtext as well as a controversial final cut of the movie that Peeters hated. Peeters, as a director, wasn't big on gratuitous gore: In 1978, Peeters said:

> I move in very closely and try to show the sensuality that creates the sexuality. There are as many different ways to do a love scene as there are people ... Ordinarily, violence repels me, yet in *Bury Me an Angel* I show a head spew blood. I did that because it's a story about a girl who slowly goes insane while looking for her brother's killer. How could I make the audience understand what she is going through unless they are shocked in the same way she was?[6]

In that same 2010 *Fangoria* interview, Corman said,

> On *Humanoids*, we stayed within the boundaries of the R rating and had no problem getting it. If I remember correctly, we had to cut very little, if anything. When I talked to Barbara about the movie initially, I told her that the premise was very simple: the humanoids rape the women and kill the men. And she said, "OK, got it," and that's what she did![7]

But according to Peeters, that is not at all what happened.

On May 6, 1980, right after the release of *Humanoids from the Deep* in theaters, an article in the Los Angeles Times was written by Andrew Epstein. "*Humanoids from the Deep*," it began, "a low-budget, sci-fi thriller about genetic experimentation gone haywire, is causing special distress for its female director and female star."[8] The article would describe how Peeters and *Humanoids* star Ann Turkel were shocked and upset by new nude rape scenes that had been added to the film after production. Entirely new scenes had been shot with the humanoid creatures and added blood, guts, gore, rape, and plenty of "tits and ass." During the shooting, Turkel and Peeters had been told that the film's title was *Beneath the Darkness*, which sounded far classier, according to Turkel, who said, "Now it's a B-title and a B-movie. I never would have made a movie with a title like *Humanoids*. That title is a joke."[9] Producer Martin Cohen, who also co-wrote the original script, said that it was initially called *Humanoids from the Deep*, but *Beneath the Darkness* was the working title during production:

> I liked the first title [*Humanoids from the Deep*] much better. I contacted Roger after the picture was done and explained that I don't want the public to be misled. I think *Beneath the Darkness* sounds like a story about a mental institution. My story is about humanoids.[10]

James Sbardellati,[11] the second-unit director on the film, was hired by Corman to film new, more sensational scenes that would later be interspersed into Peeter's original footage, and some brand-new footage was shot by uncredited director Jimmy T.

Murakami, without Peeter's knowledge. Of the new scenes in which the humanoids rape actresses, Turkel complained, "The added stuff is like out of a bad pornography movie."[12] Cohen, however, said of the humanoid rape scenes when interviewed: "What's too much T&A? How do you argue that? You and I are men and we look at women differently. A woman director just has a different point of view toward sexuality."[13]

Even as late as 2010, Corman states that he and Peeters discussed precisely his expectations for the film's violence levels. He felt that Peeters did a great job filming the death scenes of the male characters but that the rape scenes she shot were too "shadowy" and had too many cutaways.[14] While Peeters disliked the additional scenes with the humanoids, the extra blood and gore, and the film's title change, the insertion of rape and overt violence against nude women in her film for cheap thrills seemed to have hurt her the most. A *Variety* review of *Humanoids from the Deep* explicitly called her out for being a woman director making movies that were blatantly showing women being hurt as entertainment: "The irony of the entire production, which will confound feminist-minded crix (critics), is that a female director was behind one of the more woman-degrading pix to come down the pike in some seasons."[15]

Not only was Peeters criticized for her role in *Humanoids from the Deep* for the perceived offensive content she was presumed to have directed, but she was also explicitly critiqued because she was a woman director, who, according to the *Variety* review, must have an additional responsibility to make films that are devoid of material that sensualizes rape. Peeters said:

> I'm not opposed to shooting nudity. I've shot nudity before but only when it was integrated into the story. I've never shot rape or violence toward women, or things that would be mean or degrading. I've shot a lot of B-movies and I've stayed away from rape. If I was ever to shoot it I would do it as ugly and unsensual as rape is ... what frightens me the most is that if this picture makes a lot of money, someone will call me and ask me to do another. This whole thing just turned out to be an experience of horror.[16]

On May 25, 1980, a printed response from Roger Corman to Peeters and Turkel's article appeared in the *Los Angeles Times*. In it, he writes that not only did he not produce Peeters' 1974 film *Summer School Teachers* (it was produced by Julie Corman and released by New World Pictures), but he also did not produce *Humanoids from the Deep*. He says that Martin Cohen and Hunt Lowry alone produced it. He takes particular affront at the article's tone, saying that it seemed to suggest that *Humanoids* was an anti-feminist film and that he was "some sort of male chauvinist." He continued to defend the film:

> While I did not produce *Humanoids*, my company did distribute it and checking our copies of reviews, I find a majority of critics who discuss such things in their reviews felt *Humanoids* was a strong feminist statement in the guise of a horror film.[17]

Was it?

Of the final version of *Humanoids*, "It's drek," said Peeters in 2010.[18]

Only revealed years afterward was the fact that Peeters was fighting terminal-stage melanoma at the time production started. The hoops she jumped through to get a medical clearance for the film's insurance and the illness were challenging and unpleasant experiences. Peeters was also a Director's Guild of America member by the time Corman hired her—but his films were non-union. At one point, a DGA representative found her and fined her $15,000 for working on a non-union film (which meant Peeters didn't get a paycheck for *Humanoids*). "If I start a movie, I finish a movie, union or non-union," she told the rep.[19] Gary Morris has observed of *Humanoids* that:

> In spite of its success, it marked the end of her directorial career. Corman's magic touch, which catapulted Joe Dante, Jonathan Demme, and others from exploitation into the mainstream, didn't work with Peeters (or Stephanie Rothman, for that matter); after 1980, her name appears only on forgotten television shows like *Misfits of Science* and *Shadow Chasers* (both 1985).[20]

The most culturally relevant horror film directed by a woman and produced by Roger Corman is *The Slumber Party Massacre*, which, together with its two sequels, established the iconic Driller Killer character and cemented women directors as horror movie canon. *The Slumber Party Massacre* series is the first horror film series written and directed by women. "All *The Slumber Party Massacre* films were directed by women because Roger Corman thought that a female director would have more insight into teenage girl slumber parties than a male director would," said Priscilla "Sally" Mattison, the director of *The Slumber Party Massacre III* in a 2001 interview with *The Slumber Party Massacre* researcher Tony Brown:

> I'm not sure how true that theory was—given that my slumber party days ended in about third grade—but directing opportunities for women are still hard to come by and thus much appreciated. I should also credit Roger for hiring lots of women in all sorts of jobs, from running his studio to working as producers, writers, and directors.[21 / 22]

Noted feminist and lesbian author Rita Mae Brown (who now has most of her recent work co-authored by her cat Sneaky Pie Brown) wrote a screenplay parody of teen/slasher flicks called *Don't Open the Door*, which ended up at Concorde-New Horizons. Frances Doel, head of scripts at Corman's company, showed it to editor Amy Holden Jones, who wanted a chance to direct her first film and asked Corman to do so. Deciding she'd direct a short seven-minute version of the first few pages in 35mm as a proof of concept for Corman, Holden Jones filmed the first few pages of the feature script with cinematographer Michael Chapman, cut from the final feature version. She edited the short on Joe Dante's Moviola as he finished editing his feature horror film *The Howling* (1981). Dante called Corman to tell him that the seven-minute short was good and that Corman already owned the script. "What was most clever was that she structured it so that it could be used as the opening scene of a possible feature version, which naturally appealed to Roger," said Dante when asked.[23] "Plus, it was very professionally directed."

The Driller Killer stalks Trish (Michele Michaels) and Kim (Debra De Liso) in Amy Holden Jones' *The Slumber Party Massacre* (1982).

The girls strip down and dance at their slumber party in Sally Mattison's sleazy sequel, *Slumber Party Massacre III* (1990).

The film's name changed from *Don't Open the Door* to *Sleepless Night* and finally to *The Slumber Party Massacre,* and it was theatrically released in 1982. In the movie, a cast of six female characters is terrorized by a man killing them with a power drill. The drill is phallic, and it's symbolic, etc., which you can read about *ad nauseam* in Carol J. Clover's famous 1992 book *Men, Women, and Chain Saws: Gender in the Modern Horror Film*, in which archetypes, feminism, Freudian psychology, and other abstract ideologies are used to analyze *The Slumber Party Massacre* series as well as slasher films in general. "I was interviewed by a professor at UC Berkeley about slasher films," said Corman filmmaker Catherine Cyran about Clover:

"She'd done a lot of research. If a woman has had sex in a slasher film, she's definitely going to get killed. The girl who survives has never had sex, is uptight, a tomboy, and almost always has a male name."[24]

Amy Holden Jones's film is played straight for scares. Holden Jones described Brown's original script as "serious," to the point that Holden Jones added humor. If Rita Mae Brown did write the screenplay as a parody of slasher films, it wasn't directed or marketed that way. She modified Brown's original script to fulfill the "requirements of the genre" but was worried about making something "politically incorrect."[25] Holden Jones had wanted actress Jamie Lee Curtis to star in the film as Valerie, and secondly, Meg Tilly, who were both eager to do so, but Corman wouldn't offer more than $25,000 to either of them, and their agents wouldn't make the deals. The entire film itself had a budget of $250,000.[26]

High school senior Trish (Michelle Michaels) has a slumber party with her friends Kim (Debra Deliso), Jackie (Andree Honore), and Diane (Gina Mari). Her next-door neighbor, the shy Valerie (Robin Stille), doesn't attend because she feels slighted by the other girls. Teenage boys Jeff (David Millbern) and Neil (Joseph Alan Johnson) interrupt their slumber party by playing dumb pranks on the girls, like turning off all of the electricity, to scare them, and the girls are not happy about it. That's why when escaped mentally ill serial killer Russ Thorn (Michael Villella) begins killing them one by one, they believe he is part of the prank. Thorn's weapon of choice is a power drill, and the bodies pile up while the girls slowly realize they're in danger. *The Slumber Party Massacre* has a satisfying body count and violent gore; while not bathed in blood, the film shows dead bodies and the drill as it murders them. The only signs that the original script was supposed to be a satire of slashers is that writer Rita Mae Brown's book *Rubyfruit Jungle* is visible in a scene, and at the high school, there are signs saying, "Join the Drill Team!" and "Emergency Drill Instructions" posted in the background and in the scene in which Linda is drilled to death. "It was a good, solid film," said Holden Jones in an interview, "A violent film, but one that has some very funny parts. Also, I find the suspense fascinating. I think most people like suspense. Ghost stories go straight to your unconscious. There is a great release from working on them because your primal fears provide a lot of inspiration."[27]Actors Brinke Stevens and Deborah DeLiso began their careers as Scream Queens in *The Slumber Party Massacre*. They would star in films like *Slave Girls from Beyond Infinity* (1987) and *Sorority Babes in the Slime-Ball Bowl-O-Rama* (1988). Stevens played Linda, Thorn's first victim, and dies during a nude scene in the high school locker room showers. She worked on the film for three days and remembered Holden Jones as "One of the hardest working directors [she] had ever met."[28]

When *The Slumber Party Massacre* came out in theaters, it was reviled by the critics. Called "An infuriatingly stupid slasher film" by reviewer Richard Taylor "made all the more ridiculous because it was created by feminist types."[29] Holden Jones defended her film by saying:

> More boys die on camera, by far, than girls, and far more brutally, as well. This is the nature of the genre. It's not about violence against women any more than *The Omen* is about child abuse. I was a young feminist then and I'm a middle-aged one now. There were precious few strong women on-screen at that point. I've made a whole career out of trying to change that. This was the beginning, humble though it may be.[30]

Holden Jones went on to direct female-oriented films such as *Maid to Order* (1987) and *Love Letters* (1984), but never again would she direct horror.

The Slumber Party Massacre II, released in 1986, is both a return to and a far cry from the first *The Slumber Party Massacre*. Written and directed by Deborah Brock and produced once again by Roger Corman, the film stars Crystal Bernard as Courtney, the little sister of Valerie and the only survivor of the original driller killer massacres. Courtney is pained by horrific memories and new dreams of a driller killer/rock musician stalking her while singing rockabilly with a guitar weapon. Flashbacks to *The Slumber Party Massacre* provide some background on the storyline, but the killer himself (who appears only in dreams for the first seventy-five percent of the film) is completely unrelated to the antagonist in the previous film. (Incidentally, there is a quick shot of Courtney pulling back some bloody sheets on a bed in one of her dream sequences; it's not a flashback to the first film, but a bit of footage from *Sorority House Massacre*, Corman's 1986 movie about women trapped in a sorority house with a killer, and the woman pulling back the sheets is the character Beth, who also has bad dreams in *Sorority House Massacre*.)

The Driller Killer (as he is affectionately known in the second film) has returned, reincarnated as an evil rocker out to kill with his guitar, which has a drill bit on the end of it. Of course, capitalizing on the cheesy, campy rock band fetish of the late eighties,

Brock and Corman make music the main focus of this movie. Corman, never one to miss an opportunity to copy himself or promote his older films, conveniently shows a scene from *Rock and Roll High School* (1979) on the television set at the slumber party. By the time Brock was hired, Corman had already sold the rights to the film based on the title (*Don't Let Go: The Slumber Party Massacre II*) and needed it finished quickly. "As long as it was a horror movie involving high school girls and a drill, I could make it pretty much what I wanted it to be."[31] Brock believes that Corman hired her because he had a problem (no film) and needed a quick fix (someone to make it), but she also believes that Corman did give more women first jobs than anyone in Hollywood.[32]

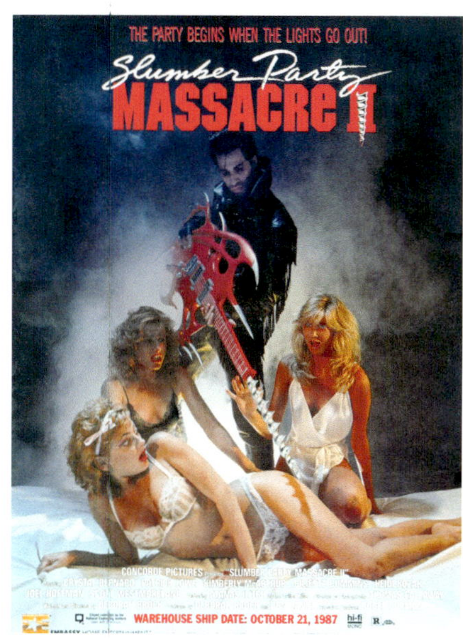

Poster art for *Slumber Party Massacre II* (1986).

The third installment in *The Slumber Party Massacre* series was released in 1990.

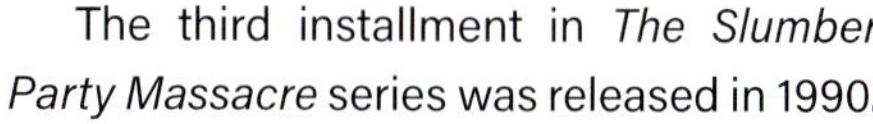

This time the script was written and produced by Catherine Cyran (who later went on to direct the mad-doctor-slasher television film *Sawbones* in 1995, also produced by Roger Corman.) and originally titled *Night Light*. "It was the first movie in which I sold my soul," said Cyran,

> It was a slasher. Roger Corman knew that I wanted to write and produce. He said, "I've got a project for you." Hahaha. He's like the Devil. "How would you like to do *Slumber Party Massacre III*?" I said, "I can't think of anything I'd like to do less." He said, "I'll let you produce it, but you have to let me know in the next hour." So, in the next hour, I decided that it was good experience.[33]

The film was directed by newcomer Sally Mattison, who, like Holden Jones and Brock, was given her first directing job with *The Slumber Party Massacre* series. "I'd been on staff with Concorde-New Horizons for a couple of years, and I had told Roger Corman that I wanted to direct," said Mattison in a 2001 interview. "One day, he suddenly asked if I wanted to direct *Slumber Party Massacre III*, and I said, gulp, yes!"[34] *The Slumber Party Massacre III* was released in 1990 to a theatrical audience. It involved the traditional driller-killer theme but emphasized the original phallic symbolism and female nudity to such an extent that the result was a comprehensive, silly, engaging, and fun film. With an all-B-star cast of women like former playmates Brandi Burkett and Maria Ford, *The Slumber Party Massacre III* involved the traditional red herrings that had been so sorely missed in the second installment of the series. It's essentially a remake of the first film in the series, with more brutality in the killings, encouraged by Corman, who wanted it to be graphic: "I decided that if I were being asked to make a slasher film, I would give people what they seemed to want—more than they wanted, maybe, to get them to think about it," explained Mattison.[35]

Though *The Slumber Party Massacre* films originally were marketed as the first slasher films written and directed by women, which they were not (Lois Weber's short *Suspense*, discussed in Chapter 1, is arguably the first, but in terms of feature films, Doris Wishman, discussed in Chapter 3, and Tonia Marketaki, discussed in Chapter 4, had made films with the essential slasher elements several decades earlier than Jones), they are important in that they all feature women in traditionally male roles; producer, director, and writer. Corman marketed the films as "feminist" because that would sell the films. The fact that there were women making movies that showed women getting naked and being murdered was, and is, fascinating to horror fans. Clover goes on about the deeply phallic and sexist, and feminist symbolism in the films. Holden Jones cites the solid and well-written female characters as an embodiment of feminist filmmaking despite the brutal and senseless murders of those characters by a man. Corman's hiring of women directors, especially for a slasher series which is usually all about appeasing male filmmakers' audience members, is, in and of itself, a feminist act. *The Slumber Party Massacre* series is a slasher film series with an interesting gimmick (women filmmakers) that serves a real function (he wanted the women to create the story about a woman's slumber party) and is open to interpretation by critics, scholars, and fans. As Cyran put it, "Certain producers ... perceive these films are about empowering women because usually, they end up killing the bad guys."[36] Unmarred by the tragic suicide of *The Slumber Party Massacre* star Robin Stille (she played "Val") in 1996, who had become a working Scream Queen based on her performance in the film, the legacy of the series lives on as some of the most well-known horror films directed by women. The film series was a major event that normalized women as horror film directors beginning in the 1980s.

After *The Slumber Party Massacre* came out in 1982, Roger soon realized that there was serious potential in making more slasher films about women and hiring women to direct them. Carol Frank, fresh off *The Slumber Party Massacre* as the Assistant Director to Amy Holden Jones, wrote the script for the film *Sorority House Massacre* (1986) and directed it. Pitting innocent, boyish Beth against a psychotic, escaped mental patient, Frank created a more intense, brooding atmosphere in *Sorority House Massacre* than had been designed in the *Slumber Party Massacre* films. Utilizing ideas from *A Nightmare on Elm Street* (1984) (dream imagery; later to appear in *The Slumber Party Massacre II* as well) and traditional slasher films, Beth (played by Angela O'Neill) is a classic 'Final Girl,' a bit tomboyish, and ultimately survives the attack. *Sorority House Massacre* never gained the traction that *The Slumber Party Massacre* films did, with either the box office or cult followings. Though it plays with the same ideas of women being murdered by a killer in a distinctly female space (a sorority house), it just doesn't make much of an impact. Many scenes from *The Slumber Party Massacre* are inserted as parts of the dream sequences, no doubt to save time and money, and it feels disjointed and uninspired. Corman gave up on the idea of this series being made by women when he hired director Jim Wynorski to direct *Sorority House Massacre II*.

This is an excellent time to mention the documentary *Some Nudity Required* (1998), co-directed by Johanna Demetrakas and Odette Springer. *Some Nudity Required* is narrated from the point of view of director Odette Springer who worked as Roger Corman's music supervisor on exploitation and horror films from 1990 to 1995 and felt compelled to make a film about her experiences as well as the experiences of various actresses, like Brinke Stevens, Maria Ford, and Julie Strain, who starred in many of Corman's films. Contemplating the nudity and violence against women in most of the slasher and exploitation films, *Some Nudity Required* explores how sex and violence may be harmful to women's psyches, especially the actresses playing the roles. The most affected of the group seems to be Maria Ford (who starred in *Stripped to Kill II*, 1989, and *The Slumber Party Massacre III*); she is conflicted about her career in many ways. In between director Springer randomly singing her compositions and discussing her childhood, actresses and filmmakers are interviewed candidly.

Some Nudity Required is interesting from a cinephile's point of view in that it provides an additional context to the female experience in B-movies, but it is shockingly one of the only documentaries (mainly) about Roger Corman and his films that features interviews with any of the women directors working for Corman. Catherine Cyran, the writer of *The Slumber Party Massacre III* and the director of the Corman-produced television horror film *Sawbones*, gives a rare interview on screen. Cyran, Mattison, Brock, Shea, and Holden Jones are not even mentioned in Alex Stapleton's 2011 documentary *Corman's World: Exploits of a Hollywood Rebel* (as I complained earlier in Chapter 3). *Some Nudity Required* is a somewhat pretentious walk into Springer's insecurities about her career and sense of self. Still, the context of this strangely narcissistic production makes it essential as a documentation of women's experiences working in horror films.

The cable television network Showtime approached Roger and Julie Corman to create a series of made-for-television original horror and science fiction films that would air exclusively on their channel. Of the thirty films made for the *Roger Corman Presents* series, several were directed by women: Victoria Muspratt's *Circuit Breaker* (1996), Catherine Cyran's *Sawbones* (1995), Katt Shea's *Last Exit to Earth* (1996, produced by Julie), and Gwenyth Gibby's *Marquis de Sade* (1996). In *Some Nudity Required*, Catherine Cyran candidly spoke about making movies in which women are murdered and nude. She doesn't have a problem making movies and, in fact, ambitiously worked her way up in Corman's school to do just that. "I also have a chip on my shoulder," she said about making horror films:

> I don't want to be prissy about doing something. I'm obviously not out to exploit women. But if someone says, "I want you to direct this sex scene, and I want lots of nudity." There's a thing that you should not hire a woman because she'll be prissy about it, and you won't get a good hard sex scene. I want to be able to do it just as well as them. I just don't want to do it at all. But if I am going to do it, I want to do it just as good as the boys do it.[37]

Cyran used this philosophy in the film *Sawbones* (also released as *Prescription for Murder*). In the film, police Detective Burt Miller (Adam Baldwin) is looking for a demented, failed medical student who kidnaps victims and performs basement surgeries to fulfill his fantasies of being a doctor. Baldwin (*Full Metal Jacket*, 1987, but known best to horror fans for his role as Jayne Cobb on Joss Whedon's short-lived science fiction series *Firefly*) does what he does best: act like a jerk while the brave and oppressed Jenny (Nina Siemaszko, Dr. Amelia Emerson in *The Haunting of Molly Hartley*, 2008) works to solve the murders with some reluctant help from Detective Miller. Don Harvey (*Creepshow 2*, 1987) is the psycho Willy Knapp, and Nicholas Sadler (*Hellraiser: Inferno*, 2000 and Professor Cooper in Stacy Title's 2017, and final horror film *The Bye Bye Man*) is Jenny's cheating, cold boyfriend Brad Fraser who she ultimately saves from Willy Knapp. Despite Harvey and Sadler looking almost identical to the point that it's hard to tell if they're supposed to be the same character for the first twenty minutes, Sawbones is a fine example of television horror from the 1990s. There's blood and a lot of violence, but the gore is tuned down. Medical equipment makes a great set of murder weapons, but Cyran was prevented, by the television medium, from going all-out on the bone cutter saw sequences, unfortunately. *Sawbones* was the Corman attempt to ride the coattails of the higher-budget theatrical medical horror movies from the same time, especially the very similar plotline of *Dr. Giggles* (1992) and the buzz around *The Dentist* (1996).

After writing *The Slumber Party Massacre III*, Cyran also directed the erotic thriller *In the Heat of Passion II: Unfaithful* (1994), the action thriller *Hostile Intentions* (1995), and the television thriller *Dangerous Waters* (1999), all for the Cormans. "It's no joke that men get a hard-on from seeing women in jeopardy" is just one of Cyran's unequivocal observances when discussing violence against women in exploitation films. Her first film was a family film (*White Wolves: A Cry in the Wild II* in 1993, produced by Julie Corman), and she returned to her roots after making films for the Cormans. "I believe that all movies affect people. That's why it's betraying yourself to make movies like that. It's the idea of working from the inside. You get to where you can make differences."[38] After making *The Prince & Me II: The Royal Wedding* (2006), it's been chiefly Christmas films for Cyran. My favorite quote from Cyran from *Some Nudity Required* is her astute observation of how random and not merit-based the entertainment industry can be, especially for directors. "Every day that I walk into a room and out of a room," she explains, "And I get a call from someone, 'Hey, that producer really liked you. He likes girls with big hair.' I'm a fucking director, but he likes girls with big hair. So guess what? I might get the job."[39]

Penelope Spheeris is one of my favorite women directors, not only because her career bounces back and forth between high-budget Hollywood comedies and self-financed, independent music documentary projects but because she remains uncorrupted by Hollywood's bullshit despite having a long career right in the thick of it. She says things in interviews like "Hollywood can blow me."[40]

After getting her master's degree in film at UCLA, Penelope Spheeris worked for a short time writing sketches for the first season of the television comedy series *Saturday Night Live* before independently directing and producing the world-famous rock n roll documentary *The Decline of Western Civilization* (1981). Her next film would be the feature narrative *Suburbia* (1983), produced by Roger Corman. *Suburbia* is a coming-of-age thriller about teenagers attending punk concerts, living on the streets, dealing with abusive parents, and committing crimes, mainly a tragic murder. Spheeris says that she wanted to make a movie about "a group of disenfranchised punk kids who had been rejected by their biological families," but at Roger Corman's urging, had put in sex and violence:

> Roger told me his formula was that his films needed either some sex or violence every ten minutes and asked me to write those scenes. I didn't want to, but it was the only way I could get the movie made. Those scenes included the toddler torn up by the dog in the opening, the girl getting her dress torn off at a punk concert, and the kids ripping off suburban garages and getting into fights. I would have preferred to have made the film without those scenes, but evidently, they worked. Flea from the [Red Hot] Chili Peppers says wherever he goes to perform around the world, *Suburbia* is referred to as the "Punk Rock Bible."[41]

Spheeris's next film, *The Boys Next Door* (1985), written by James Wong (who would go on to produce the *Final Destination* films), is also a very violent movie about teenagers. In it, two high school outcasts, played by Maxwell Caulfield and Charlie Sheen, embark on a nihilistic road trip crime spree after graduation, engaging in random acts of violence and murder until they face an eventual gun standoff with police and one of them is killed. Many people consider *The Boys Next Door* to be a horror film. "I never perceived the film as a horror film, but many people did," said Spheeris. "To me, it was an anti-violence message.[42]" It also wasn't a project Spheeris wanted to be involved with. "I really didn't want to direct *The Boys Next Door*," admits Spheeris,

"But I needed to pay the bills. I didn't realize I was so skilled at directing violence until I did that movie. We had to go many times to the MPAA, make extreme edits, in order to get an R rating instead of an X."[43]

Both films deal with hopeless youth engaging in violent acts to rebel against a world they consider unfair and meaningless. "As far as youth angst goes," said Spheeris, "it is common to every generation of late teens/early twenties kids. It must be something in our DNA. Anxiety, anger, search for identity."[44] Spheeris would have a very successful commercial career directing comedies like *Wayne's World* (1992) and *Black Sheep* (1996) while independently making two sequels to *The Decline of Western Civilization*.

Corman's most successful, constantly-working woman director hire is Katt Shea. At age nineteen, Shea drove from Michigan to Los Angeles to pursue a career in film. Working first as an actress, Shea co-starred with Lana Clarkson in the Corman-produced fantasy adventure film *Barbarian Queen* (1985). She's one of Norman Bates' victims in *Psycho III* (1986). Shea loved working in films, and she wanted to direct. While working on a film in the Philippines, she and Andy Ruben, who would become her husband, began writing together, eventually creating a creative partnership that would last for a decade. Their first script together was about a woman police officer going undercover as a stripper to catch a serial killer. This story would flesh out into the horror thriller *Stripped to Kill* (1987).

Shea explains the way the story for *Stripped to Kill* was born: one night, Shea and Ruben were having dinner when he told her that there were times of the year when mussels were poisonous. She wasn't sure she believed him. So they made a bet: if she lost, she would

The VHS cover art for *Stripped to Kill 2* (1989), directed by Katt Shea.

have to go to a strip club with him. She lost the bet. "I didn't want to go and see these women being exploited," she said,

> But we went to The Body Shop, and I fell in love with it all[45] ... I saw a girl swinging around on a pole, and I thought, "Oh my god, this has got to be in a movie!" I mean, nobody knows this goes on except a bunch of guys with dollar bills, so it just had to be exploited, I guess. I thought they were very artistic, and I just loved the girls, they were real artists, and they were just using this particular venue to explore their art.[46]

With a script written, Shea knew the next step was to get Corman to produce it and let her direct it. She waited outside his office as lunchtime approached. When he came out, she "accidentally" bumped into him and said,

> "Roger, I've got this fantastic idea for a movie, and it involves strippers! You're not gonna believe it, they fly around this pole, and here's what the poster will look like!" And his eyes are just getting bigger and bigger. So he says, "Come into my office Monday morning." Andy said to me, "When you pitch him, tell him you're gonna direct it." And unbelievably, Roger was open to it.[47]

Excitedly in the planning stages of their film, Shea and Ruben were sidelined when Corman suddenly changed his mind and didn't want to do the film anymore. When he called Shea to cancel the project, she just told him no, that's not happening. "I go, 'Yes we are. We're doing it! We're doing it!' He's going, 'I said no!' And I'm like, 'Yeah, but we are, and we're doing it.' He finally just hangs up on me and goes, 'I guess we're making *Stripped to Kill*.'"[48] And they did.

They cast Kay Lenz (also in *Trial by Terror*, 1983, directed by Hildy Brooks) as the lead: a police detective named Cody Sheehan who goes undercover at the Rock Bottom strip club as a stripper to catch a maniac serial killer targeting the dancers. Along the way, she discovers that stripping is fun, sexy, thrilling, and very dangerous when there is a serial killer on the loose killing strippers. With some truly spectacular dance performances (not the run-of-the-mill stripping but some serious acrobatics and beautiful choreography) from characters named "Cinnamon," "Dazzle," and "Angel," *Stripped to Kill* has some genuine talent glossing the veneer of gritty, noirish crime story. Detective Heineman

(Greg Evigan), Cody's partner (and sometimes boyfriend), is the only one who can know her secret identity, but as Cody is slowly seduced by the sexual power she feels on the stage from the moment she dances at amateur night, he can tell he may be losing her. Harsh but caring somewhere deep inside, Norman Fell (best known as Mr. Roper from the late 1970s/early 1980s television series *Three's Company*) is the sleazy owner of the Rock Bottom. Still, while his club is sleazy, it's filled with gorgeous young women in pristine, lacy lingerie in deep red lighting. The grim, lonely scenes of men sitting in uncomfortable chairs staring at the women as they dance are contrasted with a lively music soundtrack (every new dance is an opportunity for a new song). Shea's original impression of the dancers at The Body Shop as impressive and beautiful comes through: the dancers seem to like what they're doing, despite the men for whom they're doing it.

The murders are graphic and brutal. Cinnamon is hung by a wire and strangled to death as blood drips from her gasping mouth. Decaying victims are found wrapped in plastic. The contrast between the ugly and beautiful, the sleazy and the lovely, is pretty great. The characters are well-created and directed. *Stripped to Kill* is every bit a modern film noir as much as it is an exploitation film or a horror movie: the underworld inhabitants of a cold Los Angeles, ambiguously good or bad cops and strippers, and a confusing mystery all make it so. The major standout of *Stripped to Kill* is the exploration of transgender women, double identities, and traditionally female spaces several years before *The Silence of the Lambs* (1991) featured a transgender serial killer, and *The Crying Game* (1992), long held to be a controversial drama about gender identity, featured a transgender woman as a lead character.

Shea and Corman disagreed vehemently on the final edit of *Stripped to Kill*, but when it was released, it was a hit. It was the biggest hit Corman had had in a long time. Film critic Kevin Thomas called it a "gritty exploitation picture" with "style and substance" and wrote that "Ruben does an excellent job of turning actual strippers into actresses."[49] Before the film had been released, Corman had asked Shea and Rubin if there was anything they could do with the strip club sets before they had to be torn down: could they write and make another film incredibly quickly? They did: *Dance of the Damned* would be released in 1989. "Well, Corman wanted to use a strip club again, and he had a haunted house set that he had left over from another film," explained Shea, "so Andy Ruben and I came up with an idea to shoot in those two locations. Of course, we changed the haunted house into this really modern, amazing, great house."[50] In another interview, she said. *Dance of the Damned* was "always a process of including the elements Roger wanted into the script and story that Andy and I envisioned. We always had very high aspirations. Roger didn't discourage that; in fact, I think he was proud of it, but he wanted to make sure his style of commercial elements were included."[51]

In *Dance of the Damned*, Jodi (Starr Andreeff of *Ghoulies II*), a stripper, is followed to her club by a charismatic and mysterious vampire (Cyril O'Reilly) who has chosen her as his prey for that evening. But Jodi is suicidal, and the vampire is drawn to that sadness and is intrigued by it. He hires Jodi to keep him company throughout the night until dawn. The vampire is abusive and narcissistic but desperate for a connection, even if it is with a lowly "human." He's a romantic, Byronic character, brooding but fascinating to Jodi. Throughout

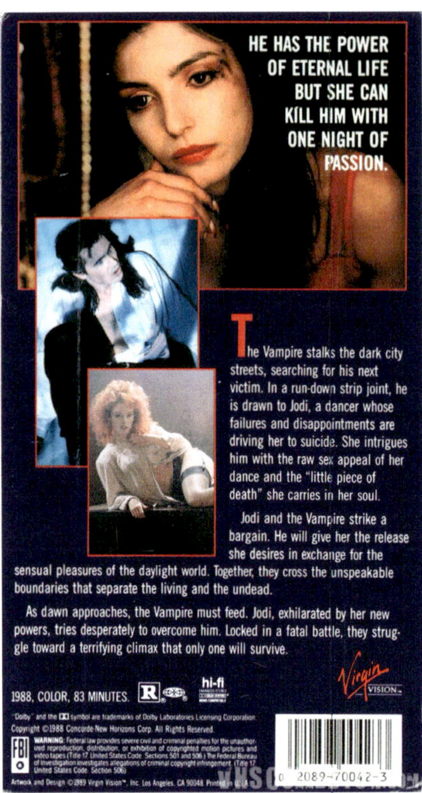

The North America VHS cover art for the release of Katt Shea's *Dance of the Damned* (1989). Image courtesy of Shout! Factory.

the night, Jodi learns she's afraid to die and wants to live. The "dance" is the back-and-forth between the two characters. In the end, the vampire offers to make Jodi a vampire, but she rejects the offer violently and exposes the vampire to sunlight, which kills him. *Dance of the Damned* is a very static film, with only two scenes outside the strip club or the house. Most of the film is dark, but we get a few glimpses of "vampire vision" through the eyes of the vampire. Shea calls *Dance of the Damned* "an oddball relationship movie," but it explores abuse and control in relationships under the guise of a fantasy film.

Shea shot for fifteen days to complete *Dance of the Damned* on an exhausting schedule. That's when Corman came to Shea and Ruben and asked if there wasn't just one more movie they could squeeze out of the strip club set. Ruben and Shea wrote the script for *Stripped to Kill II: Live Girls* and cast it over one weekend, as they had only five days to use the strip club sets before they'd be torn down. She shot all of the topless and dancing scenes in those five days and had to write a story that fit around those scenes afterward. "So we had no script and no actors," explained Shea:

> My assistant on *Damned*, an actor himself, was cast as the cop in the film, and there was this girl in the picture [*Dance of the Damned*] who had two lines—she had never acted before—she was cast as the lead. We shot for a week, and then we wrote the script around what we shot. We were ready to hide when the film came out. I wanted to take my name off it, but I didn't want to hurt Roger's feelings, and the fact is he loved it, and so did other people.[52]

That actress was Maria Ford, who would go on to star in *The Slumber Party Massacre III*. *Stripped to Kill II* was her first starring role. In *Stripped to Kill II*, Ford plays Shady, a stripper with horrific nightmares: she sees a masked killer stalking her stripper friends, and when she unmasks them, she sees herself as the killer. The real-life so-called "vampire killer" (because the victims have their throats slit and saliva has been found on their necks) continues to kill, and Shady is convinced that she's the one hurting people.

But the case is more complicated than that: Shady's innocent roommate Cassandra is a psychotic sociopath who may have multiple personalities and was once part of a murderous gang of prostitutes that killed people by hiding razor blades in their mouths and slitting throats. Shady has been drugged by her repeatedly, and in the film's final ten minutes, it all comes out, along with some gunshots.

It turns out Corman loved the film, and even director Quentin Tarantino is a known fan of the movie. But Shea herself? Not necessarily. "I was almost shooting it and making it up as I went along," she said,

> So when people tell me they love that movie so much, I just kind of go, "Why?" I didn't know what I was doing! I was flying by the seat of my pants completely! And it just amazes me because these other scripts that I've worked so hard on, I expect people to like them but *Stripped to Kill II*, I was writing it as I went, honestly.[53]

After *Stripped to Kill II* was released, Shea was ready to move on from making films for Corman. "Hopefully, we break from Corman now. It's time. Working under that kind of pressure is really exhausting," she told the *Detroit Free Press* in 1989.[54] Making three films under such grueling circumstances was tough on Shea, and she and Roger had clashed on many creative decisions throughout the entire process:

> I threatened to take my name off every movie I did for [Corman] ... At the end, he would be driving me so crazy with the editing and putting more boobs in and everything, I would go, "OK, Roger, I'm taking my name off!"[55]

When she parted ways with Corman, Shea and Ruben began making higher-profile and higher-budget movies. After finishing the murder mystery/crime thriller *Streets* (1990) for Corman, Shea and Ruben moved on to the erotic thriller *Poison Ivy* (1992). Each film was a successful vehicle for Christina Applegate (*Married with Children*) and Drew Barrymore (*E.T. The Extra-Terrestrial*, 1982), respectively, to move on to mature roles and leave their childhood acting careers behind. New Line's vice president for creative affairs, Marjorie Lewis, saw *Streets* and was impressed. She brought Shea in for a meeting, which led to her directing *Poison Ivy*. *Poison Ivy* gripped audiences for its racy V.C. Andrews-esque story about a teenage girl named Ivy (Barrymore) who moves into a rich family's house and subsequently seduces the father (Tom Skerritt) and his adolescent daughter (Sara Gilbert) and drives the mother (Cheryl Ladd) to suicide, destroying all of their lives.

A New Line Cinema release, *Poison Ivy*, was based on the true-life story of producer Melissa Goddard, who had also written the script. "We changed the ending of Melissa's story to have Ivy die," explained Shea, "but I didn't really want that:

> In reality, the girl got away with it, and I thought that's how it should have been portrayed, but the executive at New Line got her way, and Ivy died—then they made numerous sequels even though the lead character had been killed off. I had nothing to

do with the sequels because they made me kill her. We didn't even shoot the ending until after the movie was edited because I was still fighting for her to live while we were shooting. I do like the ending we shot, but I just didn't feel it was realistic, those kind of people get away with stuff.[56]

Poison Ivy, described by New Line president of production at the time Sara Risher as a "teenage *Fatal Attraction*,"[57] was controversial. Barrymore played a fifteen-year-old girl in a film with sex, "murder, incest, lesbianism, alcoholism, and suicide," but because Shea finally had a budget ($3 Million, as opposed to the under-$500,000 for the Corman pictures), she was able to make a film that the *New York Times* said had a "sophisticated look and literate script."[58]

Poison Ivy was made because of the massive success of another erotic thriller/broken home film from the previous year: *The Hand that Rocks the Cradle* (1991), which starred Rebecca De Mornay as a demented nanny who takes a woman's place in her own home as mother and wife, using nefarious tactics. But that didn't stop people from being offended by *Poison Ivy*. *Poison Ivy* played at the 1992 Sundance Film Festival, where it was one of the most controversial films in the lineup. Then, it played at the 1992 Seattle International Festival of Women Directors, where people were offended by it. The fact that a woman director had made a film in which a teenage girl is seducing a grown man was awful to them. At one screening, a woman asked Shea, "'How could you, as a woman, write a character like Ivy?" She wanted to reply:

> You can't censor art to be the way you want it depicted. Because pretty soon, no one can be bad. There can't be bad men. There can't be bad Black people. There can't be bad Chinese people. Who gets to be bad?[59]

But Shea knew that making a sexy thriller in which a devious minor has sex with a grown man would be, at the very least, outrageous to some people. During the filming of *Poison Ivy*, Shea knew that some of the sex scenes were shocking, and she felt weird filming them. "I really try to take it all the way to the edge, really try to take some risks," she said while shooting the film,

> But it's really scary, too. And you never know, I always thought I was crossing the line—I thought they were going to come and arrest me. I expected the cops to come pick me up any minute—really, I'm serious. After I shot some of those scenes with Drew, I thought they were going to be bringing in the handcuffs.[60]

The controversial nature of *Poison Ivy* also led actress Drew Barrymore down a path of playing damaged characters in following films like *No Place to Hide* (1992), *Gun Crazy* (1992), *The Amy Fisher Story* (1993), *Mad Love* (1995), and *Bad Girls* (1994). It wouldn't be until 1998, when she starred in the romantic comedy *The Wedding Singer,* and 1999 when she began producing her own films, that her image would change into that of an innocent. In 1996, Shea and Ruben ended their writing/producing partnership.

Despite the success of *Poison Ivy*, it would take six years for Shea to get another film off the ground, and when she did, it was back with Julie Corman. She hired Shea to direct the science fiction television movie *Last Exit to Earth* (1996). In it, female aliens come to Earth to find males with which to repopulate their species. It's silly. Shea didn't want to continue making low-budget films; she was talented, and *Poison Ivy* had the budget she hoped for. That's why she took the last-minute job of directing the sequel to *Carrie* (1976) titled *The Rage: Carrie 2* (1999).

A direct sequel to Brian De Palma's Stephen King story adaptation, *The Rage: Carrie 2*, was saved by Katt Shea. The film only happened because the producers fired the first director and were desperate to salvage something out of the mess rather than cancel the film entirely. Shea was brought on as the director with only two weeks to prepare for the job and two weeks of previously shot footage to include in the final version. Shea was hugely influenced by Brian De Palma as an artist and worked with him as an actress in the 1983 film *Scarface*. In a small role, she paid attention to the directing and John Alonzo's cinematography, asking questions about techniques and stylistic choices.[61] Seventeen years later, she directed the sequel to De Palma's original horror masterpiece.

It retells the original *Carrie* story: an outcast girl begins to trust people and then has her trust dashed to pieces. She gets revenge as she finally releases the powers she's been hiding, which could have given her control years ago but which she chose to hide to not draw attention to herself. She's beyond shame or embarrassment; she wants to kill and destroy. In short: they fucked with the wrong girl.

Like its thematic successor, the Oscar-winning *Promising Young Woman* (2020), directed by Emerald Fennel, also about rape and suicide, *Carrie 2* makes insightful comments about how boys from prominent families, or who are highly valued by schools for their sports prowess, are not punished for rape while women are encouraged not to report sex crimes because it will "ruin the boy's life," placing a higher value on boy's futures and lives than on girl's, even when the girl has died, been murdered, or gang-raped. *The Rage: Carrie 2* was released in 1999 as a box office failure, but by the 2020s had gained a cult following and audiences an appreciation for its progressive messages about toxicity (much like the 2009 film *Jennifer's Body* by Karyn Kusama, which we'll talk about in Chapter 7, was seen as an insightful satire an entire decade after the original release of the film).

In the early 2000s, Shea directed two television movies, but nothing after that for almost two decades. In 2019, she directed the theatrical remake of the teen mystery feature *Nancy Drew and the Hidden Staircase*. As of 2020, she was working on a remake of *Dance of the Damned*, written and produced by herself. "I've made it now into much more of a love story," she explained in 2020:

> I love the new script. I think the new script is much better than the old one. It's much more of a progression of two people over the course of a night who want to kill each other in the beginning. He's taking her to kill her later on, and she's trying to kill him as well. Then, and over the course of the night, they fall in love. They truly fall in love.

> He tries to save her at the end. He's trying to prevent himself from killing her. I think it's much more accessible.[62]

The first woman to be elected President of the American Cinema Editors (ACE) in 2000, Tina Hirsch has worked as an editor on several iconic genre films. In 1968, after working on fashion still photography, she worked, for free, as an assistant editor to learn the art. She began as an assistant editor on Brian De Palma's *Hi Mom* (1970) and worked on *Macon County Line* (1974). The Cormans recruited Hirsch to work as an editor on the Corman production *Big Bad Mama* (1974) and later *Death Race 2000* (1975) and *Eat My Dust* (1976). Hirsch was Joe Dante's editor on *Gremlins* (1984) and his *Twilight Zone: The Movie* (1983) segment. The only film Hirsch directed herself is a low-budget creature-feature rip-off of *Gremlins* called *Munchies* (1987), produced by Corman: "I went to Roger because I'd told him, years before, that when I felt ready to direct, I'd let him know,"[63] said Hirsch. Corman was ready to make a creature feature.

After the release of *Gremlins*, horror films about small, horrible creatures attacking people were very popular at the time. Just a few include *Critters* (1986), *Ghoulies* (1984), *Troll* (1986), and *Hobgoblins* (1988), so it was "a perfect fit" to have Hirsch direct, according to the Cormans. The story is simple and silly: a space archaeologist, played by Harvey Korman, finds a fossilized "munchie" monster in a cave in Peru. He takes it back home to the United States as a family pet for his son and names it Arnold. Korman's character, Simon, has an evil twin brother named Cecil, who kidnaps Arnold. Scared, Arnold fights back, attacking Cecil, so he chops Arnold into small pieces. Like in *Gremlins*, each small part of the creature turns into a whole new creature, and suddenly angry munchies are attacking people.

Munchies had a budget of $1.2 million; that was big for Corman but small as far as film budgets go. Hirsch shot the entire film in only fifteen days, relying on her editing skills and experience working on *Gremlins* to get her through the hurried production with all the shots she needed for a complete film. Hirsch:

> I was really lucky that I'd learned a lot on *Gremlins*. Mostly I learned what you could get away with. *Munchies* is not a slick movie, particularly by today's standards, but if you were a twelve-year-old boy when you saw it, chances are you liked it.[64]

Corman was, for Hirsch, a good producer. "The best producer I'd ever worked with," Hirsch said,[65] and "the reason that he turns out so many good people is that he is willing to take a chance. He gave me a chance."[66] Always practical and constructive, Corman told Hirsch and her production team not to worry so much about the film's contents. "I don't think we're going to blow anybody away with our effects or our budget," he conceded to them, "so don't let bad taste stand in the way."[67]

Munchies was released in the United States in March 1987 and played in theaters for two weeks. The promotional poster was a spoof of the iconic image of Marilyn Monroe from *The Seven Year Itch* (1955) of her white dress blowing up, exposing her thighs, but with a munchie staring up the woman's skirt. The MPAA initially rejected the poster for being too "pervy," but it ended up being the main image. Despite her incredible career, Hirsch seems to consider the role of "editor" as a female role, a support role to the (male) director. "You must be the kind of person who can stand behind the director. The ego goes away, and it's all about creating his vision for him,"[68] she said in an interview with *Variety*. And while it may very well be a support role, why it is a "woman" role is strange, considering how many male editors there are.

For Corman, Susan Shadburne wrote and directed the supernatural horror film *Shadow Play* (1986). Previously, she'd been a writer for claymation animation films, but she was hired to make this dreamy mystery horror film starring Dee Wallace as a woman named Morgan haunted by her dead fiancé who killed himself at an isolated lighthouse on the night of their engagement party. She's staying with her dead fiancé's mother, Cloris Leachman, and his brother John (Ron Kuhlman). Morgan is a playwright, and staying at the lighthouse is supposed to help her heal from this terrible incident. Visions of Jeremy (Barry Laws), her dead fiancé, begin to drive her crazy, and she is convinced that she is seeing him. Wallace puts on a marvelous performance in this emotional ghost story with its long, drawn-out scenes that Shadburne created to make a love story with some Gothic elements rather than a frightening horror film. Mirror images, dreamy sequences, tears of lost love, and ocean waves add atmosphere but no tension. *Shadow Play* lacks any exploitation elements that Corman seems to have required of his filmmakers: no racy nudity, no violence, and no blood/gore.

Of the other women Corman hired to direct genre films, several have standout horror film careers. Kristine Peterson directed the successful direct-to-video slasher *Deadly Dreams* (1988) with some backing from Roger Corman. Peterson had been working for Francis Ford Coppola and had done some editing work for Corman when, one day, she told Corman that she wanted to direct, and he agreed that she should.[69] *Deadly Dreams*, made for $400,000 to $500,000 in eighteen days, is about a man having horrible dreams that turn out to be true. The film is incredibly low-key and somber but engaging, though the scares happen mainly towards the movie's last third.

After *Deadly Dreams* came out, Corman hired Peterson to direct the first of the *Body Chemistry* (1990) erotic thriller series films, which was released in theaters. This was the only film she'd make with Corman. Peterson would immediately direct the theatrical action thriller *Lower Level* (1991), followed by the direct-to-video creature feature sequel *Critters 3* (1991, starring a young Leonardo DiCaprio in one of his first roles). She directed the theatrical crime thriller *The Hard Truth* (1994) starring Michael Rooker (*Guardians of the Galaxy*, 2014) and then the straight-to-video action sequel *Redemption: Kickboxer 5* (1995). When she made *Kickboxer 5* and after, she was hailed as "Almost certainly the only woman to direct a martial arts film" (Pao-Shu Kao was directing them in the 1970s).[70] And there, in only seven years, her entire career as a genre film director burned brightly, faltered, and sputtered out. The best of these films is her first, the horror movie *Deadly Dreams*. Before and even during the time that she directed, Peterson was an assistant director on many Corman and non-Corman films, including Janet Greek's rape-revenge thriller *The Ladies Club* (1986), horror classic *Chopping Mall* (1986), *Bill & Ted's Excellent Adventure* (1989), and, of course, the sequel film *A Nightmare on Elm Street 5: The Dream Child* (1989).

Mary Ann Fisher's science fiction ocean horror *Lords of the Deep* (1989), on the other hand, has all the necessary elements that similar, higher-budget films at the time like *The Abyss* (1989), *DeepStar Six* (1989), *The Evil Below* (1989), *Leviathan* (1989), and *The Rift* (1990) did: it's *Alien* (1979) set underwater. The highlight of this low-budget monster movie is Priscilla Barnes (*Three's Company*) as Dr. Claire McDowell and Bradford Dillman (*The Swarm*, 1978 & *Piranha*, 1978) in his second-to-last onscreen appearance. In *Lords of the Deep*, a gelatinous undersea alien life form threatens the crew of an underwater laboratory after a submarine is sent to explore the possibility of undersea mining. Stingray-like creatures transform humans into mucilaginous (it's the only synonym) messes to stop the colonization of their underwater realm. The special effects are absurdly satisfactory in a low-budget way, and the creatures are, again, oddly adorable, like little stingray candies you want to chew. A decade later, this subgenre of horror and science fiction would reemerge with films like *Sphere* (1998) and *Deep Rising* (1998), probably to exploit the success of natural disaster films like Mimi Leder's *Deep Impact* (1998), *Armageddon* (1998), and *Dante's Peak* (1997). But Mary Ann Fisher? *Lords of the Deep* was her only film as a director. She'd been producing for Corman on low-budget genre films beginning with *Forbidden World* (1982), and continued to produce films for him until *The Haunting of Hell House* (1999), when her film career abruptly ended. This may be because *Lords of the Deep* was not a big moneymaker and was not loved by critics at the time. A Canadian newspaper film writer said it had been "deep-sixed" in the United States and wondered if it would do any better in Canada.[71] Fisher stuck to producing.

Next up for Corman was Talia Shire's erotic thriller *One Night Stand* (1995). Shire is known mainly for her mainstream acting career, not her directing work. She appeared in *Rocky* (1976), *The Godfather* (1972), and *The Godfather: Part II* (1974) before eventually trying her hand, once, at directing. *One Night Stand* is, just as you thought, about Michelle Sanderson (played by Ally Sheedy), who has a one-night stand with a sexy stranger and then finds out he's an extremely dangerous person. A contemporary reviewer called Shire's direction "wobbly" and said, "Had this film not had Shire's name on it, it surely would have headed straight to video stores."[72] Shire never directed anything else but continued to act well into the twenty-first century, having a prolific career at the time of the writing of this book.

For Corman, Victoria Muspratt made the science fiction thriller *Circuit Breaker*, released in 1996. Unlike Fisher and Shire, she immediately directed one more exploitation film for Corman: the women in prison sex thriller *Macon County Jail* (1997). Then, she left Corman and made the teen fantasy movie *Teen Sorcery* (1999) for Charles Band and his Full Moon Pictures company. After working for him as an editor on several films in the early 1990s, Gwyneth Gibby was hired by Corman to direct the erotic historical thriller *Marquis de Sade* (1996), the disaster adventure film *Eruption* (1997), the adaptation of Isaac Asimov's science fiction novel *Nightfall* (2000), several episodes of Corman's adventure crime television series *Black Scorpion*, and two related features, *Black Scorpion Returns* (2001) and *Sting of the Black Scorpion* (2002). Gibby stopped directing after *Sting of the Black Scorpion* and, as of the writing of this book, works in small press publishing.

Rachel Samuels' first film was *Running Woman* (1998), produced by Corman: an action/crime thriller closely followed by the period thriller *The Suicide Club* (2000), an adaptation of the Robert Louis Stevenson story of the same name. Eight years later, Samuels would direct the theatrical musical Film Noir *Dark Streets* (2008) and describe working for Corman in a press interview for that film:

> My first job in the industry was developing scripts for producer Roger Corman, who's been a mentor to so many of the best American directors, from Coppola to Demme to Sayles. That was my film school—we made about twenty films in two years, and then Roger produced the first two films I wrote and directed. This was all kind of the antidote to my visual arts background—it was intense boot camp training in classic Hollywood storytelling and in working very, very efficiently. But what's great about starting out with Roger is that every schedule and budget you get down the road seems luxurious. Like in the case of *Dark Streets*—shooting a period musical in twenty-eight days on an indie budget sounded just wonderful to me, although many were skeptical it could be done.[73]

Charles Band is an American film producer and director with his independent production and distribution company Full Moon Pictures/Studios/Entertainment (along with a few other labels like Moonbeam Entertainment and Empire International Pictures). Like Roger Corman, Band makes low-budget movies, mainly horror but also exploitation, erotica, and even family films. Some of his most famous films include Stuart Gordon's *Re-Animator* (1985) and the *Puppet Master* series. I just mentioned Victoria Muspratt's teen fantasy movie *Teen Sorcery* (1999), produced by Charles Band's Full Moon Pictures horror banner. Band began hiring women to direct his genre films in the 1990s when his company became big and gave several women their first feature films. Please note that Silvia St. Croix, director of *Gingerdead Man 2: Passion of the Crust* (2008) and *Corona Zombies* (2020), is a pseudonym and not a real woman director, nor is Ellen Cabot (*Lurid Tales: The Castle Queen*, 1998), Mary Crawford (*My Stepbrother Is a Vampire!?!*, 2013) or Virginia Sloane (*Prison of the Dead*, 2000); all are listed directors of Full Moon films and also pseudonyms of male directors.

Beginning with director Anita Rosenberg's crime comedy road trip movie *Assault of the Killer Bimbos* (1988), Band produced and/or distributed films directed by women under his horror Full Moon Films/Studios/Pictures, Empire Pictures, and family/teen Moonbeam Productions/Films labels including the horror anthology film *The Dungeonmaster* (1984) with a segment directed by Rosemarie Turko, the horror-sci-fi family film *Pet Shop* (1994) by Hope Perello, Linda Hassani's horror fantasy *Dark Angel: The Ascent* (1994), Cybil Richards' science fiction erotica *Femalien* (1996), Jackie Garth's science fiction erotica *Dream Master: The Erotic Invader* (1996), Ellen Earnshaw's erotic thriller *Human Desires* (1997), Ellyn Michaels' erotic thriller *Rebecca's Secret* (1998), Julie Jordan's erotic thriller *Losing Control* (1998), Felicia Sinclair's science fiction erotica *The Exotic Time Machine* (1998), Adele Bertei's erotic thriller *Secrets of a Chambermaid* (2000), Tammi Sutton's horror sequel *Killjoy 2* (2002), Denice Duff's Gothic horror *Vampire Resurrection* (2001),

Jill Hayworth's crime thriller *Seducing Fina* (2000), Marcy Ronen's science fiction erotica *Sex Files: Creating the Perfect Man* (2000), and Rachel Gordon and Madison Monroe's fantasy erotica *Dungeons of Ecstasy* (2018). And many more titles by some of these women. Brinke Stevens (*The Slumber Party Massacre*, 1982) directed the sequel *Sorority Babes in the Slimeball Bowl-O-Rama 2* (2022) for Band's distribution label Delirium Films.

In 1999, Charles Band produced and directed the horror film *Blood Dolls*. During the filming, director Penelope Spheeris visited the set. She filmed some behind-the-scenes imagery and asked a few questions of the cast and crew into the camera about making *Blood Dolls*. This footage was later edited into the documentary *Hollyweird* (1999), viewable only as clips that appear as special features on the DVD release of *Blood Dolls*. On the Full Moon Pictures website, the documentary is advertised as "An in-depth documentary shot by music video director Penelope Spheeris (*Wayne's World*, 1992, *The Decline of Western Civilization Part I*, 1981) during the production of the Full Moon Features classic *Blood Dolls*."

But Penelope Spheeris insists that Band and music documentary producer Miles A. Copeland III (he made *The Decline of Western Civilization Part II: The Metal Years*, 1988, with Spheeris) wanted to make a documentary about a new girl band that Copeland had put together. Part of the documentary was supposed to be about the business relationship between Copeland and Band as they worked together on the girl band project. Copeland asked Spheeris to direct it. "I filmed some behind-the-scenes pieces on one of Charlie's cheesy horror movies," she said in an interview:

> Just a couple of days shooting. Meanwhile, Miles is trying to get the girl band to sign a very strict recording contract and be part of the documentary. The girls refused to sign the contract because it was too demanding. At that point, I decided I didn't want to be involved because I didn't want to do a movie with actors/singers that were not contractually bound. I noticed a while back on IMDb that I was listed as the director of this movie whose working title was *Hollyweird*. A title I gave it. Evidently, Charlie put the movie together, kept my name on it, and finished it. I have no idea what it looks like, but I'm sure it's totally embarrassing.[74]

Dark Angel: The Ascent (1994) is a Full Moon Entertainment picture directed by Linda Hassani. It's the only film that Hassani would direct for Full Moon, though her name would appear as a director on two horror anthologies released by the company in 2004 and 2018, respectively. The script for *Dark Angel: The Ascent* had already been written by Matthew Bright when Hassani was hired. Hassani had heard that Full Moon had created a studio in Romania, and she was very interested in working there. She said in an interview:

> The script was funny, and though it had scary moments, it did a great job of riding the tonal line between horror and comedy. The characters were clever, unexpected. The humor was off-kilter and surprising. I loved the script, and I was very happy the lead was female.[75]

Written by Matthew Bright (who also wrote *Guncrazy*, 1992, which was mentioned earlier), *Dark Angel: The Ascent* is not a sequel to the film *Dark Angel* (1990). It is a stand-alone fantasy horror set in the world of the Judeo-Christian God and Satan. It focuses on the emotional and physical journey of a supernatural creature. This demon escapes Hell and finds true love on Earth, named Veronica Iscariot (Angela Featherstone, best known to horror film fans as "Raven" from 2001's *Soul Survivors*, and who has also begun directing films as of 2021).

The film was shot in Romania, which is why the streets of the American city are all cobblestone. When they weren't shooting in the city, Hassani had found a seventeenth-century castle where she created an entire underworld for the scenes in Hell. These scenes show a great eye for directing large-scale scenes and a larger budget than most Full Moon horror films; it's on par with the Full Moon masterpieces and *Puppet Master* (1989) in terms of their production value. In Hassani's Hell, the "punishment pits" were lit with only regular fire or magnesium torches, no electric lights. "The walls were set on fire, and people were carrying torches," said Hassani in a behind-the-scenes video released on VHS in 1994. "It's quite an amazing thing to see because it's just illuminated with flame." Vivi Dragan Vasile was the cinematographer, and it was he who "thought it would be intriguing to film the Hell sequences using primarily natural fire light:

> Since the location for the opening shots, across a landscape, was very difficult to reach with trucks, it worked well to hand the extras torches and have them light the landscape as they crossed it. In the Hell sequence interiors, most, if not all, of the light was generated by flame. There may have been a few small lights for coverage, but as I recall, it was mostly flame. I think the result is absolutely beautiful ... [76]

A particularly creepy moment in the film is in the beginning Hell scenes with a trio of human torsos shaking violently in eternal agony; it was accomplished by shooting at six frames per second and "the actors sitting in boxes, covered with a black sort of cloth, so they look legless."[77] Even though there was plenty of fire in the Hell scenes, it was still cold on set. "Between shots, the extras would warm up by putting socks on with their sandals," said Hassani:

"More than once, the assistant director discovered that some extras had forgotten to remove their socks before the next shot. After that, the reminder before each shot became, 'There are no socks in Hell.'"[78]

Everything outside of the Hell scenes was filmed in regular locations in Bucharest. The recently-communist country of Romania was still experiencing some significant changes to its local and federal government. "Since Nicolae Ceausescu and his wife had been executed in 1989, just a few years before we filmed in 1993," explained Hassani, "there were still many remnants of his rule, and communism, in the country. Romania was very much in transition politically, economically, and culturally:"

> The Securitate, the secret police, still seemed to be around and gathering intelligence. While the team was filming in Bucharest, we were all housed at a hotel called the Hotel Lebada. It was located on a tiny little island outside the center of Bucharest.

> Rumor had it the building was once a monastery but had also served as a prison. When taking a taxi back home from the center of town, many of us had the experience of taxi drivers insisting they did not know where the sprawling hotel was located. "There is no Hotel Lebada" was a common response. At the end of filming, Charlotte Stewart, who played Heliken's wife, kindly assembled a little album of photographs from the set and entitled it "There is no Hotel Lebada."[79]

Dark Angel: The Ascent was released by Paramount, straight to video. Based on the title, *Dark Angel: The Ascent* may have been the first in a planned series of films with similar themes or characters, but that never manifested. Hassani would go on to direct other films and many commercials, but she never directed another horror movie. She's credited as one of the directors of the 2004 Full Moon anthology horror film *Tomb of Terror* (the first segment "Ascent From Hell") and the 2018 Full Moon horror anthology *Bunker of Blood: Chapter 5: Psycho Sideshow: Demon Freaks*, but those films feature clips from *Dark Angel: The Ascent*.

Denice Duff is famous in the world of horror films for starring in *Bloodstone: Subspecies II* (1992), released by Full Moon Pictures, and its sequels *Bloodlust: Subspecies III* (1994) and *Subspecies 4: Bloodstorm* (1998). By the early 2000s, Duff also wanted to get behind the camera. In 2001, she directed the vampire film *Song of the Vampire*, which was retitled *Vampire Resurrection* when Blockbuster Video wanted the film to have an edgier title before they'd agree to distribute it in their stores.

In the late 1990s, Duff was asked to star in a student film, an offer she had to decline because she was in the Screen Actors Guild and the film was non-union. She said, however, that she would be interested in directing it, and the students obliged. As the new director, she decided to shoot on 35mm film, make the film compatible with Screen Actors Guild union contracts, cast the film, and also star in it (now that there were no union conflicts). *Song of the Vampire* was shot over four weeks in Los Angeles, California, and Baton Rouge, Louisiana. After production, before beginning the editing and post-production process, Duff got busy. She got a part on the soap opera *The Young and the Restless*, and *Song of the Vampire* was put aside. Over two years, Duff coordinated the distribution of the movie, and it was finally released under the title *Vampire Resurrection* in 2003. "Now I know why there are so few women directors," she said in a 2004 interview about the film:

> They are busy being good mothers, raising their children, unlike me for the last year trying to finish this albatross. I wasn't around much, and when I was, I was always on the phone. But it's done, it's halfway decent, and it's at friggin' Blockbuster ... that still amazes me.[80]

As a first-time director, Duff ran into problems she didn't know she would have. Getting the film edited properly and with the effects that she wanted was a challenge. "Simple things like dissolves, color correction, musical score, and a consistent aspect ratio size," she explained. "The first time I watched the finished product, I sat in my living room crying, tears streaming down my face with disappointment." In retrospect, Duff wishes she had been savvy enough to learn to edit the film and ask for a piece of the profits. "No one knows your vision except you. Just because someone is cool and you like them and their art doesn't mean they are in your head with the same vision."[81] Duff did not direct another film, though she continued to act and was acting at the time of the writing of this book.

Vampire Resurrection is silly but very beautiful. Duff plays Victoria Thorn, a woman whose true love is a mysterious vampire named Jonathon Travers (James Horan). In 1897, they were together until she died suddenly and tragically. Now a vampire, Jonathon has finally found her reincarnated as Victoria, and he wants to make her a vampire so they can be together forever. Duff has an excellent eye for color and lighting and staging her scenes, which may explain why she became a photographer later in life. The actors and their relationships with the script, one another, and the director are not as strong. But there are a few gorgeous scenes of Duff dancing around in the colored mist that lend the film a magical aspect.

Duff does have one other directing credit. In the horror anthology film *I, Vampire* (2000), Duff stars in and is credited as director on the segment "From the Grave." It's not a different film; it's a shortened version of *Vampire Resurrection* cut to fit with two other segments. The first segment, "Spawn of Hell," is a shortened version of the feature film *Subspecies 4 Bloodstorm* (1998). The third segment, "Undead Evil," is a shortened version of the feature film *Vampire Journals* (1997). Both *Vampire Resurrection* and *I, Vampire* were distributed by Charles Band.

Hope Perello worked for Full Moon for many years in various roles: as a production coordinator on *Trolls* (1986), as a second unit director on *Puppet Master* (1989), and as a production manager on *Deadly Weapon* (1989). After leaving Full Moon to direct her first horror film feature, *The Howling VI: The Freaks* (1991), Charles Band hired her to direct the science fiction creature feature, *Pet Shop* (1994), because he felt she had enough experience to take on the job. *Pet Shop* is about extraterrestrial aliens that open a pet shop as a ruse to abduct human children, turn them into pets, and sell them as slaves to other aliens. The story is set in a small town where the FBI hides witnesses, and it's a comedy. "I felt the story was silly, but also had potential to be a fun sci-fi monster movie," said Perello in an interview.[82] It was supposed to be funny:

> We amped up the humor wherever we could, especially with Mr. and Mrs. Zim, the alien pet shop owners who were kidnapping kids and turning them into pets. We gave them outlandish costumes and big cowboy hats to emphasize their zaniness and hired a comedy duo to play their parts. We also went overboard with the Yeagher family, exaggerating their roles as fish-out-of-water New Yorkers forced to live in the Western town of Cactus Flats. I wanted to play up the blandness of the town as a contrast to the colorful family, so we had a whole street in Ridgecrest, California, painted beige: all the storefronts were drab, and all the extras had to wear beige.[83]

Perello is a director that focuses on her actors. One of her favorite actors on the set of *Pet Shop* was Terry Kiser, who had played Bernie in *Weekend at Bernie's* (1989). He "was a hoot to work with," said Perello, "He had a droll sense of humor and was totally game to play with the sci-fi drama."[84]

Pet Shop is not a well-known genre film among genre fans mainly because of its PG rating. It's suitable for kids to watch, so there's no gore, nudity, or cussing. But it's rare to find a film like that. Most genre films are rated R for an adult audience or rated G to appeal to younger kids. "I liked playing against what was expected of the genre," Perello continued. Unfortunately, *Pet Shop* had a low budget and ran out of money in, meaning that the pet shop animals couldn't be animated the way Perello had originally envisioned. "So, they seem quite stiff and silly," she regrets.[85]

Tammi Sutton's first film as director was the 2002 sequel to the 2000 Full Moon horror film *Killjoy, Killjoy 2: Deliverance from Evil.* Sutton had moved to Los Angeles from Florida in 1995 to pursue a film career with no industry connections, but soon met several influential horror filmmakers working for Charles Band: Dave Parker (*The Dead Hate The Living*, 2000), J.R. Bookwalter (*The Dead Next Door*, 1989) and Danny Draven (*Horrorvision*, 2001). She was first a production designer and later produced *Witchhouse 3: Demon Fire* (2002), *Hell Asylum* (2002), and *Dead and Rotting* (2002) for Full Moon and Charles Band. She knew she wanted to direct films, however:

> J.R. knew I was interested in getting into the director's chair. While co-producing *Witchhouse 3*, I expressed interest to him about getting financing together for an outside project I wanted to direct. *Killjoy 2* was slated to go into production shortly after these talks, and before I knew it, while I was prepping to produce, J.R. asked if I was interested in directing as well. I went home, wrote a treatment, and jumped right in. I didn't have time to doubt myself.[86]

In 2002, Sutton felt that she had "two major strikes against me when I got into this project: Being white, and being a woman was shocking to most people when they heard I was the director." However, once she got her foot into the door, "being a woman has probably been more advantageous than not."[87] *Killjoy 2* was a stressful experience for Sutton because of the low budget and her having to take on multiple jobs. Trent Haaga, who played the role of Killjoy, the clown, also acted as line producer. At the same time, Sutton worked on "wardrobe, art department, craft services, scheduling issues, location scouting, transportation, and even support in post-production."[88] Sutton would also act in the film as a trailer park resident.[89]

Killjoy 2, under Sutton's control, was a flashier (her words) and more fun version of the previous film. Haaga's Killjoy is an insane, flamboyant, supernatural clown that murders people. In the sequel, teenage juvenile delinquents from the inner city are on a bus on their way to do community service rebuilding an old rural farmhouse as part of their criminal punishment. Their bus breaks down on a lonely road out in the countryside, and when they stop to ask a white local for help (Tammi Sutton), she shoots at them in a racist rage and wounds one of the kids. The police officers transporting the teenagers shoot back and kill the crazy trailer park lady, but now one of their wards needs to get to a hospital, and they have no transportation. Luckily, they come across a voodoo priestess (played by Rhonda Claerbaut) who can help with magic. Unfortunately, the voodoo magic conjures up the urban legend of Killjoy, the killer clown, and he starts killing off the teens and the cops as he spews cheesy one-liners. Band would go on to make three more *Killjoy* films.

Sutton then directed three more genre films. In 2009, she released a slasher film called *Sutures* which stars Jason London (*The Rage: Carrie 2*) as a police detective and features a cameo from cult horror actor Andrew Prine (*Simon: King of the Witches*, 1971). In 2014, her gangster crime Giallo *Isle of Dogs*, starring Barbara Nedeljakova (*Hostel*, 2005), was released, and in 2017 her supernatural horror film about a haunting, *Whispers,* came out. When talking about horror films during her *Killjoy 2* days, Sutton said,

> I love the genre because it lets you explore fear openly and aggressively. I think it's a healthy medium to fantasize in. It allows you creative freedom to do basically whatever you can dream up. There are no rules, and no holds barred in the things you say or do.[90]

Roberta Findlay and Doris Wishman continued directing horror and genre well into the 1980s and 90s. Findlay's style shifted from pure exploitation and sex to legitimate (if low-budget) horror movies: *The Oracle* (1985), *Tenement* (1985), *Blood Sisters* (1987), *Prime Evil* (1988), and *Lurkers* (1988). Like Findlay, Wishman's thematic style evolved with the times, and she made two more films before her death, both slasher films: *A Night to Dismember* (1983) and *Each Time I Kill* (2002).

Findlay's new movie partner was Walter Sear, a sound and music engineer and composer who had worked with numerous musicians and scored several horror films, including *Let's Scare Jessica to Death* (1971). He owned and operated Sear Studios in New York City and electronically scored all Findlay's movies from the 1980s (also acting as the production manager and, sometimes, the editor). Findlay had known Sear since the *Snuff* days in the 1970s, and they'd made pornography films in the late 1970s and early 1980s before turning to mainstream horror films. They'd been distributing their pornography films in theaters, but when home video VHS became a booming new distribution avenue, it was no longer financially viable for them. Switching from pornography to horror was an economic necessity.

Tenement was made from a script that Findlay and Sear bought from low-budget genre film writers Joel Bender and Rick Marx, and it was perfect for a production set in an abandoned building in Harlem. The entire film is about the residents of a tenement building in the South Bronx defending themselves and each other against a gang of drug dealers determined to take over the building for themselves. Not only would they shoot the entire film in the building (though they would use exteriors from a different building in the South Bronx), but they would use different apartments in the building for film production department offices and sound stages. This was not a good neighborhood, and as Findlay and Sear were in preproduction in the building, two real street gangs began fighting in the street below. Instead of calling the police, Sear hired two of them to appear in the movie, one from each gang. While this sounds unsafe, they cast an actress named Olivia

Ward (Mrs. Wesley), whose husband was the police commissioner. "She had battalions of police with her all the time we were shooting. We never had a problem," said Findlay in an interview.[91] She put Olivia in as many scenes as possible so her police escort would protect the film crew from unsavory people in the neighborhood or in the nearby garage where they filmed. One day they found a dead body in an adjoining lot to the South Bronx exterior building. Findlay had chosen the building because she "hated it": "I hated the building because it reminded me of the building where I grew up. It was far worse than any place I had grown up in."[92] It was a two-week film shoot. The final result was an incredibly violent film with no intentional comedy. "If there is camp appeal in it, it's unintentional or unconscious,"[93] Findlay explained in an interview. The set was not an orderly one. Findlay tells a story about her favorite assistant cameraperson, who appears to have had an alcohol issue, and discusses his behavior as commonplace at the time:

> He was drunk a lot, at night, at any time. We were sprawled out in a hallway, shooting and shooting; we had to get a dolly track. He said, "I have to go." I said, "There's no way you can go now; we're shooting." And he proceeded to urinate all over the script and the floor. "I said I had to go," he said.[94]

Tenement, also distributed as *Game of Survival* and *Slaughter in the South Bronx*, originally received an MPAA rating of X for all the violence. Ironically, Findlay had made the film only for commercial purposes, believing that if they made a film as violent and horrible as possible, they'd be able to secure distribution because that's what people wanted to see.

R. Allen Leider wrote the script for Findlay's horror film *The Oracle* and appeared as the character Gordan Mannering at the party scene. He'd known Findlay and Sear since the 1970s and had written the scripts for several of their pornography films. Findlay and Sear owned all the camera equipment and had their own sound studio to keep their costs down, and they wanted to make another movie. Leider was originally writing a novel that he said was similar in tone to *The Haunting* (1963), but when Findlay asked him for a script and wanted him to add blood and gore, his novel fell by the wayside, and he wrote the script instead. Findlay and Sear paid him $500. They made the film non-union for $36,000. Sear wrote, produced, recorded, and edited the film's music in his studio. After screening briefly in theaters, *The Oracle* went straight to video and wasn't available on DVD until fifteen years later.[95]

The premise of *The Oracle* is that a couple moves into a new apartment in New York City, and when looking in the apartment building attic on her way to find the laundry room, Jennifer (Caroline Capers Powers, in her only film role) finds a planchette, used for writing messages from the dead, in a wooden box. The apartment manager, Pappas (Chris Maria De Koron, also in his only film role), lets her take it back to her apartment, and that night, Jennifer brings it out to play with her husband Ray (Roger Neil) and guests Cindy (Stacey Graves) and Ben (G. Gordon Cronce). Jennifer starts receiving written planchette messages from ghosts and demons, and one in particular, a man who has been murdered by his wife and two assassins. The oracle box glows an eerie green color,

Roberta Findlay's low-budget cheapie slasher *Blood Sisters* (1987) was one of her most successful horror films with audiences. Image courtesy of Media Blasters.

and sometimes it pulls people into its netherworld or eats them (not sure); sometimes it throws knives at them or stabs them, and sometimes a skeleton puppet demon comes out of it to terrorize its victims. Findlay shot one scene in an actual magic store in New York City when Jennifer goes in to ask for help with her psychotic oracle problem, and a friendly witch gives her advice. "The owner was a creepy Wiccan," according to Findlay. She continued,

> It didn't really make much sense to shoot there; it's just a crammed bookshop. It was stupid. But I did pick up *The Black Sabbath Bible* for *Prime Evil* later. And a Wiccan flag. We had to be there at dawn, four am, something like that. Of course, my AC [assistant cameraperson] was still hungover, and so was my gaffer. I was caught in the crosswind of their breath. The smell was extraordinary. I couldn't breathe ... Just to get the shot—that's all I ever wanted to do.[96]

Blood Sisters was the cheapest of Findlay's 1980s horror films and the only one that Findlay herself wrote:

> The cheapest of the cheap. I wrote the script for this one and we shot it in eight days. It was an experiment. All the tricks, the murder scenes, are practically nonexistent because those things are expensive! Walter did all the effects on BS as they were. That may be why it's boring because there's not a lot of blood in it. After all, it's an attempt to be cheap. And we made a lot of money on it; we sold it to Sony![97]

Blood Sisters is about sorority girls stalked and killed by a deranged serial killer on their pledge night. During the shoot, two German shepherd dogs wandered the house guarding it against burglars, making Findlay very nervous. It also had no heat, and they were shooting in the winter.[98]

Lurkers (originally titled *Home Sweet Home)*[99] is probably the best of Findlay's 1980s horror films. Despite an opening scene shot incredibly badly, the rest of the film and the story build into something more substantial than the other films. Ed Kelleher and Harriette Vidal wrote it; Kelleher had written one previous screenplay for a film that Findlay worked on in the early 1970s: *Shriek of the Mutilated* (1974). *Lurkers* stars Christine Moore in her first role; Moore would star in Findlay's next film, *Prime Evil,* and then several other horror films throughout the 1980s and 1990s, including the notorious Joseph W. Sarno's *Helgerån* (1988). In *Lurkers,* Moore plays an unstable young woman with childhood trauma named Cathy. The "Lurkers" are spirits trapped in the buildings of New York City, unable to leave, terrorizing the people that live within them. *Lurkers* has an intentionally surreal quality that Findlay's other films don't. Findlay plays with time, space, and reality, so we're never quite sure if Cathy is hallucinating or experiencing some of the horrors she witnesses. Like Jennifer in *The Oracle*, Cathy is made to feel crazy until the truth is finally exposed. When making *Tenement*, Findlay said she hated the building because it reminded her of the horrible building in which she grew up; she then made *Lurkers*, a movie about a woman who doesn't want to return to the building in which she grew up.

Findlay and Sears sold *Lurkers* to Crown International, who thought it was a great film. They asked them to make another film like it for them. Kelleher and Vidal had another script, the satanic horror story *Prime Evil*. They cast Moore again as the protagonist Alex. *Prime Evil* also features Amy Brentano, who played Linda in *Blood Sisters.* Alex works at a teen rescue organization and has recently been troubled by several young girls going missing. One of them she brought back to the church for the night, hoping to give her a place to rest, but the girl vanished. Two police detectives investigating the disappearances make the connection to the church and believe that they are sacrificing the girls to Satan.

Banned was Findlay's last film, but it has, as of 2022, never been officially released. Clips and trailers for the film exist. It's a comedy horror about a musician possessed by the soul of a dead punk rocker. *Banned* was made because Findlay and Sears' accountant advised them to shoot another film before the end of the fiscal year so they'd have more write-offs on their taxes and avoid a high payment to the Internal Revenue Service. "So, we grabbed the first thing we could find, and the script was just terrible," said Findlay in an interview. "I said, Walter, this thing is terrible."[100] They made it anyway. It was, in Findlay's own words, a "total disaster. It's terrible. We made no sales. It's a rock 'n' roll comedy. I know nothing about rock 'n' roll, and I'm not a comedic director."[101] Findlay added rock music scenes and some comedy, but it just didn't help:

> I remember editing the film, and every time I made a cut, I said, "This can't be sold," and I was right. So, we lost all our money on that thing. We wrote it off, of course. Walter said, "Well, you make one bad one out of thirty-six films. Let's try another one." I said, "Not with my money; you ain't doing it." And that was the end of that.[102]

In October 2020, film distributor Media Blasters announced that they had the negatives and were going to release *Banned* on Blu-ray.[103]

Some say Doris Wishman's *A Night to Dismember* (1983) was filmed in New York City in 1979, but Andrea Juno's 1986 interview with Wishman in *Incredibly Strange Films* states that she began work on the film in 1983. "There's a lot of blood in this," said Wishman of the film, "but that's what the public wants, and if you're in the business, you have to give them what they want if you have the courage."[104] A worker fired from the film lab where *A Night to Dismember* was stored burned down the entire building and all of the film prints inside it. *A Night to Dismember* had been shot on 35mm and was uninsured, so when it was gone, everyone believed it was gone forever, and Wishman lost every penny she had put into making it, forcing her to move to Florida to live with family. From then on, Wishman kept all of her films on VHS stored in a box in her garage. Wishman never finished *A Night to Dismember*, and as Michael Bowen so fittingly says, it existed in a "dismembered state"[105] until 2018 when the cinematographer uploaded a finished version that he'd made of it based on the original "burnt" version. There are two versions, officially: the supposedly "lost" original version and the refilmed version officially released in 2001. Both have been digitized, and both are available to watch. The refilmed version is about the cursed Kent family; they all seem to kill each other because of some mental illness or secret dark supernatural spell. Adult actress Samantha Fox plays Vicki Kent (with no speaking lines), who has just been released from a mental hospital for murdering two boys. The Kent family is unhappy to have her back, and soon her extended family, ex-boyfriend, and friends are murdered. Fingers point to Vicki, but her sister Mary (Diane Cummings) has been murdering everyone and blaming it on her sister all these years. The original version is also about the cursed Kent family, but the resemblance to the reshoot stops there. Both films feature Wishman's signature sound voice-overs, mismatched scenes, strange inserts of static objects, and silly music.

I've already discussed a few women directed horror film sequels at the beginning of this chapter, and *Pet Sematary II* will be discussed in Chapter 6. Sequels have been an important vehicle for filmmakers to get their foot in the director's door both in Hollywood and horror. In the 1980s and 1990s, sequels, and prequels, gave women a built-in audience for their finished product and gave studios more faith in their ability to direct in a male-dominated genre. However, sequels *usually*[106] don't match up to their predecessor's greatness. It might be that sequels usually went straight to video, the budgets were often lower, the talent second-choice, or that public interest grew wary of sequels because they tended to be so bad (a vicious cycle) that contributed to sequels' "bad reputations."

By 2020, sequels were a legitimate aspect of new franchises and great opportunities for women directors. For instance, *See No Evil 2* (2014), the sequel to the slasher film *See No Evil* (2006), was an upward career move for independent filmmakers Jen Soska and Sylvia Soska. After they'd made the low-budget, independent *Dead Hooker in a Trunk* (2008) and the higher-budget but still independent *American Mary* (2012) (we'll discuss both films in Chapter 9), they made *See No Evil 2*, which was a mainstream(ish) theatrical franchise that was heavily publicized at major horror and comic conventions. *See No Evil 2* stars Danielle Harris, herself a director (we'll discuss her work in Chapter 8 as

Either Jen or Sylvia Soska, identical twins, directing Dean Cain on the set of *Vendetta* (2015). Image courtesy WWE Studios.

A dark and scary moment from *Camera Phone 2* (2016), directed by Meosha Bean.

well), and pits her character Amy against mass murderer Jacob Goodnight (played by World Wrestling Entertainment celebrity Glenn 'Kane' Jacobs). Harris partly did the film because of her desire to work with other women horror film directors:

> I was actually a huge Soska twin fan before this film, as I loved *American Mary* ... the idea of being directed by women was something I felt had been lacking in the genre for quite a long time, considering that most of the leads in these movies, especially the ones I'm in, are usually females ... So with the women in the films having to save the day and defeat the monster, I wanted to see what it would be like to have a female's perspective on a genre story.[107]

Sylvia Soska took the opportunity of directing a sequel to improve on the first film's flaws. "We felt like we had some room to play with the character of Jacob for the sequel," she said in 2014 when *See No Evil 2* was released. "What was he missing? What could we change so that we can make him actually scary this time around?"[108]

Another example of women directors getting ahead with sequels is Meosha Bean, who had been making short, low-budget horror films and music videos and releasing them online when, in 2015, a filmmaker named Eddie Brown Jr. contacted her. He loved her work and wanted her to direct a segment in the sequel to his found footage 2012 horror movie *Camera Phone* called *Camera Phone 2* (2016). Bean and another filmmaker named Andrew Kripps both directed segments of this new found footage anthology. Bean also directed two feature-length sequels to the action series *Anatomy of an Antihero* created by Alan Delabie. After directing episodes of the series *Anatomy of an Antihero 2*, Bean wanted to direct a feature-length film version, and Delabie agreed that she should. Bean could access actors through her management that would not have been available for a limited series: Eric Roberts and Bob Wall (*Enter the Dragon*, 1973), for instance. "As a director coming from a horror background, this [action] movie was somewhat of a challenge to make," said Bean in an interview:

> I never understood martial arts until making this project. As a filmmaker, I do things

that scare me. Taking this job made me grow so much. I definitely incorporated my genre of expertise in scenes in the movie.[109]

Bean would continue to work with Delabie to direct the sequel *Anatomy of An Antihero 4: Redemption* (2018) as well as the horror film sequels *MVB Films Halloween Horror Stories Vol II* (2018), *M.V.B Films Anthology Vol III Paranormal* (2020), and *M.V.B Films Horror Vol 4: True Stories* (2022). In the 1980s and 1990s, horror sequels did not have the same prestige for directors as they do in the 2020s.

Beginning with the first film in 1988, the *Witchcraft* series features an iconic poster art of a gorgeous semi-nude woman lying down under a pentagram and a storyline that only loosely relates each of the films to one another. The series features recurring characters in our modern world and always involves black magic, satanic killings, and ritual magic. Each sequel is less coherent and less relatable to the first film than the previous entry. *Witchcraft III: The Kiss of Death* (1991) and *Witchcraft 666: The Devil's Mistress* (1994) are just two of the sequels in the sixteen-film-long (as of 2022) *Witchcraft series*. Several of the films in the series were produced by Vista Street Entertainment, which also produced other horror films directed by women like Deryn Warren's *Mirror of Death* (1987) and *The Boy From Hell* (1988), Laura Keats' *Crystal Force* (1992), Jan Marlyn Reesman's *Body Parts* (1992), and Kim Turney's *Bloodbath* (1999), along with several action and thrillers directed by women. Vista Street also produced *Witchcraft III* and *Witchcraft 666,* and Troma Entertainment distributed the films; all of the *Witchcraft* sequels went straight to VHS/DVD and skipped theaters completely.

Rachel Feldman is the director of *Witchcraft III*, and Jerry Daly wrote the script for Vista Street. Another Gerry Daly wrote *Mirror of Death* (1987) and *The Boy from Hell* (1988); these are *not* the same two people but are often confused in online databases. In the first two films, it's established that the lead character William Spanner is a baby in the first film and then a teenager in the second film. In the third, he's an adult William Spanner (played by Charles Solomon). After putting the events of the first two films behind him, William is now a district attorney, defending an accused murderer, a teenager named Ruben Carter (Ahmad Reese), and William adamantly believes in his innocence. Spanner and his girlfriend Charlotte (Lisa Toothman) sometimes go to seedy clubs, and there Charlotte meets the magical and evil Louis (Domonic Luciana). Louis is a witch and uses his powers to seduce and enslave women sexually, including Charlotte, and then kills them to steal their life force and transfer it to his evil girlfriend, Marlena (Alexa Jago). Spanner must stop this serial killer Louis and can only do so by unlocking his latent magic powers, received from the previous two films. Reverend Jondular (William L. Baker) will help Spanner unleash his magic and stop Louis.

Witchcraft III has less gore and more sex than the previous *Witchcraft* installments. There are few special effects, and the witchcraft itself is underwhelming. It also has a strange script heavily padded by many additional scenes of people traveling from one location to another, walking, or doing mundane things. The worst discrepancy is that Spanner is a district attorney, so he would prosecute people, not defend them. The Reverend is a Christian priest and a voodoo practitioner. Feldman used the pseudonym

R.L. Tillmanns for the release of *Witchcraft III*. She was a young, eager filmmaker hired for a directing job and was probably grateful for that. But her work since then has been entirely different: many episodes of mainstream television series like *Doogie Howser, M.D.* In 2022 she helmed a biopic of Fair Pay activist Lilly Ledbetter called *Lilly*.

Witchcraft 666: The Devil's Mistress, directed by Julie Davis, is more accurately a softcore pornography film than a horror movie. Written by Davis and Peter Fleming (whose only other credit is the writer of *Witchcraft 7: Judgment Hour*, 1995), it was, like Feldman's, Davis' first directing job. The story still revolves around Will Spanner, though now he is played by Jerry Spicer, usually a stuntman in genre films like Roger Corman's ill-fated *Fantastic Four* (1994). Spanner is still a lawyer, and he has been working as a psychic for the police department as well, so detectives bring him in on a new serial killer case. Someone is murdering beautiful young women wearing gold crosses, and they need Spanner's magical powers to help stop the killer. Bryan Nutter is the evil witch, Mr. Savatini, who is murdering beautiful virgins in his witchy rituals as Satanic sacrifices. Two police detectives, Lutz (Kurt Alan) and Garner (John E. Holiday), are Spencer's partners in this murder case. The characters of Lutz and Garner would go on to be featured in many of the *Witchcraft* sequels. Kelli (played by Debra K. Beatty, who also starred in Jackie Garth's softcore science fiction movie *Cyberella: Forbidden Passions*, 1996) gets naked. There is much more nudity in *Witchcraft 6* than in *III*, but the plot isn't too different from *III* (or *IV* or *V*) in that an evil person is murdering women for witchy reasons, and Spanner has to stop it.

The *Mirror Mirror* series, as is implied, is mainly about a witchcraft-infused mirror that preys upon women's insecurities to wreak unspeakable evil upon them and those around them. *Mirror Mirror*'s director, Marina Sargenti, also directed the television horror film *Child of Darkness, Child of Light* (1991). Of *Mirror Mirror*'s three sequels, two others would be directed by women. Jimmy Lifton was the producer of all four and director of the second installment. His wife, Paulette Victor-Lifton, directed the fourth installment. All the *Mirror Mirror* films were made by the Orphan Eyes production company, headed by producer Virginia Perfilii (who also directed the third film in the series). It's incestuously strange that these four people made four films in this series, each worse than the previous one, each with lower budget and fewer resources, and holding on to the franchise that would need to be pried from their cold, dead hands in 2000 when *Mirror Mirror 4* finally quashed their ambition to continue with it.

In the first *Mirror Mirror* film, a goth teenager named Megan Gordon (Rainbow Harvest) goes to live in a new house with her kooky mom (Karen Black) after her father has passed away. Megan is bullied at her new school but makes friends with her classmate Nikki (Kristin Dattilo). Nikki begins to sense that there's something strange going on with Megan aside from the fact that she's goth and looks exactly like Wynona Ryder, outfit and all, from the film *Beetlejuice* (1988). Megan's house is the site of an old murder from the 1940s when one sister stabbed the other to death. All the antiques were removed from the house by real estate agent Mrs. Perlili (Ann Hearn) and antique dealer Emelin (Yvonne De Carlo), except for this strange, huge, magic-looking mirror which is haunted by demonic forces and responsible for the murder in the house. It has attached itself to Megan, and it fulfills all of her evil wishes to kill people. In the end, Nikki helps save Megan from the forces she can't control.

Billy Drago stars in *Mirror Mirror 3: The Voyeur* (1995), directed by Rachel Gordon and Virginia Perfili.

Billy Drago also stars in *Mirror Mirror 4: Reflections* (2000), directed by Paulette Victor-Lifton.

Despite the mildly authentic moments in the film (the mirror bleeds; Megan rubs up against the mirror and licks blood off of it; a creepy demon hand comes out of the mirror; a demonic head and torso try to leave the mirror; Karen Black gets her arm stuck in the garbage disposal, and the mean teenage girl is burned by scalding hot steam in the shower room so that her skin falls off), it's impossible not to notice that *Mirror Mirror* is a rehashing of *Carrie*: a teenage girl is picked on and uses her supernatural powers to get revenge. The characters are named after people making the film: Mrs. Perlili, the real estate agent (Perfili produced all of the films), and Megan Gordon (Rachel Gordonwould direct the second one)

Sargenti shows a decent amount of blood in the movie, but in a May 1991 interview with film journalist Maitland McDonagh, she said she wanted to tone down the gore. "I like scary movies, and I'd rather show a little less and scare the hell out of the audience rather than gross everyone out with a room full of blood and body parts," she said. "Don't get me wrong—there's a scene in *Mirror Mirror* where a woman's hand gets dragged into a garbage disposal, and there's blood everywhere."[110] Weird accidents plagued the set. "At first, it was funny, but it began to spook people," said Sargenti:

> Two of the actors were having such awful nightmares that they couldn't sleep, and there was an article in the Globe while we were shooting, you know: *Disaster Hits Demon Movie Set* with a picture of our mirror monster. A terrible picture, I might add ... It was an interesting example of what your mind can do when you let it run wild.[111]

Mirror, Mirror III: The Voyeur (1995) was directed by Rachel Gordon and Virginia Perfili. Perfili was the producer of the first three *Mirror Mirror* installments and the director of *Bikini Witness*, a 1995 exploitation crime film starring Deborah Dutch (*Sorority Girls and the Creature from Hell*, 1990). Gordon also made the cheesy action film *Death Run to Istanbul* (1993). Perfili would go on to direct the horror film *Cheerleader Chainsaw Chicks* (2018). Unlike the previous two films, *Mirror Mirror III* was released straight to video and had terrible reviews. The production values, action, and direction are considerably worse than in the first two *Mirror Mirror* films.

The last film, *Mirror, Mirror IV: Reflection* (2000), was directed by Paulette Victor-Lifton. Victor-Lifton had edited *Mirror Mirror III* and been a producer on the whole series. Perfili, director of *Mirror Mirror III*, served as a consultant. But it was Victor-Lifton and James Lifton who, having begun the series, would write the last installment and push it through to the end. They wrote the film in two weeks and shot it in nine days. Victor-Lifton feels that the *Mirror Mirror* series is less like *Carrie* and more like "The Monkey's Paw," a be-careful-what-you-wish-for story. "Making the story your own is very hard," she admitted. "I think the first film was the best and I wish I had more than two weeks to write mine. I think the most important thing is to keep the spirit of the story and the main theme." One of the things that Victor-Lifton loved best about the *Mirror Mirror* series is that it all had female lead characters. "Each of the stories, especially the original, was based on female characters," she said. "The second and the fourth were female-driven, which appealed to me. All the women in the films were strong, the evil and the good." I think Victor-Lifton sees the *Mirror Mirror* series as more of an erotic female fantasy than a horror movie. She admitted that she doesn't like gore and believes that gore films mostly appeal to men.[112]

Children of the Corn 666: Isaac's Return (1999), directed by Kari Skogland, is about as late in the game as a director can get on a franchise. This sixth installment was co-written by John Franklin (he played "Isaac" in the first film) with Tim Sulka. It goes back to the roots of the first film, telling the audience how Isaac wasn't killed at the end but survived because of his magic powers. Now, the daughter of one of the original children of the corn has decided to visit the small Midwestern American town of Gatlin to find out the truth about her birth. There's a prophecy of some kind that the first-born daughter of the corn cult children will return to Gatlin and start a new pure race with He Who Walks Behind the Rows, the god they worship. "I loved seeing Isaac years later, a father and still secure in his worship of He Who Walks Behind the Rows," said John Franklin in an interview.[113]

Children of the Corn 666 was not a planned sequel. Franklin had wanted to return to the series since his character Isaac was killed off at the end of the original movie. Franklin and his co-writer, theater manager Tim Sulka (with whom he had created a comic book), came up with an idea for the sixth film and pitched it to Miramax/Dimension. The studio green-lit the film because they wanted to end the series once and for all. "However," explained Franklin in an interview, "*666* made too much money, and they got greedy and cranked out a few more after ours."[114] Director Kari Skogland was originally from Canada and worked as an editor before becoming a director. She had directed two low-budget independent films, one of which was a crime thriller titled *Men with Guns* (1997), before taking on some genre television episodes, like *La Femme Nikita* and *The Crow: Stairway to Heaven*, before making *Children of the Corn 666*, but she didn't have much experience in Hollywood.

We mentioned Kristine Peterson earlier when talking about Corman, her horror film *Deadly Dreams* (1988), and the erotic thriller *Body Chemistry* (1990). Peterson's next film was the horror sequel *Critters 3* (1991), a PG-13 film starring a young Leonardo DiCaprio as the lead. Written by David J. Schow, who also wrote *Critters 4*, *Critters 3* was shot almost simultaneously with *Critters 4*. Several scenes for both films were shot at a supermarket on Pico Blvd in Los Angeles, California, where New Line had also filmed scenes for *Suburban Commando* (1991).[115] *Critters 3* is an awful film. It continues with the same theme from the previous *Critters* films: adorable but deadly space alien creatures that love to eat humans come down to earth in a spaceship and proceed to wreak havoc in an R-rated *Gremlins* fashion. Peterson has gone on to have a great career in genre television directing.

The Howling VI: The Freaks (1991) was directed by Hope Perello, who had worked for Charles Band on numerous Full Moon films before starting her directing career. She got the job when the director the producers had originally wanted, Steve Johnson (the special effects artist for *Howling IV: The Original Nightmare* and numerous other horror films), left the project. She had initially been hired only to budget the film, but when Johnson dropped out, Perello took the initiative and pitched the producers her version of the sixth *Howling* film. "They ended up agreeing to hire me after getting a producer friend of mine to guarantee that I would deliver the goods," she said in an interview:

> One of the producers kept saying to me, "I can't believe I hired a woman director. I can't believe it!" all the time. It was unsettling and made me feel as if he was hoping I would fail. There wasn't a lot of confidence in a female director's ability to do a good job with horror, probably because the horror genre at that time, especially slasher films, was often violent and sexist.[116]

This sixth installment of the *Howling* series takes place in a carnival with a Gothic atmosphere and is less gory than the previous *Howling* films. A young werewolf becomes trapped by an evil carnival owner and is forced to join the freak show. This more magic-based and romantic *Howling* film is a result of Perello's vision for the movie:

> I treated the film like a Gothic mystery featuring a tortured soul—the werewolf—as the protagonist, which he was written to be. And having a carnival freak show as a backdrop to the story allowed for a lot of creativity with the art direction, cinematography, wardrobes, etc. And I used classic films from auteurs like Antonioni as inspiration, especially in some scenes involving the main characters of Brendan and Elizabeth, whose love story was poignant though non-traditional. I think I tried to elevate the film beyond the expectations of a low-budget sequel needed to keep the franchise going.[117]

Though it's not as gory as horror fans would have liked, Perello did have her actor Antonio Fargas bite the head off of a chicken in one scene for that authentic carnival feel. "The interesting thing about the *Howling* films is that none has anything to do with any of the others," said Perello in a 1991 interview with *Fangoria* magazine to promote the release of the film on video:

> In a way, it's their downfall; they could have had a continuing character like Freddy Krueger, but for me, it was liberating not to have to pick up a character who'd already been in five films and try to think of something new to do with him. I also had a chance

> to experiment stylistically; I did a lot of weird things that work because the whole milieu is so eerie.[118]

There had originally been no sex scene in the script Perello and writer Kevin Rock had written (Rock also wrote the screenplay for Corman's doomed 1994 Fantastic Four adaptation), but they added it later. Perello didn't want to have her lead female character get naked in the film. But she initially hadn't envisioned it as a nude scene for the actress. "One producer really wanted more skin," she said.

> I guess he felt it would increase the film's chances on tape. It got to the point where I wanted to say, "Look, if you just want someone to take her clothes off, I'll talk to the script supervisor, and she and I will strip the day you're on the set. I'll get some of my friends to come over, and they'll rip off their clothes, too, if that will thrill you." But the other producer really stood by me, and in the end, we kept it out of the film.[119]

Freddy's Dead: The Final Nightmare (*A Nightmare on Elm Street Part VI*) (1991) was supposed to be the last in the *Elm Street* series. One of the most famous horror movie franchises of all time, the series had released sequels almost every year since the first installment appeared in theaters in 1984. On every *Elm Street* film, except for number five, Rachel Talalay served officially as a crew member. Talalay started as a production assistant on John Waters' film *Polyester* (1982). Before taking up the director's chair on *Freddy's Dead*, she worked as a production manager or assistant director on genre films like *Alone in the Dark* (1982), *Android* (1982), *The House on Sorority Row* (1983), and *Return to Horror High* (1987). As an employee of New Line Cinema in the 1980s and '90s, she worked on every *Elm Street* film as either line producer, production manager, or assistant director. She directed and wrote *Freddy's Dead: The Final Nightmare* in 1991. Talalay had wanted to direct *A Nightmare on Elm Street Part 5* (1989) but wasn't given the job. Instead of working on *Part 5* under director Stephen Hopkins, she worked with John Waters on his new film *Cry-Baby* (1990). Then, she gave New Line an ultimatum: "I told them to please let me know if they were taking the request equally seriously because, if they weren't, I was going to stop hanging around waiting for a directing chance."[120]

New Line was experimenting with many new ideas and distributing films like *Reefer Madness* (1936) and filmmakers like Werner Herzog, exploring the world of pretentious art films and cult genre films as viable avenues of revenue. While Talalay was at New Line and got the job directing *Freddy's Dead*, Bob Shaye was head of the company. Talalay was precisely the kind of person Shaye wanted to hire to direct: she'd worked in the low-budget cult world of John Waters but also had a strong sense of the entire *Elm Street* series. "Bob really made the films that he wanted to make," said Talalay when discussing her first studio film as director:

> [He] is an incredibly astute businessman and also a total film lover interested in both sides of the coin. He aimed to do a wide variety of things and do it all by not working within the scope of the studio system in those days.[121]

The Head of Production at New Line was a woman, Sara Risher, something also uncommon at the time. It wasn't until Talalay left New Line that she felt any barriers to her career because of her gender. "I'm aware that people have a lot of questions about women directing horror," she said, "But I don't think gender is a major consideration ... I think a woman can bring certain things to horror films in general, things like paying more attention to the actors and characterization rather than effects."[122]

THEY SAVED THE BEST FOR LAST.

FREDDY'S DEAD
THE FINAL NIGHTMARE

TOP: Upon entering the dream world, Carlos' (Ricky Dean Logan) hearing is definitely impaired when confronted by the evil Freddy Krueger.
Photo credit: John Bramley
BOTTOM: Maggie (Lisa Zane) has the upper hand during her battle with evil dream master Freddy Krueger (Robert Englund, left) in New Line Cinema's chilling finale, *Freddy's Dead: The Final Nightmare.*
Photo credit: Suzanne Tenner

NEW LINE CINEMA

Courtesy of New Line.

In a 1991 interview about the making of *Freddy's Dead*, Talalay talked about why she was the ideal choice to direct the next sequel in the *Elm Street* series: "I can bring a whole lot to this film because of my *Nightmare* experience. I really know what works with Freddy:

> With this film, I wanted to get away from the Gothic feeling the last couple of *Nightmare* films had ... I wanted this movie to have a more gritty and urban feel and a distinctly visual style to it. I like the idea that the script spends more time on character and relationship scenes and has gotten away from funerals, teens crying over their friends' deaths, and the mandatory retelling of Freddy's back story. This script is different and definitely more adult.[123]

The film itself is an overly-cartoonish and shallow reworking of the original idea. In *Freddy's Dead*, all of the children in Springwood have been murdered by Freddy, and there is only one survivor left who was sent out of the town to protect him from the evil dream demon. The teen, named John Doe (Shon Greenblatt), has horrible nightmares that overwhelm him. After he is sent to a teen youth authority shelter for troubled kids, Freddy manages to pull him into a strange, dreamy kind of Springwood in which Freddy has a lot of control over the physical world. John and his therapist Maggie Burroughs (Lisa Zane, who is also in 2003's *Freddy vs. Jason* (2003) and other troubled youths Tracy (Lezlie Deane), Spencer (Breckin Meyer, who is in both *The Craft*, 1996, and *Clueless*, 1995), and Carlos (Ricky Dean Logan, who appears in the segment "Psycho Therapy" in the all-women horror anthology *Shevenge*, 2019, directed by Staci Layne Wilson), travel to the real Springwood in an old van to find out the mystery of who John Doe is.

Unfortunately, once they arrive in town, they're trapped by Freddy, who torments them one by one with some secret agenda.

Freddy's Dead is incredibly outlandish in terms of storyline, atmosphere, and set design. It's a very surface-level silly movie that doesn't work due to the slower, incredibly unsettling moments created by Wes Craven in the original movie. Several of the most outlandish moments include an homage to *The Wizard of Oz* (1939) when John Doe's house is flying around inside a tornado, and when he opens the window, Freddy appears riding on a broomstick like the Wicked Witch of the West. An entire segment toward the film's last act is supposed to be viewed in 3-D glasses. Breckin Meyer's character Spencer enters a dreamlike video game world (based on the Nintendo graphics of the early 1990s) that has him busting through walls and jumping to the ceiling with video game sound effects. Cameos include strange appearances by Johnny Depp, Alice Cooper, and Roseanne Barr. "We wanted to kill Freddy for good," explained Talalay in an interview. "We'd been making a film a year, and it was too much. Also, it was the time of *Twin Peaks*, so we wanted lots of cameos and weird dark humor."[124] In addition, she isn't fond of how the 3-D turned out and wishes she had been able to make the film a little later when digital graphic technology was improved from what it was in 1991:

> I wish I'd been able to make a *Nightmare* film in the digital age. But, not like *Freddy v. Jason*, which was the kitchen sink of effects, just selective use of digital, so stuff like Spencer (Breckin Meyer) in the video game would be awesome and simple now ... We didn't have the resources to test the technology well enough. So we were winging it. I think it barely worked and limited everything I could do in the end. It was pure gimmick and cost a lot of money that I would have used to make the rest of the film better and not have a lame ending take place in a room the size of my bedroom.[125]

She also isn't fond of the tone and sense of humor. She wonders if it was "a mistake to go the humorous, tongue-in-cheek route with Freddy. I wondered if we should have gone full-on horror ... We were burned out on ideas, on scripts, and horror was predictable. We were looking for something to make it different."[126]

Reviews of *Freddy's Dead* ranged from so-so to horrible. *The Spokane Chronicle* review said it was "ambitious, light-hearted, heavy-handed, and horrific ... a garish, Gothic comedy of terror,"[127] while the *Asbury Park Press* called it "by the numbers" with "grossness rather than frights."[128] The *Los Angeles Times*, in the heart of Hollywood, said it was "weirdly stylized in the wrong ways," and blamed Talalay's inexperience as a director for the hand-held camera and choppy editing.[129] It wasn't dead on arrival, though: the film did well at the box office, making $13 million in almost two thousand theaters on opening weekend, beating out the former winner *Terminator 2: Judgment Day* (1991). And while *Freddy's Dead* is not anyone's favorite horror movie, it is crucial to the story of women genre film directors because it is only the second time in film history that a woman director was hired for a big studio genre film. This wouldn't happen to another woman director until Kathryn Bigelow made the thriller *K-19: The Widowmaker* in 2002. Though Bigelow's budget was considerably higher than Talalay's (over $100 million), it is a milestone, nonetheless, prompted not only by New Line's faith in Talalay, their franchise, and horror fans but probably by the recent success of *Pet Sematary* (1989), the first studio horror film ever directed by a woman.

Internet horror films were trendy in the early 1990s through the early 2000s when the mystery of "how they worked" disappeared. Talalay would next direct the technology-horror movie *Ghost in the Machine* (1993). In it, a serial killer's soul is uploaded into a computer by an electrical surge. Other horror and thriller films that get it so funnily wrong for horror include *Brainscan* (1994), *The Net* (1995), *The Webmaster* (1998), and *FeardotCom* (2002); it was a robust subgenre that combined science fiction and horror with computer technology designed to exploit people's anxieties about using computers. In 1995, she directed the big-budget fantasy/sci-fi/action film *Tank Girl* (1995), with Lori Petty as the title character; *Tank Girl* had a budget of $25 million but brought in only $4 million gross profit in theaters. After *Tank Girl*, Talalay directed television and has not returned to studio feature filmmaking. Some of her television genre work has been highly acclaimed and gathered her attention for her directing skills in ways that her features never did. Peter Capaldi, one of the stars of the twenty-first-century *Doctor Who* series, said that "There are a lot of people directing, but very few who are really special:

> Rachel is. She will get the best out of any scene—technically, dramatically, visually, and emotionally—and is wonderfully collaborative to work with. She excels at getting beauty and drama to flourish in our punishing schedules, not a task for the timid or mean-spirited, and has the heart and eye of an edgy, smart artist.[130]

In June 2018, my film festival Etheria gave an Inspiration Award to Talalay for her work as a pioneering genre director who happens to be female. At the event, after Lori Petty presented her with her award onstage, Talalay said to the audience,

> I am constantly exasperated that my gender is even a topic of discussion. But we're on the cusp now, and I want you, all of you, to use genre as a voice to get under their skins, make your statements, tell your stories, break down their walls, and kick down that glass ceiling.

Talalay is still directing genre television as I write this.

Horror 102: Endgame (2004), *Day of the Dead 2: Contagium* (2005), and *Creepshow 3* (2006) are three horror sequels that most horror fans have never heard of (or would prefer to forget, if possible). All three were directed or co-directed by Ana Clavell, who formed the film production company Taurus Entertainment with her husband and business partner, James Dudelson. Through Taurus, Dudelson directed the films *Horror 101* (2001) and *Museum of the Dead* (2004), while Ana produced. *Day of the Dead 2: Contagium* is a direct, but not authorized, sequel to George Romero's acclaimed zombie horror movie *Day of the Dead* (1985), the third in his *Of the Dead* series of films. Clavell wrote the script in December 2003, which went into production in April 2004 in Norwalk, Southern California. Surprisingly, the film was shot on 35mm despite having a straight-to-DVD distribution plan through Anchor Bay films; perhaps Clavell and Dudelson believed it would have a theatrical run before Anchor Bay purchased the movie.[131] The awful special effects, camera work, and awkward editing have destroyed any real joy a Romero fan could get from watching the movie.

In the early 2000s, there was an explosion of low-budget, independent horror movies from amateur filmmakers inspired by the original Romero trilogy. The new digital cameras hitting the market were smaller and cheaper, and the Internet was the perfect place to distribute a horror movie one had made. Horror conventions began flourishing in cities throughout the United States, and people found a community of like-minded low-budget horror filmmakers to network with and share their films. Though women had made zombie movies before the 2000s (Jackie Kong's *Blood Diner*, 1987, Mary Lambert's *Pet Sematary*, 1989, Betty Stapleford's *Zombie Army*, 1991, Judith Priest's *Reanimator Academy*, 1992, and more), women directors such as Sue Corcoran (*Gory Gory Hallelujah*, 2003), Elza Kephart (*Graveyard Alive*, 2004), Emily Hagins (*Pathogen*, 2007), Janine Gosselin (*Killa Zombies*, 2007), and Christine Parker (*Fistful of Brains*, 2008) were making a decidedly on-purpose low-budget zombie film as a sort of homage to zombie films everywhere. These more self-aware zombie films have elements of comedy and cliché that *Day of the Dead: Contagium* does not. They also acknowledge and consider their low budgets rather than pretend they're high-budget productions, as Clavell and Dudelson seem to have done, at least with their attitudes towards fans and promotion. Taurus Entertainment later remade *Day of the Dead* (2008), unrelated to *Day of the Dead: Contagium*.

Creepshow (1982) was also Romero's original film based on the aesthetic of horror comics. The first two *Creepshow* films are beloved and acclaimed for their influence on future horror films and anthology series. While Clavell and Dudelson were making *Creepshow 3*, Romero was making a reboot of *Creepshow* with Stephen King and Matthew Leutwyler (*Dead and Breakfast*, 2004). Clavell and Dudelson's filmmaking is much lower budget than Romero's films in the early 2000s, with far less production value than the original *Creepshow* films. Having secured the rights to make both *Day of the Dead 2* and *Creepshow 3*, Taurus Entertainment made two of the worst horror film sequels ever directed by a woman to two of the best horror films ever created by a man. Shot on sets at Universal Studios in Hollywood, California, *Creepshow 3* has five separate short segments. The segments "Alice," "The Radio," "Call Girl," "The Professor's Wife," and "Haunted Dog" have subject matter like vampires, serial killers, hauntings, mad scientists, and different realities. Aside from being an anthology film with different horror segments, it can't be called a sequel in any meaningful way. Clavell's *Creepshow 3* (not to be confused with the 2001 film *Creepshow 3*, directed by Alex Wesley) is, plainly put, also terrible. Not only was the fan anticipation of the film and the reaction to its release mainly that it was going to be and was an abomination, but also that no one who isn't Romero should have been making a new version of *Creepshow* without his involvement or blessing.

The rights to the *Creepshow* and *Of the Dead* films seem like they should belong to the George A. Romero estate, but that isn't the case. According to Mike Gingold, who wrote the liner notes to the Scream Factory special edition Blu-ray of *Creepshow* (1982), the film was financed by several companies and run by parent companies that left and brought in new partners several times. One of these partners was Taurus Entertainment, owned by James Dudelson and his two sons. Taurus was supposed to act as a sales agent for the leading companies' film releases, but something unclear happened, and there were lawsuits. Presumably, in one of these lawsuits, the rights to *Creepshow* and any sequels became the property of Taurus.[132] Taurus also owns all the rights to the *Day of the Dead* film and any sequels, prequels, or remakes, presumably also won in these lawsuits. "If I had my way," said Clavell in 2005, "I'd do a *Creepshow* every year. It's a format you can get away with almost anything, and that is what I'd call storytelling freedom." She went on to describe the way she made the film her own:

The 2006 American Film Market poster art advertising *Creepshow 3* (2006), directed by Anna Clavell.

> I edited the stories together and intertwined the plots, so characters pop up in different episodes. Plus, there's animation, effects, and an extra ending sequence. One of the characters, Professor Dayton (created by James Dudelson, co-director), is a real piece of work, the kind of character you should never turn your back on. He pops up throughout, but we don't fully see the scope of his antics until the last story, "The Haunted Dog" ... Ultimately, it's the characters that compel me, and they usually try to go on by ignoring how their world is falling apart around them. I just try to stay close to them, as moral support.[133]

As is not unexpected, Clavell has experienced backlash for making bad sequels to some of the most beloved horror movies. "I shrug it off because," she explained, "in the end, I'm still the director."[134]

Yeogo goedam 3: Yeowoo gyedan, AKA Wishing Stairs (2003), is a Korean horror movie sequel directed by Yoon Jae-Yeon. Yoon had only made one short film, the thriller *Psycho Drama* (2000), when a producer scouted her at the 2000 Seoul Women's Film Festival. The company Cine 2000 was looking for a new director for the third entry in their horror film franchise *Whispering Corridors,* and they felt that Yoon was the right new talent for the job. Written by Kim Soo-Ah and Lee Yong-Yeon, *Wishing Stairs* is the third installment of the *Whispering Corridors* series of films in a creepy girls' school in South Korea. The first two films, *Whispering Corridors* (1998) and *Memento Mori* (1999), are not related directly but share a setting and general theme: supernatural horror and teenage girls at school.

Yoon is a master at suspense and shadowy images that scare, but she doesn't know

A creepy moment from *Whispering Corridors 3: Wishing Stairs* (2003), directed by Yun Jae-yeon.

The stuff of nightmares in *Urban Legends: Bloody Mary* (2005), directed by Mary Lambert.

how to make sense of the story. Yun Jin-seong (Song Ji-Hyo) and Kim So-hie (Han-byeol Park) are two teenage girls in high school who are best friends. There is an urban legend at their high school that when you climb the twenty-eight steps of the school staircase and carefully count each step, you might find that there is a secret twenty-ninth step, which, once reached, will grant you any wish you make.

Though it involves murder, ghosts, and legends, *Wishing Stairs*' teen horror morality lessons are reminiscent of the themes of films like *Heathers* (1987) and *Jawbreaker* (1999): the complex relationships between teenage girls are often nasty. There are some fabulous 'cat scares' and twisted scenes. There are also parallels to the story of "The Monkey's Paw" and the *Swan Lake* ballet, in which ghosts return to avenge their disloyal lovers.

Yoon's second feature is the 2009 horror movie *Yoga Class*, and she was a horror fan before she made *Wishing Stairs*. "*Wishing Stairs* was conceived as a genre film," explained Yoon in an interview,

"So it was in that sense easier for me, but also it was a little like a jigsaw puzzle. You know, the picture was already there, and I was looking for the pieces that fit together."[135]

Worried that the success of the first two films in the series would make things daunting, Yoon found that the most challenging part of making the sequel was creating the storyline:

> The big problem was how to find a story that did not overlap with the ones already told in *Corridors* and *Memento Mori*. That was pretty difficult. Eventually, we settled on the theme of jealousy and competition. It was decided early on that *Stairs* would follow the model of *Corridors* in the sense that a certain level of familiarity with genre conventions would be maintained. At the same time, *Memento Mori* was praised for its uniqueness, and its strong character, if you will, as a movie. For *Stairs*, we tried to create a unique look through production design.[136]

While both previous films in the series had been filmed at real school campuses during school vacation, *Wishing Stairs* was filmed on sets built from scratch. Only the exteriors were filmed at an abandoned school. The magic stairs were in a completely different location altogether. Yoon likes to put her characters in narrow, confined spaces: "I love the economy of visual composition and concentrated emotional effects I could have when, for instance, a character's backside and face are put in one shot. Mirrors were very helpful in this regard. "[137]

Urban Legends: Bloody Mary (2005), directed by Mary Lambert, is the third film in the *Urban Legends* slasher series, which began in 1998. The previous two *Urban Legend* films were popular because they were a fun example of the late-1990s teen horror resurgence that dominated horror between the release of *Scream* (1996) and the tragedy of 9/11. These late-90s films always had lead protagonists in high school or college and self-aware horror movie tropes that played out in gruesome and expected ways. Many of these films were the result of the fantastic horror script writing of Kevin Williamson, who not only wrote *Scream*, but also *I Know What You Did Last Summer* (1997), *The Faculty* (1999), and *Teaching Mrs. Tingle* (1999). The first *Urban Legend*, directed by Jamie Blanks (who also directed the horror film *Valentine*, 2001), is set at a university where students are being killed in gruesome ways that resemble the stories from local urban legends they've heard all their lives. In *Urban Legends: Bloody Mary*, the story is based on the supernatural legend of Bloody Mary: when a person looks in the bathroom mirror with the lights out and says "Bloody Mary" three times, the ghost Bloody Mary will come and take you away to Hell. It's a widespread sleepover party game that little girls play in the United States, and while no one ever has been taken away by Mary, it's still terrifying to young children.

In *Urban Legends: Bloody Mary*, girls at a high school sleepover play the game, setting off a chain of events that reveals a murder at their high school and guilty parents who have been hiding it for years. Unlike the other two *Urban Legend* films, this one is supernatural, and Mary is the ghost of the deadly high school girl seeking revenge on the people who killed her. It features deaths based on urban legends (spiders come out of a girl's cheek, a boy dies in a tanning bed, and one gets electrocuted when he pees on an electric fence). Unlike the first two films, *Urban Legends: Bloody Mary* was released straight-to-DVD and never played theatrically. Lambert herself liked the film. "I've always liked the movie and the way it turned out," she said in an interview:

> That legend, I have always liked it. I completely remember it from sleepovers when I was an adolescent, and you go in the bathroom. She always appeared, somehow. That's a legend that exists in a lot of other cultures. When I was sixteen, I spent the summer in Hawaii, and I heard it there. There's a version of that story that involves Pele, the volcano goddess, who is a really scary goddess, the goddess of wrath. If you cross her, she erupts and pours hot lava on your head. In fact, I would really like to do another version of that story in Hawaii and Pele.[138]

Urban Legends: Bloody Mary was made on a low budget. "We had no money—it was made for about $1.5 million in Utah," admitted Lambert, "But I thought the costume designer did a really good job with the 1960s flashbacks. I was in high school in the late sixties, so that was fun for me."[139]

In the 1980s, when women directors were discouraged by a lack of feature film directing jobs, they often went into television, which was churning out hundreds of television series on dozens of channels that needed content twenty-four hours a day, seven days a week, and in need of directors, male and female, for their rigorous schedules. There's disagreement about whether getting into television horror was easier for a woman than being hired to direct a feature, or vice versa, depending on which woman director you ask. "It's actually easier for a woman or a man who is brand new to directing to get a feature film than a television episode," Columbia Pictures television President Barbara Corday said in the 1980s. "I see it happening with some frequency."[140] Other women, like Sharron Miller (*The House of the Dead*, 1978), found a place directing for television in the 1970s relatively easy. "Back in those days," says Miller,

> There were not women directors, so it was just three or four of us in the 1970s. So the work was in television. So that's why I ended up going to television and having a happy and successful career there. I would have liked to do more features about things that interested me [not horror], but I never got that opportunity.[141]

Like his contemporary Corman, Norman Lear was instrumental in hiring women directors for television but insisted that he never made a conscious effort. "We went out of our way for talent, and a lot of talent belongs to women."[142] British director Lesley Manning felt that feature film and television directing jobs were just about even in terms of difficulty:

> It's the same. It was a sort of vacuum. I can't put my finger on it. I mean, why would that be? Is it mixed up with the fact that women were ... it was very hard for the industry to think that women were of note in those days. Women have to go out and do it before anyone will actually trust them to do it, whereas men will have people's trust to go out and do it.[143]

These are a few stories about the women who found a home directing horror television in the 1980s and 1990s.

Gabrielle Beaumont was a British director of compelling skill and talent with several horror films and numerous genre television series episodes on her resume. The child of actor and director Gabriel Toyne and actress Diana Beaumont (who had both starred in the 1950 British TV horror movie adaptation *Spring-Heeled Jack*), Beaumont began directing on the supernatural British television anthology series *Shadows*. The series was produced by Thames Television for Independent Television and aired from 1975 to 1978. A family-orientated show extending over three seasons, it featured ghost stories, horror dramas, and fantasy episodes that were appropriate for children. Beaumont directed an episode in season three called "The Silver Apple," a story set in a fantastical medieval land with princesses and wizards. There were two other women directors on the show: Pamela Lonsdale ("Honeyann," 1978) and Audrey Starrett ("After School," 1975 & "Time Out of Mind," 1976). Though I discussed British television horror extensively in Chapter

2, I didn't mention *Shadows* because of its family rating, nor did I cover some of the other extraordinary fantasy series directed by women at the time, such as Helen Standage's miniseries *The Lion, the Witch and the Wardrobe* (1967).

The poster art for Gabrielle Beaumont's horror film *The Godsend* (1980).

The Godsend (1980) is Beaumont's one theatrical feature horror film with full directing credit. In 1971, the low-budget horror movie *Crucible of Horror* was released with Viktors Ritelis credited as director and Beaumont as the producer. While it's true that Beaumont did produce the film, during production in 1969, she stepped in as director after Ritelis had to leave during principal photography for another job with BBC Television. Beaumont took over as director and completed all post-production from a director's and producer's point of view.[144] She did not receive a co-directing credit, however.[145] Olaf Pooley wrote *Crucible of Horror* and the screenplay for *The Godsend*. Pooley, as an actor, was in Beaumont's "The Sil1er Apple," her 1984 TV film *Gone Are the Dayes,* and her 1996 TV film *Beastmaster III: The Eye of Braxus*, indicating that they had a long and successful professional relationship.

The Godsend is based on the 1976 horror novel of the same name. It's a gorgeous film in the vein of *Burnt Offerings* (1976). *The Godsend* captures the inexplicable supernatural horror of losing children in a highly sophisticated way with a rural folk feel reminiscent of the best 1970s British horror films. Her next film, the thriller *Death of a Centerfold: The Dorothy Stratten Story* (1981), was made for television and starred Jamie Lee Curtis in an account of the life of Playboy model Dorothy Stratten, who her husband murdered at the age of twenty. As good as these films are, Beaumont's episodic horror television is most fascinating. Her *Fox Mystery Theater/Hammer House of Mystery and Suspense* episode "The Corvini Inheritance" aired in 1985, and her *Nightmare Classics* episode "Carmilla" aired in 1989. Beaumont was interviewed for the Los Angeles Times in 1986 about directing episodic television and how it differs from directing feature films. "The most difficult thing in the world to direct is episodic television," she said: "You need incredible technical knowledge and absolute endurance to shoot eight to ten pages of script a day. On a feature, you usually shoot two pages a day."[146]

Both "The Corvini Inheritance" and "Carmilla" are feature-length episodes. *Nightmare Classics* only has four episodes, one of which is Beaumont's, while *Fox Mystery Theater* has thirteen.

Fox Mystery Theater was the United States title for the British television series

Vampire Meg Tilly hovers in the air to bite her girlfriend Ione Skye in *Carmilla* (1989), Gabrielle Beaumont's episode of *Nightmare Classics*.

Eva (Jan Francis) doesn't know that she's being stalked in the *Fox Mystery Theater* episode *"The Corvini Inheritance"* (1985), directed by Gabrielle Beaumont.

Hammer House of Mystery and Suspense. Made as a response to the success of *Hammer House of Horror*, another episodic horror series, *Hammer House of Mystery and Suspense* usually didn't feature fantastical situations and was more, in general, rooted in real horrors. Beaumont's episode, "The Corvini Inheritance," was written by David Fisher, who had previously written for the fantasy series *Doctor Who* and *Hammer House of Horror*. Eva (Jan Francis) moves into a new apartment building. On her first night there, she encounters a masked man who stalks her. Her next-door neighbor Frank (David McCallum, who starred in Gloria Monty's *The Screaming Skull*)[147] is a security expert specializing in video security. He suggests that they install a camera in the hallway so they can catch the masked man on tape should he return. Reluctantly, Eva agrees. It's a slow-moving, never dull, suspenseful story with marvelous acting and strong direction. In "The Corvini Inheritance," Beaumont proves she is a superb director of her actors and the scenery, timing, and blocking. I'd highly recommend Beaumont's work to anyone who enjoys classic, well-made anthology series like *Alfred Hitchcock Presents* and *Boris Karloff's Thriller*; Beaumont would have fit right in as a director on both shows.

Nightmare Classics was promoted as the brainchild of actress and producer Shelley Duvall (known best to horror fans as Wendy Torrance in Stanley Kubrick's *The Shining*, 1980), but it was actually Bridget Terry, the unit publicist on the set of Duvall's 1980 film *Popeye*, who spearheaded Duvall's image as a producer for television. After producing the television fantasy film, *The Princess Who Had Never Laughed* (1984), Duvall, with Terry, created a series devoted to fairy tales called *Faerie Tale Theater*, which ran from 1983 to 1998, and the separate series *Tall Tales and Legends*, which followed the same pattern. Television and movie actors would guest star in her series, which were always designed for families to watch together. *Nightmare Classics*, which only had four episodes aired in 1989, was a completely different type of series. Again, horror stories from literature were adapted with recognizable actors for an adult audience. Airing on the cable channel Showtime, *Nightmare Classics* had a high budget but didn't last past the first season. Beaumont's brother, Christopher Toyne, produced the *Nightmare Classics* series and worked closely on each episode with the different directors. The episode

"Carmilla" is a television adaptation of the nineteenth-century vampire story of the same name by Sheridan Le Fanu. Screenwriter Jonathan Furst adapted the story and set it on an antebellum southern plantation in the United States.

Ione Skye plays Marie, a solitary young woman who lives on the plantation with her father, Leo (Roy Dotrice). Her mother died years ago, and Marie is very lonely. One day, Marie and her father come across a carriage wreck on their isolated road. An old woman in the carriage and the driver are both dead, but a young woman is still alive. They bring her to their home and call the doctor (John Doolittle) to care for her. The bodies they bury in their family crypt, where Marie's mother's body was placed. The young woman, Carmilla (Meg Tilly), is fascinating and strange, and soon she and Marie become very close. *Very close.* Like in the original story, Carmilla is a vampire set on seducing and transforming Marie into a monster.

A beautiful-looking film, "Carmilla" has Beaumont's classy, understated performances. Skye's Marie is incredibly naive and childlike. Meg Tilly is sweet and never menacing, but it works well and gives us a Carmilla with whom we believe Marie could have fallen in love. Beaumont's atmosphere is calm and tends towards the realistic and grounded, but when Marie and Carmilla have nocturnal love walks through the forest, she fills that atmosphere with garish blue light and fog. "I really enjoyed playing her," said Tilly in an interview. "She wasn't just a simpering mess; she had a distinct personality and energy. I remember where I was emotionally when I did it, and I was glad to have it; perhaps some of that emotion made its way into the picture."[148] Both women are wearing white dresses that flow in the air, and sometimes Carmilla defies physics by floating upside down to bite Marie's neck. The staking of the vampires gets bloody and delivers the Hammer-esque violence beloved by vampire movie fans. The doctor is splattered with blood by the end, his shirt more red than white. Marie herself, dressed in white, has a long red sash marring the perfect purity of her white gown, like a streak of blood. Beaumont sets much of the final horror during daylight hours, bringing the horror out of the dream world into reality and taking away some of the fear factors that horror fans gain from nighttime settings.

After "Carmilla," Beaumont moved on to shorter episodic series and television (except for the terrible fantasy movie *Beastmaster III: The Eye of Braxus* in 1996). After the year 2000, she didn't direct anything more. Beaumont has a "special thanks" credit on Karen Arthur's thriller feature *Lady Beware* (1987). With her brother, producer Christopher Toyne, Beaumont had optioned all the short stories of author Daphne Du Maurier, a family relation of theirs (except "The Birds"). The BBC was ready to make eight anthology episodes based on Du Maurier's works produced by Toyne and directed by Beaumont, but Du Maurier's son, Christian Browning, prevented the series from moving forward.[149] Beaumont passed away in October 2022.

In 1986, when forty-four-year-old Karen Arthur realized that she had been trying to make the erotic thriller *Lady Beware* since 1978 with no luck, she began to feel that it was because she was a woman that she wasn't getting opportunities. She had started writing *Lady Beware* at Universal in 1978, right after *The Mafu Cage* came out. "Since then," she said,

> It has had one hundred homes, seventeen drafts, and eight writers...The purseholders are men. And they attempted to make *Lady Beware* a violent picture. I am not interested in making a picture where a woman gets beat up. I want to show how a woman deals with this kind of insidious violence..."Surely now that I've done a feature, they'll let me direct," I thought. All I got were pats on the head.[150]

Arthur finally found directing work on television but felt it was a consolation prize rather than the career she had felt she deserved after her 1978 debut. Some of the older technicians on the television shoots told her that she was the first woman they'd seen directing on set since Ida Lupino. "I'm beginning to hear names of women I don't know who are directing the occasional Dynasty," she admitted. Arthur found work on television products, and so did many other female directors of her generation.

From the 1970s to the 1980s, numerous horror anthology television series ran in the United States and the United Kingdom, and women directors were continuously staffed. Actresses who had never directed before were directing episodes of these horror television shows, usually half-hour, fantastical, supernatural stories with some morality lesson attached. *Tales from the Darkside* first aired in 1983, kicking off a trend of half-hour fantasy and horror anthology series in the United States. Created by George A. Romero and producer Richard P. Rubinstein, it was originally discussed as a series called *Creepshow* to benefit from the popularity of the theatrical anthology horror movies *Creepshow* (1982) and *Creepshow 2* (1987) but ultimately was named *Tales from the Darkside* to imitate the popularity of horror comic books like *Tales from the Crypt* and to avoid any copyright issues with the film.

Five women directed episodes of *Tales from the Darkside,* including Jodie Foster, whose episode is "Do Not Open This Box." The show opened with a narration letting the audience know they were about to step over into the "dark side" and an image of a tree changing abruptly into a photographic negative along with ominous music. Short and sweet, the introduction would lead directly into the opening credits of each episode. Timna Ranon directed three episodes: "Bigalow's Last Smoke," "Mookie and Pookie," and "Dream Girl." Katarina Wittich (Romero's Assistant Director on *Day of the Dead*, 1985) directed the episode "Mary, Mary" (her only directing credit), Eleanor Gaver directed "The Apprentice," and Shelley Levinson directed the comedy horror episode "Djinn, No Chaser." Foster was a famous actress then, and directing was an experiment for her. "I wanted to be a director by the time I was six," said Foster in an interview about directing the 2017 science fiction anthology series *Black Mirror*:

> I did a television show with an actor/director, and I was just amazed that those two things could happen ... I see the *Black Mirror* piece as a stand-alone feature that is just a little shorter than what I might do on the big screen ... it says, "We're just gonna give you a movie, it's gonna have a beginning, a middle, and an end, and that's gonna be the end of it," and for me, that is the best form.[151]

"Do Not Open This Box" is about an older man, Charles (William LeMassena), and his wife, Rose (Eileen Heckart), who are in a loveless marriage. He loves to tinker in his basement and invent things, and she is constantly undermining him and criticizing him for not being successful. When a box labeled "Do not open this box" appears in the mail one day, they aren't sure what to make of it. It's the basic story of the fable "The Fisherman's Wife": a couple demands more and more money and luck from a supernatural entity until they end up with nothing. Foster's episode is pretty run-of-the-mill; it's set almost entirely in the home's basement, but Foster has control of the emotional atmosphere and the actors' interactions. "Do Not Open This Box" was released on VHS in 1985 with four other episodes of *Tales from the Darkside* as *Stephen King's Golden Tales*.

Shelley Levinson also directed several episodes of the 1980s reboot of *The Twilight Zone* and is a standout director of the series' comedy episodes. In 1982, Levinson won an Academy Award for Best Short Film for her film *Violet* (1981). The first of three reboots of *The Twilight Zone* series, this one was prompted by the success of Stephen Spielberg's *Twilight Zone: The Movie* (1983) and the popularity of the *Creepshow* films and *Tales from the Darkside*. Her episode "But Can She Type?" is about an unappreciated secretary who accidentally goes into a parallel universe where secretaries are revered when she uses the new copy machine in the office one night. "Time and Teresa Golowitz" is a poignant story about regret and traveling back to one's past to be a better person. Martha Coolidge, coming off of the success of her romantic comedy *Valley Girl* (1983), directed three episodes: the Christmas-themed "Night of the Meek," the science fiction future story "Quarantine," and the cautionary survival tale "Shelter Skelter." "Shelter Skelter," season two, episode nine, stars Joe Mantegna as Harry Dobbs, a survivalist who has built a bomb shelter filled with enough food, water, and guns to last for months, if not years, if there were nuclear war. His neglected wife, played by Joan Allen, hates his obsession with his downstairs man cave, not knowing it is actually a bomb shelter he had reinforced. Harry's employee Nick (Jon Gries), who works at Harry's gun store, is over at Harry's house while Harry's wife and kids are out of town. Drinking beer together, they contemplate what life would be like if there were a nuclear war. Just then, there's a nuclear explosion. Harry shuts him and Nick in the shelter, assuming the absolute worst, that the world is being destroyed by nuclear war. The explosion had not been caused by war but by an accidentally-detonated bomb that only destroyed their town. A dome covers what's left of the town to keep the radiation from spreading. Harry is trapped in his shelter under the dome and will never know that the world has not been destroyed. The two other women directors on *The Twilight Zone* reboot were Otta Hanus (episode "There Was an Old Woman") and actress Claudia Weill (episode "A Small Talent for War"). Weill was an acclaimed independent director; her 1978 comedy film *Girlfriends* was well-known. "A Small Talent for War" is only an eight-minute segment, but it packs a full punch and a classic *Twilight Zone* twist at the end.

Stephen Spielberg's anthology horror, science fiction, and fantasy series *Amazing Stories* (1985-1987) was higher-budget than most other anthology series in the 1980s. Almost all the stories were Spielberg's, and many of the screenplays were written by Mick Garris. The narratives were more playful and with higher production values than other series, and not every episode was meant to scare. Two women directed episodes of the series: Joan Darling (episodes "The Sitter" and "What If ... ?") and Lesli Linka Glatter (episodes "No Day at the Beach," "One for the Books," and "Without Diana"). Darling was a prolific television director, having been directing since the 1970s. In 1984, Glatter graduated from the prestigious American Film Institute Directing Workshop for Women and won numerous awards for her short film *Tales of Meeting and Parting* (1984). *Amazing Stories* was her first professional job as a director. Glatter says that Spielberg is "an incredible mentor." Right before she was to direct her first episode, "No Day at the Beach," she had a terrible nightmare about it. The next day, she told Spielberg about her dream: she was late to the set, she didn't recognize the crew, and it was nothing like she had expected, they had started shooting without her, and she was utterly unprepared. Spielberg said to her, "I have that dream before I start everything."[152] "No Day at the Beach" is one of the best episodes of *Amazing Stories*; it serves as a sort of test-run for Spielberg's most violent scenes in his later film *Saving Private Ryan* (1998) but has an added supernatural element. Shot beautifully in black and white, "No Day at the Beach" flows exactly like a Spielberg story is supposed to: it's just gritty enough to make you anxious but overflowing with sentiment. Glatter would go on to have a fantastic career directing television, with plenty of genre television series like *The Walking Dead* (2013), *True Blood* (2010–2012), and the original *Twin Peaks* (1990-1991).

Monsters (1988-1990) was created by Richard Rubinstein when *Tales from the Darkside* was canceled. It seems to have had an even lower budget than *Tales from the Darkside* and isn't nearly as polished as *Amazing Stories* and *The Twilight Zone*. Bette Gordon, whose independent, feminist film *Variety* (1983) was a critical success, directed four episodes: "Desirable Alien" (1991), "Habitat" (1990), "Jar" (1989), and "The Mother Instinct" (1989). Though low-budget, *Monsters* did attract some good actors. For instance, "Habitat" stars Lili Taylor as a woman who must spend months isolated in a room as part of an alien test. Lili Taylor was a notable actress in the 1990s, and since the entire episode takes place with her locked in one room, it was up to Taylor to make it a success. Indie director Sara Driver was hired to direct the episode "Bed and Boar" (1990), set in a motel room. Lizzie Borden, another independent filmmaker, directed the episode "La Strega" (1989) starring Linda Blair as a witch and Rob Morrow as a man who wants to kill her to get revenge for his dead mother; this episode mainly takes place in a dress shop and an apartment. Producer Debra Hill's episode "Far Below" (1990) was one of her only two directing credits. Hill was the producer responsible for the first three *Halloween* films, *The Fog* (1980), *Escape from New York* (1981), and *The Dead Zone* (1983). Before her death in 2005, she continuously produced comedy and horror films but only dipped her toes into directing. "Far Below," her episode, is the best of the *Monsters* episodes directed by women.

In one half-hour, she manages to pace a horror story about a man perfectly, Dr. Vernon Rathmore (Barry Nelson), who works in an office in the subway system of New York City with his small security team. When a city official comes to see why he has requested more funding, Rathmore shows him that a hideous, underground race of ape-like monsters eat humans live in the subway system, and he is the only one who can keep them under control. Dick Smith supervised the special effects makeup. The monsters look like the Morlocks in *The Time Machine* (1960); like the Morlocks, they live underground and can't

A promo shot for the *Amazing Stories* episode *"No Day at the Beach"* (1986), directed by Lesli Linka Glatter.

Jonas (M. Emmet Walsh) is mummified and can finally just enjoy the cats in the *Tales from the Crypt* episode *"Collection Completed"* (1989), directed by Mary Lambert.

bear any light. Rathmore explains that these creatures had always lived on the Earth and were only discovered when the New York City subway system was built. Of course, he can't let the city official leave now that he's learned the secret.

Like many other *Monsters* episodes, it is set in a small, confined area which means a smaller production cost but can be a challenge for unskilled directors. Hill knows what to show, how to show it, and how to build fun, if silly, suspense. It's a shame she didn't continue to direct. On the other hand, Lizzie Borden's episode "La Strega" is a real stinker.

The most well-remembered horror anthology series from the 1980s/1990s is *Tales from the Crypt*, developed for HBO as an original series based on the EC Comics series and adapted into a horror film anthology in 1972. Every episode is hosted by a skeletal puppet named The Cryptkeeper, who prefers to make bad jokes about the stories rather than scare the audience. Home Box Office is a pay cable channel; therefore, *Tales from the Crypt* was not subject to any network or FCC censorship for gore or nudity. Out of ninety-three episodes, three were directed by women. Only one of those women had any experience directing horror.

British director Mandie Fletcher has directed comedy most of her career, including episodes of the British series *Blackadder*; her episode "Smoke Wrings" has impeccable comedic timing. Randa Haines, who had won an Oscar for directing the drama *Children of a Lesser God* (1986), had worked a little in television since then. Her episode "Judy, You're Not Yourself Today" is a hot mess despite talent like Carol Kane playing the lead. It's mostly the incoherent script that makes the episode fail so badly, but unlike Fletcher, Haines has no comedic timing. Mary Lambert's episode "Collection Completed," from the show's first season, perfectly captures the sarcastic irony of the *Tales from the Crypt* aesthetic.

Like her work on the horror film *Pet Sematary* (1989), "Collection Completed" shows how deft she is with grotesqueness and tragedy. Anita (Audra Lindley, you'd know her best as Mrs. Roper from the television series *Three's Company*) is a middle-aged woman living with her husband Jonas (M. Emmet Walsh, who has been in hundreds of films and television series) in their comfortable home. Anita, however, loves pets, and Jonas can't stand them. The cats and dogs annoy him to no end for roughly twenty-five minutes, and then he cracks: he kills and stuffs all of Anita's pets on the sick pretext that this way, they can share their hobbies (his new hobby being taxidermy). She kills him, stuffs him, and they're much happier that way. Not only does Lindley stand out and shine in a way that she hadn't been before on a television series, but her pain is like a punch in the gut, something Lambert is excellent at delivering through human emotions on screen (we'll be covering Lambert in Chapter 6).

As with *Amazing Stories*, *Monsters*, and *The Twilight Zone*, *Tales from the Crypt*'s producers seemed to take every woman director that had a remotely successful independent film in the last five years and throw them against the wall of horror television directing, hoping some would stick. Not all of them would stick. Some would. Lesli Linka Glatter stuck, and Mary Lambert was well-prepared to make what is arguably a far less challenging finished product than *Pet Sematary*. Debra Hill knew horror and had spent so much time producing it that her directing skills were pretty tight within the horror short parameters. Martha Coolidge worked well with *The Twilight Zone*, but her career has ended up more varied, and she also regularly works with comedy and romance. Jodie Foster, well—she'd been working towards directing for years and relished the opportunity.

Many more horror and science fiction anthology series from this time hired women as directors. The series *Freddy's Nightmares*, also known as *A Nightmare on Elm Street: The Series*, was created by New Line to compete with all the other anthology horror series using Freddy Kreuger as a host and the *Elm Street* franchise fandom as an audience. Lisa Gottlieb, director of the successful teen comedy *Just One of the Guys* (1985), directed the episode "Saturday Night Special" (1988), and Anita W. Addison directed "Life Sentence (1990). Helen Shaver directed a whopping six episodes of the reboot of the 1960s fantasy & science fiction anthology series *The Outer Limits*: "Last Supper" (1997); "Lithia" (1998); "Phobos Rising" (1998); "What Will the Neighbors Think?" (1999), "Starcrossed" (1999), and "Simon Says" (2000). "Simon Says" is particularly unnerving, with human personalities being programmed into robots that look like ventriloquist dummies.

Some of the less well-known horror anthology series of the time, such as *Night Visions*, *The Ray Bradbury Theater*, *The Hitchhiker*, *Chillers*, and *The Hunger,* had episodes directed by women, but these series were not as popular as the other shows. *Night Visions* had actress JoeBeth Williams direct a segment, "The Doghouse" (2001). Anne Wheeler ("The Martian," 1992) and Eleanore Lindo ("The Concrete Mixer," 1992) directed for *The Ray Bradbury Theater*. *The Hitchhiker* had Aline Issermann ("Together Forever" & "Her Finest Hour," 1989) and Mai Zetterling (whose *Night Games* (1966) we talked about in Chapter 4) direct three episodes: "And If We Dream" (1985), "Hired Help" (1987), and "Murderous Feelings" (1985), and Patricia Mazuy directed one, "A Whole New You" (1991). Zetterling also directed two episodes of the series *Chillers*: "The Thrill Seeker" (1990) and "The Stuff of Madness" (1990), along with Clare Peploe's «Sauce for the Goose» (1990) and Nessa Hyams' «The Cat Brought It In» (1990). Patricia Rozema, who directed the feature thriller film *Into the Forest* (2015), made only one episode of *The Hunger*: "But at My Back, I Always Hear" (1997). In 2019, the streaming horror platform AMC/Shudder produced a new reboot of *Creepshow* with brand-new episodes. Two women directors,

Axelle Carolyn (*The Manor*, 2021) and Roxanne Benjamin (*Body at Brighton Rock*, 2019), both helmed episodes.

On Halloween night, 1992, director Lesley Manning and writer Stephen Volk sat in a restaurant with the cast and crew of their latest BBC production *Ghostwatch*, celebrating the film's screening that evening. Because *Ghostwatch* was set up to look like a live event, producer Ruth Baumgarten wanted the cast and crew out of sight so they wouldn't be noticed out and about town while they were supposedly in the studio at the BBC or live on location. Baumgarten hadn't arrived at the gathering yet, as she had gone to the BBC to check in on the phone lines; even though the show was scripted and prerecorded, the BBC had opted to keep the call-in lines open as they usually did during live programs to accentuate further the illusion that the show was live.

When Baumgarten did arrive at the cast and crew reception, she said ominously, "I think something is happening"[153] Unexpectedly, the call-in lines at the BBC were jammed. Three technicians watching the phone calls exclaimed, "Oh my god, it's going really wrong on studio one!"[154] The next day, no one discussed the program's quality, acting, or effects. They were talking about the reaction of the public to the show. There had been over thirty thousand complaints[155] made directly to the BBC. One viewer had soiled his pants out of fear. Three women claimed to have been so terrified that they went into early labor.[156] What was supposed to be a fun Halloween horror event had become a PR nightmare for the BBC and would only worsen in the coming days. As Manning walked in the corridors of the BBC, her colleagues would either ignore her or pull her aside and whisper that they liked the show. "Stephen and I felt like lepers for a few years afterward,"[157] admits Manning.

Ghostwatch was a show about an investigation of a haunting in a typical United Kingdom council flat where single mother Pamela Early and her two daughters Kim and Suzanne (played by actors) were experiencing paranormal activity. Their rather ordinary home was haunted by a spirit named "Pipes" (because he communicated to the family using the house's pipes to make banging noises). Actual BBC presenters Michael Parkinson, Sarah Greene, Mike Smith, and Craig Charles played themselves, acting as if they were taking part in a Halloween special live news broadcast when the show was prerecorded and fictional. Actress Gillian Bevan played the role of Dr. Lin Pascoe, a paranormal researcher studying the Early haunting for months and who appeared with Parkinson inside the studio. There was also a 'location' at the house where Sarah Greene was with the family and a cameraman, as well as a third 'location' outside the home on Foxhill Drive where Craig Charles interviewed the Early's neighbors and stood around with a crowd that had gathered to watch the spectacle. This 'live' show was intended to appear as real as possible. Still, because the subject matter was supernatural, the BBC hoped it would be clear that it was a fictional story. To make sure no one was fooled, they put credits at the beginning of the show opening, crediting Volk as the writer and other crew members. But that didn't seem to make much of a difference. After the show aired, it was compared to the Orson Welles reading of *The War of the Worlds* in 1938, which made the United States panic that an alien invasion was occurring. "These were real people that were on television. It felt very authentic in that way, and it was vital to making

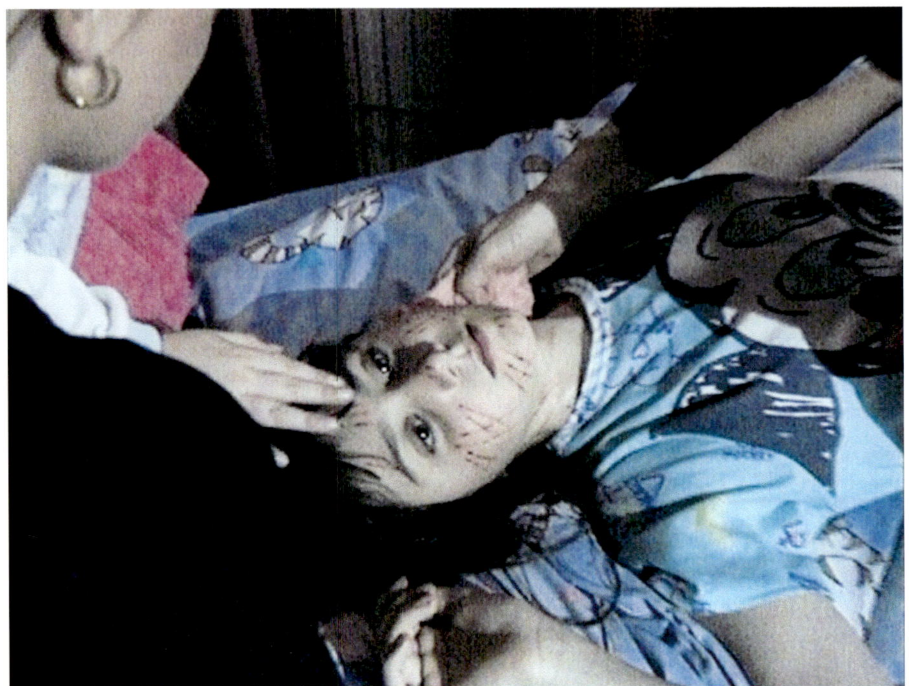

Suzanne (Michelle Wesson) suffers spontaneous claw marks on her face from the poltergeist Pipes in the TV horror film *Ghostwatch* (1992).

it what it was," says filmmaker Aislinn Clarke, whose found footage horror film *The Devil's Doorway* (2018) was heavily inspired by *Ghostwatch.*[158] Many steps were taken to make this horror story feel as authentic as possible. It was almost as if the BBC were trying to perpetrate a hoax on their audience and only at the last minute created the opening credits out of fear of the repercussions. "We never used the word hoax," scoffed Manning when asked about it.

> I would have been insulted if someone said that at the time. It was about honoring the language of the piece and the integrity that the story demanded. We didn't think it would go that distance. We thought maybe people might believe it for a bit.[159]

But many people did believe it, and when they found out it was pure fiction and not at all a live event, perhaps out of embarrassment, they felt that their trustworthy BBC (referred to lovingly as Auntie Beeb) had broken the faith of the nation and betrayed that trust. Producer Baumgarten was on board for keeping the truth a secret; she wanted the audience to be surprised. She, and Volk and Manning, had no idea how terrifying it would be to viewers. They were told by one French critic who was given a secret, early screening of *Ghostwatch* that it wasn't scary enough, so based on his feedback, they went in and sharpened up the pace and the scary parts. Likewise, the BBC itself screened it internally before airing it and said there was no drama; it was obvious they had no idea it was terrifying either. "I think they only watched the first five minutes," suspects Manning.[160]

Ghostwatch begins very slowly with the setup of the family and the investigators, just as a real live presentation would. It switches between hosts at the studio, at the house, and out on the street, with these personalities communicating as if they were all there in real time. It was all shot separately. Sarah Greene is at the house with the family and builds an initial bond with them. She is also set up by one of the crew members who pops out at her wearing a mask as a prank, and the stage is set for what unfolds. The two girls, Kim and Suzanne, describe Pipes as a ghost, especially Kim, who can see him. She draws him, a man covered in blood with a bald head, and she says she can sometimes see him, even during the presentation. Suzanne suffers from strange trances and terrors. At one point, Suzanne is caught rattling the pipes herself to make something happen so that Sarah and the audience will believe their story, which discredits her (momentarily). In the studio, Dr. Pascoe explains her research to Michael Parkinson, who adopts a dry and skeptical attitude that reinforces his role as a news reporter. Pascoe has artifacts from her research and photographs of the girls experiencing telekinetic attacks. She plays an audio recording of Suzanne during a trance-like state, in which a deep and horrible voice emanates from the child chanting nursery rhymes. The chills begin. Adopting this slow build to the eventual climax was thoughtfully calculated by Manning:

> I was very aware that so much horror at the time was all extremely tense until you found 'the thing,' and then it let itself down ... For me, it always felt too technical. But that wonderful gap—the anticipation and the fear of the unknown—is the gap that I find much more thrilling ... I do love that when horror comes into your world, into your reality.[161]

The moment that one's hairs begin to stand on end arrives when a caller is placed on the line with Pascoe and Parkinson; she seems to think she can make out a ghostly figure in the corner of the girl's room in one of the photographs that Pascoe showed the audience. Parkinson brings the photo back, and as an audience member, you can see something there. For a second. It's vague and awful, but it's there. Parkinson says, "I can't see anything." "It's there," confirms Manning. "I imagine people at the door of their sitting room saying, 'Oh my god, I see something,' and I thought that was such a magnificent conceit."[162] Pipes the ghost is scattered throughout the entire film, briefly but artfully. Regarding these cameos of Pipes, says Manning,

> My philosophy is to put him in as many times as I could as subtly and relevantly as possible. Because BBC and budgets are so tight, even if you've got a budget, it would have been on the day of the shoot. If he was booked, I tried to get him in every scene, and if it didn't work, we cut it out.[163]

We learn through presenter Craig Charles and a neighbor that he interviews that back in the nineteenth century, a baby farmer (women who took in children for money) named Mother Siddons lived right where the Early house is now. She was found to have murdered many of the children. Then, from another caller in the studio, we learn that the house used to more recently belong to a couple whose nephew, Raymond Tunstall, went mad and committed suicide in the basement/cellar (where Pipes lives, according to Kim). He was locked in there with his numerous cats, who ate his body as they waited to be let out for days and days before his body was discovered. Tunstall also had an issue with harming children, perhaps sexually, and when he was alive, he may have been possessed by the spirit of Mother Siddons to the point where he began dressing like an older woman. This explains the odd appearance of Pipes, whose eye is missing, and wears a long dark dress. Perhaps, realizes Pascoe, there is a darkness in that house that originates from far longer ago than that, perhaps even thousands of years. The Early family and Sarah Greene are harassed by the ghost on camera, as it manifests via poltergeist activity and through possessing Suzanne and leaving claw marks all over her face. The show has gone too far, and police are called to take Suzanne to the hospital. Craig Charles helps Kim, Suzanne, and their mother, Pamela, to safety outside the house.

Pascoe and Parkinson are watching from the studio, unable to help. Pascoe suddenly realizes that with all the people watching the show, the event has acted as a sort of mass séance and made Pipes more powerful. Back at the house, Sarah Greene and her cameraman are still inside. All the lights have gone out, and they are using the camera's night vision to see and record footage. Sarah, believing she can hear noises from the basement door, enters the basement, and the doors roughly shut behind her. The studio in the BBC begins to shake, and lights explode. The television camera people abandon their posts, with a disturbed Michael Parkinson attempting to stay calm and keep the show going. It's clear that Pipes has now entered the studio, has control of the cameras, and is using its destructive powers to terrify the studio crew. Soon, Michael finds himself alone, in the dark, in front of the camera, and Pipes takes possession of him. The last thing we see and hear is Parkinson chanting nursery rhymes in the same horrible voice that Suzanne had used when she was possessed.

What allowed such daring and unconventional filming to take place at the BBC? According to Manning, there was a restructuring that was going on internally at the time, from which *Ghostwatch* benefited:

> A lot of stuff at that time was maverick producers given free rein, like Ruth Baumgarten, who had burning ideas, would rush into offices, and only have one small chain of command. She only had to persuade [producer] Richard Broke, and I personally think it had a lot to do with the innovation of television at that time. The more layered and more voices, the worse it gets.[164]

Manning believes that Baumgarten was "visionary" not only in her desire to produce innovative new television but in her hiring of a woman director freelance:

"I'd come out of film school four or five years [prior]. I'd done a tiny bit of television, and they took a punt ... 'I've got this thing called *Ghostwatch*. Do you want to take a look at it?'"[165]

Perhaps the most substantial reason the film is so compelling and why so many people found themselves believing that what they saw was real is the realistic acting of both the hired actors and the real presenters: "The artifice of acting—get rid of it. We [the

BBC] had been leaning on performing tropes ... I wanted to strip it back."[166]

Ghostwatch began its development as a six-part series written by Volk. Originally only the final episode was supposed to show a paranormal investigation, and even after they were given the green light to make only one episode, which would be the investigation episode, they had many different ghost stories being told throughout. The BBC wanted only one storyline. So Manning asked Volk which of the stories he loved the most, and he decided on the Early family. In a move that was unorthodox at the time, Manning wanted to shoot on video and make it as thoroughly realistic as she could. "Everyone shot on film then," she explains,

> And if you shot on film, you were a 'proper' filmmaker. But I said, look at the story. You can't. The cameraman needs to be the actual cameraman. I am not going to have an actor pretending to be the cameraman; we have to be pure to the language. And they went along with that.[167]

Manning and Baumgarten found real parapsychologists and genuine people who wanted to talk about their experiences with the paranormal; these are the pixilated faces we see earlier in the film when Pascoe and Parkinson hear from unrelated subjects. Parkinson and Greene loved the script immediately and wanted to do it. But some others were wary of ruining their reputation as professional presenters and hesitated. Mike Smith, Sarah Greene's real-life husband and a presenter for the BBC, read it through his wife and wanted to be in it, so they wrote him a part on a suggestion from the casting director. United Kingdom Professor and horror television scholar Stacey Abbott says, "Parky [Parkinson's nickname] allows you to settle in and become very comfortable. But then he also becomes rather patrician in terms of his cynicism. Clever, it really works."[168] "Parky was not an actor," adds Clarke,

"He was a personality journalist. He really comes across as himself in it. The way he controls the tone of the conversation with Gillian [Pascoe] feels like what he really would do."[169]

Manning shot the film over several weeks. They shot everything inside the house first, then cut it into clips played on the video wall while all Parkinson's scenes were shot. "That shows his skill as a television presenter," says Manning. "He had a lot of free flow as long as he answered Gillian." Originally Parkinson was using an autocue (called a teleprompter in the United States), a standard for television presenters, and it felt a bit stiff. "We threw it away, and I talked to him, freed him up massively ... He brought that undermining cynicism that really helped."[170] Manning counted on suspense and tension to make *Ghostwatch* successful as a horror film. "The precision of horror I love," she explains:

"You are creating tension and shocks, and you're working with stress and anxiety in film, which needs a precision that is a fantastic filmmaker's skill."[171]

Though the term didn't exist yet, *Ghostwatch* was a found footage horror film—a film made with clips of audio or video recordings that are presented to the viewer as real, often a news investigation (as in *REC*, 2007), abandoned or old VHS tapes (*V/H/S/2*, 2012), personal phone recordings (*Cloverfield*, 2008), security cameras (*Paranormal*

Activity, 2007) or a film-within-a-film (*Frankenstein's Army*, 2013) is the plausible reason presented for the recordings. This real-time footage creates the illusion of reality and unedited truth. Using found footage as a premise for a horror film allows the audience to see things that are usually overlooked, according to Manning:

> Found footage is a fantastic horror tool. It catches stuff that you think you're privy to stuff, you know,[the film] *Creep*, when he puts the camera on the table, and you see stuff in the background, and you think the protagonists just dumped the camera, but the audience is just in the know. How Parkinson says there's nothing in the photo. 'There's something behind you.' It's far less mannered than drama. It has that looser feel that you can get in sideways when you zip pan or go over there, and something over there has caught your eye. That's classic horror. It facilitates a use of composition that other styles don't.[172]

According to Aislinn Clarke, found footage is a handy tool for horror filmmaking:

> That's the beauty that you can slip in some uncanny stuff in a way that the cast is not aware of. There's an intimacy with the audience, a direct link to the audience, and the cast isn't even aware. It can also make it tricky, walking that line between being subtle and hitting the mark of the horror.[173]

The complexities of constructing a drama that feels like reality was an unusual feat in 1992; this was before unscripted reality television was a trend, and Manning was at the forefront of a new kind of media:

> It was complex in the most enjoyable way. Everybody said we'd never done this before. We broke every single habit of the BBC ... I enjoyed every minute of it. Isolated cameras had never been done before; every camera went into the cutting room.[174]

Ghostwatch, as of 2021, has never been rebroadcast on the BBC. Manning and Volk have thusly paid the price for being disruptive to the mainstream television expectations of the public (and the studios). The BBC never again took the kind of risk it did with *Ghostwatch*. A few years after the *Ghostwatch* airing, however, an unlikely fandom crept up in the world made up mostly of people who had seen *Ghostwatch* originally air when they were children. As adults, they realized how groundbreaking and fun it had been. An unofficial website was created, and bootleg VHS copies were being sold in the early 2000s for £50. Visitors to the website participated in forum discussions, asking where the director was. "He's dead" was the original answer people posted, not knowing the impact Manning has had on the horror genre. *Ghostwatch* was not released on DVD until 2007 by the British Film Institute. It aired on the horror media platform Shudder from 2017 to 2019. A documentary called *Ghostwatch: Behind the Curtains* was released in 2012 by filmmaker/fan Richard Lawden, which is now out of print and hopefully will be re-released. Today, viewers who watched *Ghostwatch* when it originally aired have

TRAGEDY FOLLOWS PROTESTS OVER GHOST DRAMA

Viewers slam BBC Hallowe'en hoax

Mail on Sunday, November 8, 1992

This TV programme killed our dear son

By ANDREW CHAPMAN

GHOSTWATCH, the BBC's controversial Hallowe'en TV spoof, was blamed yesterday for a teenager's suicide.

Profoundly disturbed by last Saturday's programme, 18-year-old Martin Denham hanged himself five days later from a tree, called The Witch Tree, near his home in Beckhampton Road, Nottingham.

A suicide note on Martin's body read: 'Dear Mam, please don't worry, if there are ghosts I will be a ghost and I will be with you always as a ghost.'

The documentary style of the drama starring Michael Parkinson, Sarah Greene and Mike Smith terrified thousands of viewers who jammed BBC switchboards in protest at its reality and the gory scenes.

Yesterday distraught parents April and Percy Denham told how they tried to reassure Martin, who was slighly mentally retarded, that it was all make believe.

Mrs Denham, 41, said: 'That programme killed my dear son.

FEAR ON BILL: The Radio Times

Michael Parkinson and the BBC will have his death on their consciences.

'Michael Parkinson said later anyone who believed it must have been living under a stone for the past few weeks. Well, my boy believed it and he took his life because of it.

'Martin had watched horror films without being frightened,' said Mrs Denham, who has four other children. 'He knew the difference between reality and fantasy but this was so real.' The BBC point out the programme was billed as a drama but Mrs Denham says there should have been a specific warning.

'It would have saved Martin's life,' she said. 'I would not have let him see it if they had warned us first but it was all made out to be a true story.'

Martin had sat transfixed by the programme where the depicted haunted house was, like his own, on a council estate.

Proud

He seemed to accept his parents' reassurances but that night he slept with a lamp on in his room.

'On Sunday he didn't eat his lunch which was not like him,' said his 51-year-old father.

'He was stopping friends and neighbours in the street asking about the programme and ghosts.'

Monday morning saw Martin leave for work at a local clothing factory. He was proud of having a proper job despite his dyslexia and learning difficulties.

But factory talk about the programme upset him and he left work early.

'On Tuesday he started on about ghosts again even asking if there was one in our house,' recalls Mr Denham. 'I laughingly told him there must be a ghost in this place because all the biscuits keep disappearing. It was meant as a joke, the lads just help themselves. But Martin just went quiet.'

On Wednesday Martin gave a close friend a treasured cross and chain as a keepsake.

'The next morning he was found hanged by a length of nylon hosepipe from the Witch Tree — killed by asphyxia said a pathologist at the inquest which was opened and adjourned in Nottingham on Friday.

Mr Denham's complaints to the BBC resulted in a call from an official who said his superiors would contact the family.

'He added he was deeply sorry. But since then we haven't heard a thing,' said Mr Denham.

A BBC spokesman said yesterday that the programme was clearly advertised as fictional drama and added: 'Of course, we are very sorry to hear of this tragic event. However, we need to know more about this case before venturing any comment.'

Speaking at his riverside mansion in Berkshire last night, Michael Parkinson said: 'It is a terrible tragedy for the family and I do not want to add to their misery.'

TOO-REAL TERROR: Martin Denham

A November, 1992 newspaper says that "Tragedy follows protests over ghost drama" about the controversial *Ghostwatch* (1992), directed by Lesley Manning.

an appreciation of the complexity and dexterous production techniques that went into making it.[175] Film scholar Alexandra West describes the legacy of *Ghostwatch* with a deliberate nostalgia:

> *Ghostwatch* has become a sort of cult artifact in popular culture; it remains an anomaly precisely because of how effective it was. It managed to not only terrify but to actually traumatize its viewers. The backlash against it was so loud and forceful that it seems to have scared off any true imitators ... *Ghostwatch* worked, arguably too well, because of its reliance on the 'real'—the real presenters purporting to present facts aired on one of the most trusted names in media. *Ghostwatch* proved that sometimes even fiction can be too real.[176]

"If it wasn't so skillfully made, it wouldn't have the impact it had," says Clarke. "Landmark piece of BBC programming. Monumental piece of television"[177] In an entirely new century, what is the place of *Ghostwatch* in horror history? Scholar Stacey Abbott believes, "It's a pivotal moment of moving from traditional to contemporary Gothic. It shifted things in that direction ... It is a touchstone for a lot of recent British television horror"[178] *Ghostwatch* is the direct inspiration for the popular British television series *Most Haunted* (2002-2019), in which each episode featured a team investigating a paranormal event/place with a camera crew, specialized equipment (including an infrared camera for dark scenes) and supposedly real investigators in the form of real-life television presenter Yvette Fielding.

Surprisingly, what doesn't seem to come up in conversation with Stephen Volk or Lesley Manning in any of their interviews since the resurgence of fandom for *Ghostwatch* is the fact that while, yes, it is funny that several people were upset by the program when it aired, a disturbed young man killed himself as a result of watching the show. On November 5, 1992, troubled eighteen-year-old Martin Denham hung himself from a tree near his home in Bestwood Park, Nottingham, United Kingdom. In his back pocket was a note that read, "Please don't worry—if there are ghosts, I will be a ghost, and I will be with you always as a ghost." Martin had been glued to the television when *Ghostwatch* aired and immediately became frightened that ghosts were living in his house. He believed he could hear noises in the pipes, just like in the show, and he slept with his bedroom light on out of fear. A few days later, Martin committed suicide. His stepfather Percy Denham told the newspaper *The Independent,* "In my own mind, I hold the BBC completely responsible for his death." His mother, April Denham, told the same reporter, "I blame the BBC—it is all their fault. They said it was based on a true story, but it was all a hoax."[179] The Broadcasting Standards Commission investigated the matter and concluded that the BBC "had a duty to do more than simply hint at the deception it was practicing on the audience. In *Ghostwatch,* there was a deliberate attempt to cultivate a sense of menace."[180] Unfortunately, if viewers had paid attention to the program's opening credits, they would have immediately seen that it was fiction as it clearly stated that there was a writer.

Stephen Volk has had time to contemplate the legacy of *Ghostwatch* and its effect on audiences at the time. It was so shocking because,

> Unlike a horror movie where you pay money, and you go to see a film, the contract is "I am going to be frightened." But television is piped, if you forgive the expression, into your home. You get given it. You don't go out seeking it; that's a very different kind of transaction.[181]

Filmmaker Aislinn Clarke watches *Ghostwatch* every Halloween and cites it as a direct inspiration for her own found footage horror film, *The Devil's Doorway* (2018). Richard Lawden, the director of the *Ghostwatch* documentary *Behind the Curtains*, organizes social media watch parties for *Ghostwatch* every Halloween. The impact of *Ghostwatch* on its audience is undeniable. As one fan remembers,

> *Ghostwatch* was without doubt the scariest piece of film I've ever seen. I was thirteen when I seen [sic] it and I've never been that scared since. No other program has had such an impact on my memory. I'll never forget it. Truly brilliant.[182]

Chapter 6

Sometimes dead is better

THEATRICAL HORROR OF THE 1980S AND 1990S

Joshua Miller discovers he can't be in the sunlight in *Near Dark* (1987), directed by Kathryn Bigelow.

IN 1993, THE OSCARS HELD a special celebration called 1993 Oscars Salute Women and a tagline of "The Year of the Woman," even though no women directors or producers were nominated that year. I want to say one was nominated for Best Screenwriter, but I'd be lying to you. Only in the Best Documentary Film category were any women directors mentioned, and all of those co-directors. The Salute included a montage of women in the film industry throughout the century, put together by Oscar-winning documentarian Lynne Littman. Betty Friedan, the noted feminist author, was so disgusted that she said, "On behalf of women directors, cinematographers, and producers, I resent the travesty of calling that a tribute."[1] The ceremony was reviewed as "lackluster, including a tribute to women in film that—at a time when the industry's male bias is especially notable—seemed about as curious as celebrating the female perspective on the Supreme Court."[2]

Journalists wrote newspaper articles about women directors in the 1910s and 1920s, in the 1950s, the 1960s, 1970s, 1980s, and the 1990s. They still do in the 2020s. The story never changes: women directors are an anomaly and a curiosity. Usually, these articles support individual filmmakers or point out sexism in hiring practices; rarely are they negative because the director is a woman. Why was this phenomenon—a woman directing a film—still considered outside the norm? In the 1990s, more women-directed films were theatrically released than in any prior decade. Some incredibly impactful mainstream films like *Wayne's World* (1992) by Penelope Spheeris, *Little Man Tate* (1991) by Jodie Foster, *The Prince of Tides* (1991) by Barbara Streisand, *Clueless* (1995) by Amy Heckerling, and *Point Break* (1991) by Kathryn Bigelow became permanent fixtures of twentieth-century cinema culture. Independent films directed by women had a resurgence like that of the late 1960s: *Gas Food Lodging* (1992) by Allison Anders, *I Shot Andy Warhol* (1996) by Mary Harron, *The Piano* (1993) by Jane Campion, and *Daughters of the Dust* (1991) by Julie Dash. There were also several mainstream horror films made by women directors widely recognized as part of the current pop culture. Kathryn Bigelow's thrillers *Blue Steel* (1990), her action film *Point Break* (1991), and her science fiction thriller *Strange Days* (1995) are all fantastic movies and deserve to be watched alongside her iconic horror Western *Near Dark* (1987). *Tank Girl* (1995) was Rachel Talalay's science fiction/action/adventure movie follow-up to *Freddy's Dead* (1991). Fran Kuzui's *Buffy the Vampire Slayer* (1992) would spawn a television series spinoff that still, in the 2020s, has an enormous fandom. Jennifer Lynch's strange thriller *Boxing Helena* (1993) was the first film in Lynch's long career directing horror and thriller films in the twenty-first century but was hampered by a lengthy court case with actress Kim Basinger who was supposed to star in it originally. Lynch is an incredibly frank and outspoken, unpretentious person and tells the story of how the much-maligned *Boxing Helena* was conceived with her customary sizzle:

> I was reading poetry at a place called Helena's out in Los Angeles, and after reading one night, a man named Philippe Caland, who was one of the producers, approached me and said, "I'm interested in having a woman write a story I have into a screenplay. It's called *Boxing Helena*, and it's about a man who cuts a woman's arms and legs off and puts her in a box because he loves her." And I said, "Well, that sounds kind of terrible."[3]

Caleb (Adrian Pasdar) and Mae (Jenny Wright) fall in love in the horror western *Near Dark* (1987), directed by Kathryn Bigelow.

Antonia Bird's period cannibal thriller *Ravenous* (1999) stands out as one of the best interpretations of the horrors of the Donner Party tragedy. Mary Lambert's immensely popular Stephen King adaptation *Pet Sematary* (1989) was the first large studio-produced horror film directed by a woman.

There's a beautiful book dedicated in entirety to *Near Dark* (1987) written by Stacey Abbott for the British Film Institute Film Classics imprint; it is the most comprehensive source on the film.[4] I highly suggest it to anyone looking for a deep dive into the movie. Kathryn Bigelow's horror Western is one of the most important in women's horror history. Bigelow, an up-and-coming new director with one prior feature, and Eric Red, a horror screenwriter known for the successful film *The Hitcher* (1986), formed a filmmaking partnership. They'd co-write two films, one of which Bigelow would direct and one which Red would direct. *Near Dark* was the result of this partnership. Though it played in mainstream theaters and is considered one of the more well-known 1980s vampire movies because of the attention it received, *Near Dark* was not a studio production. Produced by Edward S. Feldman's company F/M with his partner Charles R. Meeker, Meeker produced *The Hitcher* and was familiar with Red. Impressed, they decided to produce the film within a few days of receiving the script. Made for only $5 million, *Near Dark* was, and is, considered 'low-budget' for Hollywood. When it was released in theaters, *Near Dark* did very poorly; it didn't even make back its budget. But it premiered at the 1987 Toronto International Film Festival just a month before, and the artistic and genre-bending choices made by Bigelow and Red did not go unnoticed by critics. The Museum of Modern Art hosted the film for their Cineprobe program honoring exceptional independent film productions.

Near Dark is about Caleb (Adrian Pasdar), a young man who meets a beautiful woman named Mae (Jenny Wright) in his small town in the Southwest of the United States. They spend an evening together, and Mae bites him on the neck before disappearing. As the sun rises, Caleb realizes that the sunshine is burning his skin, and he runs for cover from the hot, bright sunlight. Mae appears with a van full of other people; they rescue Caleb and drive off. Thus begins Caleb's new life as a vampire in the group made up of Mae, the leader Jesse (Lance Henriksen), unhinged lunatic Severen (Bill Paxton), the hard Diamondback (Jenette Goldstein), and the child vampire Homer (Joshua John Miller).

Abbott breaks down *Near Dark* into its elements in a way that allows us to see what made it so different from other 1980s vampire films and why it was marketed in a confusing way that may have contributed to the poor box office. First, Bigelow originally wanted to make a Western, but since no one would finance a Western, she and Red had to think of a way to "subvert" the genre to make it attractive to investors; vampires were trendy at the time, so they made it a vampire Western. The absence of traditional vampire folklore and mythology set it apart from other vampire films of the time and the past: the vampires are vulnerable to sunlight, but there are no crosses, stakes, priests, Gothic castles, or coffins. Jesse and his "family" have the dynamic of an Old West criminal gang that happens to be vampires. Even though she didn't want to make her film "Gothic," Bigelow used lighting and darkness (chiaroscuro, as Abbot refers to it) to create contrast and shadows reminiscent of traditional, Gothic horror films. Mae is not a damsel in distress; she doesn't need to be rescued, and she has agency and has found happiness with her vampire family. Even though she is "cured" in the end, she isn't a reluctant or innocent maiden. Last, the fights and the showdown have all the energy of a classic 1980s action movie. It *is* an action movie.

Bigelow would become famous for her ability to direct complicated, large-scale, violent sequences in her later films like *Point Break* (1991), *K-19: The Widowmaker* (2002), *The Hurt Locker* (2008), and *Zero Dark Thirty* (2012), seamlessly showcasing male actors in hyper-masculine cinematic stunts. The action sequence at the end of *Near Dark* was her first. Three of the prominent cast members had appeared in her soon-to-be husband's film *Aliens* (1986): Bill Paxton, Jenette Goldstein, and Lance Henriksen. Though it didn't make money at the box office, when it was released on VHS in 1990, *Near Dark* became extremely popular and gathered a big cult film fan following that it still has today.

Bigelow won the genre film-specific Saturn Award in 1995 for her science fiction thriller *Strange Days*. Partnering with Red again, they'd write the thriller *Blue Steel* (1990), directed by Bigelow. Though she kept directing steadily, most films were financial failures in theaters. But her war drama *The Hurt Locker* (2008) made her one of the most famous mainstream directors of the twenty-first-century film industry. Aside from the numerous other awards for which she was nominated or was given because of the film, she won the coveted 2010 Academy Award for Best Director. She was the first woman to ever win in that category. Also of note: in 1983, Bigelow was an actor in Lizzie Borden's feminist, dystopian film *Born in Flames*.

> *"When I'm asked, as I frequently am, what I consider to be the most frightening book I've ever written, the answer I give comes easily and with no hesitation:* Pet Sematary. Pet Sematary *is the one I put away in a drawer thinking I had finally gone too far. Time*

suggests that I had not, at least in terms of what the public would accept, but certainly I had gone too far in terms of my own personal feelings. Put simply, I was horrified by what I'd written and the conclusions I'd drawn." —Stephen King[5]

"Sometimes dead is better." How could dead be better? Let that one sink in. We've all lost someone we love to death. We all have grieved and wished that there was some way around death. (If you haven't, trust me, just wait, *you will*). If we could bring someone we love back from the dead, how could that be worse than them still being dead? Well, when the person coming back is worse than them staying dead, it must mean that things would be unimaginably horrifying. If the feelings of grief and sadness and pain are easier on us than the experience of bringing a person back from the dead, then that moment of pain and grief and anguish is the best we can hope for, ever, in terms of happiness. That's grim. It is depressing to know that every moment of happiness you have ever had is fleeting and irrevocable and that there is no way to catch it, keep it, or get it back. To parents who have lost small children, it is most likely a devastation that one can't imagine until it happens to them personally. *Pet Sematary* (1989), the film adaptation of the novel by Stephen King, is the first horror film directed by a woman and produced by a major studio (Paramount).[6] Previous horror films directed by women had all been made by small, independent studios or for television. In that sense, *Pet Sematary* is a seminal film in a trend of women directors gaining access to the mainstream horror film world that began when Mary Lambert took the helm of the production. Hollywood "broke the mold" when they hired Lambert because women were not usually offered studio directing jobs, period.[7]

Pet Sematary is considered one of the best Stephen King adaptations in cinema.[8] The book, published in 1983, was immensely popular, and plans to turn it into a movie were underway shortly after publication. It's a solid horror story with gruesome scenes, death, blood, and terror. But it's also a solid horror story about grief, regret, mistakes, love, secrets, and self-destruction. It's a story about cheating death and destroying what's left of life in the process. There are some similar themes in nineteenth-century horror novels such as *Dracula*, *The Strange Case of Dr. Jekyll and Mr. Hyde*, and *Frankenstein* (which

Gage in the blue outfit in *Pet Sematary*.

Louis (Dale Midkiff) realizes that you can cheat death, but it will always come back for you in *Pet Sematary*.

King used as an inspiration for his work): unnatural life, eternal life, and the living dead. More so, however, *Pet Sematary* includes echoes of the short story "The Monkey's Paw" (1902) by W. W. Jacobs. In it, a couple uses a cursed talisman (a dried monkey's paw) to make three wishes, each with horrific consequences far worse than anything they would have imagined. *Pet Sematary,* the story of both book and film, is about the Creed family: father and husband Louis (Dale Midkiff), wife and mother Rachel (Denise Crosby), and the two children, adolescent Ellie (twins Blaze and Beau Berdhal), and toddler Gage (Miko Hughes). Louis moves his family to a quiet town in Maine for a new job as a doctor at the local university hospital. The house and town are idyllic and charming, except for the dangerous trucks that run down the highway right past their house at various intervals. The Creeds settle in nicely and make friends with their neighbor Jud Crandall (Fred Gwynne), an old local who saves Gage's life by moving him out of the way of a speeding truck. Unfortunately, Rachel's beloved cat, Church, is not so lucky and is hit by one of these trucks. Feeling compassion for the family and young Ellie, Jud shows Louis and the family the local pet cemetery where local children have come for decades to bury their beloved pets, with an incorrectly spelled sign saying "Pet Sematary" at the entrance. But Jud tells Louis that another graveyard has unique properties, and he will show it to him if he wants to bring back the family cat. Taking Louis on a strange hike through the Maine wilderness beyond the children's cemetery to an ancient Micmac Indian burial ground, he has Louis bury the cat in the soil, which is supernatural.

Louis is dealing with a crisis when he loses a patient at his new job: student Victor Pascow who has been fatally injured in an accident, and there is no way to save him. Victor seems to channel some psychic or demonic powers on his deathbed when he says, "The soil ... in a man's heart ... is stonier." Not understanding, Louis goes home to find that Church has returned. From the dead. Only the cat is now basically evil. At this point in the story, Jud Crandall comes clean and tells us about the cursed Indian burial ground and how anyone buried there comes back to life but evil and dead. He probably shouldn't have told Louis about it, not even for a cat, because the family is devastated when Louis's son Gage is hit by a truck and dies. Unable to cope with the loss of Gage, Louis digs up his body from the real human cemetery and, despite warnings from both Jud and the ghost of Victor Pascow, takes Gage to the Micmac burial ground and buries him there. Of course, Gage comes back to life, evil like Church before him, killing Jud and Rachel as well. Louis has no choice but to kill his son purposefully to stop any further horrors from taking place. But of course, he buries Rachel in the Indian burial ground, again despite Victor's warnings, and Rachel comes back, decomposing and decidedly not the actual Rachel.

I like to refer to *Pet Sematary* as "tragedy porn": incredibly heart-wrenching, sad, suspensefully agonizing, and drawn-out misery that one can share and wallow in with the characters and other members of the audience. Scene after scene in the film is grief or pain, building up gradually but relentlessly until it's overwhelming for both the characters and the audience. *Pet Sematary* is an incredibly emotional film, one of the reasons it is so successful with horror fans. "It's a timeless story," says director Mary Lambert. "All the reasons people thought it wouldn't work is why it worked. Fear of death, confronting death, love of a parent for a child, feelings, and desires, even unhealthy, are relatable."[9]

Rachel (Denise Crosby) demonstrating grief porn in *Pet Sematary.*

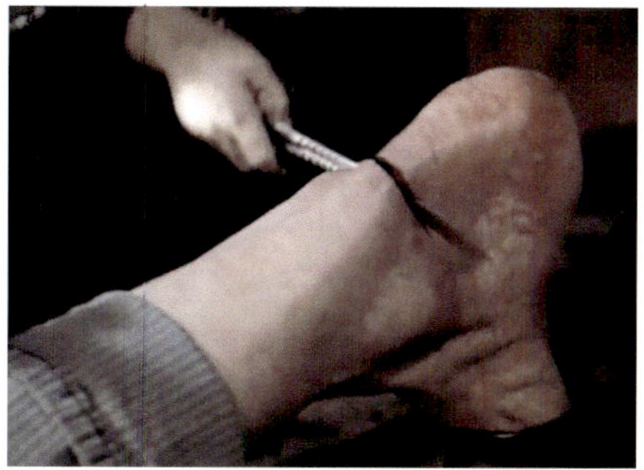
The Achilles' tendon-cutting scene in *Pet Sematary.*

Audiences and critics agree with me. *The Los Angeles Times* said after the film opened that *Pet Sematary* is:

> Americana at its most Gothic, a depiction of a normal family made vulnerable by the eternal yearning to cheat death. It cuts to the deepest human emotions, and there certainly are going to be many people who aren't going to be willing or able to take it. *Pet Sematary* is one of the most numbing mainstream American movies since *The Exorcist.*[10]

Stephen King was heavily involved in the making of the film. He had the final say on the director, wrote the script, and he had chosen Maine as the shooting location. The pet cemetery in the novel was based on a real place; near where Stephen had lived in Maine was an actual pet cemetery, with an actual misspelled sign, where children did come to bury their pets. The Micmac burial ground beyond it, hopefully, was purely a fabrication. King actively collaborated with Mary Lambert, but he didn't push his ideas on her. He also supported Lambert's creative choices and any changes she made.[11] "He's an incredible storyteller," says Lambert of King:

> He's the Dickens of our age. He is the popular storyteller ... He wanted to make sure the director [of *Pet Sematary*] was going to respect the material. There were a lot of things, visuals, that made it uniquely my project, but I never had anything but support from Stephen; he would often build on one of my ideas.[12]

Despite the film being based on a popular Stephen King creation, there seems to have been reluctance on the part of Paramount and Lambert to call the film a "horror" movie when production began. When remembering when she first considered directing the script, Lambert says, "I kept thinking that I don't really think of myself as a 'horror director.'"[13] During an on-set interview with *Fangoria* magazine during production, executive producer Tim Zinneman described *Pet Sematary* as "a psychological study," while star Midkiff referred to it as a "psychological thriller." *Fangoria* itself noticed this and stated, in the same article, "Anything that features bloody deaths, exposed and pulsating brains, Amerindian demons and rampaging zombie kids stretches the definition of 'psychological' to extremes"[14] A contemporary film reviewer admitted in their article that "movies—so far—haven't gotten much more gruesome or disturbing than *Pet Sematary.*"[15]

Most likely by design on the part of Paramount, the only media on set during the filming of *Pet Sematary* was *Fangoria* magazine. Writer Rodney A. Labbe wrote two articles for *Fangoria* based on his set visit. In the first, Labbe describes a "troubled set" during a summer heat wave in Maine, followed by freezing temperatures six weeks later, and trains passing by within range forcing breaks during the shooting.[16] In his second article, Labbe made a point of interviewing special effects artist Lance Anderson but not director Mary Lambert (though he does refer to her several times as a "novice director" in particular—she had already directed numerous music videos and the feature film *Siesta*, 1987). Lambert and her star Fred Gwynne were not participating in interviews. An "insider" told *Fangoria* that

> Mary wants to avoid controversy; that's why she won't grant interviews. George Romero was supposed to direct *Pet Sematary*, and some people still think he ought to be doing it. She's understandably shaky about the assignment since her professional reputation is riding on it. Producer Richard Rubinstein[17] supposedly had a falling out with Romero somewhere along the line...I'd heard that George was given a very short lead time on Pet Sematary. He was finishing up *Monkey Shines* and considering his immediate responsibility, he had no choice but to turn it down.[18]

This version is very different than the story Lambert herself tells. Stephen King handpicked her as the director for the film (she strongly supposes King's desire to meet her close friend Dee Dee Ramone may have been one of the major factors).[19] She was also coming off a successful streak of very popular music videos that made her "the flavor of the month" in Hollywood (in her own words).[20] In any case, King chose Lambert, and the two worked together as a team on the film, masterfully weaving King's vision into a visual experience that would go on to be easily one of his fans' favorite adaptations of his work. Lambert was insightful and fought for the things she wanted creatively, which included cast and set design decisions:

> The biggest decision I pushed for was Gage. I worked hard not only to cast ... a lot of the execs at Paramount were worried about having a child, a baby, essentially, do some of this stuff in the movie. They wanted to use a puppet, a midget, a little person, to play the child. A puppet. I felt that the humanity of a real baby would be creepier than anything we could come up with. I really pushed hard not to have any of these artifices. I felt like I could get a performance from a child. We found Miko, but I had to stand in front of the train again because the studio wanted to use twins. But Miko didn't have a twin, and I had fallen in love with him. I feel vindicated. I feel he is the beating heart of the film. Then I had to do that all over again for Fred Gwynne. There were executives who felt that he's "Herman Munster." That he's just going to make people think of the Munsters, take us out of the movie, and laugh at him. But I knew we needed Fred. I had to really exert my position as a director in order to make those things happen.[21]

The titular cemetery in *Pet Sematary* (1989), directed by Mary Lambert.

Jud (Fred Gwynne) saves toddler Gage (Miko Hughes) from a truck roaring down the highway in *Pet Sematary*.

Lambert wanted a strong actress who could pull off grief and intensity, and she found that in Denise Crosby.[22] Lambert "set up a good environment"[23] for her actors, especially young Miko. In the feature documentary film *Unearthed and Untold: The Path to Pet Sematary* (2017), it's said that Lambert was shooting scenes in sequence, which made life easier for the young cast, the crew, and the production in general.[24] However, in one of the *Fangoria* magazine articles written during the set visit, actor Dale Midkiff states, "We're not filming in sequence, so one minute I'm calm and the next I'm bananas"[25] Lambert remembers not shooting in sequence.[26] When Lambert approached directing *Pet Sematary,* she called on her skills as a painter and a visual artist (which had made her such a successful music video director). She saw the script for *Pet Sematary* as "a child's drawing. It had a mommy, daddy, house, cat, tree ... " and as a fairy tale. Truthfully, *Pet Sematary* is a fairy tale. It's about a magical place in the woods where the supernatural circles contain spirits and demons and where children should not go. Not used in the 1989 film as much as in the 2019 remake, the legend of the wendigo, a Native American spirit of death and cannibalism, is the basis for the terror that lives in the woods. Jud alludes to the demonic spirit several times throughout the film but never mentions it by name. Instead, he leaves the evil as a nebulous being with no clear motive other than to be evil, which is a staple of King's supernatural evil entities: *"Louis, sometimes dead is better,"* says Jud Crandall. *"The Indians knew that. They stopped using that burial ground when the ground went sour. Don't think about doing it, Louis. The place gets holier, but the place ... is evil."*[27]

Despite being evil, the Indian burial ground is starkly pleasant, in a way. Piles of white rocks that look like bones and concentric patterned circles echo the pet cemetery's circular burial orientation and handmade grave markers. Circular burial grounds are reminiscent of fairy rings in medieval folklore. One place is sad but beautiful and colorful, while the other is ominous, lonely, and monochrome. Lambert herself sees the film as a child's cautionary tale about a family, scary haunted woods, and otherworldly beings: "Maine is incredibly visual," she said. "It has these really dark colors and rocky shores and forests, and then in the summer, everything is really green. It's a fairy tale."[28] The nature and landscapes of the shooting location, Ellsworth, Maine, become an integral part of *Pet Sematary*. Ellsworth is only twenty minutes from Stephen King's house, and other locations include Acadia National Park (where the Micmac trail can be found) and Bangor, Maine. It's also a source of duality throughout the film: bright, sunny days with green grass and gorgeous weather contrasted sharply with gray days, the shadowy forest, and the bleak Micmac burial ground. "I can't imagine not shooting that film in Maine," said actress Denise Crosby in an interview.[29]

It's a picnic day on the green grass. The skies are blue, and the lake behind the Creed home sparkles in the distance. On this sunny day, Gage is hit by a tractor-trailer barreling down the road (the driver is listening to the Ramones' "Sheena is a Punk Rocker" on the radio). We don't see Gage's body, but we see a little bloody shoe roll across the asphalt, and we hear Louis's cry of despair. "I wanted to tear people up with it," Lambert explains about the brutality of Gage's death scene. There were discussions at Paramount about whether they should show the child's death in so blatant a fashion, but again, Mary stood her ground and insisted.[30] "The death of a small child can destroy a family," said Lambert:

> It's one of the hardest things for a marriage to survive. So there's a truth there. A really solid truth. And Stephen just expanded it into a metaphor for that truth. To me, that's what great horror movies always do, are they take a subject that's a little taboo and that people don't want to think about.[31]

The most challenging scene for the actors to film was the incredibly emotionally violent funeral scene, in which Gage's coffin is knocked off the podium when Louis and his father-in-law physically fight each other. Mary wanted this scene to be "big and ugly" because "There's not a lot of action in grief. It's a bleak landscape." Paramount was worried that having a child's body knocked around in a falling coffin was possibly in poor taste.[32] Additionally, when Lambert saw the final edits of Gage's death scenes, she was happy:

> When the truck hits Gage. I love that scene with the kite, and I love the very end when Louis has to kill Gage with the hypodermic needle, and Gage goes, "No fair, no fair!" That was my payoff for begging and pleading and demanding we cast Miko Hughes. He vindicated me.[33]

Lambert's favorite scene in the film is when Gage is seen for the first time since his resurrection when Rachel arrives at Jud Crandall's house after her furious flight from Chicago. The old-fashioned blue costume that Gage is wearing is by design terrifying to Rachel, who had to spend her childhood walking past creepy paintings in her parent's home on her way to feed her disabled sister Zelda. There is a particular painting in Rachel's childhood home in which a child is wearing that exact clothing, complete with a top hat. Mary described what she likes about it:

> I feel like the realization of that little costume was just perfect, and it was just the perfect amount of creepiness, even if you weren't watching the movie that carefully and you didn't specifically remember that there was a creepy painting on the wall that

The blue velvet painting in *Pet Sematary*.

Andrew Hubatsek as the terrifying Zelda in *Pet Sematary*.

> she had to look at every day as a little girl, it's still there subliminally. Those are the things that scared you when you were a child. Most people have a memory of being afraid of a photograph or a painting at their grandmother's house, at the museum, at the library ... because those things do have a spiritual life. In particular paintings of children ... you kind of sense that when you see the painting [in the film].[34]

Zelda, Rachel's deformed and dying sister, is played by Andrew Hubatsek in flashback scenes. After searching for an actress that could play the part, Lambert and her team decided that to give Zelda a genuinely creepy, angular look, they would be better off casting a male in the role. Hubatsek, a young man, had the tallness and thin physique that Lambert wanted, and he wanted the role. Undergoing hours of uncomfortable makeup each day and shooting for twenty-four hours straight sometimes (to avoid makeup removal), Hubatsek created a truly grotesque nightmare figure that haunts Rachel's memories and her daily present realities. "Zelda had to be terrifying because that's what drives Rachel over the edge," Lambert elaborated.[35] Throughout the film, Rachel and her daughter Ellie manifest symptoms of what seems to be "the shining" in the Stephen King universe: they have visions, second sight, can sense spirits, and are affected deeply by negative energy and events, even those happening miles away. It is through this second sight that Ellie can see the ghost of Victor Pascow and that the angry spirit of Zelda visits Rachel in her darkest times.

Church, the cat, was played by several kitties, possibly ten or so, and each cat had a different specialty on command: one could hiss, one could cuddle, one could run in a set direction, one could jump, etc. There was a different cat for each action needed by Church in the story. It was not unusual to hear Lambert say, "Quiet on the set. The cat is acting!" During one of the first scenes filmed with the cats, Lambert got the cat running across the highway and up a tree in one take, which impressed everyone and gave everyone renewed confidence in 'kitty acting.'

One of the final scenes in the film takes place in the Crandall house after Gage has reanimated from the Micmac burial ground and has killed Rachel. The house is transformed into something murky and primordial, being taken over by the wilderness, the earth, soil, and plants, but in a glistening, sick way that implies disease and decay.

Lambert believed that this house transformation scene at the end was critical because King does describe such a transformation in a detailed manner in the book. Mary was happy with the off-kilter and otherworldly mise en scène, perhaps rivaled only by the surreality of the children's Pet Sematary itself in terms of fantastical imagery in this film. As Louis searches the house for Gage and Rachel, he finds them. Her son has murdered Rachel, and Louis has to kill Gage for a second time to end the horrors finally. This part of the film ends with the house burning, symbolic of cleansing and endings, as Louis carries Rachel's corpse, wrapped in a sheet, out to safety. Lambert and her team did burn the house down during the filming; however, the original structure was protected and still standing when the facade they had built became ashes. Then, crazed, Louis buries Rachel in the Micmac burial ground, too, despite the screaming warnings of the ghost of Victor Pascow, who is actively fading away from the physical world as there is nothing else he can do to help The Creed Family.

Paramount was happy with the film and the script but believed that the film needed "one more hit" at the end to drive home the scares with the audience. They had discussed three possible scenarios for the last scene: 1) reanimated dead Rachel arrives home from the burial ground just in time to hear the phone ring. She picks up the phone and smiles evilly; 2) reanimated dead Rachel walks into the kitchen unnoticed, then extends her hand onto Louis' shoulder from behind, and then the screen goes black; or 3) Rachel walks into the kitchen directly facing Louis. He embraces and kisses her, despite her face oozing and squirting blood and goo where Gage had eaten away her left eye. The screen goes black, and all we hear is Louis screaming. This third way was how the studio ended the movie, which is incredibly impactful and "hits" the audience right where it hurts deliciously.

Ultimately, this grotesque little fairy tale with the morals of "Be careful what you wish for" and "You can't cheat death" is lyrically profound in its narrative of secrets, particularly about secrets men keep from women. As mentioned earlier, *Dracula*, *The Strange Case of Dr. Jekyll and Mr. Hyde*, and *Frankenstein* were all novels that inspired King at the time of the writing, and all three are horror stories about men keeping dark secrets from the women they love; secrets that end up destroying them and the women, ultimately destroying everything and everyone involved, with nothing gained except a new appreciation for the power of the indifferent (at best) universe and the evil forces that might wreak havoc with it. When discussing the reanimation of Church the cat with Louis, Jud makes sure he knows never to mention it to Ellie or Rachel:

> *"What we did, Louis, was a ... secret thing. Women are supposed to be the ones who are good at keeping secrets, but any woman who knows anything at all will tell you she's never seen into a man's heart. The soil of a man's heart, Louis, is stonier, like the soil up there in the old Micmac burial ground."* [36]

The secret of the burial ground's properties was passed to Jud Crandall by an old Micmac rag man when he was a child. Jud passes that knowledge on to Louis but never to his own wife or Rachel. This is a secret between men: a dirty and unnecessary secret that they should be ashamed of, and they are ashamed of it. This secrecy destroys families and tears apart the soul of the man who is keeping it, alienating him from everyone he loves and imposing an unearthly loneliness upon him. That is Louis's fate, and Rachel's (presumed) violence towards him is freeing him and allowing him the closeness his secrets have cost him, if only for one minute. In the end, Louis is free, if in despair. Rachel now has the burden of being somewhere between life and death until someone she loves dares to end her (second) life. In a review of the film after opening weekend, a journalist wrote, "You could say facetiously the moral of the story is to avoid buying a house too close to the highway. In a very real way, that is King's point, which is that all it takes is a simple misjudgment to unleash the forces of destruction."[37]

The studio production held open-call auditions during casting and actively encouraged locals to attend, with many supporting roles being cast this way. Many of the cast of *Pet Sematary* were locals from Maine, many who had never acted before, including Blaze and Beau Berdhal (Ellie Creed), Brad Greenquist (Victor Pascow), Susan Blommaert (Missy Dandridge), Matthew August Ferrell (Young Jud), Lisa Stathoplos (Young Jud's Mother), Donnie Greene (the truck driver that kills Gage), and Elizabeth Ureneck (Young Rachel), among others. *Pet Sematary* had a big premiere in Bangor, Maine, with King in attendance to show appreciation for the local support. For the end credits, Lambert's friend Dee Dee Ramone had composed the song "Pet Sematary," which, while upbeat and bouncy musically, is a sorrowful and poignant song with lyrics that embody the grief and futility of the *Pet Sematary* characters, with the lament that the song narrator doesn't want to be buried in a pet sematary and live their live again.

"He meant those lyrics," says Lambert. "He [Dee Dee] had a really sad life, and he didn't want to live it again."[38]

To say that *Pet Sematary* was a success in mainstream theaters is an understatement, as reported by the contemporary film press:

> *Pet Sematary*, the screen version of Stephen King's best-selling horror novel, spooked away its competition and clinched top box-office honors with a $12 million gross. In its first week in release, the occult story of a New England family living near an abandoned pet cemetery opened in 1,585 theaters and scared up an astounding $7,600 per-screen average. Although *Pet Sematary* lacks a marquee value cast featuring Dale Midkiff, Denise Crosby, and Fred Gwynne—it is enhanced by a screenplay crafted by King, who stuck to the original. Paramount Pictures boasted that its newest release received the biggest opening ever during the traditionally slow period between New Year's Day and Memorial Day.[39]

Despite a seeming reluctance on the part of the press to enjoy the film or give it accolades, they couldn't deny that it was resonating with audiences and that there was an artistic sensibility both simplistic and appropriate that Lambert brought to it as director:

> There's no denying that in Mary Lambert, he has a director who can go the distance and make the contradiction work ... With only one feature under her belt—and a

much-maligned one at that, *Siesta*—but various commercials and key music videos behind her, Lambert goes for strong, succinct images and never stops to worry whether there's a lack of credibility or motivation ... Elliot Goldenthal has composed a helpfully ominous score as moody as vintage Bernard Hermann, and Peter Stein's cinematography is superbly varied, from the bright hues of a glossy magazine to the dark shadows of the charnel house. No question about it, *Pet Sematary* (rated R for extreme violence) is a handsomely produced film.[40]

The sequel to *Pet Sematary*, *Pet Sematary II*, went into production soon after and was released in 1991. Of *Pet Sematary II*, Lambert said, "Well, you know what they say in Hollywood: no good deed goes unpunished. They even lowered the budget."[41] Lambert would direct several more horror films and an episode of the horror series *Tales from the Crypt*. However, she never got offered other big-budget studio films. "I don't think it was so much that women didn't direct horror," Lambert says of the phenomenon, "it's that women didn't, and still don't, get directing jobs from the big studios. After I had a very successful film, I didn't get other offers."[42] But she will make another horror movie.

"I'm gonna do another horror movie," she said in 2021. "I've tried so hard and had so many projects that I haven't been able to get off the ground that were scary movies, but maybe I'll bring out those scripts and try to sell them again."[43]

In my life, there has been one fictional blonde heroine every decade that inspires a generation of little girls to defy stereotypes that natural blondes are dumb and to never hide their strength or intelligence in a world that doesn't always value them. In the 1980s, there were two: the tough, rebellious Billie Jean from *The Legend of Billie Jean* (1985), played by Helen Slater, and the 1980s cartoon heroine She-Ra, every bit as bold as her brother He-Man. In the 2000s, there was Elle Woods (played by Reece Witherspoon) from *Legally Blonde* (2001), the intelligent lawyer who proved that everyone who doubted her was just dumb. In 2015, Furiosa (Charlize Theron) from *Mad Max: Fury Road* (2015) shaved her blonde hair entirely because you don't even need it in the future. But in the 1990s, this heroine was Buffy the Vampire Slayer. Buffy was not the small, squeaky Sarah Michelle Gellar of the television series; she was the original Buffy from the 1992 film *Buffy the Vampire Slayer*, played by Kristy Swanson, who was physically fit, mentally formidable, and full of courage. Fran Kuzui's *Buffy the Vampire Slayer* (1992) is often forgotten under the cloak of the Joss Whedon television series (1997-2003). But the film is what not only launched Whedon's career as a screenwriter but allowed him to develop the series and all of his future films.

Buffy Summers is a popular cheerleader at Hemery High in Los Angeles, California. She has a group of popular friends, including Kimberly (a not-yet-famous Hilary Swank) and her boyfriend Jeff (Randall Batinkoff). But Buffy has nightmares and discovers she is a vampire slayer from the odd, older man lurking around her high school, Merrick (Donald Sutherland). He tells her she is "The Chosen One" and it is her destiny to kill vampires; there are vampires all over town and all over her school. Buffy is reluctant to believe any of this and continues being flippant, silly, and shallow as long as she can. But she is finally

Kristy Swanson as Buffy in *Buffy the Vampire Slayer* (1992), directed by Fran Rubel Kuzui.

convinced and agrees to be trained by him in the art of killing vampires. Luke Perry and David Arquette play two high school students that Buffy must save from the vampire king Lothos (Rutger Hauer) and his sidekick Amilyn (Paul Reubens). Buffy is very silly on many levels, but there is darkness to the story and a real character arc for Buffy. Whedon's original version of the script was even darker.

Fran Kuzui was an independent filmmaker working in distribution in Japan when she directed her first feature, *Tokyo Pop* (1988). Kuzui and her husband owned their own distribution company and had been working for years to bring mainstream American films to a Japanese audience. They independently raised money for *Tokyo Pop* and released it successfully. Kuzui wanted to direct again. In 1991, she discovered Joss Whedon, a completely unknown aspiring screenwriter with a feature script no studio wanted to make called *Buffy the Vampire Slayer*. Kuzui read the script, which Whedon had sold to Dolly Parton's production company Sandollar, partnered with Whedon on refining it, and then pitched it to Fox, attaching herself as the director with big star Luke Perry as the male love interest and sold it to them. Kuzui would go from independent filmmaker to studio director in just one film. She said,

> I found the project, I developed the project, and I brought it to Fox already in script form. I didn't develop it inside of Fox, and they wanted to make it. It started out that they were just going to pick up the domestic, and as it was cast and packaged and developed, they became so enthusiastic about it that they wanted everything.[44]

Kuzui was given only five weeks to prep the entire film and six weeks to shoot it, which meant things were moving fast.[45] Though Whedon originally wanted brunette Alyssa Milano to play Buffy, blonde Kristy Swanson won the role. It was Perry who fought for Swanson to play the lead. "He said to me, 'I want you to audition for it. You have to audition for it. You're perfect for it.' He was behind me the whole time, pushing me to audition and convincing the studio and [writer] Joss Whedon that I was the girl for the part."[46] Joan Chen (Josie on the original *Twin Peaks* television series) was going to play the villain's henchman Amilyn, but it didn't work out, and Kuzui cast Paul Reubens (Pee-Wee Herman) in the role instead. Not-yet-famous Ben Affleck (*Justice League*, 2017) and Seth Green (*Austin Powers: International Man of Mystery*, 1997) make tiny appearances as a student and a vampire, respectively.[47] Kuzui was not secure in her role as a director of a major motion picture:

> I spent a long period of time thinking somehow I was going to get replaced before I could start the movie because I was so low on the food chain that I figured that eventually, they would just bring in somebody that was more high-profile than me ... And I thought I could fuck up ... I suddenly had Donald Sutherland and Rutger Hauer staring at me. I was working with two actors who, between them, had made close to one hundred and fifty movies. That's like pretty daunting.[48]

Joss Whedon was on the set and very involved with the shoot until he left and didn't come back. He did not like Donald Sutherland, and he did not like the less scary version of the film and its PG-13 rating. "Fox was very clear to me what kind of rating they wanted me to try to get," said Kuzui, who was following the guidelines set by Fox when it comes to blood and gore, and violence.[49] "I had major involvement," said Whedon:

> I was there almost all the way through shooting. I pretty much eventually threw up my hands because I could not be around Donald Sutherland any longer ... Eventually, I was like, 'I need to be away from here.' [Sutherland] would rewrite all his dialogue, and the director would let him. He can't write—he's not a writer—so the dialogue would not make sense. And he had a very bad attitude. He was incredibly rude to the director; he was rude to everyone around him. He was just a real pain. And to see him destroying my stuff ... But the thing is, he acts well enough that you didn't notice, with his little rewrites and his little ideas about what his character should do, that he was actually destroying the movie more than Rutger was. So I got out of there. I had to run away.[50]

Two of the things that Whedon was most upset about in terms of changes to the story were that, in the end, Buffy is supposed to burn down the gym with all the vampires in it and that Merrick is supposed to kill himself to save Buffy, not be killed by Lothos. "It didn't turn out to be the movie that I had written," said Whedon:

> They never do, but that was my first lesson in that. Not that the movie is without merit, but I just watched a lot of stupid wannabe-star behavior and a director with a different vision than mine-which was her right. It was her movie-but it was still frustrating.[51]

Buffy doesn't burn down the gym, and Merrick doesn't commit suicide. "It took me a long time to realize I was writing about me," Whedon told *Vulture* in 2022, "and that my feeling of powerlessness and constant anxiety was at the heart of everything."[52]

Kristy Swanson had the opposite experience of Whedon on set. To her, Donald Sutherland was "just lovely."[53] She had a good time making the film and remembers how much fun the cast had together. She shared two of her favorite moments on set in an interview:

> One is where Paul Reuben keeps dying. That scene initially lasted ten minutes longer than it does in the theatrical release. It was a fun scene, and we couldn't stop laughing. Then there's another moment where I brought my cat to the set, and it was rubbing against Luke Perry, and he was petting it back. Next thing I know, he says, "Oh my god, your cat just ate my soul patch."[54]

When Sarah Michelle Gellar, who played Buffy in the television series, said that the movie was unsuccessful, actress Kristy Swanson came to its defense: "It wasn't a blockbuster in the theatres. But it became a cult classic. I look at that as a success. And if that wasn't successful, then she wouldn't have had that series."[55]

Whedon would go on to create the version of Buffy that he wanted with his television series and followed his original script as the prequel to the series. In the first episode, Buffy says that she burned down the gym at her previous school. Whedon would also make big Hollywood movies and direct some of them, like the Marvel films *The Avengers* (2012) and its sequel *Age of Ultron* (2014). People loved his writing and films; he was hailed as a feminist because of his strong female characters. In 2017, his ex-wife Kai Cole and several actresses he had worked with, including Gal Gadot (*Justice League*, 2017) and Charisma Carpenter (*Buffy the Vampire Slayer: the series*), publicly accused him of harassment. In his own words, Whedon said, "Nobody ever fell from a pedestal into anything but a pit."[56]

Director Antonia Bird passed away from a rare thyroid cancer on October 24, 2013. To horror fans, she is known only as the director of the 1999 cannibal film *Ravenous*, which starred Robert Carlyle and Guy Pearce alongside David Arquette as nineteenth-century soldiers isolated in the Sierra Nevada during a long and deadly mountain winter. Bird's career as an award-winning film, television, and theater director began in 1968 when, at the tender age of seventeen, she began working as a stage assistant in local London theatrical productions. Eventually landing a coveted position at the Royal Court Theatre, she didn't transition to directing for the screen until the BBC asked her to recreate one of the plays she had directed at the Royal Court. From there, she directed episodes of award-winning British television series (particularly *Eastenders*) and television films. Bird's controversial 1994 feature *Priest* was the spark that ignited her passionate film career. The dark drama depicted homosexuality in the conservative Catholic Church and incest, abuse, hypocrisy, and ultimately forgiveness, with power and insight. *Priest* also solidified the lifelong friendship between Bird and star Robert Carlyle, who would be her business partner and collaborator until her death.

Bird's cannibal Western horror masterpiece *Ravenous* was not originally her project: she

Guy Pearce as Capt. John Boyd in Antonia Bird's cannibal horror western *Ravenous* (1999).

took over directing at the suggestion of Robert Carlyle (who was starring in it) when original director Milcho Manchevski was unceremoniously fired three weeks into production (for, among other reasons, arguing that co-star David Arquette didn't need any more close-ups). Bird arrived in Prague to a disorganized and unhappy cast and crew promptly energized by her on-set dynamic with Carlyle. "With Milcho, the set was heavy and untenable," said one crew member. "Now it's going on like a house on fire. The whole atmosphere has changed."[57] Bird herself believed she took on the role of mother to the confused, overworked, and bedraggled production and that part of her job was to soothe the wounds caused by the already hectic shooting schedule and manipulative studio influence.

Ravenous was inspired by the horrific story of the Donner Party and that of Alferd Packer and was written by Ted Griffin; set in 1846 in the harsh Sierra Nevada mountains of California, at a lonely military fort, men cannibalize each other not out of necessity, but out of addiction to human flesh and its regenerative properties. Sometimes supernatural and sometimes merely psychological, *Ravenous* is ambiguous and deeply personal, playing with our human drive to survive but also to flourish, possibly at the expense of those around us. Are we men, or are we monsters? That old tried-but-true cliché works so well in *Ravenous* that it's almost as if it were new again just for this movie. There's not much supernatural in *Ravenous*, but it is creepy, chilling, and well-made. Guy Pearce is Captain John Boyd, a soldier who is sent to remote Fort Spencer in the mountains in California (the same area where the real Donner Party resorted to cannibalism after being trapped in the harsh snows of winter on their way to the coast). The Algonquian Native American legend of the wendigo is the basis for the film's grotesque "wendigo psychosis": a psychiatric condition characterized by a desire to cannibalize human flesh.

Ravenous was not a massive success at the United States box office in 1999 (a different cut, monitored by Bird herself, was released in the United Kingdom to more enthusiastic audiences later that year), but it has left a mark on the psyche of modern horror film fans.

When asked how many women horror directors they can name, fans will invariably list Antonia Bird in the first five, citing *Ravenous* as, at least, very fun and, at most, one of their favorite horror films. What makes *Ravenous* so memorable is that Bird handled cannibalism in a period setting with an unabashedly dark gallows humor. *Ravenous* stirs the hearts of those who love their tragedy tinged with dark comedy, gore, and unspeakable symbolism. Forgoing the stark seriousness of historical, murderous drama in favor of intelligent, stylish, grim, and shameless violence, Bird's movie resonated with horror fans in the same way that *American Psycho* (2000) did: as a dark social satire wrapped inside many layers of blood. Bird herself once said that *Ravenous* was not a film about cannibalism but an allegorical movie about the state of Western society in the late twentieth century. Not a fan of the Hollywood machine, she once said, "LA [Los Angeles] is the most cannibalistic society I've ever spent time in."[58] Bird would have loved to eliminate the voice-over narration and the quotes at the film's beginning (which were not her idea). She called them "superfluous" and said the studio suffered from the "disease of thinking your audience is stupid—and they're not."[59] Many horror fans have found cathartic comfort in her satirical, moving, and excruciatingly powerful portrayals of the human condition.

Bird was, in 1999, considered one of the "most interesting young British directors."[60] Ken Loach and Martin Scorsese were her icons, her idols. She looked up to their genius and aspired to create films and stories that were compelling and substantial. To that end, Bird, Robert Carlyle, Mark Cousins, and Irvine Welsh created the production company 4-Way Film, which sought to develop those projects. Unfortunately, her pet horror movie *The Meat Trade*, which would have starred Carlyle and Colin Firth as "Burke and Hare"-type nineteenth-century body snatchers and was on her agenda until her death, was never produced. Right before her death, she was developing a new feature film drama called *Cross My Mind* and had an active television directing career in London. Bird had been considered for one of the segments in the all-female horror film anthology *XX* (2016) but unfortunately passed away before she could be included.[61]

Numerous low-budget horror films directed by women played briefly in theaters and drive-ins in the 1980s and 1990s that we aren't covering in this chapter—hundreds of them. A highlight is *Spookies* (1986), a horror movie with four different directors and a meandering, crazy plot that disappeared for three decades before being rediscovered in the late 2010s when the distributor Vinegar Syndrome created a Blu ray version with special features, including interviews with the much-older and much-wiser filmmakers and crew. Co-director, co-writer, and editor Eugenie "Genie" Joseph herself shed some light on what exactly happened with *Spookies* on her website in 2004:

> There were three directors (Thomas Doran, Brendan Faulkner & Frank Farel) prior to my hiring, who were fired by the producer, Michael Lee. I never met those other directors, but I'm sure they hate me. I was originally hired by the producer as an editor to fix the project. The first cut—nearly three hours long—was so unworkable that I felt we could only use bits and pieces. By the time I finished trimming the fat, the beef was only forty minutes long. The useable footage was mostly special effects, monsters, and gorey [sic] goo. Since we now had only a half a movie, we had to go shoot another forty-five

minutes. The problem was that the fired directors had used all their friends as actors, and none of them would work with us to get the film finished. But would we let that rather large problem stop us? We wouldn't be filmmakers if we would be daunted by such materialistic matters. We would simply write a new script—or more precisely, half a script—that would allow us to intercut some of the original footage with brand-new footage—using an entirely new set of actors with an entirely new storyline.[62]

For reasons unknown, *Spookies* was listed in Variety's Top 50 list for 1987 and played at the first Paris Film Festival in 1986, along with George Romero's *Day of the Dead* (1985).[63] Joseph would make a second horror movie as the sole director: *Mind Benders* (1987).

So many films from this time were released either exclusively to VHS or first played in theaters. *Dolly Dearest* (1991), a *Child's Play* (1988) rip-off with a little girl protagonist, was directed by Maria Lease, who defended her film by saying it was not like *Child's Play* because "It differs in that not only does the doll come alive, but it controls the child."[64] Lease liked the script and wanted to make the film because of the "near-universal fear people have of dolls."[65] Marina Sargenti (*Mirror Mirror*, 1990) dove into her next project, the television horror film *Child of Darkness, Child of Ligh*t (1991). She described it as "kind of like *The Omen*" and a "real serious, spooky picture: the conflict is very pure, good against evil."[66]

New York City artist Cindy Sherman was approached by a producer and asked if she wanted to direct a horror movie. "Many of them [horror movies] are so lousy," thought Sherman, " ... even if this is bad, it'll at least fit the qualifications of the genre. I thought that I could definitely have fun with it, and the fact that it was low-budget meant that I would have complete control over it."[67] She described what she wanted:

> I had wanted this woman to be working in an office and accidentally killing people at first, and then kind of becoming empowered by it, and bringing the bodies back to her basement, where she would play with them, and they would become her pets or her friends or her toys.[68]

Heather Boulton as the haunted Meg in director Gaylene Prestons' New Zealand horror movie *Mr. Wrong* (1986).

Rachel Blake as Melanie in Gaylene Preston's stalking horror movie *Perfect Strangers* (2003).

Still photographer Sherman would end up making the Carol Kane-starring slasher movie *Office Killer* (1997), playing it straight, and just having fun. "I love it," she said, "Even the scenes that I think are really kind of terrible ... "[69]

Many horror movies came from countries other than the United States during this time. The horror movie *Intensive Care* (1991), made in the Netherlands and directed by Dorna van Rouveroy, is widely considered by the Dutch to be the worst movie to ever come out of their country.[70] It stars American actor George Kennedy (*The Dirty Dozen*, 1967) as Dr. Bruckner, an American scientist in the Netherlands who is perfecting a revolutionary and dangerous new electro-shock therapy treatment for coma patients. When Dr. Horvath (Jules Croiset) fires him and pulls all his research funding, Dr. Bruckner leaves the hospital in a huff and is in a horrific auto accident that leaves him in a coma. Months later, he wakes up, totally disfigured, and goes on a murder rampage. Kennedy is only in the film for roughly ten minutes, but he gets top billing.

In New Zealand, Gaylene Preston debuted as a director with the horror movie *Mr. Wrong* (1984), in which a woman buys a haunted car; the ghosts of a murderer and his victim torment her. She'd later make the thriller *Perfect Strangers* (2003), starring Sam Neill as a man who seems a perfect love interest until he kidnaps his date and holds her hostage. Also in New Zealand, Melanie Read made *Trial Run* (1985), a thriller about a woman working in isolation who comes to be stalked by an unknown entity or person. In Australia, Aboriginal filmmaker Tracey Moffat made the supernatural horror anthology movie *beDevil* (1993) to wide acclaim. Ann Turner's extraordinarily dark and fantastical *Celia* (1989), like Moffat's *beDevil*, is set in rural Australia. *Celia* is about a little girl fantasizing about horrible creatures, immersed in gorgeous imagery, surreal design, and style. These films would be covered quite well by film and horror critics in publications such as *Senses of Cinema* and the 2014 film anthology book *Kid Power!* by editors Kier-La Janisse and Paul Corupe. A woman in Australia would not direct another horror feature until *In Memorium* (2005) by Amanda Gusack.

In Germany, *A Demon in My View* (1991) is a film set in London in which Anthony Perkins (*Psycho*, 1960) plays The Kenbourne Killer, a serial killer that the police have been tracking for twenty-five years. Based on the novel by Ruth Rendell and directed by Petra Haffter

Ann Turner's horror fantasy *Celia* (1989) stars Rebecca Smart as the title character.

Director Tracey Moffat crafts a surreal supernatural horror experience in her masterpiece *Bedevil* (1993).

from her screenplay, the movie is in English. Haffter directed episodes of the German crime/mystery television series *Tatort*. Previously, Haffter made the television science fiction movie *Exotic Pleasures* (1983), "an apocalyptic love story between a woman and a big black raven,"[71] based on a short story by the Australian writer Peter Carey and the thriller *Kiss of the Tiger* (1988) based on Francys Rieck's dark novel *Voulez-Vous Mourir Avec Moi*.

Shimako Sato made the first non-erotic horror films directed by a woman in Japan: these were *Tale of a Vampire* (1992), *Eko Eko Azarak: Wizard of Darkness* (1995), and *Eko Eko Azarak II: Birth of the Wizard* (1996). All previous genre films made by Japanese women directors were 'pink' films or pornography, essentially, until Sato's mainstream horror movies. *Eko Eko Azarak* is based on a popular 1970s Japanese manga and is best described as the Japanese *Buffy the Vampire Slayer*. It's set in a high school and is about a teenage witch who must fight to protect her classmates from being sacrificed to Satan by an evil cult. It's fun stuff. *Eko Eko Azarak* was adapted into a television series after Sato's first two films in the series, and there were further sequels made afterward. Sato would direct many more genre films in the next two decades.

Enigmatic director Jackie Kong's career as a cult icon began in the early 1980s with the gritty, heartfelt monster movie *The Being* (1981), an admitted low-budget, drive-in rip-off of *Alien* (1979) complete with slimy, dripping-jawed creatures of superhuman power and intelligence. After watching the original 1979 *Alien*, a then barely twenty-one-year-old Jackie Kong, who had just finished film school, thought to herself, "I can write that." Also inspired by a family friend who had played, uncredited, the creature in *Creature from the Black Lagoon* (1954) ("I watched the whole movie, and I didn't see him," she says of his heavy makeup and costume), she wanted to make a monster movie that would not only appeal to the drive-in crowd, but would be easily distributed in the cinematic climate of the early 1980s. "I figured, okay, I'm twenty-one," said Kong,

> What movie can I make mainstream where I can get an audience? Every distributor knows this, too: if you make a horror film, you have an audience. It's like the music

Teenage girls in high school are afflicted by evil magic in *Eko Eko Azarak* (1995), directed by Shimako Sato.

An attempt at a Gothic Poe story adaptation, *Tale of a Vampire* (1992), directed by Shimako Sato is cheesy vampire romance horror.

business with country and western: they know they have loyal fans that will come out to the concerts and buy the albums. So I thought, "Well, I am only twenty-one. I haven't lived that long. I'm not Bertolucci. But I could write a really good horror film. I know how to elicit a reaction. I know how to scare someone." I knew I had this ability, but who would give me money at twenty-one? And I couldn't make an art film. I didn't really have enough world experience. And I wanted to shock people.[72]

Originally envisioning actor Harry Dean Stanton (also a family friend and who had acted in some of Jackie's amateur films in high school) in the lead role of small-town policeman Mortimer Lutz, Kong eventually had to recast her then-husband Bill Osco (credited as Rexx Coltrane) in the role when Stanton became unavailable. Kong's tenacity brought Martin Landau (who won an Oscar in 1995 for his performance as Bela Lugosi in Tim Burton's *Ed Wood,* 1994, and is father to *Buffy the Vampire Slayer: the series* actress Juliet Landau) and José Ferrer onto the project. When Kong was casting *The Being*, Barbara Bain and Martin Landau ran an acting school in Hollywood. Pretending that she was an actress who wanted to audition for them, Kong made an appointment:

I was just using it as an excuse to meet him so that I could give him my script to see if he would be in it. So I go to the appointment, and I am in the office with him, and he wants to audition me, and I said, "No, I'm really not an actor, I wanted you to be in my film!" and I pulled out my script from my purse.[73]

Later that day, Landau called Kong at home and told her he'd not only be in the film, but he'd help her get other cast members like José Ferrer (best remembered in the 1950 film as the title character in *Cyrano de Bergerac*, 1950), Dorothy Malone (also an Oscar winner for 1956's *Written on the Wind*), and others.

Kong was determined to follow the successful path of filmmaking devised by Roger Corman for his legacy of low-budget horror releases. Stirred especially by Ron Howard's accounts of directing *Eat My Dust* (1976) and finishing ninety set-ups a day, she understood that making an independent horror film on the cheap would be a harrowing but essential experience:

Corman would give young filmmakers $100,000. He'd say he didn't care what they did, just get it done. He didn't care about their vision, etc. People used to cut their teeth, back then, Ron Howard, Jonathan Demme—everyone did horror films for Roger Corman. New World was the great distributor where everyone could learn. My experience on *The Being* was like my Roger Corman movie. Today, there isn't a training ground like that for people. He'd [Corman] give you money to make a movie, and he'd get that movie in a drive-in. That was the automatic market. Now there are no drive-ins anymore. They were basically replaced by VHS. I was on the tail end of the drive-in scene.

Kong's budget for *The Being* was limited to less than $1 million, despite being officially listed as having a budget of $4 million (which Kong attests is an outright untruth). Some

Carl Crew preparing a feast fit for a goddess in Jackie Kong's *Blood Diner* (1987).

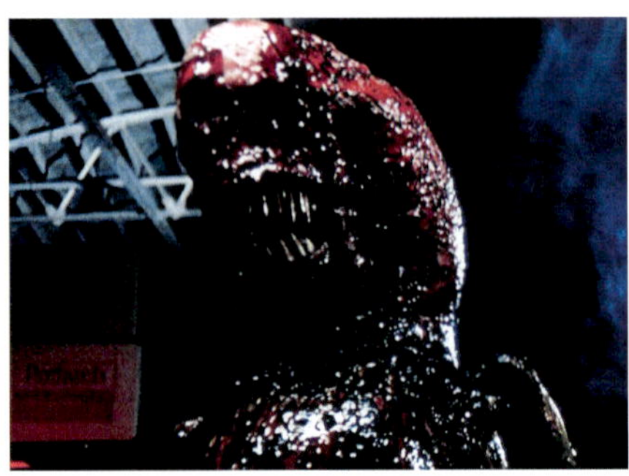

The Being in *The Being* (1983), directed by Jackie Kong.

of the money came from singer Kenny Rogers, whose wife Marianne Gordon played waitress Laurie. Shot on location, *The Being* was set in the small Idaho town of Pottsville on Easter Sunday. "We shot it in Idaho because it was set in Idaho," Kong explains. "Nowadays, I mean, you don't have to shoot in Idaho just because it is set in Idaho." Like other low-budget drive-in movies of the early 1980s, *The Being* delivers on creatures, gore, and dripping green goo. There's a teenage decapitation and a car accident in the first ten minutes. Another major gore scene also takes place in a car when a deputy's heart is ripped from his chest by the mutant monster (the movie's Being, as it were):

> We had a good DP that created some good shadows, and the monster looked okay, but quite honestly, the whole heart coming through the chest? That's a total rip-off of *Alien*. And it was fun. There's no way you could get your heart ripped through your chest and then watch it pump in your hand. But it was fun, and it freaked people out. And there's that other guy who gets his head ripped off; he's on the roof of the car, and he gets his head ripped off. That kind of stuff is fun to do in a studio. There's no reason to do it in Idaho. But I was young, I was learning, and it was a lot of fun. Half the time the monster didn't go where it was supposed to.[74]

In the scene in which Landau and Osco are flying in a two-seater airplane in a dream sequence, actor Jerry Marin, in his Being-suit, was supposed to land on the windshield, but he was flying around in front of a blue screen. "I am sure they've perfected wires since then, especially out of Hong Kong, but back then, we were just trying to figure it out ... It looked like a giant cocoon," Kong remembers,

> And we'd put it on a bungee cord and bungee it across the drive-in. We had bungee cords flying into windows across the screen—it was old-school. There were no visual effects, so we were just bungee-ing everybody all over the set.[75]

The Being also has a sort of film noir mood with some (perhaps misplaced) voice-overs and ominous (small-town Idaho) street scenes. *The Being* is Jackie Kong's attempt to make an entertaining drive-in horror film that was also an ode to all drive-in horror films. At one point in *The Being*, a group of horny teenagers is attacked by the monster in a drive-in theater as they watch a nude woman wrestle with a lumpy, misshapen monster on their film screen. Kong's snarky humor is dark and unrelenting; even the most serious scenes and characters are punctuated with a wry, dark comedy. Kong's personality made its way into her script (as it would with her second horror film, 1987's *Blood Diner*) and onto the set, too, where everyone knew that the film they were making was ultimately silly. "Martin is a major trouper," she remembers,

> Even though he was known to be a very serious actor, he has a really wicked sense of humor, and he was almost like a Catskill Hills comedian telling crass jokes all the time. It was a fun set. It was like the circus came to town.[76]

Aside from the obvious downsides of making a low-budget horror film on location, the non-union set of *The Being* was at one point visited by angry teamsters threatening to blow up the equipment trucks. Makeshift sets, questionable physics, and inconsistent performances and storylines don't take away from the movie's silly charm but do betray the low-budget and Kong's inexperience. Actual explosions and witty segues impress, but the obvious voice-overs underwhelm. Osco's lines as Lutz all had to be redubbed in the editing room. In Kong's cut of the film, actor Robert Downey's [Sr.] voice was used (but was later discarded because he played it too humorously), and in a second cut (which was used in the final version), James Keach's more serious reading was added over Osco's voice. "That was the biggest lesson in editing I ever had," says Kong of creating the two versions of the film. "You can change the tone, order, everything in the cutting room."[77]

Kong says the inspiration for *The Being* was *Alien*, but there are so many more horror films from the same time period that have the same themes, plots, monsters, and clichés (though usually without the wit), like *Tremors* (1990), *Alligator* (1980), and *The Boogens* (1981). Evil corporations, lazy police work, corrupt politicians, and environmental destruction are the downfall of a small community plagued by an evil, unstoppable, misshapen entity that is a direct result of the victims' own irresponsibility, apathy, and shallow consumerism. In the small town of Pottsville, Idaho, on Easter Sunday, a creature is born of the toxic and chemical waste that pours from unsafe factories run by dishonest officials and scientists in cahoots with the local government. Hiding the gruesome murders, the mayor leads a crusade against pornography and filth that might assail the good Christian town in the form of a local massage parlor while playing a dangerous game with the environment and the very lives of the Pottsville inhabitants. *The Being* is a *Frankenstein* tale of a monster turning on its hypocritical creators, a celebration and parody of all the axioms of early 1980s low-budget monster movies. When asked why he kept the mutant toxic waste creature a secret even though it was murdering townspeople, the mayor's response is priceless: *"Potatoes are big business."* They are, after all, in Idaho.

Kong would go on to direct the successful comedy *Night Patrol* (1984), followed by the horror film *Blood Diner* and another comedy called *The Underachievers* (1987). Kong enjoyed making horror films much more than comedies: "Making a monster movie was actually more fun than making a comedy," she said.

> Everyone watched the comedies and thinks it must have been so much fun, when in fact, that was more work than making the monster movie. There's something about getting everyone in makeup and costumes and everything that's so much more fun.[78]

Kong was a young woman with no real film directing experience who was suddenly in charge of a large set with veteran, Academy Award-winning actors at a time when women and Asians were not exactly commonplace in the early 1980s. "I didn't realize I wasn't supposed to be doing it," she explains,

> No one was handing it to me. People always say to me, "Oh, when you were doing it, it was so much easier," and it was never easy. Things have changed, but it was not easier to make a hit movie. It was harder, especially if you were female and ethnic and not part of any club. There was no female director club; there was no Asian director club. It was always just me looking like some strange anomaly. I was lucky that people liked what I wrote and wanted to participate.[79]

Deryn Warren started as a stage actress and director but decided to apply for the American Film Institute for directing. After she graduated, she made her first film: *The Dead of Night,* AKA *Mirror of Death* (1987). Written by Gerry Daly, who would also write her next two features, it's a supernatural horror story about an abused woman who discovers deadly powers through a magic spell. *Mirror of Death*, like all of Warren's films, came about because she was networking with several other women working in the entertainment industry who had what they called "ladies lunches." The newly-graduated Warren was ready for her first project, and one of the women told her about a sleazy producer of soft-core pornography who wanted to transition into mainstream horror films. Very grateful for the opportunity, Warren took Gerry's script for *Mirror of Death* to them, and they were eager to hire her to direct it. All three of Warren's directing jobs came from networking lunches with other women and the opportunities they shared with one another.[80]

Mirror of Death is the story of Sara (Julie Merrill), who has just fled an abusive relationship. Staying in her successful older sister April's house (Janet Graham) while she's out of town, Sara has to deal with the threat of her boyfriend Bobby (John Reno) harassing her. Sara finds a book that had been given to her sister—a book of Haitian voodoo and magic. Using candle magic, she believes she is casting a simple empowerment spell for herself, but instead, she conjures the spirit of Sura, an ancient Egyptian empress, with magic powers.

The shooting schedule was grueling (they once had a twenty-five-hour day on set), but the film was completed on budget and released. "My film with the sleazy guy made him so much money that he wanted to do another one," said Warren in an interview, "They both were sold around the world, and he made more money with them than with his soft-core stuff. He really was sleazy. He cheated me out of money. But he did give me my opportunity."[81]

He also immediately gave her the job of directing another horror film for him. This one, also written by Gerry Daly, was originally titled *To the Devil a Son* before changing the name to *The Boy From Hell*. Also released in 1988 as *Bloodspell*, the film was financially successful. *The Boy From Hell* is the story of Daniel (Anthony Jenkins), a young teenager sent to the St. Boniface home for troubled teens by his mother to protect him from his father. His father, it turns out, is a demon and wants to possess his son's body so he can use it to murder people, which is how the demon's family tradition is. The demon finds his son, and the other teenagers at the home are killed.

After *The Boy From Hell*, Warren had two solid features behind her and a new script she wanted to make. Also written by Gerry Daly, *Black Magic Woman* (1991) was a thriller, not a horror film, according to Warren (though it seems to have all of the elements of a horror film). At another ladies' lunch, a friend told Warren about a contact at Trimark Pictures; they agreed to make Warren's next film. *Black Magic Woman* had a much higher budget than *The Boy From Hell* or *Mirror of Death*, but the process of making the film was the same for her. She loved it. Because of the higher budget, she cast Mark Hamill as her lead, Brad, and the 1980s music performer Apollonia Kotero as a sexy witch named Cassandra. Amanda Wyss (*A Nightmare on Elm Street*) also has a role as Brad's girlfriend. In the film, Brad is a wealthy art gallery owner dating Diane (Wyss), but he has a sexual affair with a witch named Cassandra. Cassandra curses him with voodoo magic when he dumps her, and he becomes seriously ill. After doctors can't help him, Brad's housekeeper Carlita (Abidah Viera) takes him to a voodoo practitioner to cure him. But Cassandra isn't done with him yet; she terrorizes him and the people around him. Bloody eggs, snakes, and other weird voodoo imagery are interspersed with murders and a bit of soft-core sex in a bed and a shower. *Black Magic Woman* is another version of the *Fatal Attraction* story, but with black magic. Warren did some magical research for the film:

> I went to a curandero. He taught me how to break eggs after rubbing them over the person's torso and then look inside to get a message, so we did that. We also put some stuff on Mark Hamill that made his chest steam. But he was screaming in character and was actually being burned! He didn't stop the scene, though! What a good actor he was to do that. We were so sorry.[82]

Unfortunately, the producer of *Black Magic Woman* had a drug habit that made him difficult to work for. "He fired me on a Friday and rehired me on Monday to show his powers," said Warren,

"Later, I banned him from the set. He also asked me to put up my house as collateral which, as a single mom, I refused."[83]

In 2012, Warren was interviewed on a horror blog, and when asked why she loved horror movies, she said, "Why do I love horror films? Because they gave me my start. I will be forever grateful."[84] In 2022, when asked if she likes horror movies and if that's why she made them, she said, "Not at all. I don't even watch horror films. They were just what I could get."[85] Warren has since stopped directing, and, as of the writing of this book, she teaches acting skills to performers and auditioning techniques to actors. She has published several fiction books and a book about acting and performance.

Janet Greek's first feature as director was *Ladies Night*, AKA *The Ladies Club*,

AKA *The Violated,* AKA *Take Back The Night* (1986), a rape-revenge horror thriller. Immediately after being hired to direct on *St. Elsewhere*, Greek was offered an independent film, and she put off directing television until *St. Elsewhere*'s following season. The producer who approached Greek to direct had what she calls "a terrible script." He said he wanted a woman director because the film was about "a group of women in Canada who became vigilantes and would track down recidivist rapists and castrate them."[86] *The Ladies Club* is about a policewoman and a surgeon who band together to castrate their male rapists, men who the law has not justly punished for their crimes. Based on a 1977 novel by Betty Blake and Casey Bishop titled *The Sisterhood, The Ladies Club* is purportedly based on a true story in Canada in the 1980s. Policewoman Joan Taylor (played by Karen Austin) is sexually assaulted in her own home by three young thugs. Her ensuing quest for justice and revenge leads her to form an organized group of rape victims that systematically stalk, kidnap, and surgically castrate their attackers.

"The rapists who attack these women are about to have their lives permanently altered," and "rapists have two problems, and *The Ladies Club* is about to remove them both" were the film's taglines. Released on in theaters in 1986 and on VHS on in 1987, *The Ladies Club* shows its female protagonists castrating their male victims. It feels reactionary to the 1970s women's rights and anti-rape movements. Unlike other rape-revenge movies of the 1970s and earlier, it was less about hurting and killing males than rectifying the lack of justice female rape victims get. Suppose *I Spit On Your Grave* (1978) is on the far end of the low-budget, sexualized, offensive, gratuitous rape-revenge spectrum, and *The Accused* (1988) is on the other end of serious character studies of rape victims, societal attitudes towards rape and female victims, and an overhaul of the political and legal system that allows and encourages rapists and punishes victims, then *The Ladies Club* is somewhere right in the middle. However, the gratuitous nudity and sexualized violence are difficult to reconcile with the film's supposed message. There's an excellent reason that *The Ladies Club* falls short of its potential. "That film bears no resemblance to the film I made," said Janet Greek,

> And I took my name off it. It's directed by "A.K. Allen" because they [the producers] tried to make it into a soft pornography movie, and I had made this really radical, political movie about rape. I was kicked off the movie because I refused to put nudity in the movie, and I didn't ever shoot any nudity, boys![87]

Shot for violence, not for sex appeal, Greek's original film was intended to be a mature, feminist thriller with no nudity and absolutely no sexualized rape. Greek's original title had been *Take Back The Night* (for the national feminist movement to end sexual violence against women), and there was a clause in her contract stating that as long as she and the producers agreed on a final cut of the film, nothing could be changed or edited without her consent. Despite having agreed on a cut, after the producers received the finished film, they decided they wanted nudity:

The ladies of the rape/revenge film *The Ladies Club* (1985), directed by Janet Greek.

> They didn't want a political movie about rape. I am sure in their minds, they couldn't imagine how you could have rape without nudity. But I put 'no nudity' in every single actress's contract who was in a rape scene, and the rapes are shot from the point of view of the victims, so when you see the rape, you see the guys' faces hitting her, fucking her, whatever they're doing to these women.[88]

Greek's original version was so upsetting and violent that when she held an industry screening at Fox, three men in the audience walked out and threw up. Despite how effective it seemed, the producers insisted on nudity, and they recut *Take Back The Night* with more bare skin and some new salacious scenes and released it at *The Ladies Club* in United States theaters. "They wanted this movie to appeal to young guys," says Greek, "and it was promoting rape, in my view, which was completely horrifying. I was heartbroken."[89]

While the intense schedule was exhausting (the non-union crew was sometimes asked to work twenty-four hours in a row with just pizza at twelve hour intervals), Greek was proud of the film and enjoyed the crew. Cinematographer Adam Greenberg would later go on to shoot big-budget genre films such as *Terminator 2: Judgment Day* (1991), *Ghost* (1990), and *Near Dark* (1987). James Le Gros, playing one of the three rapists that assaulted Karen Austin's character, beat out then- unknown Brad Pitt for the lead on Don Coscarelli's *Phantasm II* in 1988. Le Gros would also appear as a cowboy in *Near Dark*. Le Gros did such a fine job of acting as a sociopathic, sexist rapist that his then-girlfriend broke up with him, saying that if he could act like a rapist, he must be a rapist. Dr. Constance Lewis was played by Christine Belford, who also played Regina Cunningham in the Stephen King adaptation of *Christine* (1983). Diana Scarwid, one of the rape victims, would star in *Psycho III* (1986) that same year. Composer Lalo Schifrin (*Day of the Animals*, 1977) wrote the score, but the music was not ready when Greek first screened the first cut for the producers. Instead, she and her editors put up a temporary soundtrack of circus music over the montage scenes in which the women kidnap the rapists and castrate them. "The guys were incensed," she says of their reaction. "I had a whole female team cutting the movie with me, and, boy, we all thought that was hilarious."[90]

Unfortunately, Greek's second experience in mainstream Hollywood, directing the horror feature *Spellbinder,* AKA *The Witching Hour* (1988), was not good, either. The script had originally been brought to Joe Wizan by writer Tracy Tormé. Joe brought it to Greek and said, "This script is a mess. What are we gonna do?" Greek wrote six drafts of *Spellbinder*'s script and only kept two scenes that Tormé had originally written. She rewrote the whole film but didn't take a writing credit:

> I had this noble idea that I was gonna give Tracy the credit, and I would just have the directing credit. In retrospect, I am sorry I didn't have it made a co-writing credit. I wrote every single line of dialogue in the movie.[91]

Like *The Ladies Club*, *Spellbinder*, the final distributed film, was a cut-up version of what she'd originally shot and edited. "This is what they were doing to everybody's movies," Greek said.

> The guys were trying to undermine women. They didn't really want women in the business. In the late 1970s, when there were a few actresses that were directing, like Lee Grant, and you'd hear the producers talk about them and say things like, "Yeah, well, she's just an actress."[92]

Los Angeles attorneys Jeff Mills (Timothy Daly) and Derek Clayton (Rick Rossovich of *Waxwork*, 1988) save a woman from her abusive boyfriend one evening on their way home from work. The woman, Miranda (Kelly Preston), is beautiful, and Jeff decides to take her to his house. They fall in love. But weird things happen that Jeff can't explain. Miranda wears a satanic symbol on her necklace and is probably a member of a local cult that is killing people, and Jeff is their intended sacrifice.

Audra Lindley again plays a villain as Miranda's mother. Also in the film is the awesome Cary-Hiroyuki Tagawa (Shang Tsung in the *Mortal Kombat* movies) as Lieutenant Lee. *Spellbinder* is a flawed movie with some generic thriller elements, but some special effects scenes turned out quite well. At one point, about fifty minutes into the film, Miranda and Jeff are beset by cult-member witches on all of their windows, pressing their heads and hands against the glass and looking in at them. Then, the windows explode magnificently. This scene was really fun. It was unexpectedly well-executed. "The actors were on ladders on top of each other," Greek explained,

> But it wasn't lit, so it looks like they're floating in the air. We shot them moving in, pushing, and then we cut. We left the cameras in the same spot, and then we pulled the windows with fishing line and pushed them from the side off-screen. The candy glass windows exploded in one shot.[93]

Another notable special effects moment is a scene in which a human head explodes into flames. Likewise, the sound effects are strong, and the music composed by Basil Poledouris, who also composed the scores for the films *Conan the Barbarian* (1982) and *RoboCop* (1987), add layers to the atmosphere. When MGM released the film, they cut the entire twenty-minute first reel. The original title was not *Spellbinder* but *The Witching Hour* and was changed without Greek's input two weeks before the theatrical release. Greek's then-husband Joe Wizan,[94] fresh off of a stint as an executive at Twentieth Century Fox, was one of the producers and, according to Greek, actively attempted to destroy the film:

> When MGM tested the movie, it was ninety minutes, and it tested through the roof—they were so excited about the film ... [But] they forced me to either add thirty minutes back into the movie, or they would do it themselves. I was so angry I was crying every day. And my editor was so angry too. We did it. We put in an extra thirty minutes, then we turned the print into MGM, and they cut the first twenty minutes right out of the movie, the entire first reel ... I had to extend a lot of the thriller moments when I had to put back in that extra thirty minutes, which lessened the thriller effect. It was infuriating to have them force me to do that. It was stressful to see this movie that I knew was so good get wrecked without even knowing that the whole first reel would be cut off.[95]

Spellbinder's opening scene is a shot of the downtown plaza in Los Angeles, but the original opening credit sequence was of a man jogging on Mulholland Drive at sunrise. Greek describes her original opening:

> You see that he lives all alone. He has pictures of his parents, and you find out his parents are dead and that he has no family. Then he goes to work, and he meets Rick Rossovich. He's a new hire, and he gloms onto Tim Daly. One afternoon, they're leaving work, and it's daylight, and Rossovich and Daly walk out of the building, and a woman is being beaten up in the parking lot. They stop, and Rick looks at Tim and says, "Don't get involved." They leave, and eventually, Tim goes to play basketball. The recut of the movie starts at this part.[96]

Greek's experience of having her film cut up into something she didn't recognize is not new; Barbara Peeters experienced the same thing with *Humanoid from the Deep* (1980). As the 1980s ended and the 1990s drifted closer to the new millennium, the film industry would change again, simultaneously providing numerous directing opportunities for women horror directors while putting up ever more insidious cultural barriers that prevented many women from working in the industry.

A demonic Jennifer (Megan Fox) and her prey in Karyn Kusama's *Jennifer's Body* (2009).

Chapter 7

Pieces of Jennifer's body

THEATRICAL AND MAINSTREAM HORROR OF THE 21ST CENTURY

"The horror genre is not inherently sexist, but it's an area where women have been historically misrepresented onscreen and underrepresented behind the camera. People think that by making the killer a woman or objectifying men, they are 'turning the genre on its ear' and being progressive. But those are superficial attempts at feminist horror. People ask me all the time what makes a horror film feminist. The solution is actually quite simple: all you have to do to make any movie a feminist film is portray women as actual human beings. This is symptomatic of a larger systemic issue in film, but progress has to take shape somewhere—and horror is the genre I know most intimately."
— Jovanka Vuckovic[1]

IN THE FIRST DECADE OF the 2000s, many genre films directed by women were given wide theatrical releases. Films directed by Jennifer Lynch, Catherine Hardwicke, Karyn Kusama, Laura Lau, Kimberly Peirce, Kathryn Bigelow, Lexi Alexander, Agnieszka Wójtowicz-Vosloo, and Katja von Garnier were heavily marketed to genre fans. Smaller, independent genre-adjacent films were also given critical attention, such as Karen Moncrieff's *The Dead Girl* (2006), Andrea Arnold's *Red Road* (2006), and Jane Campion's *In the Cut* (2003).

2000 was called "The Year of the Sundance Women," as forty-seven percent of the films selected that year were directed by women. "I think more women have been going to film schools for a while now, and eventually that was bound to have an effect, said Mary Harron (*American Psycho*, 2000) when she was interviewed at the Sundance Film Festival that year.[2] "There are more women in the industry now," agreed Martha Coolidge (*Valley Girl*, 1983) at that same festival, "but they're not working ... the film schools are pouring them out, but there is no room for them."[3] Producer Gale Anne Hurd (*The Terminator*, 1984) had a producer's objective view of the situation: "Being a success at the box office is crucial. If a woman's film succeeds, it will be slightly easier for her, but if a woman's film bombs, making the next feature will be twice as hard as it is for a man."[4] Catherine Hardwicke (*Red Riding Hood*, 2011) believed that:

> It's just as tough for guys on one level. But on another level, it's even tougher for women. There's just no question about that. Just look at the statistics and see that 6% of films are directed by women ... ? Of course, it's tougher, and there's a lot less respect. I really do believe that. The Michael Bays and McGs that have these big franchises, but if they had the success I had on *Twilight*, I cannot imagine that the studios would treat them the way that they're treating me on this movie.[5]

These are some of the more influential theatrically-released horror films directed by women in the twenty-first century.

The glorious violence and blood splatter of *American Psycho* (2000), directed by Mary Harron. Image courtesy of Lionsgate.

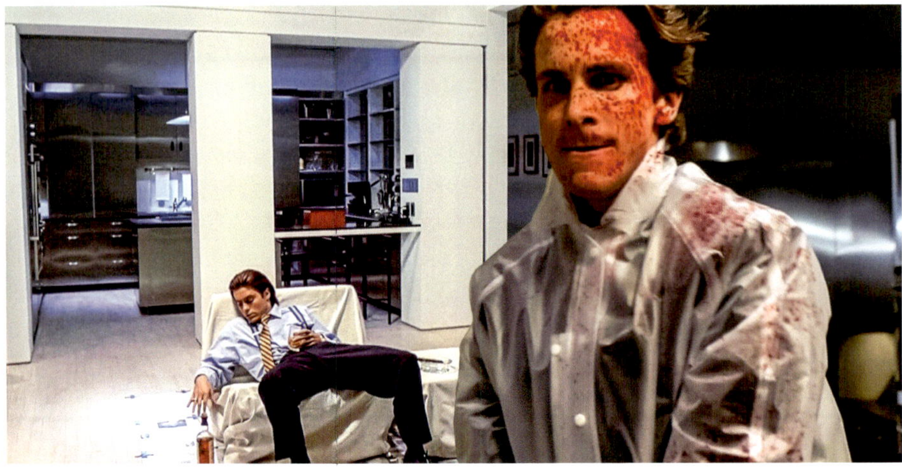

The first great horror film of the twenty-first century was *American Psycho* (2000),[6] directed by Mary Harron and written by Guinevere Turner. The cynical, funny, dark, cruel, and disturbing movie about young, successful sociopath Patrick Bateman is one of the most-seen horror movies directed by a woman of all time. Based on the novel by Bret Easton Ellis, *American Psycho* is set in the 1980s, where the empty and shallow, almost inhuman Bateman thrives as a Wall Street executive. He has a fiancée, friends, and a full-time job; in his own words, there's "nothing there" inside him. A scathing satire of the shallowness of 1980s consumerism and surface obsession, Bateman kills numerous women and men in increasingly brutal ways but fits in so well with the values of the day (he's young, good-looking, rich, goes to the right restaurants) that society can't see that he's a murderer, even when he tries to confess. *American Psycho* is slick, aesthetically stark, and devoid of empathy for its protagonist, a thoroughly unrelatable yet fascinating portrait of a madman passing as the epitome of success with minimal effort.

In 1995, Guinevere Turner and Mary Harron met during a meeting with producer Christine Vachon. Vachon had produced the 1994 independent film *Go Fish*, directed by Rose Troche, in which Turner acted. She was producing Mary Harron's first film, the dark comedy/thriller *I Shot Andy Warhol* (1996).[7] When they met, Harron told Turner that she looked so much like notorious model Bettie Page, who, at the time, was just being rediscovered by pop culture. Turner asked, "Who's Bettie Page?" and Harron told her, sparking a new friendship and working relationship that would go on for several films, including *American Psycho*. "I'm thinking about writing something," Harron told Turner about Bettie Page's life story. "Do you want to write a short piece of Bettie, a little, short bio kind of thing?" Turner replied, "Sure!"

> And then we just had so much fun writing together. You can think someone's brilliant, and you can really like them as a person, but it doesn't necessarily mean you can

collaborate with them. We just really clicked immediately. I don't know. It's like the conversation is continuous. There's a lot of trust. A) you can say something stupid; B) we somehow just trust to tell, "No, that's dumb, that doesn't work," there's no ego between us. It just clicked.[8]

Soon, they had a script for what would become *The Notorious Bettie Page* (2005), but they were having difficulty getting it made. Then, Harron was offered *American Psycho*, and Turner came on board as the screenwriter. *I Shot Andy Warhol* had shown the film industry that "This woman does crazy people," according to Turner:

So, they approached her to adapt *American Psycho*, and she asked me if I would do it. But she said, and I quote, "You're going to really hate me for this, but can you please read this book?" Because I'd never read it. I'd never even heard of it. I don't know what rock I live under, but I'd also never heard of Bettie Page. I don't know what I'd do without Mary Harron in my life. I'm always like, "What's that?"[9]

The book, written by Bret Easton Ellis and published in 1991, was dropped by its original publisher, Simon & Schuster, for too much graphic violence against women. It sparked a rather loud controversy then, including discussions about free speech and how bad taste should be protected like any other speech. And in 1992, producer Edward R. Pressman bought the film rights to it and had been working on making it since. "So, I read the book," said Turner, "and I was like, 'Yes, you're right, I'm mad at you'":

The book, for those who have not read it, makes our movie look like a Disney movie. It is really, really, really graphic. Graphic violence, graphic sex, graphic sex and violence intersect for pages and pages and pages. It's a really tough read, especially if you're someone like me, who, ironically, does not like scary movies. I mean, I appreciate it when they are well done. I'm just too scared to watch them. The only scary movies I've seen, I've been tricked into seeing them. But I did see that there was a potential really feminist satirical, funny-but-scary movie there, and so I toughed it out and said "Yes." And then, halfway through, said, "But I'm not writing another word unless you let me play this character [Elizabeth]."[10]

"I thought {the book} was hilarious," said Harron in an interview with *Rue Morgue* magazine in 2005. "When it gets violent, it gets hideously violent, but it is a satire. I was also very interested in the period. It was probably the first piece of serious fiction to turn the 1980s into a source of comedy."[11] Some of the funniest moments in the book come from Bateman's strange obsessions and the way he tries to attune himself to pop culture. "The book is full of, sometimes, just three paragraphs of talking about clothes," explained Turner, "Lists of clothes that he has, or stuff like that, and that will come through in just how they're dressed and how obsessive he is when you see him getting dressed."[12] "One thing about the book is that it switches very rapidly from one form to another," explained Harron in an interview with *Fangoria* magazine in 2000. "It goes almost arbitrarily. That was an element I wanted to keep in the film, those very abrupt transitions of comedy into horror, of light into darkness."[13]

Turner and Harron, together, began adapting to screenplay format the novel that author Ellis himself has said was "unadaptable."[14] "When we were working on the script," explained Turner, "we met Bret and hung out with him a bit":

> When the movie came out, he'd written a review of it for, I think, *GQ* [magazine] or some men's magazine, and he said that he liked it, and the only thing he didn't like was the moonwalking right before Patrick Bateman kills Paul Allen, which is funny because that wasn't in the script, that was all Christian Bale, but I thought it was amazing, it was just so '80s and so loser-ish. But then, as the decades have gone by, Bret Ellis loves to be on Twitter, just stirring up trouble, and he tweets things like, "Men are better equipped to direct movies than women," just to piss people off. He knows everyone's going to be like, "What?" And he's like, "Ha-ha, gotcha." So, he posted that *American Psycho* should never have been made into a film, to which I say, to his face, "Yeah, I guess it does get a little exhausting hearing that the film was better than the book, doesn't it?"[15]

Harron and Turner removed some of the literary violence so the film could be made, allowing Ellis's satire to come through more clearly in the screenplay. "I think that by taking away so much of the violence that takes center stage in the book," said Turner, "we could appreciate his writing more":

> I mean, he said that he knew where these long, protracted sex-turning-to-violence scenes were in the book ... He's proving a point by making it excessive, but it's just a little too much, at least for me. Although people love the book. I mean, he loves controversy; the more controversy, the better. Although, he did tell me that he was genuinely surprised that not only did he not write a feminist book, but feminists were mad at him.[16]

The first time Christian Bale spoke to Harron about the script, he said, "I spoke with her on the phone, and I said, 'I've just got to get this over with because this might end our conversation and insult you. But I find this to be one of the most ridiculous and hilarious scripts.'"[17] Bale worked out for two months to gain a perfect physique for the looks-obsessed Bateman and perfected an American accent. "Mary described Bateman to me as an alien who has landed on earth and is trying to understand humans and to assimilate with them," Bateman said in an interview.[18] There were some on-set arguments between the cinematographer Andrzej Sekuła (*Reservoir Dogs*, 1992) and Harron,[19] but despite their disagreements, the film is unusually slick and polished in a deliberate and meaningful way. Turner played a small role in the movie, Bateman's friend Elizabeth:

> It was hilarious doing the scene I have in *American Psycho* because it's a sex scene, and I get killed. It was just hilarious. Because Mary, all of a sudden, was kind of uncomfortable

directing the sex of the scene. So, that was interesting. Because she's no shrinking violet, she was like, "Um ... " I think just because it was me. So, the character is in the book, and she is like, "I'm not a lesbian," which I am. They're talking about Sarah Lawrence, which is my alma mater. So, when I was reading the book, I was like, "Mary, I want to play this character." I am not her, but I went to college with her.[20]

The films that most influenced Harron when making *American Psycho* are *The Discreet Charm of the Bourgeoisie* (1972) by Luis Buñuel and *The Tenant* (1976) by Roman Polanski.[21] The hardest part of making the film may have been figuring out how to interpret the excessive violence in the novel and translate it onto the screen. "It was about really paring down the on-screen violence," admitted Turner, "while not appearing to be afraid, just because we're girls, to put violence on the screen; finding that balance ... " But, as Mary put it:

We want one classic horror thing: Girl in nightie being chased by chainsaw. Both of us have read every feminist text ever about the representation of women and violence against women and seeing how much we could avoid that without it not being a scary movie. That said, I was at a screening once of *American Psycho*, and there was a woman at the reception beforehand. This woman said, "I'm so sorry, I can't come to see your movie; I'm too scared." And I was like, "It's actually really not that violent. There's a lot of implied violence. It's more of a satire, and some of it's funny." I talked her into seeing it. And then, sitting in the movie, the first time, I'm like, "I may have lost perspective on the film." It's still upsetting. She was pissed.[22]

In terms of the satire, which was never a problem for Turner and Harron, they got it immediately and knew exactly how to execute it on film. Harron has referred to it as a period piece set in the 1980s, even though that was only fifteen years before the film version came out. "The focus is on the satire of this kind of corporate male behavior, elite male behavior," said Harron. "It seemed quite a brilliant attack on male behavior ... and I definitely had a female take on it."[23] "And we often thought that one of the reasons that the success of *American Psycho* was such a slow burn is because we were satirizing the 1980s too soon," admitted Turner. "And I think once it was twenty years away from the 1980s,"

It's like the Peter Gabriel song, "Big Time," the lyrics are kind of the perfect way to describe the '80s. It kind of all comes from the guys on Wall Street who are making a whole lot of money all of a sudden, and there was this materialism, and hair was big, and things were shiny, and everybody wanted to have a power suit, and music was big and had lots of instruments and saxophones. So, you go to the fanciest restaurant, you spend tons of money, but you don't really even eat the food because it's just about being seen there. And that's, I think, very much what Bret Ellis was doing with the book. Although, the book got a lot more flack than our movie, he always said he thought he wrote a feminist book. [24]

Though the book had been boycotted by feminist organizations, the film version of *American Psycho* did not face any public protests when it was released. "This is a complete myth," said Harron, "There were no pickets, no protesters ... I did have to go on television and defend the book, but those were promotional events."[25] Before the release of the film, Harron had said to *Fangoria* magazine,

> *American Psycho* is very ambiguous. And because the film does have both this comedy and this very frightening and disturbing side to it, and switches between them, it becomes quite a lot for people to take. But I'd be surprised if there was a major outcry. I think that people will be rather divided.[26]

Turner agreed with Harron. "The book was really called 'disgusting pornography,' but people didn't get that upset with us":

> I actually looked up some of the reviews from back then. *The Guardian* said, "A shallow movie, as two-dimensional as its hero." *The Los Angeles Times* said, "The film's one hundred-minute running time is one hundred minutes too long." And *Newsweek* said, "*American Psycho* ends up as trapped in surfaces as its shallow antihero. It's all dressed up with no place to go"' So, people really hated it. I mean, seriously, it feels like it took at least ten years for people to start understanding it, getting it, appreciating it, and then a new generation of people, it seems like, just really loved it.[27]

Despite any critique of the film, Bale's performance was always praised in reviews for his "go-for-broke, stylized performance."[28] The *Los Angeles Times* wrote, "To be fair, *American Psycho* is not as violent as it could be; director Harron, content to be up to her ankles in bloody doings rather than hip-deep, often forgoes the most gruesome shots," then called the MPAA foolish for taking it down from NC-17 to R, and only then for removal of some sex scenes.[29] The reviewer went on to say that it was no secret that the 1980s were so shallow, so the film didn't deserve credit for pointing that out.

After *American Psycho* came out, Harron and Turner returned to their Bettie Page project. Then, in 2018, they made another film called *Charlie Says*, based on the Manson Family. Turner wrote it, and Harron directed it. "The producers of *Charlie Says* approached me and simply said they want to make a movie that centers around 'the Manson girls,'" explained Turner.

> I spent seven months thinking, "What is there original to say about these women?" They have been represented so many times over and over. So, I wanted to do that because of my own experience growing up in a cult, and I felt like I could bring a perspective to it. Those women are basically like my mother. And that was kind of exciting to me, to try to demystify Charlie, not to make him like the most evil man in the world, just show the con man and, most importantly, show the women as individuals with different paths and different reasons for being there.[30]

When Turner wrote it, she didn't know that Harron would be directing. "I actually gave it to her to read," she explained, "Because we just do that in general, give each other notes, and she was like, 'This is the best thing you've ever written. I wish I could direct it.' And I was like, 'I feel like I can make that happen.'" When Harron was preparing to direct it, Turner wanted to play the prison warden. "She was like, 'No. No one will believe you as the warden of a women's prison.'"[31]

One of the negative reviews of *Charlie Says* reminded Turner of the negative reviews they'd gotten for *American Psycho*: "It was so similar that we were like, 'Oh! We're just ahead of our time. We have to get used to being misunderstood.'"[32] "And then we have a fourth script we've written that we're trying to find the money for," said Turner. "You would think that we'd proven ourselves and that people would just be handing us money, but that's not how it works."[33]

Director Catherine Hardwicke directed the enormously successful 2008 teen horror fantasy drama *Twilight*; it made over $350 million worldwide, ten times its budget, and launched the careers of Kristen Stewart and Robert Pattinson into mega-stardom. In 2008, Hardwicke had the highest box office returns of any woman director in Hollywood history. Her next film was the fairy tale/horror werewolf movie *Red Riding Hood* (2011), which had a budget of $40 million, roughly the same budget *Twilight* had. In 2011, horror film director Karen Lam (*The Curse of Willow Song*, 2020) interviewed Hardwicke on the set of *Red Riding Hood*. Hardwicke told Lam, "I thought that after having such a success,"

> I could not believe that I wouldn't be getting a little more money, but it's actually quite the opposite. It's just as difficult and painful. In fact, now they took away so much of my salary to keep the movie going. They were going to pull the plug two weeks ago unless we found a way to come up with more money until I said, "Okay, just take it out of my salary." So now I'm getting less than I got on my last three movies.[34]

Red Riding Hood is set in a fantasy world, a medieval village called Daggerhorn in no particular European country, where magic and monsters are part of everyone's daily beliefs. A fairy tale world. Amanda Seyfried stars as Valerie, a young woman in love with a boy named Peter (Shiloh Fernandez). Her parents, Suzette (Virginia Madsen) and Cesaire (Billy Burke, who also was in *Twilight*), are forcing her to marry Henry (Max Irons), who they prefer. So Red Riding Hood and Peter must carry on their romance clandestinely. When Valerie's little sister Lucie (Alexandria Maillot) is found murdered by a wolf, the townspeople go on a rampage to find and kill it. Wolf attacks have happened in the village before, and now that they're happening again, everyone's paranoia is rebirthed, stronger than ever. A witch-hunter, Father Solomon (Gary Oldman), arrives to help them kill the wolf. "He's suffered a tragedy at the hands of one of these wolf/beasts/creatures," explained Hardwicke, "so he works through the church to go and rid people and other villages of a demon like this ... He gets a bit obsessed with the demon, too."[35] Valerie has a dream in which her grandmother, played by Julie Christie, is the werewolf, so she rushes to her grandmother's house. "The grandmother lives out in the middle of the woods by herself, and in our case, in this crazy tree house," said Hardwicke,

Catherine Hardwicke directing on the set of the werewolf fantasy *Red Riding Hood* (2011).

The bleeding, bright cloak in *Red Riding Hood* (2011) against the snow.

"And she's an herbalist, so that's a Bohemian, maybe a more independent-thinking person. So naturally, in that day, you'd be looked at suspiciously—like you could be a witch or something."[36]

Valerie finds her grandmother dead and learns about a dark family secret from her father, Cesaire, that she can't hide from.

From the beginning, *Red Riding Hood* was meant to be a PG-13 horror film. It has some scares and a few sexual moments, but there's little blood and almost no gore (except a severed hand). Hardwicke's talent for design is the film's best asset; from the sleek blood-red of Valerie's cloak on the fresh white snow to the fire-lit hearths and the blurred dreamy meadows of Valerie's mind, it's fucking breathtaking. Hardwicke captures the dark fairy tale feel better than any of the other contemporary fairy tale adaptation films of the same time like *The Chronicles of Narnia: Prince Caspian* (2008), *Snow White and the Huntsman* (2012), *Jack the Giant Slayer* (2013), and *Oz the Great and Powerful* (2013). None of these have the sexual energy of *Red Riding Hood*. As Hardwicke said:

> The wolf represents a dark sexuality—things the child may not be ready to confront yet. In the original fairy tale of *Little Red Riding Hood*, her mother tells her not to go out into the woods alone, not to stray from the path, and to go directly to her grandmother's house. But she dips into the sensuality of picking flowers and then meets the wolf, which she really wasn't ready in her development to deal with. So the wolf in our film represents an evil, a danger, the dark side of man.[37]

In this sense, *Red Riding Hood* has more in common tone-wise with much earlier werewolf adaptations like *In the Company of Wolves* (1984) and *Brotherhood of the Wolf* (2001) than it does with the cheaper, less thoughtful *Hansel and Gretel: Witch Hunters* (2013). *Red Riding Hood* made over $89 million worldwide. Hardwicke included a darker, alternate ending to *Red Riding Hood* on the DVD release.

Karyn Kusama is one of the first women directors to become widely recognized in the twenty-first century for her continuous genre work. In 2001, she debuted as a director with the boxing film *Girlfight* starring Michelle Rodriguez. Her next project was the 2005 female-led science fiction film *Aeon Flux* starring Charlize Theron and produced by Gale

Anne Hurd. *Aeon Flux* wasn't financially successful; it barely made back its $55 million budget, and critics did not review it kindly.

After the lukewarm response to *Aeon Flux*, Kusama's next feature film was the horror movie *Jennifer's Body* (2009). *Jennifer's Body* is a strange film. On the one hand, mainstream entertainment websites say it's "an example of effective feminist subversion of horror tropes and 'radical' re-examination of female sexuality."[38] On the other hand, the characters, dialogue, and pacing are awful. It's one of the most famous horror films directed by a woman in the twenty-first century. After bombing at the box office when it first came out, it's resurrected as a feminist/queer masterpiece by younger members of the horror community.

Anita "Needy" (Amanda Seyfried, also the star of Catherine Hardwicke's *Red Riding Hood*) and her best friend Jennifer (Megan Fox) live in the tiny town of Devil's Kettle, Minnesota, where there's nothing to do but go to football games and have sex. Needy is a gorgeous girl who wears glasses, so she is considered plain, while Jennifer looks like a twenty-six-year-old supermodel. Jennifer is gorgeous; every man wants to go out with her, have sex with her, and be near her. Needy has a boyfriend, Chip (Johnny Simmons), whom she loves; somehow, he is the only boy who isn't interested in Jennifer. We're told with continuous narration throughout the film how Jennifer and Needy have been best friends since they were little kids playing with Barbie together. Jennifer drags Needy to a seedy bar one night to see the band Low Shoulder play, and Jennifer has a major crush on the lead singer. Jennifer goes with the band in their van, leaving Needy to come home alone. Later that night, Jennifer comes to Needy's house covered in blood and vomits black goo all over the floor, and the boys start disappearing in their small town, eviscerated by something animal-like. Jennifer tells Needy that the band sacrificed her to Satan so they could become famous, but since she wasn't a virgin, a demon possessed her body, and now she has to feed on humans. But she only kills boys! Eventually, she goes after Needy's boyfriend, killing him the night of the school dance, and in a fit of rage, Needy kills Jennifer.

Written by Diablo Cody (*Juno*, 2007) at the tail end of her two years of fame, *Jennifer's Body* is filled with glib and tacky dialogue. Unlike her semi-poignant *Young Adult* (2011), Cody's script for *Jennifer's Body* reads like one repetitive joke. Megan Fox spews out one-liners in an affected faux Valley Girl dialect throughout the story. Jennifer, as a character, has no distinct personality. If I had to describe Jennifer without discussing her looks, I couldn't. She's pretty. That's it. When Jennifer becomes a demon, her inner self doesn't change. She's the same person she was before she was sacrificed to Satan, except now she eats boys. That's not a character arc. Needy has no major crises other than temporarily breaking up with her boyfriend to keep him away from Jennifer. She loves Jennifer, she's obsessed with Jennifer, and she will do anything, even kill Jennifer, to stop her, but we never see why. Aside from their childhood friendship, they have almost no real emotional relationship. They don't share secrets, fears, hopes, or adventures together; theirs seems to be a superficial relationship. Kusama gives the characters one connection by having Needy and Jennifer make out on Needy's bed for about forty-five seconds, which is then forgotten and never mentioned again. The only real emotional

Jennifer (Megan Fox) is a terrifying force in Karyn Lusama's supernatural horror movie *Jennifer's Body* (2009).

interaction between Needy and Jennifer is when Jennifer kills Needy's boyfriend, which causes Needy grief. Not only does Jennifer "kill boys" because it's funny only to kill boys, but she kills innocent boys who have never harmed her. She's not out for revenge, she's not out to stop the band from hurting anyone else, and she has no agenda other than "eat boys," so there is no reason to root for or against her. Unlike Needy, she has no parents; at least, they never appear on-screen. No adults ever see Jennifer or catch her acting demoniacally. Only Needy can see her, to the point where Needy having imagined Jennifer entirely, or that she's a secret personality inside Needy, would start to make some sense. But she's a real girl, and she kills boys, is incredibly vapid, and has the shallowest female relationship displayed on-screen since the film *Heathers* (1988). While Fox was okay with the kissing scene between Needy and Jennifer,[39] Seyfried said that it felt "uncomfortable" for her[40] (but then completely contradicted herself in 2014 when she said it was sexy).[41] "I remember Amanda and I were horrified that we had to make out," said Fox in an interview in 2019. "Her more so than me. I was slightly more comfortable being able to do it. She was not excited about having to film that scene at all ... that was a very stressful scene for the two of us."[42]

To the actors, the kissing scene felt just as exploitative as it felt to the audience.

Many nonsensical things happen in the film: after the third boy is killed, it's clear there's a serial killer of some kind in the town hurting people. The FBI never shows up. No curfew is enacted, no investigation occurs, and the school dance is allowed to go on. Needy's boyfriend's mother gives him pepper spray to protect himself from an attack, but then she allows him to walk alone through the woods to the school dance. It just doesn't make sense in the world that Kusama and Cody have built. The blatant exploitation of Megan

Fox's sexuality and body, along with the candy colors and unnecessary explication voice-over narrative, are not indications of a director having control over the flow of their film.

In 2018, *Vice* published an article titled "*Jennifer's Body* Would Kill if It Came Out Today" that points out the film's themes of abuse and accountability. The author writes, "It's frankly baffling that it was cast aside as B-grade genre trash" when it came out in 2009. They notice that Jennifer is demonstrably "changed" after her encounter with the band, going from a "chaste, pure, virginal, innocent teen at the start of the film" to a "bossy, has a bit of a mean streak, and comes off as self-centered"[43] girl after she is sacrificed. I remember Jennifer saying that she recently had anal sex with an adult man at the bar where Low Shoulder was playing, and that's before her transformation, so I am not sure I see that change. The only change in Jennifer is that she is nice to nerds and boys that she wants to eat to lure them into a false sense of security before she eats them. To the author, the film is a symbolic rape/revenge film (even though Jennifer doesn't seek revenge on the band but on all boys in general) that resonates with the #MeToo movement that began in 2017 that held (mostly male) people in power in the entertainment industry accountable for their sexual harassment, abuses, and rape of those around them and under their power.

Megan Fox herself has levied allegations against Michael Bay (director of the *Transformers* movies), saying that he harassed, mocked, and generally made inappropriate comments to and about her during the filming of the *Transformers* films. Hence, her presence in *Jennifer's Body* is reminiscent of her part in the #MeToo movement. Also in 2018, *BuzzFeed* posted an article titled "You Probably Owe *Jennifer's Body* An Apology," in which several other thoughtful facts were raised: the ad campaign designed to market the film during its original release was not targeted at the audience for whom the film was made. Instead of a movie about abusive female friendships, sexual tensions, and complex feminist explorations, *Jennifer's Body* was made to look like a fun, sexy horror movie starring a gorgeous woman and was targeted to straight young males. Jennifer and her sexuality were the focus of the trailers and the posters. When Diablo Cody and Karyn Kusama pointed out their concerns with the advertisements, they got an email response that brushed off their concerns thoroughly. "The response said, 'Jennifer sexy, she steal your boyfriend,'" said Cody in an interview: "As if a caveman had written it. So that's what we were dealing with." Kusama knew that the movie that was being advertised and the movie that she had made were two different films: "In those conversations, I was like, 'Oh, OK, we are seeing either we made a movie that they see completely differently,' or what's in front of them is something they don't want to see," she said in an interview nine years after the film was released. "And at the time, it was painful, but now I'm realizing this is evident of the world at large.[44]"

In 2022, the relevance of *Jennifer's Body* as more than just a shallow, silly, strangely paced movie was evident. Suppose we can look deeper than the surface, which is very shiny. In that case, we can see some of Jennifer's more abhorrent traits because she's participating in the patriarchy by exploiting herself. The fact that Jennifer and Needy have such a confusing relationship is because Cody wrote it that way on purpose:

> I wrote it for girls. If a guy wrote a movie with the line "Hell is a teenage girl," I would reject that. But I'm allowed to say it because I was one. I think the fact that we were a female creative team gave us permission to make observations about some of the more toxic aspects of female friendship.[45]

Cody also wrote the kissing scene between Jennifer and Needy not as a silly attention grab but to show that Needy is, maybe without even knowing it, in love with Jennifer. This is why she is so obsessed with her, wants to be around her so much, and will break plans with her boyfriend to be with her. This is why she will put up with Jennifer being shallow or mean to men she thinks are "losers" and is okay with the limited emotional connection they are allowed to show: inside, she's in love and lust with the character. Jennifer's exaggerated sexuality isn't for the audience, and it isn't for us. It's for Needy. Needy sees Jennifer as this beautiful creature, and maybe some of what we're seeing is Needy's interpretation of how sexy and beautiful Jennifer is rather than the true Jennifer herself.

Cody had just come off an Oscar win for her script for *Juno*; she was hot stuff in Hollywood, and people were rooting against her because of the seemingly shallow nature of her writing. "At the time, I was very aware of people's desire for me to fail, so I felt like a lot of the reviews were informed by that," she said to *BuzzFeed*. "It's less a truthful analysis of your art than it is a schadenfreude meter."[46] As I mentioned earlier, Megan Fox was a genuine victim of Michael Bay's attitude toward women. After she compared him to Hitler on the set of his films and described how she felt objectified and uncomfortable because of him, she suffered severe career setbacks. She wasn't in any of the subsequent *Transformers* films.

Fox agrees with Cody and Kusama, and many fans that the film was ahead of its time. If it had come out in 2017 instead of 2009, the #MeToo movement would have allowed people to understand better the feminist, traumatic, and emotional nuances of the story that frankly are not apparent without that context. "I genuinely don't believe people were ready for a movie like that at that time in our society and culture," Fox said in a statement to *BuzzFeed* for their article, "I also think that the film may have been overshadowed by the unrelenting vampiric nature of the media's relationship to me at that time. I'm glad that we've seen a shift in the collective conscious, and now people are able to retroactively appreciate it."[47]

In 2019, Beyond Fest in Los Angeles held a tenth-anniversary screening of the film with Kusama and Fox in person for an onstage interview moderated by journalist Jordan Crucchiola. The screening was instrumental in verifying what the articles in *BuzzFeed*, *Vice*, and several others had been saying about the film being sorely misunderstood and many of its more clever messages hidden by misplaced expectations.[48] *Jennifer's Body* subverts several horror movie clichés and women's traditional characters in horror by doing the opposite of what is expected of the female characters. As horror film journalist Meagan Navarro pointed out in 2019,

"The concept of the Final Girl is taken to task head-on, both in that the killer is female and that the surviving female isn't pure either; throughout the credits, she's become a killer as well."[49]

Since its release, *Jennifer's Body* has been studied by academics who were quicker to pick up on the cultural and social nuances of the story than many mainstream journalists.[50] On a less intellectual level, *Jennifer's Body* is liked by fans because it is satirical, campy, and unafraid of queer sexuality. The writer, the director, and the actors were aware of the subtext, but was the film itself self-aware? It doesn't come off as self-aware, which is where I believe the hatred stems. Jaded horror fans like their satire saturated in irony and over-the-top symbolism, like in *They Live* (1988), *Repo Man* (1984), *Heathers* (1988), and *American Psycho* (2000). *Jennifer's Body* isn't that easily read by audiences expecting a traditional horror film narrative. As a result, it comes off as confused, as if Kusama's straightforward direction is at odds with Cody's too-clever writing, warring with one another. The inharmonious combination sends mixed signals, simultaneously asking the audience to focus on the superficial while reading between the lines, mental gymnastics that fans and critics don't like to do. Much of this dissonance results from the failed marketing campaign because it seems that Cody and Kusama planned their movie with incredible insight. So, do we owe *Jennifer's Body* an apology? Yes, I do. I'm not a young woman as I write about this film. *Heathers*, *Clueless* (1995), and *Scream* (1996)—those teen movies make sense to me. I was the target audience. I get them. I didn't get *Jennifer's Body* the first time I watched it. So I asked a teenager how they saw the film. Nineteen-year-old (at the time of this writing) horror journalist Cory McCullough connects deeply with the film, and she explained, rather poignantly, to me that:

BJ Colangelo
@bjcolangelo

"Jennifer's Bodied" (verb): the action of a film being maligned upon release due to societal and cultural norms dictating behavior and groupthink only to be recognized as brilliant approximately ten years later.

Scaredy Cats @CatsScaredy · Jan 17, 2021
I'm eating lunch and catching up on my podcasts. I just finished listening to the Black Christmas 2019 episode by @ThisEndsAtProm and I have decided that my new favourite thing is using Jennifer's Body as a verb as in "this will be Jennifer's Bodied in 10 years." Great episode!

10:28 AM · Jan 17, 2021 · Twitter for iPhone

The social media moment when B.J. Colangelo coined the phrase "Jennifer's Bodied".

> The film treats men the way men treat women if that makes sense. They're disposable objects that Jennifer uses for her own benefit. While women are normally punished for their sexuality, Jennifer's is her power. I also love the scene where Needy finally kills Jennifer. Female friendships, especially when you're a kid, are incredibly complex. Women are told they should constantly be competing with each other for male validation, so female friendships can often become emotional minefields. Needy freeing herself from Jennifer is really empowering and shows how those types of friendships aren't healthy.[51]

As Theron said in 2017, "We've had moments like this, where women really showcase themselves and kind of break glass ceilings. And then we don't sustain it. Or there's one movie that doesn't do well, and all of a sudden, no one wants to make a female-driven film."[52]

Now that *Jennifer's Body* has been seen in a different light despite its initial, confusing release, filmmaker and journalist B.J. Colangelo coined a phrase: "'Jennifer's Bodied' (verb): the action of a film being maligned upon release due to societal and cultural norms dictating behavior and groupthink only to be recognized as brilliant approximately ten years later."[53]

Kusama's next film was a slow-burn thriller/horror set at an elegant dinner party in the Hollywood Hills (a very wealthy area). Kusama had trouble getting funding for the movie because executives kept telling her that the film needed a big star to happen. They also kept repeating to her that the film was "execution dependent," which means "you will have to direct it well for it to be successful." Kusama could only get the funding and make *The Invitation* (2015) when the female-owned and female story-driven Gamechanger Films equity fund came on board to champion the film in 2013.[54] "Interestingly, this is where we landed culturally, that there needs to be earmarked funds for women, essentially coming from politically-minded philanthropists willing to invest in women's visions of the world," said Kusama in 2017 when discussing *The Invitation*. "Amazingly, it exists, and it's completely insane that it exists."[55] *The Invitation* is reminiscent of thrillers like *The Stepford Wives* (1974) and *Rosemary's Baby* (1968): set inside at a dinner party, the personality-focused slow-burn takes time to build a sense of extreme unease. The audience, like a frog in a slowly boiling pot of water, watches events unfold, and by the time anyone in the film or the audience can admit that something is seriously wrong, it's too late, as we are all in the thick of it. Stifled rich people searching for meaning in a meaningless world among their shallow interpersonal relationships results in a very deadly outcome involving a cult mentality reminiscent of the vagueness of the Manson Family's philosophy. "It had this really stark elemental quality to the storytelling, and it felt challenging on a technical level that interested me," said Kusama: "I just felt like, hey, I can really dig into something here. It felt very mature. And I'm just ready for more mature entertainment. Not necessarily grown-up stories about grown-ups, but grown-up approaches to story."[56]

The Invitation is far more intense and personal than Kusama's prior studio-backed movies. Embracing this new independent career that allowed for more creative freedom, Kusama also directed a segment in the all-women-directors anthology film *XX* (2016), which we'll discuss in Chapter 8.

The English-language remake of *Silent House* (2012) is based on the original ultra-low-budget *La Casa Muda*, a Uruguayan horror from 2010. The script was written by Laura Lau, based on the original screenplay by Oscar Estévez. Chris Kentis and Lau, the filmmakers behind the 2004 shark thriller *Open Water*, were directors-for-hire on the remake, which purports to be all one long continuous shot, à la Hitchcock's *Rope* (1948).

Because this film takes place in one house with one main character for over one hour and a half, there are a lot of mundane moments. Sarah (Elizabeth Olsen) is a young woman helping her father renovate an old family summer home for a potential sale. Late

A rich-people dinner party gets bloody in Karyn Kusama's *The Invitation* (2015).

Elizabeth Olsen in *Silent House* (2011), co-directed by Laura Lau.

in the afternoon, the family finds themselves under attack by an unknown assailant inside the house. Sarah must navigate through the horrors of the dark and isolated mansion to survive and find a way to escape one of the many locked doors.

Silent House is a home invasion/haunted house film. Some effective jump scares, loud noises, shaky camera moments, and "I see their feet from under the bed where I am hiding" all add to a compelling little horror movie. The first three-fourths of the film follows Sarah (Olsen) as she evades the stalking attacker that has already incapacitated her father. The old house, a neglected family summer home, is ominous and horrible with its boarded-up windows and locked doors, all of which have missing keys (hence the try-the-key-in-the-lock above scenes), and the dripping, dark basements. Oh, the electricity doesn't work, and there's no phone. The camera is always on Olsen; we see what she sees when she sees it, and we travel her horrific, nightmarish journey alongside her.

The original ending of *Silent House*, which screened at Sundance early in 2012, is different from that in this theatrical release:

> We did reshoot the last fifteen minutes of the film. There were two main reasons why. Our Sundance ending adhered more to the original [Uruguayan] film in that there was a change in point of view from the lead character to one of the other characters. For our film, we realized that this broke the identification with Sarah and confused the viewer's sympathies. Secondly, some other elements were also not as clear as we would like. From the screenings at Sundance, the first time the film had been seen by anyone outside of the production, we could tell that some of our intentions were not so successful.[57]

The original Uruguayan version is based loosely on a real case. In an interview, original director Gustavo Hernández said,

> In the [19]40s, they found two mutilated bodies in a remote countryside house with a series of disturbing photographs. The crime was never solved, and the papers of the day reported different theories about the tragedy. We were inspired by these events and tried to reconstruct the last seventy-eight minutes of the bodies' lives and give our point of view about what might have caused the killings. We thought it would be

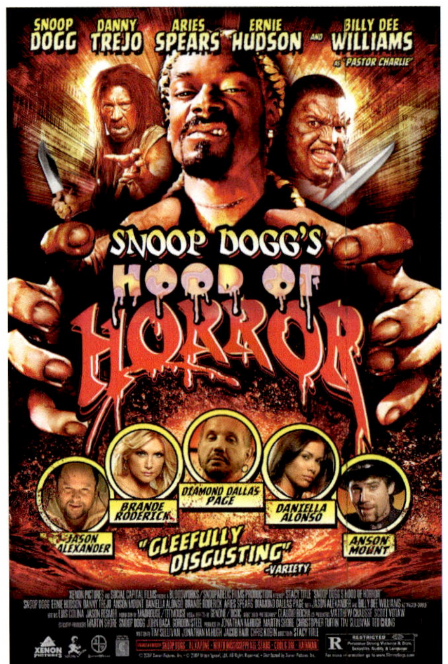

Poster for Stacy Title's horror anthology *Hood of Horror* (2006).

> interesting to explore the links and ties of the people who were together that night at the house and deepen the motivations of each one of them.[58]

Hernández spent $6,000 on his film and ended up with a festival hit. Lau and Kentis, on the other hand, made the same film with a considerably higher budget.

> We had the benefit of watching what they had trailblazed, and we were given some freedom to make it our own. The basic motivations and dynamics of the family are different in the two films; technically, we wanted to build on what they had accomplished. We do think the United States version will bring more awareness to the original, and we hope people will watch both and enjoy each on their own merits.[59]

Stacy Title was a director with a long career. She began directing thrillers in the 1990s, such as *Let the Devil Wear Black* (1999). Her first horror film was the anthology *Snoop Dogg's Hood of Horror* (2006). She told me in 2006 that "I despise the cut and how I was treated on that movie!"[60] Some issues with the Directors Guild prevented her from speaking about it. *Snoop Dogg's Hood of Horror* had segments written by one of the film's creators Tim Sullivan (*2001 Maniacs*, 2005), and stars some horror icons such as Lin Shaye (*Insidious*, 2010), Dallas Page (*The Devil's Rejects*, 2005), Billy Dee Williams (*The Empire Strikes Back*, 1980), Danny Trejo (*Machete*, 2010) and musician/actor Snoop Dogg as the host in the wraparound segments, the Hound Of Hell (H.O.H). It is mostly about racial tension, gang warfare, and crime-related horror with a supernatural twist and morality lessons in which bad people are punished, usually horribly. It's not a very good film, but it is a rare example of people of color headlining a horror film.[61]

The Bye Bye Man (2017) was Title's last film. It's a supernatural horror movie based on the short story "The Bridge to Body Island" by author Robert Damon Schneck. The screenplay was written by Jonathan Penner, with whom Title had worked on her first film, *The Last Supper* (1995), and to whom she was married. *The Bye Bye Man* follows a familiar formula for many American horror movies. There's an urban legend in a town about a supernatural entity named "The Bye Bye Man" that causes people to go insane and kill people. This is the explanation for a mass killing in the 1960s, and there are creepy signs that he is coming to haunt you: he leaves coins that magically appear, the sound of trains means he is coming, and a skinless dog, the worst of the signs, also means he's coming for you. You must forget

A creepy moment in Stacy Title's 2017 horror movie *The Bye Bye Man*.

his name and "don't think it, don't say it," or he will come for you. If anyone else knows about him, you have to kill them before they can spread the knowledge. "He is a modern version of fear," said Title in an interview when the film was released:

> He turns you into your own worst enemy, and because he's telepathic and he can come to you and figure out what your weaknesses are, he preys on your specific weaknesses. You can't stop what's coming once he's inside your head because he puts hallucinations into your life that are very real, and it's hard to figure out what you're actually seeing.[62]

The film stars Carrie Ann Moss (*The Matrix*, 1999), Faye Dunaway (*The Network*, 1976), and the iconic horror actor Doug Jones (*Pan's Labyrinth*, 2006) as the entity, but it was not well-liked by horror fans or critics. As one reviewer noted, "Aside from the poorly developed characters, the mythology of The Bye Bye Man himself is extremely fuzzy. There's just too much going on, with little explanation as to why any of this started happening in the first place."[63]

Sadly, Title was diagnosed with ALS (amyotrophic lateral sclerosis) in 2015 and quickly developed severe symptoms, losing the ability to write, speak, and walk. She was determined to finish the movie she was working on, a dark comedy titled *Walking Time Bomb*. But she never did. "I don't want to die," she said in one of her last interviews,

> But I'm going to eventually. But until then I want to live and direct—doing what I love will be part of my legacy. I don't want to sit shut away in my chair. I think this will be a beautiful, fun, challenging process for all of us, and I am happy. I want to stay happy.[64]

She passed away on January 11, 2021, at age fifty-six.

When I first saw Roseanne Liang's short action/thriller film *Do No Harm* (2018), I knew I was watching an outstanding director who intrinsically knew how to create action sequences. I screened *Do No Harm* at the 2018 Etheria Film Festival, and it premiered at the 2017 Sundance Film Festival to great acclaim. Soon after *Do No Harm* had screened in festivals, Liang was offered representation and the chance to direct a big-budget horror film, *Shadow in the Cloud*. Producer Brian Kavanaugh-Jones (*Riot Girls*, 2019) brought *Shadow in the Cloud* to her, and then producer Kelly McCormick (*Deadpool 2*, 2018) signed on. The movie was filmed in New Zealand, Liang's home country, and stars Chloë Grace Moretz as Flying Officer Maude Garrett/Johnson, a woman carrying precious, top-secret cargo on a mission that requires her to board an allied B-17 bomber crewed by a mix of British, American, Scottish, and New Zealander airmen. Trapped in the turret, she hides her true name and mission and fights a gremlin creature hell-bent on tearing the plane apart in mid-air.

Shadow in the Cloud is full of slick action sequences. One of the film's producers, Tom Hern, said in an interview that Liang "has a unique feel for the action and combat sequences."[65] Liang added, in an interview, "You see the character in the physical choices, in the way they fight. It gives you more insight into the story. It's always what I'm driving for ... I want to get into more of it. I want to get into John Wick-style action—sixty, one hundred-twenty beats of action!"[66]

There are signs of Liang's auteur directing style throughout *Shadow in the Cloud* that can be recognized from *Do No Harm*, especially in how the male characters are introduced while Moretz is in the turret and with the moment-by-moment fighting and stunts. Most of the film shoot involved Moretz alone in the turret with the seven other actors nearby so they could communicate by radio for the scenes when she is locked away from them. Because the *Avatar* sequel was being filmed on the same lot simultaneously, there were no available offices, and the actors had to be in a shipping container in the parking lot. Liang could often only communicate with Moretz by text since they were separated physically during these scenes:

> I could communicate with the men alone or Chloë alone, or all of them together. So that was quite a stressful process for our sound operator at that time, but it was valuable because Chloë's reactions were truthful and authentic. The men also formed a camaraderie that she fell on the outside of, and I personally think that comes across in the performance ... [67]

There was a synergy between Liang, the stunt coordinator, and Moretz as they worked with the visual effects supervisor in charge of animating the creature. "And the creature is really strong, obviously. It can rip up metal with its hands."[68] The Gremlin was inspired by stories told by World War II pilots about creatures, "gremlins," that would sabotage a plane in mid-air and could fly and defy gravity.

Fans and critics highly anticipated *Shadow in the Cloud*. Liang was mentioned in *Variety*'s influential 2021 "Ten Directors to Watch" feature.[69] Horror fans were excited by the idea of a new airplane horror film. And then, the original scriptwriter, Max Landis,

Chloë Grace Moretz is thrown around inside the B-17 bomber's ball turret while a monster tries to crash the plane in *Shadow in the Cloud* (2020), directed by Roseanne Liang.

was accused of sexual harassment and sexual assault publicly via the online #MeToo movement, and the film itself was tainted in the eyes of the audiences, some of whom vowed not to see it because they didn't want to contribute to a paycheck for Landis. As the director who had also rewritten large swathes of the script after Landis left the project, Liang found her film boycotted on a small, social level by the audience she had hoped to attract. She made a public statement regarding the public outcry:

> I want to support women, and I want to believe women. And if you want to boycott *Shadow in the Cloud* because of your feelings about Max Landis and #MeToo, I support you. All I can say is from my point of view; it stands for what I believe in. I believe in the power of women and the strength of women, and I think the movie does speak to this incredible well of strength that women have.[70]

Not only did the Landis controversy hurt the film's release, but the strange shift in tone midway through the movie for a more predictable characterization of a woman hurt the film with reviewers and critics. "One of the first reviews to come out about this movie was from TIFF [Toronto International Film Festival]," said Liang after the film was released,

> And I remember the logline, "A piece of garbage movie by a loathsome creator." And when I first read this review, I was like, "Whoa, you don't know me. How am I loathsome?" And then I realized that the guy was not talking about me; he was talking about Max [Landis]. He'd somehow erased me and decided that a writer who wrote an early draft of this project was the creator of this project.[71]

Landis's original script was under seventy pages. Which parts exactly were written by whom, only Liang and Landis know.

"FYI I did not say remaking The Craft *was a bad idea—I said remakes—IN GENERAL—tend to be a bad idea."* — Fairuza Balk

In 2019, Mary Lambert was asked her opinion of the *Pet Sematary* (2019) remake of her original 1989 film. "I think they did a really good job," she graciously said:

> I mean, [directors] Dennis [Widmyer] and Kevin [Kölsch], they did a great job with the script, and they gave Ellie a lot more agency in moving the plot. In the novel, she's the force behind Louis's decision to bring Church back to life, and Ellie's relationship with her father is very complex in the book, and it was important in the original movie, in the movie that I made, but it's even ... more of a dynamic in the new movie. And, as somebody who was once a young girl, I really liked that. There's a lot of things in there I really like. There's an animal parade that the children do that's a great, wonderful way of dramatizing the sort of eerie force behind the pet sematary. It's super eerie, and it shows a lot of things without dialogue. I love it when you tell a story visually, with subtext instead of with text.[72]

Remakes of beloved horror films tend to be heavily criticized or reviled by some horror fans, especially when the versions are vastly different. Mick Garris, who directed a television miniseries version of *The Shining* that aired in 1997, found that many angry fans of the original did not appreciate the remake at all. "If you are remaking a film thought of as a classic, it's kind of a no-win situation":

> In our case, *The Stand* had been so successful that ABC asked King what he wanted to do next, and he said he wanted to do *The Shining*, as he didn't feel his novel was adapted well. But remaking a highly regarded, established, iconic film can be a fool's errand. Regardless of how well it is done, there will be purists who can't accept anything that is what came before. That said, I couldn't be happier than to have had the opportunity to make it.[73]

The Stand, which Garris had directed for television, was remade as a new television miniseries in 2021. Between 2000-2020, so many classic horror films had been remade that the audience's first reaction was usually to assume it would be horrible, or at least different enough that they wouldn't like it, before going in to see it. Just some of the films that were remade include *Halloween* (2007), *The Wicker Man* (2006), *Friday the 13th* (2009), *The Texas Chainsaw Massacre* (2003), *A Nightmare on Elm Street* (2010), *Prom Night* (2008), *Black Christmas* (2006), *When a Stranger Calls* (2006), *House of Wax* (2005), *The Amityville Horror* (2005), *The Wolfman* (2010), *The Stepfather* (2009), *My Bloody Valentine* (2009), *The Omen* (2006), *The Hills Have Eyes* (2006), *The Crazies* (2010), *The Fog* (2005), *One Missed Call* (2008), *The Hitcher* (2007), *The Last House on the Left* (2009),

It's Alive (2009), *April Fool's Day* (2008), *Evil Dead* (2013), *Night of the Demons* (2009), *Mother's Day* (2010), *I Spit on Your Grave* (2010), *Suspiria* (2018), *Don't Be Afraid of the Dark* (2010), *Fright Night* (2011), and more. Most of these films were forgotten within a few years, and most people don't know they were ever made. Rarely is a remake excellent, as in *The Invisible Man* (2020) and *Dawn of the Dead* (2004), for example, and even more rarely is it exceptional and better than the original, such as *The Thing* (1982) and *The Fly* (1986). As these many remakes were churned out, horror fans began noticing that none of them, not even the ones with female leads, were directed by women. There was no specific reason that women weren't being hired for these remakes or any other horror movies. They just weren't being considered. But then horror fans began asking for them to be considered. Just because women directed them didn't mean that they were good or that they made money, but it did mean that films were being remade differently than if men had made them; in some cases, they were remade spiritually and psychologically as well as physically, taking on the aspect of an entirely new story. *Black Christmas* (2019) co-writer April Wolfe said:

> Horror is about subverting expectations at this point, because we've had a hundred and how many years of cinematic horror. And so, trying to do something new, you're always, always building on something else. One of the things that drives me nuts is when people talk about remakes for horror films, because nearly every horror film is a remake at this point. Whether or not it's in name, in actuality, or whether they're just remaking something like their idea, you know? It's just we're all remaking the same thing, so how do you go about making it different, and make it distinguishable.[74]

Agreeing that remakes are about subverting expectations, but staying true to your original vision, which may be very different than the original, Jen Soska, one of the directors of the *Rabid* (2019) remake, said in an interview:

> I'm guilty as anyone for not giving remakes or re-imaginings a fair chance. I think that is because as a horror fan we've so often been manipulated by the studios that make one that is a remake in title alone, and then it's a completely different film. I think it's important for a filmmaker to do their own thing. I think *Scream* said it best that the golden rule is, "Don't fuck with the original."[75]

Carrie (2013) was the first and highest-budget horror remake directed by a woman. Director Kimberly Peirce had directed two acclaimed films (*Boys Don't Cry*, 1999, and *Stop-Loss*, 2008) when MGM executive Jonathan Glickman approached her to direct a remake of the Brian De Palma horror film *Carrie* (1976), based on the novel of the same name by Stephen King. Her previous film *Boys Don't Cry* was a retelling of the true story of the rape and murder of Brandon Teena, a young trans man, so Glickman and the film's producer Kevin Misher believed that Peirce would understand the "outsider" story of *Carrie*.[76] In the original film adaptation of King's novel, telekinetic teenager Carrie lives with her mentally ill, abusive, and religious mother and attends the local high school

Chloë Grace Moretz stars as the title character in *Carrie* (2013), directed by Kimberly Peirce.

where the students concoct an elaborate humiliation for her by pouring a bucket of pig's blood on her when she is crowned the prom queen. Carrie snaps, telekinetically kills everyone, including her mother, and burns down the school.

Instead of trying to compete with the cinematic vision of Brian De Palma, a director of exceptional talent, Peirce went back to the source novel to see if there was anything she could adapt directly from the book in a way that De Palma didn't. "What I wanted was to capture the essence of Stephen King. I went back to King's characterizations of Carrie, her mother, and the girls and to Carrie's response to being bullied."[77] She refers to Carrie, the character, as a "superhero." Chloë Grace Moretz, from *Shadow in the Cloud*, played Carrie. She was a teenager at the time, only fifteen, unlike Sissy Spacek in the original. Peirce also added a social media element to update the story to 2013, and additional actors at the prom scene were added digitally during post-production.[78] De Palma wasn't threatened when a remake of his famous horror film was being made. Instead, Peirce contacted him "and we discussed the way she was approaching it and who she was going to cast, and I gave her my blessing. I think they're going to say it's more like the book, where it's basically Sue Snell giving testimony, which kind of puts Carrie in brackets."[79] Peirce rewrote pieces of the existing script herself, and she took De Palma's blessing and advice to heart:

> I know the original is a legacy. Brian suggested I read this book about his work and about Roman Polanski, Wes Craven, William Castle, etc. That whole move from when horror was more low-budget in the 1970s, but they really pushed the genre to new levels. Being a student of film and a fan of horror, I really didn't want to fall flat and not do a good job, but at the same time ... I saw opportunities to do things that Brian did not ... there were major things we could explore ... Stories are remade all the time, and as long as you find your way in and it's authentic, it can be really good.[80]

Zoe Saldana is Rosemary in the 2014 TV-miniseries remake of *Rosemary's Baby* (1968), directed by Agnieszka Holland.

Nicely done witchcraft in *The Craft: Legacy* (2020), directed by Zoe Lister-Jones.

The four-hour made-for-television miniseries remake of Roman Polanski's 1968 horror movie *Rosemary's Baby* was directed by Agnieszka Holland (*In Darkness*, 2011). Polanski, like De Palma, is a notable talent who has made some of the most influential horror movies of all time, including *Rosemary's Baby*. Like *Carrie* (2013), *Rosemary's Baby* (2014) has the original novel subject matter to turn to for retelling the story with Ira Levin's 1967 novel of the same name. In the updated television version, Zoe Saldana plays Rosemary. In the original film, willowy housewife Rosemary has just moved to New York City with her attractive actor husband Guy. Their new neighbors in their apartment building are a little strange but friendly. One evening, Rosemary is drugged and has visions that a strange man is raping her. She finds out she's pregnant, and her strange neighbors become increasingly involved in their lives and the pregnancy until Rosemary realizes that Guy has made a deal with Satan that Rosemary will have the Devil's child in return for fame and money with his acting career. Unable to get help or to make anyone believe her, Rosemary is at the mercy of the satanic forces.

The 2014 version differs significantly from the novel, which has more in common with the 1968 film. Instead of being set in New York City, writers Scott Abbott and James Wong have set it in Paris, France. Guy is a writer, not an actor, who has been teaching at the Sorbonne for one year, and Rosemary has suffered a miscarriage and is emotionally recovering from it. It is set in 2014, so the technology is updated: computers, phones, and Internet searches are all different than the dusty books the original Rosemary used to do her research. The creepy neighbors, Roman and Margaux Castevets (Jason Isaacs and Carole Bouquet), meet them before they come to live in their new apartment building; it is the Castevets who helped them get the apartment. There are some small touches, such as hidden rooms and creepy occult books stored in secret places, but the satanic coven and its goals remain the same. The story feels stretched over four hours, and even though it has the dynamism of Saldana, it's easily forgettable. Holland is a Polish director and usually makes dramas, like her semi-famous historical film *Europa Europa* (1990), and has only one other horror/thriller credit, the relatively unknown *Spoor* (2017).

Another remake from Blumhouse, *The Craft: Legacy,* is a "soft reboot" and a sequel, referred to as a "requel," to the 1996 horror movie *The Craft*. The 2020 film was written and directed by Zoe Lister-Jones, although Leigh Janiak (*Honeymoon*, 2014) had been initially hired in 2015 to direct the film. After *The Craft* lingered in development for a few years, Janiak signed on to direct the *Fear Street* horror trilogy (2021) instead, and Lister-Jones signed on. When it was announced that a woman would be directing the horror movie about high school girls who practice witchcraft and dangerously play with forces beyond their control, *The Hollywood Reporter* wrote:

> The news of a female director coming on board to direct a female-centric feature project is welcome news to Hollywood, as it breaks after the studios have come under fire from the American Civil Liberties Union for "systemic failure to hire women directors at all levels of the film and television industry." Janiak's hiring was already weeks in the works; the filmmaker impressed execs with her take on a female empowerment tale.[81]

The original was a mesmerizing piece of teen 1990s horror. Very similar to the original, the synopsis of *The Craft: Legacy* is:

When three aspiring witches—Lourdes (Zoey Luna), Frankie (Gideon Adlon), and Tabby (Lovie Simone)—invite Lily (Cailee Spaeny) to join their coven, she accepts. However, as their powers increase, the quartet soon discovers the hefty price of messing around with unknown forces.

Lister-Jones wanted her film to reach the hearts and souls of unhappy and struggling, witchy teenage girls everywhere, just as the original had done, "Creating a world that really feels current and fresh," but also changing things and updating everything "while still paying homage to everything that was incredible about the original, which was about centering voices of those people who were considered outsiders."[82]

One of the ways Lister-Jones updated the story is by having a trans character, Lourdes, played by Zoey Luna. "Obviously, I am trans," said Luna in an interview,

> And there's not that many trans people, who are in film, that aren't just [playing] a sex worker who gets killed at the end ... There isn't a lot of children that have inspiration to look up to. And my character ... I think she is opening up a lot of doors.[83]

Lister-Jones created entirely new characters:

> These are very much their own young women, living in their own fictional universe ... [My film] is about what it means to be an outsider and a young woman—and when I speak of young women, of course I am also speaking to young trans women—in today's landscape.[84]

Unlike the original, there are bisexual characters and a new villain, Lily's stepfather Adam, who is a practicing witch and wants Lily's powers for himself; ultimately, the girls have to defeat him, not one of their own, like in the original (the evil Nancy). Lister-Jones also felt that magic and witchcraft were shown as evil in the original film, which is not in the remake:

Fairuza Balk
@fairuza

FYI- I did not say I thought remaking The Craft specifically was a bad idea- I said remakes -IN GENERAL-tend to be a bad idea.

3:44 PM · May 20, 2015 · Hootsuite

41 Retweets 136 Likes

Fairuza Balk (star of *The Craft*, 1996) expressing herself on social media in 2015 about remakes.

> No shade to the original—and women are allowed to be villains—but ultimately, it was about women whose power was too overwhelming for them to harness and was turned on each other. The message that I want to put into the universe is that there is no power too great for women to harness and that we always need to be wary of turning that power on each other.[85]

Lister-Jones also ensured that there were real witches on set, occult consultants, to maintain authenticity and respect for the religion and beliefs portrayed onscreen. "The divine feminine is something that has been so suppressed for so long," said Lister-Jones, "And I think the suppression of witchcraft and witch hunting and the history that those traditions have had are so much about the institution of patriarchy being terrified of women's power."[86]

One thing that Lister-Jones did keep in the film was Fairuza Balk's character Nancy (even after what Balk said about remakes). Reading between the lines, it feels like something Lister-Jones was told to do by the studio rather than something she wanted to do with her script. "It was definitely a challenge to figure out how to incorporate [Fairuza Balk's Nancy Downs]," Lister-Jones told *The Hollywood Reporter*,

> Of course, as a character, she's so iconic and important to that cinematic history of women villains. And she is very much the original *Craft*. So I definitely knew that I wanted her to be a part of this reimagining of the story ... But, yeah, it was definitely a tough needle to thread, and there were many different incarnations to get us there.[87]

Nancy appears at the film's end as Lily's birth mother; she'd been adopted originally and never knew it, which explains where all her powers came from. Spaeny, who played the newcomer witch Lily, was the embodiment of what Lister-Jones recognized about herself as a teenager. "And in working on *The Craft* with her," said Lister-Jones, "we talked a lot about my younger self because that was her entry point into the character."[88] Lister-Jones would next direct the feel-good apocalyptic comedy film *How it Ends* (2021).

In 2018, Sophia Takal (*Always Shine*, 2016) was hired to direct a remake of *Black Christmas* (1974) for the film studio Blumhouse. Takal had previously directed the horror movie *New Year, New You* (2018) for Blumhouse's *Into the Dark* feature film series. *Black Christmas* had been unremarkably remade once before, in 2006, but the original is considered a classic slasher film. In the original, several sorority sisters at their house on Christmas Eve encounter a maniac who makes obscene phone calls and kills the girls gruesomely. In Takal's own words during a promotional interview for the film's release, the synopsis of her remake sounds very much like the original:

> My version of *Black Christmas* is about a group of women who are sorority sisters at a college, who start to disappear one by one. The remaining sisters have to figure out why these women are disappearing and who's responsible for it. And eventually, once they figure out who the bad guy is, they have to fight for survival.[89]

There are several key differences between the 1974 version and the 2019 version: in the original, the real killer is never discovered or defeated; the original has no supernatural aspect; the remake was set in 2019, so the technology used is different, and last, the remake focuses around rape culture, misogyny, and trauma, which would ultimately lead to many horror fans being upset by the new story. There are other differences, cleverly calculated by Takal and her co-writer, April Wolfe. It touched a nerve with audiences. "You know, this movie," said Takal:

> Even though it's very, very loosely based on *Black Christmas*, I'd say the plot is extremely different. It's more inspired by the feeling that *Black Christmas* made me feel watching it, this idea of misogyny always being out there and never totally eradicable ... I wanted to make something that reflected our time right now, drawing more from what the original evoked for me rather than great plot points. For me, it was about what does it feel like to be a woman in 2019? ... I didn't just want to make a movie about a bunch of women getting slaughtered. I call this movie a fiercely feminist film, so I don't mind being asked about that at all.[90]

Brought to Takal in March 2019 by Blumhouse and slated for a release date in December 2019, the movie had a swift turnaround. Takal brought Wolfe on board as a co-writer when she needed creative input. "It's an opportunity to write *Black Christmas*," said Wolfe, "and that's amazing, and you're not going to say no to that";

> But the thing is, we also had a really short amount of time to develop and write this story. So that meant that within two months, we didn't really have time to question ourselves or to waste any time. So, if something wasn't working, then it wasn't working. And we were both experienced enough to know when something was just not quite right.[91]

The supernatural element was Wolfe's addition to the story:

A black-masked killer threatens Kris (Aleyse Shannon) in *Black Christmas* (2019), directed by Sophia Takal. Image courtesy of Blumhouse.

Writer/Director Sophia Takal directing Imogen Poots on the set of *Black Christmas*. Image courtesy of Blumhouse.

> Before I came on, Sophia was writing the film solo and was hitting a wall, because she was killing off a bunch of women and just not feeling it or feeling good about it. It was a weird time in American life. I gave her some notes on her script. I offered a few suggestions for ways she might be able to create some healthy distance from murdering women and lean into campier/thematic/metaphorical bits that would allow her to complete the project. She shined to one of my suggestions, which was the supernatural element, and we took it from there and started writing together. So as soon as I came onto the project, I knew that was my directive.[92]

In Takal and Wolfe's version, there's less gore and blood than in the original or the 2006 remake: it was rated PG-13 by design so that younger teenagers could see the film in theaters. In *Black Christmas* (2019), the students of Hawthorne College are shocked when one of the students, Lindsay, is found murdered. The audience knows that three masked people in black cloaks killed her. Riley (Imogen Poots) is a student struggling with having been raped; many people don't believe her allegations about the popular DKO fraternity member Brian. At the fraternity, Riley sees the statue of Calvin Hawthorne, the university's sexist founder, being worshipped by the frat boys while black ooze emerges. A few more murders later and it's clear that the frat house is killing women. Riley, having publicly accused Brian of rape, is now a target; one by one, her sorority sisters are killed by people in cloaks and black masks. She and her sisters fight back, but only Riley and her friend Kris make it out alive with their friend Landon. DKO was using black magic to have the spirit of the sexist Calvin Hawthorne possess university pledges and kill women on campus who "get out of line." The girls smash the statue, of course, ending the terror.

While the entire film does center around women being victimized by sexist, insane frat boys using black magic to murder uppity feminists, it's not any more sensational than a movie like *I Spit on Your Grave* (1978) in which a woman goes on a murderous rampage against the men who raped her or *Hard Candy* (2005) in which a young woman tortures a man who molested her friend. It's a horror movie, and the gendered combat is extreme and completely unrealistic. It's a purgative, satiric style of horror in which

The thing I'll say is the price I paid for co-writing what I thought was an innocuous low-budget movie was death threats, rape threats, harassment from political figures, & now seasonal harassment. I don't feel comfortable talking about BC on here cuz of that so I rarely do. 🤦‍♀️

9:48 AM · Jan 18, 2022 · Twitter for iPhone

The co-writer of *Black Christmas* (2019), April Wolfe, confirmed harassment from fans that didn't like the feminist leanings of the remake in a Twitter update.

exaggerations and absurdity allow significant social issues to be viewed without any danger of real extremism because it's *so out there. The Purge* (2013), in which Americans are allowed one night a year to kill one another with no legal repercussions, *The Hunt* (2020), in which politics and social media cause a wealthy woman to round up people who tweeted about her and hunt them like helpless animals, and *Get Out* (2017) in which a Black man finds out his white girlfriend's family kidnaps Black people and inserts old rich white people's souls into their bodies, taking over their existence, are all examples of this. It's supposed to be upsetting and heavy-handed. It's horror satire. With *Black Christmas* (2019), some combination of the film having been made by a woman director, with feminist lead characters challenging rape culture while frat boys murder them for it, and the fact that it was a remake at all (which always pisses some people off because they don't believe anyone should remake good horror films) made some people on the Internet very angry. Wolfe related,

> I don't so much mind people who give negative feedback, because they hate remakes—that's par for the course, and it's a perennial rant I find amusing. But we are women, and so, of course, we got rape and death threats. The studio had to shell out cash to make sure our personal information was scrubbed from the web ... [angry people] defaced every poster in NYC to write 'cunts' on Imogen Poots' body. It was pretty relentless and remains so through every holiday season so far. Most of these trolls don't really know how to specify what it is that angered them. A good number of the people who got so angry would not consider themselves to be misogynist ... That a seemingly normal person would be that angry about a movie we thought was a pop exercise in camp feminism with some hammer-to-the-nose catharsis. I don't mind if people don't like it or give it a bad review, but the anger ... Making this movie really showed me the dark side of quite a few people. Also, super fun to have an entire marketing team comprised of men who don't seem to understand your movie at all.[93]

There was also positive feedback, however, from people who love "pop exercises in camp feminism with some hammer-to-the-nose catharsis," as Wolfe put it. There were audience members that connected with the movie:

> I got a significant number of women writing to tell me about their experience with rape and how it actually felt cathartic being able to watch this film and actually have fun. Whenever I got letters like that, I was always honored these people would reach out to tell me their stories. A lot of them appreciated that there was a woman character who'd experienced trauma but wasn't defined by it. And that was a goal Sophia and I had had from the beginning. There were other women who reached out and said it was like a secret message movie for them like they'd seen it with their boyfriends, and they had to explain a bunch of shit to their boyfriends, which I thought was fucking hilarious.[94]

It made $18 million, and the budget was $5 million. *Black Christmas* got *Jennifer's Bodied*.

In 2018, Jordan Peele (*Get Out,* 2018) announced that his production company Monkeypaw would produce a remake of the 1992 *Candyman* horror film along with Universal Pictures and MGM and that Nia DaCosta had been attached as the director. Both the 1992 and the 2021 versions take inspiration from horror author and artist Clive Barker's short story "The Forbidden." However, the 2021 version is more of a sequel to the first film than a remake, as it includes events in the past in the earlier movie as factual. The two additional *Candyman* films, *Candyman: Farewell to the Flesh* (1995) and *Candyman: Day of the Dead* (1999), are not included in the canon of the 2021 version.

Candyman (2021) follows the story of the spirit of a murdered Black artist, Daniel Robitaille, who, in 1890s Chicago, was tortured and killed by the local white community for having a relationship with a white woman. The stories of Robitaille, now called "The Candyman," persist a century later when he returns when anyone says "Candyman" five times in a mirror to keep his memory alive and to terrorize the community. In DaCosta's version, the legend has continued, involving every Black man unjustly killed in the Cabrini-Green Chicago tenements. In 1977, a man named Sherman was killed by the police, and his spirit now also appears as the Candyman. Many other men have been absorbed into the evil entity, the Candyman, and an artist named Anthony (Yahya Abdul-Mateen II), an infant in the first movie, is also targeted. A man named Burke (Colman Domingo), who remembers the 1977 murder, wants to reclaim the Candyman as an act of racial empowerment, using him to make the Black community stronger rather than a source of terror in their community. He kidnaps Anthony and cuts off his hand, which is what happened to the original Candyman (and was replaced with a hook), but his girlfriend Brianna (Teyonah Parris) arrives to save him from Burke. When the police arrive, they shoot Anthony, seeing only a Black man at the crime scene. Anthony is absorbed into the Candyman legend, which will never end as long as Black men are unjustly murdered in the community.

DaCosta had previously directed the 2018 Western thriller *Little Woods*, but just a few shorts before that. In 2018, she heard Peele was interested in doing a *Candyman* movie, and she pitched her version to him. "I love *Candyman*, the original film, and I just wanted to be involved."[95] When writing and directing a remake of a very beloved horror film with one of the only Black main characters in mainstream horror movie history, DaCosta had to make sure the original fans didn't hate it while also making sure that the studio got what it wanted. "For me, as a fan," she said, "I just did what I would do as a fan of the story."[96] She made changes: in the 2021 version, the Candyman is no longer a single entity; he's a phenomenon, and the Candyman is more significant than any person. He's a manifestation of trauma. She knew there were parts of the film that she wanted and needed to keep, too:

> What I wanted to keep was the romantic nature of *Candyman*. There's something really interesting about that, that they did in the first film. I really loved the way he was this darkly romantic, Gothic, antihero character, so I really wanted to keep those layers to him. It was also important to expand on who he was and what that meant.[97]

Unlike the 1992 version, the 2021 version expands on who the Candyman is and what motivates him. It's complex; DaCosta simultaneously makes him out to be a monster, an antihero, a villain, and a martyr. She deconstructs the monster and tells us where he came from. "*Candyman*," she shared on social media during the production, is "at the intersection of white violence and Black pain is about unwilling martyrs. The people they were, the symbols we turn them into, the monsters we are told they must have been."[98] DaCosta is a Black woman director who made a movie about a Black horror movie character with a predominantly Black cast set in a Black community; she doesn't believe Black artists are expected to deal with issues of Black trauma, she happens to have made a film that does that, and she happens to be a massive fan of the original film and horror as a whole.[99]

When the film was released in August 2021, it was marketed heavily as "Jordan Peele's *Candyman*." Many fans made a point on social media to insist that it was Nia DaCosta's *Candyman*. Peele's fame and reputation as a horror filmmaker with his work on the remarkable *Get Out* (2018) made it appealing to market the film using his name as much as possible, but it almost erased DaCosta initially.[100] That kind of marketing also happens to male directors when a much more famous producer is the focus of their film's marketing campaign. DaCosta immediately went into production on the $100 million Marvel superhero film *The Marvels* (2023) after shooting *Candyman*, an enormous leap in budget.

The Slumber Party Massacre (2021) was Danishka Esterhazy's second film for SyFy. *The Banana Splits Movie* (2019), a gory and surreal adaptation of the 1970s children's cartoon, was her first. Like *The Banana Splits Movie*, *The Slumber Party Massacre* has an element of satire that is missing in her earlier genre film work, like the Gothic drama *Black Field* (2009). "I didn't choose satire as much as it chose me," said Esterhazy when asked about this transition in her style as a filmmaker,

"My films caught the attention of a network executive at SyFy channel—Josh Van Houdt. He liked my visual style, commitment to telling women's stories, and ability to build tension and suspense. He hired me to direct *The Banana Splits* and *Slumber Party Massacre*."[101]

With screenwriter Suzanne Keilly, Esterhazy created a new version of the woman-directed, low-budget slasher series of the 1980s. Distributor Shout! Factory owns the

It's drill vs. guitar in this homage moment to *Slumber Party Massacre 2* in *Slumber Party Massacre* (2021), directed by Danishka Esterhazy.

One thing is the same in both the original and the remake of *Slumber Party Massacre: the slumber party*.

three original films and worked with SyFy and Esterhazy on this version. For Esterhazy, this was her opportunity to make the version of *The Slumber Party Massacre* that she had always wanted to see. From the fan's point of view, she could take all the things she loves about the original films and then put in all of the things she wishes had been in the original films. She wanted a lot of gore and blood and had complete support from the network. "I was already familiar with the trilogy—as a woman horror fan, how could I not be?"[102] said Esterhazy. She had a love/hate relationship with the original film:

> I wanted to celebrate all the woman writers and directors who made those films. Yet I was so disappointed by the leering male gaze that defined the franchise. But as I rewatched the first film, again and again, I became a deep fan of [original *The Slumber Party Massacre* director] Holden Jones. A fan of her pacing and her visual compositions. *The Slumber Party Massacre* was her first feature film, but her background as an editor is very clear in her smart staging and skillful intercutting. I also became a fan of her frank no-nonsense attitude in interviews. She makes no apologies. She has a healthy feminist rage for the nonsense in the film industry and the hypocrisy of male film critics.[103]

There were some things from the original film that she absolutely would not change. One was the character Diane's death in the garage. Holden Jones had Diane (Gina Mari) slide down between Russ's (Michael Villella) legs as he was about to impale her with the drill, which was the inspiration for the original poster. She used a similar framing in one of the early kills. There were also scenes she would not even attempt to recreate out of respect for the original, like the death of Neil (Joseph Alan Johnson) cut with Valerie (Robin Stille) watching an old horror movie in her living room:

> The intercut between her watching this scream fest and Neil being murdered outside. It's so beautifully put together, and you can really tell that Amy Holden Jones was an editor before she became a director because the pacing and editing in that sequence are so good. So I knew I wasn't even going to touch that one. I was

like, "That cannot be improved. I will not mangle that beautiful sequence. I will just continue to enjoy it as a fan."[104]

Esterhazy did make some changes, though. For one, there are nude men in the movie, something absent from the original. She described the original, a famous feminist horror film series, as "all boobs all the time."[105] It made her feel erased as an audience member, that no horror film story was speaking to her. Instead of a remake, this version of *The Slumber Party Massacre* is more of a sequel, with the character Trish, from the original, being grown up with a daughter. It's this daughter, Dana (Hannah Gonera), who rallies her friends Maeve (Frances Sholto-Douglas), Breanie (Alex McGregor), and Ashley (Reze-Tiana Wessels) to revisit the location (now a cabin instead of a house) where Russ Thorn (Rob Van Vuuren) originally attacked Trish (Schelaine Bennett) and her friends back in 1993 with the express purpose of finding Thorn and killing him. They meet four young men staying in a nearby cabin. These young men get shirtless and attacked by Russ Thorn, so the boys and the girls must band together to survive the night and ensure Thorn doesn't. Unfortunately, Thorn's mother, Kay (Jennifer Steyn), is the owner of the cabin where the boys are staying. She isn't going to allow her son to be mercilessly murdered by a group of girls at a slumber party without a serious fight. It's a satire, much like the original was supposed to be (see Chapter 5), updated for a modern audience that appreciates irony. Esterhazy's changes seem to have been less grating towards critics and audiences than the ones Takal and Wolfe made for their version of *Black Christmas,* as the criticism was nowhere near as vehement or virulent, instead reserved for negative reviews attacking the jokes that don't work rather than the gendered changes to the story. "I was really gratified by the fan response," said Esterhazy:

> I knew that I wanted to make a bold feminist remake. I fought to include the gender reversal scenes. I would not have made the film if I wasn't allowed to mock those original shower scenes and pillow fights. But I knew that my approach would piss off some of the fans. It would be unavoidable. I hoped that my satirical tone would allow horror fans to laugh at the glaring sexism of the 1980s while still loving the original films.[106]

There was criticism on social media, however. One person declared that the film ruined the franchise because women don't understand horror. Another post claimed that the movie tries to force homosexuality onto the male horror fan. "That is such a bizarre (and homophobic) statement that it makes my head spin," said Esterhazy. "But the fact that some viewers can only imagine male nudity as a homoerotic scene *shows* how invisible the female gaze remains to many."[107]

Part of the overall and comparative acceptance of *The Slumber Party Massacre* remake as opposed to some recent others may be the way Esterhazy approached the original: not as something that needed to be changed, but something that should be updated and as an opportunity to fix the problems inherent in the original while keeping what worked and even respectfully declining to copy the things that would work better in the original:

> I love the original trilogy, and I have huge respect for the women writers and directors who made them, and I don't want to dismiss what they achieved, the barriers they faced becoming women horror directors in the 1980s. That's no small feat. It's huge. I wouldn't be here today if women hadn't made that series because they opened so many doors. I absolutely recognize that. But I want to continue the conversation.[108]

The version of *The Slumber Party Massacre* that was screened at film festivals versus the one that aired on the SyFy Channel does differ, mainly in profanity being replaced. But both versions keep the small homage that Esterhazy wanted to include, like original film character Kim's (Debra Deliso) "Space Baby" t-shirt, original character Courtney's (Jennifer Meyers) nightstand goose lamp, and new character Sean's (Nathan Castle) guitar, which is the same one used by the rock 'n' roll Driller Killer (Atanas Ilitch) in the original *The Slumber Party Massacre II*.

Jen and Sylvia Soska are twin sisters who write and direct films together. After making several short horror movies in 2006 and 2007, they burst into the Canadian independent horror film scene with the gritty action/horror movie *Dead Hooker in a Trunk* (2009). Shortly after, they made another horror movie, *American Mary* (2012), a segment for the horror anthology *The ABCs of Death 2* (2014), the horror movie sequel *See No Evil 2* (2014), and the action/thriller *Vendetta* (2015). After *Vendetta*, they became attached to write and direct the remake of David Cronenberg's creepy *Rabid* (1977). *Rabid* is about a woman named Rose (Marilyn Chambers) who gets into a motorcycle accident. In the hospital where emergency surgery is performed, the doctors have implanted a parasitic creature inside her that bites and infects other people with a strange illness that turns them into zombies.

Rabid (1977) is a milestone film in the development of Cronenbergian body horror films. Body horror, described by Jen Soska, is "scientifically based, or medicine-based, horror.[109]" Body horror can sometimes have a supernatural or spiritual aspect too, but in most body horror films, the cause is a virus, scientific aberration due to experimentation gone awry, or self-mutilation/mutilation of others. A better phrase may be "biological horror"—the horror of losing bodily autonomy to another person, creature, or entity. The Soskas experimented previously with body horror in their films *Dead Hooker in a Trunk*, which involves an arm being torn off and sewn back on later, and *American Mary*, in which a medical student performs underground body modifications, some of which are horrifyingly extreme.

Just like Cronenberg, the Soskas have come out of the Toronto independent and underground film scene. They were nervous to touch such an iconic director's work by directing a remake. One of the main reasons they went ahead is because Cronenberg directed a remake: *The Fly* (1986). "His 1986 version was a complete reimagining that took the story in places no one but Cronenberg could have with his sensibility for body horror and physical transformations," said Jen. "Of course, it's terrifying to remake a Cronenberg

Some of the expected blood and violence in Jen and Sylvia Soska's *Rabid* (2019).

film," agreed Sylvia. "If he hadn't made *The Fly*, I don't think it would've been kosher."[110] By sticking to their guns that their version of *Rabid* would be an homage to Cronenberg, the Soskas decided on a self-aware reboot with updated technology.

Jen and Sylvia were contacted by the people who had bought the rights to the original *Rabid* and found them when conducting an Internet search about Cronenberg. Their work popped up in their results, and the producers compared their work with Cronenberg's. The producers assumed that the Soskas were the right people for the job. "And a lot of people on the internet seemed to draw that as a comparison,[111]" said Sylvia, regarding their work and Cronenberg's. "I was very skeptical when I heard someone was remaking this film," admits Jen,

> But when I realized we'd be working with [John Serge] a real author, I was like, "Well, I hate remakes, but it's really important for someone who gives a shit about David's body of work, the fans of the original film, to revamp it." I thought, "Oh, god, what if it's just one of those soulless remakes?" I don't need to name any of them, but you know what I'm talking about. I was afraid this would be *Rabid* in title only with nothing to do with the original.[112]

Focusing on what they can do to update the story without changing the underlying atmosphere of the movie, the Soskas decided to add stem cell research and transhumanism (which means that their characters not only mutate due to the parasite but mutate in non-human ways)."Forty-one years ago, stem cell manipulation wasn't even a term that had been coined, but David was already anticipating it," said Sylvia:

> And what he was really talking about was transhumanism experiments. He talked

about how we were going to normalize how our technology is going to connect us, but keep us actually farther apart. So, everything he saw, it was almost like the seeds already existed forty-one years ago. And it actually blossomed into more of a horror story that's very appropriate for today.[113]

Because the original film had starred adult actress Marilyn Chambers, it was a quite unusual casting for the time. In the new version, actress Laura Vandervoort plays the lead, Rose Miller. "Even though Laura worked hard to make the character her own," said Jen, "there are scenes that she would watch Marilyn Chambers' performance over and over again beforehand because she'd be like, 'Okay, this is one of the big Marilyn moments, so we definitely want to emulate her, and we want to pay tribute to her.'"[114] Rose in the Soskas' version was meant to be different than Cronenberg's Rose. "In his original, Rose didn't have a career, she didn't have a last name, and she was very much an appendage of her boyfriend, Hart. In our version, Rose is very much driving her own story," said Jen.[115] "David originally wanted to hire Sissy Spacek for the role of Rose, but they refused to hire her because of the accent," said Sylvia, giving some background and context to their choices about Rose. "They ended up having Marilyn Chambers instead, and both of them are awesome actresses in their own right. So we wanted to have somebody who was like a blend of the two."[116] The Soskas' *Rabid* is set in fashion design, highlighting the cut-throat competition for survival that their characters face in more than one way.

"I think the big difference between our *Rabid* and David's *Rabid* is," explained Jen, "firstly, we're female, so it's going to be from a female gaze. As much as I feel in touch with the male side of myself, it will be seen through the eyes of a lady."[117] Just because they feel they have a "female gaze" does not mean the Soskas shy away from violence, gore, blood, or horrific imagery. Quite the contrary, their films are known for their disturbing imagery. Some of their ideas were vetoed by the producer for being too extreme. For instance, Sylvia wanted to include a tentacle between Rose's legs but was forced to change the scene so that it comes from Rose's armpit instead. "And then I found out that was David's original idea as well," she said. "Both of us got shot down."[118] In another scene, they had actor Stephen Huszar (Dominic) ripping someone's face. "As we were doing it, it was so specific," said Huszar about their directing of the violent moment. "We were even adjusting the skin that I was ripping off, and how it was flinging off his face, so we were really trying to get that shot ... "[119]

Despite their efforts to pay homage to Cronenberg, there was negative criticism. "This *Rabid* strives to emulate the striking body horror of the original but mainly comes across like a half-baked imitation,"[120] wrote *The Hollywood Reporter*. But some critics saw the self-awareness and appreciated it: "They have a wickedly funny sense of humor," wrote a reviewer for Rogerebert.com, "and a few winningly nasty ideas about how their obsessive characters would only grow more selfish during a crisis."[121] Sylvia Soska doesn't have an issue with negative criticism but disagrees with people who say the film is not considerate of the original:

We got a cast and crew who had worked with Mr. Cronenberg. So not only were we trying to do the most respectful job, we had people that we could ask literally who had worked on his original films. I don't know if there's any film like this that is a remake that is so respectful to the original because every aspect of it does grow from the original one in some way.[122]

"I am a fan like the rest of you," said Jen,

And I'm just lucky to be directing films and trying to make them what us, as fans, would like to see. I was terrified of somebody misusing and abusing *Rabid*. My god, it could have been about rabid dogs and rabies. It could've gone really, really far from transhumanism and weird body horror.[123]

Japanese filmmaker and artist Kei Fujiwara made horror history when she released her gory, disturbing horror movie *Organ* in 1996. Fujiwara was an actress in some of the most extreme Japanese horror films of the 1990s and was a main aspect of the cult horror films of director Shinya Tsukamoto beginning in the 1970s. After appearing in the violent experimental film *Tetsuo: The Iron Man* (1989), Kei Fujiwara created an experimental theater troupe called the Organ Vital Company. They performed a play about two organ thieves that would remove high-demand body parts from the victims while they were still alive. Fujiwara adapted the play into a film she wrote, directed, and starred in. Fujiwara is originally a theater actress and makes films as art; her films don't follow mainstream narrative rules and are experimental in many ways. In an interview, she explained that her films "need to lock in perfectly with someone's desire to watch it, or else watching it has no meaning. It just appears as a confusing, grotesque film."[124]

In *Organ*, two police detectives go undercover to infiltrate a black-market organ-harvesting cartel. They discover the criminals' lair, where Saeki and his one-eyed sister Yoko (played by the director Kei Fujiwara) are performing disgusting and horrifying surgeries on live patients. One of the detectives is captured, and Saeki has to protect himself and Yoko from the angry yakuza gang members for whom they are working. The police come to rescue the captured detective only to find that he has been wholly mutilated and is now just a deformed torso. On a deeper level, *Organ* is about good versus evil and how it doesn't always make sense in the context of killing. "The police represent upholders of this regulation. And then there are those who defy this regulation, who lie in a realm completely different from this conventional morality. *Organ* is a clash between these two groups."[125] It's also about portraying deep, agonizing pain to the audience. The pain is horrifying, grotesque, and exquisite. "Desire and slaughter are inescapable. My fear and sorrow regarding this, and my questioning what are they anyway. That's what I wanted to portray."[126]

Fujiwara's disregard for mainstream notions of horror movie entertainment stems from her background as an experimental artist in theater. "Theater is an impermanent art, and that's why it's such a luxurious art form," explained Fujiwara in an interview. "But film is like capturing a world in a crystal ball. The joy of creating film is like making your

Just some gratuitous body gore in Kei Fujiwara's *Organ* (1996).

own universe."[127] She directed her actors just as if they were in a play during the ultimate and only performance of the piece:

> I don't give actors multiple takes. If there's a camera or equipment problem that requires another take or two, I'll do it. But I won't do it for the actor. The actor has one chance, the take. But, on the offhand that the actor makes a mistake and requires a take two, I tell them they need to buy their own film roll. So, no one ever made a single mistake ... [128]

Used to performing in one location and changing the stage setting as needed, Fujiwara and her cast shot the entire film in the same theater space they used for performances, just re-dressing the sets when the scenes were in a new location. She'd written the script and asked her theater actors to pool their savings with her so they could fund the film. "Between the seven of us we had 200,000 yen, so I thought, 'Great, if we have 200,000 yen and one reel of film is 5,000 yen, and even if we bought lights, we can make thirty minutes of footage.'"[129] Counting on favors and loans of equipment from other filmmakers and artists, they were able to shoot an entire film by doing all of the set design by themselves. "All those organs in that scene were worked from what was supposed to be our dinner for the day [laughs]. We used real food. We took some gelatin and konjac noodles and thought, 'This can look like veins!'"[130] Their dinner was covered in fake blood that night, so they didn't have anything to eat, but the sacrifice meant that they had the gore they needed for the scenes. She also used random household items, anything that could work. "I don't have any background knowledge of special effect makeup. I just have a gut feeling of what can and can't be used."[131]

The smallness of the shooting space and the limited crew made the film a difficult one. "The most difficult challenge was the first scene, in the warehouse," she said. Shooting in the middle of summer, the small, cramped location became unbearably hot and suffocating. There was an incident with the police during which the cast and crew of *Organ* were almost shot:

> The characters got all bloody and we were shooting, and the police came. They thought it was a real yakuza fight and took off the safety on their pistols and were about to shoot at us. So, he came out from the ditch all bloody and with a sword in him, screaming, "We're shooting a film!" terrifying the police even more ... The police just told us to be safe and left, but it was all thanks to him for putting his life on the line.[132]

Fujiwara's next film, *Id* (2005), also had a disturbing plot: a series of murders occur at a rural pig farm. The film has people hearing voices, cannibalism, murder, and sexual abuse (among other horrible visuals) but, like *Organ*, is fascinating as an exercise in putting trauma and emotional horror into visuals in a film and justifies its extreme ugliness. On a deeper level, the film is about the human id, the part of us inside that can manifest actions and realities in our world.

In 2004, Japan saw the breakout director Mari Asato direct over ten horror films over a decade. Beginning with her action film *Samurai Chicks* (2004), she swiftly directed the horror movie *The Boy From Hell* (2004). *The Boy From Hell* is a zombie adaptation of the short story "The Monkey's Paw," in which a woman deals with a mysterious stranger to resurrect her dead son, only to find that he's a reanimated rotting corpse. She needs fresh, new organs to restore him, but she can't stop him from killing and eating people as she desperately tries to save him.

Her second horror film, *Twilight Syndrome: Dead Go Round* (2008), is based on a popular video game franchise about high school girls investigating urban legends. In Asato's film, the teenagers explore a haunted amusement park under the influence of a horrible demon. Not only was it Asato's game adaptation, but it was also her first sequel; two previous *Twilight Syndrome* films had been released.

Asato's next film is a sequel to *Ju-on: The Grudge* (2002), one of the world's most well-known horror movie franchises. *Ju-on: Black Ghost* (2009) is the fourth film in the series originated by director Takashi Shimizu and seems only to be a sequel in name. "The Grudge" becomes a personified entity that can affect people when they undergo trauma or horror in real life; in *Black Ghost*, a mother who loses a child (a recurring theme from *The Boy from Hell*) is distraught, so The Grudge begins to possess her.

Cellular Girlfriend (2011) is also a sequel to the film *Keitai kareshi,* AKA *Mobile Boyfriend* (2009). A character from a deadly phone game is murdering all the boys at a high school, and students must solve the mystery. Asato's *Ring of Curse* (2011) is also set in high school but is based on a novel by Yuka Hidaka written entirely on his cell phone texts. It stars the popular Japanese girl group Buono! in their first acting roles, and is about an unpopular girl at school placing a curse on her bullies by writing it into a script for the school play. Next, Asato made *The Chasing World 3* (2012), *The Chasing World 4* (2012), and *The Chasing World 5* (2012), which are all sequels to *The Chasing World* (2008), a dystopian horror novel in which everyone with the last name "Sato" is targeted for death by a dictatorial future Japanese government.

One twin has a reflection. And the other doesn't! Mari Asato's *Bilocation* (2013).

LiLiCo (Erika Sawajiri) starts to fall apart emotionally and physically in Mika Ninagawa's 2012 *Helter Skelter*.

Bilocation (2013) is widely considered to be Asato's masterpiece. *Bilocation* is a phenomenon during which one person is simultaneously in two locations, defying the laws of physics. Based on a famous horror novel by Harukea Hôjô, the premise of the science fiction horror film is that a doppelganger is out to destroy the protagonist's life and take her place. *Bilocation Ura* (2014) is the direct sequel directed by Asato.

Like most of her films, *Fatal Frame* (2014) is a horror movie set in a high school and features a curse and a mystery that must be solved to save everyone. *Under Your Bed* (2019) departs from her work with teenage characters. Based on the novel *Andâ yua beddo* by Kei Ôishi, *Under Your Bed* is about a man who becomes obsessed with a woman to the point that he secretly moves in under her bed. The producer approached Asato to make the film on the pretext that it was challenging and broke many rules, something that Asato was craving. She took inspiration from director Yasuzô Masumura and his film *Seisaku's Wife* (1965), in which an unreliable narrator tells the story from his point of view.[133]

We mentioned Shimako Sato in Chapter 6; her feature horror film *Tale of a Vampire* (1992) and her fantasy horror series *Eko Eko Azarak* and its sequel are popular Japanese teen horror movies. In the twenty-first century, she has continued to direct horror and thriller movies. Her action thriller *K-20: Kaijin nijû mensô den* (2008) is one of the best superhero movies that is unknown in the West. The protagonist is a Robin Hood-like figure that robs the rich invented by author So Kitamura in his novels *Kaijin Nijû Mensô Den* and *Kaijin Nijû Mensô Den: Seidô no Majin*. Master criminals duke it out in a fictional 1949 Tokyo in a world in which World War II never happened. Sato continued directing action and thriller films with the *Unfair* series about a hard-boiled female police detective played by Shinohara Ryoko in *Unfair: The Answer* (2011) and *Unfair the End* (2015). *Yo ni mo Kimyô na Monogatari: Eiga kantoku-hen* (2015) is a television anthology horror sequel to the original *Yonimo kimyô na monogatari,* AKA *Tales of the Bizarre* anthology series that ran on Japanese television from 1990 to 1992. There were numerous television sequels to the *Yonimo kimyô na monogatari* series, but Sato is the only woman who has directed a segment in any of them.

Mika Ninagawa's horror film *Helter Skelter* (2012) was a departure from her photography work; since the 1990s, Ningawa's photographs have been seen in art galleries in Japan and worldwide. She was approached by a producer who asked her if she might be interested in making a film, and after wrangling with the rights, she made the film version of the manga *Helter Skelter*.[134]

In *Helter Skelter*, an ugly woman has multiple drastic plastic surgeries and becomes beautiful. She starts a new career as a beautiful model named LiLiCo (Erika Sawajiri). The clinic where she had her surgeries has been operating illegally and comes under fire for unethical practices that may have harmed their clients. As LiLiCo's personal life starts falling apart, so does her body, which can't handle the many procedures she has undergone. She unravels as her body does, descending into a "helter skelter" hellish nightmare. Ninagawa's tremendous photographic skills come through with the intense color design and beautifully framed scenes. Ninagawa loved the original manga and wanted to keep as much of it in her film version as possible:

> The original manga is a very highly acclaimed work, therefore, I took care not to get too caught up in its reputation. The manga was published in the 1990s, so I tried to draw out the universal elements that link Tokyo in those days to the present. I also strived to keep the original's female perspective, to fully express those senses that are unique to women that are not necessary logical and sometimes difficult to explain. I also did my best not to submit to pressures that "films must be such and such" that exist in the Japanese film industry.[135]

Ninagawa had to wait seven years for the film to be greenlit finally; she made an entirely different film while she was waiting for *Helter Skelter* to happen, "the longest time I've waited for anything in my entire life," she joked to the British Film Institute in a 2012 interview. "But I felt I had to do this, if only because I am a woman and an artist, and if this material wound up in the wrong hands, well ... one shudders to think what could happen."[136] While waiting for the financing to come together, Ninagawa thought about the film all the time, deciding that actress Erika Sawajiri should play LiLiCo. She wanted someone physically beautiful who could also project depth and sadness. Ninagawa was the daughter of a famous film director, Yukio Ninagawa, and her mother, Tomoko Mayama, was an actress, so she understood the dark side of fame and beauty in the entertainment industry. While there is glamour and fame, there is also horror behind the lens, "those that consume these women's images":

> And between the consumer and the consumed, there is a rift so wide they may as well be in different galaxies ... There's rage in me as well. As a photographer, I'm always in the middle of this dilemma about wanting the best expression, the most beautiful shot, but on the other hand, I know what these models and actresses are going through, how lonely it is to be on the other side of the lens, ruthlessly reflected and then manufactured for mass consumption.[137]

Helter Skelter was popular in Japanese theaters and in other parts of Asia, like Hong Kong, Taiwan, and Korea. "Surprisingly," said Ninagawa, "the majority of our audiences were women."[138] Her next feature was the horror movie *Diner* (2019). Like *Helter Skelter*,

Ninagawa directing Erika Sawajiri on the set of *Helter Skelter*.

The disturbing death is about to begin in Lisa Takeba's highschool horror movie *Signal 100* (2019).

it was made with an eye for design and color, sliding into the surreal and absurdist sometimes with a story about a woman who gets a job in a diner run by a former professional hit man who only serves other professional killers.

Lisa Takeba's films are more magical and whimsical than the other horror films made by contemporary Japanese women directors. Her film *Haruko's Paranormal Laboratory* (2015) has just a dash of the silliness that her successful romantic comedy about cloning criminals from small body parts, *The Pinkie* (2014), had. Her first film, *The Wandering Alien Detective Robin* (2012), has weird imagery and a premise that was just the beginning of her blossoming style as a genre filmmaker. "I like to put a certain amount of absurdity in my films,"[139] said Takeba in a 2014 interview. The premise of *The Pinkie* derives from a grim romantic tradition in Japanese prostitution traditions:

> To prove to a special customer that he was the only real lover for her, the geisha or prostitute would cut off her little finger and give it to him. In this way, it is basically a connection between lovers, like connecting a red string between two persons' pinkies; it is a body part where someone's heart is located.[140]

Haruko's Paranormal Laboratory is about a woman named Haruko (Moeka Nozaki) who sits and watches television all day, often talking to it. One day, her television begins talking back to her; it morphs into a man/television hybrid (Aoi Nakamura), and falls in love with Haruko. Believing that this happened because of her hidden paranormal abilities, Haruko tries to keep the man at home with her, but eventually, he gets outside and creates chaos while Haruko looks for and saves him from sticky situations. "My aunt used to talk to the television a lot while watching it. I thought that she talked to it so much that the television might get feelings," she explained at the 2015 Rotterdam International Film Festival, about where the inspiration for her movie came from.[141]

Takeba's 2019 film *Signal 100* is a horror/thriller. Set in high school with lead teenage characters facing a supernatural curse, the film is part of the same horror subgenre as Sato's *Eko Eko Azarak* and Asato's *Cellular Girlfriend*. Like *Eko Eko Azarak* and *Helter Skelter*, *Signal 100* is an adaptation of a popular manga of the same name. In the film, a high school teacher hypnotizes his classroom of kids and embeds 100 signals or actions they are not allowed to make in their subconscious, on penalty of death by forced suicide. Actions like laughing, crying, vomiting, being late, and looking at someone else for too long, for instance, which are almost impossible for humans to avoid, are forbidden. The worst part is that the victims don't know the signals and only find out when one of them dies from performing one. While Takeba's earlier films were "quirky and cute,"[142] she said in an interview, *Signal 100* is gory, bloody, violent, and unrelenting.

I first met Kayoko Asakura when I showed her short supernatural horror film *Hide and Seek* (2013) at the first Etheria Film Festival in 2014. Asakura made five horror features and several horror shorts between 2010 and 2020. Her first feature, *Kuso subarashii kono sekai,* AKA *It's a Beautiful Day* (2013), is a slasher film. *It's a Beautiful Day* was first brought up by producer Mr. Yamaguchi in 2010, only several months after Asakura had contributed a short segment to the horror film anthology *Kaidan shin mimibukuro hyaku monogatari* (2010), which he produced. Two years later, in the spring of 2012, she was filming the feature.[143] When asked where the concept for the film came from, Asakura simply said, "I thought I would like to make a slasher horror film, which had a main female character being a serious killer."

Shot in Los Angeles, where Asakura had never been until she filmed *It's a Beautiful Day*, the film is set in the United States with Japanese and Korean student main characters, some of whom do not speak English, and two psychopathic American killers. When asked what she hoped audiences would take away from the movie, she answered, "For both Japanese and foreign audiences, I would like them to feel the stateless chaos, which is mingled with many nations and races."[144] Asakura's next four films would all be horror/thrillers: *Girls, Dance with the Dead* (2015), *Dokumushi: Toxic Insects* (2016), and *Love and Murder of Sheep and Wolf* , AKA *My Girlfriend Is a Serial Killer* (2019). *Girls, Dance with the Dead* (2015) is about five girls working part-time at a cleaning company who discover the body of a beautiful girl. They use a black magic ritual they learned from listening to Norwegian black metal to reanimate the corpse. The corpse was a suicidal woman who was murdered and who regrets not being able to die by her own hand. The girls help the corpse to die the way she wants to. Asakura's favorite part of the film is where the corpse is run through with a chainsaw without being able to die, for comedic effect. "Everyone cheers for the corpse to die over and over again," she said. "The body gets cut in half by a chainsaw, or the body gets dismembered by jumping off a building. However, because of the fairy tale aspect for teenagers, the gore in the movie is understated. I thought of the corpse as an allegorical being, more like a mannequin than a real human body."[145]

Dokumushi: Toxic Insects, based on a novel and a manga, is about a man who wakes up to find himself in a classroom at an unknown school. He's trapped in the building with seven other strangers, and they can't find food. Because of suspicions and paranoia, they end up turning on each other. The gore is inspired by Italian giallos, especially the scene in which a neck is sliced open, and blood spurts out profusely.

My Girlfriend Is a Serial Killer is based on a comic book. In it, a man tries to commit suicide by hanging himself at home but fails. He leaves a big hole in the wall, though, and when he looks through it, he sees a beautiful woman in the next apartment and becomes

Etsuro (Yôsuke Sugino) has found the perfect girlfriend: serial killer Rio (Haruka Fukuhara) in Kayoko Asakura's *My Girlfriend Is a Serial Killer* (2019).

obsessed with her. He witnesses her commit murder. She wants to kill him when she finds out, but when he reveals his feelings for her, she decides to be his girlfriend instead. It's a mix of romantic comedy and humor, and "It's also aimed at teenagers," said Asakura, "so the gore is understated. There are many scenes of murder, but half of them are light and comic-like."[146]

The first feature-length horror film directed by Thai women in the twenty-first century is the true crime movie *Zee-Oui* (2004), co-directed by Buranee Rachjaibun and Nida Suthat Na Ayutthaya. *Zee-Oui* is based on the infamous murders of seven people in the Rayong province of Thailand between 1954 and 1958 by a Chinese immigrant named Si Oui Sae-Ung. The murders were subsequently linked to several more in other areas, and most horrible is that organs were missing from the bodies, presumably eaten.[147] *Zee-Oui* was released as *The Man Eater* in English-speaking nations.

The films that follow *Zee-Oui* include the relatively unknown horror movies *Secret Room No. 7* (2006) by Kirati Nak Intanond, *Perng Mang: Glawng phee nang manut* (2007), co-directed by Sranya Noithai and Chomsri Nuttapeera, and *9-9-81* (2012) directed by Rapeepimol Chaiyasena. It's not until Anucha Boonyawatana's *The Blue Hour* (2015), a supernatural horror romance film about two young men who meet and fall in love at a haunted swimming pool, that film festivals and Western horror fans noticed the new horror films directed by women coming out of Thailand. *The Blue Hour* was followed closely by Kanittha Kwanyu's widely-known *Arpat* (2015), about a reluctant monk and the horrors that haunt his psyche. Boonyawatana also directed three episodes of the Thai horror television series *After Dark* in 2020. Thirati Kulyingwattanavit's short horror film *Kumal* (2017), about horrific cults that sacrifice babies for magical powers, played in film festivals internationally. *Sad Beauty* (2018), directed by Bongkot Benjarongkakul, features a spoiled model and her friend who go on a drug-fueled road trip after a violent family encounter that leaves someone dead.

The cinema of mainland China in the twenty-first century became increasingly profitable in the 1970s when the People's Republic loosened its reins on film content and became more liberal towards the arts. While Hong Kong and Taiwan, often considered a part of Chinese cinema, had many women directing genre films throughout the twentieth century, mainland China did not have women horror directors until after 2000. It wasn't until Fanfan Zhang's horror/thriller *Mi shi zi bu ke gao ren*, AKA *Lost in Panic Room* (2010), that mainland China made a significant contribution to the list of women horror film directors. The film is about a group of people in an isolated hillside manor who are being stalked and murdered Agatha Christie-style while a mystery writer scrambles to discover the murderer before they are all dead.

Zhang directed the sequel, *Lost in Panic Cruise* (2011), shortly thereafter, in which the same mystery novelist-turned-detective helps solve murders on board a cruise ship. These two films, both in Mandarin, were very successful in Chinese theaters. Filmmaker Jil Wong Pak-Kei (also known as Jill Wong) made the film *Moonlight*, released in China in 2011, about a small Chinese town in the 1930s plagued by vampires. Like the *Lost in Panic* films, it follows a familiar Western-style story present in many North American and British horror films but makes the hero a Taoist priest rather than a Catholic or a stake-wielding Dutch doctor. *Inside: A Chinese Horror Story* (2017), directed by Lili Bai, is about an author who is hired to create a horror comic series. He does, and it's wildly successful, but he has several other personalities that begin creeping back into his brain; he hasn't heard from them since his days at the mental asylum. Convinced that the stories he's writing are inspired by his extra personalities, the writer faces a gut-wrenching trauma. At the time of the writing of this book, Fanfan Zhang is set to direct a film version of the science fiction novel *The Three-Body Problem*. But in regards to Taiwan, director Alice Wang released two Taiwanese horror films so far in her career in the new millennium, *Hu gu po* (2005) and *Killing 7* (2013), as well as numerous action movies.

Despite previously having only two women horror film directors throughout the twentieth century, Indonesia has produced several new women-directed horror films since 2000: Arie Azis's ghost stories *The Secret: Suster Ngesot Urban Legend* (2007) and *Lawang Sewu* (2007) and Viva Westi's *Suster N* (2007), a retelling of an Indonesian urban legend about the ghost of a dead Dutch woman that haunts people. Arie Azis has directed dozens of genre films in the decade following 2010. *Marlina the Murderer in Four Acts* (2017), Mouly Surya's rape-revenge horror Western, seems to be the most famous Indonesian horror film directed by a woman, as it was distributed on streaming services in North America.

In France, the 'New French Extremity horror' film movement (a series of highly gory new horror films made at the turn of the century by new French filmmakers) began in earnest in 2000 with the violent rape/revenge film *Baise-Moi* directed by Virginie Despentes and Coralie Trinh Thi and followed soon after by Marina de Van's breakout body horror *Dans ma peau*, AKA *In My Skin* (2001) and Claire Denis's erotic horror *Trouble Every Day* (2001). The movement would continue through the first decade of the twenty-first century, these being the most famous films directed by women, along with Marina de Van's *Ne te retourne pas* (2009).

Baise-Moi, AKA *Fuck Me,* was originally a 1993 novel written in French and published in France by author and feminist theorist Virginie Despentes. Drawing on her own experiences with rape and sexual trauma, Despentes wrote a story about two women who are brutally gang-raped and then go on a killing spree, traveling across France in their car, a sort of *Thelma and Louise* with hardcore penetration and violent revenge murders. In 1995, she sold the rights to the film version to producer Philippe Godeau; it was Godeau who suggested that Despentes herself direct it. The two leads, Nadine and Manu, were cast as French pornography actresses Karen Lancaume and Raffaëla Anderson after Despentes saw them in a documentary called *Exhibitions 1999—Exhibitions X* (1998) which featured interviews with both of them. Writing the screenplay was Despentes' friend, pornography actress Coralie Trinh Thi, and Despentes asked Coralie to co-direct it with her as "she and I shared the vision of a feminist battle, an avant-garde battle, as well as certain fondness for provocation." Despentes described Nadine and Manu as "outlaws" and said they were not "bad girls." She said that they were pushed across a boundary and "No excuses, no explanations, no intellectualization" of their murders and crimes can be made at all. They are "beyond judgment," and their "blood-soaked road movie" is "a sure way to avoid the worst fate of all: obedience, submission, renunciation of the self—boredom." It's the actual hardcore rape scenes that "return their complete bodies to women, of which they have always been deprived" and "reclaim women's rights over their true sexuality, to seize it back from the male gaze."[148] The film was given an X-rating in France and banned from mainstream theaters there for twenty-eight years.

In My Skin (2001) was Marina de Van's first feature-length film as a director. The story is simple; a French woman named Esther, played by de Van, accidentally hurts her leg at a friend's party. She doesn't feel it, but when she sees it, she goes to the doctor for it and isn't too concerned. The wounds begin to fascinate her, and her boyfriend and best friend become very concerned that she can't feel the pain and is harming herself further. Eventually, the idea of harming herself becomes an obsession, to the point where she fakes a car accident to explain the numerous self-inflicted injuries. However, the people that love her are still upset. Finally, she locks herself in hotel rooms, avoiding work, avoiding everyone, spending time alone in her skin, and physically tearing herself apart slowly, eating pieces of herself, mutilating herself. It's a highly bloody film and takes body horror to a new, dissociative level; most body horror films are about losing control of yourself, being experimented on by someone else against your will, and changing into something other than yourself, but Esther is entirely comfortable in her transformation. She is the agent of change and makes the decisions to modify herself. The fact that she can't feel pain adds to the disturbing aspect of the story; is she disassociated from the pain? Can she truly not feel pain, and is her self-harm a way to try to feel something? It's a complicated movie with a straightforward narrative, exploring so many different and inexplicable angles of personal horror that it resonated with audiences not only in France but worldwide, becoming one of the most talked about horror movies of 2002. De Van's film is based on a vague truth: when she was eight, she was in a car accident that hurt her leg badly. She lost feeling in the part of her leg where a bone had been surgically removed in the repair, and she would sometimes stick needles in it to see if she could feel it:

> As I grew up, I began to think that in our society we are utterly alienated from our bodies. Think of the work we do in offices—it's as though our bodies could have their own lives and we wouldn't necessarily know about it. There is a split, and sometimes our bodies are utterly absent from us.[149]

De Van's Esther is wholly alienated from herself, and this sick self-mutilation is a way of owning her own body, bringing it back where it had been lost to existential dread. It's a sick film, and de Van ingeniously directs the grotesqueness of the entire story.

De Van's next film, *Ne te retourne pas* (2009), had a much bigger budget and starred Sophie Marceau (Jeanne) and Monica Bellucci (Jeanne/Rosa Maria) in an unbelievable story of identity and self. Jeanne, a married woman with a family, feels that her home is being altered in small ways. Things are in different places; she remembers things differently. She feels alienated (again, that theme from de Van) from her family and, therefore, more agitated as time passes. She visits her mother to see if she can make sense of these altered perceptions and changed memories. At her mother's, she finds an old photograph of herself as a child with her two parents in Italy and a strange woman; this prompts her to go to that exact location in Italy and figure out who this strange woman is and what exactly she has to do with Jeanne. Sophie Marceau's Jeanne becomes Monica Belluci's Jeanne in a normatively experimental manner that is not easy to describe even after one watches the film. *Ne te retourne pas* premiered out of competition at the 2009 Cannes Film Festival. "I found it an interesting challenge to change one woman into another," said de Van:

> I can't commit to a project unless it presents a challenge, something spectacular to accomplish. I need an ambitious goal. Even if I fail to reach it, it's something that drives my desire and my dream. I'm not interested in showing the audience a formula, something easy or already done. I hope my film will touch people. It involves challenges, daring, and also negative reactions.[150]

Though officially past the first decade of the twenty-first century into which French Extremity films are confined, de Van's third feature film, *Dark Touch* (2013), is a real horror movie. Set in Ireland, the film is about an eleven-year-old girl named Niamh (Missy Keating) who believes that the house she lives in is trying to hurt her and her parents. She shows up to school with bruises, but her parents insist that she is doing it to herself, and no one believes Niamh. Then, Niamh is found as the only living member of her family alive after what looks like a terrifying home invasion massacre; even her baby brother is dead, found suffocated. The police can only imagine the ruthless people that must have perpetrated this crime, but Niamh can't help them, claiming that the house killed everyone.

Because they're in a very rural part of Ireland and Niamh has no one, her neighbors take her in, expecting her to have some trauma and to need time to adjust after the incident. But it turns out, Niamh has incredible psychic powers that she can't control and it was her paranormal energy that killed everyone and harmed her. Like de Van's other films, *Dark Touch* leaves many questions unanswered and values the poetry of horror over logic. *Dark Touch* was released theatrically in numerous countries, including the United States, and won several awards, including Best Film at the 2013 Neuchâtel International Fantastic Film Festival in Switzerland.

Claire Denis, one of the most famous French directors of all time, occasionally makes a genre film. Her horror movie *Trouble Every Day* (2001) is regarded as one of the most brutal erotic horror movies ever made. An American doctor named Shane (Vincent Gallo) and his wife June (Tricia Vessey) are on their honeymoon in Paris, but Shane secretly has another motive: he's obsessed with a woman named Coré (Béatrice Dalle), who is married to his former doctor colleague Léo (Alex Descas). Shane discovers where Léo and the supposedly "unwell" Coré live, but when he does, Coré is revealed to be a cannibalistic sexual maniac who has already killed many people. Cannibalism, addiction, sex, fetishes, gore, animalistic tendencies, inhuman urges, the combination of sex and death, and blood: this movie has a lot to unpack. Most of it can easily be left up to interpretation. Do they have a disease? A mental illness? Are they just weird? Is it a metaphor for a social problem? Are they vampires? Denis never gives us the full explanation. It's a gruesome movie, and the mix of sexuality with violence and blood feels alien and abhorrent, but to Shane and Coré, it's delightful.

Trouble Every Day screened at the 2001 Cannes Film Festival, out of competition, and apparently, several people walked out, and several fainted due to the appallingly dark imagery.[151] Denis herself doesn't think it's that violent and never saw anyone faint at the screenings. "There's not much violence in my film," she said to the BBC, "but what there is springs from something very deep. I would say it's about love in a way. And what happens when you tangle with something that is stronger than you are."[152]

Denis would go on to make the thriller *Bastards* (2013 film) and the science fiction drama *High Life* (2018), set in a space prison.

Caroline du Potet co-directed the film *Dans Ton Sommeil*, AKA *In Their Sleep* (2010), with her brother Éric du Potet. It's a relentless, nerve-wracking, desperate horror film, gritty and dark, taking place during one evening. *Dans Ton Sommeil* goes back and forth in time, showing events from different characters' points of view; the narrative is about deception and constantly challenges the audience's ability to predict what happens next. Films as brutal as *Dans Ton Sommeil* were only able to be made in France because of the success of the earlier French Extremity films. "Ten years ago, it was almost impossible to make a horror film in France," admitted du Potet in 2009. "There were only comedies or dramas. Then, a new generation of filmmakers, like Alexandre Aja, started to initiate the movement."[153]

The film stars Anne Parillaud as a troubled woman grieving the death of her teenage son. When she runs into a young stranger at night on a dark road, she immediately feels responsible for his well-being. He tells her he's running from a burglar and lives close by

Hee-eun (Seon Yu) in Soo-youn Lee's ghostly horror film *Uninvited* (2003).

with his parents. She believes him and takes him home. Then the story gets nightmarish and violent, and the woman is too blinded by grief to see the young man is not who he says he is. "We wanted to make a very realistic film, a dark story about a young killer," said du Potet. "I have always been convinced that the stories which could happen to us, to anybody, are much more frightening for the audience than imaginary monsters."[154]

Though made more than a decade later, the French horror films *Revenge* (2017) by Coralie Fargeat and *Raw* (2016) by Julia Ducournau are the natural inheritors of the French Extremity's proclivity for unexplained and metaphorical bloody violence.

We already talked about *Whispering Corridors: Wishing Stairs* (2003) by Yun Jae-yeon in Chapter 5, but South Korea's film industry in the early 2000s was thriving, especially within the horror genre. Lee Soo-youn's *Uninvited* (2003) is a broody, atmospheric horror movie about a troubled man named Kang Jeong-won (Park Shin-yang) who begins hallucinating after coming across two dead little girls in the subway one evening. He bonds with a woman named Jung Yeon (Jun Ji-hyun) who has recently lost her child: a friend of hers murdered both of their children and is now on trial for the crime, so she is seeing the psychiatrist for sessions to help her cope. Yeon has psychic powers and can see flashes of Jung-won's childhood and other's people's lives, thoughts and trauma. When the trial of her child's murderer is over, and the killer has been found innocent, it is revealed that it was Yeon who killed her child. Yeon commits suicide by jumping off of a building. Jung-won goes home, where he finds the two poisoned girls and Yeon sitting at his dining room table. It's a punch in the gut, a really moody, dark, sad, and engaging piece of cinematic horror.

Yoga Hakwon by Yun Jae-yeon (2009) is her follow-up to *Whispering Corridors:*

Wishing Stairs. It's a horror movie set in a yoga retreat! The incredibly stressed-out Hyo-jeong (Eugene) has just lost her job, and her friend Seon-hwa (Lee Young-jin) suggests a one-week yoga retreat. When she gets there, Hyo-jeong meets her fellow yogis and their instructor Na-ni (Cha Soo-yeon), who tells them what the strange rules are for this yoga course: no eating; no bathing within an hour of taking a yoga class; don't leave the premises; don't call anyone. Of course, everyone has a difficult time following these rules, and, one by one, each of the yoga students dies brutally as a result. It turns out that the yoga retreat is owned by the famous 1970s Korean actress Kan Mi-hee (Lee Hye-sang), and she is an immortal demon that needs the souls of the perfectly prepared in order to live forever, and Na-ni is her loyal servant. Hyo-jeong kills Na-ni and leaves, only to run into all of the dead yoga students on her way to the subway, where Kan Mi-hee finally gets her. It's a silly film with a silly premise, some funny moments, and some really good horror imagery.

Yoga is just like doing pilates except you're in a cult. Poster art for *Yoga Hakwon* (2009), directed by Jae-yeon Yun.

There are dozens of thrillers, mysteries, and science fiction movies directed by Korean women directors. Just a few are *Orora gongju* and *Yong-eui-ja X* (Bang Eun-jin, 2005 and 2012), *Shadows in the Palace* (Kim Mi-jung, 2007), *Myeong-wang-song* (Shin Su-won, 2012), *Helpless* (Byun Young-Joo, 2012), *Teukjong: Ryangchensalingi* (Noh Deok, 2015), *Bi-mil-eun eobs-da* (Lee Kyoung-mi, 2016), *Yoorijungwon* (Shin Su-won, 2017), and *TRANS* (Do Naeri, 2021).

Malaysia (the films of Eyra Rahman), Panama (*Diablo Rojo: PTY*, 2019, by Sol Moreno), the Philippines (the films of Joyce Bernal), Portugal (*Lovely, Dark, and Deep*, 2022, by Teresa Sutherland), Russia (*Stray*, 2019, by Olga Gorodetskaya), Slovakia (*Socialistický Zombi Mord*, 2014, by Zuzana Paulini), Spain (the films of Yolanda Torres), Sweden (*The Stockholm Bloodbath*, 2015, by Stephanie Ohlsson), and even Bahrain (*Dead Sands*, 2013, by Ameera Al-Qaed) and Benin (*Larmes de sang*, 2011, by Laitan Faranpojo) have contributed to the modern horror genre, along with numerous other nations that previously did not have vital film industries.

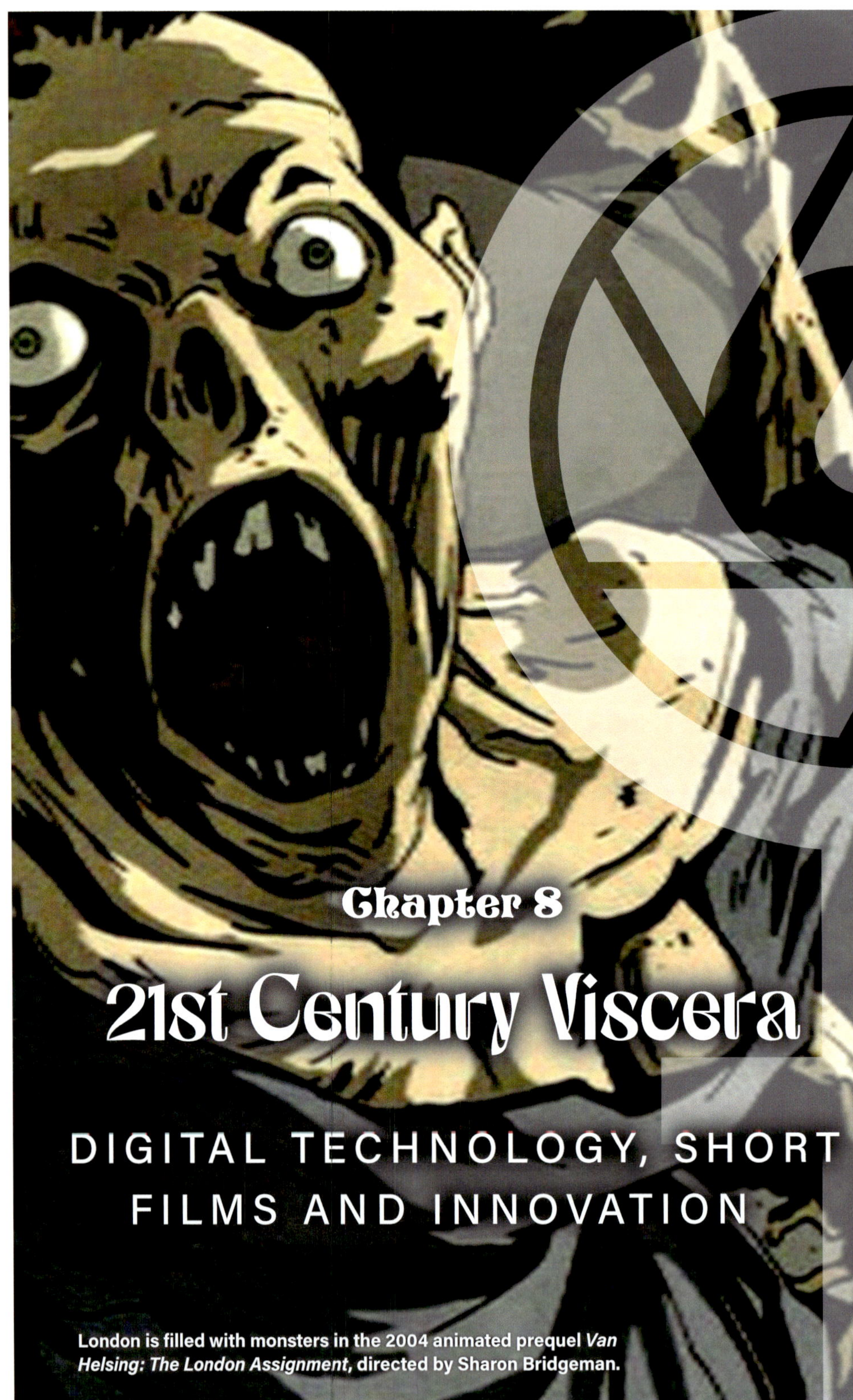

Chapter 8

21st Century Viscera

DIGITAL TECHNOLOGY, SHORT FILMS AND INNOVATION

London is filled with monsters in the 2004 animated prequel *Van Helsing: The London Assignment*, directed by Sharon Bridgeman.

THE DIGITAL REVOLUTION, THAT SWEET, special time between the mid-1990s and about 2005, was a fantastic time for filmmakers. Not only was the digital format finally a viable option for filming, but it was cheaper, easier to edit, and physically smaller and more dynamic than traditional film cameras. Thousands, possibly hundreds of thousands, of horror fans made no-budget horror movies during this period, some of which have been forgotten and some of which are still celebrated.

In 2000, Barbara Kopple, director of the crime thriller *Havoc* (2005), said, "In five years, they won't be writing articles about the increase of women filmmakers. By then, we'll be talking about children breaking into film with their digital cameras."[1] Kopple wasn't entirely correct, as articles about women directors are still very prolific, but children certainly do make their movies, like Emily Hagins, who made a zombie movie at age twelve in 2006 called *Pathogen*; there's a documentary about the making of the film called *Zombie Girl: The Movie* (2009) that I highly recommend. Hagins continued to make horror and comedy films throughout the 2010s and the 2020s.

The digital revolution, as well as social media, changed the nature of horror filmmaking and horror fandom forever. Many filmmakers were created and fostered during the last twenty years that we consider staple horror filmmaking icons today. I'll talk about some of them in this chapter. "I think the internet gives us all so much potential to do so many things," said director Lola Wallace in 2009: "It will be interesting to see what starts to happen in the next few years. From Amazon and CreateSpace, making it so easy for anyone to sell their own films online, to sites like Hulu.com providing so much studio content, I think that everyone is really trying to figure out where they can fit in and how they can profit from it."[2] "Digital technology allows us to shoot scenes and edit here in Tulsa and mail the scenes to another filmmaker," said horror feature director Darla Enlow in 2005. "The filmmaker can then edit the scenes right into his editor/movie. I am in a movie shot in Pennsylvania, and I never had to leave Tulsa."[3] Anya Camilleri's horror film *Incubus* (2007) premiered on the web-based streaming service AOL Red. "I think it's unusual that the film is being released in this way," said Camilleri at the time, "but I am excited about it."[4]

There was also a fantastic networking phenomenon among women in horror; social media spurred the change, and filmmakers connected to like-minded artists around 2008-2009. Film festivals found their content. People became friends. After she made the film *Dead Hooker in a Trunk*, Sylvia Soska didn't know what to do with it. Filmmaker Eli Roth (*Hostel*, 2005) connected Sylvia and Jen Soska to Hannah Neurotica, the creator of *Ax Wound* zine and the Ax Wound Film Festival, "And he said we were going to love each other, which is true," said Sylvia Soska, "We got on like sisters from the get-go, and she was starting something called Women in Horror Recognition Month, which was going to start the next year! We were stoked, and we had no idea how much it would change our lives."[5]

Women in Horror Recognition Month would be an informal online celebration of all things women and horror in the month of February and ran from 2010 through 2020. Women in Horror Recognition Month connected women filmmakers more than any networking group.

The unhinged feminist psychopath Mary (Kristin Bree Calabrese) in Sarah Jacobson's *I Was a Teenage Serial Killer* (1993). Image courtesy of The American Genre Film Archive.

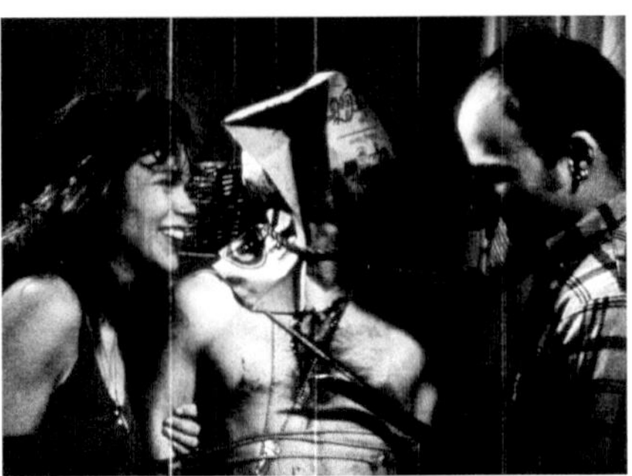

A still from *I Was a Teenage Serial Killer*. Image courtesy of The American Genre Film Archive.

In 2010, crowdsourcing became an amazing way to raise money for low-budget, independent films, leading to many more horror films being made. Horror web series were prevalent in the 2010s. Even seasoned horror film directors like Mary Lambert (*The Dark Path Chronicles*, 2008), Martha Coolidge (*The Unknown*, 2012), Lexi Alexander (*Aidan F/X*, 2012), Devi Snively (*Martini Mom and Devil Spawn*, 2012), Letia Clouston (*Broken Toy*, 2009), and L.C. Cruell (*31*, 2011) directed genre series made initially to air online.

I Was a Teenage Serial Killer (1993) is, at first glance, another black-and-white, low-budget, 16mm student film. It is that, but it is also so much more than that. Sarah Jacobson's semi-surreal and semi-experimental story of a nineteen-year-old woman who keeps murdering the men that invalidate her feelings has a tangible and palpable sarcastic and defeatist tone that only could have come from the early 1990s. The black-and-white, gritty story of Mary (Kristin Calabrese), a nineteen-year-old murderer who harbors deep anger for having been molested by her father and the men she murders, was made by Jacobson when she was only twenty years old. Mary deals with catcalling, a man removing a condom during sex without consent, and is blamed for her childhood abuse by a stranger. She kills every man that wrongs her, but it doesn't alleviate her pain. Mary briefly enters a relationship with Henry (Gorey), who is also a serial killer; he only kills straight, white males because it's the only way he feels he can get back at the patriarchy, even though he is a straight, white male. Mary kills him when he brings home a woman for them to murder, torture, and rape.

At the end of the twenty-five-minute movie, Mary has a realization while she's holding a broken bottle against a man's throat as she believes he is victim blaming her for the childhood abuse: she can just be angry, and if people invalidate her shit, then fuck them, she can still tell her story. She will not murder anyone anymore because when people push her story aside, it doesn't make it any less true.

I Was a Teenage Serial Killer, a play on the 1950s teen horror films like *I Was a Teenage Werewolf* (1957) and *I Was a Teenage Frankenstein* (1957), has a level of camp perversion that only John Waters has also mastered as well as the ironic, scathing social critiques of Gregg Araki's films and the natural flow of Kevin Smith's *Clerks* (1994). There's a punk rock, trashy feeling to the characters and the story, and the city in which they live, much like *Repo Man* (1984) conjures up a wasteland of disgruntled youth and constant passing car noises.

Jacobson is the natural heir to Doris Wishman and Roberta Findlay. She represented an underground rejection of mainstream culture and an embracing of third-wave feminism that would usher in the Riot Grrrl movement, zine culture, and girl rock bands like Bikini Kill. Like Jennifer M. Kroot (a documentarian discussed later in this chapter), Jacobson was inspired by George Kuchar, who she met while attending the San Francisco Art Institute and who encouraged her to make *I Was a Teenage Serial Killer*. Because of its powerful feminist message and eccentric, underground style, the San Francisco Art Institute declined to show it at the end-of-year student film showcase.[6] However, numerous film festivals, magazines, and critics soon discovered the film and noticed what the Institute had tragically missed: it was good, and people would like it.

Jacobson's feature film *Mary Jane's Not a Virgin Anymore* (1996) is less surreal and experimental and more a straightforward narrative, but it shows that Jacobson, while a member of the angry and disgruntled youth of my generation, was funny and wanted to entertain people. Jacobson was very successful in film festivals and was written about in mainstream magazines like *Variety* and independent zines like *Film Threat*. Like feminist psychopath murderer Valerie Solanas and her S.C.U.M. manifesto, Jacobson wrote her own manifesto called S.T.I.G.M.A (Sisters Together in Girlie Movie-Making Action) in 2002, which was all about women making their own films.

Jacobson knew the power of women filmmakers revolutionizing art, and she understood how women like Guy-Blaché were cut out of the history of film for about a century. She understood that some women, like Laura Lau, weren't given the directing credit their husbands got and were forced to take only producing credit. Jacobson passed away at age thirty-one from uterine cancer.

If Jacobson had lived the full extent of her natural life, she would be in the ranks of Quentin Tarantino, John Waters, Robert Rodriguez, and other revered independent filmmakers. Her mother, Ruth Jacobson, was incredibly supportive of her daughter's aspirations as a director. When Jacobson wanted to raise money for her feature *Mary Jane's Not a Virgin Anymore*, Ruth moved to San Francisco and dedicated herself to helping raise funds. Ruth traveled with Jacobson to film festivals and marketed the film when it was finished. And Ruth preserved Jacobson's films and ran a dedicated website for her daughter after she passed away. "My mom wanted me to have all the opportunities she never had for herself," said Sarah Jacobson in a 1999 interview.[7]

A film grant in Jacobson's name was created after her death to support young women filmmakers "whose work embodies some of the things that Sarah stood for: a fierce DIY approach to filmmaking, a radical social critique, and a thoroughly underground sensibility."[8] Jacobson's death is reminiscent of that of filmmaker Adrienne Shelley (*Sudden Manhattan*, 1996), who was on the verge of a fantastic filmmaking career when she was murdered at the age of forty.

SHORT FILMS

WHEN DIGITAL FILMS FOUND distribution online and on streaming services, the short film industry boomed. Before the Internet and streaming, there were very few distribution avenues for short films; fewer people made them, and fewer people saw them. That all changed in the early 2000s. Some of the first distribution platforms for short films directed by women, including horror, were iFilm.com and Undergroundfilm.org. Then, beginning in 2005, YouTube and Vimeo, followed by the dedicated websites Popcorn Horror, Fun Sized Horror, and YouTube channels such as Alter, Omeleto, and numerous others. In the mid-2010s, Amazon streaming allowed short films to be independently distributed on their platform. By 2020, during the worldwide pandemic, when most film festivals shut down for at least a year, most went fully digital and aired all of their films, including shorts, online for a wider audience.

Some shorts are made as a calling card to showcase the director's skills, and others were made as proofs-of-concept for feature-length films that the director wanted to make. For instance, in 2009, Senegalese filmmaker Mati Diop made the short film version of *Atlantiques*, a supernatural fantasy made into a feature in 2019. Roseanne Liang was only hired to direct *Shadow in the Cloud* because her short film *Do No Harm* exquisitely showcased her skills in directing action and horror. "You can create a whole world really fast," said director Jenn Wexler about the short horror film format. "How can you pull the viewer in really quick and get them to identify with these characters and then shock them in some way?" Wexler made a short horror film called *Slumber Party* (2012) about two roommates that play a game of Bloody Mary in the mirror of their bathroom:

> It was really just me putting all my roommate frustrations out onto the screen and doing it in three minutes. But what was really important for me is that I really needed it at that time. I was a couple of years out of college and I was trying to figure out, like, what I wanted to do with my life and everything. And this was a creative thing that I funneled myself into because it was only three minutes. I finished it. I shot a thing. I finished it. I got it into festivals, and I met other filmmakers ... And it was just really important; it helped me prove to myself that I can do this. I can complete this creative endeavor. And then once you do that, you just become obsessed, and you just want to keep doing it.[9]

Women directors have been making short films since the beginning of the film industry, but by the twenty-first century, making a short was a choice rather than a necessity. Some short horror films are just made for fun, and some are to experiment. These are some notable horror film shorts directed by women in the twenty-first century.

The short horror film *Cursed Part 3* (2000) is the only directing credit of actress Rae Dawn Chong. Having starred in the action film *Commando* (1985) and the horror anthology *Tales from the Darkside: The Movie* (1990), Chong is a familiar face to horror fans. She is the daughter of legendary comedian Tommy Chong, and she not only wrote and directed a horror film but she launched the career of actor Chris Pratt (*Guardians of the Galaxy*, 2014). *Cursed Part 3* was his first movie. Chong met Pratt in Hawaii when he was homeless. "He is gorgeous, and that was the first thing (I noticed)," she said in an interview, "I was casting my film, and I needed a beautiful kid to play the Brat, an actor who complains out loud about having to make out with an older actor, played by Donna Mills."[10]

Amy Lyndon, who plays the lead, Mavis, would go on to star in the horror movie *Signed in Blood* (2006), which is also about a series of murders on the set of a horror film. She's also directed several short genre films herself. Annie Little, who plays Xuxa, would go on to have a great career in both film and television, but *Cursed Part 3* was only her second acting job. Ben Reed already had a substantial career when he starred in *Cursed Part 3*. Donna Mills, of course, was famous for her role in the 1980s television series *Knots Landing* and was the big star of Chong's movie.

At twenty-five minutes long, *Cursed Part 3* is a short film and was never adapted into a feature, nor was it intended to be. It's the story of Mavis (Amy Lyndon), a delusional woman who finances her film so she can direct and star in it. Her film is a rip-off of *The Blair Witch Project*, and while she and her actors are out in the woods making their film, a real killer is stalking them. Like *Scream Queen* (2002) by director Tatiana Bliss, *Cursed Part 3* is a movie within a movie and a biting critique of show business and Hollywood while also showcasing the predictability of the modern slasher film. After appearing in several big studio films, Chong knew she wanted to take the next step in her career, which meant directing. She was eager and hungry to try it. *Cursed Part 3* was conceived when a producer asked Chong to write a screenplay version of a three-page horror movie treatment for their client. Chong agreed and met with the woman but soon realized that the three-page treatment was a rip-off of the recent horror movie hit *The Blair Witch Project* (1999). "Plus, she was the star of the thing, and every man in the three pages was in love with her," said Chong. So instead of writing a screenplay for her, Chong wrote a three-page spoof treatment for a horror film about a woman who shoots a vanity project without a full script. "In my version," said Chong,

> I have Mavis being cagey about her wealth and hating her breast job—two things that the original lady dealt with. She hated her boob job, and her money was an inheritance from a husband who passed away in a shady way … She was hurt and offended, but I owned the material since she didn't pay me. I had some money, and we liked what I came up with, and so I thought, "let's shoot it."[11]

Having trouble finding actors through the traditional agents Hollywood usually uses, Chong instead went with her gut and hired people who hadn't been given a break in acting yet. "Chris [Pratt] was a magical meet-up," she recalled. "He had a psychic tell him a woman who was brown was going to save him, and he would be very successful if he did everything she said. This was a day before I walked into his restaurant where he worked."[12] The film consists of actors playing actors out in a remote location; they're shooting a horror movie, and as the shoot goes on, they are killed, making their story within a film a slasher film. A deconstruction, a parody, a meta experiment in horror ideology—you can call it what you want as it is open to interpretation.

Cursed Part 3 was filmed in California, near Santa Barbara, at the same location where *Creature from the Black Lagoon* (1954) was shot, on a new technology: digital cameras. Camera problems and the latest technology were two main reasons *Cursed Part 3* did not turn out to be a good horror movie despite a talented and fresh cast, a funny story, and a great shooting location. "I love this movie," Chong said, despite believing it's an "epic fail." "An epic fail that was an intensive filmmaking school," she added. "Back then, digital was new. My cameraman had only shot with film prior," she explained:

> We used a Canon XL6 which, in 2000, had a bug which was you set focus, and the moment you pressed to shoot, it jumped to autofocus. So that meant my A camera was unusable. We were sequestered 2.5 hours away from electricity or a hotel. We shot in a campground without dailies. So I did a catastrophic thing. I trusted my producer, who said he was watching dailies, and they were amazing. I trusted him. This rookie mistake is on my shoulders. The producer was a sleaze, lying creep. I was a lazy newbie who didn't check her footage. Just because we are remote and didn't have a way to watch dailies myself? I should have humped down to the nearest town and set them up. Had we done that, we would have seen that all the A stuff was out of focus. Luckily, we had a B camera, which was all we had to properly use. I spent a fortune trying to fix it up, and I mastered a beautiful sound design, and I decided since it was a bust, I may as well learn everything I could about filmmaking using Cursed 3.[13]

Anna Biller made the 2016 horror romance fantasy film *The Love Witch* and the 1970s housewife *Playboy* fantasy sex comedy *Viva* (2007). Biller's style is complicated, intricate, and beautiful. Biller had been making films since 1994, but it was her twenty-six-minute short *A Visit From the Incubus* (2001) that fully showcased her artistic vision in its most mature form before she shot *Viva*. *A Visit from the Incubus* allowed Biller to fine-tune the details that she would need to have complete mastery of moving forward onto her ambitious feature film.

This monstrously creative and funny short film is mostly about what happens after an incubus pays a visit to Miss Lucy McGee (Anna Biller), a chaste young woman living in the American Old West in the late 1800s. Lucy, feeling violated and rather un-virginal after the incubus (a sex demon) ravishes her night after night, decides to take a familiar and yet surprisingly constructive and nearly feminist stance against her rape and ends up coming out a winner.

Biller's wild taste and eccentric attention to detail make *Visit* a theatrical experiment in color, costume, style, and genre. Biller, dramatist and independent filmmaker, writes films and plays that involve a creative edge a notch above even the most decisively "artistic" independent projects. Anna Biller wrote, directed, produced, and creatively controlled everything from the costumes to the sets and the makeup. The acting, camerawork, pacing, and choreography are reminiscent of the 1940s and 1950's Western films and Hammer horror movies. Lucy (probably named after the character in *Dracula*) is played

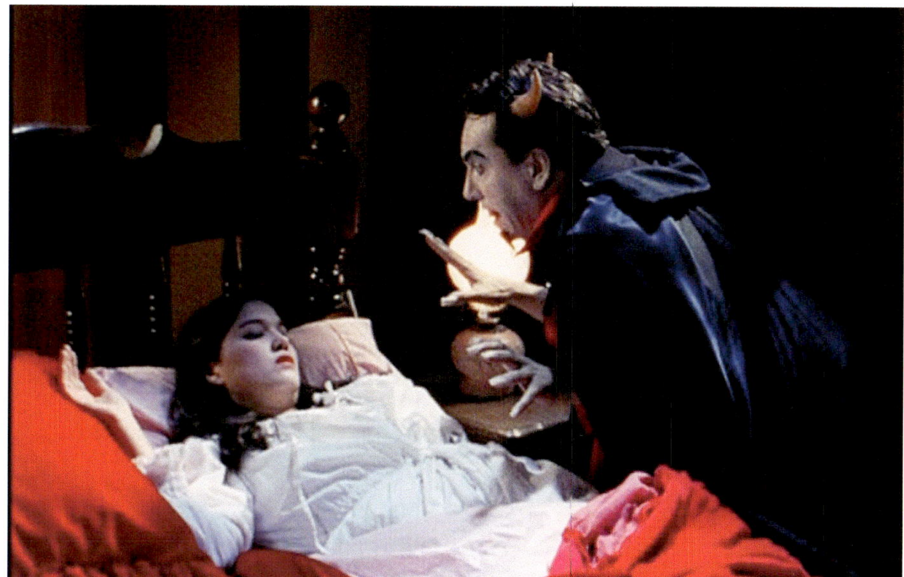

Still image from Anna Biller's short film *A Visit from the Incubus* (2001).

by Biller with subtle humor and unfailing, deliberate blandness. Natalia Schroeder is Madeleine, the best friend, who also has been a victim of nightly incubi visits.

The main message of *A Visit From the Incubus* is unconventional for vampire stories: although Lucy has been raped by the incubus, she has been awakened sexually. When she decides that she finally "feels like a woman," she takes a job in the local saloon as a dancing girl, a profession that was considered shocking in the late 1800s but common in 1950s Western musical films. The incubus, her terrorizer and rapist, follows her to the saloon and attempts to put together an act to compete with Lucy's successful one. Lucy knocks him out of the water. It's Lucy's femininity that made her vulnerable to incubus in the first place, but now she uses that femininity to gain the love of the audience and get the incubus thrown out of the saloon. The incubus becomes ineffective, impotent, and powerless to hurt her. Biller can fully recreate an immersive film experience set in any decade she chooses; she manages to emulate the Technicolor staging of films like *Gentlemen Prefer Blondes* (1953) and *Show Boat* (1951), giving the audience an incredible contemporary experience of the 1950s through a twenty-first-century lens.

Jennifer Kent's 2014 horror movie *The Babadook* was released to overwhelmingly positive reactions from horror film fans. The film, in which a terrifying creature called the Babadook haunts a single mother and her demanding child, was an allegory about the horrors of parenthood and the emotional toll being a mother can take on one. But *The Babadook* was originally a short film called *Monster* in 2005, long before Kent could bring it to her full vision of a feature film. The original inspiration for *Monster* and *The Babadook* was a real-life situation. "My friend who's a single mother was having real trouble with her three-year-old son," said Kent in an interview in 2005:

> He kept seeing a man everywhere in the house, a monster man. It was driving my friend nuts because her son was absolutely terrified, would wet the bed, scream, that kind of thing. So she started to talk to this monster, pretended it was real, and included it in their daily life. This made the son a lot better because he was taken seriously and started to calm down after that. I got to thinking ... 'what if that monster was actually real? What if the son was being terrorized and the mother was too tired and overwhelmed to see that this force was seeping through the house and in danger of taking over?' And that's how *Monster* came about.[14]

Starring Susan Prior as the mother and Luke Ikimis-Healey as the boy, *Monster* is far less structured than its feature film counterpart. It's black and white and has surreal and even experimental moments that are only present in the feature film when the Babadook is onscreen. *Monster* is as graceful as a horror movie from the silent era; fantastic and with adept use of shadows and light. Kent's description of the short gives a good idea of the emotional construction of the narrative:

> *Monster*, for me, is about the mother waking up from a deep somnambulistic state, coming into some sort of awareness and strength. She's asleep at the beginning, totally oblivious to this evil presence in the house. And not happy as a result. Her child is running amok! She's overworked, overstressed and wishing she wasn't where she is in life. Totally disconnected from herself ... But through the course of the film, she is forced to wake up. And although this is terrifying for her, ultimately, it's a good thing. The monster is definitely HER monster. It comes to her through the boy. Because she's so unaware of things, the only way for it to get to her is through the child. When she is brought face to face with this force, the force that is about to tear open and eat her son, she has two choices. One is to let it happen, and the other is to wake up and match the monster's energy. To bring it under her control.[15]

Monster is just a slice of horror from a larger story that would someday be the horror movie *The Babadook*:

> I have always been fascinated by the film as dream, and I suppose the monster, if I was going to get deep and meaningful about it, is the mother's shadow. That's why I couldn't kill it off at the end; it's a part of her psyche, an important part. It just needs to be kept in check, put back in its box, so to speak. But we can't do without this aspect in ourselves. We can't kill off that shadow side. We need it to be balanced and whole. I really believe that light and dark exists in all of us, and we need to integrate both sides into life. If we suppress the shadow, ignore it, it can actually become more huge, take over, and run the house! Of course, that's what it's about for me. Now that I've made it will be about whatever people get out of it when they see it.[16]

Making the film was not easy. No one knew, in 2004, that the film Kent would make would end up getting picked up for a legitimately funded feature. An independent filmmaker, Kent had to find the money and the distribution for her short just like everyone else:

> I was going to make *Monster* whether I got funding or not. There is only one avenue for funding in this country. It comes from the government and is in short supply. We don't have 'private' funding of any sort because there are no studios, and no corporations/individuals are interested in funding films because they don't get any tax incentives. Having said that, there IS one great state-run government scheme for shorts that the NSW Film and Television Office runs called 'The Young Filmmakers Fund.' It offers assistance for those filmmakers starting out (under thirty-five years of age) to make a short (or feature if you're game!) Their maximum award is 30,000 Australian dollars. You have to have had some experience in the industry, and you have to reside in NSW. $30,000 still means pulling in a hell of a lot of favors, but it is indeed money to make a short film! And most people have to pay for their first short, so every man, woman, and their dog puts into this scheme in the hope to get lucky. I submitted and just had my fingers crossed. It is very competitive, and they only choose four or five projects a year. I really wasn't holding out hope as *Monster* is in the horror realm, and I thought they would be more interested in funding non-genre projects, you know, 'serious film.' But everyone at the FTO loved the script and was confident in what I wanted to achieve with it all, so they gave us the cash. I was, needless to say, thrilled. It's much easier to beg for equipment etc. when you have a base of $30,000 to play with. The whole project, if paid for fully, would have cost us over $200,000. We really had a lot of help from amazing companies here who really support their short filmmakers.[17]

Heidi Lee Douglas's *Little Lamb* (2014) is an astonishing short Gothic horror/thriller film. Like *Monster*, *Little Lamb* is an Australian movie, but unlike *Monster*, it is set in the 1940s during Australia's turbulent colonization when British convicts were forcibly brought to Van Diemen's Land (modern-day Tasmania) as indentured servants and slaves. The costumes, locations, and setting are vibrant and convincing. The story, loosely based on the *Bluebeard* fairy tale, is about a newly-transplanted convict named Louisa (Georgia Lucy). The convicts are allowed to pick their new master, and Louisa, knowing no reason why not, chooses Mr. Black (James Grim) as her new employer and owner so she can leave the horrible prison. "I named the main character after my own ancestor," said Douglas,

> Who died in childbirth about that time, leaving my great-great-grandmother an orphan. So the connections to these women felt strong, and they didn't have a chance to tell their own stories. I felt like they wanted me to tell them for them.[18]

It's a part of Australia's darker history that doesn't get very much attention, and Douglas was the first woman director to tell this kind of story about convict women. "I lived just up the road from the derelict ruins of a nineteenth-century women's prison," she said:

> I used to sit amid the ruins and hear the ghosts of the rebel women wanting to have their stories told. The stories about the convict women detained in Tasmania reminded me of my own rebellious, strong-willed friends, and I imagined that if we had been born 200 years earlier, we might well have got in trouble for some little thing and been convicts too.[19]

Douglas wrote the script for *Little Lamb* for a feminist Gothic horror screenplay competition at the first Stranger with My Face International Film Festival in Hobart, Tasmania. She won the contest, and the festival judge (and horror filmmaker Donna McRae, *Johnny Ghost*, 2011) urged her to make it as a film. Using Tasmania's preserved nineteenth-century ruins as sets, authentic touches, such as cut marks on the buildings from the convicts, added to the film's atmosphere in a way that no fabricated set could have. "It was like traces of their blood and pain are still living beside you every day."[20] The rugged rural setting and the nineteenth-century farmhouse convicts had built were luckily available for filming. All the props were handmade to ensure authentic quality. Douglas's mentor, historian, and documentarian Roger Scholes (*The Human Journey*, 2000), encouraged her to make it as well and helped her determine how to film the more ambitious aspects of the story: the burning barn, chopping off an arm, and the real-life lam, for instance. "It was only when we were shooting the short that the cast and crew started saying I should make it into a feature," she said.[21]

After she made the film, it screened at numerous film festivals, including the prestigious Fantasia Film Festival in Montreal, Quebec, where producers became interested in a feature version of *Little Lamb*. Douglas wrote the feature film script, *Unnatural Conduct*, funded by the Australian Screen Agency. When it was complete, and she was seeking financing, Douglas was told by the agency that there was another film a lot like it that was already going into production and "there can't be two convict women films" and "women don't like violence." Jennifer Kent, who we talked about just before Heidi Lee Douglas, was making a new film shockingly similar to *Little Lamb*: *The Nightingale* (2019).

Though it wouldn't be released until 2019, *Nightingale* is also set at the same time in the same location. It also has a lead female who is a convict (Clare, played by Aisling Franciosi) and an evil enslaver that abuses her (Lieutenant Hawkins, played by Sam Claflin). The woman also seeks revenge. Kent began writing it as soon as *The Babadook* was released (2014), also the year that *Little Lamb* was released. *The Nightingale* has a more extensive story structure; it has wholly original characters, such as Clare's husband and an Aboriginal guide that helps Clare when she runs away.

Coming from the same country, it's probably true that Kent was fascinated by the same history that Douglas had been; she felt the same affinity for the same women and wanted to explore her country's darker, colonial past in a way that didn't glorify the violence against those who were dominated and controlled. But I know that Kent and Douglas are both independent filmmakers in a smaller Australian horror film community that shares the same film festivals. Before *The Babadook*, like Douglas, Kent was a short horror filmmaker. How many other filmmakers in Australia were also thinking of making films in that same setting with a similar storyline? Kent has said she wouldn't direct

A chilling still from director Melanie Light's short horror film *The Herd* (2014); it shows us the horror of animal exploitation through a feminist and vegan lens.

Hollywood franchises (she turned down *Wonder Woman*) and will stick to independent films. *The Nightingale* is a prime example of the film Kent wants to make.[22]

Disappointed that the Australian Film Agency rejected the feature film version of *Little Lamb*, Douglas made another horror short not long after, *Devil Woman* (2017), which featured an angry woman protagonist through which she could creatively and constructively channel her frustrations.

Melanie Light's *The Herd* (2014) is one of the most frightening and visceral films I've ever seen. British Light had always been a fan of horror films and dark, grotesque art and video. She was able to start working in the art department on horror movies like *The Devil's Chair* (2007). After working on several more films, directing a few music videos, and finishing her first horror short, *Escape* (2012), Light directed *The Herd*. Written by Ed Pope, *The Herd* takes an ordinary woman and places her in a filthy prison where she is milked for breast milk. Other women, all recent mothers, have had their children taken away and are being used to manufacture milk. Pope approached Light with the script and the idea, wanting her to direct it. "After he brought it to me," said Light in an interview,

> It kind of sat on the shelf for a while, and then we focused on it, and we worked together quite a lot on shaping the script. We had to make it shootable, and it was very important that there had to be a reason that these things were going on; it was very important to make sure that it wasn't strictly an animal rights story but that it was a horror story as well. We needed something that would cater to everybody but still get the message across.[23]

The message was relating the lives of human women to the factory farm dairy industry. "Ed wrote it out of his frustrations of having to explain to people why he doesn't drink milk, why he doesn't eat cheese," explained Light, "The purpose was always to show women in cages being milked and impregnated to represent the dairy cow and dairy industry."[24] Light, like Pope,[25] is a vegan: a person who chooses not to eat any food products that come from animals. By representing human women being exploited for their reproductive systems the way cows are, Pope and Light created a horror film that makes feminism transhuman: cows and chickens, these creatures are also female and are being sexually assaulted, imprisoned, and tortured so that their bodies can produce milk for other people to drink. In the film, a human woman wakes up on the factory farm; cramped in tight cages, filthy, prodded, and treated like objects, the women suffer greatly. But in Light's version of this true horror, the women fight back against their captors and rapists, ultimately gaining freedom through violence. Said Light,

> It is a political film, and there are people who may not agree with it or may be offended, but I think if you're going to make a film with a message, you want that message to be clear.[26]

The gritty and bloody film doesn't hold back from showing how graphic dairy farms are in terms of blood and pain. The film begins with Paula (Victoria Broom), a human woman, being forcibly impregnated by a technician in a dark, unfriendly makeshift farm clinic. Her hands are tied as semen is inserted into her via a plastic tube (the technician is played by Pollyanna McIntosh, who would go on to direct the horror movie *Darlin'*, 2019). She is shackled and led by workers to her tiny pen next to many other pens filled with women like her. The women's breasts are hooked up to milking apparatus, uncomfortable-looking, pumping a continuous stream of milk while they sit and stare, defeated and broken. One of the pregnant women, Sarah (Charlotte Hunter), goes into violent labor in her cage at night. The farm workers disappointedly point out that the baby is a boy and take it away despite the mother's cries. Looking for a way out among the dark, dimly lit, dingy hallways of the factory farm, Paula comes across a room filled with dozens of women hooked up to giant milking machines. The women sway to the hum of the machines, completely enveloped, unable to detach from the Gigeresque nightmare of pumps, tubes, and sounds. Running in horror, she steps into another room where adolescent girls, barely thirteen or fourteen, are being kept. Paula realizes they will be impregnated soon and live their entire lives inside the farm.

It's a brutal, uncomfortable watch. It's a fearless film with a message that many people don't care to hear and will hate. Light's intense camera work involves emotional touches, such as showing us the point of view of the women in the cage and the energetic, bloody killings, the worst of which is Pollyanna McIntosh having her tongue sliced out of her mouth by the two crazed women. Her agonizing, muffled moans, screams, and blood-drenched mouth and throat as the camera moves away from her are the stuff of genuine horror. When I first saw *The Herd*, I knew I was looking at something good but was too afraid to show it at the 2015 Etheria Film Festival because it had a political message. I didn't want the films we screened to have a political or feminist stance in any way, necessarily. I regret that now because *The Herd* is a brilliant piece of finely-crafted terror from an incredibly passionate filmmaker who absolutely should be making more films. The 'political' message is up to the viewer to reject or accept, not me, the programmer. If you enjoy that almost-vomiting, nightmare feeling that only the most intense and well-made horror movies can give you, *The Herd* should hit the spot.

Gigi Saul Guerrero has always been inspired by filmmakers like Rob Zombie, Robert Rodriguez, and Quentin Tarantino. "They were just not afraid to be upfront about it all," she said in an interview about violence in her horror films:

> Like they would not be scared of crossing the line, not just in gore ... they will show you everything. Even if it's Kill Bill with a lot of blood everywhere, and it's super cheesy and exaggerated. I feel like he was upfront about it, like, "Nah, this is how it's going to be shown." I could really be upfront about some stuff, and it led me to really be gritty and handheld. And really, I just got really into it, really invested in that style of filmmaking.

Having made numerous short films and two features, Saul Guerrero's work is firmly rooted in Mexican folklore and legends, usually in the Spanish language, and always extraordinarily dark and violent. "I was like, wow, he's [Rodriguez] Latino. And he's bringing that folklore too. So I felt like, okay, I can do it too."[27] Saul Guerrero began making short horror films about more serious topics, such as immigration and other 'realistic' social horror from Mexico. Her short film *Dead Crossing* (2011) was about immigrants from Mexico attempting to illegally enter the United States by covertly crossing the border at night.

> "I was like, well, you know what? Mexico has incredible things to offer too. And that is in amazing folklore and culture. So I was like, if I'm keeping this Latino trend in the horror, I should start also bringing the positives of all the stuff I love of where I'm from."

With her company Luchagore, she made short horror films about bullfighting (*El Matador*, 2013), the cult of Saint Mary (*Madre De Dios*, 2015), lycanthropy (*Bestia*, 2017), Day of the Dead (*Día de los muertos*, 2013), Aztec graves (*Mistress of Bones*, 2020 and *Dulce Muerte*, 2020), and what is perhaps her best short film, *El Gigante* (2014). *El Gigante* is the film that best shows Saul Guerrero's talent with gruesome imagery. Truly fucked up, the film features some of the most demented physical effects in a short that I have ever seen. The premise is simple, and there is very little dialogue: a man is kidnapped, and a giant, hulking man wearing a lucha libre mask named El Gigante savagely assaults him in a mock wrestling match.

Saul Guerrero has an exceptional natural talent for a gritty, cartoonish style that generates an intense feeling of dread and disgust in the viewer. Saul Guerrero brutalizes her victims. She tortures this poor man. She pounds him into oblivion like a piece of meat. The gore and horror retain that cartoonish quality absent in torture pornography, but it leaves one with an enjoyable sense of existential dread. The camerawork and production design, along with Saul Guerrero's auteur talent for the grotesque, is a rare blend. After *El Gigante*, she would continue to fine-tune that talent for future short films and for her two features, *Culture Shock* (2019), another immigration horror movie, and *Bingo Hell* (2021), which tackles the gentrification of a Latino community as a horror film. Both films were made for Blumhouse's television horror film production arm. *El Gigante* premiered at the Etheria Film Festival in 2015 to a live audience. "And I still remember," said Saul Guerrero,

El GIgante, the horrifying murderous wrestler from Gigi Saul Guerrero's *El Gigante* (2015).

> Which is by far the most glorious thing I think I've made ... it was the best audience reaction I've ever heard. It was a world premiere. I was like, "This is what winning an Oscar must feel like." It was incredible. In that screening, at one point during the intermission, I went to the bathroom and, you know, did my business. And there were two older ladies washing their hands and talking, and they were talking about all the movies. And then one of them says, "I don't know who Gigi Guerrero is, why they would want to make that, about that wrestling thing. It was so atrocious and visceral." And I passed out. "Who, who in their mind must be so dark and violent?" And I'm in the stall, enjoying every second of it. So since then, I was like, this is my signature. Like, it makes me so happy. It makes me so happy.[28]

In modern horror movies, Saul Guerrero's work has normalized Latino actors and Mexican-American culture.

Jill Gevargizian directed a short horror film titled *The Stylist,* released in 2016. It won Best Film and the Audience Award at the 2016 Etheria Film Festival. Four years later, a feature film version of *The Stylist*, also directed by Gevargizian, expanded on the first film while keeping so much of what made the original such a memorable movie. "It was always my hope that this story or concept would be told in feature-length form when I first started to think about it," said Gevargizian:

> ... I didn't go to film school. I feel like I learned everything as I made *The Stylist*. But it was always my hope to turn it into a feature, but we started just by writing a short and thought that it was a concept that could easily be told both ways because we would learn so much more about Claire [the stylist] ... In hindsight, I wish we had written the feature and short maybe together, and it would have been this packaged thing, maybe would have happened sooner.[29]

The Stylist, the short, is an evening in the life of Claire, a hairstylist in a respected salon. Her last client of the night, a busy, bright woman with a great career and long blonde hair, finds out that Claire likes to scalp her victims and wear their hair over her own so she can experience what it's like to be them. The scene is particularly gruesome, with the victim waking up to see her own red and bloody head. Of course, Claire has to kill her to keep her silent. "I had this idea," explains Gevargizian,

> I've been a hairstylist for fifteen years, or at the time, I feel like I first wrote these notes down almost six/seven years ago [2013] about a hair stylist that kills people. It's like, "How does this not already exist?"[30]

Director Jill Gevargizian on the set of *The Stylist* (2016). Photo credit: Daniel Hinkle.

Like Saul Guerrero, Gevargizian is inspired by Robert Rodriguez and his stories of making the action film *El Mariachi* (1992) for less than $8,000. "This kind of came from that Robert Rodriguez thinking," she explained,

> Many people read his book when they first start, of what you have access to that's unique to you, from locations to props to cars, people, anything that's unique and can make your thing look cooler, look like it has money in it. I especially took the location thing to heart with everything I've made. I realized that makes something look huge when you don't have the money to build a set from scratch. So, I'm a hairstylist, and I have access to so many different types of salons, and it seemed like something that hadn't happened before. I just felt like I had to make it. I was like, "I can make this, and hair stylists can watch it." It was important to me from that perspective, too. I could make something personal and unique. So, that's why this was the thing that I wanted to be a feature from the start.[31]

"She really stuck with me," said actress Najarra Townsend about her character in both the short and the feature, Claire:

> I don't exactly know how to explain it. I usually have a lengthy process when it comes to developing a character, but that's always for features. I downsize for shorts, which might not be a good thing. But, with *The Stylist*, I just found her so interesting, and I wanted to dive in more, and I knew that Jill had the intention of, hopefully, one day, we can make this a feature, so I was like, "Hey, I hope that's true." But when you make short films, and people have that intention, you never know if it's going to happen. And

> then, when I saw the short, I was like, "Hey, this has a chance of becoming a feature. This should become a feature." People responded so well to the short. I feel like a whole community of people wanted this film to be a feature film ... I was like, "Oh my gosh, we have to make this movie." I could visualize it so well. So, I was really excited to make this film.[32]

But when a producer attached to help make the feature couldn't get the funding together, Gevargizian had an idea: to raise the funds themselves using Kickstarter, the popular crowd-sourcing platform. "I was like, 'Heck yes. We have to do this,'" said Townsend:

> I think that was when Jill asked me to be a producer. It kind of just happened naturally and organically. And I wanted to help in any way I could, so the opportunity to be more than just an actor in the film was so exciting, especially for this film because I loved Claire, I loved the movie, I love Jill, I just wanted to do as much as I could for it.[33]

Looking back on it, Gevargizian realized she should have had a feature script version ready to show people when she released the short film. But she was able to keep what made the short so captivating and, instead of losing it in a larger story, amplify it and improve upon it; this is what ultimately makes the feature film version so successful. The short and the feature were both designed to be made from Claire's perspective, explained Gevargizian, "for everything to feel that way like we're leaning on to Claire's side always, even the camera, how everything's designed."[34] The color palette stayed true to the original short while expanding on the themes and elegance of the production design. "Yeah, we geeked out about styling the movie to the extreme," said Gevargizian:

> From the short, we always thought that's what this movie should be. We always wanted to have this elegance to it; even the gross scenes, we wanted to still have an elegance to it. In hindsight, we were lucky to have all this time between the feature and the short. The things that we had already done in the short, we were wondering, "How do we go back to this, make it better, but not make it obvious we're just trying hard to make it different, when we already liked how it looked?" So, we wanted to do more. But her lair might be my favorite, which I learned Sarah described to her whole team as a "nest," which makes sense ... But since we want you to like Claire and be on her side, and everything is supposed to tell her story, and how she feels, so, down there, we wanted it to feel warm and safe. The only color in that room is brown and gold, and I love it. The gold came to me as some weird destiny thing in the short, and then I became obsessed with it. But I became obsessed with yellow at that point, and I remember googling 'redheads in mustard-yellow clothing' because Najarra's hair was red at the time, and I was like, "This is beautiful." I wanted a classic baby doll dress. Her wardrobe, I also always had it in my head. But the color, once we found that dress, inspired the whole thing, and we became psychotically obsessed with it in the feature. We call it 'Claire yellow,' and every time we'd find something yellow anywhere, we'd all start screaming. We put yellow benches in the movie everywhere.[35]

Censor (2021) is a feature-length horror film directed by United Kingdom filmmaker Prano Bailey-Bond with surreal overtones in a beautiful gore-soaked homage to low-budget slashers and banned video nasties. *Censor* is the unsettling tale of film censor Enid, who discovers an eerily familiar horror film that speaks directly to her past. As she unravels the mystery behind the film, she is dragged into a twisted fairytale, blurring the lines between fiction and reality. Steeped in a 1980s aesthetic, *Censor* is an atmospheric and suspenseful love letter to the horror classics of the past.

In 2016, Bailey-Bond submitted her short film *Nasty* to Etheria, and it was an official selection that year, screening alongside Anna Biller's *The Love Witch* and *The Stylist* short. The story of how *Nasty* was made and became the *Censor* feature is very similar to that of *The Stylist*. "I put this film together to try and get the attention of a financier who might be able to support the short and then support the feature," said Bailey-Bond in an interview,

> But they didn't support the short. So we ended up crowdfunding. I was obsessed with the film by that point and then made *Nasty*, but it was always with sight to the feature. I think it's hard for me to say exactly what ideas were in the feature before making *Nasty* and exactly what ideas came out of *Nasty*. Things were evolving, I guess, side by side, but many of the techniques I explored in *Nasty* and the kind of character's journey. So the search for missing family members and the kind of color journey from peak 1980s, Britain and the video nasties. They were 'nasty' as well, using techniques like shooting on film and vision effects, kind of how we get from the real world into the video nasty world. So, you know, using a steady cam or visual effects, moving through the television and things like that, I just really loved working on. They naturally folded into *Censor*. So there was a little bit of, like, back and forth echo going on between the two projects.[36]

Nasty is about a young boy in 1980s Britain obsessed with watching 'video nasties': a list of banned horror movies considered too extreme for regular audiences. As the boy watches these videotapes of horror movies, he and his family are sucked into the world of the films, where they experience the terror and horror firsthand. It's a very disorienting film halfway between a dreamscape and a narrative story; much of the movie is experienced on a visceral level of noise, color, and atmosphere.

Nasty blew the audience away at the Etheria Film Festival in 2016. It is, to this day, one of the most disturbing and surreal short films I have ever seen. *Nasty* is a predecessor to *Censor* both in subject matter and visual style. Possibly the most striking difference between the two films is the transition from a child to an adult's point of view. For the short, "the idea of telling a child's story came out of the research looking at this period and the fear around what these films were going to do to kids," said Bailey-Bond,

> That was what inspired me to want to explore a child's perspective during this period. And actually, it was great. I absolutely loved making Nasty, but I was really excited to then be in the perspective of an adult and to be able to do something maybe, like, more complex, I think, with Censor, because as adults, we are all more complex

because we've got more backstory and we've spent more time getting screwed up or repressing parts of ourselves or liking or disliking parts of ourselves and all of those kinds of things that happen as an adult.[37]

In *Censor*, the lead character is now Enid Baines (Niamh Algar), an adult working at the British Board of Film Classification in charge of film censorship. Many of the video nasty horror movies come through the office, and Enid recommends that violence of any kind be cut out before a film can be approved. But Enid slowly slips into some mental illness, her reality and fantasy worlds clashing and mixing. Believing she will save her long-lost sister from the horrors of exploitation film acting, she infiltrates a film set, not understanding that it isn't real. Bad, gorgeously horrible things happen. Enid failed to protect her sister when she disappeared as a child and "is trying to make up for something through her work," said Bailey-Bond. "It gets further and further out of control that it's this woman on a mad mission … stuff that you can't get into with a child protagonist."[38] The same films and filmmakers influenced Bailey-Bond for both *Nasty* and *Censor*: *Twin Peaks*, *The House by the Cemetery* (1981), *The Beyond* (1981), *Suspiria* (1977), *Opera* (1987), *The Player* (1992), *Black Swan* (2010), *The Machinist* (2004), and *Let's Scare Jessica to Death* (1971), everything from lighting to the blurring of reality and film industry, or just the blurring of reality in general. Bailey-Bond once told me that the best way to describe *Nasty* is that it takes place in an "off-kilter world." Shifting the perspective of the audience and the protagonist from the 1980s into the actual video nasty world via a color journey using lights and dream sequences drenched in purples and pinks, *Censor* weaves these things into our real world.

Devi Snively's recognizable style can't be deterred despite her subject matter. Her short films *Teenage Bikini Vampire* (2004), *Confederate Zombie Massacre!* (2005), *Raven Gets a Life* (2006), *Meat Is Murder* (2009), *Death in Charge* (2009), and *Bride of Frankie* (2017), as well as her feature horror comedy, *Trippin'* (2011), all share a calculated sense of heightened reality; while the camera, the costumes, the makeup, the music, and special effects are exaggerated, the characters themselves often deliver their lines in a dry, deadpan manner that is at odds with the rest of the film. The result is funny and endearing, even when the subject is horror, gore, or murder. Snively can't make a film that doesn't look like a Devi Snively film; even in black and white, her vision remains unhindered. Some piece of her always comes through; it's what an auteur director does.

Bride of Frankie is the most sophisticated version of her artistic vision, a black-and-white love song to *Bride of Frankenstein* (1935). It was altogether more comedic and fantastical than its predecessor. Inventing a new character in the Frankenstein universe named Frankie (Rachel Sledd), Snively creates a lead woman character on equal footing with the obsessed Doctor Stein (Circus-Szalewski). *Bride of Frankie* is whimsical but dark and intentionally funny without downplaying the ominous nature of monsters or their scientists. "My all-time favorite film is dark comedy as opposed to horror," admitted Snively in a 2011 interview,

But it was my 'gateway movie' to the dark side—*Harold & Maude*. It showed me that social commentary combined with humor, the macabre, romance, tragedy, a touch of

In Devi Snively's *Bride of Frankie* (2017), Frankie (Rachel Sledd) meets Shelley (Jessica Ridenour).

> gore, and the occasional dance number is the perfect storm for me when it comes to storytelling.[39]

In *Bride of Frankie*, Snively's intense art design and particular aesthetic are at their masterful height, complete with homunculus in glass jars and other fantastical touches.

In the 1990s, a cult film fan named Tom Smith recognized Doris Wishman working in an adult sex shop called The Pink Pussycat in Coconut Grove, Florida. She had moved to Miami from New York in the late 1980s to live with her sister Pearl because she lost all of her money when *A Night to Dismember* burnt up. He asked her if she was Doris Wishman, and she said yes. He responded, "You are a genius!" She immediately asked him for $50,000 to make a new film. Instead, he took her to dinner. Tom convinced Doris that she should be making films again.

At this point, the films of Doris Wishman had become something of a curiosity among cult film scholars and academics. Filmmaker Peggy Ahwesh, a professor at Bard College at the time, became interested in her films. Ahwesh's work was experimental and sometimes sleazy; her short horror films *The Deadman* (1987), *The Scary Movie* (1993), and *Nocturne* (1998) show Ahwesh to be an artist who would be drawn to the strange work of Wishman and other filmmakers like the Kuchar Brothers[40], George A. Romero, and Jennifer Todd Reeves (*Shadows Choose Their Horrors*, 2005). During this renaissance of Wishman scholarship and appreciation, Wishman would make three more films: the pornography *Dildo Heaven* (2002) (on which Rodney Ascher, director of *Room 247*, 2012, was a cameraperson), a 2001 thriller remake of her previous pornography film *Satan Was a Lady* (1975) starring Honey Lauren (director of period thriller comedy *Wives of the Skies*, 2020), and the supernatural horror film *Each Time I Kill* (2007).

Each Time I Kill is Wishman's last film. It was filmed in 2002 but was not released until 2007, after her death. It has an uncomfortable, shot-on-digital look that is absent from all of Wishman's previous films, which were shot on film stock. Ellie Saunders (Tiffany Paralta in her only lead role) is a woman who finds a magic necklace in a haunted house that allows her to steal beauty from the women she murders. There's excessive soft-core sex and breast nudity. There's cheap blood. The film looks like a cat made it: every scene is shot either by the actors' feet or from high above them looking down. The sound is off, sometimes, the characters are inaudible, but other times all the dialogue is dubbed. It's an inconsistent mess. Fred Schneider of the band The B-52s and cult filmmaker John Waters both make cameos, and it's heartwarming to know they were Wishman supporters. The film's producer, Michael Bowen, was Wishman's primary supporter and friend. Bowen is not the actor Michael Bowen who played the lousy boyfriend Tommy from Martha Coolidge's romantic comedy *Valley Girl* (1983). This is Michael J. Bowen, the film scholar, and expert on underground cinema. He wrote an academic paper on her films titled "Embodiment and Realization: The Many Film-Bodies of Doris Wishman," published in the journal *Wide Angle* in 1997, one of the first to bring attention to Wishman's career in the twenty-first century.

What I find most fascinating about Doris Wishman is that from her first film in 1960 through her death on August 2, 2002, she never improved as a filmmaker in any capacity. Her style was that she had no style at all and had no technique or art when it came to directing, lighting, or editing a film. Her films are endearing, funny, and silly but pretty terrible. Tom Smith put it best when he said that her films have "no irony, no analysis, no lingering in the interstices" and that she was "unencumbered by craft, chasing dollars."[41] In 2021, an academic film book titled *ReFocus: The Films of Doris Wishman* was published by Edinburgh University Press and features articles about Wishman. I highly suggest it for further reading about this strange and wonderful woman filmmaker.

Many new short horror movies directed by women come from film school graduates. The Florida State University College of Motion Picture Arts, the University of Southern California School of Cinematic Arts, the Australian Film, Television and Radio School, and the American Film Institute have facilitated the horror thesis films of more women directors than any other universities or film school programs in the world. In particular, the American Film Institute's Directing Workshop for Women has produced so many genre films, many of which I have shown at my film festival, that it's astounding how many women will choose to make a genre movie when given the option. The AFI DWW, as it is known for short, has produced a plethora of women directors and their genre shorts, and here's a list of some the women horror film and television directors that the program has graduated: Heidi Miami Marshall (*A Through M*, 2006), Liz Adams (*Air Collision*, 2010), Devi Snively (*Bride of Frankie,* 2017), Kimberly McCullough (*Nice Guys Finish Last*, 2011), Sarah Doyle (*You, Me & Her*, 2014), Neema Barnette (*Spirit Lost*, 1996), Lily Mariye (*The Walking Dead,* 2022), Tricia Brock (*Breaking Bad,* 2008), Hanelle M. Culpepper (*Star Trek: Picard,* 2020), Annetta Marion (*The Doll Collector*, 2003), Valerie Weiss (*The Archer*, 2016), Michelle Steffes (*Summoned*, 2020), Joy Gohring (*Date A

Human, 2013), Meredith Berg (*Void*, 2009), Maggie Kiley (*American Horror Story,* 2017), Rachel Goldberg (*American Horror Story,* 2017), Bridget Savage Cole (*Blow the Man Down*, 2019), Aubree Bernier-Clarke (*The Night is Ours*, 2014), Erin Li (*Kepler X-47,* 2014), Lesli Linka Glatter (*The Walking Dead,* 2013), Bola Ogun (*Lucifer,* 2021), Thoranna Sigurdardottir (*Zelos*, 2015), Kantu Lentz (*Jack and Jo Don't Want to Die*, 2019), Tessa Blake (*American Horror Story,* 2021), Christine Boylan (*The Punisher,* 2019), Courtney Hoffman (*The Good Time Girls*, 2017), and Amber Sealey (*No Man of God*, 2021).

ANTHOLOGIES

THE ANTHOLOGY HORROR FILM has been popular since the silent era of cinema. The first widely-accepted horror film anthology is considered to be Richard Oswald's *Unheimliche Geschichten* (1919), made up of five short films. An earlier horror anthology film is *Trilby,* AKA *Three Tales of Terror* (1912), directed by Louise Kolm-Fleck in what was then the Austrian Empire, as discussed in Chapter 1. The lost film had three separate segments, but only one, that of evil hypnotist Svengali (Paul Askonas) and his musical thrall Trilby (Frau Galfres-Hubermann), is confirmed by documentation to have been included. We may never know what the other two stories were, nor what their wraparound segment may have been. Another early anthology horror with a woman director is *Three Cases of Murder* (Wendy Toye's segment "In the Picture") (1955), also discussed in Chapter 2. And we discussed the horror anthologies *House of the Dead* (1978) in Chapter 3, the Filipino *Katotohanan o guniguni?,* AKA *Fact or Fantasy?* and *Mga alamat ng sandaigdig,* AKA *Legends of the World*, both from 1960, in Chapter 4, and *The Dungeonmaster* (1984) in Chapter 5. The next significant achievement of women directors in horror film anthologies would not come until the 1990s when filmmaker Asia Argento, daughter of Dario Argento, the famous horror film director, would direct her very first piece for the Italian horror anthology film *DeGenerazione* (1995) with the segment "Prospettive" In fact, it was the first thing she would ever direct at all; she went on to have a career as a director, most notably with the drama/thriller *The Heart Is Deceitful Above All Things* (2004). Director Eleonora Fiorini also contributed to *DeGenerazione*, directing the segment "Finalmente insieme."

Argento's is the fifth short in the film, coming right after "Vuoto a rendere," and it's a surreal, strange, very short little film about a woman who takes hold of an umbrella for a strange man standing there at his "new job." He's in his underwear, wearing a sheet wrapped around his waist and nothing else. He said he's got "prospects" and asks the woman to hold the umbrella for a minute. She does, and it flies her through the air over two men carrying a mirror and a windmill. "Perspettive" can mean both "prospects" and "perspectives" in Italian, so this has to be a clever pun that doesn't translate as well into English.

"Finalmente insieme" is a bit longer and has some vital horror elements, but it's just as weird and far more surreal than narrative-based. A man and a woman are working on a home renovation together. When they sleep, they both have horrible nightmares about the other; he that she is a nurse in a torture hospital who drills a hole in his head and then drinks his blood through a long tube; she that he is a bloody, disfigured monster who has eaten her cat. When they wake up, he tries to rape her, and in their struggle, a bookcase lands on top of them. The next scene shows them sitting at a small table in the snow, having tea. Your guess is as good as mine.

There's an underground, anarchist flavor to the entire anthology as it follows zero rules; it's an art film with horror elements. It's an expression of angst and attitude from the 1990s, and it was not overly ambitious and therefore is accessible to a horror movie fan. A contemporary review spoke about the collective of filmmakers all having the same "cultural roots." "A passion for music, non-politicization and the absence of labels, tolerance, respect for B-movie production, the very strong desire to do 'new' things but not 'against' anything, hoping to reach the public."[42]

Horror film anthologies were popular in Europe; though, in the United States, they'd be relegated to straight-to-VHS releases, in Europe and Asia, they would be aired on television and in theaters. *Todesvisionen—Geisterstunde* (1989) is a horror film anthology from West Germany that played on television but has never had a proper DVD release in the United States. Susanne Aernicke's segment "Julia" is a doppelganger story with lots of violence. *Todesvisionen—Geisterstunde* was released in the United States as *Visions of Death: Witching Hour*. The French horror/fantasy anthology *Adrénaline* (1990) also had very surreal horror segments, thirteen of them, in its feature-length running time.

Three of these segments were directed by Anita Assal. Assal's segment "Television Buster" is an energetic, surreal account of a French couple watching television one evening. As the night progresses, they watch themselves appearing in all of the news stories, as terrorists and hated criminals, and finally, the new French president makes a speech about how they must be destroyed. A television exorcist comes in to help them, eventually subduing the television with a cross-shaped antenna and a bible made up of remote control buttons and removing the set's beating heart. It feels a lot like a segment of an American horror television anthology such as *Monsters,* with plenty of influence from *The Exorcist* (1973) and *Videodrome* (1983).

Another segment directed by Assal, "Cyclope," is a science-fiction horror piece in which a walking AI security camera attacks a security guard at his post while a baseball game announcer speaks in the background about the ongoing "game." Assal employs social commentary about media and surveillance in both segments while imposing a Gilliamesque absurdity to the editing, sound, lighting, and exaggerated human reactions. Assal also directed the wraparound segment, "Les aveugles," a black-and-white series of clips showing blind people in a dystopian future city. In 1994, the same group of filmmakers, again including Assal, made another absurdist horror anthology film: *Parano, N'Ayez Pas Peur d'En Rire,* AKA *Wacko.*

Also in 1994, the United States horror film anthology *Twisted Tales* was released. It featured only three shorts and three filmmakers (Rita Klus, Kevin J. Lindenmuth, and Mick McCleery). Klus's segment, "Nothing but the Truth," is a fantasy horror set in mundane reality, much like many of the *Tales from the Crypt* morality lesson episodes. In the segment, a man named Joey (Freddie Ganno) has a reputation for lying to make himself look good. After being mugged, he lies to everyone, embellishing the story to make himself sound like a hero. He is mugged a second time, but in this instance, everything happens exactly the way described when he was lying. So he embellishes that version as well, and when he is mugged a third time, his fake version comes true once again. So, if Joey doesn't stop lying, he'll keep getting mugged over and over again, forever, until he tells the truth. Lindenmuth was also the producer of the anthology through his company Brimstone Media Productions LLC, and Klus had previously worked for him as an assistant on other films. This is her only directing credit.

After 2000, there are so many horror film anthologies with women directors that we can't go through each one. While larger studios backed some (VH1's short-lived *Strange Frequency*, a rock 'n' roll-themed *Twilight Zone*-style series for which Mary Lambert directed the segments "Disco Inferno" and "More Than a Feeling"), the most exciting horror anthologies, to me, are the low-budget, independent ones. In the early 2000s, it was widespread for ambitious filmmakers who the Internet had loosely connected to band together to create a horror anthology that would feature work from each one of them. These filmmakers networked and pooled their resources: if they each made one short segment and stayed within a theme or concept, they could string all of the shorts together and make a 'horror anthology feature' that would get more traction, attention, and possibly even distribution, than their shorts ever could alone. Usually, aside from a theme like 'vampires,' 'werewolves,' or 'zombies,' there was no control for budget, filmmaking style, or consistency of sound design or editing, making these anthologies challenging to appreciate in a purely cinematic fashion. But there is a particular do-it-yourself, anarchist enthusiasm associated with these films that occasionally showcased a spectacular talent who would go on to make better films and eventually have a career in filmmaking because of these early efforts.

Examples of this type of anthology include the films *Around Midnight* (2004) and *After Midnight* (2005). Laura Giglio and Isabelle Stephen were actresses who would direct horror anthology segments. Giglio appeared in 1990s straight-to-video horror like *Sorority Slaughter* (1994) and *Psycho Sisters* (1998). *Around Midnight* (2004) was a super low-budget effort from feminist auteur Andrew Shearer, first-time filmmaker Christopher Kahler, and veteran feature director Gary Whitson. Whitson had directed Giglio in several films, and he presumably brought her in as the fourth director. *Around Midnight* was produced by prolific low-budget horror movie producer Phil Herman. A sequel, *After Midnight* (2005), came out soon after. This sequel would again have a segment directed by Giglio and also segments directed by Isabelle Stephen ("The Perfect Subject") and Tiffany Warren ("A Moment of Darkness"). Quebecois Stephen, like Giglio, had acted in dozens of horror movies between the mid-1990s and 2005. Warren, however, had already made her short "A Moment of Darkness" when she was asked to include it in the final anthology as it fit the theme. Because Herman did not exclusively purchase the rights to her short for *After Midnight*, "A Moment of Darkness" also appears in the horror film anthology *Vampyre Tales* (2005). This non-exclusive distribution for short films was standard practice for anthology DVD releases.

A still from the segment "E is for Exterminate," directed by Angela Bettis, in the horror anthology film *The ABCs of Death* (2012).

Miho Yabe was another actress who directed a segment in a horror anthology. Yabe had starring roles in horror films like *Ghost Gate* (2003) before she was asked to direct the segment "Kafuka no yoru" of *Chô' kowai hanashi the movie: yami no eigasai* (2005) in which she also acts. All of the segments are based on short stories by horror author Yumeaki Hirayama. In China, the horror film anthology *Visits: Hungry Ghost Anthology* (2004) included one woman director as well: Low Ngai Yuen with her segment "1413." The anthology's premise is set during the Chinese Hungry Ghost Festival, and the gates of Hell have opened up to all the malevolent spirits. The stories are all set in contemporary China, and "1413" is set in a hospital, in room 1413. Teenager Mai Ling wakes up there and discovers that she survived the suicide pact that she made with her best friend, Jia Chyi. Her friend's ghost is now angry and is haunting her room, the hospital bed next to her, and chases her down the long hospital hallways.

Numerous omnibus anthology films followed. Most notably, two anthology franchises from North America, *The ABCs of Death* and *V/H/S*, dominated the decade of 2010-2020 and spawned dozens of similar projects. *The ABCs of Death* (2012) was an internationally produced project from Drafthouse Films, the same people that created the Texas-based international film festival Fantastic Fest, with directors and producers from various countries to develop twenty-six segments, one for each letter of the Roman alphabet.

Angela Bettis was one of the few woman directors featured in the first *ABCs of Death* project. Bettis had acted in some extremely influential 2000s horror movies like Lucky McGee's *May* (2002) and *The Woman* (2011), the *Toolbox Murders* remake (2004), and directed the horror film *Roman* in 2006. Bettis's segment of *The ABCs of Death*, "E is for Exterminate," is a simple story about a man who attempts to kill a spider, only to later find that the spider laid eggs in his ears when it bit him. The spiders pop out.

Inspired by a short story from the beautiful mind of Brent Hanley,[43] "O is for Orgasm" was directed by Hélène Cattet, with Bruno Forzani, and Cattet is the only other woman director in the first installment of that franchise.

The ABCs of Death 2 followed shortly after that in 2014. Kristina Buožytė (co-directing with Bruno Samper) made the segment "K is for Knell," in which a strange black floating sphere makes people in an apartment building go insane and fight one another. At the same time, a girl painting her toenails begins to bleed, and her blood touches a puddle of oozing black goo. Jen and Sylvia Soska were asked to make the segment "T is for Torture Porn," in which an actress (Tristan Risk, who starred in their 2012 horror feature *American Mary*) is aggressively filmed and abused by several male filmmakers. When she is undressed, it is revealed that she has tentacles where her clitoris should be, and she kills them with those tentacles.

The dreaded Raatma in Chloe Okuna's segment "Storm Drain" in the anthology horror film *V/H/S 94* (2021). Photo by Derrick Childers.

In 2016, *The ABCs of Death 2.5* came out, featuring twenty-six shorts, all for the letter "M," that had been submitted to a 2014 contest they'd held. *2.5* showcases the twenty-six best shorts from that competition. "M is for Matador," directed by Gigi Saul Guerrero, is about a deranged matador that kills women after forcing them to wear a decapitated bull's head; Ama Lea's "M is for Mermaid" shows a deadly, murderous mermaid dragged out of the water unwillingly, and Australian filmmaker Mia'Kate Russell's "M is for Muff" is about a man who dies of suffocation when an obese prostitute dies on top of him during sex. Distributor Magnet Releasing released the first two *ABCs of Death* films in theaters internationally. The first film was considered a financial success, but the second was not. The third was only distributed on DVD. It didn't escape the notice of women horror film directors that there were far more male directors being asked to participate in the three anthologies than women directors.

Also in 2012, a found footage horror anthology developed by the horror media site Bloody Disgusting was released. It was produced by Roxanne Benjamin, an aspiring film director and film executive at the time, and Brad Miska, the owner of Bloody-Disgusting.com. There were no women directors in the original *V/H/S* film. In 2012, when promoting the project, Miska said, "For V/H/S, we went to people that I have a relationship with via Bloody Disgusting—a group of trusted filmmakers who we thought would want to take part in this. They pitched their ideas and came to us with treatments and scripts. It was like, 'If you like this, go do your thing.'"[44]

In 2011, a few well-known women directors, like the Soskas, were working on *The ABCs of Death*, a competing project. *V/H/S 2* followed swiftly in 2013, also with only male directors. *V/H/S: Viral* (2014), the third in the series, had no female directors involved. It was also not produced by Roxanne Benjamin. A decade later, *V/H/S/94* (2021) came out, the fourth entry into the series, and it had two women directors: Chloe Okuno (*The Watcher*, 2022) and Jennifer Reeder (*Knives and Skin*, 2020). Okuno's segment was "Storm Drain," and Reeder created the wraparound, titled "Holy Hell."

Like the previous installments, all of the segments were found footage horror, with Okuno's featuring a creature named Raatmaa: an urban legend monster being investigated by a local news team. After being taken prisoner by sewer people who worship a Rat Man, the newscast is interrupted by a commercial for something called "The Veggie Masher" and then cuts back to the live footage. Okuno explains how she became involved in the project:

> I went in to meet with [writer] David Bruckner quite a few years ago when they were interviewing filmmakers to potentially come onto the project. I believe I pitched a couple ideas, one of which was an early version of "Storm Drain." Simon [Barrett] and Timo [Tjahjanto] were also involved with the project pretty early as veterans of the series. Ryan Prows and Jennifer Reeder came on a little later. I'm pretty sure the producers, Brad Miska and Josh Goldbloom, were fans of their work, so it seems like it was really a conversation between them, and it all proceeded pretty organically.[45]

In 2015, Roxanne Benjamin produced the horror anthology film *Southbound* (2016), on which she was a segment director, also produced by Miska of Bloody-Disgusting.com. Benjamin's segment, "Siren," is about several young women becoming the victims of a crazy cult. The segments, like in *V/H/S/94*, were interconnected and set in a Southern California desert atmosphere. Benjamin agreed to be a part of *Southbound*, but with the stipulation, "Only if I can direct":

> I had been working for the production companies that had financed the *V/H/S* movies, but I was also the head of acquisitions for the horror label that Brad and I were doing, Bloody Disgusting Selects, and head of development, so I had a full-time job on top of that ... we were all so influenced by *The Twilight Zone* and EC Comics and just hadn't really seen a lot of that tone set out in the desert.[46]

"Siren" is a road trip horror movie about an all-girl band. "I lived in Nashville for a great number of years," said Benjamin,

> So a lot of the people that I interacted with were musicians who were out on tour all the time, living in vans. So I had a lot of those stories to draw from on. ... I feel like I don't have enough of those kinds of stories, female-driven coming-of-age stories. There's all the male-driven ones, so that was definitely was something I wanted to bring![47]

After the success of *The ABCs of Death* and *V/H/S* series, dozens of new low-budget horror anthology films were made between 2012 and 2020, ranging from underground and exploitation to highbrow and auteur-focused. In 2017, Jovanka Vuckovic, who had directed several short genre films by this time, produced a new horror movie anthology with only female directors. In 2016, she explored different options about how to make it happen. Ultimately, Vuckovic wanted experienced directors,[48] and one of them, Antonia Bird, was interested in directing a segment. Sadly, Bird passed away before *XX* could be filmed, and she had to be replaced by another director. The original lineup of directors was Jen and Sylvia Soska, Mary Harron, Jennifer Lynch, and Vuckovic. The Soskas couldn't make a Director's Guild film, so they had to pull out; Mary Harron had a television series offer and had to drop out and was replaced by Annie Clark (AKA St. Vincent), and last, Jennifer Lynch had to withdraw because of a demanding television directing schedule. She was eventually replaced by Roxanne Benjamin, who produced Annie Clark's segment. Rose McGowan and Lana and Lilly Wachowski were also considered.[49] Vuckovic was upfront with her reasons for making the anthology:

Director Roxanne Benjamin behind the scenes of her segment "Don't Fall" in *XX* (2017).

> We created *XX* because there were no all-women horror anthologies. I had been thinking about crowdfunding one on Kickstarter when out of the blue, Todd Brown of XYZ called me and asked me if I wanted to produce an all-women horror anthology with him—which was an amazing coincidence. We had both noticed women being passed over for jobs in the recent spate of horror anthologies, so we put our heads together and decided to do something about it ... So we started making a list of directors we wanted to approach. *XX* is a direct response to the lack of opportunities for women in film—in the horror genre in particular.[50]

"The only thing that's going to change it is if women start hiring other women," she said in another interview, "and *XX* was something functional that we could do to address this problem."[51] The wraparound segment was made by Spanish horror animator Sofia Carrillo; it's a series of creepy images involving a dollhouse and doll's eyes. Carrillo had been making animated horror movies for a decade when she was approached to participate in *XX*. Vuckovic's segment was based on a Jack Ketchum story, "The Box," a surreal exercise in family dynamics. Kusama's segment, "Her Only Living Son," was written by Kusama and shows an alternative to the end of *Rosemary's Baby* (1968), in which the mother took the child and raised them away from the satanic cult. The son is still Satan's, however, and the mother finds she can't keep that side of him hidden.

Benjamin's "Don't Fall" is a classic creature story set in the desert,[52] and Clark's "The Birthday Party," which stars famous indie actress, Melanie Lynskey, is a strange *Weekend at Bernie's* (1989)-style dark comedy about a mother who hides a dead body so as not to ruin her daughter's birthday party.

The film came out with support from the horror community. It inspired aspiring women directors that they, too, could hire and support other women directors while collectively making a name for themselves and drawing attention to their work. Several other all-women horror anthologies would soon be completed.

The obscure *13 Chambers* (2017) was the next all-women-directed horror anthology. Thirteen short films from Seattle, Washington-based women directors that are mostly surreal and experimental rather than actual straight horror make up the movie. Smarthouse, a distributor in the Netherlands, released it on Amazon Prime in 2017, but it is no longer available.

Dark Whispers: Volume 1 (2019) was produced by Australian directors Briony Kidd and Megan Riakos and featured an all-Australian-horror-director roster, including the well-known Kaitlin Tinker ("The Man Who Caught a Mermaid") and horror stop-motion animator Isabel Peppard ("Gloomy Valentine"), with Riakos directing the wraparound segment about a book of *Dark Whispers* that contains each of these stories. Unlike *XX*, *Dark Whispers* was a collection of existing shorts rather than a production of brand-new material, including Kidd's critique of celebrity and Hollywood, "Watch Me." Riakos explained what she believed her anthology brought to horror when she said, "What I love most about this collection is that it dispels the myth that there is just one kind of 'women's horror' by showcasing eleven very different perspectives. These are all stories told through the female gaze, but in terms of tone, subgenre, and style, there is a great diversity."[53]

In the United States, an intrepid group of women directors created the short anthology (only thirteen minutes long) *Fatale Collective: Bleed* (2019). These shorts were, again, existing pieces that were put together to make one larger short anthology to showcase the work of these individual women directors. Megan Rosati ("ASMR"), Lola Blanc ("The Safe Space"), and Natasha Halevi ("Boxed") were among the producers and members of an informal group that called themselves The Fatale Collective, a band of women horror directors with ambitions to direct horror features, which produced and released the collection. *Bleed* is the title of their first collection of several to be made.

Veteran horror film writer, journalist, and filmmaker Staci Layne Wilson produced the all-women anthology horror film *Shevenge* (2019), which has segments directed by influential independent horror film filmmakers Izzy Lee ("For a Good Time, Call ... ") and Karen Lam ("Doll Parts"). Wilson herself directed the segments "Karma is a Bitch," "Psycho Therapy," and the wraparound. The films were collected, not made exclusively for the release, and all have a connecting theme: women getting revenge. "I came up with the idea to make a compilation of kickass horror shorts directed by women after a couple of my own films had run the festival circuit and really had nowhere to go after that," said Wilson in an interview,

A still from Lola Blanc's segment "The Safe Space" in the all-women-directors short horror anthology *Fatale Collective: Bleed* (2019).

> Around the time I decided to pull the trigger on this project, I had a couple female friends who were going through some tough times in relation to sexual harassment and assault, which made me think of the old adage: 'Living well is the best revenge.'[54]

The profits from the release of the anthology were donated to the Time's Up Legal Defense Fund for victims of sexual assault and harassment.

This decade of anthologies opened up dedicated collections of specific types of films and filmmakers to horror fans, making short films more accessible and connecting filmmakers with similar bonds of culture, gender, and thematic talent. Anthologies like *Dark Place* (2019) provided a place for niche women directors to showcase their talents and ethnicity without specifically joining a "woman's" anthology. *Dark Place* is a collection of short horror films made by Aboriginal Australian filmmakers about colonialism and traditional folklore, including director Kodie Bedford's "Scout," about a group of Indigenous women sold by colonists as sex slaves who decide to get revenge and escape, in that order. *Mexico Bárbaro* (2014) is an anthology of Mexican horror filmmakers with distinctly Mexican horror shorts. There are two segments directed by women: "Tzompantli" (Laurette Flores) and "Día de los Muertos" (Gigi Saul Guerrero). Saul Guerrero met *Mexico Bárbaro*'s producer while competing with short films for *The ABCs of Death 2*. "He started telling me about his new project *Mexico Bárbaro* and the other directors involved, and I immediately saw the opportunity," said Saul Guerrero, a Mexican Canadian. "My dream has always been to be able to represent where I am from, and this project was exactly what I wanted to take part in. Not only that, but the idea was so different and unique. I loved how it was all about Mexico's memorable traditions and legends." She continued to talk about the inspiration for her segment:

> Also, another thought I had in mind was all the issues happening in border town Mexico where many women are going missing, are being abused, raped, killed, you

name it. I was, in general, getting sick of seeing so many films about this topic where the women that are victimized in the film weren't even considered as a secondary character. It was always about an agent trying to find them or about a family member coping with the situation, for example. I wanted to take the Tex-Mex humor I always love bringing on screen and changing the stereotype of victimized women in border towns in my segment. So I figured ... hell! On the night of Day of the Dead, these women come together to take revenge on those who have abused them. At the same time, for those who watch my segment will notice all the details within the colors, the tradition, and the story is just a great blend of many things I wanted to execute.[55]

Anthologies provide an outlet for short filmmakers to pool resources and execute a larger project that can reach larger audiences: there is strength in numbers. Like the horror television anthologies of the 1980s, twenty-first-century horror anthologies have provided opportunities for amateur directors to be a part of a larger film project. Even Caroline Kennedy, daughter of John Fitzgerald Kennedy and Jacqueline Kennedy, co-directed a segment (with Jan Bernotat) in the horror anthology film *Maldoror* (2001), which also featured segments from women directors Colette Rouhier and Veronika Dimcke.

DOCUMENTARIES

THERE ARE HUNDREDS OF long and short-form documentaries about horror movies or the paranormal. Many of them I consider "required viewing" for horror scholars and anyone interested in the work of women directors.

Joel DeMott shot all of the footage for the documentary *Demon Lover Diary* (1980), a behind-the-scenes story of the film *The Demon Lover* (1976) (also known as *The Demon Master* on VHS). DeMott was the girlfriend of cinematographer Jeff Kreines, who had been hired to shoot *The Demon Lover* by co-directors Donald G. Jackson (*Hell Comes to Frogtown*, 1988) and Jerry Younkins, and DeMott joined them on the road trip and subsequent film set to document the making of *The Demon Lover* in gritty realism. Jackson and Younkins are temperamental, bad filmmakers with no vision and no idea what they're doing. The precious truths that DeMott captured on her own camera are a testament to the power of the documentary in the horror genre. Making of documentaries would soon be common, *Demon Lover Diary* being one of the first made by a woman director.

Ever since Reba Merrill made the short documentary *The Witching Hour* (1996) as part of the official promotion of the feature horror film *The Craft* (1996), and Sarah Kelly made *Full Tilt Boogie* (1997) which details the making of the horror film *From Dusk till Dawn* (1997), women directors have been heavily involved in making documentaries about horror films and television series commissioned by the studios as special features content on their DVD releases. Some women directors have made entire careers out of chronicling the history of horror filmmaking, like Michelle Palmer (also sometimes credited as Michelle Palmierro); since the early 2000s, she has directed behind-the-scenes films for the DVD releases of the horror movies *Bones* (2002) (*Diggin' Up Bones,* 2002), *Final Destination 2* (2003) (*The Terror Gauge*, 2003), *Jason X* (2002) (*By Any Means Necessary: The Making of 'Jason X,'* 2002), and *The Texas Chainsaw Massacre* remake (2003) (*Ed Gein: The Ghoul of Plainfield*, 2004). Sarah Elbert, the producer of all Hatchet films, including *Victor Crowley* (2018), documented behind-the-scenes 'making of' featurettes for every single movie in the series over a roughly fifteen-year period. Julie Ng documented the horror movies *Final Destination 3* (2006), *The Black Christmas* remake (2006), and the 2018 reboot of *The X-Files* television series (*Implanted Memories: 25 Years of the X-Files*, 2018), among many others. This documentary filmmaking is a godsend to future researchers writing about these films and to horror fans who can enjoy the movie and how it was made.

Naomi Holwill is a prolific documentarian whose individual works include *Brain Food: Analysing Late Day Fulci* (2018) on the Blu-ray restored release of Lucio Fulci's *A Cat in the Brain* (1990) and *Jorge Grau: Catalonia's Cult Film King* (2020), which was shot right before Grau passed away and was released on the restored Blu-ray edition of his horror movie *Living Dead at Manchester Morgue* (1974). *You're Invited: The Making of Night of the Demons* (2014) by director Aine Leicht and *Christopher Lee: A Legacy of Horror and Terror* (2010) by director A. Susan Svehla are other examples of the 'making of' documentation, the effects of which won't be fully felt for another few decades when new generations of horror fans find they can easily access the stories of their favorite horror movies from the twenty-first century onward in ways that are lost to films made before DVD special features. In the case of low-budget independent releases of the early 2000s that are out of print or hard to find, such as those by director Robin Garrels, documentaries like *Rehab: The Post-Production of 'China White Serpentine'* (2004) by director Jessie Seitz may be the only record we have of how some of these movies were made.

Other women horror documentarians make full feature-length horror movies chronicling a specific aspect of the horror genre. Sarah Appleton, co-director of *The Found Footage Phenomenon* (2021), a documentary about how found footage horror films like *The Blair Witch Project* (1999) and *REC* (2007) came to dominate early twenty-first-century horror culture, believes that fans of horror fiction are also fans of horror fact and history:[56]

> The audience for horror docs seems to be the same audience as is for horror fiction. These people are often fascinated by how the horror film is made, and I'd imagine it has something to do with the way horror films stay with you. Most people started watching horror from a young age, and these curious stories get people wondering how and why did someone come up with this monster.[57]

The *Found Footage Phenomenon* documentary began as a special feature for the Blu-ray release of the found footage horror movie *Lake Mungo* (2008) and turned into a much larger project.

Ashley Fester's *Celluloid Horror* (2004) is one of the most intense and exciting documentaries about horror films that I have ever seen. Long before I actually met Kier-

La Janisse, the director of *Woodlands Dark and Days Bewitched: A History of Folk Horror* (2021), I saw the documentary film *Celluloid Horror* which was about Janisse and her horror film festival CineMuerte (1999-2005) that Fester made over the course of seven years. Taking sixty hours of footage from seven years of following Janisse as she created, programmed, and attended the CineMuerte Film Festival into only ninety minutes of story still couldn't prevent the film from having an extremely personal and touching, nuanced portrayal of a dedicated film fan and programmer who accomplished extraordinary things by sheer will and effort. "When I started CineMuerte," said Janisse,

> I had no idea what I was doing. I'd barely even been to a film festival before. I started the festival with my student loan. I still haven't finished paying back the student loan. But I like to think that people have benefited more culturally from this transgression than if I'd finished that Medieval Studies degree.[58]

It's a documentary about horror in that Janisse is a horror fan, but it's also about dedication, determination, and, honestly, Janisse as a person. The documentary gets very personal, going into Janisse's childhood, marriage, and dissolution. Janisse openly wrote about personal topics in her 2011 non-fiction book about horror movies *House of Psychotic Women*, and that, along with *Celluloid Horror,* provides a beautiful insight into the mind of one of the most influential curators and historians of horror's most artistic films. Fester herself would devote years to making the documentary, which first played at the Fantasia Film Festival in Montreal in 2003. In 2007, she finally acquired distribution for the film.

Fester believes that one of the essential things *Celluloid Horror* does for horror fans is that it introduces them to movies they may not have ever heard about in North America: "The film exposes audiences to a history of horror from a European perspective," she said. Many of the filmmakers that are celebrated at CineMuerte are not mainstream Hollywood filmmakers. Janisse has an intellectual and artistic sensibility that horror fans exposed only to studio horror movies will not have; *Celluloid Horror* introduces those films to horror fans in the course of telling Janisse's story of navigating a strange new world of film festivals, grant funding, distributors, and the press. Fester herself is a narrative horror filmmaker with several award-winning genre films on her resume as a director, but making *Celluloid Horror* was transformative for her in many ways. "You get addicted to documentaries," she said. "You start filming everything."[59]

It Came from Kuchar (2009), directed by Jennifer M. Kroot, is a fascinating look at the relatively unknown low-budget horror films of George and Mike Kuchar, members of the 1960s New York City underground film scene. Kroot first met George Kuchar when she was a young film student at the San Francisco Art Institute, where he taught, and took one of his film classes. With his brother Mike, he made films that influenced filmmakers like Guy Maddin, John Waters, and Atom Egoyan. "I had always sort of fantasized about making a film about him mostly because I could never describe how insane the class was or how funny and charismatic he is and the inspiration he is as a teacher," said Kroot when asked why she made this documentary. "When I learned about all these more mainstream characters that he influenced, it seemed like an idea I really wanted to pursue."[60]

Director Jennifer M. Kroot with George and Mike Kuchar on the set of the documentary It *Came From Kuchar* (2009). Photo credit: Patrick Siemer.

I Am Nancy (2011) is a feature-length documentary directed by Arlene Marechal about Heather Langenkamp and how playing the role of "Nancy" in the *Nightmare on Elm Street* movie franchise transformed her life. Over two years, Marechal follows Langenkamp to horror conventions and speaks to horror fans about the character of Nancy and what she means to them. She talks to the franchise's creator Wes Craven and asks questions about Nancy's appeal compared to Freddy Krueger's. When Langenkamp was asked to compare *I Am Nancy* to another documentary about the *Nightmare on Elm Street* series that she had recently been in, *Never Sleep Again* (2010) from Daniel Farrands and Andrew Kasch, she said,

> It's so much more of an autobiography of my character Nancy and me. It's much more of a personal project. I've always felt it was as if I wrote a diary of what it's like to be me on a weekend at a convention.[61]

Director Trish Geiger was inspired to make *Beast Wishes* (2012), the documentary about Bob and Kathy Burns, a couple who have a long history of collecting horror movie props and involvement in classic and iconic horror movies, after meeting Kathy Burns while making a behind-the-scenes featurette shoot for the Larry Blamire horror comedy film *Dark and Stormy Night* (2009). Directors Frank Dietz and Geiger interviewed Bob in the Burns' legendary basement filled with rare and priceless science fiction, horror, and fantasy film and television props and artwork for the special features section of the film's release. Dietz interviewed Bob while Geiger worked the camera, and Kathy Burns sat off-camera quietly. "I'd notice her smiling and listening," said Geiger:

> I turned the camera on Kathy, and she said something like, "It's the creative spark

> that I love. When like-minded people come together, the creative spark explodes into something wonderful." It was at that moment that I thought the story of these two would be a great documentary. I thought everyone would like to know Bob and Kathy ... I wanted to make a film about two creative people that were not afraid to be who they truly are and shared that love freely with others.[62]

In 2010, filmmaker Penny Vozniak was on her way to Kabul for a directing job when she visited an old producer friend in India. He was frustrated by a new project he was working on—a multi-million dollar fantasy horror movie called *Hisss* (2010) that Jennifer Lynch was directing. Lynch's twelve-year-old daughter was on set with the crew, and he needed someone to watch her. He begged Vozniak to do it. She relented. She was so fascinated by Lynch and her daughter Sydney that she stayed on the set for eight months and decided to document the film production instead of taking the job in Kabul. Lynch was making a hybrid horror fantasy Bollywood film about a woman who can turn into a snake. The production, unfortunately, went wrong in many ways, becoming a nightmare for Lynch and everyone involved. "Anything that can go wrong on a film set goes wrong," said Vozniak:

"In the course of that, Jennifer has a fascinating personal breakdown and a series of personal breakthroughs along the journey."[63]

After filming more than two hundred hours of footage, Vozniak spent eight months editing it into a cohesive, narrative documentary called *Despite the Gods* (2012). "Who knows how the fuck it'll turn out," says Lynch in the documentary, speaking of the horror movie *Hisss*. "No biggie. It's only my third, and hopefully not last, film," says Lynch in the film while dealing with a frustrating day on the set of the movie. *Hisss* didn't turn out very well, but thanks to Vozniak, we have a meticulous record of a woman director making a horror movie, which is priceless to me. "It's just so absurd. I'm making a movie about a fucking snake that turns into a woman that turns into a snake," says Lynch in the film.

There are broader, more general documentaries about horror, such as Johanna Salomäki's *Into the Dark: Exploring the Horror Film* (2008), Ursula Macfarlane's television miniseries "A-Z of Horror" (1997), and Katharina Klewinghaus's *Science of Horror* (2008), and ones that focus on specific geographical areas, like *Something Wicked This Way Comes* (2018) directed by Stacy Buchanan and Jessica Barnthouse, which is only about horror filmmakers in the New England area of the United States. Some documentaries directed by women explore the darkest aspects of horror culture. Jessie Seitz (*Devotion*, 2017) directed *Beyond Horror: The History and Sub-Culture of Red Films* (2020); red films are movies too extreme to be distributed in the mainstream entertainment world and usually pass hands as bootleg copies to bypass censors. Underground filmmaker Heidi Moore (*Dolly Deadly*, 2016) made the documentary *More Blood!* (2018) to explore why people like watching horror and gore in movies. It goes "beyond horror," she said in an interview, to explore ideas of death in general with those that consume horror movie media,

> So I think it's for anyone who ever wondered why watching death and gore is so entertaining. It's fun to realize it's everywhere, and to put some thought into how

something like that could be funny, cool, exciting, therapeutic, etc. In retrospect, it seems so dark, but the world isn't black and white.[64]

Kier-La Janisse made her feature directorial debut with the documentary *Woodlands Dark and Days Bewitched: A History of Folk Horror*, one of the most heavily promoted horror films of 2021. After it premiered at the South By Southwest film and music festival in Austin, Texas, that year, it was recognized immediately as an essential contribution to an ill-defined horror movie subgenre. Like Appleton's *The Found Footage Phenomenon*, Janisse's film began as a short featurette for the *Blood on Satan's Claw* (1971) Blu-ray release from distributor Severin, and from there spiraled into a three-hour movie documentary. At first, she only planned on interviewing six people for the featurette. "But what would inevitably happen every time I interview somebody was that they would bring up something I hadn't thought about," said Janisse:

> And that would then make me go, "Okay. I just need to interview one more person who's an expert in that particular thing so that I have somebody to be the transition between these two ideas," you know? So that it makes sense ... Just filling in to make these things—these ideas—fit together. That just kept happening for, like, three years, where ... everybody I interviewed was so amazing, but they would always bring up ideas or perspectives I hadn't thought of. Then that would lead to another month of research ... [65]

Janisse was also involved in the short featurette *Celia & Me* (2021), directed by Briony Kidd. Janisse commissioned it from Kidd for *All the Haunts Be Ours: A Compendium of Folk Horror* Blu-ray box set released by Severin Films, which contains Ann Turner's horror fantasy movie *Celia* (1989). Kidd, an Australian filmmaker like Turner, screened *Celia* in 2014 at the Stranger With My Face Film Festival. Kidd knew Turner from film school, where she had been a lecturer when Kidd was a student. The short *Celia & Me* is a recorded interview with Turner about making *Celia* and how it fits into the subgenre of folk horror.

Though I've heard people say otherwise for the last decade (2010 through 2020), there are more than several documentary films made by women about women in horror and women horror filmmakers. In 2009, three documentaries about women in horror were released: *Pretty Bloody: the Women of Horror*, directed by Donna Davies, *Bloody Breasts,* directed by Maude Michaud, and *Welcome to My Dark Side — Women in Horror,* by Reyna Young. *Pretty Bloody: the Women of Horror* was commissioned from television documentarian Davies by Canadian cable network Space and aired on television.

Bloody Breasts is a web-based documentary series made independently by horror filmmaker Maude Michaud (*Dys-*, 2014), inspired by her time in academia and the idea that feminism and horror movies are not compatible. She made *Bloody Breasts* counter that assumption, wanting to profile various feminists working actively in the horror film industries. *Welcome to My Dark Side — Women in Horror* is also an independent production. Filmmaker Reyna Young (*Forgotten Tales*, 2016) explores the general enthusiasm some women have for all things horror. In 2010, horror filmmaker

Belinda Green-Smith released *Women in Horror*, an hour-long documentary about women in horror movies, both behind and in front of the camera. Amy Lynn Best made a pseudo-documentary called *Spicy Sisters Slumber Party* (2004). It was shot in a hotel room at a horror convention with low-budget horror movie actresses discussing their opinions on independent horror. In 2022, Vancouver filmmaker Becca Kozack released a documentary titled *Girls with Guts*, focusing only on women horror filmmakers from the Vancouver area, including Gigi Saul Guerrero.

Ever since true crime and paranormal television series became popular in the early 2000s, numerous horror documentaries about real life and supernatural events have been made by women directors. I believe it was co-director Barbara Brancaccio's 2009 true crime film *Cropsey* that was the first to be marketed as a horror movie to horror fans. *Cropsey* combines local urban legends with a series of real-life disappearances in the filmmaker's local Staten Island community. Women directors would make documentaries about the paranormal while also making narrative horror films; this mixing of the paranormal and true crime documentary into the horror genre became very prevalent in the 2000s and 2010s. Belinda Nicole Bentley directed the paranormal web series *Belinda Bentley's Raw Fear* (2007). It was about her psychic abilities, the afterlife, and ghosts in the context of horror. Kalila Katherina Smith's *Journey into Darkness* (2003) is based on her book *Journey into Darkness ... Ghosts & Vampires of New Orleans,* which recounts her experiences running New Orleans Haunted History Tours, including stories about ghosts, vampires, and voodoo. The usual stories come up: hotels, tragic fires, and lost loves that walk the streets of New Orleans searching for a reprieve from their haunting. Vampire tales about legends roaming the city streets searching for new victims to bleed. Cemetery visits to the grave of Marie Laveaux, the Voodoo Queen of nineteenth-century New Orleans, coffee shop stops under haunted hotels, and wispy "proof" of the supernatural phenomenon are just a few of the touches. "After working extensively with television crews, I decided to write and direct my own documentary using my experiences and stories from my book," explained Smith,

> Not only did I develop a passion for filming, but the work turned out so well. Future shows used my footage rather than shoot their own reenactments for the stories. I had always been a horror fan and had hoped at some point to write horror fiction, but loved filming so much decided I'd rather make movies than write novels.[66]

Another example of true crime documentary marketed towards horror fans is Michelle Palmer's *Ed Gein: The Ghoul of Plainfield* (2004). Palmer makes sure to delve into how Gein was sensationalized in comic books like *Tales from the Crypt* and films like *Psycho, The Texas Chainsaw Massacre*, and *The Silence of the Lambs*. Likewise, horror and true crime combine in the short horror documentary *Suicide Bridge* (2003), co-directed by Misty B. Beck. "Suicide Bridge" refers to the nickname of the Colorado St. Bridge in Pasadena, California (a suburb of Los Angeles), which it received after being the site of numerous suicides. Misty Beck, the film's producer and director made the film because she experienced something chilling as she crossed the bridge one night. With the insights of psychic Peter James (famous for his insights into the spirits aboard The Queen Mary in Long Beach, California), the short film traces the lives that were lost on the Colorado St. Bridge by conducting fact-based and first-person accounts from the police department, Pasadena residents, near-victims, and eyewitnesses to crimes and suicides on the bridge and combining it with unprovable urban legends and psychic phenomenon. A historical account of the known (and unknown) deaths from 1913 to the present and psychic musings combines history and horror stories. Documentary horror is journalism; it's a chronicle of the horror film industry, the changing nature of horror movies, and the preservation of stories and struggles that otherwise would be lost behind the polished, finished product of a narrative film. Blood, sweat, and tears are essential pieces of the horror film genre that I hope continues throughout the century.

ANIMATED HORROR

WOMEN DIRECT HORROR ANIMATION commercially and independently, traditionally and experimentally, using mainstream and alternative animation methods. We talked about animators Claire Parker, Mary Ellen Bute, and Joan Foldes in Chapter 1, Caroline Leaf in Chapter 3, and Russian animation in Chapter 4. Irish animator Jean Mathieson co-directed two animated television horror films for the BBC with Al Guest: *Ghost Stories* (1987) and *The Phantom of the Opera* (1988). *Ghost Stories* is an adaptation of Charles Dickens' "Ghost Stories" from *The Pickwick Papers* and features several shorter stories in an anthology. Although very close in the narrative to the original novel by Gaston Leroux, *The Phantom of the Opera* has clunky animation and is relatively unknown to horror fans.

Amber Benson's animated BBC series *Ghosts of Albion: Legacy* (2003) and Sharon Bridgeman's movie prequel *Van Helsing: The London Assignment* (2004) both use traditional forms of animation. *Ghosts of Albion* employs a comic book-style art design by animation studio Cosgrove Hall while the Japanese anime format heavily influences *Van Helsing*. *Ghosts of Albion* is set in an alternate London in 1838 and follows two heroes who use magic as they save the world from demons with the help of the ghosts of Queen Boadicea, Lord Byron, and Admiral Lord Nelson. *Van Helsing* is a prequel to the 2004 Universal live-action *Van Helsing* film in which Van Helsing (voiced by Hugh Jackman, who plays him in the live-action version) travels to London to battle Dr. Jekyll's evil alter-ego, Mr. Hyde, as Jack the Ripper interferes. Benson had never worked in animation before or since, but she had directed the live-action science fiction comedy *Drones* (2011) and the short horror film *Shevenge* (2015). Bridgeman has worked in the Art Department on dozens of animated feature films. In 2021, Bridgeman joined Spire Animation, a company created to make animated films with diversity and gender equality in mind.[67]

In 2004, animator Jennifer Shiman created a series called *30-Second Bunnies Theatre,* in which animated rabbits would reenact critical scenes from famous films in only thirty seconds. In 2004, she debuted the series with a thirty-second version of *The Exorcist,* reenacted by bunnies, which caught the attention of distributor Starz!, who commissioned episodes in 2005. The series would continue through 2016 with numerous horror movie episodes, including *The Shining* (2004), *Hellraiser* (2004), and *Cannibal Holocaust* (2015). Shiman won a Webby Award in 2008, but in 2015, after making sixty-eight episodes, many of them horror movie parodies, Shiman ended the series and was ready to move on to different projects.[68] It was also in 2004 that Ann-Marie Denham's short animated horror comedy *Frankenchicken* (2004) came out in film festivals; the short is told from the point of view of a chicken made of patchwork body parts that have been created to make chicken nuggets.

Animator Marie Caillou contributed a segment to the French horror animation feature *Peur(s) du noir,* AKA *Fear(s) of the Dark* (2007), which is comprised of six horror-themed black-and-white animated segments. Caillou doesn't have an individual title, but the clean, Japanese-influenced art style stands out from the sketchy and chaotic art of the other artists. In Caillou's segment, a little girl lives in an insane asylum. She constantly relives a nightmare sequence where she encounters a multi-eyed snake demon woman and various preserved heads in jars in a laboratory setting. Caillou was invited to a residency/fellowship at the Maison des Auteurs (the House of Authors) in Angoulême, where she animated the sequence for the movie. The IFC label in North America distributed the movie.

While women directing in mainstream animated horror has been limited (because mainstream horror itself does not exist in animation), experimental, independent horror animation has thrived. Martha Colburn, an experimental artist and animator, uses horror imagery in her short films because she feels that animation can "illustrate those things impossible for the human eye to see. In my case, that includes the imagination."[69]

Colburn's short horror film *Evil of Dracula* (1997) is a collection of images from advertisements in the 1960s and 1970s with smiling women. "The women in these ads appeared to me as the dead searching for the dead,"[70] she said. She painted over the ads to transform the women into vampires, created "filters" (acetate sheets painted with spirals/ blood drops) to place over them, and had musician Jad Fair (from the band Half Japanese) record a hypnotic, aggressive pop song called "The Evil of Dracula" which played over the animated images to create "a mad consumer vampiric world."

Her next horror film is *Spiders in Love: An Arachnogasmic Musical* (1999). Colburn heard a record from the early 1980s with a song about spiders being in love. She sought out one of the band members in Holland, who said that he was a professional clown and wanted "nothing to do with avant-garde music ever again" and allowed her to use the music freely. The film has images of creatures that are half-glamour models and half-spider that dance in crazy routines, eat candy, and spin and weave. She watched many Busby Berkeley films and studied spider behavior to get the look and vibe she wanted. "Collecting piles of spider books and pornography, my work area resembled *The Island of Doctor Moreau*," said Colburn.[71]

Skelehellavision (2003) contains meticulous detail and showcases Colburn's obsession with it. A film initially set to be about the afterlife, it mixes sexual and death imagery and characters functioning in an imaginary landscape. She hand-scratched hundreds of tiny skeletons over strips of discarded pornography film strips she'd found. She created the

The H.P. Lovecraft story of the same name gets the claymation treatment in *Die Musik des Erich Zann* (2006), directed by Anna Gawrilow.

soundtrack from different music she'd composed and removed the images from both the horror and the pornography world, so they exist in a kind of nether-realm. "Much of my work comments on popular culture, consumerism, politics, and sexuality," said Colburn.

> Though they sometimes contain the symbolism of the conventional horror genre, they are personal horrors that I wish to rid myself of, visualize, and exorcise somehow. My 'horrors' resonate with others, I think, on some level, because I focus (usually) on contemporary topics. Interwoven themes of duality surface in my films, many of which I never consciously conceived of. Beauty and ugliness, horror and humor, disgust and pleasure: all of which are themes in the horror genre.[72]

Another form of animation that horror directors have used is stop-motion animation, or claymation, in which clay or other objects are animated motion-by-motion in the camera to create the illusion of movement. Czech animator Vlasta Pospíšilová directed the animated fantasy horror films *O Marysce a Vlcím hrádku* (1979) and *Fimfárum Jana Wericha* (2002). *O Marysce a Vlcím hrádku,* set in a fantasy world with haunted castles and princesses, was made with stop-motion animated clay figures, as is *Fimfárum Jana Wericha.*

Inspired by the horror claymation Rankin/Bass parody film *Mad Monster Party* (1967), in which Dracula, Frankenstein, the Mummy, and other horror characters from pop culture interact, Brazilian artists Eliana Fonseca and Cao Hamburger co-directed the short stop-motion horror parody *Frankenstein Punk* (1986) in which Frankenstein searches for happiness. When he finds it, he dances to the song "Singin' in the Rain."

German animator Anna Gawrilow wrote, directed, and animated the H.P. Lovecraft short film adaptation *The Music of Erich Zann* (2005). *The Music of Erich Zann* was her film school thesis project at Bauhaus University in Weimar, Germany. She needed a short story with only two characters that included music and a horror element. A friend who had recently read Lovecraft's short story *The Music of Erich Zann* (1921) suggested it to her. She loved it. "I was very excited about this story because I associated at the first read a lot of interesting problems with this character, and it is a truly mysterious story," said Gawrilow.[73] In the story, otherworldly music from a cello breaks the line between our world and that of another dimension filled with horrible creatures.

Gawrilow grew up in East Germany. Her childhood was dominated by Eastern European children's series, including one called *Unser Sandmännchen*, in which slightly-animated puppets would showcase amazing socialist inventions that didn't exist, such as flying cars. The Sandman would put sleepy sand in the children's eyes to make them fall asleep. When she saw *Clash of the Titans* (1981), she was only four and was in awe of Harryhausen's work but scared by the snake-haired monster Medusa. "I didn't realize that it was not a real person," she said,

> Twenty years later, I was amazed to see that this ugly woman that caused me a lot of nightmares when I was a little girl wasn't anything else than my favorite project these times: Stop Motion Animation.[74]

Sofia Carrillo is a Mexican animator from Guadalajara whose short films are tinged with an unearthly and unsettling type of slow-breathing horror. *Prita Noire* (2011) is the first short film of Carrillo's that I saw, and it's breathtaking. A combination of live-action and stop-motion, it's a surreal story of a woman whose tinier sister controls her life; the sisters live in a dark fantasy world of horror imagery. Carrillo was chosen to create the wraparound and title sequences for the horror film anthology *XX* (2017), which we mentioned earlier in Chapter 8. Again, those segments use childlike and found object footage mixed with animation to create a genuinely unsettling, experimental setting. Asked by *XX* producer Todd Brown to use a dollhouse in her animation, Carrillo was given that and only a brief logline from the other segments. "I have this obsession with the 'hidden energy' of objects," explained Carrillo,

> Since creating my short film *The Sad House [La Casa Triste*], that energy that goes from the person to their objects. When objects survive their owners, what happens then with those beloved belongings? The answer became almost natural to provide life to the dollhouse. This house is kind of lost and sad, without her master, walking around an old house searching for something and finding it in the tiny doors to other worlds, the live-action worlds. I wanted to make it very feminine, mysterious.[75]

Like Carrillo, Isabel Peppard is known as a great woman stop-motion horror director. Also, like Carrillo, Peppard uses Gothic imagery, fairy tale narratives, and handmade and symbolic elements to "tell humane stories of existential horror and personal transformation.[76]" Her two short animated works, *Gloomy Valentine* (2006) and *Butterflies* (2012), both tend towards the absurdist more than Carrillo's work and are more energetic and less haunted. But they're creepy, nonetheless. *Gloomy Valentine* appears in the anthology horror film *Dark*

Time and space have no bounds in the horrifying world created by animator Sofia Carrillo in her short film *Prita Noire* (2011).

Animated gore in Lauren Marie Morrison's short animated horror film *Viscera* (2014).

Whispers, discussed earlier in Chapter 8. "...from an early age, I was inspired by Japanese Fairy Tales, ghosts and demons," recalled Peppard in an interview,

> I remember being initially terrified by the monstrous temple guardians or 'Nio' that stood at the temple gates in our hometown of Kamakura. This fear started to become a fascination, and at some point, I stopped being afraid and started emulating them ... I'm pretty sure that this is where my love of and kinship with horror and dark surrealism began.[77]

Laura Whyte's master's thesis film *Nursery Crimes* (2010), in which a stop-motion Little Bo Peep embarks on a murderous rampage when she cracks from the pressure of herding sheep, and Lauren Morrison's master's thesis film *Viscera* (2015), which is about a creepy little girl, monsters in the walls, and moving food, both stand out as extraordinary examples of modern stop-motion animated horror. Whyte's is more whimsical and sick, whereas *Viscera* is disturbing on a more emotionally traumatic level. "Mostly, I just have a twisted sense of humor, and I won't apologize for it," said Whyte in an interview.[78] Sophie Lagues' animated short *Barbee Butcher* (2009) is only twenty-five seconds long and much more crudely animated. Still, its depiction of a green clay monster chopping off Barbie's limbs and sticking them onto itself is marvelously effective.

The only feature-length, fully stop-motion animated horror movie directed by a woman is the fantasy story *Blood Tea and Red String* (2006) from animator Christiane Cegavske. It took Cegavske thirteen years to design, animate, edit, and complete it. Painstakingly animating each sequence by hand, Cegavske is an artist with a savage passion. Red-eyed white mice dressed in velvet and lace, The Creatures Who Dwell Under the Oak (some strange cross between foxes, birds, and weasels), skull-headed ravens, and a hand-sewn doll with an egg sewn inside of her inhabit a bizarre fairy tale world that is unsettling and otherworldly. *Blood Tea and Red String* is a groundbreaking example of surrealism in modern fairy tales and a testament to the dedication of the driven female visionary embodied by Cegavske.

It's an unsettling film, a modern interpretation of Victorian children's horror. There's a

The bird rips its way through the doll's torso in Christiane Cegavske's stopmotion feature horror/fantasy *Blood Tea and Red String* (2006).

distinct emphasis on drug use, intoxication, and obsessive misguided love and jealousy. The chilling score by Mark Growden adds to the horror of *Blood Tea and Red String* with its harsh tones. It is one of those once-in-a-lifetime films: something that comes along so incredible and awe-inspiring that it breathes new life into decrepit subgenres. Cegavske's second animated feature, *Seed in the Sand*, is set in the same dreamland. In this story, creatures called The Nest Dwellers must cross a sandy desert to find trees with leaves while they're haunted by images of dolls on a dark ocean. *Seed in the Sand* is currently in production at the time of the writing of this book and is a spiritual sequel to *Blood Tea and Red String* and may be followed by a third film: "There is an element that transforms from beginning to end that is passed to the next film," explained Cegavske,

> In *Blood Tea and Red String*, an egg is sent into the animated world and returns to the live-action world as a large golden gem. It is that gem that is sent into the animated world of Seed in the Sand by the live-action masked woman, and it will be transmuted, returning to the live-action world as something new at the end that will be useful in the beginning of the third film.[79]

HORROR PORNOGRAPHY

WOMEN HAVE BEEN MAKING erotica and pornography since the beginning of film (that's another book). In the 1960s and 1970s, Doris Wishman and Roberta Findlay, both included in Chapter 3, made soft-core and hardcore thriller and horror films before shifting to directing pure horror movies. Roberta Findlay's *A Woman's Torment* (1977) and Doris Wishman's *Come with Me, My Love* (1976), AKA *The Haunted Pussy* and *Satan was a Lady* (1975), are hardcore pornography. *Baise-Moi* (2000), which we discussed in Chapter 7 when we talked about French Extremity films, is the result of two pornography actresses who decided to make a horror/thriller film depicting real sex and violence. In the twenty-first century, women are still making horror pornography as directors. Some are inspired by mainstream horror movies like Jane Waters' *The Coven 2* (1993) and Lizzy Borden's *Cannibalism* (2002), and *Creature Feature* (2010), but pornography parodies are usually the way horror seeps its way into pornography. Just a few of my favorite hardcore horror film parody titles include Cybil Richards' *The Exotic House of Wax* (1997), Skye Blue's *Spankenstein* (1998), Véronique Lefay's *Le Projet Blair Bitch* (1998), Anastasia's *The Pervert Witch Project* (2000), Zenova Braeden's *The Taunting* (2007), and my favorite horror pornography director, Joanna Angel's films *Fuckenstein* (2012), *The Walking Dead: A Hardcore Parody* (2013), *The Craft XXX: Welcome to the Dicking Hour* (2014), and *I Know Who You Fucked Last Halloween* (2018). Sebrina Bedard is a prolific pornography director who uses horror themes and imagery in her work. Most of her films as director feature women in dangerous situations in which they are tortured, raped, and sometimes murdered as part of the narrative. In 2013 alone, she directed eight adult films involving women being hurt or killed by slashers, killers, rapists, stalkers, professional criminals, and johns: *Witness Protection Breakdown*, *Escort Erased*, *Deadly Dreams*, *Doomed Dom*, *Last Night Forever*, *Hitman Cumeth*, *The Reporter*, and *She Picked the Wrong Guy*.

Joanna Angel first started taking directorial control over her horror pornography movies in 2009 when she made the short hardcore film *Dong of the Dead* (2009), in which she also stars. In 2007 she directed a segment of the interactive horror video game *Slumber Party Slaughterhouse* (2008), which is not a hardcore film; it starred mainstream horror actresses Tiffany Shepis-Tretta and Masuimi Max, who have never appeared in pornography films. *Slumber Party Slaughterhouse* is an interactive film about a geek named Paul Tard who is killed on the night of his high school graduation; selling his soul to Satan, he gets the power to exact revenge on his former friends while they are at a massive party with hookers and drugs. The game aspect was that every time Paul wanted to kill one of his friends, the demon would ask the viewer a horror movie trivia question from a multiple-choice menu. If the viewer gets the correct answer, the protagonist kills his friend. The wrong answer sends him back to Hell, and you must start over again. This game didn't get much traction in the horror or pornography community, but it's a great piece of art that showcases the crossover between the pornography industry and horror filmmakers.

In *Cindy Queen of Hell* (2016), a teenager finds out Satan is her father. Directed by Joanna Angel. Image courtesy of Burning Angel Films.

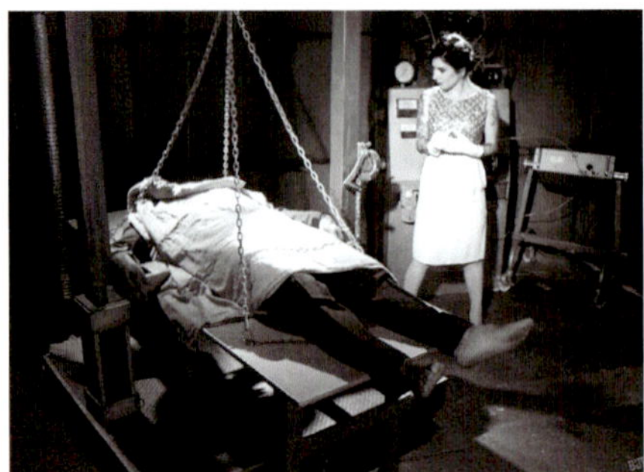

in *Fuckenstein* (2012), Angel plays the scientist's sexually unfulfilled wife. Directed by Angel. Image courtesy of Burning Angel Films.

In 2002, Angel founded her pornography website, BurningAngel.com, to compete with the popular SuicideGirls.com; both sites showcased alternative-looking models in the nude ('alternative' in this context means that they have tattoos, piercings, and often hair inspired by the punk or goth music aesthetic).[80] Angel is mainly responsible for the phenomenon of the 'alternative' hardcore pornography movement. "I think it's a movement," she told *Hustler* magazine in 2006:

> I think I've started something. I didn't know anything about the Internet. I didn't know anything about pornography. I didn't know anything about film. It was just me and my friends experimenting and doing what we wanted and seeing what happened. I think that's what punk rock is all about. It's not about doing something because it's going to sell. We didn't make a punk pornography site to cash in on some untapped market.[81]

But she did cash in on an untapped market nevertheless and has been the most successful female pornography director of probably all time. Her penchant for hardcore horror parodies is evident, as she's made eight of them. SuicideGirls.com was founded in 2001 as a community of alternative-minded people seeking to connect with others who value non-conformist examples of female beauty, and a soft-core pornography site. Website creator Missy Suicide and model photographer Sawa Suicide made *Suicide Girls Must Die* (2010), a reality show-style horror movie showing young, nude women being stalked and killed. It showcases the alternative pin-up models of SuicideGirls.com but does not include hardcore sex, only soft-core, topless-in-the-hot-tub-style sex.

Sawa Suicide directed while Missy produced. The cast features an array of tattooed, beautiful models being stalked in real-time during a photo shoot. None of the cast was in on the joke; they all thought they were participating in a creative location photo shoot. But the producers started pulling individual models to the side, letting them know they were filming a horror movie and instructing them to pretend to be murdered, scream, or get covered in blood for the other models to find. Sawa and Missy wanted their next Suicide Girls movie to be horror because "We love horror movies," said Missy in an interview,

Murder, mystery, intrigue, and lots of sex in *I Know Who You Fucked Last Halloween* (2018), directed by Angel. Image courtesy of Burning Angel Films.

In *Three Cheers for Satan* (2019), Satan hangs out at a high school in order to get sexy cheerleaders to sign away their souls. Directed by Angel. Image courtesy of Burning Angel Films.

> We love [19]80's campy horror movies, and we really wanted to do an homage to that. But you know, we can't write a horror movie, and the girls can't act, so we ended up doing this.[82]

"This" is supposed to be a routine shoot for the girls in a nice summer cabin in Maine. Still, the filmmakers orchestrated disappearances and strange encounters and did their best to terrify the women and get their natural reactions on camera. "We had done an Italian villa film prior," explained Sawa, "which worked out really well, so we decided to send these girls to a nice cabin in Maine, so they'd think they were going to a similar type of shoot."[83] When Missy and Sawa were deciding who to cast, they "did want girls who were going to enjoy it," insisted Sawa. "One of the girls, Fractal, loves horror! We wanted women who would scream and freak out when something went wrong! Girls that had an appreciation of horror or who could build a fire and had some survival skills. But we also wanted girls that we knew we would get a reaction from them." Horror filmmaker Paul Solet (*Grace*, 2009) was on set to suggest brutal ways of terrifying the models, one involving bloody sheets with "someone's blood" on them, and according to Sawa, the plot changed a bit every day because it was impossible to predict how the women would react. "A few girls had a few ideas, but no one had a clear idea of what was happening," explained Sawa,

> I think it drove them crazy that I wasn't talking to them when things were going on. I would tell them what to do and then keep silent. I had to keep a straight face and not give anything away because I was shooting it.[84]

"The naked girls are mixed in," answered Missy,

> It's funny, and it's interesting to see how people react to things in this film. It is an interesting sort of character study to see how different people react to different stresses. There are places to laugh, too. Other horror films have plenty of skimpy clothes and boobies.[85]

The promotional poster for the release of *Suicide Girls Must Die!* (2009).

The movie came and went without much fanfare, but it's a strange little piece of woman-directed sleaze core horror that Doris Wishman would have loved to have made.

PINK FILMS

'PINK FILM' IS A broad term for any sensational Japanese genre film that shows nudity and is a genre phenomenon unique to Japanese cinema with no exact Western equivalent. The closest Western terms are probably 'sexploitation' or 'erotica,' but they don't fully describe what a 'Pink' film is. Pink films materialized in March 1962 when the film *Nikutai no ichiba,* AKA *Market of Flesh,* opened in Japanese cinemas; hundreds of films would follow well into the twenty-first century despite changing social norms and the advent of modern pornography VHS and DVDs in the 1980s and 1990s. Most Pink films include elements of crime, rape, revenge, action, violence, and other thrilling narratives designed to accompany the soft-core sex and the nudity of the actors. The Western film company that seems to embody what the Pink films of Japan do is Alternative Cinema, a low-budget horror and exploitation film distributor whose catalog includes their production company Seduction Cinema's films with titles like *Satan's School for Lust* (2001), *Lustful Addiction* (2002), and *Dr. Jekyll and Mistress Hyde* (2003), all of which star erotica actress Misty Mundae (she directed *Lustful Addiction*). These films, like Pink films, are meant to titillate. They present a fantasy of sex and violence, and women direct very few. But there are some.

One of the first Pink films was directed by a woman. In 1965, Kyôko Ôgimachi's sex/crime thriller *Yakuza Geisha* came out in Japanese theaters. Ôgimachi had been an actress, appearing in almost fifty horror, exploitation, and thriller films between 1959 and 1966 before she directed *Yakuza Geisha*. It was the only film she directed, and the Japanese newspapers accused her of only pretending to have directed the movie as a publicity stunt.[86]

Sachi Hamano is the most well-known of all women Pink film directors, directing three hundred erotic and pornography films between 1972 and 2019, only one of which is a horror film: *Kageki honban: Midareru,* AKA *Drifting Into Chaos* (1989), which is a rape film inspired by the original *Texas Chainsaw Massacre*. Two young women are ambushed by a family out in the forest who then forces the women to have sex and sit next to their

Death by lightbulb in Sachi Hamano's *Drifting into Chaos* (1989).

An eerie shot of the bad guys in *Drifting Into Chaos*.

demented, disabled old grandfather. After being sexually abused for nearly an hour, the two girls murder their captors and escape. It's a ruthless film with simulated rape and forced sex acts highly depraved by most mainstream standards. The women are abused and used; even though they have revenge upon their abusers at the end and escape, the entire film is a rape fantasy that deliberately degrades the two main characters. Hamano disagrees with me; she believes that her films showcase women in ways Pink films directed by men don't, for instance, in the way the main characters in *Kageki honban: Midareru* manage to kill the antagonists:

> A pink film is all about fulfilling the distorted desires of men, so the sexuality is only perceived from the male point of view; so, for instance, if a woman has been raped, she has to appear like she's having a good time straight after, and obviously that's not the reality. Male directors always use the same line when they shoot a rape scene—the male character always says something like this at the end: "Oh, you hated it before, but five minutes later, you're having a good time." So I decided that I really wanted to turn that around so that women would not be sex objects for men.[87]

When she first started making Pink films at age twenty-one, Hamano reluctantly changed her first name from Sachiko to Sachi so no one would know that she was a woman:

> At that time, if men saw a woman director's name on the poster of a Pink movie, they were not going to get excited. They would go, "Woman director, I'm not going to watch it."[88]

In 1998, Hamano made her first mainstream, non-Pink film and would continue to make commercial films through 2021. She decided to do this in 1997 when, at the Tokyo International Women's Film Festival, director Kinuyo Tanaka was said to be the Japanese woman director who had made the most films. Tanaka had only made six films while Hamano had made hundreds, and Hamano realized that nobody mentioned her because "Pink film doesn't count," she said,

> Up until then, I really enjoyed shooting Pink films, but I realized that if I kept making only Pink movies, nobody would ever know about me, and I couldn't actually call myself a woman director. That's why I had to make at least one normal movie.[89]

Rumi Tama, an actress for the Pink film studio Nikkatsu as well as a pornography director for the studio Shintoho, made the rape/revenge horror/thriller Pink film *Joshigakusei: Karenna Ikenie,* AKA *College Girl: Pretty Sacrifice* (1983) through the Pink film production company Million Films. This is the first rape/revenge film directed by a woman to come out of Japan. A college girl (played by Kyoko Hibiki) is raped by her father and her professor. She seeks vengeance for these unjust, misogynistic violations in gruesome, horror-film ways.[90] *Seikan zenkai onna* (1986) was a Pink film directed by erotic actress Keiko Arisugawa. The title translates into English roughly as *The Last Surviving Woman*. It was the only film directed by Arisugawa.

In the twenty-first century, Yumi Yoshiyuki is directing Pink films. She's an actress and a prolific director, having made hundreds of films since 1993, many of which have genre elements. Yoshiyuki directed the erotic horror movies *Shinkon tsuma no seiyoku: Motomeru shiroi hada* (2012) and *Uwakizuma: Shinshitsu no nozoki ana* (2015) as well as the romantic mainstream horror movie *Mayonaka kimi wa kiba o muke,* AKA *Midnight Screening with the Vampire* (2014).

EXPERIMENTAL HORROR

GERMAINE DULAC'S *THE SEASHELL and the Clergyman* (1927) and Maya Deren's *Meshes of the Afternoon* (1943), covered in Chapter 1, influenced so many women horror filmmakers over the last century. From Valie Export (mentioned in Chapter 4) to Christina Hornisher (Chapter 3), the influences of experimental and surreal filmmaking techniques are in every horror movie to a greater or more significant extent. When the Internet became available to the general populace, many previously-unseen shorts were digitized and put online, and many new experimental shorts were made because they could now be shared easily online. Cecelia Condit's 1983 experimental horror movie *Possibly in Michigan* became a viral sensation in 2015 on social media when the public rediscovered it in digital form; its uncanny, creepy story of two women stalked by a slasher is accompanied by uncomfortable music and sing-song musical lyrics that are entirely at odds with the masked man holding a knife, waiting to kill them as they wander around the local mall, unaware of their danger.[91]

Instead of focusing on all surreal horror movies directed by women, which I could write an entire other book about, I'd like to include a few films that are seriously influenced by the work of Deren and Dulac in style and substance.

The first experimental horror film that I saw in the twenty-first century was Alison Maclean's *Kitchen Sink* (1989). Alison Maclean began what would become a mainstream directing career with this skillful 35mm, black-and-white short about grief, rejection, and love. In 1989, *Kitchen Sink* made its way through film festivals but never into the eyes of the general public through distribution; it was elusive to horror fans until its re-release on the official DVD of the 1992 thriller film *Crush*, which Maclean directed.

In the film, a woman (Theresa Healey) finds a trail of gunk sticking up out of her garbage disposal one day while doing the dishes. Naturally, she pulls on the thread, and a pile of slop emits itself from the reaches of her disposal pipes. The nasty stuff increases in size until, finally, a creature steps out of the sink. The woman, glad to be rid of it, immediately throws the ugly thing into the garbage. As a few moments pass, she reconsiders. Perhaps all the gunk monster needs is a little cleaning up. While it is in the bathtub, we see a fundamental transformation. While the monster is still covered in gunk, it is a human figure. A little shaving action with the razor does the trick, and soon what the woman has in front of her is not a monster at all but an attractive man (Peter Tait). The woman, however, is still unsettled, even when her creature becomes a man, and she chooses not to be intimate with her conception and to destroy it instead.

This twelve-minute short is all about one woman's fear of intimacy; the protagonist is only able to tolerate the creature once she fashions it into what she believes it ought to be, and once she has it, she rejects her feelings for it and relegates it to less-than-human in order to alleviate her guilt at its death. There is almost no dialogue in the movie, but *Kitchen Sink*'s emotional impact about fear and passion in close relationships is pretty moving. *Kitchen Sink* was nominated for the Cannes Film Festival's Palme d'Or for Best Short Film in 1989.

Lisa Hammer, a New York City-based filmmaker, has a long resume of films ranging in genre from horror, fantasy, comedy, experimental, and a combination of these. Of all her many pieces, *Empire of Ache* (1996) is a collaboration with underground artist Dame Darcy. It has a silent movie aesthetic: it is shot in black and white and uses interstitials instead of spoken dialogue. Hammer filmed it on the now-discontinued Super 8 4x film; the dissolves are in-camera. A beautiful and weird celebration of silent horror film expressionism from the 1910s and 1920s, *Empire* stars Dame Darcy as Clara, a one-armed girl who a demented-looking nurse torments in an enclosed bedroom space. "I was feeling like a Victorian girl trapped in an asylum at that point in my life," said Hammer, "haunted by my own childhood ghost, so I made a film about my inner insanity."[92] Outside Clara's abstract window, puppets harass her. Ghosts, a terrifying nurse with a long needle, and a talking platter of meat visit her in succession. Musicians in demented costumes provide a distraction, so Clara has a chance to escape through the tiny door in the wall.

Hammer had been working with Dame Darcy on a cable access television series at the time, so they partnered on *Empire of Ache*. Shooting it in the basement of an old vintage store on the corner of 5th Avenue and 5th Street in New York City called "The Kasbah," they had access to its props, fabric, and costumes. "Kasbah was closing, and it had a basement full of costumes, dresses, and all kinds of things going back for decades. Even Victorian and wedding dresses. So *Empire of Ache* is literally an underground movie," said Darcy.[93] Darcy dominated two Wall Street executive gimps[94] with money that funded part of the film. Hammer participated in medical testing for money to fund the rest of it. "We found some supplies in the garbage and had a great

Kathryn Briggs Hobbs as "the Nurse" in the short experimental horror fantasy *Empire of Ache* (1996), directed by Lisa Hammer.

Erin Brown stars in and directed the experimental short horror film *Voudon Blues* (2004).

team of artists draw the surreal sets on cardboard and sheets," explained Hammer,

> I laid the actors down on sheets then drew around their bodies and cut out their costumes, the artists painted buttons, and I stapled the costumes around the actors.[95]

Empire of Ache premiered at the New York Underground Film Festival in 1996, Masters of Super 8 World Tour, and toured with independent film director Miranda July's "Big Miss Moviola" show. The Getty Museum purchased the film to preserve it for all eternity. "We were trying to make an impact with these movies," said Darcy,

> But didn't understand at the time how the echoes of our art would resonate into the future. Though we have been celebrated, we have also been marginalized. But regardless, nothing can silence or stop us, for we planted the seeds of what we produced. They continue to grow, and we relentlessly shadow forth and survive in the underground.[96]

Voodoun Blues (2004) is one of my favorite experimental horrors. Written and directed by Erin Brown under her stage name Misty Mundae, the six-minute film school short was released by El Cinema (now known as Pop Cinema) with the short film *Night of the Whorror Whoppers* (2004) by Katie Bordeaux. Brown has been an actress in primarily soft-core, low-budget movies since the late 1990s; she's known for the erotic creature features *Bite Me!* (2004), *Screaming Dead* (2003), and *Spiderbabe* (2003). *Voodoun Blues* is a silent film about a woman and her stray lover. Brown plays a woman who is the victim of actress Katie Bordeaux's voodoo magic, which eventually causes Brown's disturbing death. Bordeaux, dressed scantily and at the fortune-teller's table, performs black magic rituals that make Brown bleed and eventually die painfully. The simple set features candles, voodoo dolls, and blood, but the film's best part is the highly stylized, choppy movements during the ritual achieved by Brown's creative eye, giving the short a grotesque and unreal feeling.

There's an element of the underground filmmaking styles of the 1960s, with which

Brown would have been very familiar due to her work with underground film director William Hellfire. *Voodoun Blues* was shot on a Blackmagic camera, filmed on 16mm. At the high point of her acting career and in college at the time, Brown wanted to gain experience in other areas of production. "I was on the fence about the direction in which I wanted to take things given that I was, to my mind, an overestimated B-movie/soft-core actress who was now given a platform to direct films as well," she said. Mainly inspired by the films of Jan Švankmejer, Brown checked out a 16mm Bolex camera from school, "And I took the opportunity to do some camera tests and experimental things ... All in the name of homework/independent study, And study and experiment ... independently ... I so did."[97]

Brown continued to describe the origin of the imagery in *Voodoun Blues*: a strange, dark rendition of Hollywood voodoo that she'd been introduced to by her ex-boyfriend, and "A shoebox under the bathroom sink ... Containing a doll lying atop a brown, bloodstained maxi pad mattress adorned with a wisdom tooth" which was the catalyst to "break the spell" the filmmaker had over her:

> Coincidentally, being in college at the time, I was also studying different factions of religion, spirituality, and folk medicine. I suppose it all coalesced in my mind ... The stop-motion animation of Švankmejer (as I understood it at the time, and still to this day, a rebellion against censorship and governmental corruption), the grotesque and beautiful dichotomy of horror films, fetish films, video exploitation 'movies' and, ultimately, the weird and fantastical purgatory in which I found myself engrossed within and betwixt ... and, all of the above.[98]

Brown is also the writer, director, and star of the 2002 remake of *Lustful Addiction* (1969), a film by underground filmmaker Nick Phillips. Brown's version of the sexploitation movie about a drug addict who will do anything, including stealing her dealer's stash, to get her fix of sex and drugs, stars Brown and Ruby Larocca and is a vast improvement upon the original. Larocca, incidentally, would go on to direct the horror films *Belated by Valentine's Lover* (2010) and *Sociopathia* (2015), both of which feature surreal elements and a gritty, artistic style that also reminds me of the independent women directors of the 1970s. Other horror actresses like Kristina Klebe have made experimental horror for their film school projects (*As Human as Animal*, 2012).

Two other horror shorts that draw on Deren's and Dulac's work are *Le Jeu de Kinderspiel* (2003) by a filmmaker who only goes by the name of Augusta, and *Replacing Delphine* (2003), directed by Kasia Kowalczyk. Based on Marcel and Helmut Himmel's nineteenth-century stories, *Le Jeu de Kinderspiel* is about twin dolls that come to life in a child's playroom. *Le Jeu de Kinderspiel* stars two twin burlesque performers, Fifi and Bibi Poubelle (Vera Duffy and Barbra Duffy). With no dialogue at all, the playroom fantasies are told from the point of view of the two strangely beautiful twin ballerina dolls named Les Deux Filles (The Two Girls). Slightly sad and dangerous-looking, Les Deux Filles encounter other toys, strange demons, and even dreamlands in their non-linear fantasy journey. Augusta calls up those dreams we all had, playing with our dolls, that

A stranger stalks a woman in the mall in the experimental musical horror *Possibly in Michigan* (1983), directed by Cecelia Condit.

A still image from Shayna Connelly's experimental horror film *Quiver* (2018).

perhaps, when we weren't looking, they walked around, talked, danced, played, made mischief, maybe even plotted bad things to happen, perhaps even plotted our demise. *Le Jeu* makes you feel like a frightened child in a Victorian nursery, which is probably precisely what the Himmels wanted their readers to feel.

Replacing Delphine is also an entirely silent film, in black and white, about a man, Professor Paroux, who loses his wife and daughter in a tragic fire. Twenty-five years later, the loneliness consumes him, and he can no longer discern right and wrong in a world without his child, Delphine. He kidnaps a little girl and locks her in Delphine's old room in his house, where she finds the magic of Delphine's past can help her in time to save her from being preserved forever as one of the professor's taxidermy experiments. *Replacing Delphine* also reminds me of Bergman's *Wild Strawberries* (1957) in many ways. For example, it's mostly static, but the surreal sensation of imagery moving forward in the narrative is both unnerving and beautiful.

There are so many beautiful works of surreal horror; it would take a separate book to mention everything necessary that women horror directors in the experimental and surreal genres have made:[99] Stacie Ponder's feature horror film *Ludlow* (2010) starring Shannon Lark as a woman maybe, or maybe not, being stalked by an abusive partner in a seedy hotel room in a desert town in Southern California; there's the painful, experimental, bloody short *A Fever and a River* (2011) by artist Rachael Deacon; Carina Dielissen's eerie short *Nightmare of the Fisherman's Wife* (2003); the prolific and obscure catalog of filmmaker Victoria Prince's work including *My Heart the Slayer* (2003), and Staci Layne Wilson's experimental retelling of Edgar Allan Poe's Gothic poem *The Key to Annabel Lee* (2011), among many more.

Shayna Connelly's *Quiver* (2018) is a moving and tortuous experimental horror short film made up of a series of sharp, clear images and sounds. The result is something strong and stabby, like a knife, that shows a woman's suffering as she lives with the ghost of the person she loves. *Quiver* is set in an abstract world where time and narrative don't follow the laws of physics; much more abstract than most horror films that usually find their way into film festivals. "All my work feeds off dread rather than revulsion or terror," explained Connelly in an interview about her work,

"I also chose to visualize the ghost, which throws people off, as does the fact that the film is a distinctly female experience of the world, which is considered 'other' in cinema."[100]

Her previous short film, *Gardening at Night* (2016), is also experimental and deals with grief and loss and ghosts.

Some feature horror films succeed at being purely experimental and/or surreal; most of these films live underground in the art world. German director Julia Ostertag's moving urban nightmare set in Berlin, *Saila* (2008), and her fantasy-threaded surreal follow-up *Dark Circus* (2016); Susannah Gent's uncomfortable British body horror movie, *Jelly Dolly* (2004), Abigail Child's Mary Shelley home movie experiment, *A Shape of Error* (2012), and the earlier work of horror/thriller directors Josephine Decker (*Butter on the Latch*, 2013), Elza Kephart (*Go in the Wilderness*, 2013), and Danishka Esterhazy (*H & G*, 2013) all showcase an experimental influence from the earlier surrealist/experimental movements in horror film history, even if it's just a tiny touch.

LOST BUT NOT FORGOTTEN

ONE OF THE MOST tragic aspects of making my whole life's work about women horror directors is learning about the films that disappear and are never distributed or, worse, never finished. So many silent horror movies directed by women have been lost, as we saw in Chapter 1, and so many foreign horror movies lost, as discussed in Chapter 4. These lost films are a beautiful part of the story of women making horror films. Since the advent of the Internet, more films have been digitized and preserved. Still, sadly, some horror movies from the early days of the Internet existed only on servers of now-defunct distribution websites. Some films never get finished for the same reason they have always not been completed: the money falls through. We'll never know why some were never finished or released.

But, sometimes, women's 'lost' films become found. For instance, Doris Wishman's *A Night to Dismember* (1983), as discussed in Chapter 5, is an example. Another is Astrid Frank's short films *Red* (1976) and *The Jealous Mirror* (1982), which were locked away in a box, never having been digitized or seen outside their initial distribution runs in the U.K. One film that had disappeared but was saved and distributed twenty years later is Tina Krause's *Limbo* (1999). When researching a 1990s follow-up to his book *Bleeding Skull: A 1980s TrashHorror Odyssey*, horror journalist Joseph Ziemba realized he needed to find out more about *Limbo*, a feature horror film directed by famous underground horror film actress Krause. Krause has appeared in hundreds of horror films, primarily low-budget, since the mid-1990s, and it was pretty early in her film career that she decided to make her feature horror film debut as a director.

The shot-on-video horror movie is about a woman who wakes up in bed to find that the man she picked up the previous night is dead. The woman then descends into a surreal, experimental nightmare for three days that involves hallucinations, nightmares, and abstract visions. "I wanted to see if it was possible to make a true horror without it becoming a slasher film or a titty flick," she said in an interview in 2001.

> I had this story, and I wanted to put it out, so I figured if you want something done, you've got to do it yourself... It's called *Limbo*, and it is about exactly that... limbo. The denial of one's self so that she may never become free and the souls that she trapped all this time are coming back to haunt her in her own limbo.[101]

Limbo could easily fit in the 'experimental horror films' discussion, the 'actresses-turned-horror-directors' section, or the general twenty-first-century independent films discussion in Chapter 9. But I believe that the way Ziemba and the American Genre Film Archive resurrected *Limbo* makes it a perfect example of a 'lost' film that was found and given back to audiences. Said Ziemba,

In the realm of shot-on-video horror from the 1980s and '90s, you can count the number of women filmmakers on one hand. So we knew Limbo was important from the outset for that reason.[102]

Limbo was shown at the 2019 Fantastic Fest genre film festival in Austin, Texas, with Krause in person. Krause told a story to the American Genre Film Archive that after she completed the film in 1999, she submitted it to several film festivals and was rejected. She resubmitted the movie using a man's name, "Stephen Krause," and it was accepted. When "Stephen" was called onto the stage for a question and answer session, Tina walked up. She then told the festival to go to hell and told the audience about the toxic gender politics of the film industry.[103] In 2015, the independent film distributor Sub Rosa Studios printed thirty copies of a VHS/DVD combination of *Limbo*, but until 2019, that was the only distribution it had received. She only directed one other film, the short *Answering Machine* (2001).

Lost Not Found was an Australian feature horror film that was to be directed by Efisia Luce Fele and Phoebe Meyer. In 2007, the two filmmakers tried to raise funds for the film by creating a short, two-minute teaser, but the project fizzled despite online buzz. It was going to be set in the Australian outback, but little else is known. There's also the *Halloween* feature-length fan fiction movie *Thorn*, which was to be co-directed by Katie Taylor Bullock with Mark Goles in the United States in 2004. "*Thorn* is a movie that is kind of a 'silent sequel' to *Halloween 6*," said Taylor Bullock in a 2004 interview, "It describes the mark of Thorn in more detail and explains what it is and demonstrates how it can be used."[104] Jennifer Nichol was going to direct the horror movie *Deserted Chaos* in 2006, but her Geocities website was removed, and now there is no information about it anywhere online.

Ruth Elizabeth's horror movie web series *The Chronicles of Gatri* was in motion in September 2001, collaborating with British company MalleUs Independent Motion Pictures. Based in Worcester, England, MalleUs consisted of a troupe of performers who released their horror movies online for free. The film was to be made in thirteen separate segments, the first four called "Looking for Gatri," "Waking Gatri," "Echoes of Gatri," and "Gatri Ex Machina." "Looking for Gatri" was released in 2000, and Ruth Elizabeth was hired to help direct several scenes. She was asked to direct the next three episodes.

Director Tina Krause's experimental horror film *Limbo* (1999) was unavailable to the public until the American Genre Film Archive distributed it in 2020. Image courtesy of AGFA.

When the film file of the first episode, "Looking for Gatri," was lost when a computer drive died, shooting was delayed for the second episode, "Waking Gatri." "This gave director Ruth Elizabeth time to secure the loan of a genuine coffin for the morgue scene and supervise the creation of the morgue set and some explicit effects," said producer Andrew John Morris on their website in 2001,

> She made fantastic use of the locations and framed the performances beautifully. She's most proud of the Mummy footage, particularly the panning and zooming of the opening pursuit. In fact, so good is Ruth with a camera that Andrew has asked her to direct further installments of *The Gatri Saga*.[105]

The stories of the episodes are a bit confusing, but the general gist is this:

> "Looking for Gatri" is the first episode in a series of short movies featuring our hapless hero Alex as he uncovers secrets concerning the Ancient Evil that looms over his world, and more startling revelations concerning himself and his place in the greater scheme of things ... Directing each episode will be Ruth Elizabeth, who proved invaluable during the shooting of the flashback sequence in episode one. Morris-Henshaw has agreed provisionally to play Alex Monday throughout the series.[106]

These episodes were all released for free online, but when the website ceased to exist in 2006, the episodes were removed from the server.

And who is the mysterious horror director GDragonAF, whose short horror films were made in 2000-2002 and also posted on her website? In 2002, she announced a new series of shorts to be published online:

> Written and Directed by GDragonAF, *The Detective Series* introduces the detective who is trying to hunt down and capture The Stalker. Tired of her misdeeds, the detective vows to stop the chaos, putting an end to The Stalker once and for all. This new series is a collection of five shorts, feeding off one another, in a continuation style; without seeing them in order, it will not make much sense. The new shorts are guestimated to be approximately three to ten minutes in length for each, and a roundabout twenty-five to fifty minutes in total length. Special features for this collection should include: pics, "The making of ... " featurette, and some out-takes; plus, a lot more.[107]

But then—poof! They never appeared, Geocities disappeared, and GDragonAF disappeared.

Horror author Gwendolyn Kiste (*The Rust Maidens*) was making horror movies in the 2000s: she made two horror film features, *Outside of Nowhere* (2004) and *Edge of Midnight* (2006), but they were never publicly distributed. *Outside of Nowhere* is on IMDb, and the director is listed only as "Gwendolyn." Kiste developed a strong career as a horror fiction author in the 2010s and 2020s, but I interviewed her in 2005 when she was actively making movies through her company Deadly Underground. "When I was in the process of filming *Outside of Nowhere*," said Kiste,

> *Edge of Midnight* is about two supernatural bounty hunters (played by the lovely Tina Jane Goldfarb and myself) who are sent on several assignments at once and ultimately end up dealing with a well-guarded vampirism cure, a runaway teenage werewolf, and even the Devil herself. Although those could make for some heavy issues, it is definitely a dark comedy. The supporting cast includes Robyn Griggs (as Satan), Amy Lynn Best, and Lilith Stabs, along with newcomers Steff Mascaro, Leslie Ann Kuder, and Xan Heaton.[108]

Edge of Midnight was never released.

In 2010, I wrote an article about a new horror feature in production called *The Torture of Delva Mills,* directed by Jill Gatsby. Gatsby is the daughter of cult filmmaker Larry Cohen (*The Stuff*, 1985) and was a horror filmmaker at the time. She was to write, direct, and star in *The Torture of Delva Mill*s, which was supposed to be out in 2010. In 2005, Jill directed *Xis*, a terrifying short horror film about a serial killer and his victims, and she co-produced the movie *Captivity* in 2007. In 2015, *The Torture of Delva Mills*' title was changed to *Social Distortion,* and Gatsby released a trailer on YouTube. Gatsby based *The Torture of Delva Mills*/ *Social Distortion* on a real-life murder case, in which Hollywood publicist Ronni Sue Chasen was shot and killed on her way home from a film premiere in 2010. Chasen is Gatsby's aunt, the sister of her father. *The Torture of Delva Mills/Social Distortion* never manifested.

Mary Miracle is another mystery of a filmmaker. Between 1997 and 2002, she directed five feature-length low-budget horror movies: *Zombies Ate My Neighbors* (2001), *Junkies* (2001), *The Santa Claus Killer* (1998), *World Unknown* (1997), and *Vacation of Blood* (1997), all by age twenty-three, with help from her twenty-year-old sister Donna Miracle. *Zombies Ate My Neighbors* (2001) is a fan film version of the early 1990s Nintendo horror video game of the same name but was not officially affiliated in any way. Donna Miracle played the lead, Karen, in *Zombies Ate My Neighbors,* while Mary Miracle played Vicky.[109] Miracle has an IMDb page, but none of these films are listed. I doubt "Miracle" is her real last name, so we may never get to see these lost horror films by the Miracle Sisters.

And where are Stephanie Aldridge and all of her horror films? In 2003/2004, a teenage horror film director named Stephanie Aldridge was making feature after feature and showing them at horror conventions all around the United States. In 2004, she was interviewed by an online horror magazine and said,

> I am sixteen years old, soon to be seventeen, though, and am a fan of all low-budget horror films. I started making films when I was twelve years old, and have watched horror movies ever since I was five. So far, I have filmed two movies and am currently working on a new vampire film, which is titled *Descend Into Darkness.*[110]

She had already filmed the horror features *Blood Beneath the Moon* (2004) and *Slice 'N' Dice* (2003). In the same interview, she said that none of her horror films had official distribution and would be available to purchase directly from her website, which, unfortunately, stopped working in 2004.[111] Aldridge described *Descend into Darkness* as a "modernistic vampire film:"

> About Amy - an innocent young woman who was bitten by a 500-year-old vampire. She now struggles to survive her battle with the curse that has been bestowed upon her vampirism. Her friends must try and save her soul before it is damned to all eternity and before the battle of the undead begins. Will Amy's friends save her soul in time, or will she forever be cursed as being a creature of the night?[112]

Slice 'N' Dice is about: *"A world of terror unleashed upon a group of friends in a small, suburban town"*[113] and starred Stephanie Beaton (*Evil in the Bayou*, 2003). *Blood on the Moon* is a story about an evil scientist in a haunted house and the young girls that get trapped there, starring Lilith Stabs as "Darla Death".[114] *Descend Into Darkness 2: Battle of the Undead* was "almost completed"[115] as of 2004. It stars Suzi Lorraine (*Model Hunger*, 2016), Isabelle Stephen (*After Midnight,* 2005), Heather Leigh Davis (*Slashers Gone Wild!*, 2006), and Dawn Desiree. Beaton and Stephen would both go on to direct their own horror films not long after making *Descend Into Darkness 2*. So where are these films now? Where is Aldridge? Did she ever complete *Descend Into Darkness 2*?

And Brandy Hines, whose feature horror *The Maze* was stuck in preproduction in 2009 due to funding issues—did she ever make the film with her company, Sicko Filmz? *The Maze* starred someone named Peggo Thy Leggo from something called the 999 Eyes Freak Show, but after 2009, there's no mention of Hines or *The Maze* anywhere.[116]

Another fascinating lost film is Julia Davis's *Room and Board*, which was announced on horror news websites in 2010 and was supposed to star Burt Reynolds (*Boogie Nights*, 1997), Robert Patrick (*Terminator 2*, 1991), and Kane Hodder (*The Devil's Rejects*, 2005). The movie was going to be about a bunch of Russian cannibals running a bed and breakfast inn.[117] It may have been released with a different cast, but there is no definite information about the release available. And then there's *The Bottom of Fallow Lake*, for which director Elizabeth Arends shot a sizzle reel in 2014 to get funding for the project. Unfortunately, the funding never came in, and *The Bottom of Fallow Lake* is in a perpetual state of development.

In 2005, Melinda Marroquin set out to make the horror film *Lycan Rising*, a werewolf feature that she would shoot in the Rio Grande Valley in Texas, United States. C.H. Morris, who wrote the script, and Carter Robinson, the producer, both men, started Phoenix Productions to make films in the Rio Grande Valley region and had hired Marroquin because they liked her short horror film *Dancing with the Devil* (2004), about an old Mexican folklore about the Devil being seen at a disco in McAllen, Texas in 1979. *Lycan Rising* was planned as a straight-to-DVD release. At the San Antonio Underground Film Festival in 2005, she told filmmaker Tiffany Warren what *Lycan Rising* was going to be about:

> A Gothic band of young werewolves are on the run from private investigators that believe they are serial killers. Only a shady music producer who has illegally burned a CD of their music knows what they really are. Fearful of this kind of publicity, the pack heads to Grandma's house for refuge and to plan their next move. With one of their own seriously injured, the pack must come together not only to protect their identities but also to save themselves from a mysterious sickness that has plagued their community for decades. The lives of the werewolves and the humans determined to hunt them down intertwine and culminate in a classic battle of good versus evil.[118]

And that was the last time I heard about *Lycan Rising* until 2022. "It just never happened," explained Marroquin. South Texas media had written about the film production, and Marroquin and Phoenix Productions held auditions for actors in San Antonio, Austin, and Dallas. Actress Lar Park-Lincoln (*Friday the 13th Part VII: The New Blood*, 1988) met with Marroquin in Corpus Christi in the spring of 2005, and she was interested in co-starring in *Lycan Rising*. "But sadly," related Marroquin, there was a disagreement about how the producers represented themselves to investors. Park-Lincoln heard rumors that "the director walked," and no one on the project ever contacted her again. Marroquin did leave the film, and so did the entire crew, who believed in Marroquin and the project but felt that there had been unethical practices regarding financing.[119]

Susanna Lo's thriller about the Manson Family, *Manson Girls*, starring Bill Moseley as Charles Manson, was in development as early as 2011. After Lo shot a teaser and raised some funding, the film fell apart when the production was accused of not following through when they sold walk-on acting roles in the film as a fundraising effort. The film sits in limbo, unmade but developed, like so many others.

ACTRESSES DIRECTING HORROR

"We're not just women making movies, women making chick flicks. Someone like myself, who's been doing horror for a million years, is actually stepping behind the camera for the first time and making a movie that I want to make."[120] *— Danielle Harris*

MANY FILMMAKERS BEGAN THEIR careers as actors before becoming directors; this was the case with many early women horror film directors in Chapter 1, which is true of Ida Lupino, the most prolific woman horror director of the 1960s. Katt Shea dipped her toes into acting in low-budget genre films before she directed *Stripped to Kill* for Roger Corman, and so many actresses directed episodes of television horror anthology series, as we discussed in Chapter 5, like Jodie Foster's episode of *Tales From the Darkside*, "Do Not Open This Box" (1988), Rebecca De Mornay's *The Outer Limits* episode "The Conversion" (1995), and Catherine O'Hara's *The Outer Limits* episode "Glyphic" (1998). Some actors direct only once or twice as an experiment, and others transform their entire careers, as we saw Roxann Dawson do when she began directing episodes of the late 1990s *Star Trek* spinoff series. Another actress, Shannon Doherty, starred in the horror fantasy TV series *Charmed* from 1998 to 2001 and directed three episodes in seasons two and three ("Be Careful What You Witch For," "The Good, the Bad, and the Cursed," and "All Hell Breaks Loose"). We've also talked about some actresses who directed horror like Mai Zetterling (*The Hitchhiker*: "And If We Dream," 1985), Astrid Frank (*Red*, 1976), Kei Fujiwara (*Organ*, 1996), Denice Duff (*Vampire Resurrection*, 2001), Rae Dawn Chong (*Cursed Part 3*, 2000), Asia Argento (*De Generazione*, 1994), Laura Giglio (*After Midnight*, 2005), Isabelle Stephen (*After Midnight*, 2005), Angela Bettis (*The ABCs of Death*, 2012), Amber Benson (*Drones*, 2010), Kristina Klebe (*As Human as Animal*, 2012), Erin Brown (*Voodoun Blues*, 2004), Ruby Larocca (*Sociopathia*, 2015), Tina Krause (*Limbo*, 1999), and Talia Shire (*One Night Stand*, 1995). Just a few more of the mainstream actresses that have directed horror movies include Rie Rasmussen (*Human Zoo*, 2009), Rose McGowan (*Dawn*, 2014), Kirsten Dunst (*Welcome*, 2007), Lily Mariye (*Err*, 2002), Heather Hemmens (*Designated*, 2010), Emma Bell (*Between the Pines*, 2019), Robin Wright (*The Dark of Night*, 2017), Katie Aselton (*Black Rock*, 2012), Amy Seimetz (*She Dies Tomorrow*, 2020), Heather Langenkamp (*Washed Away*, 2019), and Ileana Douglas (*Devil Talk*, 2003). Even Melissa Joan Hart, best known for playing both title characters in the television series *Clarissa Explains It All* (1991–1994) and *Sabrina the Teenage Witch* (1996–2003), directed a remake of the horror/thriller *The Watcher in the Woods* (2017) for the women's television network Lifetime. The *Watcher in the Woods* is an adaptation of the 1976 young adult horror novel *A Watcher in the Woods* by Florence Engel Randall and was made into a film in 1980 starring Bette Davis.

Low-budget horror film actresses and 'Scream Queens' have also directed horror movies; just a few include Stephanie Beaton (*Bloody Bender's Return*, 2003), Amy Lynn

Best (*Splatter Movie: The Director's Cut*, 2008), Melantha Blackthorne (*Sinners and Saints*, 2004), Raine Browne (*No Rest for the Wicked*, 2011), Pamela Sutch (*Trakked*, 2015), Debbie D (*Clownsploitation*, 2018), Deborah Dutch (*Hollywood Warrioress: The Movie*, 2016), Dawn Murphy (*Backwoods Marcy*, 1999), Jessica Cameron (*Mania*, 2015), Devanny Pinn (*cathARTic*, 2011), Jennifer Blanc-Biehn (*The Girl*, 2016), Phoebe Dollar (*Sunset Society*, 2018), and Genoveva Rossi (*Attack of the Killer Chickens: The Movie*, 2022).

Danica McKellar is an actress best known for her role as Winnie Cooper in *The Wonder Years*, who branched into directing. Her second short film is a surreal horror movie called *Broken* (2005). The six-minute short is written and directed by Danica McKellar, produced by Danica McKellar and Timilee Romolini, and stars Timilee Romolini. "*Broken* started as a dream that Timi had that involved a real broken heart," said McKellar in an interview about the gory and bloody movie that shows a real heart being pierced, "I was so taken by that image that I wrote a script around it and asked Timi to star in it." *Broken* uses real lamb hearts from the grocery store as the movie's centerpiece. Near the end of their twenty-one-hour shooting day, the police were called to the production twice. The crew was almost arrested for not having filming permits for a scene at the morgue. "I was terrified we would be shut down before we finished, but Timi was great with them, and after a minute or two, they were laughing and just told us to keep it down and finish up," said McKellar. Romolini had told the police that, since they were filming in October, it was just a home movie for her niece's Halloween party, and they let her go.[121]

Juliet Landau, daughter of actor Martin Landau, began her directing career with a horror-themed music video for Godhead titled *Hero*. Landau is known for acting in the horror television series *Buffy the Vampire Slayer* and *Angel* and Tim Burton's *Ed Wood* (1995) and is a filmmaker. *Hero* is inspired by silent horror films like *Nosferatu* and *The Cabinet of Doctor Caligari* with black-and-white, silent expressionism. The music video's loose narrative is a captivating and tragic love story under Landau's directorial vision. "We wanted to do it to be about a dysfunctional relationship," she explained,

"But we wanted the way that we shot it to be at odds with that. We wanted it to have a very luminous 1930s feel and for the subject matter to be very dark in opposition."

After *Hero*, Landau embarked on a highly ambitious project that ended up becoming two different films: *A Place Among the Dead*, which was to be about the fantasy of vampirism in crime and reality, and *A Place Among the Undead*, which was to explore every aspect of vampires in myth and pop culture: movies, television, art, literature, comics, music, video games, and young adult literature. *A Place Among the Dead* (2020) became a scripted, fiction film shot documentary-style, and *A Place Among the Undead* became the documentary series titled *The Undead*. *A Place Among the Dead* is a scripted film that explores the repercussions of growing up under the sway of narcissism and evil in a natural, powerful way. The official synopsis is: "*An actress/filmmaker confronts her own dark past when she begins an investigation into the link between narcissism in the film industry and vampirism*." Landau herself stars, and the cast includes Gary Oldman, Ron Perlman, Robert Patrick, Lance Henriksen, Joss Whedon, and Anne Rice (in her first and only film appearance). In 2015, Landau began working on the project, *A Place Among the Undead*, to explore the cultural obsession with vampires and what they reveal about the human psyche but developed into a narrative film with scripted interviews and a documentary-style presentation. With plenty of amazing leftover footage of celebrities discussing vampires, Landau created an entirely separate series that features the interviews in their pure form:

"We set out to make a genre-bending, entertaining art film and to give voice to what has affected many, to open up a dialogue, which is exactly what keeps happening."[122]

Danielle Harris is one of the most famous horror film actresses in the world, having played Jamie Lloyd in *Halloween 4: The Return of Michael Myers* (1988) and *Halloween 5: The Revenge of Michael Myers* (1989), Annie Brackett in Rob Zombie's *Halloween* (2007) and *Halloween II* (2009), and Marybeth Dunstan in *Hatchet II* (2010), *Hatchet III* (2013), and *Victor Crowley* (2017). Harris has also been a horror director since 2008, when she directed the short segment "Madison" for the horror anthology feature *Prank*. *Prank* was to have two other parts directed by Ellie Cornell (*Halloween 4* and *Halloween 5*) and Heather Langenkamp (*A Nightmare on Elm Street 1*, *3*, and *7*). At the time, she described "Madison" by saying, "It's a lot like the plot of *When a Stranger Calls*. It was definitely a learning experience, and I loved it, and I'm dying to do it again." In 2009 she said, "I'm tired of working for the man, in other words ... I had been in so many low-budget horror films, and I thought to myself, 'Gosh, why aren't I doing this? I know how to do this. I'm getting hired by these guys—I'm doing this on my own.'"[123] In 2011, Harris did not only star in the vampire movie *Stake Land*, but she also directed a short backstory for one of the characters, "Willie," played by Sean Nelson. It appeared on the *Stake Land* DVD release.

In October 2010, she was interested in directing a feature horror film. Harris created a production team including actress/producer Jennifer Blanc-Biehn, writer/actress Alyssa Lobit, and producer Athena Lobit. Blanc-Biehn reached out to writer Alyssa Lobit, who had written *Among Friends* (2012, and gave it to Harris, who loved it and wanted to direct it. Harris took a pass at the script and made it a bit more fucked up and twisted. According to Harris, it was a "radically, awesomely hardcore, dark, twisted psychological thriller with a comedic element (depending on how fucked up and twisted you are) about a group of friends at a dinner party gone wrong."[124] The official synopsis says the film is:

> *Set against a 1980s backdrop, the good time takes a dark turn when one in the group hijacks the evening in an attempt to help the others come clean about their secret betrayals against one another—and is willing to cut through the bone in order to expose the truth.*

Harris thought it was fun, twisted, and fucked up. "As fucked up as these characters are," she said, "they're all pieces of characters that I've played and pieces of myself and my friends as well. I felt that I wanted to get on board with it pretty early on."[125] Heavily inspired by dark comedies like *Heathers* (1988) and *American Psycho* (2000), *Among Friends* is filled with striking, sharp colors like vivid turquoise and bright pink, inspired by 1980s horror, but not set in the 80s, exactly. "It's timeless," said Harris, "Color and style and tacky-hip, and super-cool ... It's stylized, which I think most of these movies are not."[126]

By playing with style and time and choosing to explore crazy scenarios in the plot,

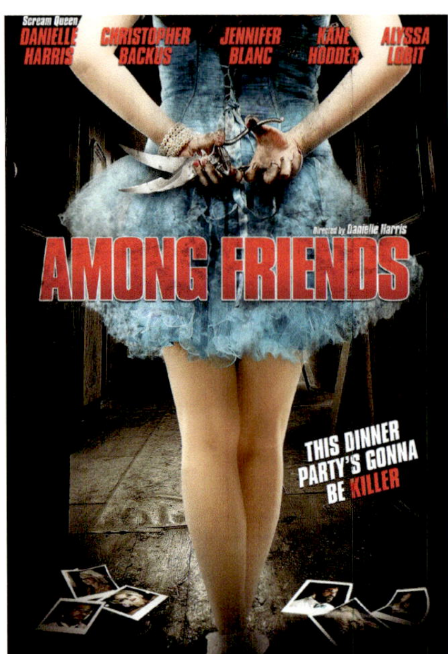

The poster for Danielle Harris' horror comedy feature film *Among Friends* (2012).

Harris said she and her team are not "locking ourselves into a typical horror format. All the things that make a good horror film are present, but there are so many things that most horror movies lack that I think we have here." Modern horror is "so typical," as far as Harris is concerned:

> Dialogue is so typical. Characters are so typical. The shoot goes so typical. I'm so bored out of my fucking mind doing these movies ... Fans want to be excited by something different ... I wanted to take a chance and have fun with it; I don't want to make movies that aren't fun ... I'm not interested in making some gritty, arty, art-house slasher movie ... I wanted to exploit women a little bit, and men, and there's a lot of sexual tension, drugs, and all kinds of fucked up perversion and deliciousness and all the things I like and like to see.[127]

Harris has worked with other women directors: In 2011, she starred in Kimberly McCullough's AFI Directing Workshop for Women horror movie *Nice Guys Finish Last*, and she starred in Jen and Sylvia Soskas' horror sequel *See No Evil 2* (2014). Jennifer Blanc-Biehn, the producer of *Among Friends*, directed the horror movies *The Girl* (2016) and *The Night Visitor* (2013).

In 2015, actress/writer Alice Lowe (*Garth Marenghi's Darkplace*) was six months pregnant and had pretty much given up on directing a feature horror film. She'd made several short films over the past decade, including the short horror movie *Solitudo* (2014), but couldn't seem to get a feature. Then, seemingly out of nowhere, Western Edge Pictures offered Lowe a fully-financed low-budget movie as the director. The catch was she had to make it as soon as possible. While pregnant. Lowe wrote a script about a pregnant woman who murders people because she believes her unborn baby is telling her to get revenge on those who killed its father. She shot the entire film in eleven days and also starred in it. "I'm very pragmatic," she said in an interview in 2017 to promote the movie. "I don't like to dick around."[128] Lowe is great with comedy, and the dark funniness of *Prevenge* is precisely what one would expect from the co-writer of the serial killer comedy movie *Sightseers* (2012). Of the title, *Prevenge*, Lowe said,

"It just popped out. I seriously just went with it should be a pregnancy revenge thriller. And I just went 'Prevenge,' and for a while, it is a bit of a jokey title. We didn't think we would actually use it, but it just stuck."[129]

Pollyanna McIntosh, who starred in the short film *The Herd*, directed her first feature horror film called *Darlin'* (2019). It's a sequel to the movies *Offspring* (2009) and *The Woman* (2011), in which McIntosh stars. The series is based on the Jack Ketchum novel *Off Season* (1980), in which feral cannibals exist in the forests of Maine. McIntosh plays a character known only as The Woman in all three films: a wild cannibal who, in various instances, interacts with regular humans with horrific results. Andrew van den Houten, who directed *Offspring* and produced *The Woman*, asked McIntosh to board a third film, *Darlin'*, and to direct it. "It was a shock," said McIntosh in an interview,

> I was thrilled with the idea, but *The Woman* is a film I respect so much, and when I first heard about it, I was like, "How the fuck is this going to work?" Because the Woman is so quiet and we need to bring her into a new scenario, so I asked, "Who is going to be writing it?" And he said, "Well, we're going to be looking at different writers," and I said, "Well, can I write it?" Because then I can live with it for two years, and I knew I'd make it into something I wanted to do.[130]

Because *The Woman* had been received with such intensity by offended audiences (her character is imprisoned and abused), McIntosh suspected that one of the reasons van den Houten wanted her to direct is that having a woman in charge would make any violence against her character less offensive, somehow, "not that I think that was necessary, but I just was ready to step up to the challenge and to do it."[131]

In 2013, actress Brea Grant released her first feature film as director, the apocalyptic buddy road trip movie *Best Friends Forever*. She wrote and directed with Vera Miao, and they both starred in it. In 2020, Grant released her second film as director, the horror/dark comedy *12 Hour Shift,* and the film *Lucky*, directed by Natasha Kermani, which Grant had written and stars in, and *The Stylist*, directed by Jill Gevargizian, in which Grant stars. In 2018 she worked with Izzy Lee on the short horror comedy *My Monster*. In 2018 she appeared in Rebekah McKendry's Christmas-themed horror anthology *All The Creatures Were Stirring*. Grant's *12 Hour Shift* stars Angela Bettis, who directed the 2006 horror movie *Roman*. "I have worked with a few women directors," admitted Grant in an interview, "but not nearly enough."[132] She directed *Best Friends Forever* because the original director had backed out:

> And so I will be the director, never having directed anything, which is a lot; it tells you a lot about me. I am a person who tends to jump in face first and to anything that I do. I learned a lot on that set, but I had a really great crew, and it was really hard. And then I kind of took a step back and was like, maybe this is too hard for me. Maybe I don't know what I'm doing.[133]

Though it was shot on a shoestring budget in West Texas, Grant is proud of *Best Friends Forever* but isn't sure it's successful as a feature. Later, she worked in several television writers' rooms, was a producer and director on the *Eastsiders* series, and gained a lot more experience directing several short films. Feeling more confident in her abilities, she thought to herself,

I'm going to do everything I want to do. I'm going to do all the weird stuff. I'm going to do all the cool stuff. I'm going to make the movie that I want to see and quit worrying about what everyone else thinks, which was kind of what *12 Hour Shift* ended up being.[134]

Inspired to set her horror movie in a hospital because she spent a lot of time in one caring for her sick father, Grant watched the nurses, in particular, and how they worked around the clock taking care of patients. She began writing the script for *12 Hour Shift* with that in mind, set in one night at a hospital. Producers at HCT Media had seen Grant's short film *Megan, 26* (2019), and they were impressed. They read *12 Hour Shift*, and they liked it. They shifted the location from Texas to Arkansas, where they could go into production immediately.

Grant filmed *Lucky* and *12 Hour Shift* just weeks apart. *12 Hour Shift* is about two unscrupulous people, one a nurse (played by Bettis), who participate in an underground black market organ theft. At the same time, a dangerous criminal is being held in one of the hospital rooms. *Lucky* is about a woman who finds that the same man breaks into her home and tries to kill her every night, and almost no one will help her. *12 Hour Shift* has a darker sense of humor than *Lucky*, and both have some abstract/surreal elements (just a few) that seem to be Grant's signature touch. It's an unusual film that presents a heightened reality to the viewer and has an expressionist feel. It's Grant's take on modern storytelling, wavering in and out of a dreamy heist film and operatic theatrical tragedy. Or is it a comedy? *12 Hour Shift* is both and neither while solidly maintaining a violent sensibility.

One of the ways Grant created this delicate atmosphere was by having her actors improvise in the supporting roles. "I love to let people improvise on set," she said, which is where many of the dark jokes in the movie came from. "Yeah, I kind of did whatever I felt like, which was great," she said about directing the actors, "'cause I just don't know if I'll ever have that opportunity again. So I felt like, you know, just go balls to the wall and make something cool, something that I would be interested in seeing."[135]

12 Hour Shift's lead character, the troubled nurse Mandy, is played by Angela Bettis, best known to horror fans as Lucky McGee's *May* in the film of the same name. "She portrays this character in such a dark way. We rarely see women characters play these kinds of dark, funny roles," said Grant:

I wanted to write a female antihero because I don't think we see them. I mean, the Final Girl in the movie is always kind of perfect. She has no flaws. And I think I like seeing women with flaws. I always write women with flaws. And obviously, Mandy has quite a few. I met with Angela, I got the script to Angela and met with her, and she totally got it from the go. She was like, "I get it." Angela is from Texas. So she knew that kind of no-nonsense attitude of having lived a hard life.[136]

Debbie Rochon is known as an actress, primarily. She had had an uninterrupted acting career since the 1980s when she was in Findlay's *Lurkers* (1987) and *Banned* (1989). She directed her first horror film feature, *Model Hunger* (2016), based on a script by writer James Morgart and herself. Morgart produced the film, and Lynn Lowry (*Shivers*, 1975) stars as Ginny Reilly, a former model who kills all the young models that forced her out

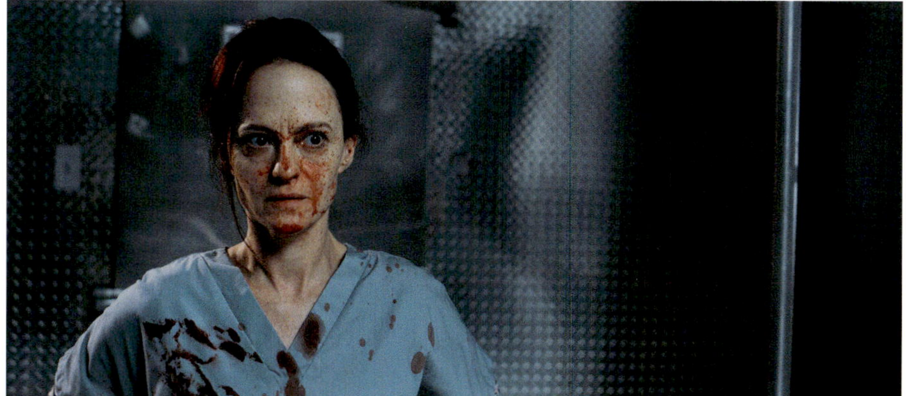

Angela Bettis stars in Brea Grant's crime/horror movie *12 Hour Shift* (2020).

of the industry for being too old. She lures them to her home and then cannibalizes them while her nervous neighbor, played by Tiffany Shepis, grows increasingly suspicious.

Rochon kept an ongoing diary of the making of *Model Hunger* throughout 2014 in *Fangoria* magazine in her column "Diary of the Deb," which provides a fantastic, detailed account of this particular film and how it was made. After Rochon read what Morgart sent her, she told him she loved it, to which he replied, "Then why don't you direct it?"[137] "Knowing how Debbie felt about the script," explained Morgart,

> Knowing she had two hundred-plus films under her belt as an actor, knowing her taste in films, knowing that she knows so many people, I figured that there was no one else really qualified that I knew who could shoot this movie. So I asked her if she'd direct it, and I was lucky enough for her to agree.[138]

At first, Rochon felt some trepidation about directing. After the first few days, she felt that there was "an impending tsunami on the horizon."

> Even with all my experience making films, I wasn't ready for what was about to be thrown in my path. I didn't know it at the time, but I was about to go through a life changing experience that still sends shockwaves through my entire body. I was about to venture into the fire and come out the other side a victor ... but not without third-degree burns. What I was about to discover for myself was that this would be my first and last time helming a movie.[139]

The eighteen-day production was smooth until the third day when there was confusion about the schedule and the start of what Rochon called "a series of flying-by-the-seat-of-our-pants" shooting styles. She explained, "I was getting mad, though. I had spent so much time trying to keep the peace behind the camera that it had started to piss me off how many people couldn't see that nothing mattered but the movie."[140]

After the film was finished and the DVD was released, Rochon was much more

Horror icon Lynn Lowry stars in horror icon Debbie Rochon's directorial debut horror film *Model Hunger* (2016).

optimistic about a future as a horror film director. "I definitely will be directing again," she said in 2016,

> There are a couple of different things that I'm working on right now, and I'm sifting through; we're going to see which one actually flourishes because, as we all know, it's difficult financially to get the projects made.[141]

In 2018, Rochon and Morgart would embark on a second horror film as director and producer: *Torment Road*. Rochon came up with the plot for the film and wanted to make a road movie: a woman gets out of jail and has to find her child, who has joined a gang of drug dealers and pimps. They were going to shoot *Torment Road* in the spring of 2020, but the Covid-19 pandemic began when almost all film and television productions were shut down. As of the writing of this book, *Torment Road* is still waiting for the go-ahead to begin production.

One of the most well-known scream queens has played with the idea of directing horror but, as of the writing of this book, hasn't yet. Tiffany Shepis-Tretta was set to direct a horror film titled *The Devil's Pies* in 2008. The film "tells the story of two beautiful dumb blondes who get accepted into the hottest sorority on campus only to be chosen as virgin sacrifices for a demonic creature that the sorority sisters worship for their continual wealth, beauty, and power."[142]

Other horror film actresses are turning to short film directing to hone their craft before possibly directing a feature. Genre film actress Tristan Risk (*American Mary*) directed the short horror film *Reptile House*, released in 2020, as the proof of concept for a feature film.[143]After Brinke Stevens directed the short horror film *Personal Demons* (2018), it was announced in 2019 that Stevens would be co-directing *Sorority Babes in the Slimeball Bowl-O-Rama 2*, which would star original cast members Stevens and Michelle Bauer.[144] Full Moon Features released *Sorority Babes in the Slimeball Bowl-O-Rama 2* in November 2022.

Anna Biller's *The Love Witch* (2016) is a meticulous study of ingenious art direction, Gothic imagery, and character creation.

Chapter 9

Promising young women

THE CHANGING NATURE OF HORROR

"In a lot of ways, 'Dead Hooker In A Trunk' was our 'Desperado,' but also our version of 'Weekend At Bernie's.' The world does tend to beat you down as an artist, but it's vital to keep that insanity and energy alive in you." [1] *— Jen and Sylvia Soska*

SO FAR, THE NUMBER OF horror films made in the twenty-first century is staggering, and women directors make a staggering number of them. "We're living in a horror renaissance right now that I hope I am part of,"[2] said director Danishka Esterhazy (*The Slumber Party Massacre*, 2021). Not only have women become an integral part of the modern horror film as creators, but horror itself has evolved to tell stories from many different viewpoints that hit viewers harder, right where it's supposed to. "Fear is a basic and normal emotion," said director Veronika Franz (*Goodnight Mommy*, 2014), "everyone has it, and we have to talk about that. I think you can make a horror film about almost any issue. You can confront people with things they don't want to see because we can, in a compelling way."[3]

When asked about the horror elements in her film *The Attic* (2007), Mary Lambert said, "I have always been enthralled by supernatural phenomena. In a secular society, demonology is one of the only avenues open to the transcendental. Working in the horror genre gives me the opportunity to explore taboo subjects."[4] Taboo subjects, political opinions, conversations, dreams, and memories are the inspiration for numerous horror films directed by women.

Stained (2010), a horror film directed by Karen Lam, a Vancouver-based genre film and television writer/director, was the first feature film script she had ever written. She was trying to make a short horror film at the time, *Cabinet* (2007), but was inspired to make a horror movie when she overheard a conversation between her friends' young daughters discussing finding romance with "the one:"

> It's amazing how young girls will soak in these cultural myths: you're not complete until you find your soul mate, or you can't have a happy life unless you're married with kids, or that life only begins on your wedding day. One of the girls asked me, "Well, what if you're all alone, and it's just you and your cats?" And I cheekily responded, "Well, maybe I'm crazy, and if I drop dead, my cats will eat me." Which was the kernel for the script. I thought about all the relationships single women form that take the place of traditional relationships and decided to have a bit of fun with it.[5]

Her next horror feature, *Evangeline* (2013), she described as a "female revenge fantasy" that started as a superhero movie. Her follow-up to *Evangeline*, *The Curse of Willow Song* (2020), is, as Lam describes it:

The unholy mash-up of Lovecraft, watching *The Dead Files* as marathon viewing, Japanese ghost stories, and Butoh dance, interviewing female inmates at a firefighting

A terrifying image from director Karen Lam's horror movie *Evangeline* (2013). Photo credit: Michael Balfry.

program in Portland, Oregon, and a lot of personal experiences.[6]

Evangeline was the result of Lam reading stories about women being brutally raped and murdered in the newspaper; she crafted a story in which one of the women this happens to, Evangeline, gets revenge from beyond the grave. "I think as a society we need it," said Lam about horror as a genre:

> It's a place where we channel all our darkest fears and nightmares ... And you can use evil in a metaphoric way with human monsters rather than having to deal with the documentary version, which, I think, is pretty harsh.[7]

The Curse of Willow Song also features a female protagonist who faces abuse; Willow (played by Valerie Tian) has psychic and telekinetic abilities with which she can learn to defend herself, however. *The Curse of Willow Song* also features Asian lead actors, which stands out when most genre films (and films in the genre) have white characters as leads. "I think the moment that I decided Willow would be Chinese and in an Asian gang family, everything stemmed from there," she said:

> I wasn't thinking representation, to be honest, but to write from a cultural and political place I had never explored before, which was my own cultural heritage. I create a character on the page rather than through casting, and Willow was actually written with Valerie Tian (Willow Song) in mind. I had worked with her on a web series and had always wanted to make a film that highlighted her abilities.[8]

Inspiration for their horror films comes from many different places. Danishka Esterhazy, for instance, didn't just draw on the original Hanna-Barbera live-action kids' show for her horror film version of *The Banana Splits Movie* (2019); she also drew on her memories from childhood and watching television:

> The story has a contemporary setting, but I drenched the set and costumes in colors from the 1960s and 1970s: harvest gold, avocado green, almond, and copper brown. I wanted to evoke memories of children's television from an era when hippy writers ran amok in studios with little to no network oversight. Those wacky shows, like *The Banana Splits Adventure Hour*, seemed more psychedelic than educational. I wanted to evoke nostalgia for that zaniness.[9]

Elza Kephart also drew on memories for her killer-slacks horror movie satire *Slaxx* (2020):

> We were on a road trip with another friend of ours, going from Gainesville to New Orleans, and we were really irritating each other by repeating words that we hated. So our friend Andrea hated the word slacks, so we kept going, "Slack, slack, slack, slack." And it just naturally ended up sounding like a horror movie villain. The first draft we wrote—we were pretty young, we were in our mid-twenties—it was really terrible. It was high school girls being killed by pants. We knew it just didn't hold up. Then years later, we set it in a store—because Patricia worked retail—but there was still an element missing. It still felt like a one-note joke. And then, I think four or five years ago, we finally decided to really get serious and rewrite it. We wanted to finally get it out there.[10]

Ana Lily Amirpour also was inspired by memories when she conceived the short *A Girl Walks Home Alone at Night* (2011) and then the feature film version in 2014. In both films, a vampiric woman is walking alone through dark streets at night in a fictional Iranian town called Bad City, entirely created out of Amirpour's imagination. Memories of world-creating drove her as a child and her early love of vampires. "I had the same exact core feeling when I was nine years old," she said in an interview:

> Building a fort in my house and naming shit. I don't know—I fucking want to make my own universe, and a film is the opportunity to do that ... Vampires were one of my first major obsessions. I loved Anne Rice; I got way into her.[11]

Sometimes, a creative partnership spurs a woman to direct when she otherwise may not have made that choice. Angela Bettis directed the feature film *Roman*, released in 2007. Bettis had worked with director Lucky McKee on the horror movie *May* (2002), in which she had the starring role, and a creative partnership developed that would see her directing McKee. Shot over twenty-three days in Los Angeles, *Roman* is about the titular man, played by McKee, a lonely recluse who nevertheless is pursued by several women who end up dead at his hands. McKee entirely wrote the script, but he had placed the direction in the hands of Bettis: "Angela and I had established such a strong creative and personal relationship that it just made sense to challenge each other in a different way."[12]

Audrey (Anna Walton) spends time in a haunted house in Axelle Carolyn's ghost film *Soulmate* (2014).

Women filmmakers sometimes find themselves with all-women crews for the first time. For example, Cheryl Dunye's thriller *The Owls* (2010) had an all-female cast and crew. They can reinterpret the horror clichés that women horror fans have been watching for years, like in Alexandria Perez's short film *The Final Girl Returns* (2019), in which a young man is the main character tasked with helping the Final Girl, and in Jenn Wexler's horror feature *The Ranger* (2018). "It was fun thinking about the Final Girl and thinking about, like, what my version of the Final Girl would be," said Wexler,

> Especially having been a, you know, a child of these late nineties slashers and being obsessed with *Buffy the Vampire Slayer* when I was ten years old, all these things were just like living inside the recesses of my brain. And so it was fun, like putting it out onto the page.[13]

When she made *The Babadook* (2014), Jennifer Kent was making a film about a taboo subject. "When I was working on the script," she said, "I would Google things like 'mothers who can't love their kids,' and there was nothing online. It's seen as a big failure if you talk about it; it's kind of an unspoken thing that women don't discuss."[14]

Axelle Carolyn's Gothic horror *Soulmate* (2013) is an independent film that led her to a career directing horror. "To me," she said, Ghosts are continually sad. To be stuck here on earth after something traumatic has happened is something I wanted to explore: the 'weirdness' of being a ghost.[15]

Carolyn would go on to direct the ghostly episode of *The Haunting of Bly Manor*, "The Romance of Certain Old Clothes," the only black-and-white episode that deals with the spirits' origins.[16] She would also direct the ghostly *The Manor* (2021) for Blumhouse and other horror television.

The future is made up of innumerable horror movies directed by women, and many of them will be on streaming platforms and will be produced exclusively for streaming platforms. Gigi Saul Guerrero, for instance, was hired to co-write and direct the feature-length horror film *Culture Shock* (2019) for Blumhouse's television series *Into the Dark*, which streamed on the platform Hulu. Guerrero's talents and ideas as a Latina filmmaker making horror movies about Mexican people and issues were made widely available to horror fans in a way that Spanish-language and Mexican horror had not been before. "I was so excited when I read the script of *Culture Shock*," said Saul Guerrero,

> First thing, here is a movie for me, not only as a Latina but as an immigrant. I couldn't help but see a lot of meat. And that's never really happened before ... Having people like [lead actor] Richard Cabral, whose parents have an immigration story, or like our lead actress, Martha Higareda, whose story is that she immigrated to the United States and worked there, and for myself from Mexico, immigrating to Canada, we all have those experiences of what it's like just to want a fair chance in life ... *Culture Shock* was to let the audience, for one moment, let go of what we're seeing and experiencing. And by the end of it, you know, we've had our scares, we had our squirming moments. And as soon as the movie's over, we can actually think about what's happening.[17]

The impact of film festivals on women horror directors' work has been significant, as well as mainstream awards shows like The Oscars awarding horror films more seriously. Director Emerald Fennell won a Best Original Screenplay Oscar for rape/revenge thriller *Promising Young Woman* (2020), while Julia Ducournau's strange horror movie about a serial killer who fucks a car, *Titane* (2021), won the Palme d'Or at the Cannes Film Festival the year of its release.

Both films had been introduced to the public at film festivals and gained a fan base before their official release in theaters. Many independent horror movies directed by women have had the same trajectory (though not usually ending with those highest accolades), especially among the international fantastic and genre film festivals. Films such as *Strigoi* (Faye Jackson, 2009), *Black Rock* (Katie Aselton, 2012), *American Mary* (Jen and Sylvia Soska, 2012), *Vanishing Waves* (Kristina Buožytė, 2012), *The Strange Colour of Your Body's Tears* (Hélène Cattet and Bruno Forzani, 2013), *Blood Punch* (Madellaine Paxson, 2014), *The Babadook* (Jennifer Kent, 2014), *A Girl Walks Home Alone at Night* (Ana Lily Amirpour, 2014), *Midnight Swim* (Sarah Adina Smith, 2014), *Honeymoon* (Leigh Janiak, 2014), *The Lure* (Agnieszka Smoczyńska, 2015), *Evolution* (Lucile Hadžihalilović, 2015), *She Dies Tomorrow* (Amy Seimetz, 2020), *Blue My Mind* (Lisa Brühlmann, 2017), *Berlin Syndrome* (Cate Shortland, 2017), *Revenge* (Coralie Fargeat, 2017), *Tigers Are Not Afraid* (Issa López, 2017), *The Ranger* (Jenn Wexler, 2018), *Level 16* (Danishka Esterhazy, 2018), *The Lodge* (Veronika Franz and Severin Fiala, 2019), *St. Maud* (Rose Glass, 2019), *Braid* (Mitzi Peirone, 2018), *The Stylist* (Jill Gevargizian, 2020), *Relic* (Natalie Erika James, 2020), *Bloodthirsty* (Amelia Moses, 2020), and *Censor* (Prano Bailey-Bond, 2021) are just a handful of the hundreds of feature genre films that have been screened at major film festivals to audiences of genre fans in the 2000s, 2010s, and 2020s. *Goodnight Mommy* (Veronika Franz and Severin Fiala) was Austria's official 2016 Oscar entry for Best Foreign Language Film. It's a heady mix of European slow burn and classy shocking violence. There's never been a better time to be a woman horror film director.

Jen and Sylvia Soska, mentioned elsewhere, are twin sisters and co-directors (self-

Katharine Isabelle as "Mary" performing surgery in *American Mary* (2012), directed by Jen and Sylvia Soska.

The Bad Ass (Sylvia Soska) and The Geek (Jen Soska) in *Dead Hooker in a Trunk* (2009), which they also directed.

dubbed as "The Twisted Twins"). They began making short films in Vancouver, Canada, in the early 2000s. Their short film *bad GirLs* (2009) was made for *Bloodshots*, a forty-eight-hour horror film competition for which filmmakers are given a line of dialogue, a weapon, a subgenre, and a prop that must all be included in the film, and they have a maximum length of seven minutes. *bad GirLs*, in many ways, feels like a precursor to their first feature film, *Dead Hooker in a Trunk* (2009), which is a wild ride and launched the directing careers of the Soskas after it played in dozens of international film festivals.

Dead Hooker in a Trunk came as a response to a place of frustration experienced in film school and the film industry, said Sylvia Soska:

> We decided to make a faux trailer as an artistic response with our own money on our own time. The school had a list of everything inappropriate for school projects, so we made sure to have all of them. Inspired heavily by the multi-collaborative *Grindhouse* (2007), Jen came up with a perfect title that matched Eisener's *Hobo with a Shotgun*. We would call ours *Dead Hooker in a Trunk*. It was a trailer, so we just had to shoot the money shots, then we presented it dead last at graduation to a loud response of walkouts and people cheering at the screen. When we were asked when the whole film was coming out, we lied and said we were getting to work on it now—which is actually what started us working on it.[18]

Once they actually started writing the film, however, the narrative was also inspired by something much darker: the missing and murdered First Nations Women in Canada. "There were ongoing cases of sex workers going missing in British Columbia, and the rumor was that because they were primarily First Nations women who were going missing, the police did not make it a priority," said Jen Soska. "Ultimately, the serial killer dubbed the Pickton Pig Farmer Killer was found out as a murderer who looked for those many already saw as lost."[19] Despite the "fun" violence in most of the film, there is a moment when all of that craziness dies out, and the titular hooker is murdered; that is a tonal shift to a cold, horrible, long, intentionally uncomfortable scene. The film's four heroes give the woman the respect she deserves, even if they can't seem to respect anyone else.

Jen and Sylvia Soska star in their film as sisters: The Bad Ass (Sylvia Soska) is completely ruined as a person, and The Geek (Jen Soska) has managed to handle the trauma they both experienced as children. The Geek hangs out with The Goody Two Shoes (C.J. Wallis), while the Junkie (Rikki Gagne) hangs out with The Bad Ass. Their lives usually don't intersect until one night when The Junkie and The Bad Ass get high and party at a club, and they somehow wake up with a dead hooker in their trunk.

The pace of the movie is smoking fast, even when the characters are reflecting or talking; the sense of insane urgency is the kind that can only come from a genuine, adrenaline-filled fever dream of inspiration. "I loved the tone of that film," said Sylvia Soska, "and I feel we've been toning ourselves down ever since to fit into the industry." The mixture of spontaneous art and calculated chaos work together to produce a movie debut so impressive that it's absolutely a modern exploitation film deserving of cult status.[20]

The Soskas played the film festival circuit with *Dead Hooker in a Trunk. They* established themselves as major independent horror film industry players, but finding distribution was complex. "Having a film with a title like *Dead Hooker in a Trunk* closed many doors as much as it garnered attention," said Sylvia Soska. "Many people didn't know that the film was a satire. You would have to have lost your mind to think of releasing a film with such a title if you couldn't defend it."[21] "The fans made *Dead Hooker in a Trunk* what it is," explained Jen Soska:

"They got our weirdness. I honestly feel IFC Midnight [the distributor] eventually picked up the film because of that huge fan reaction. By the time they picked it up, they said the film already felt like a cult classic. That was a great feeling."[22]

Like so many independent genre filmmakers, Jen and Sylvia Soska learned about filmmaking from the example of Robert Rodriguez. "So much of the way we created the film was based on Robert Rodriguez and his ten-minute film schools," said Jen Soska:

> A lot of filmmakers give back, but Robert was really the patron saint of indie filmmaking. We took a lot from the way he would shoot his action. He directed, shot, and edited it all, so he really taught you to think about how your shots were going to fit into your edit. And shoot accordingly. Rodriguez is a master of putting together great fight scenes.[23]

By 2012, they had a second feature film: *American Mary*. Actress Katharine Isabelle reappears after a long absence from horror films like *Ginger Snaps* (2000) as the stoic, cold, and incredibly charismatic Mary Mason. The higher production value and professional performances put it in a different budget class than *Dead Hooker in a Trunk*, but *American Mary* remains, like its predecessor, a pure exploitation film. The film is about troubled medical student Mary Mason who, in need of money, performs unlicensed, extreme, and illegal underground body modification surgeries for underworld lowlives and modification enthusiasts. The lines between modification, mutilation, and torture blur. The Soskas have referred to *American Mary* as another allegory for their experiences in the film industry; is that why so many characters in the film are shallow, disconnected sociopaths pathologically obsessed with their looks, exploiting people for profit, or both? It's dark.

One of the film's highlights was the inclusion of actress Tristan Risk (who would end up directing the horror film *Reptile House*) as Beatress, a woman who has modified her face and body to resemble Betty Boop. Risk became aware of the Soskas when she went to see *Dead Hooker in a Trunk* at the Rio Theater in East Vancouver. After watching eyeballs pop out, people getting shot point-blank in the head, and an arm getting torn off by a passing car only to be sewn back on later, Risk contacted the Soskas and told them, "I threw up watching your movie. If you guys need anything from me, if I can help in any way, let me know." Then they sent her the screenplay for *American Mary*.[24]

Chanthaly (2012) is Laotian director Mattie Do's first horror film. It's also the first horror film from Laos directed by a woman. *Chanthaly* was extremely popular in fantastic film festivals like Fantastic Fest because of its novel approach to East Asian horror (which abounds with supernatural and folkloric tales of possession, ghosts, and witchcraft) but also represented cultural and industrial changes in the nation of Laos: changes that are putting film and independent filmmakers on the map in a way that the country's structure did not permit in decades prior.

Chanthaly is a ghost story about a young girl named Chanthaly, who her overprotective father raises in their home in Vientiane, Laos. Chanthaly suffers from a heart condition and is not allowed to go out alone, have friends, or experience everyday teenage life because of her father's intense protection. When she begins seeing a ghostly figure around the house, she believes she is either hallucinating or witnessing the ghost of her long-dead mother, who may be trying to send her a message from the afterlife. Chanthaly's visions may be a result of her heart medication, or they may be real; she doesn't know. Vague memories of her mother's suicide, which her father said did not occur, trouble her and make her question the truth about her life and her relationship to her parents.

Laotian superstition provides a culturally different backdrop to the film that Western audiences will not find familiar. The film opened in Vientiane, Laos, in May 2013 and shortly after that in other major cities in Laos. It was in theaters in Cambodia and Vietnam in the fall of 2013 and many horror film festivals in Western nations.

Chanthaly is a milestone for Southeast Asian horror films because it is only the ninth feature film produced in the country since the tumultuous government turnover in 1975. Between a lack of movie theaters (the capital city, Vientiane, has one cinema with two screens, thin walls, and a bowling alley right next door where they play nonstop, deafening techno music), bootlegs and piracy, a poor production and post-production infrastructure for filmmakers, and lack of equipment resellers and repair services, it can be far more challenging to make a film in Laos than in other surrounding countries. "So any film immediately becomes a costly proposition with virtually no chance of breaking even at the end of the day," said Do. "So it's actually kind of impressive that there's anybody making Lao films."[25]

But Do made a few, beginning with *Chanthaly*. The inspiration for the film was Jules Perrot's one-hundred-and-fifty-year-old classical ballet "Giselle." "My idea," explained Do, "was to take the ballet, add some personal experience, turn it into a horror film, set it in Vientiane, and then shoot it with Lao actors." Do went on to explain how she had been a ballerina before becoming a filmmaker and that most ballets are horror stories:

> I was a ballerina, and most of our stories are horror. I don't think a lot of people realize that, but most of our classical ballets are all horror films. The most famous ballet is *Swan Lake*—she's a freaking werewolf! The light of the full moon comes out, and she turns into a human, and then when the full moon goes away, she turns into a swan ... The best part of making those stories is [that] fear is so universal.[26]

Chanthaly was made for a Lao audience on a budget of only $5,000. "It genuinely creeps them out," said Do:

> We showed a rough cut of the film at the Luang Prabang Film Festival ... and it was a very rough cut, but they screamed through the jumps, covered their eyes, pulled away from the screen. I don't know why, but Lao people burst into riotous laughter when they're scared or unsettled. And they laughed, which, again, I need to qualify. I can't tell you how strange it is to have an audience laugh through your horror film and then have everybody tell you how scary they thought it was.[27]

Do had to get the script approved by the Ministry of Information and Culture, which censors all media in the country. "I know that everybody probably wants some sort of horror story about working with a communist censorship system," said Do:

> But the Department of Cinema here is run by people that have a genuine interest in the development of the Lao film industry. There were hurdles—including a firm rejection the first time we submitted the film because "Marxists don't believe in an afterlife, and therefore, no ghost stories" —but in the end, the script remained right in line with what I'd wanted in the pre-censorship draft, albeit with less gore and I had to cut a kiss out between the bride and groom at the end of the wedding scene ... I knew that this was Laos' first horror film.[28]

The "next" time was her horror film *Dearest Sister* (2016), the nation's first submission for a Foreign Language Oscar nomination, and a horror movie about two sisters, one of which is blind but has psychic abilities and can see ghosts. The script was selected for La Fabrique des Cinémas du Monde, a section of the Cannes Film Festival with partner L'Institut Français au Festival de Cannes that selects ten scripts each year to highlight to potential investors. After that, her next horror movie, *The Long Walk* (2019), premiered at Venice Film Festival and was released in North America in February 2022. In this film, Do's main character is a man who can travel back fifty years in time to when he witnessed a woman's death because that woman's ghost is guiding him.

The Love Witch (2016), by Anna Biller, is, with all its pieces put together, one of the most beautiful films of the last decade and most likely of the twenty-first century. It's also a love story, a fantasy, and a horror movie made by one of my generation's most inspired and talented filmmakers. The combination of delicate direction with an astounding aesthetic is almost unparalleled in modern cinema except in very few auteur filmmakers such as Wes Anderson and Quentin Tarantino. I don't believe

Samantha Robinson stars as the narcissistic, love-hungry witch Elaine in Anna Biller's *The Love Witch* (2016).

another woman director's genius in filmmaking comes close to that of Anna Biller, except perhaps Christiane Cegavske (*Blood Tea and Red String*, 2006). It won numerous awards for cinematography at film festivals and was nominated for Best Film at the Sitges—Catalonian International Film Festival and the Strasbourg European Fantastic Film Festival.

I first met Anna Biller when she was editing her first feature film, *Viva* (2007), on physical 35mm film and magnetic sound. I'd contacted her for an interview about her short horror movies, such as *A Visit from the Incubus* (2001), and found out that she'd devoted several years to the film *Viva*, painstakingly sewing the costumes, acquiring the props, painting background images, and creating from scratch an entire world made up of 1970s *Playboy* ads in which she set her characters.

Proving that *Viva* was not a freak occurrence but a result of innate talent and obsession with a specific vision, Biller released *The Love Witch* in 2016 after years of additional work putting the pieces in place. The film's overriding theme is love and how Elaine (played by Samantha Robinson), the main character, uses love to further her interests and fulfill what's missing in herself. "Elaine is a toxic narcissist," said Biller in an interview:

> She's really a sociopath. And she's a heroine, but she's also the villain because she's using love as a weapon. Historically, that's the kind of weapon women have used, socially and with men. It's love and sex and seduction and subterfuge—a more passive-aggressive type of weapon. I liked the idea of creating a female villain that uses female types of weapons against men. It's not that she's just purely evil and was born that way; she's been used by men. She's been objectified. She says, in the end, "*Men have thrown me in the garbage except when they wanted to use my body.*" She's very bitter about that, and she's getting back at men for it.[29]

Elaine, a beautiful woman desperate for love, uses witchcraft to make men fall in love with her. But it never works properly, and sometimes they die, causing her to do horrible things like bury their dead bodies. "She's kind of like this monster, this Frankenstein monster of patriarchy," explained Biller:

> She was created by patriarchy because she's been valued only for her beauty and her looks her entire life. She's never been valued for herself. So, she's put on this disguise and costume and kind of female drag, which are her tools and weapons. She goes out and tries to find these men, and I think that's the comical part of the movie, how it's never going to work, you know?[30]

Elaine is a toxic narcissist, but the men in the film are also horrible. They only like Elaine for her looks and don't care who she is or what she wants. And they're limited, the men she chooses. She puts on a show of being the perfect woman who will fulfill a man's every desire, but that only leaves her own needs unfulfilled. Biller's inspiration for the story came from her personal experiences—not as a toxic narcissist, but as a woman who has tried to be perfect in relationships:

> Women try to be perfect, a perfect cook and housekeeper, to be patient and kind. To listen and never argue, criticize, or complain. But you lose yourself, you lose yourself, and you become weird inside. You become sort of like a monster because you've got all of this anger built up. I'm kind of talking about that with Elaine... It's sort of funny. It's not funny, really, but it can be funny. The idea that it falls apart because you're trying too hard. Sometimes, the man doesn't even want you to do it. He just thinks you're a freak when you do it. You know what I mean? It's like you're putting this on yourself.[31]

Biller said that Elaine is wearing "female drag" in that she's dressing up as a character of the hyper-feminine, but she resorts to witchcraft rather than just using makeup and beauty and affected ways of speaking. Elaine finds herself through witchcraft as a way to cope with life. The way Biller uses the actual aesthetics of witchcraft and the occult is one of the most striking things about this film: how it looks, feels, and sounds. The way the characters speak. Everything is exceptionally detailed and planned. When Elaine visits the Victorian tea room, Biller films in an actual tea room. "I couldn't believe it," she said,

> It was all women. They wore flowered hats and they were all very precious about themselves. I was thinking, "This is interesting. This is a feminine space, and these women are having self-fantasies that are extremely intense" ... I thought it was bizarre and off-putting, but I also loved it because these women were having fantasies about themselves as fairy princesses. They were like little girls playing with tea sets. It didn't have to do with the male gaze at all. They were just having their own bridesmaid, wedding, whatever, fantasies.[32]

When Biller makes a film, she's all there: there's her heart, her soul, her brain, her mind, in the movie. There are elements of the film that she manages that perhaps in mainstream movies, the director would not, or have other people do, or that wouldn't be as important to them. Biller sees each scene in her film as an art installation. The visual tableau is so essential to her. She makes a list of all the things she wants in her movie, and then she makes them, one by one, even if it takes years to make or find all of the pieces. "That takes the longest," said Biller. "I spent a lot of time writing, but I also spent a really, really, really long time designing and thinking about colors and themes and dresses and clothes and stuff. I spent two years sewing for *The Love Witch*. Two years."[33]

Biller's philosophy is that if she is going to get to make a film, which she considers an incredible privilege, she will create what she wants. "I like hard lighting; I like glamour; I like beautiful women. I like objects; I like the texture of the walls; I like horses. There's just things I want and I like."[34]

Because of the nudity and sexuality in her feature films and because they're set in the 1960s/70s, many modern horror fans assume Biller is a fan of exploitation films. But it's not just that *The Love Witch* has the occult and murder and sex in it; it's because when people make low-budget movies now, they look a certain way. But when people made low-budget movies in the 1960s, they looked a certain different way. "My movie doesn't look like a low-budget movie from now," she explained,

> It looks like a low-budget movie from the 1960s. That's why they associate it with low-budget movies from the sixties because it's got all the same kinds of issues. Whatever issues you get with hard lighting, for example, you get weird double shadows, or you get things that people think are funny ... But it's only just because I have a low budget. It's not because I'm trying to make it look like I have a low budget.[35]

Biller wants her audience to feel sad after they watch the film. "Sad that this beautiful young woman was destroyed by the patriarchy," she said.[36] I think one can't get away from the way feminism works into that, when she mentioned the patriarchy and the way women are subject to some of the treatment regarding their beauty and their physical value.

Lucky is a 2020 horror movie written by and starring Brea Grant (*12 Hour Shift*, 2020) and directed by Natasha Kermani (*Imitation Girl*, 2017). *Lucky* is not a straightforward horror film; it's surreal in many ways, and it sends strong social signals to the audience about gender and violence in ways that are not always easily accessible to the average fan. Grant and Kermani were familiar with each other's work before making *Lucky* together and, in fact, shared the same manager. But it was an executive at Epic Pictures, Robert Galluzzo, who had read the script and wanted to make it. He'd recently released *Imitation Girls* on the Epic label and contacted Kermani to see if she'd be interested in directing *Lucky*. "This script was doing something that I had been looking for," said Kermani in an interview, "which was complexity and layers and humor and horror."[37] In addition, the producer and Kermani saw Grant as the lead actress in her own script. "It's funny," said Grant, "'cause I never intended to be in it. That was never my intention. But he had it in his head, and then Natasha got it in her head."[38] "I see Brea in this role," confirmed Kermani.

Brea Grant as the tortured May in *Lucky* (2020), directed by Natasha Kermani.

"I see her delivering these lines. I feel like I can take this project to the next level visually and thematically."[39]

Lucky was shot in the East Los Angeles area, in a city called Altadena, California. It's a multi-faceted horror film with elements of slasher, home invasion, and tongue-in-cheek horror comedy, but it is based on Grant's personal experiences. It's a drama and a satire, she said, in the skin of a slasher movie. "It's not a slasher movie," agreed Kermani. "It's a satire wearing the coat, the hide of a slasher movie." The narrative and stylistic influence on *Lucky* includes *Scream* (1996). When it comes to *Lucky*, Kermani says that "a lot of elements of it don't exist without *Scream*" and continued to find other horror influences:

> There's some visual stuff we didn't do intentionally, but afterward, I realized this is my John Carpenter shot. Okay, there's the shot from *Halloween*. We didn't intentionally do it, but the DNA of being horror fans made its way into the film, just in the way that you're setting up frames and you're setting up shots, the stuff that I really do love just sort of came through ... I would say the only references really came in are very nitty-gritty technical details. For example, the man's costume was inspired by the Bryan Fuller *Hannibal* television show, the Mads Mikkelsen Hannibal, that idea of like the posh and beautifully groomed villain.[40]

Some other technical influences include the work of cinematographer Natasha Braier's work on *Neon Demon* (2016) in terms of lensing choices and focal length, and the dynamics of the original Argento *Suspiria* (1977), in which color is used as a tool of expressionism while the cinematography reflects how unhinged the film is becoming narratively.

Lucky's plot is about May (Grant), a successful self-help author married to Ted (Dhruv Uday Singh); they have marriage troubles, but they're working on repairing them. May has just released a new book and goes to readings at bookstores. In the middle of the night, a man breaks into her house and tries to kill her. She manages to fight him off and calls the police. Ted and the police are there to help her, but they don't help. Ted seems unfazed by the event and acknowledges that women being attacked is normal. The attacks continue, and May can fight off the unknown assailant and kill him every time, only to have his body disappear, and he shows up again the following night.

The plot comprises time loops and a *Groundhog Day*-like reliving of the same situation over and over, only there's no real solution. The men in her life (her husband, her publisher, the police detectives) prefer to call her hysterical when she tells them about the attacks; her publisher even calls her "lucky" to be a published author, completely downplaying any of the hard work May put into her career. At the last attack, May stabs the attacker with a shard of glass; his face changes to the faces of every man in her life. "There's a normalization of violence against women," explained Kermani, "You get stalked every night; someone tries to kill you every night. This is just what happens in the world we live in. So I think it was a real setup for what was to come, which is a world in which it's like, right, this is normal."[41] But Kermani means it's expected in the sense of absurdist theater, not truly real that we're all attacked by the same man every night because we're women. It's symbolic and surreal.

Lucky tends to absurdism. It plays with the rules of reality and takes a satirical vision of the self-help industry. It looks at the normalization of violence against women through an expressionist lens. *Lucky* is more concerned with what the audience feels than if it has a logical, realistic rule book for the audience to follow. Ultimately, the film presents a series of feelings and ideas that don't necessarily have an actual resolution, leaving it up to the audience to decide if what they just saw is an exaggeration or a true reflection of what society as a whole has come to accept as just "the way it is." *Lucky* also reimagines the Final Girl trope by giving all women a chance to fight like hell for survival and win or lose, depending not on her actions but on whether or not she's *lucky*. It removes the blame that slasher films have placed on women for their own deaths and reframes the survivors not as stronger or purer than other women but simply able to defend themselves in the right way at the right moment.

It was announced in June 2021 that Kermani would next direct the horror film *Abraham's Boys,* based on the original *Dracula* spinoff story written by Joe Hill.

UNDER THE RADAR

SOME INDEPENDENT FILMS DON'T play on the festival circuit for whatever reason; some are extremely low-budget, some are too offensive, and some are better suited to smaller festivals and horror conventions where their filmmakers have a following. The festivals they screen at will tend to be underground or horror film festivals open to alternative and low-budget content. Some of the weirdest and best films in the world fall into this category. "The underground film world is where you can make art without worrying if your vision will be widely accepted," explained independent horror filmmaker Heidi Moore:

Anything you dream up that you want to share with the world is on the table. I feel indie horror is where I've seen the most creative stories, monsters, and kills. You really get to see the filmmakers pour their hearts and souls into their movies, and it's a beautiful thing.[42]

Moore's first horror feature is *Dolly Deadly* (2016), which is about including "emotions, creepy visuals, psychological trauma, and comedy," she said, "I like to make people feel uncomfortable ... of course, I like to throw in some fun gore, but when you make the audience feel weird, you know you've done your job."[43]

The pace of shooting an underground horror film is much faster than that of a mid-size budget movie. "We were casting before the script was done, and we started production as soon as we got the insurance and the okay from the owners of the location," said Amy Lynn Best of her horror feature *Splatter Movie: The Director's Cut* (2007). They were shooting the film in an active Halloween Haunt attraction, and "the haunt's workers were beginning construction for the upcoming Halloween season, so we had no time to lose."[44]

Transgressive, underground filmmaker Amy Hesketh's horror film *Olalla* (2015), based on the Robert Lewis Stevenson vampire story, created and supervised every detail of her horror film. She made her gory, violent film because "Vampirism has been very romanticized in film as of late, and I want to show the darker, disgusting aspects,"[45] she said.

Staci Layne Wilson described her first feature, the trash/art *Cabaret of the Dead* (2017), as "a live-action *Scooby-Doo* cartoon. Those who get it will love it, I hope."[46] Elza Kephart's (*Slaxx*, 2018) first feature was the low-budget zombie movie *Graveyard Alive* (2002); she came up with the idea after she bought a slutty nurse costume at a garage sale:

"We decided that the film would be about a nurse who turns into a zombie and has to go around the hospital, eating corpses to keep from decomposing."[47]

So many beautiful films fit into the 'underground' subgenre of horror movies: Holly Dale's *Blood and Donuts* (1995), Aimee Stevenson's *Grave Matters* (2004), Heidi Burrowes' *Breakfast of Imbeciles* (2005), Anette Ashlie Slomka's *The Secret Life of Sarah Sheldon* (2006), Rena Riffel's *Trasharella* (2009), October Kingsley's *The Seduction of Dr. Fugazzi* (2009), Lindsay Denniberg's *Video Diary of a Lost Girl* (2012), Jessica Cameron's *Mania* (2015), Kansas Bowling's *BC Butcher* (2016), and Donna McRae's *Lost Gully Road* (2017) are just a *few*. They're all glorious and rarely seen outside smaller horror film festivals.

Modern folklore lends a mix of magic and metal to the everyday devices we rely on so much. Asian horror films in recent years have merged the world of ghosts and the world of machines quite effectively, and the resulting prospect is frightening; technology won't keep you safe from the supernatural. *Videodrome* (1983), *The Ring* (1998), *Ju-on: The Grudge* (2002), and less spectacular but equally relevant, *Feardotcom* (2002) and *Pulse* (2001) inspired Melanie Ansley's *Watch Me* (2006), the aptly-titled modern ghost story about vengeful spirits and illegal pornography. A snuff film clip is being passed via email amusingly titled "Watch Me." Not so scary, except that the emails all come from people who have died. Think that's bad? You better not watch the email film clip attachment 'cause if you do, an uber-creepy redheaded ghost comes to wreak her revenge upon you. You never see the person behind the ghost, and she never gives her victims a chance. There's no way to redeem her, and there's no way to save yourself once you've watched the clip (if you enjoyed it). The protagonist of *Watch Me* is a female sleuth who tries to save her own life as well as solve the mystery of the ghost email. She, along with an underground pornography-savvy film student, devises a way to keep the emails from being sent to anyone else. It's the only way to stop the killings.

Already you might notice a similarity to the plot of *The Ring*. And there is a strong resemblance in many ways. Despite this drawback, Ansley has a great understanding of the manner and subtlety that camerawork, editing, and a tremendous soundtrack of eerie, grating, and pulsating music can do to generate fear. An unresolved ending and a vengeful, unreasonable spirit are reminiscent of Asian horror movies. *Watch Me* is also a testament to the growing talent coming out of Australia in the twenty-first century.

Writer/Director Amanda Gusack might have some 'mother' issues. At least, the lead character in her horror movie *In Memorium* (2005), Dennis (Erik McDowell), certainly does. When his mother was diagnosed with leukemia, he couldn't even bring himself to visit her on her deathbed. Perhaps he feels guilty, not having seen her before she died, because now that he's been diagnosed with the same illness, he is very thankful for the support of his younger brother, Frank, and devoted girlfriend, Lily (Johanna Watts). He only has six months to live, and no treatment could successfully help him. The situation is pretty grim. Still free of symptoms, Dennis documents his death by placing motion-activated cameras all over the house he and his girlfriend share. He's paid an editor to put all the footage into a film after he passes, and it seems he must only sit and wait for his death. But soon, Lily and Dennis have a distraction; their motion-detector cameras pick up strange movements and images when no one is in the room. They start picking up sounds.

Staying up all night analyzing the video and stressing enormously, Dennis begins to weaken under strain. He begins to feel sick. He begins to think more and more about his dead mother, whom he hated, and how he let her down. Dennis finds that he is haunted by regrets and personal weaknesses, as well as family lies. And he's also haunted by something else far worse, as it turns out. *In Memorium* is a haunted house story with substance and emotion. The ever-present memory of Dennis and Frank's mother is a resentful female spirit. Rather than an overprotective and, therefore, vengeful and dangerous mother figure, she's an oppressive and angry woman whose death is bitter and lonely.

It's all shot documentary-style, with stationary cameras placed throughout the house where Lily and Dennis experience their strange encounters. At the end of *In Memorium*, the cameras cut out conveniently at the crucial moments. Despite this shortcoming, *In Memorium* is an intriguing and well-made movie released a full two years before the found footage horror ghost phenomenon of *Paranormal Activity* (2007).

In 2005, Lola Wallace and Tom Devlin produced and wrote the feature-length horror movie *Legend of the Sandsquatch*, an ultra-low-budget creature feature shot on MiniDV, through her company Waltzing Devil Productions/1313 FX. They would make three horror films together with Wallace as director: *Legend of the Sandsquatch* (2006), *Creek* (2007),

The poster for Lola Wallace's low-budget horror film *Legend of the Sandsquatch* (2006).

and *The Trek* (2008). *The Trek* begins with two young, recently married people setting out on a honeymoon hike across what looks like the California hills. Kim (Erin Fleming) and Keith (Brett Hundley) are a sweet pair, as acknowledged by their family in true-crime documentary flashbacks narrated by an *Unsolved Mysteries*-style actor (Trent Haaga) with a black suit and a matter-of-fact tone. We're shown the last place the couple was known to have been and the grisly discoveries made by the cops. What we don't know is what happened to Kim and Keith. But we're about to find out. Wallace said,

> *The Trek* is the result of a crazy experiment in filmmaking that I began in July 2007. It›s the story of Keith and Kim Russell, these two really down-to-earth people, spending their honeymoon on a camping trip in the mountains. In the movie, we spend the first day watching them as they have a great romantic time with each other. Then they wake up the following day, and the mood completely changes when we find out that there are savage cave people who live in these mountains.
>
> Tom convinced me we could improvise the whole thing. During production, though, I said to Tom almost every day that I would never do it again! There were a lot of pros and cons to shooting this way. Being on such a short shooting schedule made it even harder. There wasn't enough time to take too many [risks] or try different things. But that was also the best part about shooting this way—to let the actors surprise me.[48]

In 2009, Wallace and Devlin were wrapping up principal photography on a film called *Halfway to Hell*, which Wallace said was "the story of two friends who unintentionally make a deal with the Devil while taking a road trip to Florida for spring break. It's full of motorcycles, monsters, and mayhem."[49] As of 2022, *Halfway to Hell* has not been released.

Scottish filmmaker Kerry Anne Mullaney's *The Dead Outside* (2008) is a story we've heard before: a virus runs rampant, affecting most of the population. It turns you into a maniac or a living virus carrier, but either way, you're doomed. Individuals who have escaped infection band together to survive while dealing with the breakdown of civilization, society, and their relationships. *The Dead Outside* is set in rural Scotland's bleak, desolate, frigid rocky landscape. Survivors Daniel (Alton Milne) and April (Sandra Louise Douglas) must also contend with weird wandering lunatics who have had their brains turned into mush by the infection. The infected are unpredictable and violent. When civilization collapses, there is no standard of sanity any longer.

The Dead Outside takes advantage of the gorgeously morbid landscape. Slow-moving and character-driven, the surreal drama is often cut abruptly with images of stark farmlands and impending rainclouds in the distance, as tattered clothing blows in the wind, gripping the barbed wire. It's highly claustrophobic, locking all the characters in this cold, depressing world and keeping them muffled up for heat, warmth, and common sense in the chilly confines of the creaky farmhouse.

Hundreds of independent horror films were made by women from the year 2000 through the early 2020s, most unknown, undistributed, and unavailable. The same is true for horror films directed by men. Countless finished movies float unseen in the atmosphere of the horror film underground.

QUEER INNOVATION

THE SECOND MILLENNIUM NORMALIZED queer characters and filmmakers in horror movies. From parody to serious "elevated horror," genre movies provide a cathartic release of frustrations related to the queer experience and onscreen representation that had never previously been seen in mainstream or even underground films.

Writer/director Jane Clark spent a lot of time figuring out appropriate ways to murder the bitches in her slasher film *Crazy Bitches* (2014). In it, Clark kills off seven sisters of the Alpha Kappa Pi sorority in an isolated, cursed cabin with a bloody history of mass murder, and the audience enjoys watching these vain, self-centered, and severely insecure characters get what's coming to them. Darkly funny, irreverent, twisted, and sordid, *Crazy Bitches* is also poignant and mysterious. Set against a gorgeous Malibu hills backdrop, an ensemble cast plays out a dirty, violent little murder mystery with plenty of blood. Guinevere Turner (she plays "Belinda") commented on the satirical aspect of the movie:

> I think that horror films themselves have a hard time not being somewhat ironic—we've seen it all, and so there always has to be something fresh that takes us out of on-the-nose horror. It's just like pornography in that way. In *Crazy Bitches*, the premise—people being killed by their vanities—is already inherently tongue-in-cheek. Just add a whole bunch of bitches and one gay man, and BOOM—gold.[50]

Crazy Bitches is a horror film about underhanded friendships and insecure people that stem from a conversation Clark had with a friend. She explained, "She said something meant to build up her own self-esteem but inadvertently cut me down with something I was insecure about. And I thought, 'what the fuck?' ... it started the wheels spinning."[51]

Crazy Bitches features gay characters and stars well-known gay actors. But it isn't necessarily a "gay horror movie." "I wrote each of the roles for a friend to play," she said,

> Some of my friends are LGBT, so writing those characters and their storylines into the film simply reflects my world. I do recognize that the film industry likes to slot films into categories. It makes it easy on them. And I have been very conscious of introducing Crazy Bitches into straight festivals to make sure the perception of the film stays neutral. But the world (and audiences) continues to change in attitude about gay at warp speed, and the film industry hasn't caught up.[52]

New York City underground filmmaker Lola Rocknrolla's films are a play on horror movies with a queer twist, and all of them are campy, funny, and comedic: *Dragzilla* (2002), *Night of the Living Gay* (2006), and *I Was a Trannie Werewolf* (2009). It was in *I Was a Trannie Werewolf* (2009) that we first see the allegory of being a werewolf linked to being a trans woman. This wasn't a secretly queer-coded horror film like *Psycho* (1960); this was an overt and comedic look at the feelings of a trans woman who is desperate to hide her growing hair from her high school peers. Scholars and critics have linked werewolves and trans characters in films,[53] but in 2009, this was a new way of telling a horror story from a unique perspective to straight audiences.

Amy Lynn Best's short horror film *Weregrrl* (2002), also a comedy, is about a woman who is transformed into a butch lesbian by the light of the full moon due to an ancient curse. But does she want to be cured? *Weregrrl* was Best's directorial debut, and all of her films as a director would have a satirical or comedic element.

Werewolves and monsters have also been a euphemism for the straight female experience, like in *Ginger Snaps* (2000) and Jackie Garry's *The Curse* (1999), but using horror to convey the internalized anxieties of a person living in a homophobic society is also a twenty-first-century phenomenon.

Meta (2019) is a short horror film directed by Sydne Horton and written by Savannah Ward in which a young trans boy named Artie attends the senior prom with his best friend. Unprepared, Artie is caught off guard when he gets his period, and his perfect night is suddenly filled with anxiety. The transformation that Artie then goes through parallels the emotional and physical change of the transmasculine experience but with werewolf imagery. Likewise, January Jones' short film *Lone Wolf* (2019) is about a fifteen-year-old girl named Sam who is bullied and deals with her attraction to her friend Willow with a bodily transformation from a girl into a wolf.

Queer identity in horror would also be explored in slasher films. In the early 2000s, director Sharon Ferranti and writer/producer Lauren Johnson were advised to make a horror movie "because it is a very popular genre, but no lesbian horror film had been made," explained Ferranti in a 2004 interview. "The genre also does not require a star, and the low-budget look is still acceptable to horror fans. This is when Ferranti's lesbian slasher movie *Make A Wish* was born. This was, in fact, the first lesbian horror movie ever made.

Ferranti felt that the story for *Make A Wish* was particularly good for a lesbian film because of "the cheating? The fact that the characters are camping? An opportunity to use a machete? There are so many elements to this screenplay that are quintessentially lesbo."[54] *Make a Wish* takes place during a camping trip for Susan's (Moynan King) birthday with five of her lesbian friends and one bisexual one (to add erotic tension). Of course, the women are killed one by one, and no one knows who is doing it or why they are being targeted. The characters are lesbian clichés: the sexy blonde bisexual Linda (Melenie Freedom Flynn), the hardcore Wiccan Dawn (Hollace Starr), the militant vegetarian Chloe (Lava Alapai), and the sweet couple Monica (Virginia Baeta) and Andrea (Amanda Spain).

In the short *Meta* (2020), director Sydne Horton uses werewolf imagery to show a trans teenager's fears that his period will ruin prom night.

Ferranti and Johnson made this horror film for a lesbian audience in particular. "Lesbians don't really like to be all that scared," said Ferranti,

> They're not crazy about gore. But they love an efficient story. They much prefer character-driven stories. So we had to temper certain elements usually found in great horror flicks and enhance elements not usually bothered with, like character. A great horror flick, like any other movie, really, is one that you can't stop watching for whatever reason ... The most fun thing I've gotten to do in my whole career, besides helping a kid, is sitting in an audience watching *Make A Wish*. It's a movie that plays best in a group because it's so ridiculous. Everybody gets in on the joke.[55]

Lyle (2014), directed by Stewart Thorndike, has been called a "modern-day *Rosemary's Baby*"[56] because it's about a couple that experiences terror and grief over losing one child and potentially a second to paranoia. Set in Brooklyn, New York, Leah (Gaby Hoffmann) and June (Ingrid Jungermann) move into a new building with their toddler daughter, Lyle, and are eagerly awaiting their second child as Leah is pregnant. Then, Lyle dies in a tragic accident. Still pregnant but facing her days alone as June goes to work and experiences life in a way Leah can't, Leah develops a paranoia that the neighbors are part of a Satanic cult. Thorndike described the way the story was born:

> I've always liked horror and genre stuff, but *Lyle* came really fast. The whole story was I was in the shower—I was dating Ingrid (Jungermann) at the time, and I wanted kids, and she didn't. She had just gone on some vacation, or she'd left town, I remember—and all of a sudden, in my head, I thought, "She's bad; she's stopping me from having kids." I suddenly had this whole story, and I just wrote it down really fast. When I looked at it, I realized that I had just written like a gay-lesbian *Rosemary's Baby*.[57]

A still image from director Stewart Thorndike's horror movie *Lyle* (2014). Photo credit: Mary Cybulski.

The relationship between Leah and June is just a normal part of the story, not a subject of the film, which is exciting as an example of the normalization of queer characters in horror movies.

Kelli Breslin's *Man in the Corner* (2019) also explores gay relationships in horror, having one of her characters enter a very unsettling hookup with the man of his dreams. My favorite example of the normalization of queer characters in horror by a woman director is the television horror miniseries *The Haunting of Bly Manor* (2020), which has a queer romance as a crucial part of the narrative. Axelle Carolyn directed the episode "The Romance of Certain Old Clothes."

LOW-BUDGET BLOOD

SOME HORROR FILMS DIRECTED by women are highly dark and blood-soaked. In addition to the enthusiasm needed to shoot a low-budget film, these filmmakers don't fear exploring themes and stories that will make their films unreleasable on mainstream platforms. Darla Enlow is an atypical horror movie director from small-town America, as she has never worked within the traditional entertainment industry system, even on a small level. Enlow grew up in the United States in Tulsa, Oklahoma, and got into acting right after high school. "I had met several people through the years on various movie sets in the Tulsa area," Enlow explains:

> Tulsa is not the moviemaking mecca of the world, so finding a set to work on was always challenging. Several low-budget movies I participated in, whether in front of

Dead Rachel (unknown actress) is creepily posed in *Branded* (2006), directed by Darla Enlow.

> the camera or behind, never came to be. Finally, I said, enough of this crap. I worked on a movie as the lead actor and met the writer on the set. The guy producing this particular movie could not seem to make it happen. A year went past, and nothing ever became of the movie. I contacted the writer and producer and asked if I could produce and reshoot the movie. I liked the story, and it was a fun horror piece. I obtained legal permission, and *Toe Tags* was born.[58]

Enlow had that strange passion for making a film that so many artists seem to have, an unyielding need to create despite opposition. With two of her friends from the low-budget film scene in Oklahoma, Larry Scott and Dana Pike, she formed a small production company called Next Monkey Productions. They shot the slasher *Toe Tags* (2003) over eight months, mainly on weekends because of work schedules, and they edited and scored the film in another six months.

Toe Tags is about a serial killer and a woman who must reassess her life choices and better herself to escape him. *Toe Tags* was accepted into a few horror film festivals and was offered distribution from Brain Damage Films, which specializes in low-budget and extreme horror movies. "It was a dream come true to know that people around the world were watching our movie," said Enlow.[59]

Her second film, *Branded* (2006), is about Mitch (Trey Fillmore), the leader of a very successful rock band, and his colorful bandmates as they struggle to complete their next album in very close quarters in an old mansion, under a lot of pressure. Comprised of flashbacks, memories, and visions, the dream world is difficult to grasp fully, as is the complicated and often unclear plot. There is a documentary-style feel to *Branded*, especially in the treatment of the crime scene discoveries, human remains, and blood, adding to the film's grittiness and low-budget quality. Enlow herself (who also starred in *Toe Tags*) appears as Skat, a slutty groupie who meets a bad end. *Branded* had a nine-month shooting schedule and a nine-month editing schedule, of which Enlow was in charge. Local Tulsa bands Dark Set Theory and Last Exit donated their music for the movie soundtrack. *Branded* was technically superior to *Toe Tags* but still unmistakably low-budget horror. "We worked the camera angles a lot harder and perfected our lighting during *Branded*," said Enlow. "We were successful in taking our technical abilities to another level."[60]

Enlow's third feature, *The Stitcher* (2007), is set in a small town in the Midwest of the United States where a young woman inherits her dead aunt's house. She and her friends are stalked by a supernatural slasher entity known in the town as The Stitcher. The Stitcher likes using needles and thread on his victims, hence his nickname. "You have to be a little twisted," Enlow explained about making gory, low-budget horror movies,

> And I love being twisted! I will always do horror. Next Monkey Productions has several movies slated to start shooting, and we are going back to the Toe Tags kind of stories. The blood, boobs, and chase ... you know, the big scary killer with the even bigger knife![61]

Unfortunately, Enlow never did direct another horror feature. Her films are available for purchase through Brain Damage Films.

Gory Gory Hallelujah (2003), written by Angie Louise and directed by Sue Corcoran (calling themselves the Von Piglet sisters), is a comedy/horror film with a fantastical storyline and outrageous, mismatched protagonists fighting against stereotypes, religious fundamentalism, corporate conspiracies, and, of course, zombies. *Gory Gory Hallelujah* is flamboyant with an intensely symbolic premise, like a big, colorful cartoon resulting in a tongue-in-cheek social commentary on racism, religion, shallow consumerism, and feminism. The film is about "The greed of man for money and power cloaked in the robes of religion," said Corcoran,

> I think our government and the rise of the religious right have gained momentum because people are greedy. I believe our country likes to dominate other cultures and rob and kill other people so that we can maintain our standard of living. It's much easier to do this when we have God on our side, and we are doing these shameless acts in his name ... These crimes inevitably will come back and eat the citizens who have committed these crimes. Zombies are the past coming back to roost.[62]

Despite the zombies, *Gory Gory Hallelujah* is also a film about self-respect, repentance, and ultimate salvation through belief. The four protagonists are on trial for their beliefs. They must go through temptations to become heroes, just as Jesus did in biblical tales. There are some shockingly dark scenarios, such as a Black man acting as an enslaved person in the home of a white family as his "punishment" and burning a radical feminist at the stake as a witch. In the end, the characters seem to find out who they are, and their beginning audition monologues make a little more sense.

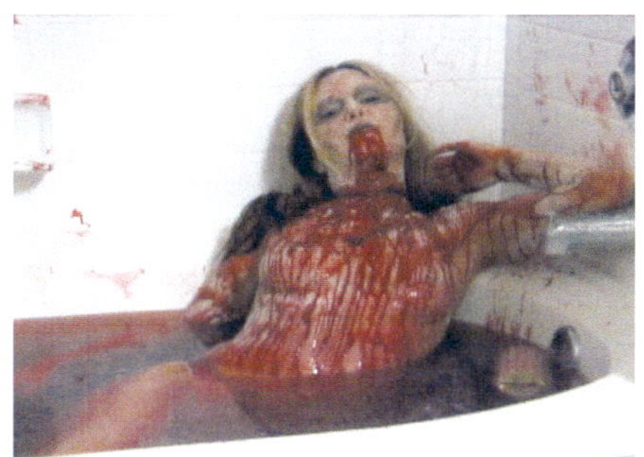

Sam (Danielle Britton) is horribly murdered in *Toe Tags* (2003), directed by Darla Enlow.

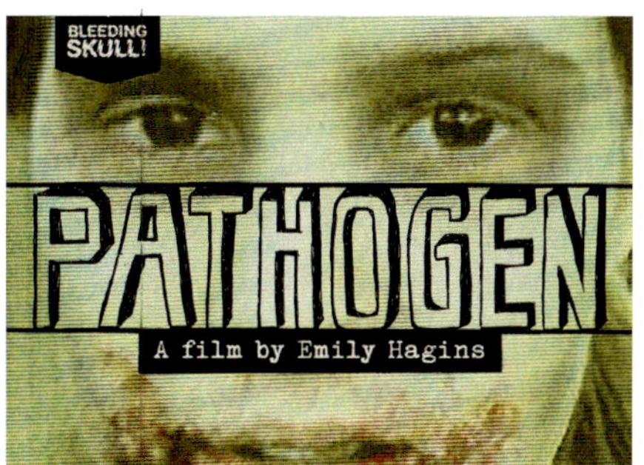

Emily Hagins made the low-budget horror film *Pathogen* (2006) when she was 12 years old. Image courtesy of AGFA.

When she was only fourteen, Emily Hagins finished her feature-length horror film *Pathogen* (2006). She'd completed the script at age twelve. With tons of support from her local Austin filmmaking community, she'd been featured in *Teen Vogue* as an up-and-coming filmmaker and was the youngest recipient of the Texas Filmmakers' Production Fund Grant. Austin, Texas, has many resources for independent filmmakers, and at the time that Hagins released *Pathogen*, Robert Rodriguez and Quentin Tarantino were there working on *Grindhouse* (2007). "When I figured out I was going to make a zombie movie, my mom and I were brainstorming ideas, but none of them seemed like they'd make a good feature," said Hagins. "But one day, I was talking with my friend on the phone, and she was telling me about a dream she had, and it triggered something in my head that helped me come up with the idea."[63]

The plot of *Pathogen* is straightforward and familiar to horror fans: a terrible (synthetically created) bacterium is accidentally released into the Austin community's water supply, and the unsuspecting citizens ingest the bacteria, which causes them to become zombies. It's not a completely original idea, but Hagins has some original ways of telling her zombie story. All the main characters in *Pathogen* are adolescents. Hagins was scared of horror until she saw the film *Undead* (2003): "*Undead* taught me that zombie movies don't have to be serious and scary all the time, and it looked like a lot of fun to make."[64] But making *Pathogen* was a long and arduous road, despite community and parental support. Though principal photography was only ten days, not including pick-up shots, the film took two years to make because Hagins had to start over twice with a different lead cast each time. It was also challenging for her to film the vast groups of zombies needed. "We didn't have as many zombies as I was hoping for," explained Hagins,

> And we had to figure out a way to make it look like there were more than there were. This was actually a problem that we encountered in a lot of zombie scenes. We also had to keep everyone entertained when we were running behind schedule and had to film another scene ... I actually lost friends over this project. I originally started out with a cast that was all my friends from school. But over the course of two years, we

had to start over a couple of times, and the cast was changing. Only one of my friends, Alec Herskowitz, stayed with the film the whole time.[65]

The documentary *Zombie Girl: The Movie* (2009) is a complete recording of Emily's journey as a filmmaker and as a horror director making *Pathogen*. Hagins would go on to make the ghost story *The Retelling* (2011), the comedies *My Sucky Teen Romance* (2011) and *Grow Up, Tony Phillips* (2013), the crime thriller *Coin Heist* (2017), and the short horror films "Touch" in the anthology *Chilling Visions: 5 Senses of Fear* (2013) and "Cold Open" in *Scare Package* (2019), and the feature horror-comedy *Sorry About the Demon* (2022). In 2022, The American Genre Film Archive would restore and distribute *Pathogen* on DVD with extra features, including a commentary by an adult Hagins.

In 2009, Australian filmmaker Ursula Dabrowsky released the disturbing horror movie *Family Demons* (2009). An indie that combines atmosphere and storyline for one hell of a mindfuck, *Family Demons* takes alcoholism and child abuse to chilling consequences for teenaged Billie (Cassandra Kane) and her abusive mother (Kerry Reid)—she drinks, beats Billie, chains her to the bathroom, brings home vile men for cheap sex, and never even bothers to stock the cabinets with any food. No longer able to exist with quiet desperation, Billie decides to take steps to remove herself from her abusive situation.

Billie, forbidden to leave the house, is always taught by her mother to fear the outside world—to fear the men out there who want to hurt and harm. Mom seems to have a good reason. But this doesn't prevent Billie from wanting to escape the chaotic and unhappy home to which she is confined, even if it means stepping out into that terrible world outside. With the surprising help of a sweet teenage boy who represents Billie's salvation, Billie concocts a plan to escape. And Billie's mother decides to interfere in any way she can to keep Billie from leaving.

The indirect sequel, *Inner Demon* (2015) (not to be confused with Seth Grossman's 2013 horror film *Inner Demons*), premiered at A Night of Horror International Film Festival in Sydney and won three awards: Best Australian Film, Best Australian Director, and Best Female Performance for newcomer Sarah Jeavons. Jeavons stars as Sam, a teenager abducted by two hardened serial killers. Trapped in their isolated farmhouse, huddled in a small closet while slowly bleeding to death and fighting desperately for survival, Sam knows it is only a matter of time before the kidnappers murder her little sister. Brimming with tension and scenes of profound physical and mental agony, *Inner Demons*' wooded landscapes and hardened, bogan psychopaths impress a gritty feeling that can only come from an independent Australian horror film.

There were plans for a third film in the series, *The Devil's Work*. Dabrowsky explained the nature of the trilogy by saying,

> In *Family Demons*, Billie is a prisoner in her own home, at risk of dying from starvation and neglect, subject to a horribly abusive authority figure, her mother. In *Inner Demon*, Sam is trapped in a closet, all the while experiencing a sick and twisted co-dependent relationship with a serial killer. Both films show the manifestation of horror, despair,

Sarah Jeavons in *Inner Demon* (2015), directed by Ursula Dabrowsky.

> and rage in the form of a supernatural entity, the "demon," whether real or imagined. The third film, *The Devil's Work*, is about a father/daughter relationship. All three horror films revolve around family dynamics, but they are all three separate stories. They also all have a vulnerable main female character that is female in her teens, physically trapped in a space, or figuratively trapped within a psychological space, and is battling with a "monster," one that is real or a figment of her imagination.[66]

The Devil's Work was completed in 2024.

There are many lesser-known horror filmmakers with prolific resumes. Rebecca Matthews is a British filmmaker who has produced and directed dozens of horror films since 2015 via her company Proportion Productions; most of them seem to escape North American theaters but seem perfect for streaming, such as *Exorcist Vengeance* (2022). In 2018, Louisa Warren began directing horror films and, by 2022, had directed twenty-two and was planning on more. Some of her films include the *Scarecrow* trilogy: *Bride of the Scarecrow* (2018), *Curse of the Scarecrow* (2018), and *Scarecrow's Revenge* (2019). Like Matthews, she is a British independent filmmaker with her own company, ChampDog Films. But before Warren and Matthews, there were other women directors with many horror film credits. Dorothy Booraem directed *Wake the Witch* (2010), *Blood Rites* (2012), and *Corruptor* (2017). Erica Summers directed *Rag Doll* (2011), *Loverboy* (2012), *Mister White* (2013), and *Obsidian* (2020). Tricia Lee made *Silent Retreat* (2013), *Clean Break* (2013), and *Blood Hunters* (2016). PJ Woodside directed the horror films *Widow* (2009), *The Creepy Doll* (2011), *Lucid* (2013), and *Frances Stein* (2015). Hanelle M. Culpepper directed *Within* (2009), *Deadly Sibling Rivalry* (2011), *Murder on the 13th Floor* (2012), and *Hunt for the Labyrinth Killer* (2013) for television before she began directing episodes of big-budget studio television such as *Lucifer*. Tommy Brunswick has directed twelve full-length feature horror movies in as many years. April Mullen's zombie horror comedy solo directorial debut feature *Dead Before Dawn 3D* (2012) led to a career directing genre television as well as several other genre movies.

Women directors of horror movies have become familiar enough that they are written as characters in actual horror films. The frequency with which fictional female directors appear as characters in horror movies seems to increase with the increase in women directing horror movies in real life, meaning that their presence has not gone unnoticed by horror movie writers and fans.

Here are some horror movies and media that feature fictional women horror film directors: Anny Papa as "Sandra" in *La Casa con la scala nel buio*, AKA *A Blade in the Dark* (1983); Anais Granofsky as "Lucy Fernandez" in the *Degrassi Junior High* episode "It Creeps" (1990); Heather Donahue as "Heather Donahue" in *The Blair Witch Project* (1999); Véronique Lefay as herself in *Ensorceleuses: Le Projet Blair Bitch* (1999); Jan Bryant as "Clara Bartok" in *Bloodbath* (1999); Amy Lyndon as "Mavis" in *Cursed Part 3* (2000); Kylie Minogue as "Hilary Jacobs" and Jessica Napier as "Raffy Carruthers" in *Cut* (2000); Jennifer Morrison as "Amy Mayfield" in *Urban Legends: Final Cut* (2000), Lisa Gordon as "Allison" in *Horror 101* (2000); Lisa Dean Ryan as "Mary Wilson" in the short television film *Cut* (2000); Debbie Rochon as "Stevie" in *Witchhouse 3: Demon Fire* (2001); Amanda Beck as "Amber Johnson" in *Bleed* (2002); Lyla Sullivan as "Angel Corman" in *Cutting Room!* (2005); Amy Lynn Best as "Amy Lee Parker" in *Splatter Movie: The Director's Cut* (2007); Juliet Landau as "Mary Shelley" in *Hack!* (2007); Kathy Butler Sandvoss as "Maya" in *G.H.O.S.T.* (2012); Alice Bahlke as "Diane Graves" in *Hell House LLC* (2015), Vanessa Paradis as "Anne Parèze" in *Knife+Heart* (2018); Alexandra Slade as "Diane" in *Friend of the World* (2020); Gillian Horvat as "Gillian" in *I Blame Society* (2020); Ayelet Zurer as "Alice" in *Losing Alice* (2020), Lauren Crandall as "Sarah" in *The Wild Man: Skunk Ape* (2022), and Aisling Franciosi as "Ella Blake" in *Stopmotion* (2023).

For those of you who are curious and want to seek out some of these movies, I assure you that you can find them. Some you'll have to work hard for, and many others are available as DVDs or on streaming platforms. But there are a few that I have never been able to get my hands on: Lilly Grote's *Daily Chicken* (1997) exists; it's just not actively distributed by anyone, and the filmmaker doesn't have a copy. *Cootie Garages* (1990) and *Junior* (1984) by Marcy Hedy Lyn, Julie Strain's mysterious directing debut *Vampire Child* (1999), Anna Procházková's *Lokis* (1987), and the German horror movie *Rungholt* (2002) by Mila Beck are elusive. If you can find these films, please let me know, and may God have mercy on your soul if you go down the rabbit hole like I did.

NOTES

FOREWORD

1 Totenberg, N., & McCammon, S. (2022, June 24). *Supreme Court overturns Roe v. Wade, ending right to abortion upheld for decades*. NPR. https://www.npr.org/2022/06/24/1102305878/supreme-court-abortion-roe-v-wade-decision-overturn

INTRODUCTION

1 Andrew Epstein, "Humanoids' Haywire, Women Say", *Los Angeles Times.* May 8, 1980.
2 Haskell, Molly. "Are Women Directors Different?" *Women and the Cinema: A Critical Anthology.* Eds. Karyn Kay and Gerald Peary. New York: E. P. Dutton, 1977. 429–435.

CHAPTER ONE
Mother of All Evil

1 *Reel women: pioneers of the cinema, 1896 to the present, the herstory*, VHS, directed by Ally Acker, Reel Women Trust Foundation.,1993.
2 Roberta and Simone Blaché, *The Memoirs of Alice Guy Blaché* (Lanham, Maryland: Scarecrow Press, 1996), 43.
3 Blaché, 26.
4 Ally Acker, *Reel women: pioneers of the cinema, 1896 to the present* (New York, New York: The Continuum Publishing Company, 1991), 10 & David A. Cook, *A Narrative History of Film* (USA: W.W. Norton & Company, Inc., 1981).
5 Blaché, 35.
6 Blaché, 131.
7 Blaché, 70.
8 McMahan, 168.
9 Blaché, 72 & 73.
10 *Shadows of the Moulin Rouge*, AFI Catalogue of Feature Films, http://www.afi.com/members/catalog/AbbrView.aspx?s=&Movie=13665.
11 The film is, unfortunately, lost.
12 *The Woman of Mystery*, AFI Catalogue of Feature Films, http://www.afi.com/members/catalog/DetailView.aspx?s=&Movie=13841.
13 *The Dream Woman*, AFI Catalogue of Feature Films, http://www.afi.com/members/catalog/AbbrView.aspx?s=&Movie=16320.
14 AFI Catalogue of Feature Films.
15 Hal Erickson, *The Woman of Mystery*, Fandango, http://www.fandango.com/thewomanofmystery_v117502/plotsummary
16 Blaché, 110.
17 Musidora. *Comoedia illustré*, "Vincenta". February 15, 1920, pp 207-208.
18 Robert von Dassanowsky, Personal interview with Walter Kolm-Veltée, Vienna, June 1997.
19 Roger Corman's 1962 film *Three Tales of Terror* is not a remake of this 1912 movie.
20 The Opera Ghost: A Phantom Unmasked. Special Feature on DVD release of *Phantom of the Opera*. Universal Studios, 2000.
21 Two films with similar subject matter by the same directors and released so closely together are most likely two different edits of the same movie. It has also been suggested that Svengali may be a remake of a segment of *Three Tales of Terror*. No copies of the films survive today.
22 Filmarchive - Die Ahnfrau. *Diagonale*. (n.d.). Retrieved December 8, 2021, from https://www.diagonale.at/filmarchiv/?fid=9433.
23 Ballhausen, T. (2011). The Many Faces of Expressionism. In Friesinger Günther (Ed.), *Mind and matter: Comparative approaches towards complexity* (p. 91). essay, Tran-

script Verlag.

24 *Anita*, The Missing Link, http://www.classichorror.free-online.co.United Kingdom/a.htm.

25 Von Galitzien, F. (2010, December 4). *"Die Yacht Der Sieben Sünden" (1928) By Luise Fleck*. Nitrateville.com. Retrieved March 10, 2022, from https://nitrateville.com/viewtopic.php?t=7768

26 Bruno, G. (1993). In *Streetwalking on a ruined map*: Cultural theory and the city films of Elvira Notari (p. 306). Essay, Princeton University Press.

27 Tomadjoglou, Kim. "Elvira Notari." In Jane Gaines, Radha Vatsal, and Monica Dall'Asta,

eds. Women Film Pioneers Project. New York, NY: Columbia University Libraries, 2013. <https://wfpp-test.cul.columbia.edu/pioneer/ccp-elvira-notari/>

28 Daniel Eagan, *America's Film Legacy: The Authoritative Guide to the Landmark Movies in the National Film Registry* (A&C Black, 2010), 56.

29 The digital version of *Hell-Bound Train* was released in 2016 with music by Samuel D. Waymon as part of an early African American film preservation project, Pioneers of African American Cinema, from Kino Lorber. James Gist wrote and filmed an initial version of the film, but Eloyce Gist re-wrote and re-edited the film, making her second version the official release version. S. Torriano Berry, a film historian, painstakingly reconstructed the film from thirty-five pieces of 16mm in the Library of Congress.

30 Blaché, 79.

31 Before 1925, Dorothy Arzner, Frances Marion, Lillian Gish and Mabel Normand in the United States, Lottie Lyell in Australia, Elvira Notari in Italy, and Dinah Shurey in the United Kingdom were actively directing mainstream silent film. After 1930, only Dorothy Arzner and Lois Weber were making films released in mainstream theaters, and from the early 1940s through the 1950s no women were actively making mainstream theatrical films until Wendy Toye and Ida Lupino broke into directing.

32 *Suspense* is preserved both in print, at the British Film Institute, and digitally.

33 The Museum of Modern Art, *MoMA Highlights, (*New York: The Museum of Modern Art, revised 2004, originally published 1999), 93.

34 A copy exists in the United States Library of Congress.

35 Published in *Live Stories Magazine.*

36 *The Mysterious Mrs. M.*, AFI Catalogue of Feature Films, (http://www.afi.com/members/catalog/DetailView.aspx?s=&Movie=18098)

37 *The Moving Picture World* 25, 7-9, Chalmers Publication. Co., 1915, 1162.

38 Foote, L. (2016, September 25). *Week of October 28th, 1916*. Grace Kingsley's Hollywood. Retrieved February 28, 2022, from https://gracekingsley.wordpress.com/2016/10/28/week-of-october-28th-1916/

39 The Library of Congress/FIAF American Silent Feature Film Survival Catalog: *The Mysterious Mrs. M.*

40 Cooper, 17.

41 "Bluebird's New Director." *Universal Weekly* 4.13 (12 May 1917): 27.

42 "Bluebird's New Director."

43 "Ida May Park Director." *Moving Picture World* (14 July 1917): 222.

44 Mirsalis, Jon C. *"THE FLASHLIGHT."* The Flashlight (1917), LonChaney.org, lonchaney.org/filmography/91.html.

45 Harris, Genevieve. "The Flashlight." *Motography*, May 1917, p. 1120.

46 Denton, Frances. "Lights! Ready! Quiet! Camera! Shoot!" *Photoplay: The Aristocrat of Motion Picture Magazines*, Feb. 1918, p. 49.

47 Park, Ida May. "The Motion-Picture Director." *Careers for Women*. Ed. Catherine Filene. Boston: Houghton Mifflin Company, 1920. 335-37.

48 Willis, R. (1915). "Chats With The Players/ Grace Cunard , of the Universal Company. *Motion Picture Magazine*, 9 (Feb-Jul), 98.

49 Willis, 100.

50 Bean, Jennifer M. "Grace Cunard." In Jane Gaines, Radha Vatsal, and Monica Dall'Asta, eds. *Women Film Pioneers Project*. New York, NY: Columbia University Libraries, 2013. <https://doi.org/10.7916/d8-zpaq-rp55>

51 Brownlow, Kevin; Stamp, Shelley; Dixon, Bryony; Day, Karen; Giese, Maria; Field, Tania; Stephens, Francesca; Cheshire, Ellen; Oughton, K. Charlie (2017-01-10). *Silent Women: Pioneers of Cinema*. Aurora Metro Books. ISBN 9780993220708.

52 AFI, American Film; Gevinson, Alan; Institute, American Film (1997). *Within Our Gates: Ethnicity in American Feature Films, 1911–1960*. University of California Press. ISBN 9780520209640.

53 Laight, J. M. (n.d.). *Maria P. Williams*. Retrieved October 21, 2020, from https://www.imdb.com/name/nm0931241/bio

54 Barbara Creed, "Women's Cinema in Australia", in Hawthorne, Renate Klein, eds., *Australia for Women: Travel and Culture* (Australia: Spinifex Press, 1994), 185.

55 Brian McFarlane, *Australian Cinema*, (New York, NY: Columbia University Press, 1988), 9.

56 Michael Burge, *"Lottie Lyell, A Sentimental Girl"*, http://burgewords.wordpress.com/tag/the-blue-mountains-mystery/

57 Harrison Owen, "London Life: A Commentary", *The West Australian* (May 15, 1922), 10.

58 Marilyn Dooley, Screen Sound Australia, Alani Publishing and Printing,

59 Williams, T. (2014). *Germaine Dulac: A cinema of sensations* (Women and Film History International). Urbana, IL: University of Illinois Press.

60 Williams, 134.

61 For anyone who wants to know everything about this filmmaker and her film, (and can read Portuguese) there is a jaw-dropping PhD. Thesis by Marcella Grecco de Araujo at the University of São Paulo titled *Cleo de Verberena: uma cineasta brasileira* published in November 2019.

62 de Araujo, M. G. (n.d.). Cleo de Verberena. *Women Film Pioneers Project*. Retrieved November 8, 2021, from https://wfpp.columbia.edu/pioneer/cleo-de-verberena/.

63 Foster.

64 *"A Woman Condemned (1934)"*, March 21, 2012, (http://dfordoom-movieramblings.blogspot.com/2012/03/woman-condemned-1934.html)

65 Joan R. McDonald, *Der Teufelsanbeter*, Carldevogt.com, http://carldevogt.org/teufelsanbeter.html.

66 Joan R. McDonald, Das *Fest Der Schwarzen Tulpe*, Carldevogt.com http://carldevogt.org/SchwarzenTulpe.html.

67 M.P. Musorgskiy, *M. P. Musorgskiy: Letters*, Ye Gordeyeva, Ye, ed. (Moscow: Muzïka), 1984.

68 Cecile Starr, *Claire Parker*, Film Directors Site, http://www.filmdirectorssite.com/claire-parker.

69 Starr.

70 Emile Vuillermoz, *Le Temps*, in Giannalberto Bendazzi, *Alexandre Alexeieff.* The Japanese Journal of Animation Studies 5 1A, (2004), 32.

71 Stefan Priacel, *Regards*, in Giannalberto Bendazzi, *Alexandre Alexeieff.* The Japanese Journal of Animation Studies 5 1A, (2004), 32.

72 John Grierson, Cinema *Quarterly*, in Giannalberto Bendazzi, *Alexandre Alexeieff*, The Japanese Journal of Animation Studies, 5 1A, (2004), 32.

73 Cecile Starr, "Remembering Claire Parker" in Giannalberto Bendazzi , ed., *Alexeieff — Itinterarie of a Master* (Paris, France: Dreamland, 2004).

74 Giannalberto Bendazzi , "Claire Parker, An Appreciation", *Online Animation World Magazine*, May 1996, http://www.awn.com/mag/issue1.2/toc1.2.html.

75 Pinscreen illustrated novels of Dr. Zhivago and several Dostoyevsky stories.

76 Starr.

77 Mary Ellen Bute managed to create an animated feature-length version of James Joyce's *Finnegan"s Wake*.

78 Mary Ellen Bute, *Reaching for Kinetic Art*. Field of Vision, ed. Robert Haller, No. 13, Island Cinema Resources: Spring 1985.

79 Mary Ellen Bute, *ABSTRONICS: An Experimental Filmaker Photographs The Esthetics of the Oscillograph.* Films in Review Vol. 5, No. 6 (June-July 1954).

80 Mary Ellen Bute, *Light * Form * Movement * Sound*. Design Magazine, 1956.

81 Cecile Starr, *Ideas on Film*. Saturday Review, Vol 35, No. 50 (Dec. 13, 1952)

82 Bruce Bennett, *Experiments In Love and Film: The Wondrous Work of Movie Explorers Mary Ellen Bute and Ted Nemeth.* The Wall Street Journal, December 10, 2010. https://www.wsj.com/articles/SB10001424052748703766704576009590243579406

83 Giannalberto Bendazzi, Animation*: A World History: Volume II: The Birth of a Style - The Three Markets*. CRC Press: 2015, 31.

84 Geerhart, B. (1970, January 01). *A short vision: ED Sullivan's Atomic show stopper*. Retrieved February 15, 2021, from http://conelrad.blogspot.com/2011/06/short-vision-ed-sullivans-atomic-show.html

85 Geerhart, B., & Mode, M. (1970, January 01). *A short vision: Legacy project*. Retrieved February 15, 2021, from https://conelrad.blogspot.com/2011/06/short-vision-legacy-project.html

86 Brooke, M. (n.d.). BFI Screenonline: *Short vision, A* (1956). Retrieved February 15, 2021, from http://www.screenonline.org.United Kingdom/film/id/442000/

87 Geerhart.

88 5. (2009, August). *The Appetite of a Bird*. Retrieved February 15, 2021, from http://50watts.com/filter/film/The-Appetite-of-a-Bird

89 Artaud, 84.

90 First Alexander Hammid, and later her composer Teiji Ito.

91 Claude Mathews, "Meshes of the Afternoon", Dec. 30, 2009 (http://claudemathews.com/2009/12/30/film-guide-to-maya-derens-and-alexander-hammids-meshes-of-the-afternoon/) & Gwendolyn Audrey Foster, *Women Film Directors: An International Bio-Critical Dictionary* (Westport, Conneticut: Greenwood, 1995).

92 Maya Deren. "A Statement of Principles", *Film Culture*, Summer, 1961.

93 Maya Deren, *Essential Deren: Collected Writings on Film by Maya Deren* (Klingston, New York: McPherson & Company, 2005), 246.

94 *Essential Deren*, 253.
95 *Essential Deren*, 253.
96 *Essential Deren*, 190, 194, 204 & 219.
97 *Essential Deren*, 124.
98 *Essential Deren*, 174.
99 *Essential Deren*, 169.
100 *Essential Deren*, 190.
101 *Essential Deren*, 152.
102 *Tres Dias Sem Deus*. Festival de Cannes. (2023, March). https://www.festival-cannes.com/en/f/tres-dias-sem-deus/
103 *Tres Dias Sem Deus*. Festival de Cannes. (2023, March). https://www.festival-cannes.com/en/f/tres-dias-sem-deus/

CHAPTER TWO
A Land of Both Shadow and Substance

1 Wheeler Winston Dixon, *Collected Interviews: Voices from twentieth-century Cinema*, (Illinois: Southern Illinois University Press, 2001), 179.
2 Wendy Toye, "Toye, Wendy," interview by Linda Wood, *BECTU History Project*: 8.
3 Dixon, 179.
4 Dixon, 179.
5 Wendy Toye, "Toye, Wendy," interview by Linda Wood, BECTU History Project: 6.
6 Toye.
7 Caroline Merz, "The Tension of Genre: Wendy Toye and Muriel Box" in Wheeler Dixon, ed., *Re-Viewing British Cinema, 1900-1992: Essays and Interviews* (New York, NY:SUNY Press, 1994), 126.
8 Dixon, 180.
9 H.H.T., "The Teckman Mystery Review", *The New York Times*, http://movies.nytimes.com/movie/review?res=9905E1D7113EE63BBC4A51DFBE66838E649EDE. [Original Source: *The New York Times* (August 22, 1955)].
10 Bosley Crowther, "Three Cases of Murder (1955)", *The New York Times*, http://movies.nytimes.com/movie/review?res=9D03E5DE153EE53ABC4E52DFB566838E649EDE&pagewanted=printRed Shoes. [Original Source: The New York Times (March 16, 1955)].
11 Dixon, 183.
12 Dixon, 183.
13 Noteworthy for horror fans is that actress Jennifer Connelly (*Labyrinth*, *Dark Water*) makes one of her first onscreen appearances in "A Stranger in Town" as one of the rapt children fascinated by The Stranger's magic tricks and eccentric appearance.
14 Dixon, 183-184.
15 *Peter Toye Interview*, http://www.youtube.com/watch?feature=player_embedded&v=M1ScoLRFoo8 via http://www.bigredbook.info/wendy_toye.html, (July, 2010).
16 Dixon, 182.
17 Merz, 126.
18 Muriel Box, *Odd Woman Out*, (London: Leslie Frewin, 1974), 219.
19 Muriel Box, "Muriel Box (director, producer, screenwriter) 22/9/1905 - 18/5/1991," interview by Sidney Cole, BECTU History Project: page 26.
20 Such as the play *Matilda Shouted Fire* and its subsequent film version starring Doris Day entitled *Midnight Lace*.
21 "New Deal For Star," *The Australian Women's Weekly* (http://nla.gov.au/nla.news-article44803823). [Original Source: *The Australian Women's Weekly* (April, 1956)], 52.
22 Box, 219
23 Arzner directed her last studio film in the 1930s.
24 Bette Davis, for instance.
25 Laura Wagner, *Killer Tomatoes: Fifteen Tough Film Dames*, (Jefferson, North Carolina:McFarland, 2004), 113.
26 Though there were European noirs as well.
27 Norway's first female director.
28 Seven, if you count Cook's execution in 1953.
29 As Truman Capote would with the later killing-spree "true story" film *In Cold Blood*.
30 *The Texas Chainsaw Massacre*, 1974, begins with a similar motif, as does the docu-horror shock fest *Cannibal Holocaust* (1980).
31 Anderson, 59.
32 Lauren Rabinowitz, "The Hitch-Hiker," in Annette Kuhn, ed., *Queen of the 'B's: Ida Lupino Behind the Camera*, (Westport, CN: Praeger, 1995), 96.
33 In the 1950s, Communism was a foreign and subversive political agenda that terrified everyone.
34 Robin Wood, "The American Nightmare: Horror in the 70s", in Mark Jancovich, ed., *The Horror Film Reader*, (New York, NY: Rutledge, 2002).
35 A.W., ""The Hitch-Hiker", *The New York Times*, (http://movies.nytimes.com/movie/review?res=9A06EED71F3AE23BBC4850DFB2668388649EDE). [Original Source: *The New York Times* (April 30th, 1953)].
36 Dixon, "Ida Lupino."

37 Ida Lupino, "Ida Lupino Retains Her Femininity as Director", feature article in press book of *The Hitch-Hiker*, 1953, 4. [Courtesy http://sensesofcinema.com/2009/great-directors/ida-lupino/]
38 Dixon, "Ida Lupino."
39 Barbara Scharres, "Ida Lupino", *The Film Center Gazette* 16.2, 4.
40 William Donati, *Ida Lupino: A Biography*, (Lexington, Kentucky: University Press of Kentucky, 2013), 227.
41 Debra Weiner. *Interview with Ida Lupino*, in Kathryn Kay, Gerald Peary, eds., Women and the Cinema: A Critical Anthology (Canada: Clarke, Erwin & Company, 1977), 176.
42 Mary Celeste Kearney and James M. Moran, "Ida Lupino as director of television," in Annette Kuhn, ed., *Queen of the 'B's: Ida Lupin Behind the Camera,* (Westport, CN: Praeger, 1995), 147.
43 Jo Gabriel, July 19, 2013."Boris Karloff's anthology television series: it's a thriller!", *The Last Drive-In*. http://thelastdrivein.com/2013/07/19/boris-karloffs-anthology-television-series-its-a-thriller/
44 Based on the short story "The Extra Passenger" by August Derleth.
45 Based on the story by Wilkie Collins.
46 I cannot imagine a case in which showing a giant rooster pecking someone to death could possibly have been successful in 1961 for anything other than a laugh.
47 The story "Mr. George" is from his anthology collection *Mr. George and Other Odd Persons*. It first appeared in the March 1947 issue of *Weird Tales*.
48 Gillespie was also known for playing a young Joan Crawford in *Whatever Hap pened to Baby Jane?*
49 Evelyn is best-known for her roles in Alfred Hitchcock's *Rear Window* and Willian Castle's *The Tingler*.
50 The short story first appeared in *Weird Tales*, July 1948.
51 Based on the short story "Men Must Die" by Cornell Woolrich.
52 Alan Warren. *This Is a Thriller: An Episode Guide, History and Analysis of the Classic 1960s television Series* (Jefferson, North Carolina: McFarland, 2004), 123.
53 Warren agrees with me.
54 Warren, 182.
55 Donati, 230.
56 Stewart Stanyard, *Dimensions Behind the Twilight Zone: A Backstage Tribute to television's Groundbreaking Series*, (ECW Press: 2007), 125.
57 Donati, 229.
58 Siegel later directed the original *Invasion of the Body Snatchers* the Clint Eastwood vehicle *Dirty Harry*.
59 *"Lela Swift television Director."* She Made It. http://www.shemadeit.org/meet/biography.aspx?m=55
60 Craig Hamrick & R. J. Jamison, *Barnabas and Company: The Cast of the television Classic Dark Shadows* (iUniverse, 2012), page 3.
61 Lela Swift, "Interviews," disc 4, *Dark Shadows*, Collection 3, DVD, directed by Lela Swift & Dan Curtis (Oak Forest, Illinois: MPI Home Video, 2002).
62 Jeff Thompson. The *television Horrors of Dan Curtis: Dark Shadows, The Night Stalker and Other Productions*, 1966-2006 (McFarland, 2009), 60 & R.J. Jamison. *Grayson Hall: A Hard Act to Follow* (iUniverse, 2006), 146.
63 Hamrick & Jamison, 3.
64 Lela Swift, "Interviews."
65 Swift.
66 Hamrick & Jamison, 206.
67 Swift.
68 Hamrick & Jamison, 19.
69 "Jonathan Frid Interview Part 2 of 4" Plott interview." YouTube video. Posted by EMMYtelevisionLEGENDS.ORG, 21 July 2008. http://www.emmytelevisionlegends.org/interviews/people/jonathan-frid
70 Jamison, 175.
71 Jamison, 175.
72 Jamison, 175.
73 So is Gloria Monty's "The Screaming Skull".
74 *The Classic Ghosts: "The Haunting of Rosalind"*. UCLA Film & television Archive. (2021, October 8). Retrieved from https://www.cinema.ucla.edu/events/2021/10/07/classic-ghosts-haunting-of-rosalind.
75 Chitwood, A. (2020, October 12). *Haunting of Bly Manor episode 8 explained by Mike Flanagan*. Collider. Retrieved October 10, 2021, from https://collider.com/haunting-of-bly-manor-episode-8-explained/.
76 Amanda Reyes, July 15, 2012. "Wide World: Mystery - Alien Lover (1975)", *Made for television Mayhem*. http://madefortelevisionmayhem.blogspot.com/2012/07/wide-world-mystery-alien-lover-1975.html
77 Robert Richardson, November 7, 2004. ALIEN LOVER (1975)", Mobius *Home Video Forum*. http://z8.invisionfree.com/MHVF/index.php?showtopic=473.
78 Nany Mills, April 7, 1986. "When Gloria Monty Talks, ABC-television Listens." The Los Angeles Times. http://articles.latimes.com/1986-04-07/entertainment/ca-21899_1_gloria-monty
79 "Gloria Monty She's Behind the Biggest Bubble in Showbiz: Soap Operas." *People*. December 28, 1981.
80 Adam Bernstein. "Gloria Monty; Producer Revived 'General Hospital", *Washington*

Post. April 5, 2006.

81 Irv Letofsky. "Gloria Monty Returns to GENERAL HOSPITAL 1991", *Los Angeles Times*. February 13, 1991.

82 *The Post-Standard*. August 12, 1973. Syracuse, New York, 97.

83 *The Odessa American*. December 23, 1973. 79.

84 *The Odessa American*.

85 Sarah Hellings would be the second, with episodes "The Mark of the Rani" parts one and two in 1985.

86 Plautus' *Mostellaria* (*The Haunted House*) set in ancient Athens.

87 Jerry Roberts, "Naomi Capon" in *Encyclopedia of television Film Directors* (London, United Kingdom: Scarecrow Press, 2009), page 74.

88 "1968," *Sixties City*. http://www.sixtiescity.net/Culttelevision/television68.htm

89 "Ringing in the Changes" was also remade for the CBC Radio drama series *Nightfall* on Halloween in 1980 and for BBC Radio Four on Halloween in 2000. http://hell-notes.com/ron-breznays-masters-of-horror-robert-aikman

90 Colin Cutler, 2004. "The Bells of Hell," *The Mausoleum Club*. http://www.the-mausoleum-club.org.uk/

91 Cutler.

92 Cutler.

93 Cutler

94 *Missing Episodes*. http://missingepisodes.proboards.com/thread/1720

95 Kemp-Welch, 74.

96 "The Open Door" was published as a short story in 1918.

97 Helen Wheatley, "Mystery and Imagination: Anatomy of a Gothic Anthology Series" in Janet Thumin , ed., *Small Screens, Big Ideas: television in the 1950s,* (London, United Kingdom: I.B.Tauris, 2002), 171, 172.

98 Wheatley, 172.

99 Anthony Davis, "Screams Behind the Door," *Playbill* (February 19, 1966).

100 For those who wish to read all about it, Thomas Potts' contemporary account of the trials can be read in his book *The Wonderfull Discoverie of Witches in the Countie of Lancaster.*

101 She also had a history of criticizing *Doctor Who* in the 1970s.

102 Arsineau.

103 Judge Adam Arseneau, June 28th, 2006. "The Omega Factor: The Complete Series." *DVD Verdict*. http://www.dvdverdict.com/reviews/omegafactor.php

CHAPTER THREE
A Woman's Place is in Exploitation Films

1 Nastasi, A. (2017, December 30). *Flavorwire interview: Exploitation and adult cinema ICON ROBERTA Findlay on Making "cheap" movies, getting arrested with John Holmes, and Times square's X-Rated Past*. Flavorwire. https://www.flavorwire.com/609580/flavorwire-interview-exploitation-and-adult-cinema-icon-roberta-findlay-on-making-cheap-movies-getting-arrested-with-john-holmes-and-times-squares-x-rated-past.

2 *Tank Girl State of Mind: An interview with Rachel Talalay*. Institute of Contemporary Arts. (2014, November 19). Retrieved January 25, 2022, from https://archive.ica.art/bulletin/tank-girl-state-mind-interview-rachel-talalay/

3 Leaf, C. (n.d.). *Work biography*. Caroline Leaf. Retrieved February 28, 2022, from http://www.carolineleaf.com/work_bio.php

4 Graeme Harper, "Drive-in horror across the Outback" in Gary Don Rhodes, ed., *Horror at the Drive-in: Essays in Popular Americana*. (McFarland, 2003), 33.

5 Stephen Saito, December 17, 2011. "Interview: Alex Stapleton Talks About Breaking Into "Corman's World". *The Moveable Fest*. http://moveablefest.com/moveable_fest/2011/12/alex-stapleton-cormans-world-interview.html

6 Gross, L. (1982, March 7). Gross' Sleaze Favorites. *The Los Angeles Times*, p. M4.

7 Sher, B. *"Q & A with Stephanie Rothman".* UCLA Center for the Study of Women. UCLA: UCLA Center for the Study of Women, 2008. Retrieved from: http://escholarship.org/uc/item/4jx713vz

8 Roger Corman. *How I made a hundred movies in Hollywood and never lost a dime.* (NYC, New York:De Capo Press, 1990), 124.

9 Issues number 4, 5, and 7 of 1991

10 Linda Gross. "A Woman's Place Is in... Exploitation Films?" *Los Angeles Times* (1978).

11 Colleeen Kelsey, "The Cult of Stephanie Rothman," *Interview Magazine*, March 9, 2016, http://www.interviewmagazine.com/film/stephanie-rothman/#_

12 Scher.

13 Corman, 181.

14 Corman, 181.

15 Gross.

16 Gross.
17 Lucas, 28.
18 Dannis Peary. Stephanie Rothman: R-Rated Feminist, in Kathryn Kay, Gerald Peary, eds., *Women and the Cinema: A Critical Anthology* (Canada: Clarke, Erwin & Company, 1977), 185.
19 Scher.
20 Peary, 185.
21 Tom Lisanti, "Celeste Yarnall", *Femme Fatales* 11.4 (April 2002), 53.
22 Lisanti, 53.
23 Scher.
24 Stephanie Rothman, July 27, 2010. *"Stephanie Rothman sets the record straight"*, Temple of Shlock. http://templeofschlock.blogspot.com.au/2010/07/stephanie-rothman-sets-record-straight.html
25 Gross.
26 Other science fiction, action, and thriller films directed by women made during this time period, like Barbara Peeters' *Bury Me an Angel* (1971) and *Star Hops* (1978), Virgina L. Stone's *Treasure of the Jamaica Reef* AKA *Evil in the Deep* (1976), and Beverly Sebastian's *Gator Bait* (1973) won't be covered in this chapter, or this book. *Terminal Island* is the only modern non-horror film we'll look at in-depth, mainly because it was Rothman's final genre film as director and because it is one of the most studied and cited films in academic discussions of 1970s feminist exploitation films. As this book moves from the 1970s forward, only horror films will be included, though I may make mention of other genre films made by women directors.
27 Stephanie Rothman. "A New Beginning on Terminal Island." *Omni's Screen Flights/ Screen Fantasies: The Future According to Science Fiction Cinema* (Garden City, New York: Doubleday, 1984), 138
28 Peary, 188.
29 Jenkins.
30 Honeycutt, H. (July 2006) Barbara Leigh. Personal Interview.
31 Honeycutt.
32 Gross.
33 Gross.
34 Gross.
35 Gross.
36 Alicia Kozma, "Stephanie Rothman Does Not Exist." 2014 Film & History Conference *Golden Ages-Styles & Personalities, Genres & Histories,* Institute of Communications Research University of Illinois, Urbana-Champaign, October 2014.
37 *Third Eye Cinema 6/17/12 with Roberta Findlay* [Audio blog interview]. (2012, June 17). Retrieved April 4, 2015, from http://www.blogtalkradio.com/bigpoppaonline/2012/06/17/third-eye-cinema-61712-with-roberta-findlay
38 Third Eye Cinema.
39 *Roberta Findlay: A Respectable Woman - Podcast 53*. (2015, August 16). Retrieved from http://www.therialtoreport.com/2015/08/16/roberta-findla
40 Third Eye Cinema.
41 Petrucci, L. (2019, August 8). *Grand Dames of the Grindhouse: The Films of Roberta Findlay and Doris Wishman*. Lecture presented in The Miskatonic Institute of Horror Studies, Los Angeles.
42 Third Eye Cinema.
43 Third Eye Cinema.
44 Third Eye Cinema.
45 Third Eye Cinema.
46 Laliberity, J. (2017, November 2). *Vinegar Syndrome's A Woman's Torment Blu-ray Release*. Retrieved October 18, 2019, from http://paracinema.net/2017/11/vinegar-syndromes-a-womans-torment-Blu-ray-release/.
47 Findlay, R. (Director). (2017). *A Woman's Torment (Director's Commentary)* [Motion picture on DVD]. USA: Vinegar Syndrome.
48 Third Eye Cinema.
49 Vinegar Syndrome. (2017). *Q&A with Roberta Findlay from the Quad Cinema Screening in 2017* [DVD]. USA.
50 Vinegar Syndrome.
51 Vinegar Syndrome.
52 *Whatever Happened To Sandi Foxx?* The Rialto Report. (2015, May 18). Retrieved from http://www.therialtoreport.com/2014/06/22/whatever-happened-to-sandi-foxx-actress-swinger-party-girl-porno-agent
53 Third Eye Cinema.
54 Vinegar Syndrome.
55 Vinegar Syndrome.
56 Third Eye Cinema.
57 Scherer
58 Kissell.
59 Thanks to Lisa Petrucci of *Something Weird* for this marvelous explanation of sub-genres.
60 Kissell.
61 Michael Bowen. "Doris Wishman Meets the Avant-Garde" in eds., Xavier Mendik, Steven Schneider *Underground U.S.A.: Filmmaking Beyond the Hollywood Canon*. (New York, NY: Columbia University Press, 2012), pg 117.
62 May 11, 2014. "Whatever Happened to Gigi Darlene?," *The Rialto Report*. http://www.therialtoreport.com/2014/05/11/whatever-happened-to-gigi-darlene/
63 Jerry Renshaw, July 13, 1998. "Sexploitation Queen", *The Weekly Wire*. http://weeklywire.com/ww/07-13-98/austin_screens_feature1.html
64 *"Fred Olen Ray & Doris Wishman." The*

Incredibly Strange Film Show*. IBA. Channel 4, United Kingdom. September 29, 1989. television.
65 Nathaniel Thompson. *Mondo Digital*. http://www.mondo-digital.com/chesty.html
66 Bowen.
67 *The Incredibly Strange Film Show*.
68 Douglas Martin, August 19, 2002. ""Doris Wishman, 'B' Film Director, Dies", *The New York Times*. http://www.nytimes.com/2002/08/19/movies/doris-wishman-b-film-director-dies.html
69 Kissell.
70 Juno, 110-111.
71 Renshaw.
72 *The Incredibly Strange Film Show*.
73 Acker, 281.
74 Knight, J. (1999). Murphy, Brianne. In A. L. Unterburger (Ed.), *The St. James Women Filmmakers Encyclopedia* (p. 299). essay, Visible Ink Press.
75 Weaver, T. (1996, June). The Search For Bri Murphy. *Fangoria*, 12, 13, 72–73.
76 In Acker's *Reel Women*, Murphy says that Bancroft hired her as Fatso's cinematographer because, "she couldn't give orders to men...I was a woman and not fat [so] she chose me."
77 Honeycutt, H. (2014). The Myth of the Two Percent. *Moviemaker Magazine*, 56, 57, 77.
78 Knight & Unterburger.
79 Acker, 281.
80 Erickson, H. (2010). Movie reviews. *The New York Times*. http://www.nytimes.com/movies/movie/31070/Man-Beast/overview.
81 Erickson.
82 Teel. (2001, June 17). *The films of jerry warren*. THE FILMS OF JERRY WARREN. http://www.angelfire.com/ca3/jerrywarren/. & Reis, G. R., & Casey, J. R. (n.d.). *The Wild World of Batwoman*. Jerry Warren Collection Volumes 1 and 2 (vci entertainment). http://www.dvddrive-in.com/reviews/t-z/jerrywarren646566.htm.
83 Knight, 299.
84 See Chapter Two.
85 SkiPretty. (2007, July 15). *What's it like today?* IMDb. https://www.imdb.com/user/ur16057835/reviews.
86 Hes an old friend.
87 Harding, B. (2014, November & 2015, February). Retrospective: Messiah of Evil Parts 1 & 2. *Fangoria Magazine*, (338 & 339).
88 Harding.
89 Harding.
90 Harding.
91 Harding.
92 Harding.
93 Harding.
94 The posters at http://monsterkidclassichorrorforum.com are some of the most intelligent, insightful, and best sleuths alive when it comes to finding out about obscure horror films. Much of my insight about *The Ghosts of Hanley House* comes directly from discussions on this forum.
95 Harmetz, R. (1967, December 8). New Blood Sought by Dracula Society. *Los Angeles Times*.
96 [In my opinion.]
97 Slinger, P. (2009) *The Other Side of the Underneath* [DVD]. United Kingdom. BFI. Insert booklet, essay by Penny Slinger.]
98 Janisse, K. L. (2014). *House of PSYCHOTIC women: An AUTOBIOGRAPHICAL topography of Female neurosis in horror and exploitation films* (p. 148). Fab Press.
99 Slinger.
100 Morgan, N. (2009). *Natasha Morgan Interview*. Unfinished Histories. Retrieved September 18, 2021, from https://www.unfinishedhistories.com/interviews/interviewees-l-q/natasha-morgan/.
101 Slinger.
102 Miller, A., & Raynor, B. (2009, September 1). Jack Bond. *Vice*. Retrieved September 18, 2021, from https://www.vice.com/en/article/ppzbwz/jack-bond-144-v16n9.
103 Matty Stanfield. (2015, December 30). *The dot as identity or the films of JANE Arden and JACK BOND*. Matty Stanfield. Retrieved September 18, 2021, from https://web.archive.org/web/20151231015325/http://mattystanfield.com/2015/12/30/the-dot-as-identity-or-the-films-of-jane-arden-and-jack-bond/.
104 *The suicide of my best friend Martin Pullinger*. (n.d.). Web of Stories. Retrieved September 18, 2015, from https://www.webofstories.com/play/redmond.ohanlon/17.
105 Morgan.
106 Stanfield.
107 JANE ARDEN & JACK BOND. *The worldwide Celluloid MASSACRE*. (n.d.). Retrieved September 18, 2015, from http://thelastexit.net/cinema/arden.html.
108 Kaye-Smith, S. (2007, December). *Arden and DALI loiter in the streets*. VERTIGO . Retrieved September 18, 2015, from https://www.closeupfilmcentre.com/vertigo_magazine/issue-14-december-2007/arden-and-dali-loiter-in-the-streets.
109 Miller, A., & Raynor, B.
110 Hueck, M. E. (2015, December 17). *Christina Hornisher: Alone with that obscene image of yourself.* Retrieved February 22, 2021, from https://projectorhasbeendrinking.blogspot.com/2015/12/christina-hornisher-alone-with-that.html
111 Legacy.com, & Legacy. (2003, May 04). Christina Hornisher Obituary - (2003)

- Los Angeles, CA - *Los Angeles Times*. Retrieved February 23, 2021, from http://www.legacy.com/obituaries/latimes/obituary.aspx?n=christina-hornisher-tina&pid=985088
112 Whitehead, K. (n.d.). *Insanity - Go VIDEO LTD*. Retrieved February 22, 2021, from http://go-video-ltd.co.United Kingdom/62.html
113 Poggiali, C. (1970, January 01*). HOLLYWOOD 90028 (1973).* Retrieved January 18, 2009, from https://templeofschlock.blogspot.com/2009/01/every-picture-tells-story-and-someday.html
114 Adelman, F. (n.d.). *Thriller part 2*. Retrieved February 23, 2021, from http://www.critcononline.com/thriller%20part%202.htm
115 Whitehead.
116 *Alternative projections.* (n.d.). Retrieved February 23, 2021, from https://www.alternativeprojections.com/people/christina-hornisher/
117 Alternative projections: *Experimental film in Los Angeles*, 1945-1980. (2012). Retrieved February 23, 2021, from https://web.archive.org/web/20161220024529/http://www.cinefamily.org/films/alternative-projections-experimental-film-in-los-angeles-1945-1980/
118 *Alternative projections.*
119 Adelman.
120 Miller, S. (Director). (2018). *The House of the Dead* [Film; special features audio interview with director Sharron Miller by Joe Rubin, on Blu-ray]. Vinegar Syndrome
121 This never happens anymore.
122 Miller, S.
123 Wooley, J., & Price, M. H. (2009, April). Forgotten Horrors: 'Alien Zone". *Fangoria*, 282, 72–73.
124 According to most horror scholars and fans, Ruggero Deodato's *Cannibal Holocaust* (1980) is the first found footage horror film, but *House of the Dead came* out in 1978, beating that record.
125 Wooley, J., & Price, M. H., 73
126 Miller, S.
127 Miller, S.
128 Wooley, J., & Price, M. H., 73
129 Egner, D. (1978, June 17). Sooner the Better Says Movie Mogul. *Tri City Herald*.
130 Over 200 Attend Bow of 'Alien Zone,' Enjoy Bizarre Evening in Stillwater. (1978, November 27). *BoxOffice*.
131 Miller, S.
132 Wooley, J. (2011). *Shot in Oklahoma: A century of Sooner State cinema*. University of Oklahoma Press, 211.
133 Miller, S.
134 *BoxOffice*.
135 Miller, S.
136 Arthur said that the original quote is "Kid, you got talent. You're going places." Spheeris says, since Arthur was in fact older than her, there's no way she would have called Arthur "kid" but the rest of that sentence is correct.
137 Mills, N. (1986, May 29). Lady Beware Warning Never Intimidated Her. *The Los Angeles Times*, p. 97.
138 Lowry.
139 Mills, N. (1986, November 19). Film Directing is Open to Women - Why Now? *The Los Angeles Times*, p. 64.
140 Lowry.
141 Lowry.
142 Gross, L. (1978, April 16). Karen Arthur. *The Los Angeles Times*, p. 54.
143 Champlin, C. (1978, December 1). Madness, Horror in 'The Mafu Cage. *The Los Angeles Times*, p. 26.
144 Tully, J. (1979, October 2). 'Mafu Cage' is powerful, hypnotic - and flawed. *Arizona Daily Star*, p. 5.
145 YouTube. (2017). Mafu Cage 1978 Cannes *Entretien avec Karen Arthur et Carol* Kane. YouTube. Retrieved September 22, 2021, from https://www.youtube.com/watch?v=TDobn9S3f4Y
146 Ebert, R. (2007). In *Roger Ebert's four-star reviews*, 1967-2007 (pp. 323–324). essay, Andrews McMeel.
147 Ebert, R. (2007)
148 Ebert, R. (1981, January 24). *Declarations of INDEPENDENCE: BEFORE Sundance was sundance*. Festivals & Awards | Roger Ebert. https://www.rogerebert.com/festivals/declarations-of-independence-before-sundance-was-sundance.
149 Gross, L. (1981, September 21). Problems of Women Filmmakers. *The Los Angeles Times*, p. 69.
150 Honeycutt, H. (January 15, 2022). Personal Interview.
151 Honeycutt.
152 Honeycutt.
153 Thomas.
154 Gross.
155 Ebert, R. (2010, April 11). *Anna Thomas: HONEY, there's a love in my SOUP*. Interviews | Roger Ebert. https://www.rogerebert.com/interviews/anna-thomas-honey-theres-a-love-in-my-soup.
156 Honeycutt.
157 Ebert, R. (2010)
158 Honeycutt, Heidi. (August 2021). Astrid Frank. Personal Interview.
159 Honeycutt, Frank.
160 Honeycutt, Frank.
161 Honeycutt, Frank.
162 Honeycutt, Frank.
163 Honeycutt, Frank.
164 Honeycutt, Frank.
165 But it's difficult to verify this without a

name or an outlet.
166 At the time of the writing of this book's section in 2021..
167 *The Jealous Mirror* (1982). BFI. (n.d.). Retrieved October 14, 2021, from https://www2.bfi.org.United Kingdom/films-television-people/4ce2b7310affe.
168 Honeycutt, Frank.
169 Honeycutt, Frank.
170 Leaf.
171 Mark Olsen, July 24, 2009. *Female-exploitation films seen in new light*. Los Angeles Times Retrieved from http://search.proquest.com/docview/422266838?accountid=44675
172 Colleeen Kelsey, "The Cult of Stephanie Rothman," *Interview Magazine*, March 9, 2016, http://www.interviewmagazine.com/film/stephanie-rothman/#_
173 Gross
174 Gross.
175 Mollie Gregory. *Women Who Run the Show: How a Brilliant and Creative New Generation of Women Stormed Hollywood,* (New York, NY: St. Martin's Press, 2002), 52.
176 Third Eye Cinema.
177 Olsen.
178 Gross.
179 Gross.
180 Sher.
181 Baumgarten, M. (April 9, 2010) "Exploitation's Glass Ceiling: Feminist filmmaker Stephanie Rothman on her short but brilliant run making B-movies". *Austin Chronicle.*
182 Fox.
183 Orcutt, B. (1997, September). Doris Wishman Interviewed by Bill Orcutt. Muckraker Magazine, (8), 30–35.
184 Author Parrish Randall posted on Facebook on October 8, 2022, that in his unpublished biography of Marilyn Burns, *From the Memoirs of Marilyn Burns: Tales Beyond The Saw*, that she told him that she had to direct half of the film due to "circumstances beyond her control."

CHAPTER FOUR
Obras maestras del terror

1 Lenin, V. I. (n.d.). *Lenin: Directives on the Film Business*. Marxists.org. https://www.marxists.org/archive/lenin/works/1922/jan/17.htm.
2 Kennedy, H. (1982, May). "Berlin Film Festival — 1982." *American Cinema Papers*. Retrieved October 1, 2021, from https://www.americancinemapapers.com/files/BERLIN_1982.htm.
3 *Die letzten tage von gomorrha (the last days of gomorrah)*. 1974. written and directed by Helma Sanders-Brahms: Moma. The Museum of Modern Art. (n.d.). Retrieved October 1, 2021, from https://www.moma.org/calendar/events/3286.
4 Roschy, B. (2014, July). *"germany pale mother".* Goethe Institut. Retrieved October 1, 2021, from https://www.goethe.de/en/kul/flm/20397223.html.
5 Spiegel, D. (1985, January 6). "Der Biß" Der Blonden Bestie. *DER SPIEGEL*. Retrieved December 3, 2021, from https://www.spiegel.de/kultur/der-biss-der-blonden-bestie-a-14e6551f-0002-0001-0000-000013511103.
6 When the film was in development, MGM called Stephanie Rothman for a meeting to discuss how they could pick her brain to make a seductive vampire film like *The Velvet Vampire* When she suggested that they hire her, they told her that they had already hired the director and just wanted to talk to her about how to make a vampire film. The film they ended up making was *The Hunger*.
7 Youtube. (2015). *Marianne Enzensberger - Making of "Der Biß".* Retrieved from https://youtu.be/Rb5KYToCeOc.
8 Enzensberger.
9 Enzensberger.
10 He is also a nephew of German horror actress and screenwriter Luzi Kryn.
11 Sorfa, D. (2015). Ester Krumbachová. In J. Nelmes, & J. Selbo (Eds.), *Women Screenwriters: An International Guide* (pp. 253-262). Palgrave Macmillan.
12 Sorfa.
13 Facets. (n.d.). Daisies - Description. Facets DVD Catalogue. Retrieved from https://www.facetsdvd.com/ProductDetails.asp?ProductCode=DV62817
14 Field, M. (1994, February 1). "Interview with Vera Chytilova." *Europe of Cultures*. Retrieved January 7, 2022, from https://fresques.ina.fr/europe-des-cultures-en/fiche-media/Europe00213/interview-with-vera-chytilova.html
15 Unlike *Daisies*, *Fruit of Paradise* wasn't banned in Czechoslovakia because the government did not understand it. "The subject wasn't really a murder mystery," said Chytilová in an interview. "It wasn't that simple." However, Chytilová was banned by the Czech government from making any more films after *Fruit of Para-*

dise for seven years and only then on the condition that her films are "more realistic."

16 "The cinematheque / the anarchic cinema of Věra Chytilová." The Cinematheque. (2020, 6). Retrieved January 7, 2022, from https://thecinematheque.ca/series/the-anarchic-cinema-of-vera-chytilova

17 Guardian News and Media. (2000, August 11). "Interview: Vera Chytilova." *The Guardian*. Retrieved January 7, 2022, from https://www.theguardian.com/film/2000/aug/11/culture.features2

18 Guardian News and Media.

19 I had originally covered *Le roi des aulnes* in this book's first chapter but had to remove it for space.

20 IMDb.com. (n.d.). *La Mort du cygne*. IMDb. Retrieved December 13, 2021, from https://www.imdb.com/title/tt0143749/.

21 Filmography, telefilms and television series. Lucile Costa . (n.d.). Retrieved January 4, 2022, from http://www.lucilecosta.com/Filmography_EN.html

22 At the time of this book's publication.

23 *Casa del Buon Ritorno, LA (1986)*. CASA DEL BUON RITORNO, LA (1986) de Beppe Cino, Giuseppina Marotta, Cinefania. (n.d.). Retrieved December 14, 2021, from http://www.cinefania.com/movie.php/48008/

24 IMDb.com. (n.d.). *The House of the blue shadows*. IMDb. Retrieved December 14, 2021, from https://www.imdb.com/title/tt0090800/

25 Los Angeles Times. (1993, March 19). *Movie Review: 'breath of life': Love among the ruins in postwar Italy : Franco Nero and Lucrezia Lante della Rovere discover romance in a Palermo TB Sanitarium in 1946.*. Retrieved December 14, 2021, from https://www.latimes.com/archives/la-xpm-1993-03-19-ca-12711-story.html

26 *The House of the blue shadows* - standard DVD edition. TetroVideo. (2021, July 7). Retrieved December 14, 2021, from https://tetrovideo.com/shop/the-house-of-the-blue-shadows-standard-edition/

27 Horton, A., & McDougal, S. Y. (1998). Feminist Makeovers: The Celluloid Surgery of Valie Export and Su Friedrich. In *Play it again, Sam: Retakes and re*makes (p. 218). essay, University of California Press..

28 Staff, F. N. E. (2015, September 8). *Austria selects Goodnight Mommy as Oscar bid*. Film New Europe. Retrieved December 14, 2021, from http://www.filmneweurope.com/news/austria-news/item/111179-austria-selects-goodnight-mommy-as-oscar-bid

29 Jusrud is, as of 2021, the dean of Den Norske Filmskolen (The Norwegian Film Scool).

30 Ebert, R. (1969, April 10). *Night games movie review & Film SUMMARY (1969):* | Roger Ebert. Retrieved September 30, 2021, from https://www.rogerebert.com/reviews/night-games-1969.

31 Guardian News and Media. (2016, October 27). *Previously unknown Ingmar Bergman script to be filmed by former antagonist.* The Guardian. Retrieved December 16, 2021, from https://www.theguardian.com/film/2016/oct/27/unknown-ingmar-bergman-script-filmed-fellini-kurosawa

32 Osten, S. (2021, May 28). "Gerd drömde om att regissera." nordicwomeninfilm. Retrieved December 16, 2021, from https://www.nordicwomeninfilm.com/gerd-dromde-om-att-bli-filmregissor/?lang=en

33 Sveriges Radio. (2016, April 7). *Director wins appeal on film's age* limit . Radio Sweden | Sveriges Radio. Retrieved December 16, 2021, from https://sverigesradio.se/artikel/6406266

34 Guardian News and Media.

35 YouTube. (2021, October 21). *Knocking*. YouTube. Retrieved December 16, 2021, from https://www.youtube.com/watch?v=IQau-4vD5v5U

36 rizospastis.gr | Synchroni. (2009, December 1). *Ακροβατώντας στο ... παράλογο. ΡΙΖΟΣΠΑΣΤΗΣ*. Retrieved November 13, 2021, from https://www-rizospastis-gr.story.do?id=5384461.

37 Corp, E. (2021, July 20). *Why is there no horror film directed by women in Spain?* Digis Mak. Retrieved November 3, 2021, from https://digismak.com/why-is-there-no-horror-film-directed-by-women-in-spain/.

38 *La Brujita* was brought to my attention by filmmaker Diego López-Fernández at the 2022 Sitges Film Festival in Catalonia, Spain.

39 Reyes, A. (2019, February). *Big Scares On The Small Screen: A Brief History Of The Made-for-television Horror Film.* Miskatonic Institute of Horror Studies. Los Angeles; The Philosophical Research Society.

40 Deltell Escolar, L., & Muñoz Giner, A. (2020). *Vera, un Cuento Cruel (1973) Josefina Molina.* El Cine de Terror Visto por una directora. Fotocinema. Revista Científica De Cine y Fotografía, (21), 403–424. https://doi.org/10.24310/fotocinema.2020.vi21.10018. This paper is one of the only resources available that mentions the series *Hora Once* and Josefina Molina in any meaningful context. Much of the information about the show itself as a series is taken from this paper, with full credit to the original researchers.

41 Triana-Toribio, N. (1998). *In Memoriam: Pilar Miró (1940-1997).* Film History, 10(2), 231–240. http://www.jstor.org/stable/3815284

42 Escolar & Giner, 12.

43 Escolar & Giner, 13.

44 Escolar & Giner, 14.

45 Escolar & Giner, 17.

46 Galan, D. *Vera, un cuento cruel. El Triunfo*, XXIX, n. 615, June 13, 1974. p. 50.

47 Hopewell, J. (2019, September 22). Josefina Molina: Still battling after all these years. *Variety*. Retrieved November 11, 2021, from https://variety.com/2019/film/news/josefina-molina-still-battling-after-all-these-years-1203344271/.

48 *Josefina Molina, paving the way: Timeless women*. Fascinating Spain. (2021, April 22). Retrieved November 11, 2021, from https://fascinatingspain.com/spanish-culture-fascinating/spanish-culture-in-andalusia/josefina-molina-paving-the-way-timeless-women-6/.

49 If you're a big nerd and want more, I highly recommend following academic papers about Molina which do focus on some of her horror work.

50 Chowdhury, E. H., & De, E. N. (2020). In South Asian filmscapes: Transregional encounters (p. 167). University of Washington Press.

51 Santos, S. (2014, January 14). *The fifties #502: Nestor de Villa and Charito Solis in Susana C. de Guzman's "Villa milagrosa" (1958)/* re-posted. Video 48. Retrieved November 1, 2021, from http://video48.blogspot.com/2014/01/the-fifties-502-nestor-de-villa-and.html.

52 Santos, S. (2014, June 17). *The sixties #87: An all-star cast, 4 stories, 4 directors in "Mga alamat ng sandaigdig" (1960).* Video 48. Retrieved October 21, 2021, from http://video48.blogspot.com/2014/06/the-sixties-87-all-star-cast-4-stories.html.

53 Santos, S. (2013, May 30). *The sixties #42: An all-star cast, 4 stories, 4 directors in "Katotohanan o guniguni?" (1960).* Video 48. Retrieved October 21, 2021, from http://video48.blogspot.com/2014/05/the-sixties-42-all-star-cast-4-stories.html.

54 Gonzalez, K. (2000). *Superstar Nora Aunor Komiks*. Superstar Nora Aunor. Retrieved October 18, 2021, from http://www.oocities.org/ken_gonzales2000/superstarnora.html.

55 For a comprehensive and concise understanding of women directors in Indonesian history, I highly recommend Grace Swestin's article *IN THE BOYS' CLUB: A HISTORICAL PERSPECTIVE ON THE ROLES OF WOMEN IN THE INDONESIAN CINEMA.1926-MAY 1998* from 2012 which can be found on various academic research document websites and databases.

56 Badai-Selatan (1962). BFI. (n.d.). Retrieved November 7, 2021, from https://www2.bfi.org.United Kingdom/films-television-people/4ce2b6f109661.

57 Dewi, C., & Rehatta, Y. (n.d.). *Penunggang Kuda Dari Tjimande*. Film Indonesia. Retrieved November 7, 2021, from http://catalogue.filmindonesia.or.id/movie/title/lf-p026-71-672776_penunggang-kuda-dari-tjimande.

58 Chitra Dewi. (n.d.). *Bertjinta Dalam Gelap*. (1971). Retrieved November 7, 2021, from http://filmindonesia.or.id/movie/title/lf-b019-71-686304_bertjinta-dalam-gelap#.YYgv-WDMK39.

59 Dewi, C. (n.d.). *Dara-Dara. Film Indonesia*. Retrieved November 7, 2021, from http://filmindonesia.or.id/movie/title/lf-d009-71-929871_dara-dara#.YYgwWmDMK38.

60 Michalik, Y. (Ed.). (2013). *Indonesian women filmmakers*. Regiospectra.

61 Honeycutt, H., & Samundra, T. (2021, September 23). Personal Interview.

62 Raje, A. (2017). *Freedom: My story*. HarperCollins Publishers India, pg 90.

63 Raje, 91 & 92.

64 Raje, 97.

65 Raje, 99

66 Raje, 97.

67 Raje, 94.

68 Raje, 100.

69 Raje, 102.

70 Raje 102.

71 D'Silva, N. (2015, May 15). *Gehrayee (the depth - 1980).* Neildsilva.com. Retrieved October 1, 2021, from https://www.neildsilva.com/2015/05/15/gehrayee-the-depth-1980/.

72 Raje, 98.

73 Raje, 102.

74 Raje, 13

75 GOODTiMES. (2020). *Decoding Female Representation in Bollywood.* YouTube. Retrieved November 23, 2021, from https://www.youtube.com/watch?v=OngVQ_IRbHE.

76 Shih Kuang Creative. (2005). *Taiwan Black Movies*. Taiwan.

77 *Taiwan Black Movies.*

78 *Taiwan Black Movies.*

79 *Taiwan Black Movies.*

80 For anyone interested in learning more, I highly encourage you to read the paper by Ting-Wu Cho 卓庭伍, *"From Avengers to Desperate Wives: Women's Movement, Taiwan Pulp, and the Transformation of Female Star Image (1979-1985)"* 女性復仇與母性回歸： 1970年代後期臺灣新女性主義與社會寫實女星的形象轉變 in the Journal of Art Studies 藝術學研究 volume 23, December 2018.

81 Yau, K. S.-ting. (2011). *In Japanese and Hong Kong film industries: Understanding the origins of East Asian film networks* (p. 99). Routledge.

82 Wang, L. (2011). *Chinese women's cinema: Transnational contexts*. Columbia Univ. Press.

83 Norapoompipat, A. (2019, March 8). *Girls just wanna make movies*. https://www.bangkokpost.com. Retrieved March 15, 2022, from https://www.bangkokpost.com/life/arts-and-entertainment/1641244/girls-just-wanna-make-movies

84 Milne, T., Hardy, P., & Willemen, P. (1995). *The Overlook Film Encyclopedia*. Overlook Press & Ricalde, M. C., & Hind, E. (2004). Popular Mexican Cinema and Undocumented Immigrants. Discourse, 26(1/2), 194–213. http://www.jstor.org/stable/41389696

85 Galbraith, M. (2021, March 11). *Isela Vega dies at the age of 81, an emblem of Mexican cinema and the first Latina woman to appear in Playboy Magazine*. Globe Live Media. Retrieved December 12, 2021, from https://globelivemedia.com/world/mexico/isela-vega-dies-at-the-age-of-81-emblem-of-mexican-cinema-and-the-first-latina-woman-to-appear-in-playboy-magazine/.

86 Loreti, N. (2007, December). The Rules of the Game: An Interview with Isela Vega. *Shock Cinema*, (34), 34–35.

87 Monster, S. (2011, June 6). *El fantasma de la ópera* (1960) Lost miniseries. Phantom Reviews. Retrieved November 1, 2021, from https://phantomreviews.proboards.com/thread/277.

88 Valenti, T. F. (2019, June 7). *Narciso Ibáñez Serrador: Cartas de Amor Al Fantástico. Dirigido por*. Retrieved November 2, 2021, from https://www.dirigidopor.es/2019/03/01/narciso ibanez serra dor-cartas-amor-al-fantastico/.

89 Itkin, S and Sirvén, P. (1999) *De Estamos en el aire, una historia de la Televisión en la Argentina, de Carlos Ulanovsky*. Planeta, Buenos Aires, 179.

90 Itkin and Sirvén, 179.

91 Valentini.

92 Monster, S. (2011, June 6). *El fantasma de la ópera* (1960) Lost miniseries. Phantom Reviews. Retrieved November 1, 2021, from https://phantomreviews.proboards.com/thread/277.

93 *"a finely developed idea in the libretto and an exercise of happy imagination in its exposition".* Antologia del Miedo (1959-1959). Cinefania Online. (n.d.). Retrieved November 2, 2021, from http://www.cinefania.com/television/serie.php?id=1447&l=.

94 .[Marcelino, A. (n.d.). *Rosangela Maldonado*. Mulheres do Cinema Brasileiro. Retrieved November 8, 2021, from https://www.mulheresdocinemabrasileiro.com.br/site/mulheres/visualiza/453/Rosangela-Maldonado/4.]

95 Review published in O Estado de S. Paulo on 11/19/78 and retrieved from a reprint: Andrade, S. L. (2009, January 22). *A DEUSA de marmore, Escrava do diabo*. INDICAÇÃO DO BIÁFORA.*Críticas de Rubem Biáfora, selecionadas por Sergio Andrade*. Retrieved from http://indicacao-rubembiafora.blogspot.com/2009/01/deusa-de-marmore-escrava-do-diabo.html.

96 Museo Nacional Centro de Arte Reina Sofía. (2011). *Lygia Pape Magnetized Space*. Madrid, Spain; Museo Nacional Centro de Arte Reina Sofía.

97 Januszczak, W. (2012, January 16). *A cry in the dark*. Waldemar Januszczak. Retrieved November 8, 2021, from https://waldemar.television/2012/01/a-cry-in-the-dark/.

CHAPTER FIVE
Some Nudity Required

1 McDonagh, M. (1991, May). Scare Sisters. *Fangoria*, (102), 37.

2 Corman R., & Jerome, J. (2006). In How I made a hundred movies in Hollywood and never lost a dime (p. 216). Da Capo.

3 Alexander, C. (2010, September). When Roger Corman Cleared the Beach. *Fangoria*, 51.

4 Rosenberg, A. (n.d.). *Barbara Peeters — Don't Ask her about 'Humanoids from the Deep'*. Retrieved from https://ashlandplayreviews.com/barbara-peeters-dont-ask-her-about-humanoids-from-the-deep/

5 Gross.

6 Gross.

7 Alexander.

8 Epstein, A. (1980, May 8). Humanoids' Haywire, Women Say. *The Los Angeles Times*.

9 Epstein.

10 Epstein.

11 He would later direct *Deathstalker*.

12 Epstein.

13 Epstein.

14 "The Making of Humanoids from the Deep", *Humanoids from the Deep*. Dir. Barbara Peeters. Perf. Vic Morrow, Ann Turkel, Doug McClure. Shout Factory, 2010. Blu-ray.

15 Epstein.

16 Epstein.
17 Corman, R. (1980, May 25). Corman on 'Women in Power.' *The Los Angeles Times.*
18 Rosenberg.
19 Rosenberg.
20 Morris, G. (2000). Roger Corman's New World Pictures: Notes Toward a Lexicon. *Bright Lights Film Journal.* Retrieved from http://brightlightsfilm.com/roger-cormans-new-world-pictures-notes-toward-lexicon/
21 Brown, T. (2001, December 6). *The Sally Mattison Interview.* The Old Hockstatter Place. Retrieved from http://www.project73.net/oldhockstatterplace/interviews/sallyinterview.shtml
22 Most of the information available to horror fans about *The Slumber Party Massacre* series comes from the work of journalist and filmmaker Jason Paul Collum. His August 2000 article *The Slumber Party Massacre Saga* for *Femme Fatales* magazine, and subsequent documentary, *Sleepless Nights: Revisiting the Slumber Party Massacre* (2010), are the primary resources I'd recommend to anyone who wants to make a deep, dark dive into the abyss of the films. Collum has extensively interviewed the cast and crew and documented the inception to the re-release of the three films in the series with meticulous detail. In addition, journalist April Snelling's article "Only Women Bleed" in the November 2010 issue of *Rue Morgue* magazine (inspired by the 2010 Blu-ray re-release of all three films featuring Collum's documentary as a special feature) has updated interviews with all three films' directors, several cast members, and an intelligent look at the legacy of the 'feminist' horror film. Tony Brown's website Old Hockstatter Place, no longer online but active between 2001 and 2004 (and accessible via Internet archives), was the first digital information source about *The Slumber Party Massacre* movies and featured interviews, photographs, and trivia. I highly encourage horror fans to look these up and enjoy them. I'm not going to do a deep dive into this series; these researchers have already done that. I will give you a basic rundown of the series and why it's important to the horror genre.
23 I asked him.
24 *Some Nudity Required.* (1998). [DVD]. USA.
25 Snellings, A. (2010, December). *Only Women Bleed.* Rue Morgue Magazine, (106), 30.
26 Corman & Jerome, 216.
27 Collum, J. P. (2000, August 11). *Slumber Party Massacre,* Femme Fatales, 9(3), 8.
28 Collum, 13.
29 Collum
30 Snellings, 32.
31 Snellings, 31.
32 Snellings, 31.
33 *Some Nudity Required.*
34 Brown, *The Sally Mattison Interview.*
35 Snellings, 32.
36 *Some Nudity Required.*
37 *Some Nudity Required.*
38 *Some Nudity Required.*
39 *Some Nudity Required.*
40 Rife, K. (2019, March 12). *Wayne's world director Penelope Spheeris on leaving Hollywood behind: "They can blow me".* The A.V. Club. Retrieved January 9, 2022, from https://film.avclub.com/wayne-s-world-director-penelope-spheeris-on-leaving-hol-1833211775
41 Honeycutt, Heidi. (2021) Penelope Spheeris. Personal Interview.
42 Honeycutt, Spheeris.
43 Honeycutt, Spheeris.
44 Honeycutt, Spheeris.
45 Konda, K. (2019, April 27). *From stripped to kill to Nancy Drew: Katt Shea's graduation from Roger Corman University.* We Minored in Film. Retrieved December 30, 2021, from https://weminoredinfilm.com/219/03/15/from-stripped-to-kill-to-nancy-drew-katt-sheas-graduation-from-roger-corman-university/
46 televisionSO, B. E. J. B. (2021, February 23). *Director Katt Shea talks about her 1980's Roger Corman-produced films.* televisionStoreOnline. Retrieved December 30, 2021, from https://www.televisionstoreonline.com/blogs/television-movie-news-updates/katt-shea-interview
47 Konda.
48 Konda.
49 Thomas, K. (1987, July 14). Stripped to Kill. *Sacramento Bee*, p. 23.
50 televisionSO.
51 From Corman to classes: A conversation with Katt Shea. *Fülle Circle Magazine.* (n.d.). Retrieved December 30, 2021, from https://www.fullecirclemagazine.com/2009/02/conversation-with-katt-shea.html
52 Detroit Free Press.
53 televisionSO.
54 Detroit Free Press.
55 Konda.
56 Trembath, R. (2017, November 1). *Katt Shea [interview].* TRAINWRECK'D SOCIETY (2011-2021). Retrieved December 31, 2021, from https://trainwreckdsociety.com/2017/10/30/katt-shea-interview/
57 Benenson, L. H. (1992, May 3). *Film; how 'poison ivy' got its Sting.* The New York Times. Retrieved December 31, 2021, from https://www.nytimes.com/1992/05/03/archives/film-how-poison-ivy-got-its-sting.html

58 Berenson.
59 Berenson.
60 Porter, D. (1992, June). *Katt Shea, June 1992*. The Occasional Critic.
61 televisionSO.
62 televisionSO
63 Borseti, F. (2016). Munchies. In *It came from the 80s!: Interviews with 124 cult filmmakers* (pp. 165–167). chapter, McFarland & Company, Inc., Publishers.
64 Borseti, 165.
65 Borseti, 165.
66 LoBrutto, V. (1991). Tina Hirsch. *In Selected takes: Film editors on editing* (pp. 189–195). chapter, Praeger.
67 Borseti, 165.
68 Kowalski, E. (2001, November 14). Tina Hirsch. *Variety*. Retrieved December 28, 2021, from https://variety.com/2001/biz/news/tina-hirsch-1117855804/
69 "Kristine Peterson Returns to Deadly Dreams". Code Red. 2016.
70 Johnson, H. (1994, November 27). Film Noir… or with Cream? *The Los Angeles Times*, p. 257.
71 Walsh, M. (1989, April 8). We're Kept Guessing. *The Province*, p. 10.
72 Thomas, K. (1995, November 1). Movie Review : 'one night stand' runs out of steam. *Los Angeles Times*. Retrieved January 9, 2022, from https://www.latimes.com/archives/la-xpm-1995-11-01-ca-63681-story.html
73 Indiewire. (2008, December 9). *Film noir as bad dream: "dark streets" director Rachel Samuels*. IndieWire. Retrieved January 9, 2022, from https://www.indiewire.com/2008/12/indiewire-interview-film-noir-as-bad-dream-dark-streets-director-rachel-samuels-71230/
74 Honeycutt, Spheeris..
75 Honeycutt, Heidi (February 7, 2022). Linda Hassani. Personal Interview.
76 Honeycutt, Hassani.
77 Full Moon Pictures. (1994). *Dark Angel: The Ascent Behind-the-scenes* (Full Length Videozone). YouTube. USA. Retrieved January 14, 2022, from https://www.youtube.com/watch?v=V-q0vKE-IYs.
78 Honeycutt, Hassani.
79 Honeycutt, Hassani
80 (2004, August 19). *Denice Duff: Accidental vampire*. Film Threat. Retrieved January 10, 2022, from https://filmthreat.com/interviews/denice-duff-accidental-vampire/
81 Martinuzzi, H.
82 Honeycutt, H. (2022, January 20). Hope Perello. Personal Interview.
83 Honeycutt, Perello.
84 Honeycutt, Perello.
85 Honeycutt, Perello.
86 Collum, J. P. (2002, April). Tammi Sutton. *Femme Fatales*, 11(4), 23.
87 Collum, 24.
88 Collum, 24.
89 Honestly probably the most fun part of making this movie.
90 Collum, 25.
91 Third Eye Cinema.
92 Third Eye Cinema.
93 Third Eye Cinema.
94 Third Eye Cinema.
95 Borseti, F. (2016). Roberta Findlay. In *It came from the 80s!: Interviews with 124 cult filmmakers*. essay, McFarland & Company, Inc., Publishers.
96 Third Eye Cinema.
97 Third Eye Cinema.
98 Third Eye Cinema.
99 Not to be confused with Nettie Peña's 1981 slasher film *Home Sweet Home*.
100 Third Eye Cinema.
101 Third Eye Cinema.
102 Third Eye Cinema.
103 *Banned* (1989) Blu-ray Coming soon. Media Blasters. (n.d.). Retrieved January 17, 2022, from http://media-blasters.com/banned-1989-Blu-ray-coming-soon/
104 Juno, 110-111.
105 Bowen.
106 Yes, *Aliens* is great.
107 Benardello, B. K. (2015, March 7). *Interview: Danielle Harris talks see no evil 2* (exclusive). Shockya.com. Retrieved January 17, 2022, from https://www.shockya.com/news/2015/03/07/interview-danielle-harris-talks-see-no-evil-2/
108 Wixson, H. (2014, August 6). *Exclusive interview: The Soska sisters & WWE's Kane Talk See No Evil 2*. Daily Dead. Retrieved January 17, 2022, from https://dailydead.com/exclusive-interview-soska-sisters-wwes-kane-talk-see-evil-2/
109 Honeycutt, H. (2022, January 16). Meosha Bean. Personal Interview.
110 McDonagh, M. (1991, May). Scare Sisters. *Fangoria*, (102), 36.
111 McDonagh, 36.
112 Honeycutt, H. (2006, January 10. Paulette Victor-Lifton. Personal Interview.
113 DiVincenzo, A. (2015, November 19). Interview: John Franklin (children of the corn, The Addams Family). Broke Horror Fan. Retrieved January 21, 2022, from https://brokehorrorfan.com/post/133536750618/interview-john-franklin-children-of-the-corn
114 DiVincenzo.
115 Honeycutt, H. (2022, January 20). David J. Schow. Personal Interview.
116 Honeycutt, H. (2022, January 20). Hope Perello. Personal Interview.
117 Honeycutt, Perello.
118 McDonagh, 36.
119 McDonagh, 37.

120 Shapiro, M. (1991, May). *One Woman's Nightmare*. Fangoria, (102), 39.
121 Garcia, K. (2016, July 28). *Director Rachel Talalay talks tank girl and a career of dreams and nightmares.* Westword. Retrieved January 26, 2022, from https://www.westword.com/arts/director-rachel-talalay-talks-tank-girl-and-a-career-of-dreams-and-nightmares-8140107
122 Shapiro.
123 Shapiro.
124 Exclusive interview: *Rachel Talalay.* Nightmare on Elm Street Companion Ultimate Online Resource to Horror Series A Nightmare on Elm Street. (2005, March 22). Retrieved January 25, 2022, from http://nightmareonelmstreetfilms.com/site/exclusive-interview-rachel-talalay/
125 Ultimate Online Resource to Horror Series A Nightmare on Elm Street.
126 Ultimate Online Resource to Horror Series A Nightmare on Elm Street.
127 Rea, S. (1991, September 16). Freddy's back for one more bloodfest. *Spokane Chronicle*, p. 17.
128 O'Sullivan, E. (1991, September 14). The last of Freddy and good riddance. *Asbury Park Press*, p. 26.
129 Willman, C. (1991, September 16). 'Freddy's Dead' is DOA at a box office near you. *The Los Angeles Times*, p. 280.
130 Collis, C. (2016, July 19). From 'tank girl' to 'Sherlock': The less-than-elementary return of director Rachel Talalay. *EW.com*. Retrieved January 26, 2022, from https://ew.com/article/2016/07/19/sherlock-doctor-who-rachel-talalay-tank-girl/
131 "The arrow interviews… James Dudelson and Ana Clavell! Joe Blo." (2004). Retrieved January 26, 2022, from https://web.archive.org/web/20160303220134/http://www.joblo.com/arrow/interview125.htm
132 Burnette, B. (2018, October 27). *A review of Creepshow III (a.k.a. creepshow 3).* The Truth Inside The Lie. Retrieved January 26, 2022, from http://thetruthinsidethelie.blogspot.com/2012/10/a-brief-review-creepshow-iii-aka.html
133 Honeycutt, H. (2006, January 10). Ana Clavell. Personal Interview.
134 Honeycutt, Clavell.
135 Kim, K. H. (2003, November 7). *An Interview with Yun Jae*-yeon. Korean Film. Retrieved February 12, 2022, from http://www.koreanfilm.org/yunjaeyeon.html
136 Kim.
137 Kim.
138 Honeycutt, H. (2021, February 3). Mary Lambert. Personal Interview.
139 Honeycutt.
140 Mills, N. (1986, November 18). *Rough going in television for women directors*. Los Angeles Times. https://www.latimes.com/archives/la-xpm-1986-11-18-ca-8146-story.html.
141 Mills.
142 Mills.
143 Manning, L. (2021). *A Conversation with Lesley Manning, Director of Ghostwatch* [Interview by A. Clarke, S. Abbott, & S. Lupher]. The George Romero Foundation.
144 *An Interview with Assistant Director Nicholas Granby. Crucible of Horror* (Blu-ray interview short). Scream Factory. 2018.
145 Honeycutt, H. (2022, September 15). Christopher Toyne Personal Interview.
146 Mills, N. (1986, November 18). *Rough going in television for women directors*. Los Angeles Times. https://www.latimes.com/archives/la-xpm-1986-11-18-ca-8146-story.html.
147 McCallum also starred in Gabrielle Beaumont's 1993 action/thriller *Fatal Inheritance*.
148 Alexander, C. (2013, June). Tilly, Endurable. *Fangoria*, (324), 47–48.
149 Honeycutt, Toyne.
150 Mills, N. (1986, May 29). *Lady Beware Warning Never Intimidated Her*. The Los Angeles Times, p. 93.
151 BBC. (2017, December 29). *Jodie Foster on directing Black Mirror and her childhood dream*. BBC. Retrieved January 29, 2022, from https://www.bbc.co.United Kingdom/programmes/articles/mtzhDm9g1g5N-NZHtbXLrGl/jodie-foster-on-directing-black-mirror-and-her-childhood-dream
152 The Television Academy Foundation. (2018). *Lesli Linka Glatter Interview Part 1 of 3* - televisionAcademy.com/Interviews. YouTube. Retrieved from https://www.youtube.com/watch?v=XUY8pCt5g88.
153 Manning, (2021).
154 Manning.
155 Inside a Mind (Producer). (n.d.). *The BBC's Most Controversial television Show* [Video file]. Retrieved February 28, 2021, from https://www.youtube.com/watch?v=uO2oeiGdGIM
156 "The BBC halloween spoof that led to a teenage suicide." (2017, October 31). https://www.independent.com/uk/arts-entertainment/television/news/ghostwatch-bbc-halloween-spoof-boy-suicide-television-michael-parkinson-complaints-25th-anniversary-a8027231.html
157 Lines, C. (2016, October 31). *Ghostwatch: Director Lesley Manning Interview*. https://www.denofgeek.com/television/ghostwatch-director-lesley-manning-interview/
158 Manning.
159 Manning.
160 Manning.
161 Lines.

162 Manning.
163 Manning.
164 Manning.
165 Manning.
166 Manning.
167 Manning.
168 Manning.
169 Manning.
170 Manning.
171 Manning.
172 Manning.
173 Manning.
174 Manning.
175 McCallum, S. (2013, December 4). *Why i love... ghostwatch*. https://www2.bfi.org. United Kingdom/news-opinion/news-bfi/features/why-i-love-ghostwatch
176 West, A. (2015, November 06). *Remembering notorious British television Shocker GHOSTWATCH*. https://www.comingsoon.net/horror/news/747658-remembering-notorious-british-television-shocker-ghostwatch
177 Manning.
178 Manning.
179 Parents blame television programme for son's death. (1992, December 23). https://www.independent.com/news/uk/parents-blame-television-programme-son-s-death-1565122.html
180 "The BBC Halloween spoof that led to a teenage suicide"
181 *The Ghost That Spooked a Nation* [Video file]. (2012, December 3). https://youtu.be/YBqIpjTDlzU
182 The gloryhole. (n.d.). http://www.ghostwatchbtc.com/p/the-gloryhole.html

CHAPTER SIX
Sometimes Dead is Better

1 Wiley, M., Bona, D., & MacColl, G. (editor). (1996). *Inside oscar: The unofficial history of the academy awards* (5th ed.). Ballantine Books.
2 Rosenberg, H. (1993, March 30). Calendar goes to the Oscars : Oscar sets new record for hype : Crystal is funny, but salute to women comes up short in bloated telecast. *Los Angeles Times*. Retrieved February 5, 2022, from https://www.latimes.com/archives/la-xpm-1993-03-30-ca-17049-story.html
3 Webber, J. (2012, September 25). *More than david's daughter: An interview with Jennifer Lynch*. VICE. Retrieved February 22, 2022, from https://www.vice.com/en/article/mvpkex/more-than-davids-daughter-an-interview-with-jennifer-lynch
4 Abbott, S. (2020). Near Dark. Bloomsbury Publishing Plc.
5 From the September 2000 introduction to a new edition of the book.
6 *Near Dark* directed by Kathryn Bigelow was released in theaters in 1987, but was made by an independent company.
7 Campopiano, J., & White, J. (Directors). (2017). *Unearthed & Untold: The Path to Pet Sematary* [Motion picture on DVD]. USA: Synapse Films.
8 The others being Kubrick's *The Shining* and DePalma's *Carrie*
9 Campopiano & White.
10 Thomas, K. (1989, April 24). Movie Reviews: A Chilling Vision in Pet Sematary. *Los Angeles Times*, p. 5.
11 Campopiano & White.
12 Honeycutt, H. (2021, February 3). Mary Lambert. Personal Interview.
13 Campopiano & White.
14 Labbe, R. A. (1989). *Paying Respects at Pet Sematary*. Fangoria, (81), 18-21.
15 Thomas, K.
16 Labbe, 18-21.
17 Rubinstein was a close collaborator with George Romero, working with him on numerous films and television series beginning with the 1978 horror movie *Dawn of the Dead*, the sequel to Romero's 1968 ground-breaking zombie movie *Night of the Living Dead* as well as adaptations of other Stephen King books with both *The Stand* miniseries, *The Night Flier*, and *Thinner*.
18 Labbe, 19 & 20.
19 Honeycutt, Lambert.
20 Campopiano & White.
21 Honeycutt, Lambert.
22 Denise Crosby also stars in the horror film *Dolly Dearest* (1991) directed by Maria Lease and the action sci-fi film *Deep Impact* (1998) directed by Mimi Leder.
23 Campopiano & White.
24 Campopiano & White.
25 Labbe,19.
26 Honeycutt, Lambert.
27 *Pet Sematary* (1989)
28 Honeycutt, Lambert.
29 Campopiano & White.
30 Campopiano & White.
31 Weiner, D. (2019, April 02). *How 'Pet Sematary' Director won Over Stephen King*. Retrieved February 13, 2021, from https://

www.hollywoodreporter.com/heat-vision/how-pet-sematary-director-won-stephen-king-1198107
32 Campopiano & White.
33 Honeycutt, Lambert.
34 Honeycutt, Lambert.
35 Honeycutt, Lambert.
36 *Pet Sematary* (1989)
37 Thomas, K.
38 Honeycutt, Lambert.
39 Easton, N. J. (1989, April 25). Pet Sematary Buries the Competition. *Los Angeles Times*, p. 2.
40 Thomas, K.
41 Honeycutt, Lambert.
42 Honeycutt, Lambert.
43 Honeycutt, Lambert.
44 Morgan, D. (1992). *Fran Rubel Kuzui.* Wide Angle / Closeup: Interview with Director Fran Rubel Kuzui. Retrieved February 6, 2022, from http://www.wideanglecloseup.com/kuzui.html
45 Yahoo! (2015, May 5). *Remembering the 'buffy the vampire slayer' movie and Joss Whedon's first superhero*. Yahoo! Retrieved February 6, 2022, from https://www.yahoo.com/entertainment/joss-whedon-buffy-the-vampire-slayer-118217991342.html
46 Kristy Swanson, as told to B. S. (2019, March 8). United Kingdom *e Perry's 'buffy' co-star Kristy Swanson recalls how he "Always had my back"*. The Hollywood Reporter. Retrieved February 6, 2022, from https://www.hollywoodreporter.com/movies/movie-news/lUnited Kingdome-perrys-buffy-star-kristy-swanson-recalls-how-he-had-my-back-1193157/
47 Lang, N. (2013, January 2). *25 little-known facts about 'buffy the vampire slayer'*. Thought Catalog. Retrieved February 6, 2022, from https://thoughtcatalog.com/nico-lang/2013/01/25-little-known-facts-about-buffy-the-vampire-slayer/
48 Morgan.
49 Morgan.
50 Robinson, T. (2001, September 5). *Joss Whedon.* The A.V. Club. Retrieved February 6, 2022, from https://www.avclub.com/joss-whedon-1798208181
51 Robinson.
52 Pfluger, R. (2022, January 17). *The undoing of Joss Whedon*. Vulture. Retrieved February 6, 2022, from https://www.vulture.com/article/joss-whedon-allegations.html
53 Volmers, E. (2015, March 20). *Calgary comic expo: The original buffy, Kristy Swanson, talks about her days battling vampires*. Calgary herald. Retrieved February 6, 2022, from https://calgaryherald.com/entertainment/movies/calgary-comic-expo-the-original-buffy-kristy-swanson-talks-about-her-days-battling-vampires
54 Halen, A. (2011, December 26). *Interview: Kristy Swanson (Buffy Vampire Slayer, highway to hell) - horror news: HNN*. Horror News | HNN. Retrieved February 6, 2022, from https://horrornews.net/45728/interview-kristy-swanson-buffy-vampire-slayer-highway-to-hell/
55 Halen.
56 Pfluger.
57 Anita M. Busch, "Director's Cut", *Entertainment Weekly*, April 10, 1998.
58 Roger Clarke, "They All But Ate Me Alive!", *The Independent* , Sept 3, 1999.
59 Clarke.
60 Clarke.
61 Personal experience.
62 Joseph, E. (2005) Personal Website. Retrieved from www.geniejoseph.com
63 Joseph.
64 McDonagh, 37.
65 McDonagh, 37.
66 McDonagh, 63.
67 Puchalski, S. (1998, January). *Office Killer Slays 9 to 5.* Fangoria, (169), 54–56.
68 Puchalski.
69 Puchalski.
70 IMDb.com. (n.d.). *Intensive Care* Reviews. IMDb. Retrieved February 12, 2022, from https://www.imdb.com/title/tt0104515/reviews?ref_=tt_urv
71 Petra's biography. Petra Haffter. (n.d.). Retrieved February 12, 2022, from http://petrahaffter.com/biography.html
72 Honeycutt, Heidi. (2015) Jackie Kong. Personal Interview. Portions of this interview originally appeared in *Fangoria* Magazine, from an article that I wrote in 2015.
73 Honeycutt, Kong.
74 Honeycutt, Kong.
75 Honeycutt, Kong.
76 Honeycutt, Kong.
77 Honeycutt, Kong.
78 Honeycutt, Kong.
79 Honeycutt, Kong.
80 Honeycutt, H. (2022, January 20). Deryn Warren. Personal Interview..
81 Honeycutt, Warren.
82 Honeycutt, Warren.
83 Honeycutt, Warren.
84 Serrano, N. (2012, March 20). *Horror Genre and Women Who sCare!* Hallows Outpost. Retrieved January 28, 2022, from http://nishiserrano.blogspot.com/2012/03/
85 Honeycutt, Warren.
86 Honeycutt, H. (2013, September). Janet Greek. Personal Interview..
87 Honeycutt, Greek.
88 Honeycutt, Greek.
89 Honeycutt, Greek.
90 Honeycutt, Greek.
91 Honeycutt, Greek.
92 Honeycutt, Greek.

93 Honeycutt, Greek.
94 He previously produced the horror film *Audrey Rose*.
95 Honeycutt, Greek.
96 Honeycutt, Greek.

CHAPTER SEVEN
Pieces of Jennifer's Body

1 Alexander, C. (2017, January 17). *Director Jovanka Vuckovic talks XX*. ComingSoon.net. Retrieved February 21, 2022, from https://www.comingsoon.net/horror/features/803659-exclusive-interview-director-jovanka-vuckovic-talks-xx#/slide/1
2 Clark, John. (2000, January 25). 'It' Topic: Women Behind the Cameras. Los Angeles Times, p. 7.
3 Snead, E. (2000, January 21). Women directors get better role at Sundance. The Ithaca Journal, p. 13.
4 Snead.
5 Lam, K. (2011, January 25*). An interview with Catherine Hardwicke: On the set of 'red riding hood.' An Interview with Catherine Hardwicke: On the set of 'Red Riding Hood'* | FanGirlTastic. Retrieved February 7, 2022, from https://web.archive.org/web/20110129021041/http://fangirltastic.com/content/interview-catherine-hardwicke-red-riding-hood
6 Fear, D. (2020, April 16). *This is not an exit: 'American psycho' at 20*. Rolling Stone. Retrieved February 5, 2022, from https://www.rollingstone.com/movies/movie-features/american-psycho-twentieth-anniversary-983645/
7 Vachon would also produce Mary's next film, The Notorious Bettie Paige (2005) as well as Kimberly Peirce's first film Boys Don't Cry (1999).
8 Honeycutt, H. (2021, April). Guinevere Turner. Personal Interview.
9 Honeycutt, Turner.
10 Honeycutt, Turner.
11 Alexander, C. (2005, June). Memoirs of an American Psycho. Rue Morgue, (46), 36.
12 Honeycutt, Turner.
13 Kendzior, S. (2000, April). "American" Pyre. *Fangoria*, (191), 38.
14 Jagernauth, K. (2013, August 8). *Bret Easton Ellis explains why 'American psycho' is unadaptable, talks about his film with Kanye West*. IndieWire. Retrieved February 5, 2022, from https://www.indiewire.com/2013/08/bret-easton-ellis-explains-why-american-psycho-is-unadaptable-talks-about-his-film-with-kanye-west-95013/
15 Honeycutt, Turner.
16 Honeycutt, Turner.
17 Molloy, T. (2020, September 25). *American Psycho* Oral History, 20 years after its divisive debut. MovieMaker Magazine. Retrieved February 5, 2022, from https://www.moviemaker.com/american-psycho-anniversary-oral-history-christian-bale-mary-harron-bret-easton-ellis/
18 Stuart, J. (2000, April 13). Movies; Bale's 'Psycho Analysis; The actor and activist adjusts to portray a 'horrific but ridiculous' character. *Los Angeles Times*, p. 12.
19 Molloy.
20 Honeycutt, Turner.
21 Alexander.
22 Honeycutt, Turner.
23 Kendzior.
24 Honeycutt, Turner.
25 Alexander.
26 Alexander.
27 Honeycutt, Turner.
28 Turan.
29 Turan, K. (2000, April 14). *Movie Review: A 'Psycho Carves Path From Novel to Screen*. Los Angeles Times, p. 167.
30 Honeycutt, Turner.
31 Honeycutt, Turner.
32 Molloy.
33 Honeycutt, Turner.
34 Lam.
35 Lam.
36 Lam.
37 Lam.
38 Thigpen, H. (n.d.). *How "Jennifer's body" smashed its way through the male gaze and into queer, feminist cult status*. BUST. Retrieved February 1, 2022, from https://bust.com/movies/198518-jennifers-body-feminist-queer-cult-status.html
39 Rosenberg, A. (2009, August 31). *Megan Fox talks about her 'jennifer's body' kiss with Amanda Seyfried*. Mtelevision News. Retrieved February 1, 2022, from http://www.mtelevision.com/news/2433528/megan-fox-talks-about-her-jennifers-body-kiss-with-amanda-seyfried/
40 Wightman, C. (2018, November 6). *Seyfried: 'kissing Megan Fox was weird.'* Digital Spy. Retrieved February 1, 2022, from https://www.digitalspy.com/movies/a180342/seyfried-kissing-megan-fox-was-weird/
41 Yahoo! (2014, March 17). *'we kissed really well together': Amanda Seyfried speaks out*

on Megan FoxSex scenes. Yahoo! News. Retrieved February 1, 2022, from https://United Kingdom.news.yahoo.com/news/kissed-really-amanda-seyfried-speaks-megan-fox-sex-154218117.html

42 Nichols, M. (2019, September 11). *'Jennifer's body' turns 10: Megan Fox, Diablo Cody and Karyn Kusama reflect on making the cult classic*. Variety. Retrieved February 1, 2022, from https://variety.com/2019/film/news/jennifers-body-10th-anniversary-megan-fox-diablo-cody-1203323111/

43 Blichert, F. (2018, October 23). *'Jennifer's body' would kill if it came out today*. VICE. Retrieved February 1, 2022, from https://www.vice.com/en/article/qv99y3/jennifers-body-would-kill-if-it-came-out-today

44 Peitzman, L. (2018, December 9). *You probably owe "Jennifer's body" an apology*. BuzzFeed News. Retrieved February 1, 2022, from https://www.buzzfeednews.com/article/louispeitzman/jennifers-body-diablo-cody-karyn-kusama-feminist-horror

45 Peitzman.

46 Peitzman.

47 Peitzman.

48 Beyondfest (2019, September 12). *Jennifer's body*. Retrieved February 1, 2022, from https://beyondfest.com/class/jennifers-body/

49 Navarro, M. (2018, August 22). *Hell is a teenage girl: 'jennifer's body' deserves a cult classic status*. Bloody Disgusting! Retrieved February 1, 2022, from https://bloody-disgusting.com/editorials/3516475/hell-teenage-girl-jennifers-body-cult-classic-making/

50 Kooyman, B. (2011, September 8). *Whose body? auteurism, feminism and Horror in hostel part ii and Jennifer's body*. Retrieved February 1, 2022, from https://www.ingentaconnect.com/content/intellect/ajpc/2011/00000001/00000002/art00006

51 Honeycutt, H. (2022, January 31). Cory McCullough. personal.

52 Setoodeh.

53 Colangelo, B.J. (2021, January 17). Twitter.

54 I applied for a job in development at Gamechanger Films in December 2021 with a personal reference from one of the founders Mynette Louie and I never heard back. It's okay, I'll still write about you, Gamechanger.

55 Yamato.

56 Yamato.

57 Honeycutt.

58 Martin, P. (2011, August 4). *The silent house: Uncut Horror from Uruguay*. IndieMoviesOnline. Retrieved February 4, 2022, from https://web.archive.org/web/20130415162320/http://www.indiemoviesonline.com/news/the-silent-house-uncut-horror-from-uruguay-040811

59 Honeycutt.

60 Honeycutt, Heidi. (June 05, 2006) Stacy Title. Personal Interview.

61 But a much better option is *Tales from the Hood* (1995)

62 Wixson, H. (2017, January 13). *Interview: Director Stacy Title talks the bye bye man*. Daily Dead. Retrieved February 8, 2022, from https://dailydead.com/interview-director-stacy-title-talks-the-bye-bye-man/

63 Corrigan, K. (2017, January 14). [review] *'The bye bye man' - the "why why was this made man".* Bloody Disgusting! Retrieved February 8, 2022, from https://bloody-disgusting.com/movie/3421070/review-bye-bye-man-dont-think-dont-say-dont-see/

64 Kit, B. (2018, September 21). *Director stricken with ALS vows to finish her final movie: "doing what I love will be part of My Legacy".* The Hollywood Reporter. Retrieved February 8, 2022, from https://www.hollywoodreporter.com/movies/movie-news/director-stacy-title-stricken-als-vows-finish-her-final-movie-1145218/

65 Davids, B. (2021, January 5). *'shadow in the cloud' filmmaker Roseanne Liang sets the record straight on her film's writing credits. The Hollywood Reporter*. Retrieved February 8, 2022, from https://www.hollywoodreporter.com/movies/movie-news/shadow-in-the-cloud-filmmaker-roseanne-liang-sets-the-record-straight-4110598/

66 Davids.

67 Davids.

68 Davids.

69 Debruge, P. (2021, February 25). *10 directors to watch: Roseanne Liang launches action ambitions with 'shadow in the cloud'.* Variety. Retrieved February 8, 2022, from https://variety.com/2021/film/features/10-directors-to-watch-roseanne-liang-shadow-in-the-cloud-1234914996/

70 Davids.

71 Davids.

72 Evangelista, C. (2019, April 1). *Mary Lambert interview: Making the original pet sematary*. SlashFilm.com. Retrieved February 8, 2022, from https://www.slashfilm.com/565351/mary-lambert-interview/

73 Honeycutt, H. (February 2, 2022) Mick Garris. Personal Interview.

74 Wixson, H. (2019, December 13). *Interview: Black Christmas (2019) co-writer April Wolfe on subverting expectations and PG-13 horror*. Daily Dead. Retrieved February 10, 2022, from https://dailydead.com/interview-black-christmas-2019-co-writer-april-wolfe-on-subverting-expectations-and-pg-13-horror/.

75 Kaye, D. (2019, December 13). *Getting rabid*

with horror's Soska sisters. Den of Geek. Retrieved February 11, 2022, from https://www.denofgeek.com/movies/getting-rabid-with-horrors-soska-sisters/
76 Production Notes. Carrie. 2013. MGM & Screen Gems..
77 MGM & Screen Gems.
78 MGM & Screen Gems.
79 Alexander, C. (2013, March). Spilling Blood and Splitting Screens. *Fangoria*, (231), 44–45.
80 Spiderbaby, L. (2013, March). The New (Pig's) Blood. *Fangoria*, (231), 60.
81 Kit, B. (2015, May 14). *Cult horror movie 'the craft' to get remake by Sony (exclusive)*. The Hollywood Reporter. Retrieved March 9, 2022, from https://www.hollywoodreporter.com/movies/movie-features/cult-horror-movie-craft-get-795479/
82 Cairns, B. (2021, October 22). *The craft: Legacy is bringing back that cult-classic magic for a new era*. SYFY Official Site. Retrieved February 10, 2022, from https://www.syfy.com/syfy-wire/the-craft-legacy-sequel-cult-classic-magic-witches-set
83 Cairns.
84 Valentini, V. (2020, October 13). *Exclusive: How Zoe Lister-Jones reimagined the craft's iconic Teen Witches*. Vanity Fair. Retrieved February 10, 2022, from https://www.vanityfair.com/hollywood/2020/10/the-craft-legacy-remake-sequel-zoe-lister-jones
85 Valentini.
86 Valentini.
87 Davids, B. (2021, July 17). *Zoe Lister-Jones on 'how it ends' and 'the craft: Legacy' ending*. The Hollywood Reporter. Retrieved February 10, 2022, from https://www.hollywoodreporter.com/movies/movie-news/zoe-lister-jones-on-how-it-ends-and-the-craft-legacy-ending-4156317/
88 Davids.
89 Collis, C. (2019, November 26). *Director Sophia Takal calls her 'Black Christmas' remake a 'fiercely feminist film.'* EW.com. Retrieved February 10, 2022, from https://ew.com/movies/2019/11/26/black-christmas-remake-sophia-takal-interview/
90 Collis.
91 Wixson.
92 Honeycutt, Heidi. (February 10, 2022) April Wolfe. Personal interview.
93 Honeycutt.
94 Honeycutt.
95 Radish, C. (2021, August 26). 'Candyman' director Nia DaCosta on working with Jordan Peele and keeping the romantic nature of the character. Collider. Retrieved February 11, 2022, from https://collider.com/candyman-director-nia-dacosta-interview/.
96 Radish.
97 Radish.
98 Riley, J. (2021, August 18). *With 'Candyman,' director Nia DaCosta puts a killer spin on A horror classic*. Variety. Retrieved February 11, 2022, from https://variety.com/2021/film/features/nia-dacosta-horror-classic-candyman-1235044045/
99 Guardian News and Media. (2021, August 26). *Candyman director Nia DaCosta: 'it is shocking the way people have talked to me.'* The Guardian. Retrieved February 11, 2022, from https://www.theguardian.com/film/2021/aug/26/candyman-director-nia-dacosta-this-should-be-happening-for-more-people-like-me
100 Dervishi, Y. (2021, September 3). *'Candyman' director Nia DaCosta made box office history - but some people are still calling it Jordan Peele's movie*. YourTango. Retrieved February 11, 2022, from https://www.yourtango.com/entertainment/candyman-nia-dacosta-jordan-peele
101 Honeycutt, H. (February 13, 2022) Danishka Esterhazy. Personal Interview.
102 Honeycutt, Esterhazy.
103 Honeycutt, Esterhazy.
104 YouTube. (2021). "Slumber party massacre" interview with Danishka Esterhazy, Director & Executive producer - syfy. Fanversation. Retrieved from https://www.youtube.com/watch?v=-ugegUMe8IA.
105 Fanversation.
106 Honeycutt, Esterhazy.
107 Honeycutt, Esterhazy.
108 Fanversation.
109 Millican, J. (2018, March 27). *Interview: Jen and Sylvia Soska talk rabid, David Cronenberg, and transhumanism*. Dread Central. Retrieved February 11, 2022, from https://www.dreadcentral.com/news/269430/interview-jen-and-sylvia-soska-talk-rabid-david-cronenberg-and-transhumanism/
110 Kaye, D. (2019, December 13). *Getting rabid with horror's Soska sisters*. Den of Geek. Retrieved February 11, 2022, from https://www.denofgeek.com/movies/getting-rabid-with-horrors-soska-sisters/
111 Wixson, H. (2021, March 29). *Interview: Jen and Sylvia Soska talk Cronenberg and representing Canadian Horror For Rabid*. Daily Dead. Retrieved February 11, 2022, from https://dailydead.com/interview-jen-and-sylvia-soska-talk-cronenberg-and-representing-canadian-horror-for-rabid/
112 Millican.
113 Wixson.
114 Kaye.
115 Wixson
116 Kaye.
117 Millican.
118 Millican.

119 Swope, M. (2019, December 10). *Interview: Stephen Huszar on the insanely realistic practical effects in rabid and working with the Soska sisters*. Dread Central. Retrieved February 11, 2022, from https://www.dreadcentral.com/news/314996/interview-stephen-huszar-on-the-insanely-realistic-practical-effects-in-rabid-and-working-with-the-soska-sisters/
120 Scheck, F. (2019, December 11). *'rabid': Film review*. The Hollywood Reporter. Retrieved February 11, 2022, from https://www.hollywoodreporter.com/movies/movie-reviews/rabid-1262019/
121 Abrams, S. (2019, December 19). *Rabid Movie Review & Film Summary (2019)*. Roger Ebert. Retrieved February 11, 2022, from https://www.rogerebert.com/reviews/rabid-movie-review-2019
122 Kaye.
123 Kaye.
124 Noé, A. (2019, November 27). *Capturing a world in a Crystal Ball: A conversation with Kei Fujiwara*. MUBI. Retrieved February 13, 2022, from https://mubi.com/notebook/posts/capturing-a-world-in-a-crystal-ball-a-conversation-with-kei-fujiwara
125 Noé.
126 Noé.
127 Noé.
128 Noé.
129 Noé.
130 Noé.
131 Noé.
132 Noé.
133 Nippon Connection Film Festival. (2020). Interview with Mari Asato. YouTube. Retrieved from https://www.youtube.com/watch?v=1ffCxyjPAWg.
134 *In focus: Mika Ninagawa on Helter Skelter*. British Film Institute. (2012). Retrieved February 14, 2022, from https://www2.bfi.org.United Kingdom/news/in-focus-mika-ninagawa-helter-skelter
135 Helter Skelter: Dare: 56th BFI London film festival. London Film Festival. (n.d.). Retrieved February 14, 2022, from https://whatson.bfi.org.United Kingdom/
136 British Film Institute.
137 British Film Institute.
138 British Film Institute.
139 Thor, T. (2014, March 10). *IFFR: An Interview with director Lisa Takeba*. Asian Movie Pulse. Retrieved February 14, 2022, from https://asianmoviepulse.com/2014/03/iffr-interview-director-lisa-takeba/
140 Thor.
141 Noh, J. (2015, January 22). *Tiger directors: Lisa Takeba, Haruko's Paranormal Laboratory*. Screen Daily. Retrieved February 14, 2022, from https://www.screendaily.com/rotterdam/tiger-directors-lisa-takeba-harukos-paranormal-laboratory/5082097.article
142 Wong, S. (2019, October 4). *Busan Q&A: Yerlan Nurmukehambetov & Lisa Takeba, 'The Horse Thieves. roads of time.'* Screen Daily. Retrieved February 14, 2022, from https://www.screendaily.com/interviews/busan-qanda-yerlan-nurmUnited Kingdomhambetov-and-lisa-takeba-the-horse-thieves-roads-of-time/5143424.article
143 Dimagmaliw, B. (2018, December 23). *Killer smile — Asakura Kayoko*. Indievisual Digital Magazine. Retrieved February 16, 2022, from https://read.indie-visual.net/killer-smile-asakura-kayoko/
144 *Interview: Director Kayoko Asakura talks 'it's a beautiful day'*. Diverse Japan. (2013, November 20). Retrieved February 16, 2022, from https://diversejapan.wordpress.com/2013/11/20/interview-director-kayoko-asakura-talks-its-a-beautiful-day/
145 Honeycutt, H. (February 25, 2022) Kayoko Asakura. Personal Interview.
146 Honeycutt, Asakura.
147 Kruethong, P. (2003, October). *"Si Oui" cannibals or victims of society?* Silpa Magazine. Retrieved April 6, 2022, from https://www.silpa-mag.com/history/article_9091
148 Virginie Despentes personal statement.
149 Guardian News and Media. (2004, September 15). *In the cut*. The Guardian. Retrieved February 16, 2022, from https://www.theguardian.com/film/2004/sep/15/features.stuartjeffries
150 *Press conference: 'don't look back'*. Festival de Cannes 2009. (2009, February 13). Retrieved February 16, 2022, from https://www.festival-cannes.com/en/74-editions/retrospective/2009/actualites/articles/press-conference-don-t-look-back
151 BBC. (2001). *Films - interview - Claire Denis* BBC. Retrieved February 16, 2022, from https://www.bbc.co.United Kingdom/films/2002/12/24/claire_denis_trouble_every_day_interview.shtml
152 BBC.
153 Honeycutt, H. (2009) Caroline du Potet. Personal Interview.
154 Honeycutt, du Potet.

CHAPTER EIGHT
21st Century Viscera

1 Snead, E. (2000, January 21). Women directors get better role at Sundance. *The Ithaca Journal*, p. 13.
2 Brown, N. (2008) *Lola Wallace Interview*. Pretty/Scary. http://www.Pretty-Scary.net.
3 Honeycutt, H. (2007, October 18). *Anya Camilleri's Incubus*. Pretty/Scary. Retrieved March 4, 2022, from http://web.archive.org/web/20071018205320/http://www.pretty-scary.net/modules.php?name=News&file=article&sid=671
4 Honeycutt, H. (2007, October 18). *Anya Camilleri's Incubus*. Pretty/Scary . Retrieved March 4, 2022, from http://web.archive.org/web/20071018205320/http://www.pretty-scary.net/modules.php?name=News&file=article&sid=671
5 Honeycutt, Heidi. (February 2022). Jen Soska and Sylvia Soska. Personal Interview.
6 Flesh, H. (2004). New York News - New York Press: New York's premier news source and alternative newspaper. New York Press. Retrieved February 23, 2022, from https://web.archive.org/web/20080406023816/http://www.nypress.com/17/7/nyc/
7 "Girl power". *Jewish Journal*. (1999, March 11). Retrieved February 23, 2022, from https://jewishjournal.com/old_stories/1518/
8 freehistoryproject.org/sarah-jacobson-film-grant
9 Honeycutt, H. (July 2021) Jenn Wexler. Personal Interview.
10 Sacks, E. (2019, January 9). *Chris Pratt was star in the making in never-before-seen photos from first role in director Rae Dawn Chong's 'cursed part 3'.* nydailynews.com. Retrieved January 30, 2022, from https://www.nydailynews.com/entertainment/movies/chris-pratt-director-rae-dawn-chong-recalls-discovering-future-star-article-1.1896582]
11 Honeycutt, H. (February 2022) Rae Dawn Chong. Personal Interview
12 Honeycutt, Chong.
13 Honeycutt, Chong.
14 Honeycutt, H. (2005) Jennifer Kent. Personal Interview.
15 Honeycutt, Kent.
16 Honeycutt, Kent.
17 Honeycutt, Kent.
18 Honeycutt, H. (February 2022). Heidi Lee Douglas. Personal Interview.
19 Honeycutt, Douglas.
20 Honeycutt, Douglas.
21 Honeycutt, Douglas.
22 Kohn, E. (2019, August 5). *Jennifer Kent: 'the Nightingale' explores the 'epidemic' of rape around the world*. IndieWire. Retrieved February 17, 2022, from https://www.indiewire.com/2019/08/jennifer-kent-the-nightingale-rape-epidemic-1202162992/
23 Yanick, J. (2015, November 9). *Interview: Director Melanie Light on her vegan, feminist horror film The herd*. ComingSoon.net. Retrieved February 19, 2022, from https://www.comingsoon.net/horror/pb_article_type/747686-interview-director-melanie-light-vegan-feminist-horror-film-herd
24 Yanick.
25 And like myself.
26 Yanick.
27 Honeycutt, H. (April 2021) Gigi Guerrero. Personal Interview.
28 Honeycutt, Guerrero.
29 Honeycutt, H. (June 2021) Jill Gevargizian. Personal Interview.
30 Honeycutt, Gevargizian.
31 Honeycutt, Gevargizian.
32 Honeycutt, H. (June 2021) Najarra Townsend. Personal Interview.
33 Honeycutt, Townsend.
34 Honeycutt, Gevargizian.
35 Honeycutt, Gevargizian.
36 Honeycutt, H. (June 2021) Prano Bailey-Bond. Personal Interview.
37 Honeycutt, Bailey-Bond.
38 Honeycutt, Bailey-Bond.
39 Barton, S. (2011, September 26). *Shriekfest 2011: Exclusive Q&A with filmmaker Devi Snively*. Dread Central. Retrieved February 19, 2022, from https://www.dreadcentral.com/news/27246/shriekfest-2011-exclusive-q-a-with-filmmaker-devi-snively/
40 There is a fantastic documentary on the work of the Kuchar brothers low-budget film career directed by Jennifer Kroot, who also made the science fiction fantasy comedy *Sirens of the 23rd century* (2003)
41 Pickman, K. (2013, September 12). *When I die I'll make films in hell: Doris Wishman in Miami*. The Miami Rail. Retrieved January 18, 2022, from https://miamirail.org/performing-arts/when-i-die-ill-make-films-in-hell-doris-wishman-in-miami/
42 Fusco, M. P. (1994, June 9). *Dieci piccolissimi incubi - la repubblica.it*. Archivio - la Repubblica.it. Retrieved February 20, 2022, from https://ricerca.repubblica.it/repubblica/archivio/repubblica/1994/06/09/dieci-piccolissimi-incubi.html

43 Beggs, S. (2017, April 22). *'abcs of death' director Angela Bettis talks fake blood, spiders and the scariest thing about human... Film School Rejects*. Retrieved February 21, 2022, from https://filmschoolrejects.com/abcs-of-death-director-angela-bettis-talks-fake-blood-spiders-and-the-scariest-thing-about-human-6556277140dc/
44 Smith, N. M. (2012, January 22). *Bloody Disgusting founder and 'V/H/S' producer Brad Miska on why the found-footage movie is here to stay*. IndieWire. Retrieved February 21, 2022, from https://www.indiewire.com/2012/01/bloody-disgusting-founder-and-vhs-producer-brad-miska-on-why-the-found-footage-movie-is-here-to-stay-49609/
45 Honeycutt, H. (February 15, 2022). Chloe Okuno. Personal Interview.
46 Hatfull, J. (2016, August 15). *Roxanne Benjamin talks southbound and making female-driven horror*. SciFiNow. Retrieved February 21, 2022, from https://www.scifinow.com/interviews/roxanne-benjamin-talks-southbound-and-making-female-driven-horror/
47 Hatfull.
48 I had direct involvement in the process of Vuckovic connecting with directors.
49 Alexander, C. (2017, January 17). *Director Jovanka Vuckovic talks XX*. ComingSoon.net. Retrieved February 21, 2022, from https://www.comingsoon.net/horror/features/803659-exclusive-interview-director-jovanka-vuckovic-talks-xx#/slide/1
50 Alexander.
51 Wilson, S. L. (2017, May 27). *XX - Jovanka Vuckovic exclusive interview*. Dread Central. Retrieved February 21, 2022, from https://www.dreadcentral.com/news/231334/xx-jovanka-vuckovic-exclusive-interview/
52 I'm glad she got to shoot there again.
53 Mack, A. (2021, January 19). *Dark whispers: Australian horror anthology by women gets an AUS & United Kingdom digital release*. Screen Anarchy. Retrieved February 21, 2022, from https://screenanarchy.com/2021/01/dark-whispers-australia-release-horror-anthology.html
54 Millican, J. (2019, July 22). *Shevenge is sweet! new horror anthology produced by Staci Layne Wilson coming soon!* Dread Central. Retrieved February 21, 2022, from https://www.dreadcentral.com/news/297683/shevenge-is-sweet-new-horror-anthology-produced-by-staci-layne-wilson-coming-soon/
55 Honeycutt, H. (2015, October 6). *Interview: Gigi Guerrero Talks Sex, Shock and Terror in Mexico Barbaro*. ShockTillYouDrop.com. Retrieved from http://www.shocktillyoudrop.com/news/articles/386879-interview-gigi-guerrero-talks-sex-shock-terror-mexico-barbaro/
56 I certainly hope so or no one is going to read this book.
57 Honeycutt, H. (February 2022) Sarah Appleton. Personal Interview.
58 Janisse, K.-L. (2020, October). The CINE-MUERTE Film Festival. Kier. https://www.kierlajanisse.com/2020/10/10/the-cine-muerte-film-festival/
59 United Kingdom News. (2008, February 9). *Creativity with blood, Cannibals and Zombies*. YUKON News. Retrieved February 22, 2022, from https://www.yukon-news.com/news/creativity-with-blood-cannibals-and-zombies/
60 Harris, B. (2011, January 2). *Jennifer Kroot, "it came from kuchar": Filmmaker Magazine*. Filmmaker Magazine | Publication with a focus on independent film, offering articles, links, and resources. Retrieved February 22, 2022, from https://filmmakermagazine.com/6690-jennifer-kroot-it-came-from-kuchar-2/#.YhU63pTMK38
61 Cayer, A. E. (2011, June 1). *I am nancy — an interview with Heather Langenkamp" Spectacular optical*. Spectacular Optical RSS. Retrieved February 22, 2022, from http://www.spectacularoptical.ca/2011/06/i-am-nancy-an-interview-with-heather-langenkamp/
62 This small bit of text about *Beast Wishes* is talen directly from a 2012 *Famous Monsters of Filmland* magazine article that I myself wrote, so it's okay.
63 Michelmore, K. (2012, June 4). *Despite the gods, a documentary emerges*. Despite the Gods, a documentary emerges - ABC (none) - Australian Broadcasting Corporation. Retrieved February 22, 2022, from https://www.abc.net.au/local/stories/2012/06/04/3517424.htm
64 Honeycutt, H. (February 2022) Heidi Moore. Personal Interview.
65 Blem, T. (2021, August 19). *Fantasia Fest 2021: Interview with Kier-La Janisse for 'Woodlands Dark and days bewitched'*. PopHorror. Retrieved February 22, 2022, from https://www.pophorror.com/fantasia-fest-2021-interview-with-kier-la-janisse-for-woodlands-dark-and-days-bewitched/
66 Honeycutt, H. (2005) Kalila Smith. Personal Interview.
67 Hofferman, J. (2021, November 19). *Spire Animation Studios helps lead the way for gender equality*. Animation World Network. Retrieved March 3, 2022, from https://www.awn.com/animationworld/spire-animation-studios-helps-lead-way-gender-equality
68 Shiman, J. (2016). *Thank you for six amazing years. Thank you for six amazing years of 30-second bunnies theatre!* Retrieved March 3, 2022, from http://www.angry-

alien.com/bunniesbyefornow.asp
69 Honeycutt, H. (2005) Martha Colburn. Personal Interview.
70 Honeycutt, Colburn.
71 Honeycutt, Colburn.
72 Honeycutt, Colburn.
73 Honeycutt, H. (2005) Anna Gawrilow. Personal Interview.
74 Honeycutt, Gawrilow.
75 Author. (2017, May 25). *Sofia Carrillo is making horror out of dollhouses*. Strung. Retrieved March 3, 2022, from https://histrung-com.wordpress.com/2017/01/25/sofia-carrillo-is-making-horror-out-of-dollhouses/
76 *Bio*. ISABEL PEPPARD. (n.d.). Retrieved March 3, 2022, from https://www.isabel-peppard.com/bio
77 Interview with Isabel Peppard. Beinart Gallery. (2017, November 9). Retrieved March 3, 2022, from https://beinart.org/blogs/articles/interview-with-isabel-peppard
78 Duncan of Jordanstone College of Art & Design. (2010). *Nursery Crimes*. YouTube. Retrieved from https://www.youtube.com/watch?v=NxhduJVoASw.
79 Frampton M. (2019, August 9). *Christiane Cegavske interview: The alchemy of animation*. Skwigly Animation Magazine. Retrieved March 3, 2022, from https://www.skwigly.com/christiane-cegavske-interview-alchemy-of-animation/
80 In fact, Angel was a former Suicide Girl.
81 *HUSTLERWORLD INTERVIEW: JOANNA ANGEL*. Larry Flynt's HUSTLERWORLD. (2006, March). Retrieved February 25, 2022, from http://www.hustlerworld.com/news/2006/03/hustlerworld_interview_joanna.html
82 Honeycutt, H. (2009) Missy Suicide & Sawa Suicide. Personal Interviews
83 Honeycutt, Suicide & Suicide.
84 Honeycutt, Suicide & Suicide.
85 Honeycutt, Suicide & Suicide.
86 Zahlten, A. (2017). *The end of Japanese cinema: Industrial genres, national times, and media ecologies*. Duke U.P.
87 Sélavy, V. (2009, December 1). *Interview with Sachi Hamano*. Electric Sheep. Retrieved on Feb 22, 2019 from http://www.electricsheepmagazine.co.uk/2009/12/01/interview-with-sachi-hamano/
88 Sélavy.
89 Sélavy.
90 Joshigakusei: Karenna Ikenie (1983) - Rumi Tama: Synopsis, characteristics, moods, themes and related. AllMovie. (1983, January 1). Retrieved December 20, 2021, from https://www.allmovie.com/movie/joshigakusei-karenna-ikenie-v249675
91 Gat O. (2019, July 19). *How Cecelia Condit's video art became a viral curse for teens on TikTok*. Frieze. Retrieved February 23, 2022, from https://www.frieze.com/article/how-cecelia-condits-video-art-became-viral-curse-teens-tiktok
92 Honeycutt, Heidi (February 25, 2022) Lisa Hammer. Personal Interview.
93 Honeycutt, H. (February 26, 2022) Dame Darcy. Personal Interview.
94 This is exactly how it was explained to me by Hammer.
95 Honeycutt, Hammer.
96 Honeycutt, Darcy.
97 Honeycutt, H. (2022) Erin Brown. Personal Interview.
98 Honeycutt, Brown.
99 Maybe I'll do that. Not sure.
100 Danielle, T. (2019, February 25). *Women in Horror Month 2019: Interview with Shayna Connelly*. PopHorror. Retrieved March 3, 2022, from https://www.pophorror.com/women-in-horror-month-interview-shayna-connelly/
101 *Tina Krause Interview*. Secret scroll digest. (2001). Retrieved February 26, 2022, from https://web.archive.org/web/20061107132325/http://www.secretscrolldigest.com/articles/tinak.html
102 Honeycutt, H. (February 26, 2022), Joseph Ziemba. Personal Interview.
103 Limbo. American Genre Film Archive. (n.d.). Retrieved February 25, 2022, from https://www.americangenrefilm.com/home-videos/limbo/
104 *Secret scroll digest interviews Katie Taylor Bullock*. Secret Scroll Digest. (2004). Retrieved February 26, 2022, from https://web.archive.org/web/20070101091202/http://www.secretscrolldigest.com/articles/katietaylorbullock.html
105 Malleus Aforethought. (2001). Retrieved February 25, 2022, from https://web.archive.org/web/20050205190916/http://www.gatri.5u.com/shooting.htm
106 Malleus. (2001, November 25). Retrieved February 25, 2022, from https://web.archive.org/web/20011211212633/http://www.malleus.com/news.htm
107 Year of the dragon - dragon films - 2000. (2002). Retrieved February 25, 2022, from https://web.archive.org/web/20021012012613fw_/http://www.geocities.com/dragon_films_2000/Article6.html
108 Honeycutt, H. (2005). Gwendolyn Kiste. Personal Interview.
109 *Cast & Crew*. Zombies Are My Neighbors. (2001). Retrieved February 26, 2022, from https://web.archive.org/web/20060622052219/http://zombie-movie.com/id3.html
110 Spellcaster Of Fear. (2004, May 4). *Interview: vamp queen Stephanie Aldridge*. Unspeakable mag. Retrieved February 26, 2022, from http://web.archive.org/

web/20040812085419/http://www.unspeakablemag.com/site/article.php?sid=96&mode=&order=0
111 Spellcaster Of Fear.
112 Synopsis, *Descend into Darkness*. (2004). Retrieved February 26, 2022, from http://web.archive.org/web/20050208064545/http://www.spookyart.com/blackie/dscn.htm
113 Synopsis, *Slice 'N' Dice*. (2004). Retrieved February 26, 2022, from http://web.archive.org/web/20050208064545/http://www.spookyart.com/blackie/sldc.htm
114 Synopsis, *Blood on the Moon* (2004). Retrieved February 26, 2022, from http://web.archive.org/web/20050208064545/http://www.spookyart.com/blackie/bldm.htm
115 Synopsis, *Descend Into Darkness 2: Battle of the Undead*. (2004). Retrieved February 26, 2022, from http://web.archive.org/web/20050208064545/http://www.spookyart.com/blackie/dcsn.htm
116 *Sicko filmz*. SICKO FILMZ. (2009). Retrieved February 26, 2022, from http://www.sickofilmz.com/
117 Hernandez, M. (2010, November 1). *Julia Davis' room and board gets its first one sheet and partial cast photo*. JoBlo. Retrieved February 26, 2022, from https://www.joblo.com/julia-davis-room-and-board-gets-its-first-one-sheet-and-partial-cast-photo/
118 Synopsis. *Lycan Rising*. (2005). Retrieved February 26, 2022, from http://web.archive.org/web/20050410050035/http://www.lycanrising.com/
119 Honeycutt, H. (November 6, 2021) Melinda Fontinos. Personal Interview.
120 All of the quotes from Harris come from an artilce I wrote for *Fangoria* in 2013.
121 Honeycutt, H. (2005) Danica McKeller. Personal Interview.
122 Honeycutt, Landau.
123 Honeycutt, H. (2009) Danielle Harris. Personal Interview.
124 Honeycutt, H. (2011) Danielle Harris. Personal Interview.
125 Honeycutt, Harris (2011).
126 Honeycutt, Harris (2011).
127 Honeycutt, Harris (2011).
128 Erbland, K. (2017, May 25). *How a pregnant actress overcame her frustrations with the industry and directed her first feature*. IndieWire. Retrieved February 27, 2022, from https://www.indiewire.com/2017/03/alice-lowe-prevenge-horror-interview-1201795842/
129 Independent Digital News and Media. (2017, February 8). *Prevenge's Alice Lowe interview: 'it was originally a jokey title but it stuck'*. The Independent. Retrieved February 27, 2022, from https://www.independent.com/arts-entertainment/films/features/prevenge-alice-lowe-interview-sightseers-beehive-the-mighty-boosh-horrible-histories-a7567076.html
130 Mentaculist, T. (2019, July 14). *Interview: Pollyanna mcintosh on going wild with the possibilities of "Darlin'"*. The Moveable Fest. Retrieved February 27, 2022, from https://moveablefest.com/pollyanna-mcintosh-darlin/
131 Menticulist.
132 Honeycutt, H. (June 2021) Brea Grant. Personal Interview.
133 Honeycutt, Grant.
134 Honeycutt, Grant.
135 Honeycutt, Grant
136 Honeycutt, Grant.
137 Rochon, D. (2014, August). Diary of the Deb: "Model Hunger," Part One. *Fangoria*, (335), 64–65.
138 Honeycutt, H. (February 27, 2022) James Morgart. Personal Interview.
139 Rochon.
140 Rochon, D. (2014, October). Diary of the Deb: "Model Hunger" Part Two. *Fangoria*, (336), 67.
141 Wilson, S. L. (2016, July 18). *Exclusive: Debbie Rochon Talks model hunger*. Dread Central. Retrieved February 27, 2022, from https://www.dreadcentral.com/news/177038/exclusive-interview-debbie-rochon-model-hunger/
142 Turek, R. (2008, March 31). *Shepis directing Devil's Pies this June*. ComingSoon.net. Retrieved February 27, 2022, from https://www.comingsoon.net/horror/pb_article_type/709243-shepis-directing-devils-pies-this-june
143 IMDb.com. (n.d.). *The Reptile House*. IMDb. Retrieved February 27, 2022, from https://www.imdb.com/title/tt14826366/
144 *Welcome to the deadly 10!* Deadly Ten. (n.d.). Retrieved February 27, 2022, from https://deadlyten.com/feature/16

CHAPTER NINE
Promising Young Women

1 Honeycutt, Soska & Soska.
2 Fanversation.
3 Honeycutt, H. (2015). Veronika Franz. Personal Interview.
4 Honeycutt, H. (2007). Mary Lambert. Personal Interview.

5 Honeycutt, H. (2010) Karen Lam. Personal Interview.
6 Honeycutt, Lam.
7 Leiren-Young, M. (2014, March 5). *Thriller scores opening slot for Vancouver's Women in Film Festival (with video).* vancouversun. Retrieved March 3, 2022, from https://vancouversun.com/entertainment/movies/thriller-scores-opening-slot-for-vancouvers-women-in-film-festival-with-video
8 Dabielle, T. (2021, October 15). *Interview with Karen Lam, Director of 'The Curse of Willow Song.'* PopHorror.com. Retrieved March 3, 2022, from https://www.pophorror.com/interview-with-karen-lam-director-of-the-curse-of-willow-song/
9 Honeycutt, H. (February 2022) Danishka Esterhazy. Personal Interview.
10 Clarke, C. (2021, March 23). Slaxx director Elza Kephart destroys the evils of fast fashion. CBR. Retrieved March 3, 2022, from https://www.cbr.com/slaxx-director-elza-kephart-interview/
11 Zimmerman, S. (2014, December). A Girl Walks Home Alone at Night: I Ran From Expectations. *Rue Morgue*, (338), 47.
12 Bowen, J. M. (2007, April). Love Will Tear Us Apart. *Rue Morgue*, (66), 39.
13 Honeycutt, H. (July 2021) Jenn Wexler. Personal Interview.
14 Gingold, M. (2014, December). Dare You Look at the Babadook? *Fangoria*, (338), 29.
15 Thorpe, A. (2013, September). A Little Bit of Soulmate. *Fangoria* (326), 54.
16 See Chapter Two's *The Haunting of Rosalind* by Gloria Monty.
17 Honeycutt, Guerrero.
18 Honeycutt, Heidi. (February 2022). Jen Soska and Sylvia Soska. Personal Interview.
19 Honeycutt, Soska & Soska.
20 Honeycutt, Soska & Soska.
21 Honeycutt, Soska & Soska.
22 Honeycutt, Soska & Soska.
23 Honeycutt, Soska & Soska.
24 Alexander, C. (2016, April). Risky Business. *Fangoria*, (344), 46.
25 Honeycutt, Heidi. (2015) Mattie Do. Personal Interview. Note: some pieces of this interview were published in a 2015 article in Fangoria Magazine.
26 Hatchett, K., & By. (2017, January 19). *Mattie do talks horror film 'Dearest sister'.* The Mary Sue. Retrieved March 1, 2022, from https://www.themarysue.com/interview-mattie-do-dearest-sister/
27 Honeycutt, Do.
28 Honeycutt, Do.
29 Honeycutt, Heidi. (January 21, 2021) Anna Biller. Personal Interview.
30 Honeycutt, Biller.
31 Honeycutt, Biller.
32 Honeycutt, Biller.
33 Honeycutt, Biller.
34 Honeycutt, Biller.
35 Honeycutt, Biller.
36 Honeycutt, Biller.
37 Honeycutt, H. (June, 2021) Brea Grant & Natasha Kermani. Personal Interview.
38 Honeycutt, Grant & Kermani.
39 Honeycutt, Grant & Kermani.
40 Honeycutt, Grant & Kermani.
41 Honeycutt, Grant & Kermani.
42 Honeycutt, H. (February 2022) Heidi Moore. Personal Interview.
43 Honeycutt, Moore.
44 Best, A. L. (2007). Splatter Movie: The Director's Cut - My Return to Directing. *Sirens of Cinema*, *2*(9), 35.
45 Burke, B. (2015, March). Olalla Palooza. *Fangoria*, (340).
46 Alexander, C. (2015). Weird Wilson. *Fangoria,* (341), 52.
47 Kephart, E. (2002). The Genesis of *Graveyard Alive*. *Hollywood Is Burning*, *1*(1), 6.
48 Honeycutt, H. (2006) Lola Wallace. Personal Interview.
49 Honeycutt, Wallace.
50 Honeycutt, Heidi. (2015) Guinevere Turner & Jane Clark. Personal Interview.
51 Honeycutt, Turner & Clark.
52 Honeycutt, Turner & Clark.
53 I recommend the paper *Werewomen: An Exhumation of Transness in Horro*r (2020) by Sam Miller
54 Harrison, P. (September 17, 2004) *Sharon Ferranti Makes a Wish*. OutinAmerica.com
55 Harrison.
56 Just about every review of this film.
57 Yanick, J. (2014, September 16). *"Lyle" director, Stewart Thorndike, talks pregnancy horror and gendered genre discrimination*. Diabolique Magazine. Retrieved March 1, 2022, from https://diaboliquemagazine.com/lyle-director-stewart-thorndike-talks-pregnancy-horror-gendered-genre-discrimination/
58 Honeycutt, H. (2006) Darla Enlow. Personal Interview.
59 Honeycutt, Enlow.
60 Honeycutt, Enlow.
61 Honeycutt, Enlow.
62 Honeycutt, H. (2005) Sue Corcoran. Personal Interview.
63 Honeycutt, H. (2007) Emily Hagins. Personal Interview.
64 Honeycutt, Hagins.
65 Honeycutt, Hagins.
66 Honeycutt, H. (2014) Ursula Dabrowsky. Personal Interview.

INDEX

A4
4
1
24
0.43.38.08
A
THE BOX
DECEMBER 12, 2014
Slates for Sarah
02.42.50.06
1
23.98
91J
A
THE STYLIST
J. GEVARGIZIAN
R. STERN
TIP

PussBucket
The Complete POX Collection
The Invisible Life of Thomas Lynch
HAMMER MUSIC VIDEOS
The Sis
POX
PROD.
SCENE
TAKE
LISA HAMMER
DATE:
Day.Night Int Ext
Filter
ROLL A3
SCENE 2
TAKE 1
FPS 23.98
12 HOUR SHIFT
BREA GRANT
MATT GLASS
DATE 4/3/19
16.A
3
Lady Hunters
A. ATWOOD
L. Prevost
23.9
INT EXT DAY NITE SYNC MOS
B39
128
3
24
11:31:46:24
A
HURT
B.STEPANSKY
R. KAECHELE
6/7/07
MOS
FPS
09:16:14:06
DATE
CAM
PETE SOTO
ROLL
A0024
SCENE
SA/12D
TAKE
1
DIR
VANESSA NEWELL
PROD
Bull MOUNTAIN LOOKOUT
FAMILY DEMONS
SLATE
258
TAKE
1
SCENE 77
27/1/06
DIR: URSULA
CAM: FRAYTAG